New Perspectives on

MICROSOFT®
WINDOWS® 2000

MS-DOS Command Line

Comprehensive Enhanced

HARRY L. PHILLIPS

ERIC SKAGERBERG

THOMSON
™
COURSE TECHNOLOGY

Australia • Canada • Mexico • Singapore • Spain • United Kingdom • United States • Japan

THOMSON

COURSE TECHNOLOGY

**New Perspectives on Microsoft® Windows® 2000
MS-DOS Command Line—Comprehensive Enhanced**

is published by Course Technology.

Managing Editor:
Rachel Crapser

Senior Editor:
Donna Gridley

Senior Product Manager:
Kathy Finnegan

Product Manager:
Karen Stevens

Technology Product Manager:
Amanda Shelton

Associate Product Manager:
Brianna Germain

Marketing Manager:
Rachel Valente

Production Editor:
Danielle Power

Composition:
GEX Publishing Services

Text Designer:
Meral Dabcovich

Cover Designer:
Efrat Reis

Preface

New Perspectives

Course Technology is the world leader in information technology education. The New Perspectives Series is an integral part of Course Technology's success. Visit our Web site to see a whole new perspective on teaching and learning solutions.

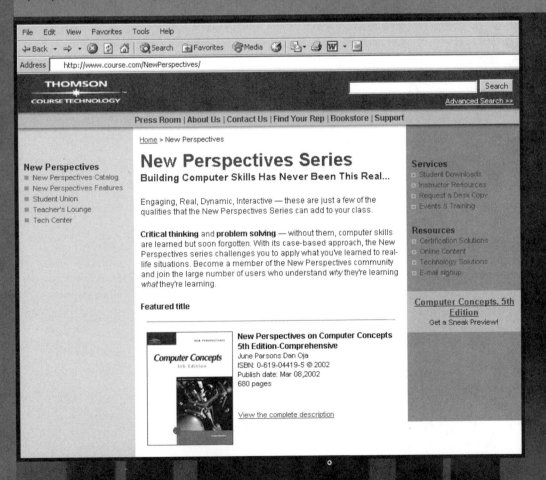

New Perspectives—Building Computer Skills Has Never Been This Real

Why New Perspectives will work for you.

Critical thinking and **problem solving**—without them, computer skills are learned but soon forgotten. With its **case-based** approach, the New Perspectives Series challenges students to apply what they've learned to real-life situations. Become a member of the New Perspectives community and watch your students not only **master** computer skills, but also **retain** and carry this **knowledge** into the world.

New Perspectives catalog
Our online catalog is never out of date! Go to the Catalog link on our Web site to check out our available titles, request a desk copy, download a book preview, or locate online files.

Complete system of offerings
Whether you're looking for a Brief book, an Advanced book, or something in between, we've got you covered. Go to the Catalog link on our Web site to find the level of coverage that's right for you.

Instructor materials
We have all the tools you need—data files, solution files, figure files, a sample syllabus, and ExamView, our powerful testing software package.

How well do your students know Microsoft Office?
Experience the power, ease, and flexibility of SAM XP and TOM. These innovative software tools provide the first truly integrated technology-based training and assessment solution for your applications course. Click the Tech Center link to learn more.

Get certified
If you want to get certified, we have the titles for you. Find out more by clicking the Teacher's Lounge link.

Interested in online learning?
Enhance your course with rich online content for use through MyCourse 2.0, WebCT, and Blackboard. Go to the Teacher's Lounge to find the platform that's right for you.

Your link to the future is at
www.course.com/NewPerspectives

What you need to know about this book.

- Students learn the Windows 2000 and Windows XP Command Line through a practical, step-by-step approach

- The Appendix contains an overview of Windows XP and addresses any differences a student may experience if using Windows XP while learning from this book

- Technically-oriented students will enjoy learning the more advanced features of a command-line environment, such as using troubleshooting tools, batch programs, and the Windows Registry

- Coverage provides a basis for comparison of the DOS, Windows 2000, and Windows XP operating system command-line environments

- Designed for a full-semester course on the Windows 2000 or Windows XP Command Line

CASE	TROUBLE?	SESSION 1.1	QUICK CHECK	RW
Tutorial Case Each tutorial begins with a problem presented in a case that is meaningful to students. The case sets the scene to help students understand what they will do in the tutorial.	**TROUBLE? Paragraphs** These paragraphs anticipate the mistakes or problems that students may have and help them continue with the tutorial.	**Sessions** Each tutorial is divided into sessions designed to be completed in about 45 minutes each. Students should take as much time as they need and take a break between sessions.	**Quick Check Questions** Each session concludes with conceptual Quick Check questions that test students' understanding of what they learned in the session.	**Reference Windows** Reference Windows are succinct summaries of the most important tasks covered in a tutorial. They preview actions students will perform in the steps to follow.

www.course.com/NewPerspectives

Tutorial 7   DOS 301

Using Batch Programs

Automating Routine Operations at SolarWinds

Tutorial 8   DOS 353

Enhancing the Power of Batch Programs

Improving Productivity with Batch Programs at SolarWinds

Appendix   DOS 529

Windows XP Command-Line Update

Acknowledgments

Dedicated to Neal Stephenson, author of *In the Beginning ... was the Command Line*

Many people were involved in all stages of the planning, development, and production of the original version and revised update of this book, and their combined efforts reflect Course Technology's continued commitment to the instructors and students who use this textbook.

We would like to thank our reviewer, Floyd Winters, Professor of Computer Science, Manatee Community College, whose valuable comments and insight helped shape this book. We would also like to thank him for providing us with photos of jumper blocks and DIP switches for use in Tutorial 1.

Thanks to all the members of the New Perspectives team who helped in the development and production of the original version of this book: Catherine Donaldson, Product Manager; Sandra K. Kruse, Developmental Editor; Rachel A. Crapser, Series Technology Manager; Greg Donald, Managing Editor; Donna Gridley, Senior Editor; Melissa Hathaway, Associate Product Manager; Rosa Maria Rogers, Editorial Assistant; John Bosco and Alex White; QA Managers; Anne Valsangiacomo, Production Editor; Nancy Ludlow; and the QA testers, John Freitas, Justin Rand, and Nicole Ashton, for their contributions in their areas of expertise. We would like to extend our special thanks to Ellen Skagerberg, who freely offered her invaluable time and expertise as a copy editor.

—Eric Skagerberg and Harry Phillips
28 August 2000

My deepest and heartfelt thanks go to my parents, David and Wanda Skagerberg, and my sister Andrea, for their love and immeasurable support through the years. My profound love and gratitude goes to my wife Ellen, for the astounding extent of practical support and encouragement she provided me throughout this process.

Thanks as well to Gary Brown, who saw some potential in a young man and hired him to teach a DOS class at Santa Rosa Junior College's CIS department over a decade ago, and to Lloyd Onyett, who gave so generously of his time and materials to mentor and work with me through those early years. I am grateful to each person in SRJC's CIS department who helped to create a warm, sharing, and cooperative working environment, particularly department chairs Metha Schuler, Cyndi Reese, and Ellindale Wells, and fellow UNIX instructors Pat Grosh and Sean Kirkpatrick.

—Eric Skagerberg
28 August 2000

Thanks to all the members of the New Perspectives team who helped in the development and production of the revised update of this book: Amanda Shelton, Technology Product Manager; Donna Gridley, Senior Editor; Rachel A. Crapser, Managing Editor; Kathy Finnegan, Senior Product Manager; Brianna Germain, Assistant Product Manager; Emilie Perreault, Editorial Assistant; Danielle Power and Jennifer Goguen, Production; Paul Griffin, Copyeditor; John Freitas, John Bosco, and Heather McKinstry, Quality Assurance; and the QA testers, John Freitas and Burt LaFountain, for their contributions in their areas of expertise.

—Harry Phillips and Eric Skagerberg
16 September 2002

New Perspectives on

MICROSOFT® WINDOWS® 2000

MS-DOS Command Line

Read This Before You Begin

To the Student

Data Disks

To complete the Tutorials, Review Assignments, and Case Problems in this book, you need 3 Data Disks. Your instructor will either provide you with the Data Disks or ask you to make your own.

If you are making your own Data Disks, you will need 3 blank, formatted high-density diskettes. You will need to execute self-extracting files on a file server or standalone computer to create your Data Disks. Your instructor will tell you which computer, drive letter, and folders contain the files you need. You can also download the files by going to www.course.com, clicking Data Disk Files, and following the instructions on the screen. If you download the files for the 3 Data Disks from the Course Technology, Inc. Web site, then you will find that there is one executable program file for each Data Disk. Each of these files is a self-extracting image file that contains an exact image of all the files and folders for each Data Disk stored in the order in which they were originally placed on the disk.

To extract the files and folders for each Data Disk, insert a blank, formatted high-density diskette in drive A, and then double-click the image file's icon. In the resulting command-line window, press the letter **A** (for drive A). The utility then extracts the files and folders to the diskette in drive A. When the operation is complete, close the command-line window if it does not automatically close.

The following list shows you which folders go on each of your disks:

Data Disk 1

Write this on the disk label:
Data Disk 1 – Tutorials 1, 2, 3, 4, 6, 8 & 9

Contents – The self-extracting image file will put 41 files on the disk (no folders).

Data Disk 2

Write this on the disk label:
Data Disk 2 – Tutorials 5 & 6

Contents – The self-extracting image file will put these folders on the disk: My Documents (which in turn contains the Company Templates, Designs, Memos, Overhead Transparencies, and Training folders).

Data Disk 3

Write this on the disk label:
Data Disk 3 – Tutorials 8 & 10

Contents – The self-extracting image file will put these folders on the disk: SolarWinds (which in turn contains the Graphic Designs, Memos, Presentations, and Templates folders) as well as the Employees.csv file.

When you begin each tutorial, be sure you are using the correct Data Disk. See the inside front or inside back cover of this book for more information on the Data Disk files, or ask your instructor or technical support person for assistance.

Appendix

The Appendix at the end of the book will help you complete the tutorials in this book if you are using Windows XP Professional or Windows XP Home Edition. The Appendix contains information on new Windows XP features related to what is covered in the textbook for Windows 2000. The Appendix also contains updates and Help information to assist you with the tutorials. As you step through each tutorial, you can consult the corresponding tutorial in the Appendix for additional topics, updates, and Help. At the end of the Appendix is a supplemental glossary with additional terms covered in the Appendix.

Using Your Own Computer

If you are going to work through this book using your own computer, you need:

- **Computer System** Windows 2000 Professional, Windows XP Professional, or Windows XP Home Edition must be installed on your computer. This book assumes a complete installation of Windows 2000 Professional, Windows XP Professional, or Windows XP Home Edition.

- **Data Disks** You will not be able to complete the tutorials or exercises in this book using your own computer until you have the Data Disks.

Visit Our World Wide Web Site

Additional materials designed especially for you are available on the World Wide Web.
Go to http://www.course.com.

To the Instructor

The files for the Data Disks are available on the Instructor's Resource Kit for this title. Follow the instructions in the Help file on the CD-ROM to copy the Data Disk image files to your network or standalone computer. For information on creating Data Disks, see the "To the Student" section above.

You are granted a license to copy the Data Files to any computer or computer network used by students who have purchased this book. The Instructor's Resource Kit and Test Bank have also been updated for Windows XP Professional and Windows XP Home Edition.

In this tutorial you will:

- Examine the role and importance of operating system software

- Learn about the importance of command line skills to Windows 2000 users

- Examine some of the basic functions of operating system software

- Open a command line session

- Identify the version of the operating system installed on a computer

- Set the date and time

- Use the Help switch

- Format a diskette

- Open a Command Prompt window

OPENING
COMMAND LINE SESSIONS IN WINDOWS 2000

Building MS-DOS Command Line Skills at SolarWinds Unlimited

CASE

SolarWinds Unlimited

SolarWinds Unlimited is a California corporation that uses state-of-the-art turbines to harness wind power—the world's fastest growing energy source—so it can provide clean energy to its growing base of environmentally conscious customers. Several months ago, Isabel Navarro Torres, the company's computer systems specialist, supervised the installation of Windows 2000 on computers at SolarWinds' southern California headquarters. To increase the background skills of the company's technical resource staff, Isabel recently scheduled a series of workshops on the use of command line sessions under Windows 2000. This investment in staff training will provide the company's technical support staff with the skills they need to set up and configure computers, and troubleshoot computer problems. Because Isabel recently hired you to provide technical support to other staff members and to assist her with administering the company's network, she asks you to participate in the workshops along with the rest of the company's employees.

SESSION 1.1

In this session you will examine the role and the importance of operating system software, the types of operating systems used on PCs, and the importance of developing a skill set that enables you to work with different operating systems in today's multifaceted business environment.

The Role and Importance of Operating System Software

At the start of the first workshop, Isabel provides an overview of the role and importance of operating system software on the different types of computer systems used by businesses, entrepreneurs, "dot com companies," and individuals.

An **operating system** is a software product that manages the basic processes within a computer, coordinates the interaction of hardware and software so all components work together, and provides support for the use of other types of software such as application software, utilities, and games. Although specific operating systems vary in the scope of tasks they manage, all operating systems play a role in the following tasks:

- **Booting a computer** The operating system participates in the later phases of the boot process. **Booting** refers to the process of powering on a computer system and loading the operating system into memory so it can configure the computer system and manage the basic processes of the computer, including providing support for other software.

  After you power on a computer, and before the operating system is active, the microprocessor executes a series of startup **routines**, or programs, stored on a special type of computer chip called the **ROM BIOS (Read-Only Memory Basic Input/Output System)**. The first routine, the **Power On Self Test** (or **POST**), checks to make sure your computer contains the components necessary for booting the computer and that these components are functional. The next routine searches the outside sector of the boot devices to locate the operating system and start the process of loading the operating system into memory. After the core operating system files are loaded into memory, the PC's operating system loads the remainder of the operating system and completes the boot process. From this point on, the PC's operating system manages the computer system.

- **Configuring a computer** During booting, the operating system configures itself by loading the additional software it needs to interact with the hardware and software on the computer. Newer operating systems can detect hardware automatically and load the appropriate device drivers. A **device driver** is software used for managing a specific type of hardware component and is essential for the proper functioning of your computer.

- **Customizing a computer** Near the end of the booting process, the operating system loads specific types of software that you install and use on the computer. For example, if you have installed antivirus software on your computer, the operating system will load that software during the latter stages of booting so it can check your computer for the presence of viruses as early as possible during the boot process. **Computer viruses** are programs designed to interfere with the performance, or even damage, of your computer. The antivirus software then continues to monitor your computer while you work. Although the operating system can function without this software, users increasingly depend on antivirus software, and other types of software, to customize their computers. Software for configuring your computer is required by the operating system, whereas software for customizing your computer is optional software.

- **Displaying a user interface** Once your computer boots, the operating system displays a **user interface**, the combination of hardware and software that lets you interact with the computer. This interface has become increasingly important to users because they rely on it to simplify the tasks they perform on the computer. Current operating systems typically display a **graphical user interface** (**GUI**) that uses **icons**, or images, to represent system components such as hardware and software; separate **windows** for displaying the interface used by application software and for viewing portions of documents; **menus** with task-related options for performing different types of operations, such as opening a software application; and **dialog boxes** with options for completing tasks, such as changing the appearance of the user interface; as well as colors, fonts (character styles), and special design elements, such as shading, which all provide a visually rich working environment. The different versions of the Windows operating system also require a mouse.

- **Providing support services to programs** The operating system provides important support services to programs that you use. Since almost every program must provide an option for saving files to disk and for retrieving files from disk, it makes sense to delegate this function to the operating system to avoid duplication and to provide consistency across different programs. Whether you are saving or retrieving a file, you must provide the program with the names of the disk drive, folder (if applicable), and file that contains your data. When saving data to a file on disk, the operating system handles the transfer of a copy of the document from Random Access Memory (RAM) to the disk. This document may be a new document you created from scratch, or it may be a document you opened and modified. **RAM**, the predominant type of memory within a computer, stores programs that you open and documents you create or open, and therefore provides a temporary workspace for you, the user. Because this memory is **volatile** (dependent on the availability of power), it is important to periodically save data to disk. When retrieving a file from disk, the operating system handles the transfer of a copy of the file from disk to RAM so you can use the data in that file with a program.

- **Handling input and output** The operating system manages all input and output. In addition to retrieving files from disk (input) and saving files to disk (output), the operating system also interprets keyboard and mouse input, and assists with other types of output, such as printing and displaying the image you see on the monitor. For example, when you press a key on the keyboard, the keyboard produces an electronic **scan code**, which the operating system interprets so the program you are using displays the correct character on the monitor. When you print a document, operating systems use a process called **spooling** to store the processed document in a temporary file on disk called a **spool file**, and to transmit the spool file to the printer in the background, so you can continue to work in your program, or even start a new task. Also, with spooling you can send several documents to the printer at once. The operating system stores the documents in a **print queue** (a list of print jobs) and prints the documents in order. Without spooling, you would have to wait until each document printed before you could do anything else.

- **Managing the file system** The operating system manages the disks, drives, directories (or folders), subdirectories (or subfolders), and files so it can find the software and documents you need to use. Disks are divided into one or more **partitions** (sometimes called drives), which provide storage for subdirectories and files. **Subdirectories** group related directories and files.

A **file** is the storage space on disk allocated to a program or data, such as a word processing document or a spreadsheet.

■ **Managing system resources** The operating system manages all the hardware and software so everything works together properly. This is a major feat today because of the wide spectrum of hardware and software products installed on any given computer. One important resource managed by the operating system is memory, or RAM. When you open a program, the operating system looks for that program on disk and allocates memory to the program as it loads that program. When you exit a program, the operating system should reclaim the memory used by that program so it can allocate that memory to the next program you open. Some applications leave program code in memory, however, and the operating system does not reclaim that memory. As a result, the amount of available memory actually decreases (a problem called a **memory leak**) overtime, and you need to reboot your computer system to clear memory and start fresh.

■ **Resolving system errors and problems** The operating system must handle and, if possible, resolve errors as they occur. For example, if you save a document to the floppy disk drive, but do not put a diskette into that drive, the operating system informs you of the problem so you can resolve it by inserting a diskette and trying again. If you print a document, but forget to turn the printer on, the operating system may inform you that the printer is off, off-line, or out of paper.

■ **Providing Help** Operating systems typically include a Help system that provides you with information about the use of the operating system and its features. Some Help systems provide troubleshooting assistance by stepping you through operations with wizards and hyperlinks. A **wizard** is a tool that asks a series of questions about what you want to do, what settings you want to use, or what problems you are experiencing; suggests options from which to choose, and then completes the operation for you or provides suggestions of options you should try. A **hyperlink** is a link to an object on your local computer, such as a Help Troubleshooter, a document, or a Web page.

■ **Optimizing system performance** Operating systems typically include a variety of **utilities**, or programs, for optimizing the performance of your computer. For example, you might use a utility to check the file system and the surface of the hard disk for errors and, where possible, to repair those errors. You might use another utility to improve the speed of accessing data on a disk by rearranging how folders, software, and document files are stored on it. Although these utilities are optional, many users depend on utilities to maintain and optimize the performance of their computer.

■ **Providing troubleshooting tools** The operating system on your computer provides you with a variety of tools for troubleshooting problems. For example, you can prepare a **boot disk** (also called a **system disk**) that contains the core operating system files needed to start your computer from drive A, so you can troubleshoot problems with the operating system (such as a failure to boot from drive C), or with the hard disk itself (such as a failure of the hard disk), and if necessary, replace your hard disk and reinstall the operating system. You can view settings assigned to hardware and software components if you need to troubleshoot a problem.

The operating system is an indispensable component of your computer. You cannot use a computer without an operating system. As you work with software, the operating system manages the moment-to-moment operation of your computer in the background, from the point you turn the power on until you shut down your computer. Furthermore, because the operating system handles important operations, such as disk, drive, directory, and file management, as well as all input/output functions, software can focus on what it is designed to do, and the operating system can focus on core functions required of all programs.

PC Operating Systems

Like many other businesses today, SolarWinds relies on a wide variety of computers, software, and PC operating systems. Some staff members use one operating system at work, and another on their home computer. Many of the technical staff members at SolarWinds set up a multi-boot configuration on their work and home computers so they can use one of several different operating systems. Because of the company's dependence on different operating system technologies, Isabel decides next to present a quick overview of the important operating systems that staff members use.

The predominant operating systems used on PCs today were developed by Microsoft Corporation. They share a common history, similar features and ways of working. Therefore, it's important for you to be familiar not only with Windows 2000, but also with other operating systems, such as Windows 98, Windows 95, Windows NT Workstation 4.0, and DOS.

Note: This book assumes that the student already has a working knowledge of the Windows 2000 operating system from a comprehensive Windows 2000 course. While the tutorials provide some summary information for context and step the student through certain operations in the graphical user interface, it is beyond the scope of this book to instruct the student in the operation of Windows 2000. Rather, this book focuses primarily on the features and uses of the MS-DOS subsystem under Windows 2000.

The DOS Operating System

Following the explosion of mass-marketed computer technology in the early 1980s that made PCs indispensable in offices, schools, and homes, the most commonly used operating system was **DOS**, an abbreviation for Disk Operating System. Disk refers to one of the more important hardware resources managed by this operating system. DOS is actually a generic name for three related operating systems: PC-DOS, MS-DOS, and IBM-DOS. PC-DOS is designed specifically for the hardware in IBM microcomputers, whereas MS-DOS is designed for the hardware in compatible PCs.

In 1981, IBM contracted with Microsoft Corporation (then a small company in Washington State) to provide the operating system for its first IBM PC. Over the years, Microsoft and IBM worked cooperatively to develop different versions of PC-DOS and IBM-DOS for use on IBM microcomputers, while Microsoft also worked independently to develop different versions of MS-DOS for use on compatible PCs, or IBM compatibles. IBM now develops its own versions of IBM-DOS for IBM microcomputers, but Microsoft no longer develops new versions of MS-DOS. However, Microsoft provides an MS-DOS command line system as an application within different versions of Windows, including Windows 2000. Although there are subtle differences between PC-DOS, MS-DOS, and IBM-DOS, all manage the hardware and software resources within a computer in similar ways, provide access to similar types of features, and include similar utilities for enhancing the performance of a system. Once you know how to use MS-DOS, you can also use PC-DOS and IBM-DOS, and you have a head start on working with command line sessions under the different versions of Windows, including Windows 2000.

DOS and other operating systems, such as UNIX, VAX/VMS, and Linux, use a **command line interface**, in which you communicate with the operating system by typing a command after an **operating system prompt**, or **command prompt**, as shown in Figure 1-1. A **command** is an instruction to perform a specific task, such as format a disk. Once you see the operating system prompt (usually C:\>), you know that the computer booted successfully, that the operating system loaded into memory, and which drive the operating system uses as a reference point (usually drive C). There are no other on-screen visual clues to help you figure out what to do next. You must know what command to use, the proper format for entering each command, and what options are available for modifying how each command works. After you enter a command, DOS attempts to locate and load a **routine**, or program, that enables you to perform a specific task. When you exit that routine or program, DOS redisplays the command prompt so you can enter another command to start another program. For these reasons, in the past, users commonly relied on technically oriented coworkers or friends to customize their computers so DOS automatically started Windows 3.1 or displayed a menu from which a user could open an installed program, or perform some task, such as formatting a disk.

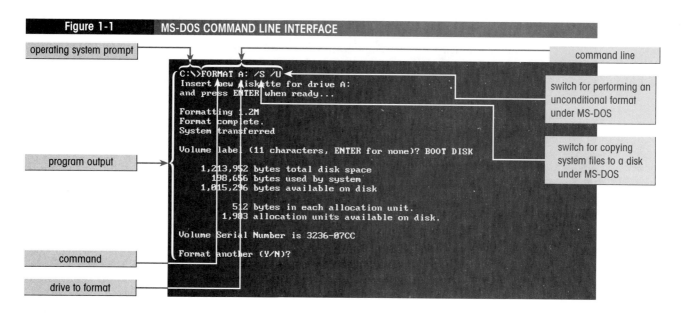

Figure 1-1   **MS-DOS COMMAND LINE INTERFACE**

Unlike Windows and other graphical user interface systems, command line interface operating systems operate in text mode rather than graphics mode. In **text mode**, the computer monitor displays only text, numbers, symbols, and a small set of graphics characters, using either white, amber, or green characters on a black background. Because text mode does not display a user interface with graphics, DOS functions were performed quickly and required far less memory or RAM than present-day operating systems that display a graphical user interface.

DOS still is important today. If Windows 2000 will not boot, you must work in a DOS-like command line interface to fix the problem. This is important especially for network administrators, specialists, and *technicians*, as well as telephone support *technicians*, troubleshooters, computer consultants, trainers, and tweakers (people who specialize in fine-tuning and optimizing computers). All of these professions find knowledge of DOS an invaluable resource. Furthermore, as noted earlier, the different versions of the Windows operating systems support the use of DOS commands in an MS-DOS command line window, or in a full-screen mode that emulates the DOS operating environment.

UNIX, Linux, and GNU

DOS and Windows owe much to UNIX, a command line operating system whose development began in 1969 at AT&T's Bell Laboratories by Ken Thompson and Dennis Ritchie. Many of its features have been adopted by DOS, particularly its hierarchical, directory-oriented file system and related commands. If you have used UNIX before, you will find many elements similar to, or derived from UNIX, as you learn more of the Windows 2000 command line interface.

In 1991, Linus Torvalds of Finland created Linux as a **kernel**, or core operating system program, that works like, or is a **clone** of, UNIX. The full operating system actually consists of the Linux kernel and software from the GNU (GNU's Not UNIX) project of Richard Stallman's Free Software Foundation. (GNU is a recursive acronym and an example of programmer wit.) The system is therefore more accurately referred to as GNU/Linux. A worldwide network of volunteers maintains and revises it, and GNU/Linux is freely distributed under the GNU Public License (GPL), which requires that programmers who distribute changes to Linux also make their source code public. (**Source code** is the original human-readable program code prepared by a programmer.)

GNU/Linux is a complete multitasking network operating system, which provides a powerful, stable, and inexpensive alternative to Windows 2000.

The Windows Operating Environment

In 1985, Microsoft introduced the Windows operating environment. An **operating environment** is a software product that performs the same functions as an operating system, except for booting a system and handling the storage and retrieval of data in files on a disk. Windows 3.1—the most commonly used version of the Windows operating environment in the past—was dependent on DOS to handle basic file functions in the background. Instead of displaying a command line interface in text mode, Windows 3.1 (and previous versions) used a graphical user interface. See Figure 1-2.

Figure 1-2	WINDOWS 3.1 GRAPHICAL USER INTERFACE

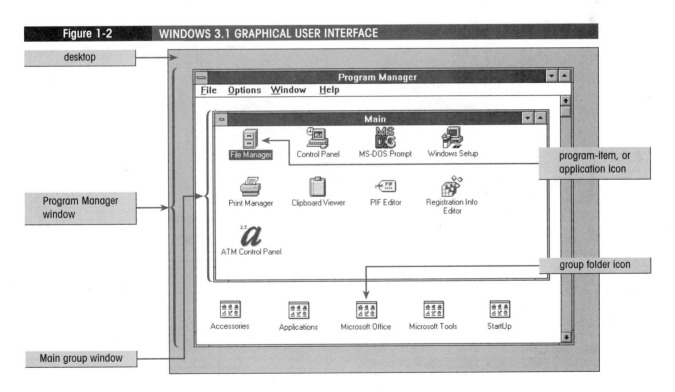

Over the years, many people used Windows 3.1, Windows 3.11, or earlier versions of Windows in conjunction with the DOS operating system. Although DOS was the predominant PC operating system from 1981 through 1995, the Windows 3.1 operating environment led to the development of the newer operating systems that most people depend on today. These new operating systems, including Windows 2000, no longer require DOS to boot and manage the computer.

The Windows 95 and Windows 98 Operating Systems

Microsoft's release of Windows 95 in the summer of 1995 marked a revolution in operating system technology, and opened the door to the development of more sophisticated operating systems like Windows NT Workstation 4.0, Windows 98, and Windows 2000. When you install Windows 95 onto a computer that contains DOS as the operating system, Windows 95 completely replaces DOS (and your previous version of the Windows operating environment) as the new operating system, unless you specify a dual-boot configuration. For example, in a Windows 95 **dual-boot configuration**, your computer would have two operating systems (such as Windows 95 and MS-DOS), and you can choose which operating system you would want to use during booting. If you chose MS-DOS, you could then launch a previous version of Windows (such as Windows 3.1). One important advantage of a dual-boot configuration is that you can still boot your computer if one of the operating systems does not work.

Like previous versions of Windows, Windows 95 displays a graphical user interface, as shown in Figure 1-3. Although its graphical user interface is different in appearance from those of previous versions of the Windows operating environment, you still interact with the Windows 95 operating system and other software using icons, windows, menus, and dialog boxes. In Windows 95, Microsoft added many new features to the operating system, some of which are available in Windows NT Workstation 4.0, and all of which are available in Windows 98 and Windows 2000.

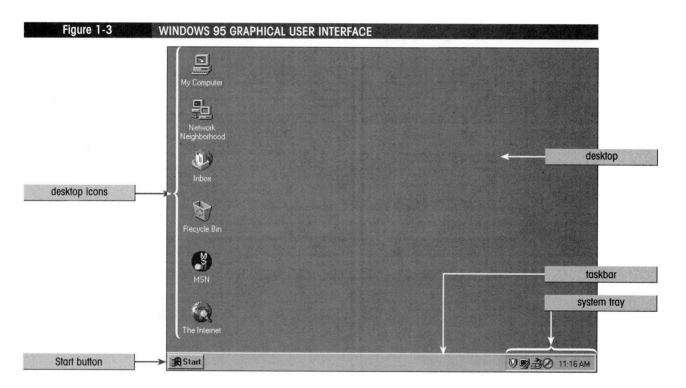

Figure 1-3   WINDOWS 95 GRAPHICAL USER INTERFACE

After introducing the original version of Windows 95, Microsoft introduced four other versions, listed in Figure 1-4. The first upgrade, Microsoft Windows 95 Service Pack 1 (also called OSR 1 or Windows 95a), included fixes to the original version of Windows 95, as well as additional components. OSR 2 (OEM Service Release 2 or Windows 95B), included Internet Explorer 3.0 and support for newer types of hardware, as well as a new file system called FAT32 that maximized the use of storage space on a hard disk. The FAT32 filing system, however, was not compatible with the FAT16 filing system used in previous versions of

Windows 95. Therefore, you could not upgrade your computer from the original version of Windows 95 (or Windows 95a) to Windows 95B by attempting to install it over your existing copy of Windows 95 (or Windows 95a). Instead, Windows 95B was installed only on new computers starting in the fall of 1996. Because some of the components in Windows 95B also worked in Windows 95 and 95a, Microsoft posted those components (called downloadable components) on its Web site. When added to Windows 95, the downloadable components make the Windows 95 interface similar to that of Windows 95B and Windows 98. OSR 2.1, a minor upgrade of Windows 95B, adds support for the universal serial bus (USB)—a high-speed communications port. OSR 2.5, or Windows 95c, included Internet Explorer 4.0, support for other online services (including an MSN 2.5 upgrade), another USB upgrade, and Internet components now found in Windows 98 and Windows 2000. (**MSN** is an abbreviation for The Microsoft Network, an Internet Service Provider, or ISP.)

Figure 1-4	VERSIONS OF WINDOWS 95		
WINDOWS 95 VERSION	**POPULAR NAME**	**WINDOWS VERSION**	**RELEASE DATE**
Original	Windows 95	Windows 4.00.950	August, 1995
OSR 1 (Microsoft Windows 95 Service Pack 1)	Windows 95a	Windows 4.00.950a	December, 1995
OSR 2.0 (OEM Service Release 2)	Windows 95B	Windows 4.00.950 B	August, 1996
OSR 2.1	Windows 95B		November, 1996
OSR 2.5	Windows 95c		January, 1998

Microsoft introduced Windows 98 in the summer of 1998. The Windows 98 graphical user interface, shown in Figure 1-5, is very similar to that of Windows 95. With Windows 98, Microsoft included all of the service pack/service release additions and expanded the role and capabilities of the Windows operating system.

Figure 1-5	WINDOWS 98 GRAPHICAL USER INTERFACE

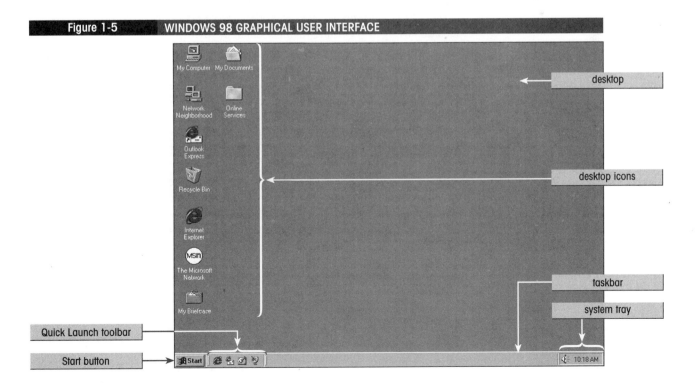

The following features are available in both Windows 95 and Windows 98:

- **Enhanced graphical user interface** The enhanced graphical user interface in Windows 95 and Windows 98 starts with the desktop. The desktop, which appears right after booting, replaces Program Manager in Windows 3.1 and is simpler in design and use. The desktop icons, such as My Computer, Network Neighborhood (or just Network), and the Recycle Bin, represent specific components of the Windows 95 and Windows 98 operating systems. The **taskbar** at the bottom of the desktop displays buttons for open programs and windows. By clicking the Start button on the taskbar, you can display a Start menu from which you can access programs, accessories, folders, files, and the Internet.

- **Document-oriented** The graphical user interface facilitated the use of a document-oriented approach rather than a program-oriented approach to opening documents. When using a **program-oriented** approach (also referred to as an application-oriented approach), you first open the software program you want to use, and then locate and open the document you want to use. This approach was required with the DOS operating system. Using a **document-oriented or docucentric** approach, you locate and open the document you want to use, and then the operating system opens the program associated with that type of document. Although this approach was available with earlier versions of Windows before Windows 95, most individuals were not aware of this approach, and therefore used the same program-oriented approach they had used under DOS. Under Windows 95, Windows 98, Windows NT Workstation 4.0, and Windows 2000, the document-oriented approach has become increasingly important to the ways in which individuals work.

- **Object-oriented interface** Windows 95 and Windows 98 (as well as Windows NT Workstation 4.0 and Windows 2000) treat components of the graphical user interface and computer as **objects**, each having discrete **properties**, or settings, that you can view and change. Hardware and software components, such as disks, drives, folders, files, and programs, are objects. As you work, you select and open objects and perform other types of operations on those objects, such as moving or renaming them, or changing their properties.

- **New system architecture** Microsoft introduced a new **system architecture**, which is the internal design and coding of an operating system, in Windows 95 and continued it in Windows 98, Windows NT Workstation 4.0, and Windows 2000. The improved system architecture takes advantage of newer types of microprocessors, such as the Pentium III, Pentium MMX, and Pentium II, as well as providing support for operating modes of earlier microprocessors, such as the 8088, 8086, 80286, 80386, and 80486 microprocessors. This system architecture also supports **multitasking**, the simultaneous or concurrent use of more than one program; **task-switching**, the ability to switch from one open task to another; and **multithreading**, the processing of separate segments of program code (called **threads**) within the same program. Multithreading is important because it allows the same program to perform multiple tasks at the same time. Even the operating system depends on multithreading for operations it performs. For example, every time you open a new window, Windows spawns a new thread from the same program (Explorer). Although you could multitask and switch from one task to another under versions of Windows earlier than Windows 95, those earlier versions of Windows did not support multithreading.

To further increase the effectiveness and reliability of Windows 95 and Windows 98, the system architecture included new design features that increased the **robustness**, or stability, of the operating system and protected important system resources. For example, the operating system allocates memory to each program you open and provides protection for that memory, so other open programs cannot access the memory used by another program. Also, each time you open a DOS program, Windows creates a **virtual DOS machine (VDM)**, which is a complete operating environment for that particular program. The DOS program thinks it is the only program running on the computer, and that it has access to all the computer's hardware—a feature typical of DOS programs. These features ensured that a single malfunctioning program did not crash other running programs or the entire computer.

■ **Backward compatibility** Windows 95 and Windows 98 support the use of DOS programs, utilities, and games developed for all microprocessors from the original 8088 to the newest type of microprocessor. Both versions also support the use of software designed for prior versions of Windows, as well as older types of hardware devices. This ability to handle hardware and software designed for earlier systems is called **backward compatibility**. Windows 2000 continues to support the use of DOS programs, utilities, and games, as well as DOS commands.

■ **Plug and Play** Windows 95, Windows 98, and Windows 2000 support Plug and Play hardware and legacy devices. **Plug and Play (PnP)** refers to a set of specifications for automatically detecting and configuring hardware. Once you add a Plug and Play hardware device to your computer, the operating system automatically detects and configures the hardware device during booting, with little or no intervention on your part. In contrast, **legacy devices** are older types of hardware components that do not meet Plug and Play specifications and often require manual installation through setting jumpers or DIP switches. A **jumper** is a small metal block used to complete a circuit for two pins on a circuit board, which specifies a configuration. See Figure 1-6.

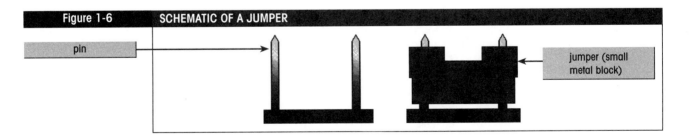

Figure 1-6   **SCHEMATIC OF A JUMPER**

pin

jumper (small metal block)

In contrast, a **DIP (dual in-line package) switch** is a set of toggle switches mounted on a chip, which is in turn mounted on an add-in board. See Figure 1-7. You flip a switch on or off to specify a setting. In some cases, you have to set a combination of switches to specify a setting, such as a **baud rate** (the transmission speed of a modem).

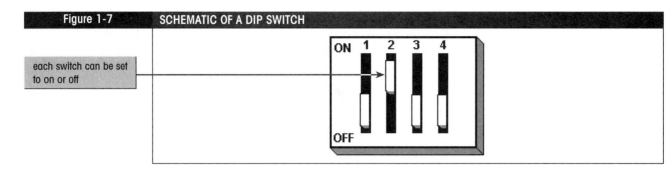

Figure 1-7   SCHEMATIC OF A DIP SWITCH

each switch can be set to on or off

ON 1 2 3 4

OFF

It is important to note that, depending on the type of hardware support built into your version of Windows 95 and Windows 98, these operating systems may or may not automatically detect legacy hardware devices during booting. If legacy devices are detected, then the operating system may only be able to configure the device as a generic, or standard device. Although the device will more than likely work, you will not have access to all the features included with that specific model.

■ **Multimedia support** Windows 95 provided increased support for the use of multimedia programs and multimedia hardware (such as CD-ROM drives and sound cards), video and audio recording and playback, and the integration of graphics, video, sound, and animation within documents, as well as the user interface. Windows 98 supported even newer technologies for improving gaming, multimedia, and 3-D rendering. It also included broadcast software to receive television programming via cable, satellite, or the World Wide Web.

■ **Hardware support** Windows 95 and Windows 98 provide support for existing hardware, as well as for newer types of hardware technologies. Both provide increased support for display adapters, monitors, printers, modems, and CD-ROM drives, as well as support for new Plug and Play hardware devices, **PCMCIA** (Personal Computer Memory Card International Association) devices (credit-card sized interface cards), and ECP (enhanced capabilities port) devices, such as modems.

Windows 98 also supports new features of the Pentium III, Pentium MMX (Multimedia Extensions), Pentium II, and later microprocessors; the accelerated graphics port (AGP) for handling 3-D graphics **throughput** (the speed with which a device processes and transmits data); the **universal serial bus** (USB) for connecting multiple devices and for fast data transfer rates; digital video discs (DVDs) for storage and playback of movies; IEEE 1394 ports (also called FireWire) for connecting multiple devices and for handling throughput of video cameras, VCRs, stereos, and other consumer electronic devices; IrDA (infrared) ports for wireless communication; multiple display (the use of up to nine monitors for a "SurroundView" effect); and improved power management of desktop and portable PCs.

■ **Network support** Both Windows 95 and Windows 98 are network operating systems that provide enhanced support for connecting to networks and working with network operating software, including Novell NetWare. These operating systems can interact with network program software and hardware, and access documents, e-mail, and other types of information on networks. By using Windows 95 and Windows 98, you can set up a **peer-to-peer network**, a simple network in which each computer can access other computers and share hardware, such as printers, hard disk drives, removable storage devices (such as CD-ROM, Zip, and DVD drives), as well as software, folders, and files.

A peer-to-peer network does not require a server. A **server** is a high-performance computer that manages a computer network with the use of network operating system software, such as Novell NetWare or Windows NT.

- **Support for portable computers** Windows 95 and Windows 98 include support for Dial-Up Networking (DUN) so employees traveling on business or working out of a home office can connect their portable computers to their company's network. They also include a component for linking Direct Cable Connection to a portable and desktop computer by means of a parallel or null modem cable, file synchronization between computers using My Briefcase, Advanced Power Management for managing power on a portable computer, Quick View for viewing the contents of files, Microsoft Exchange (and later Windows Messaging) for e-mail access, Microsoft Fax for sending and receiving faxes, and deferred printing.

- **Support for online services** One of the features introduced with Windows 95 (and still available in Windows 98) is the inclusion of software for access to Microsoft's own online service, The Microsoft Network (MSN). By joining MSN (or any other online service or Internet service provider), you gain access to the Internet, the World Wide Web and to other features such as e-mail, online chat rooms, and file libraries with downloadable software and multimedia files.

- **Web integration** Microsoft integrated Internet Explorer 3.0 into the Windows 95B user interface, and later integrated Internet Explorer 4.0 and 5.0 into the Windows 98 user interface. As a result, you have the option of switching the user interface to **Web style**, which supports single-click selection and launching of programs. Using Active Desktop technology, you can place the active content of Web pages on the desktop. **Active content** refers to information provided from a content provider's Web site and delivered to your desktop. For example, you may subscribe to The Weather Channel, and that Web site will periodically deliver updates on weather conditions in your local area to your desktop and display the information within a window. These versions of Windows also include other tools, such as Outlook Express, an e-mail tool; FrontPage Express, a personal Web page editor; NetMeeting, for Internet conferencing; and NetShow, for delivering streaming multimedia across the Internet. If you have an earlier version of Windows 95, you can download and install a more recent version of Internet Explorer and enjoy the benefits of Web style as well as the Active Desktop technology.

In the summer of 1999, Microsoft introduced Windows 98 Second Edition (or Windows 98 SE) as an upgrade to the original version of Windows 98. Windows 98 SE included Internet Explorer 5.0; **Internet Connection Sharing** for setting up and configuring computer networks at home so more than one computer can share a single Internet connection; new and improved hardware support such as USB modems and improved support for other types of hardware, such as IEEE 1394 and USB high-speed connections for peripherals; new and improved accessories, including a new version of NetMeeting; as well as improved support for WebTV, DirectX, and ACPI (Advanced Configuration and Power Interface), Year 2000 patches, and Service Pack 1 with "bug" fixes.

The diverse range of features in Windows 95 and Windows 98 not only expanded the role of an operating system, but also emphasized the importance of integrating programs and features to optimize the performance of a computer, to more effectively manage its resources, and to increase productivity.

The Windows NT Workstation 4.0 Operating System

In 1993, prior to the release of Windows 95, Microsoft introduced an advanced network operating system named Windows NT (for "New Technology") that supported computers with different types of microprocessors and different types of file systems. Unlike prior versions of Windows, Windows NT was an operating system in its own right and it did not require DOS to boot and manage the computer. Over the years, this operating system gained a favorable reputation, particularly in corporate and industrial programs, for its security features and its stability, as well as its ability to handle multithreading in real time.

In the summer of 1996, a year after it released Windows 95, Microsoft introduced Windows NT Workstation 4.0 for use on desktop computers. Microsoft included the Windows 95 interface in Windows NT Workstation 4.0. After you boot, you see the Windows NT Workstation 4.0 desktop which looks identical to the Windows 95 desktop. However, parts of the user interface, such as Administrative Tools, look and respond like the Windows 3.1 interface and therefore are not object oriented (you cannot right-click). Because Windows NT contains extensive security features for protecting the file system, such as not permitting DOS programs to write directly to disk, running DOS programs under Windows NT Workstation 4.0 is more difficult than under Windows 95 and Windows 98. Furthermore, Windows NT Workstation 4.0 does not support Plug and Play, has limited multimedia support, and does not support as many hardware devices as Windows 95. This release, however, introduced a network operating system for use on desktop computers that was previously used only on servers. Because of the security features available in the Windows NT product line, its history as a stable operating system, and its advanced networking features, businesses preferred Windows NT over Windows 95 and Windows 98 for use on employees' desktop computers.

The Windows 2000 Professional Operating System

The Windows 2000 Professional operating system originally started out as Windows NT 5.0, an upgrade to Windows NT Workstation 4.0, but Microsoft changed its name to Windows 2000 Professional Edition. Windows 2000 Professional incorporates the features of the different versions of Windows 95 and Windows 98 into the Windows NT product line for use on desktop computers. Among the many new features now available in Windows 2000 are the following:

- **Improved graphical user interface** All of the components of the Windows 2000 graphical user interface are similar to those of Windows 95 and Windows 98. The entire user interface is now object oriented. Like previous versions of Windows 95 and Windows 98, Internet Explorer 5.0 is integrated into the user interface so it supports Active Desktop technologies and features.

- **Support for Intel's Pentium III and Pentium III Xeon processors** Windows 2000 provides support for newer processors as well as other emerging hardware technologies. In fact, rapid changes in hardware technologies now require frequent upgrades to operating systems so the operating systems support these newer technologies.

- **Plug and Play support** Unlike its predecessor, Windows NT Workstation 4.0, Windows 2000 now supports Plug and Play hardware devices.

- **Advanced power management** Like Windows 98, Windows 2000 allows you to select or define power management schemes that control power to components on your computer, such as the monitor and hard disk, as well as consumer devices (such as VCRs) attached to your computer.

- **Device Manager** Windows 2000 now includes Device Manager, a tool for examining the hardware configuration of your computer. Device Manager was available in Windows 98 and Windows 95, but not in Windows NT Workstation 4.0.

- **Support for different file systems** Windows 2000 supports NTFS, the Windows NT native file system, as well as the FAT16 and FAT32 file systems supported by Windows 98 and Windows 95. If you are using NTFS, you can set disk quotas that control the amount of space used on a hard disk by individuals and workgroups.

- **Utilities for system maintenance and system recovery** Windows 2000 includes Disk Defragmenter, a utility for optimizing the arrangement of programs and data on disks. This utility is not available in Windows NT Workstation 4.0, but is available in Windows 95 and Windows 98.

- **Windows Update** Like Windows 98, Windows 2000 includes a Windows Update wizard that connects you to Microsoft's Web site, examines the installed software on your computer, and recommends software updates, device driver updates, and add-on components for your computer.

Upgrading to Windows 2000 from Windows NT Workstation 4.0, Windows 98, or Windows 95 affects users in other important ways as well, such as:

- **Computer compatibility** Before you install Windows 2000 on your computer, you should check Microsoft's Windows 2000 Update Web site to determine if your computer can run Windows 2000.

- **BIOS compatibility** In order to take advantage of the new power management features in Windows 2000, your computer must have an ACPI (Advanced Configuration and Power Interface) BIOS. You might need to obtain a BIOS update from the manufacturer of your BIOS.

- **Hardware compatibility** Windows 2000 has strict hardware requirements. In fact, prior to installing Windows 2000, you need to compare the information you have about your computer's hardware components with Microsoft's Hardware Compatibility List (HCL) (on the Windows 2000 CD or at Microsoft's Windows 2000 Update Web site) to make sure Windows 2000 will support those hardware devices. Windows 2000 does not support the use of Windows 98, Windows 95, Windows 3.x, and DOS device drivers, but instead requires new device drivers for many peripheral devices and hardware controllers. When you install Windows 2000 as an upgrade to Windows 95 or Windows 98, the Setup program examines your computer and prepares a report that identifies which hardware devices will not work with Windows 2000 and recommends that you obtain upgraded drivers from the manufacturer of those hardware devices. If you are upgrading from Windows NT Workstation 4.0, Setup identifies hardware that is not supported by Windows 2000 at the beginning of the upgrade process.

- **Software compatibility** You might need to upgrade your software and obtain versions designed specifically for Windows 2000. Programs that work under Windows 95 or Windows 98 might not work under Windows 2000. When you install Windows 2000 as an upgrade to Windows 95 or Windows 98, the Setup program examines your computer and prepares a report that identifies which programs and utilities will not work with Windows 2000.

You can download and install a program called the Readiness Analyzer from Microsoft's Windows 2000 Update Web site to check whether your computer is compatible with Windows 2000. The Readiness Analyzer will analyze the hardware and software on your computer, and provide a detailed report on incompatibility problems that it finds.

Windows 2000 Professional is the next important step in operating system technology and, not surprisingly, it builds on the successes of previous versions of Windows.

The Importance of the Command Line

Before upgrading the company's computer systems to Windows 2000, Isabel learned that Windows 2000 not only offers many new features for enhancing and optimizing the performance of computers, but also provides support for the DOS programs that businesses and companies have used over the years.

As noted earlier, from 1981 through 1995, DOS was the primary operating system used on PCs by both businesses and millions of home users around the world. During that time, DOS programs, utilities, and games proliferated.

Here are some reasons why an understanding of DOS and command line skills remains important:

- **Understanding Windows 2000 concepts and features** Windows 2000, like all other versions of Windows, relies on a feature called the full path to locate and open programs and other types of files, such as documents, on the hard disk. The **full path** identifies the exact location of a file and includes the name of the drive, and the sequence of folders to locate and open that file. For example, when you click a program shortcut on the desktop, Windows 2000 uses the full path of that program to locate and open the program. The full path is a feature first introduced with the DOS operating system, which is essential to the proper functioning of Windows 2000 (and all other versions of Windows). You will examine the full path in more detail in Tutorial 4.

- **Backward compatibility with DOS program** Windows 2000 provides backward compatibility with the DOS operating system, as well as software originally designed for DOS and Windows version 3. Some DOS programs did not function properly under Windows 3.1 because they needed direct access to system resources, including memory, and therefore you had to start the program from the DOS prompt rather than from Windows 3.1. DOS games, in particular, did not function well under Windows 3.1 because the software for these games assumed they were the only program running on the system. Furthermore, they placed heavy demands on the resources within a computer. Although DOS and Windows 3.1 handled access to hardware within a computer, the software for DOS games attempted to bypass DOS and Windows 3.1 and interact directly with the computer's hardware, thus creating conflicts with Windows 3.1. Under Windows 2000, you can open DOS programs from a Command Prompt window (known as the MS-DOS Prompt window in Windows 98 and Windows 95). Depending on how you set up your system, you can even open DOS programs from the Start menu or by using a desktop shortcut.

- **Configuring legacy devices** The MS-DOS subsystem is important in configuring legacy devices, or what are now called non-Plug and Play devices, for use under Windows 2000. Although Windows 2000 provides support for Plug and Play technologies, many individuals still have legacy devices, such as CD-ROM drives, modems, and sound cards, installed on their computers. For these legacy devices to work properly, you may need to configure these devices by using Device Manager and perhaps even by modifying the MS-DOS system startup or configuration files (called Config.sys and Autoexec.bat) and the Windows 2000 system startup or configuration files (called Config.nt and Autoexec.nt). Also, knowing how DOS interacts with hardware components is invaluable when using Windows 2000 components, such as Device Manager, to evaluate and assign resources to hardware.

- **Removing computer viruses** With some operating systems, if a computer virus infects your hard disk drive, you may need to start your computer from a boot disk in drive A, and then run a DOS-based program from a command line interface to scan drive C and remove the computer virus. Because many programs and utilities cannot run from either a command line interface or from a disk with limited storage space, you may need to rely on a program that operates in a command line environment to clean your system. However, you need to make sure that program supports the use of long file-names and the type of file system used on the drive you check.

- **Troubleshooting system, software, and hardware problems** Command line skills are important for troubleshooting Windows 2000 problems. If Windows 2000 does not start or if you experience a problem with your hard disk drive, you can boot your computer to a command prompt from the Windows 2000 Advanced Options Menu. Then you can attempt to troubleshoot problems, make backups, and restore important Windows 2000 system files. If you use Windows 2000 Help Troubleshooters (for example, to identify and resolve a printing problem), you may find that it recommends you open a Command Prompt window and use DOS commands to troubleshoot the problem. If you contact technical support to help you with a problem, you may be asked to examine, and perhaps change configuration settings and configuration files, and work with a command prompt. Likewise, if you have to rebuild a computer system from scratch, you need to know how to work in a DOS environment, use DOS commands, configure your startup system files, and install device drivers in order to gain access to your computer and reinstall Windows 2000.

- **Managing the use of different types of computer systems with different operating systems** To maximize their investment in computer systems, businesses typically retain computer systems as long as is feasible, and then gradually replace much older systems with newer ones. Therefore, some employees work on older computer systems that do not support more recent versions of Windows, which require a minimum type of microprocessor (such as a Pentium chip), a minimum clock speed (such as 133 MHz), and a minimum amount of RAM (such as 64 MB). **Clock speed** is the speed at which a microprocessor executes instructions, and it is measured in megahertz (MHz)—millions of cycles per second. Technical support staff and employees, therefore, must be familiar with different operating systems, including MS-DOS.

- **Training** If you are a corporate trainer or an educator, you should know how to use the command line in the event you need to troubleshoot problems on computers used for training employees or students; you may be the only person with the knowledge of the command line necessary to resolve problems that occur immediately prior to, or during, a training session.

- **Network administration, setup, installation, configuration, and troubleshooting** If you are a network administrator, specialist, or technician, you will need to know MS-DOS commands and how to work in a command line environment under Windows 2000 so you can install, configure, and troubleshoot network problems. At many colleges, knowing command line skills is a requirement for taking a networking course and learning how to use network operating systems—including Windows NT, Novell NetWare, and UNIX.

- **Professional certification** To acquire certification in certain specialties, such as a microcomputer specialist, a network specialist, or even as a Windows 2000 specialist, you have to prove competency in the use of DOS commands and a command line operating environment.
- **Power user skills** **Power users** are more advanced users who gradually develop a broad base of skills that are invaluable in many different types of situations, such as designing and automating the use of custom programs, troubleshooting problems, providing support for other users, and setting up computer systems from scratch.

Since the introduction of Windows 95, there has been a gradual transition from computers that use the DOS operating system to those that use Windows 95, Windows 98, Windows NT Workstation 4.0, and now Windows 2000. DOS concepts and skills, however, still remain important no matter which operating system you use.

The Windows XP Appendix at the end of the book provides additional information about the Windows ME, Windows XP Professional, and Windows XP Home Edition operating systems. The Appendix also includes updates to the topics covered in this textbook, and Help information on how to complete the tutorials with Windows XP. As you step through the tutorials, you can turn to the Appendix if you have questions about completing part of a tutorial and to also learn about new features in Windows XP.

Session 1.1 QUICK CHECK

1. A(n) _____ is a software product that manages the basic processes that occur within a computer, coordinates the interaction of hardware and software, and provides support for the use of other types of software.

2. _____ refers to the process of powering on a computer system and loading the operating system into memory.

3. Operating systems typically include a variety of _____, or programs, for optimizing the performance of your computer.

4. The DOS operating system uses a(n) _____ interface in which you communicate with the operating system by typing a command after a(n) _____.

5. In a(n) _____ configuration, your computer has two operating systems (such as Windows 2000 and MS-DOS), and during booting, you can choose the operating system you want to use.

6. The _____ identifies the exact location of a file on a disk, and includes the name of the drive and the sequence of directories to locate and open that file.

7. The ability of an operating system to handle hardware and software designed for earlier systems is called _____.

8. A(n) _____ is a complete operating environment under Windows for a DOS program.

9. In _____, the computer monitor displays only text, numbers, symbols, and a small set of graphics characters, using white, amber, or green characters on a black background.

10. A(n) _____ is an instruction to perform a specific task, such as format a diskette.

SESSION 1.2

examine the difference between internal and external commands, and you will use both types of commands in the command line session. You will customize the Command Prompt window, display the current Windows 2000 version, change the date and time, clear the window, and format a diskette. After evaluating the use of storage space on the formatted diskette, you will make a copy of a diskette. Finally, you will close the Command Prompt window, and then log off your computer.

Starting Windows 2000

So her technical support staff and other employees can develop the practical skills they need for working in command line sessions under Windows 2000, Isabel asks you and the other employees in the workshop to start Windows 2000 and set up your computer for the hands-on portion of the first workshop.

How you start Windows 2000 will depend on whether your computer's power is already on, whether your computer uses a dual-boot (or multi-boot) configuration, whether you are connected to a network, whether Windows 2000 requires you to provide a user name and password to log onto a network, and whether someone else has already powered on or logged onto the computer previously (if you are working in a computer lab or an environment where users share the same computer).

If you need to power on your computer first, complete the next section, entitled "Powering On Your Computer." If your computer is already on, and if you see the Windows 2000 desktop, then skip the next section ("Powering On Your Computer"), and complete the section entitled "Logging Onto a Network."

Note: As mentioned earlier, this book assumes that the student already has a working knowledge of the Windows 2000 operating system, such as logging on to Windows 2000 under different user accounts.

Powering On Your Computer

Complete this section only if you need to power on your computer. If your computer is already on, skip this section and continue with the next section, entitled "Logging On to a Network."

> *To power on your computer and start Windows 2000:*
>
> 1. Turn on the power to your computer. During the boot process, your computer may display technical information about your computer (such as information about the drives in your computer) as well as startup operations (such as the results of the POST memory test) before the operating system actually starts loading.
>
> 2. If you see a Startup Menu prompting you to select the operating system to use, select **Microsoft Windows 2000 Professional** from the menu (it may already be selected as the default operating system to use), and then press **Enter** (it may automatically start after 30 seconds). Then, you will see a Windows 2000 progress indicator. The next screen displays the Microsoft Windows 2000 Professional logo and another Starting up progress indicator. The following screen displays a Please wait dialog box, and you finally see a Log On to Windows dialog box that prompts for your user name and password.
>
> 3. If your computer does not require you to log on, and if you see the Windows 2000 desktop, skip the next section, entitled "Logging On to Windows 2000," and continue with the section entitled "Opening a command line Session"; otherwise enter your user name (if necessary) and password, and then press Enter (or click OK)."

REFERENCE WINDOW RW

<u>Powering On Your Computer and Starting Windows 2000</u>
- Turn on the power switch.
- If you see a Startup Menu prompting you to select the operating system, select "Microsoft Windows 2000 Professional" from the OS Choices Startup Menu (it may already be selected as the default operating system to use), and press Enter (it may automatically start on its own after 30 seconds).
- If Windows 2000 displays a Log On to Windows dialog box, enter your user name and password, and then press Enter (or click OK).

Logging On to Windows 2000

If you work on a shared computer, or if you are using a computer in a computer lab, you may need to log off that computer and then log on to the network under your own user account so you have access to the resources and files you need to use. Rather than restart your computer, you can use log off, and then log on again under your user account.

To log off, and then on to, Windows 2000:

1. Click the **Start** button and, if there is a Log Off option on the Start menu, click **Log Off**; otherwise, click **Shut Down**.

2. If you chose the Log Off option, click **Yes** in the Log Off Windows dialog box. If you chose Shut Down, click the **What do you want the computer to do?** list arrow in the Shut Down Windows dialog box, click the **Log off** option for your user name, and then click **OK**.

   TROUBLE? If the Shut Down Windows dialog box does not contain an option for logging off the current account (whatever its name may be), click Cancel to interrupt the Shut Down process and return to the desktop.

3. If you are prompted to "press Ctrl-Alt-Delete to begin", press and hold the **Ctrl** and **Alt** keys, press the **Delete** key, then release all three keys.

4. After Windows displays the Log On to Windows dialog box, enter your user name and password, and then click the **OK** button or press **Enter**. You may see a Restoring Network Connections dialog box before Windows 2000 displays the desktop, shown in Figure 1-8. Because you can customize the Windows 2000 desktop, your desktop view may differ from that shown in this figure.

   TROUBLE? If you are working in a computer lab, your instructor and lab support staff will tell you what user name and password you should use. Your network connection may also require a server name.

   TROUBLE? If Windows 2000 displays a "Welcome to Windows 2000" dialog box with options for registering Windows 2000, connecting to the Internet, discovering Windows 2000, and maintaining your computer, click the Close [X] button.

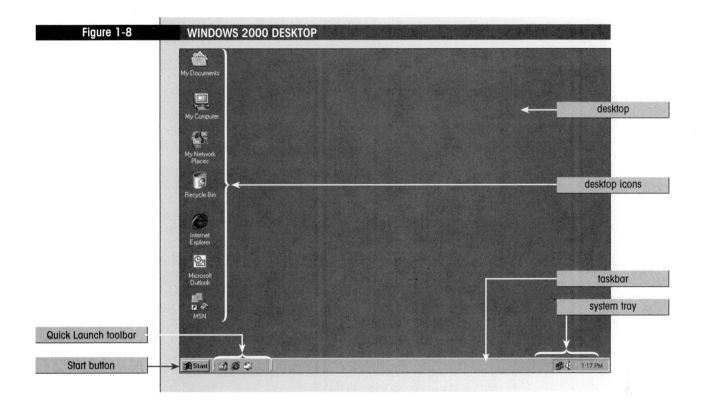

Figure 1-8 · WINDOWS 2000 DESKTOP

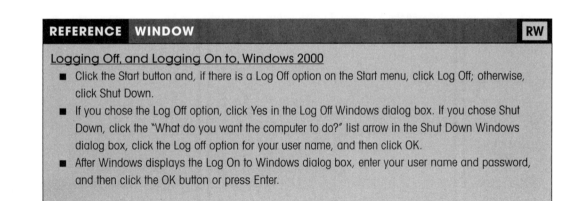

REFERENCE WINDOW · RW

Logging Off, and Logging On to, Windows 2000
- Click the Start button and, if there is a Log Off option on the Start menu, click Log Off; otherwise, click Shut Down.
- If you chose the Log Off option, click Yes in the Log Off Windows dialog box. If you chose Shut Down, click the "What do you want the computer to do?" list arrow in the Shut Down Windows dialog box, click the Log off option for your user name, and then click OK.
- After Windows displays the Log On to Windows dialog box, enter your user name and password, and then click the OK button or press Enter.

As noted earlier, if you work on a computer network, it's important to log on to the network under the proper account so you can access the resources you need. Windows 2000 supports different user logons (or accounts) and different user groups. For example, if you are working in a college computer lab, the network administrator may set up your class logon for a Standard User or a Restricted User. Both types of users can use software and create and save documents. A **Standard User** is part of the Power Users Group and can modify computer settings and install software. In contrast, a **Restricted User** is part of the Users Group and cannot install software or change system settings. Finally, an **Administrator** is part of the Administrators group and has complete access to, and control over, all parts of the Windows 2000 system, including creation and management of user accounts and permissions.

Opening a Command Line Session

Next, Isabel shows you and the other workshop participants how to open a command line session under Windows 2000.

There are several ways in which you can start a command line session, or work in a command line environment under Windows 2000. The most common way is to open the Command Prompt window from the Accessories menu. Then, you can work from within a window on the desktop.

To open a command line session:

1. Click the **Start** button, point to **Programs**, point to **Accessories**, and then click **Command Prompt**. Windows 2000 opens a Command Prompt window. See Figure 1-9. Within the Command Prompt window, you first see the name and version of the operating system—in this case, the original version of Windows 2000. As noted earlier, C:\> is called the operating system prompt, or command prompt, and it is your reference point as you work in this command line interface. This command prompt, which used to be known as the **DOS prompt**, is now called the **Windows prompt**. Many people also referred to this prompt as the "C prompt." To the right of the command prompt is a small blinking underscore called a **cursor**. The cursor identifies your current working position on the screen. If you type a character, that character is displayed on the screen where the cursor was positioned. The cursor then appears after the character you typed.

| Figure 1-9 | COMMAND PROMPT WINDOW |

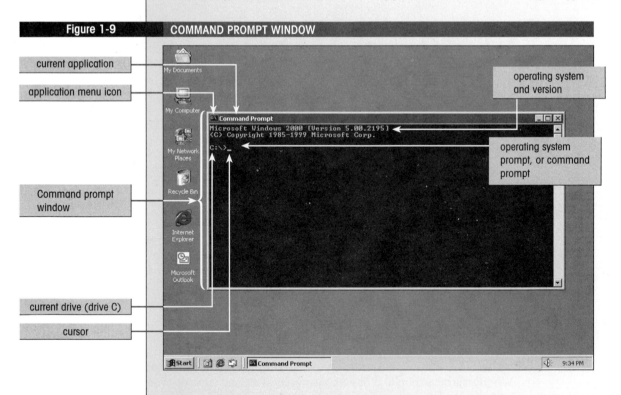

current application

application menu icon

operating system and version

operating system prompt, or command prompt

Command prompt window

current drive (drive C)

cursor

The operating system prompt identifies the default drive and default directory. The **default drive** is the drive currently in use—in this case, drive C (represented by "C" in C:\>). The default drive is important because Windows 2000 automatically checks that drive for the appropriate program file when you issue a command. When working in a command line environment (whether MS-DOS or a

Command Prompt window under Windows 2000), **directory** is the term commonly used to refer to a folder. The **default directory**, represented by the backslash symbol (\ ) in C:\>, is the top-level folder of the drive. This top-level folder is called the **root directory** when working in a command line environment. It's also important to emphasize that the view you see within the Command Prompt window is typical of that found in a command line interface. In contrast to the Windows 2000 graphical user interface, the command line interface is a very simple user interface in which text is displayed in light grey against a black background.

2. While pressing and holding the **Alt** key, press and release the **Enter** key, and then release the **Alt** key. Windows 2000 switches to full-screen view. See Figure 1-10. Certain programs, such as graphics programs, work better in full-screen view than in windowed view, or you might prefer more space on the screen for working in a command line session under Windows 2000. However, if you want to use the Windows 2000 Clipboard to copy information from a DOS program to a Windows 2000 program, or vice versa, you have to work in the windowed view. (The **Clipboard** is an area of memory where Windows 2000 stores data that you want to copy or move.)

| Figure 1-10 | FULL-SCREEN VIEW |

```
Microsoft Windows 2000 [Version 5.00.2195]
(C) Copyright 1985-1999 Microsoft Corp.

C:\>
```

3. Press **Alt+Enter** again to switch back to windowed view. The Alt+Enter shortcut key combination lets you quickly switch from a windowed view to a full-screen view, or vice versa.

4. Keep the Command Prompt window open for the next section.

| REFERENCE | WINDOW | RW |

Opening a Command Line Session
- Click the Start button, point to Programs, point to Accessories, and then click Command Prompt.
- If you want to switch from windowed view to full-screen view (or vice versa), press and hold the Alt key, press and release the Enter key, and then release the Alt key.

After Windows 2000 opens a Command Prompt window, you are working in **MS-DOS mode**—a shell that emulates the MS-DOS operating environment using Windows 2000's MS-DOS subsystem. A **shell** is a program that acts as an intermediary between you and the underlying operating system. It provides an interface that allows you to issue commands or activate functions, and then translates your directives into more basic instructions the computer can carry out. In the MS-DOS command line subsystem, you are communicating with the Windows 2000 operating system underneath. You are not actually working with a version of DOS installed on and directly controlling your computer.

Using Windows 2000 Commands

Before introducing employees to some basic commands, Isabel first describes the two types of commands available for use in a Command Prompt window.

When you open a Command Prompt window, Windows 2000 opens and runs a program called Cmd.exe. The "exe" in the filename is a file extension that identifies the file as an "executable" program file. This type of program is called a **command interpreter**, **command processor**, or **shell**, because it is responsible for displaying the user interface, interpreting commands entered at the command prompt, and locating and loading the program for a specific command.

Once you open a Command Prompt window, you can then enter commands at the command prompt to perform specific operations. These commands used to be called DOS commands, but now they are called Windows 2000 commands. The commands fall into two groups: internal commands and external commands.

The program code for **internal commands** (also called built-in commands) is stored as a set of subprograms within the command interpreter program file, Cmd.exe. These subprograms are used for common types of operations, such as viewing information about files stored on a disk. When you open a command line session, Windows 2000 loads, or copies, Cmd.exe from disk into RAM. Then, Cmd.exe displays a command line user interface with a command prompt. Once Cmd.exe loads into memory, you can access the program code for any of the internal commands it contains. Since the operating system does not have to go back to disk to locate and load the program code for an internal command (it's already in memory), internal commands execute more quickly.

In contrast, the program code for **external commands** (also called utilities) must be located and loaded from disk. The program code for these commands resides in a specific file on disk in the System32 folder, which in turn is below your Windows directory (or folder). Depending on how Windows 2000 was installed on your computer, the Windows directory might be named WINNT, Windows, or perhaps have some other name. When you type an external command at the command prompt, you type the first part of the filename—the part before the file extension—as the actual command. The command interpreter locates the file on disk, and then loads the program into memory so that it can perform its intended function. Since the program code must be located and loaded from disk, external commands are slower.

Customizing the Command Prompt Window

In addition to customizing the Windows 2000 desktop, Isabel explains to you and the other workshop participants that you can also customize a Command Prompt window so the command line environment is easier to use and, at the same time, more interesting.

One simple way to customize the Command Prompt window is to change the title displayed on the title bar. To make this change, you use the TITLE command, which is an internal command. Like every other type of command, the TITLE command has a specific syntax.

Syntax refers to the proper format for entering a command, including how to spell the command, and whether the command uses required or optional parameters. A **parameter** is an item of data used with a command to change the way the command works. The TITLE command has the following syntax:

TITLE string

This command consists of two parts: the command itself (TITLE), and a parameter called a string. A **string** consists of a set of characters that are treated exactly as you enter them. For example, to change the title on the title bar from "Command Prompt" to "DOS Session," you would enter the following command:

TITLE DOS Session

In this example, "DOS Session" is a string that is used as the parameter for the TITLE command. When you enter a command, you can use uppercase, lowercase, or mixed case for the command itself. Windows 2000 will display the string in whatever case you prefer to use. This setting is not permanent. If you exit a Command Prompt window, and then open the Command Prompt window again later, Windows 2000 displays "Command Prompt" on the title bar. The TITLE command is found in Windows 2000 and Windows NT; Windows 95 and Windows 98 do not include this command.

Another way to customize the Command Prompt window is to change the background and foreground colors of the console with the use of the COLOR command—another internal command. The term **console** refers to the video display device—in this case, the monitor. The COLOR command is another command found in Windows 2000 and Windows NT. The syntax for this command is as follows:

COLOR [attribute]

After you enter the command, you specify an optional parameter called an **attribute** that determines the background color of the Command Prompt window and the foreground color of the text within this window. This command does not affect the desktop, only the Command Prompt window. Optional parameters are commonly indicated by including a reference to the parameter (in this example, "attribute") within square brackets. Therefore, you can enter the command with or without the optional parameter. If you enter the command COLOR without the optional parameter, Windows 2000 restores the console to the original colors used when you first opened the Command Prompt window. If you want to change the background and foreground colors in the Command Prompt window, you enter two hexadecimal digits (or values) for the attribute. A **hexadecimal digit** is a value in the hexadecimal, or base 16, numbering system. The values include 0-9 and A-F (for a total of 16 values). Figure 1-11 lists the hexadecimal digits for the background and foreground colors.

| Figure 1-11 | COLOR ATTRIBUTES |

hex digits

0	Black		8	Gray
1	Blue		9	Light Blue
2	Green		A	Light Green
3	Aqua		B	Light Aqua
4	Red		C	Light Red
5	Purple		D	Light Purple
6	Yellow		E	Light Yellow
7	White		F	Bright White

corresponding color

For example, if you want to change the background color to blue and the foreground color to bright white, you would enter the following command:

COLOR 1F

Unlike the TITLE command, the COLOR command uses two parameters instead of one. When you next open a Command Prompt window, Windows 2000 reverts back to the original background color (black) and the original foreground color (light gray).

In the next set of steps, you are going to change the title in the title bar, and change the background and foreground colors of the Command Prompt window.

To customize the Command Prompt window:

1. At the command prompt, type **TITLE DOS Session** and then press **Enter**. The TITLE command changes the title on the title bar to "DOS Session," as shown in Figure 1-12, and then displays another command prompt so you can enter another command. The new title more clearly identifies what you are doing. If you make a typing mistake and notice it before you press the Enter key, you can use the Backspace key to correct the error. When you press the Enter key after entering a command at the command prompt, Windows 2000 locates and executes the instructions for the command. If you type a command and do not press Enter, nothing will happen.

   TROUBLE? If Windows 2000 informs you that the command you entered is not recognized as an internal or external command, operable program, or batch file, then you misspelled the command. Don't worry though; Windows 2000 displays another command prompt so you can try again. Just type the command again with the correct spelling and then press Enter.

Figure 1-12   **CHANGING THE WINDOW TITLE**

new title   command

```
DOS Session                                                    _ □ ✕
Microsoft Windows 2000 [Version 5.00.2195]
(C) Copyright 1985-1999 Microsoft Corp.

C:\>TITLE DOS Session

C:\>
```

string

2. At the command prompt, type **COLOR 1F** (the number "1" followed by an upper-case "F") and then press **Enter**. Windows 2000 changes the background color to dark bright blue and the text color to bright white. See Figure 1-13.

   TROUBLE? If Windows 2000 displays Help information on the use of the Color command, you typed the lowercase letter "l" instead of the number "1". Press the Spacebar to continue (if necessary) and, at the next command prompt, repeat the step.

Figure 1-13   **CHANGING THE BACKGROUND AND FOREGROUND COLORS**

color attributes   command

```
DOS Session
Microsoft Windows 2000 [Version 5.00.2195]
(C) Copyright 1985-1999 Microsoft Corp.

C:\>TITLE DOS Session

C:\>COLOR 1F

C:\>
```

foreground color of text (bright white)

background color (dark blue)

3. Type **COLOR F0** (an "F" followed by a zero) and then press **Enter**. The Color command changes the background to bright white, and the foreground text to black. See Figure 1-14.

Figure 1-14	CHANGING THE BACKGROUND AND FOREGROUND COLORS

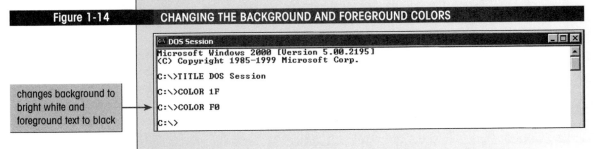

changes background to bright white and foreground text to black

```
DOS Session
Microsoft Windows 2000 [Version 5.00.2195]
(C) Copyright 1985-1999 Microsoft Corp.

C:\>TITLE DOS Session

C:\>COLOR 1F

C:\>COLOR F0

C:\>
```

4. Keep the Command Prompt window open for the next section.

In a Command Prompt window, the default screen colors are hard to read when demonstrating some programs and programming languages. By changing these colors, however, you can make your presentation easier to view.

Displaying the Windows 2000 Version

Isabel reminds you and the other staff members that, if you need to contact Microsoft technical support for assistance with troubleshooting a problem, one of the first questions the technical support representative will ask is what version of Windows you are using on your computer. You should therefore be able to check and verify the Windows version quickly so the technical support representative has an essential piece of information to help identify the source of the problem and find a solution to that problem.

Knowing the version of the operating system used on a computer is useful for several reasons. First, each operating system, and each version of an operating system, has different features and capabilities. If you attempt to perform a certain operation and experience difficulties, you should check the version of the operating system you are using so you can determine whether it contains the feature you want to use.

Second, if you are experiencing difficulties in using a program on your computer system, you should verify that the program is compatible with the specific version of the operating system installed on your computer. Likewise, when you purchase a new software product, the instructions for that new software product may indicate that the product is designed for a specific version of Windows. Before you install the software, you should check the Windows version on your computer to make sure the product will work properly.

If you are working in a Command Prompt window, you can quickly identify the version of Windows used on your computer using the Version (VER) command, which is an internal command.

To check the Windows version:

1. At the command prompt, type **VER** and then press **Enter**. Windows 2000 displays the version number of the operating system used on your computer. See Figure 1-15. This information should match what you see when you first open the Command Prompt window; however, that information may scroll off the screen as you continue to work, so you can always check the version using the Version command. Version 5.00.2195 is the original version of Windows 2000. Your version number may differ. You can also locate this same information by viewing properties of My Computer. Windows 2000 then lists the current version of the operating system on the General property sheet in the System Properties dialog box.

Figure 1-15	CHECKING THE WINDOWS VERSION

```
DOS Session                                                    _ □ ×
Microsoft Windows 2000 [Version 5.00.2195]
(C) Copyright 1985-1999 Microsoft Corp.

C:\>TITLE DOS Session

C:\>COLOR 1F

C:\>COLOR F0

C:\>VER  ◄─────────────────────────────────────────  command

Microsoft Windows 2000 [Version 5.00.2195]  ◄───────  operating system and
                                                       version number
C:\>_
```

2. Keep the Command Prompt window open for the next section.

The Version command provides similar information under different versions of MS-DOS, Windows 95, Windows 98, and Windows NT Workstation 4.0.

Changing the Date and Time

Isabel next illustrates how to check and change the date and time quickly in a Command Prompt window. She emphasizes that the correct date and time are important because Windows 2000 records the date and time with the filename when you save a file. Then, for example, if you have two versions of a document stored in two different files, you can check the date and time saved to each file to determine which file contains the most recent version of that document. Therefore, you want to make sure that any files you create and save have the correct **date stamp** and **time stamp**. If you notice that the date or time is incorrect on your computer, you can use the DATE and TIME commands to change the date or time setting.

The DATE and TIME commands are internal commands, and their syntax is as follows:

DATE [/T | *date*]
TIME [/T | *time*]

The vertical bar (|) in this syntax diagram indicates that you can use one of the two optional parameters, but not both at the same time (they are mutually exclusive). A **Syntax diagram** is notation used in the Help system and computer reference manuals when you are looking up the options for using a command. The two optional parameters are the /T switch and the setting for either the date or the time.

For example, the syntax for the DATE command indicates that you can enter this command in one of three ways:

DATE
DATE /T
DATE *date*

If you just enter the command DATE, this program displays the current date and prompts you for a new date. If you enter the DATE command with the /T switch, this program displays the current date—it does not prompt you for a new date. A **switch** is an optional parameter that changes the way in which a command works.

If you enter the DATE command and include a specific date (such as 9-22-2003), this program will change the date. As shown, when you enter a specific date you use the general format *mm-dd-yy*. Type one or two digits for the month, a dash, one or two digits for the day, a dash, and the last two digits of the year. You can also use four digits for the year.

If you want to change the time setting on your computer, you can enter the command TIME, and wait for the command to prompt you; or you can enter TIME followed by a specific time in the format *hours:minutes:seconds.hundredths* A | P . The "A | P" means that you can specify A for "AM" or "P" for PM, but not both at the same time.

In the next set of steps, you are going to look at different ways to use these commands.

To view and change the date setting on your computer:

1. Type **DATE /T** and then press **Enter**. On the next available line, the DATE command reports the date setting on your computer and also includes the day of the week. See Figure 1-16.

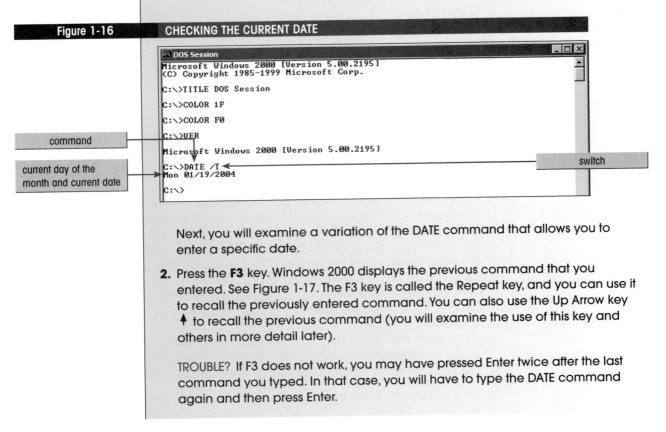

| Figure 1-16 | CHECKING THE CURRENT DATE |

command

current day of the month and current date

switch

Next, you will examine a variation of the DATE command that allows you to enter a specific date.

2. Press the **F3** key. Windows 2000 displays the previous command that you entered. See Figure 1-17. The F3 key is called the Repeat key, and you can use it to recall the previously entered command. You can also use the Up Arrow key ↑ to recall the previous command (you will examine the use of this key and others in more detail later).

TROUBLE? If F3 does not work, you may have pressed Enter twice after the last command you typed. In that case, you will have to type the DATE command again and then press Enter.

Figure 1-17   **RECALLING THE PREVIOUS COMMAND**

```
DOS Session                                                      _ □ ×
Microsoft Windows 2000 [Version 5.00.2195]
(C) Copyright 1985-1999 Microsoft Corp.

C:\>TITLE DOS Session

C:\>COLOR 1F

C:\>COLOR F0

C:\>VER

Microsoft Windows 2000 [Version 5.00.2195]

C:\>DATE /T
Mon 01/19/2004

C:\>DATE /T
```

command recalled with F3

press Backspace to delete this switch

3. Press the **Backspace** key *three* times to delete the /T switch and the space (see Figure 1-18), and then press **Enter**. Again, the DATE command displays the current date, with the day of the week. On the line after the one with the current date, the DATE command displays a prompt for you to enter a new date. See Figure 1-18. The DATE command also shows you the proper format for entering a date—namely, mm-dd-yy.

Figure 1-18   **CHANGING THE DATE**

```
DOS Session - DATE                                              _ □ ×
Microsoft Windows 2000 [Version 5.00.2195]
(C) Copyright 1985-1999 Microsoft Corp.

C:\>TITLE DOS Session

C:\>COLOR 1F

C:\>COLOR F0

C:\>VER

Microsoft Windows 2000 [Version 5.00.2195]

C:\>DATE /T
Mon 01/19/2004

C:\>DATE
The current date is: Mon 01/19/2004
Enter the new date: (mm-dd-yy)
```

edited command

current day with the month, day, and year

prompt to enter a new date

format for entering a new date

4. Type the date of your next birthday. For example, if your next birthday is September 22, 2004, type **9-22-04** and then press **Enter**. Windows 2000 displays a command prompt again. You have just recalled and edited a previously-entered command so you can use it in a different way. Notice that you do not type the day of the week. The operating system has a calendar that determines the day of the week from the date (for example, September 22, 2004 is a Wednesday).

TROUBLE? If you enter the date in the incorrect format, the DATE command will prompt you for the date again.

If you now open a program, and then create and save a file, Windows 2000 would record your birthday as the date the file was saved. That date would be incorrect. Let's change the date back to the current date.

5. Type **DATE**, press the **Spacebar**, type the current date in the format *mm-dd-yy*, and then press **Enter**. Even though it does not show you the change, the DATE command changed the date to the date you specified.

6. Type **TIME /T** and then press **Enter**. Windows 2000 displays the current time on the computer. See Figure 1-19. If the time were incorrect, you could use F3 to recall this command, delete the /T switch, and then enter the correct time.

| Figure 1-19 | CHECKING THE CURRENT TIME |

```
DOS Session                                                    _ □ ×
(C) Copyright 1985-1999 Microsoft Corp.

C:\>TITLE DOS Session

C:\>COLOR 1F

C:\>COLOR F0

C:\>VER

Microsoft Windows 2000 [Version 5.00.2195]

C:\>DATE /T
Mon 01/19/2004

C:\>DATE
The current date is: Mon 01/19/2004
Enter the new date: (mm-dd-yy) 9-22-04

C:\>DATE 04-24-03

C:\>TIME /T
 8:26p

C:\>_
```

command →

current time →

7. Keep the Command Prompt window open for the next section.

| REFERENCE   WINDOW | RW |

Viewing or Changing the Date and Time

■ To view the date used on the computer, type DATE /T and then press Enter.

■ To change the date on the computer, type DATE, press Enter, and when prompted for the new date, enter the date in the format *mm-dd-yy*, and then press Enter. Or, type DATE, press the Spacebar, type the new date in the format *mm-dd-yy*, and press Enter.

■ To view the time on the computer, type TIME /T and then press Enter.

■ To change the time on the computer, type TIME, press Enter, and when prompted for the new time, enter the time in the format *hours:minutes:seconds.hundredths* A I P, and then press Enter. Or, type TIME, press the Spacebar, type the new time in the format *hours:minutes:seconds.hundredths* A I P, and then press Enter.

As noted earlier, if you know in advance what date you want to use, you can type the DATE command followed by the date. For example, if you want to change the date to July 9, 2003, you enter DATE 7-9-03. Windows 2000 will not prompt you for the date and will not show you the date change.

The DATE and TIME commands work in the same way under MS-DOS, Windows 95, Windows 98, and Windows NT Workstation 4.0; however, MS-DOS, Windows 95, and Windows 98 do not have the /T switch.

The date and time stamps are quite important in today's business world, where networked offices are located in different time zones, and the most recent versions of documents that people have worked on at multiple locations need to be determined.

Clearing the Screen

Isabel asks you and the other employees in her workshop to stop for a minute to examine the Command Prompt window. She comments that, by now, the Command Prompt window is cluttered with commands, messages, prompts, and your responses to the prompts, and that you are now entering commands at the bottom of the window.

To clear the window so you can work more easily, you use another internal command, the CLS command (for "Clear Screen").

To clear the window:

1. Type **CLS** and then press the **Enter** key. Windows 2000 clears the window and displays the command prompt and cursor in the upper-left corner of the window. See Figure 1-20. If you were working in full-screen mode, this command would clear the entire screen (not just a window).

Figure 1-20	OUTPUT CLEARED FROM WINDOW

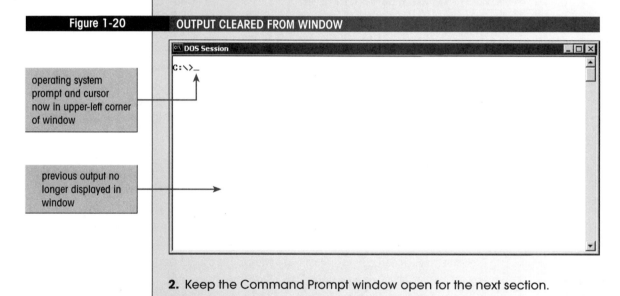

operating system prompt and cursor now in upper-left corner of window

previous output no longer displayed in window

2. Keep the Command Prompt window open for the next section.

The CLS command functions in the same way under MS-DOS, Windows 95, Windows 98, Windows NT Workstation 4.0, and Windows 2000.

Clearing the screen before issuing commands is a good habit to develop because it helps you to focus on one command operation at a time.

Formatting Diskettes

Isabel is now ready to show everyone how to format a diskette in a Command Prompt window.

Most diskettes sold currently are preformatted, and you can use them immediately, without formatting. If you purchase unformatted diskettes, you must format them before the operating system can store files on them. If you find you no longer need the files stored on a diskette, you can reformat the diskette, erasing whatever is stored on it so you can reuse the diskette. Even if you purchase preformatted diskettes, it is a good idea to reformat those diskettes on the computer that contains the operating system you intend to use with those diskettes, because they will last longer. Preformatted diskettes are formatted with an IBM-DOS or MS-DOS utility instead of Windows 2000. This means you might encounter difficulties if you use preformatted diskettes on a computer with Windows 2000, Windows 98, or Windows 95. Certain programs (like backup utilities) may not work with a diskette formatted using another operating system, the diskette may fail far earlier than you would typically expect (especially if you switch back and forth from a computer with Windows 2000 and one with DOS), or Windows 2000 may not be able to work with the diskette at all.

If you reformat preformatted disks, you should perform a full format, not a quick format, of the diskette. A **Quick Format** removes file entries from a diskette without checking it for defects. Also, if you are formatting a brand new (unformatted) diskette, you must perform a **Full Format**, which lays down new tracks and sectors and verifies the integrity of each sector on the diskette by performing a surface scan. When formatting a diskette, the operating system creates concentric recording bands, called **tracks**, around the inner circumference of the disk, as shown in Figure 1-21. Then, the formatting program subdivides each track into equal parts, called **sectors**. Although not all of them are shown in this diagram, there are 80 concentric tracks on a 3½-inch high-density diskette, and each track is divided into 18 sectors. Each sector in turn contains 512 bytes. A **byte** is the storage space required on a disk for one character. Assuming a single-spaced page contains approximately 3,500 bytes of data, then a sector stores approximately one-seventh of a page. If you create a one-page report, the operating system will use approximately seven sectors to record the contents of that document in a file on the diskette.

Figure 1-21	TRACKS AND SECTORS ON A FORMATTED 3½-INCH HIGH-DENSITY DISK

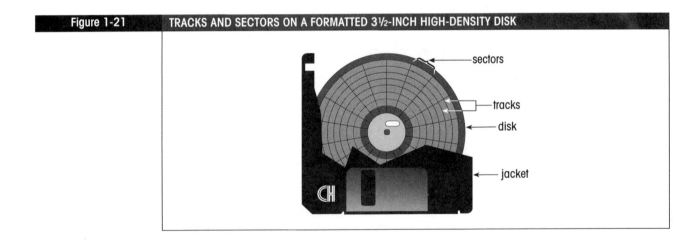

If you want to figure out the total storage capacity of a diskette, you can perform the following computation:

Number of sides formatted × Number of tracks per side × Number of sectors per track × Number of bytes per sector

2 sides × 80 tracks/side × 18 sectors/track × 512 bytes/sector = 1,474,560 bytes (or 1.44 MB)

During the **surface scan**, the operating system or Format utility records "dummy" data to each sector of the disk and reads that data back to verify that the sector supports read and write operations. If it encounters a problem reading or writing to a sector, it marks the cluster that contains that defective sector and does not store data in the defective sector. A **cluster**, or **allocation unit**, consists of one or more sectors of storage space on a disk, and the number of sectors per allocation unit or cluster varies with the type of disk. On a high-density diskette, an allocation unit is the same size as a sector.

To format a diskette, you use the FORMAT command. Although there are many different ways in which you can use this command, the basic syntax is as follows:

FORMAT *volume*

The **volume**, or drive name, is a required parameter or item of information. Therefore, you must specify the name of the disk drive that contains the diskette you want to format. If you use this syntax, you also must use a diskette that has the same storage capacity as the disk drive you are using. For example, if you want to format a diskette in a high-density disk drive, you would use a high-density diskette. If you want to format a double-density diskette (720 K) in a high-density drive, you must use the Format capacity switch (/ F) and specify the number of kilobytes that the disk supports.

The FORMAT command is an external command, so Cmd.exe must locate the program instructions for this command in a file on the disk and then load the program into memory so you can use it.

To complete the next set of steps, you will need either a preformatted or an unformatted high-density diskette. If you use a formatted diskette with files, the FORMAT program will erase all the files from the diskette.

To format a diskette:

1. Insert a high-density diskette into drive A.

2. Type **FORMAT A:** and then press **Enter**. The FORMAT utility prompts you to insert a new diskette in drive A, and then press **Enter** when you are ready. See Figure 1-22.

Figure 1-22	PROMPT TO INSERT DISK TO FORMAT

command

```
DOS Session - FORMAT A:                                              _ □ ×

C:\>FORMAT A:
Insert new disk for drive A:
and press ENTER when ready...
```

required parameter

prompt to insert disk to format

3. Because you have already inserted a diskette, press **Enter**. The FORMAT utility identifies the type of file system used on the disk (always FAT for diskette), it shows you the format capacity (1.44 MB), and it shows the percentage complete. See Figure 1-23. The file system known as FAT is the same as the one used under MS-DOS. The **format capacity** is the storage capacity of the disk once formatted.

Figure 1-23	STATUS OF FORMAT OPERATION

```
DOS Session - FORMAT A:

C:\>FORMAT A:
Insert new disk for drive A:
and press ENTER when ready...
The type of the file system is FAT.
Verifying 1.44M
35 percent completed.
```

type of filing system on disk

format capacity of disk

percentage of format complete

After the format is complete, the FORMAT utility notes that it is initializing the File Allocation Table (FAT), which keeps track of space used on the disk, and then prompts you for a volume label. See Figure 1-24. The **volume label** is an electronic label assigned to the disk. You can use up to 11 characters, including spaces, for the volume label. Certain symbols, such as a period, are not allowed. If you attempt to use an invalid or unacceptable character, the FORMAT utility will inform you of this problem and will prompt you again for the volume label. For the volume label, you typically use a label that identifies the type of files you intend to store on the diskette. If you do not want to use a volume label (it is optional), you just press Enter.

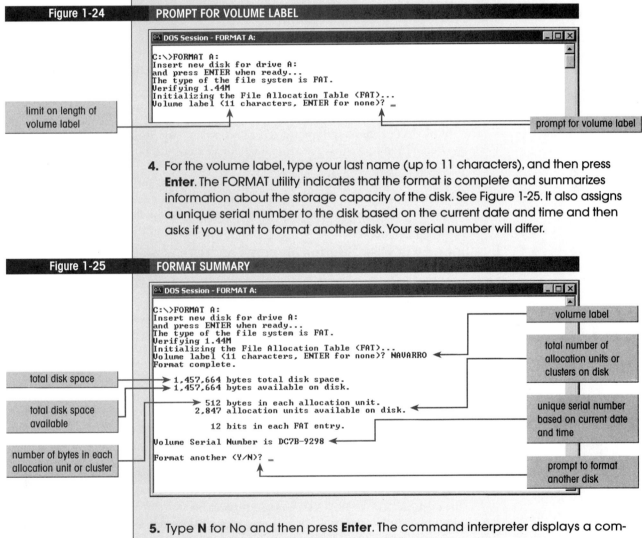

| Figure 1-24 | PROMPT FOR VOLUME LABEL |

limit on length of volume label

prompt for volume label

4. For the volume label, type your last name (up to 11 characters), and then press **Enter**. The FORMAT utility indicates that the format is complete and summarizes information about the storage capacity of the disk. See Figure 1-25. It also assigns a unique serial number to the disk based on the current date and time and then asks if you want to format another disk. Your serial number will differ.

| Figure 1-25 | FORMAT SUMMARY |

volume label

total number of allocation units or clusters on disk

total disk space

total disk space available

unique serial number based on current date and time

number of bytes in each allocation unit or cluster

prompt to format another disk

5. Type **N** for No and then press **Enter**. The command interpreter displays a command prompt.

During the formatting operation, the diskette spins in the disk drive unit at approximately 300 to 360 rpm's (revolutions per minute) and the drive light is on. You should *not* remove a diskette from a disk drive when the drive light is on. When the drive light is off, you can safely remove a diskette and insert another one.

REFERENCE WINDOW   **RW**

Formatting a Diskette
- Click the Start button, point to Programs, point to Accessories, and click Command Prompt.
- Insert an unformatted or preformatted, but blank, diskette into drive A.
- Type FORMAT A: and then press Enter.
- When prompted for a volume label, type a label no longer than 11 characters, and press Enter; if you do not want to assign a volume label to the disk, just press Enter.
- When prompted as to whether you want to format another disk, type N if you do not need to format another disk. If you want to format a set of disks, type Y to repeat the process and format each disk.

The FORMAT command functions in a similar way in MS-DOS, Windows 95, Windows 98, Windows NT Workstation 4.0, and Windows 2000; however, Windows 2000 includes more switches.

It is a good idea to apply exterior labels to your diskettes, and write your name and the diskette's contents on them. This is especially important if you are working in a computer lab, because it's easy to forget to remove your diskette from the drive unit when you leave.

Evaluating the Disk Storage Space Report

Next, Isabel explains the information displayed by the FORMAT utility after it completes the process of formatting a diskette.

The first value listed shows the total amount of storage space on the diskette in bytes. The second value shows how much of this storage space is available for use, again, in bytes. Usually, these two values are identical and indicate that you can use all of the formatted storage space available on the diskette. If these values are different, you will also see a message that indicates the diskette contains a certain number of bytes in bad sectors. Although you can still use the rest of the storage space on the diskette, many people will discard the diskette rather than risk losing valuable data later. Diskettes are invariably certified to be error-free, and if you find that newly formatted diskettes contain bad sectors, you can return them for new ones. The disk drive unit may also be defective. If you format another diskette and if the FORMAT utility does not report any bad sectors for that diskette, the first diskette you formatted was probably defective. If subsequent diskettes you format also are reported to have bad sectors, you might need to have the disk drive replaced.

On the next line, the FORMAT program reports on the size of each allocation unit and the total number of allocation units on the diskette. Although a sector is the basic unit of storage on a diskette, Windows 2000 allocates storage space on a cluster-by-cluster basis rather than a sector-by-sector basis when it records the contents of a file to a disk.

Formatting a diskette is an important operation that ultimately determines how Windows 2000 interacts with the file system on the diskette, how it utilizes the storage space on the diskette, how it opens and retrieves files, and how it saves and writes files to the diskette.

Copying a Diskette

Isabel distributes an extra diskette to each of the individuals in the workshop. She explains that these diskettes contain files that you will use in upcoming sessions, and that each of you should make a copy of the diskette as a precautionary measure.

When you copy a diskette, the operating system makes a sector-by-sector copy of the original diskette, called the **source disk**, and records the exact information onto another diskette, called the **destination disk** or **target disk**. The source and destination disks must be the same size and same storage capacity. If your computer only has one floppy disk drive (which is the case on most computer systems today), you must use the same disk drive for both the source and destination disks, and copy from drive A to drive A. Even if your computer has two floppy disk drives—one for 3½-inch floppy disks and one for 5¼-inch floppy disks (found on much older computer systems)—you *cannot* use one drive for the source disk and the other drive for the destination disk. Likewise, you cannot perform a disk copy from drive C to drive A (or a Zip drive).

Since you typically use the same drive for both the source and destination disks, Windows 2000 asks you for the source disk first, then it copies the contents of the diskette. Next it asks you for the destination disk, and then copies the contents of the source disk onto the destination disk. The disk copy operation replaces any information already stored on the destination disk with the contents of the source disk. After the disk copy is complete, the source and destination disks are identical, except for their serial numbers. To protect your original diskette during the disk copy operation, write-protect it beforehand. When you **write-protect** a diskette, you prevent the operating system or any other program from recording data onto the diskette. Otherwise, if the destination disk is a preformatted diskette, and if you insert the diskettes in the wrong order, you end up with two blank diskettes! After the disk copy operation, you can remove the write-protection from the source disk. To write-protect a 3½-inch high-density disk, use your fingernail to move the plastic write-protect tab in the write-protect notch on the back of the disk so you can see through the write-protect opening. To remove write-protection, reverse this process and cover the rectangular opening in the write-protect notch.

To copy a diskette from the command prompt, use the DISKCOPY program. To familiarize you with how to examine Help information on a command, you will display Help for the DISKCOPY program in the next section.

Using the Help Switch

So that everyone will know how to find information on how to use various Windows 2000 commands, and therefore be able to work independently, Isabel next recommends that each of you view Help information on how to make a copy of a diskette with the DISKCOPY command.

You can use the **Help switch**, (/?), to display Help information for a specific command. The syntax for this switch is as follows:

[*command*] /?

You enter the command followed by /?. Windows 2000 extracts Help information from the command's program itself. The Help switch works with almost all commands.

To obtain Help information on the Diskcopy command:

1. Type **CLS** and then press **Enter**.

2. Type **DISKCOPY /?** and press **Enter**. Windows 2000 displays Help information on the DISKCOPY command. See Figure 1-26.

TROUBLE? If Windows 2000 displays the message "Invalid parameter - \?," then type a backslash (\ ) rather than a slash (/). Repeat this step, but use the slash instead of the backslash for the switch.

Figure 1-26	VIEWING HELP INFORMATION ON DISKCOPY

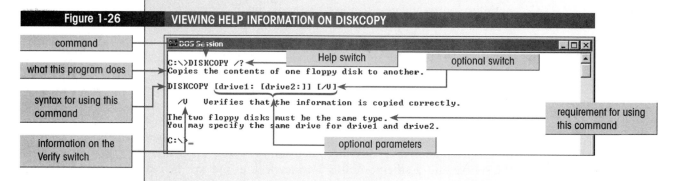

The Help information reminds you that this command copies the contents of one diskette to another (floppy disk). As shown in the Help information for the Diskcopy command, the syntax is as follows:

DISKCOPY *drive 1: drive 2:* [/V]

As noted earlier, the brackets enclose optional parameters. *Drive 1:* is the drive that contains the source disk; *drive 2:* is the drive that contains the destination disk. If you do not specify the source and destination drives (they are optional parameters), then the DISKCOPY utility assumes you want to use the current drive as both the source and the destination. If you specify only *drive 1:*, the Diskcopy command assumes you want to use the same drive for the source and target disks. Because the Diskcopy command requires that both diskettes be the same size and the same storage capacity, you must use the same drive for both the source and target disks, and you *must* switch diskettes during the disk copy operation. If you have two drives of the same size *and* the same storage capacity, you can perform the disk copy using both drives. Insert your source diskette in one drive and your target diskette in the other drive. If you are performing a disk copy from a command prompt on drive C, you have to specify both drives. The Verify switch, /V, verifies that the data is copied correctly to the destination disk. The Help information also informs you that the disks must be the same type.

The Help switch (/?) is available in MS-DOS, Windows 95, Windows 98, Windows NT Workstation 4.0, and Windows 2000.

You are now ready to copy a diskette. To complete the next set of steps, you will need a copy of Data Disk #1 and your newly formatted diskette. Your instructor or technical support staff will provide you with a copy of this diskette, or instruct you how to copy the files for this disk from your computer network to a diskette. You can then use that diskette with the files for Data Disk #1 in these steps. If you have already made a copy of Data Disk #1 using a technique preferred by your instructor and technical support staff, then read, but do not keystroke, the following steps and examine the figures so you are familiar with the use of the procedure for copying a diskette.

Although you will not work with the files on Data Disk #1 until Tutorial 2, you can use that diskette for the following disk copy operation.

To make a copy of a diskette:

1. Make sure the source disk of Data Disk #1 is write-protected.

2. Insert Data Disk #1 into drive A. This is the source disk from which you will make a copy.

3. Type **DISKCOPY A: A:** and then press **Enter**. The DISKCOPY utility prompts you to insert the source disk in drive A (Figure 1-27), which you have already done.

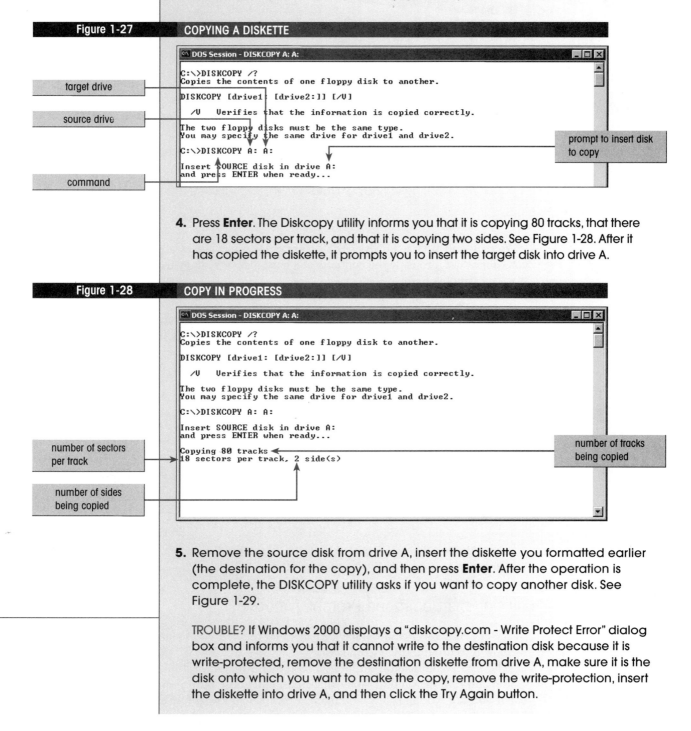

| Figure 1-27 | COPYING A DISKETTE |

4. Press **Enter**. The Diskcopy utility informs you that it is copying 80 tracks, that there are 18 sectors per track, and that it is copying two sides. See Figure 1-28. After it has copied the diskette, it prompts you to insert the target disk into drive A.

| Figure 1-28 | COPY IN PROGRESS |

5. Remove the source disk from drive A, insert the diskette you formatted earlier (the destination for the copy), and then press **Enter**. After the operation is complete, the DISKCOPY utility asks if you want to copy another disk. See Figure 1-29.

TROUBLE? If Windows 2000 displays a "diskcopy.com - Write Protect Error" dialog box and informs you that it cannot write to the destination disk because it is write-protected, remove the destination diskette from drive A, make sure it is the disk onto which you want to make the copy, remove the write-protection, insert the diskette into drive A, and then click the Try Again button.

Figure 1-29   **PROMPT FOR TARGET DISK**

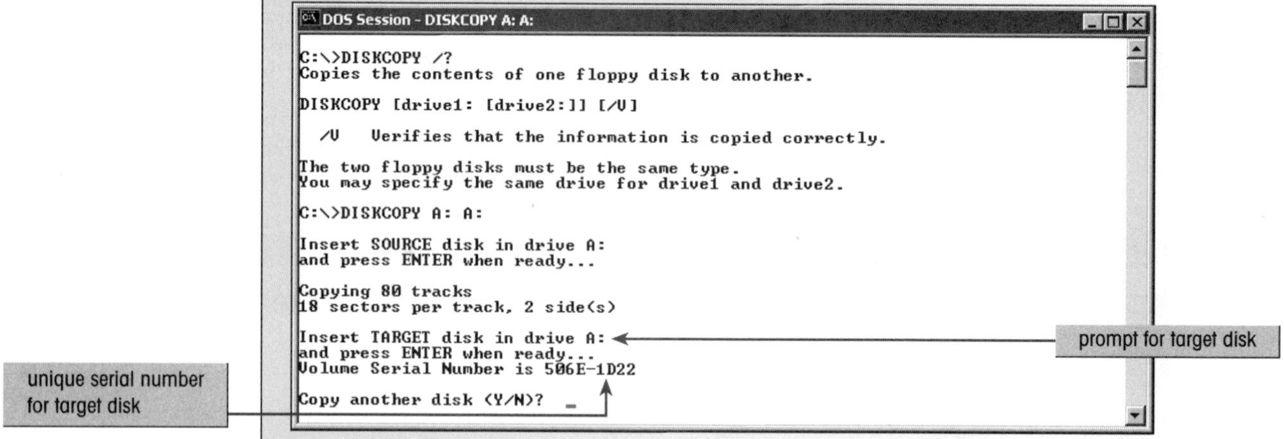

```
DOS Session - DISKCOPY A: A:                                    _ □ ×

C:\>DISKCOPY /?
Copies the contents of one floppy disk to another.

DISKCOPY [drive1: [drive2:]] [/V]

   /V    Verifies that the information is copied correctly.

The two floppy disks must be the same type.
You may specify the same drive for drive1 and drive2.

C:\>DISKCOPY A: A:

Insert SOURCE disk in drive A:
and press ENTER when ready...

Copying 80 tracks
18 sectors per track, 2 side(s)

Insert TARGET disk in drive A: ◄───────────────────    prompt for target disk
and press ENTER when ready...
Volume Serial Number is 506E-1D22

Copy another disk (Y/N)?  _
```

unique serial number
for target disk

6. Type **N** for No, and then press **Enter**. The command interpreter displays a command prompt.

7. Remove your new copy of Data Disk #1 from drive A.

You can only use the DISKCOPY command to make copies of diskettes. As noted earlier, you cannot use it to copy the contents of a hard disk or to copy to a diskette with a different storage capacity or size.

REFERENCE   WINDOW   **RW**

Copying a Diskette
- Click the Start button, point to Programs, point to Accessories, and then click Command Prompt.
- Write-protect the source disk, and then insert the source disk in drive A.
- At the command prompt, type DISKCOPY A: A: and then press Enter.
- When prompted to insert the source disk, press Enter.
- When prompted to insert the target disk, remove the source disk from drive A, insert the target disk, and then press Enter.
- When prompted as to whether you want to copy another diskette, type N and then press Enter if you are finished. If you want to make another copy of the same diskette, type Y and then press Enter.

The DISKCOPY command functions in a similar way in MS-DOS, Windows 95, Windows 98, Windows NT Workstation 4.0, and Windows 2000.

Closing the Command Prompt Window

At the end of the workshop, Isabel explains that the best way to close the Command Prompt window is to use the EXIT command.

The EXIT command is an internal command that closes the program that opened the Command Prompt window. You can also use the Close button on the right side of the title bar if you are working in a Command Prompt window (but obviously not in full-screen mode because there is no window). If you use the Close button to close the window, and if Windows 2000 displays an End Program dialog box and reports that it cannot end a program that is still active, you should click the Cancel button, close the program, and then type the EXIT command to close the Command Prompt window. You can also close the Command Prompt window by clicking the program menu icon on the left side of the title bar and then clicking Close.

Your instructor and technical support staff will explain the procedure for using the computers in your computer lab. Some computer labs require you to log off the computer you are using so the next person who uses that same computer is not logged on under your account (and therefore unable to access their class files). Other computer labs do not have a logon procedure, and therefore prefer that you not attempt to log off, restart, or shut down the computer. If you do not know what your computer lab procedures are, ask the technical support staff in your computer lab.

To close the Command Prompt window and log off your computer:

1. Type **EXIT** and then press **Enter**. Windows 2000 closes the Command Prompt window.

2. If your computer lab requires that you log off or restart the computer once you finish your work, click the **Start** button, click **Shut Down**, and if you do not see the Log off option in the "What do you want the computer to do?" list box in the Shut Down Windows dialog box, click the list arrow for this list box, click the **Log off** or **Restart** option, and then click **OK**.

You can also use the EXIT command to close an MS-DOS Prompt window in Windows 95, Windows 98, and Windows NT Workstation 4.0.

Before you return to your offices, Isabel emphasizes that operating system software is an indispensable component of a computer system. Although DOS was the predominant operating system software used on PCs until 1995, businesses and individuals now rely on the Windows 95, Windows NT Workstation 4.0, Windows 98, and Windows 2000 operating systems. Even so, DOS skills, concepts, features, and techniques are still important for understanding how Windows 2000 works and for evaluating and troubleshooting problems with a computer system.

Session 1.2 QUICK CHECK

1. The _____ is the drive that is currently in use, and that is identified in the command prompt.

2. When working in a command line environment, a(n) _____ is the term commonly used to refer to a folder.

3. The top-level folder is called the _____ when working in a command line environment.

4. Cmd.exe is an example of a type of program that is referred to as a(n) _____ .

5. The program code, or routine, for _____ commands is stored within the program file Cmd.exe.

6. The program code for _____ commands resides in a specific file on disk.

7. _____ refers to the proper format for entering a command, including how to spell the command, and whether the command uses required or optional parameters.

8. A(n) _____ is an optional parameter that changes the way in which a command works.

9. A(n) _____ is an electronic label assigned to a disk.

10. In a Command Prompt window, you can use the _____ key to repeat or recall the previous command.

COMMAND REFERENCE

COMMAND	USE	BASIC SYNTAX	EXAMPLE
/?	Displays Help information on the use of an internal or external command	*command* /?	FORMAT /?
CLS	Clears the window or screen of previously displayed output	CLS	CLS
COLOR	Sets the background and foreground colors of a Command Prompt window	COLOR [*attribute*]	COLOR F0
DATE	Displays or changes the system date	DATE [/T | *date*]	DATE /T DATE 7-21-03
DISKCOPY	Copies the contents of a source disk to a destination disk	DISKCOPY *drive1: drive2:*	DISKCOPY A: A:
EXIT	Closes a Command Prompt window	EXIT	EXIT
FORMAT	Formats a disk for use with Windows 2000	FORMAT *volume*	FORMAT A:
TIME	Displays or sets the system time	TIME [/T | *time*]	TIME /T TIME 10:30 a TIME 4:30 p
TITLE	Displays a title on the title bar of the Command Prompt window	TITLE *string*	TITLE DOS Session
VER	Displays the Windows 2000 version	VER	VER

Items shown in italics and *not* enclosed within square brackets are required parameters. See Format command.

Items shown in italics and enclosed within square brackets are optional parameters. See Color command.

Items separated by a vertical bar (|) are mutually exclusive; you can use one or the other, but not both at the same time. See Date and Time commands.

REVIEW ASSIGNMENT

As part of its community outreach, SolarWinds participates in a student enrichment program with its local community college. Isabel and her staff hire students as interns so the students can gain valuable on-the-job experience that can be applied toward their degrees. During this next college session, Isabel hires Angelina Barrett, a student in the Computer Sciences department at the community college. Although Angelina is familiar with the basics of using Windows 2000, she is not familiar with working in a command line environment. Isabel asks you to work with Angelina to show her how to use basic internal and external Windows 2000 commands.

As you perform the following steps, record your answers to any questions so you can submit them to your instructor.

1. After you log on to your computer, open a Command Prompt window using the Start menu.

2. Change from a windowed view to a full-screen view. How did you perform this operation?

3. What is the default drive and directory (or folder) used by Windows 2000? How did you obtain this information?

4. What version of Windows 2000 is used on your computer? Use the Version command to verify that this is the correct version. What command did you use to perform this operation? Is this command an internal or external command?

5. Clear the screen. What command did you use?

6. At the command prompt, type COLOR 31 and then press Enter. What is the background color? What is the foreground color of the text?

7. At the command prompt, type COLOR 9F and then press Enter. What is the background color? What is the foreground color of the text? How does this combination of colors differ from the previous set of colors?

8. At the command prompt, type COLOR and then press Enter. What happens?

9. Clear the screen.

10. Type DATE /T and then press Enter. What is the current day of the week? What is the current date?

11. Type TIME /T and then press Enter. What is the current time?

12. Name two reasons why it is important to make sure that the date and time are set correctly on your computer.

13. Insert an unformatted, or blank, diskette into drive A. *Note*: You can use the same diskette you used in the tutorial.

14. Clear the screen, maximize the Command Prompt window, and display Help on the FORMAT command. What command did you use to display the Help information?

15. What does the /V:*label* switch do?

16. At the command prompt, type FORMAT A: /V: and immediately after /V:, type your last name (no more than 11 characters), and then press Enter. When prompted to insert the diskette, press Enter again. What format capacity is the Format utility using for the diskette? When prompted as to whether you want to format another diskette, type N (for No) and then press Enter.

17. Why didn't the FORMAT utility ask you for a volume label?

18. Use the Help switch to display Help information on the VOL command. What does this command do? What is the syntax of this command?

19. Type VOL A: and then press Enter. What information does Volume provide you?

20. Remove the diskette that you just formatted from drive A.

21. Obtain a copy of Data Disk #1, make sure this diskette is write-protected, and then insert it into drive A.

22. Display Help information on the DISKCOPY command. What does the /V switch do?

23. At the command prompt, type DISKCOPY A: A: /V and then press Enter. When prompted for the source disk, press Enter again. How many tracks is the DISKCOPY command copying? How many sectors are there per track? How many sides is it copying?

24. When prompted for the target disk, remove the copy of Data Disk #1 from drive A, insert the diskette you just formatted, and then press Enter. This step takes more time. What additional operation occurs during this phase?

25. When prompted as to whether you want to copy another diskette, type N (for No) and then press Enter. Remove your disk from drive A.

26. Type EXIT and then press Enter. What happens?

CASE PROBLEMS

Case 1. Customizing the Command Prompt Window at The Perfect Match The Perfect Match is an employment agency that specializes in temporary assignments for individuals with computer skills. One of their employees, Corey Tanner, recently decided to supplement his retirement income with part-time, temporary work. Many years ago, Corey worked on IBM PCs that used the MS-DOS operating system. Recently, he started a temporary assignment at the employment agency itself. While talking with one of the company's other employees, he learns that it is possible to customize the Command Prompt window with the COLOR command. Because he prefers to use a command line environment whenever possible, he decides to use part of his lunch break to experiment with the COLOR command. He asks you to show him how to use it.

As you perform the following steps, record your answers to any questions so you can submit them to your instructor.

1. Open a Command Prompt window and maximize the window.

2. Display Help information on the COLOR command.

3. What is the primary function of the COLOR command?

4. What is the syntax of the COLOR command? Does it use any optional or required parameters? Explain.

5. How many colors are available for the background and foreground colors?

6. Try the following combinations of background and foreground colors. Also, note the command that you used for each color combination.

   - Background = Blue, Foreground = Bright White
   - Background = Red, Foreground = Bright White
   - Background = Light Yellow, Foreground = Black
   - Background = Light Purple, Foreground = Bright White
   - Background = Light Aqua, Foreground = Black
   - Default background

7. Which of the above color combinations do you prefer, and why? Were there any other color combinations that you tried which you preferred over the ones in the previous step? What were they?

8. Restore the original background and foreground colors. How did you perform this operation?

9. Is there any way in which you might find this feature useful? Explain.

Case 2. *Formatting Diskettes at Fast Track Trainers* Fast Track Trainers provides contract training in the use of Microsoft Excel 2000 for its corporate customers in St. Paul, Minnesota. Samantha Kuehl, Fast Track Trainer's lead training specialist, works with you to prepare diskettes that contain copies of Excel 2000 files for employees to use during the hands-on workshops. To speed up the process of preparing these training diskettes, Samantha recommends you use the FORMAT and DISKCOPY commands in a Command Prompt window.

As you perform the following steps, record your answers to any questions so you can submit them to your instructor.

1. Open the Command Prompt window and then maximize the window.

2. Display Help information on the FORMAT command. Although there are five different approaches you can use for the syntax of the FORMAT command, which is the one required parameter for each of these approaches?

3. If Samantha wanted each of the student training diskettes to contain the volume label "Fast Track," would it be possible to add that volume label during the formatting process without being prompted for the information? If so, how would she specify that label when she used the FORMAT command?

4. If Samantha needed to format double-density diskettes that have a format capacity of 720K, what switch would she need to use with the FORMAT command? What command would she enter?

5. After returning from a workshop, what FORMAT switch could you use to reformat the diskettes quickly and erase the information contained on the diskettes? What command would you specify to perform this operation?

6. Perform a Quick Format of your diskette to test this use of the FORMAT command.

7. Are there any safety precautions you might want to keep in mind when using the FORMAT command? Explain.

8. Is there any way in which you might find this feature useful in your line of work? Explain.

Case 3. *Assigning Volume Labels at HiPerform Systems* HiPerform Systems is a small business that sells computer systems and hard disk drives, and also troubleshoots hard disk problems for its customers in Ipswich, Massachusetts. James Everett, the owner of HiPerform Systems, employs high-school students as technical support staff during the summer. As they customize or troubleshoot computers for their customers, they assign volume labels to newly-formatted hard disk drives or to drives that they restore. Because James Everett and his staff typically work in a command line environment as they are troubleshooting, restoring, and building systems, they use Windows 2000 commands for assigning labels to disks. As a way of thanking their customers for their business, they also provide them with a diskette that contains some useful command line utilities. James asks you to become more familiar with the use of the FORMAT, VOLUME, and LABEL commands so you can prepare these customer diskettes quickly.

As you perform the following steps, record your answers to any questions so you can submit them to your instructor.

1. Open the Command Prompt window, and maximize the window.

2. Display Help on the FORMAT command. What command did you enter?

3. Using this Help information, can you perform a Quick Format of a diskette and also assign a volume label to the diskette at the same time (without being prompted for it during the formatting operation)? If so, how would you perform this operation?

4. To test your answer to the previous question, perform a Quick Format on an unformatted or blank diskette and assign the volume label HPS to the disk. What command did you enter?

5. Display Help information on the VOL command. What does the Volume command do?

6. Using this Help information, check the volume label of the diskette you just formatted. What command did you enter? What volume label is assigned to the diskette?

7. Use the Volume command to view the label assigned to drive C. What command did you enter? What is the volume label (if any)?

8. Display Help information on the LABEL command. What does this command do?

9. Use the LABEL command to change the volume label on your disk to HiPerform. (*Note*: Make sure you do not change the volume label of drive C.) What command did you enter?

10. Use the Volume command to verify that the Label utility changed the volume name. Is the volume label different in any way from what you specified in the previous step? Explain.

11. Is there any way in which you might find these features useful in your line of work (or play)? Explain.

Case 4. Changing the Time at Turing Enterprises   Melissa Turing operates a small independent business called Turing Enterprises that specializes in planning outings, camping adventures, whitewater rafting, hang gliding, travel tours, and other outdoor adventures for women in her local area. She uses her home computer for her customer mailing list, her schedule of events, business contacts, and the financial records for her business. She has observed that the time on her computer system gradually falls behind the actual time, and has to correct it periodically.

As you perform the following steps, record your answers to any questions so you can submit them to your instructor.

1. Open the Command Prompt window and then maximize the window.

2. Display Help information on the DATE command. What command can you enter to display the current date setting without displaying a prompt for a new date?

3. Check the current date on your computer. If the date were incorrect, how would you change it?

4. If you wanted to change the date on your computer to July 21, 2003, how would you do it?

5. Display Help information on the TIME command. What command can you enter to display the current time without displaying a prompt for a new time?

6. Check the current time on your computer. If the time were incorrect, how would you change it?

7. If you wanted to advance the time by 15 minutes from 9:00 am to 9:15 am to get an early start on keeping appointments, how would you do it?

8. If the time on your computer was set for 10:30 am, but it was actually 10:30 pm, how would you change the time?

9. Enter the commands TIME /T and TIME at the command prompt, and compare the differences. Why might you prefer to use the /T switch?

10. Is there any way in which you might find these features useful in your line of work (or play)? Explain.

QUICK | CHECK ANSWERS

Session 1.1

1. operating system
2. booting
3. utilities
4. command line, command prompt
5. dual-boot
6. full path
7. backward compatibility
8. virtual DOS machine *or* VDM
9. text mode
10. command

Session 1.2

1. current drive *or* default drive
2. directory
3. root directory
4. command interpreter
5. internal
6. external
7. syntax
8. switch
9. volume label
10. F3

In this tutorial you will:

- Display a directory listing of filenames on the default drive and other drives

- Use switches with the Directory command to control scrolling, arrange files in alphabetical order, and produce a wide directory listing

- Display files by name, extension, size, and date and time

- Examine the use of long and short filenames

- Display files by attributes, date stamps, and short filenames

- Use wildcards to select groups of files

- Combine wildcards and switches

- Examine the Windows environment

- Specify default switches for the Directory command

DISPLAYING DIRECTORIES

Streamlining the Process for Locating Files at SolarWinds, Unlimited

SolarWinds Unlimited

One of your job responsibilities, as Isabel's assistant, is to keep an updated copy of all template files used by the staff to prepare documents. **Templates** are files that contain the general format, or layout, of a document, and may also contain data, such as text or formulas, commonly found in a specific type of document. In the case of SolarWinds Unlimited, these templates contain the company logo and specific document formats that provide consistency in preparing various types of documents for the company.

Although you are familiar with Windows, you have little experience with DOS. Because DOS skills are crucial to providing staff support, Isabel's first task is to show you how to work with the Directory command (DIR) under the Windows 2000 command prompt.

She points out that you might also need to use the command line environment to obtain information about files unavailable in the graphical user interface, such as type extensions for certain types of files.

In this section of the tutorial, you will examine the concept and use of the command history, and learn how to display files in a directory (or folder). You will use the most common switch options of the DIR command, including options for displaying an alphabetical list of filenames. You will also examine the component parts of a filename.

SESSION 2.1

In this session you will display directory listings on different drives, use switches with the Directory command to control scrolling, arrange files in alphabetical order, and produce a wide directory listing. You also will display files by name, extension, size, and date and time; examine the use of long and short filenames; and display files by attributes, date stamps, and short filenames.

Using the Command History

After showing you how to use the F3 function key to recall a command, Isabel explains that, although this key is useful, it allows you to recall only the last command you entered. When you open a Command Prompt window, however, the command processor automatically incorporates features of a program called DOSKEY to make it easier to recall and, if necessary, modify commands you've already entered. The command processor keeps track of the last 50 commands entered at the command prompt and stores them in an area of memory known as the **command history** (or **command stack**). You can recall commands from the command history and edit those commands. When the command history fills up, the command processor eliminates the oldest commands so it has room for the new commands you enter.

Using these features, you can recall commands stored in the command history. If you want to recall the previous command, press the Up Arrow key ♦. Each time you press ♦, you move back one step in the command history and retrieve and display the previous command. If you press the Down Arrow key ♦, you advance to the next command in the command history following the one currently displayed. You can also use the Page Up key to recall the oldest command in the command history and Page Down to recall the most recently issued command.

You can also edit the current command line so you do not need to enter it again from scratch, and you can recall and edit previously entered commands. Use the Left Arrow ◄ and Right Arrow ► keys to move the cursor one character to the left or right on the command line so you can position the cursor at the point where you want to insert, edit, or replace text. Pressing the Home key will move the cursor to the beginning of the command line, and pressing the End key will move the cursor to the end of the command line.

By default, the command processor operates in **insert mode**. If you position the cursor anywhere on the command line and then start typing, it inserts the text you type. If you want to switch from insert mode to **overtype mode** so you can replace text by typing over the text, press the Insert key. After making changes, press the Insert key to switch back to insert mode. The Insert key is a **toggle key**—a key that alternates between two related uses each time you press it.

The F7 function key displays a list of commands from the command history in a pop-up box. You can then use the Up Arrow and Down Arrow keys to select the command you want. To execute the selected command, just press the Enter key.

Under MS-DOS, Windows 95, and Windows 98, one had to enter the command DOSKEY to access these features. In the Windows 2000 Command Prompt window, they are always available. Using DOSKEY, you can create macros that perform command operations. A **macro** is a user-defined program often used to automate routine procedures by storing commands for an operation or set of operations.

Displaying a Directory Listing

Isabel explains to you that the Directory (DIR) command is an internal command that displays information about files stored on disk, and that it is therefore an important tool for tracking the contents of a disk. You will rely on the Directory command, as well as other utilities that operate on files to maintain and update template files. Isabel provides you with a copy of a diskette containing the company's template files. She asks you to examine the files using the Directory command and become familiar with the contents of the disk.

Listing a Directory on the Default Drive

The Directory command shows you a directory listing of the drive you specify. If you do not specify a drive name, the Directory command will refer to the **default drive** shown in the command prompt and display the directory listing for that drive. Many Windows 2000 commands operate in the same way, using the default drive and directory if you don't specify otherwise.

To view the root directory of drive C:

1. Open the Command Prompt window.

2. Type **color f0** (an "F" followed by a zero) and then press **Enter**. The COLOR command changes the background of the window to bright white and the text to black. Note that you can type a command line in lowercase when convenient. From now on, all instructions steps will be in lower-case.

   TROUBLE? If you see help text for the COLOR command beginning with "Sets the default console foreground and background colors," you may have typed the letter "o" instead of a zero (0). Press a key to view the remainder of the Help display, if necessary. Then, retype the command in this step.

3. Type **dir** and then press **Enter**. The Directory command displays a **directory listing** containing information on the subdirectories and files in the root directory on drive C. See Figure 2-1. A **directory**, or folder, acts as a container for files and other directories. The **root directory** is the top-level folder on drive C. When drive C was originally formatted, the operating system or a formatting utility created the first directory on that drive—the top-level folder, or root directory—as the primary container for the drive's files and directories. Because you did not specify a drive, DIR assumes you want to view a directory listing of the current drive (drive C) and the current directory (the root directory). On the computer used in this figure, it appears as though there are no files in the root directory of drive C— only subdirectories of the root directory. A subdirectory (also known as a subfolder) is a directory that is contained within, and subordinate to, another directory. After you examine a directory listing of your diskette in the next section, you'll examine the parts of a directory listing in more detail. Because different systems are configured differently and contain different types of installed software, your directory listing for the root directory will differ from that shown in the figure and might appear in alphabetical order.

| Figure 2-1 | DIRECTORY LISTING OF DRIVE C ROOT DIRECTORY |

```
Command Prompt                                              _ □ ×

Microsoft Windows 2000 [Version 5.00.2195]
(C) Copyright 1985-1999 Microsoft Corp.

C:\>color f0 ◄

C:\>dir
 Volume in drive C is WIN2000 ◄
 Volume Serial Number is BC31-588C

 Directory of C:\

02/28/2003  01:33p    <DIR>          WINNT
02/28/2003  01:36p    <DIR>          Documents and Settings
02/28/2003  01:37p    <DIR>          Program Files

              0 File(s)              0 bytes
              3 Dir(s)   1,007,897,600 bytes free

C:\>_
```

Directory command →
drive and directory name →
directory markers →

← change window to black on white
← volume label
← unique serial number
← directory listing

REFERENCE WINDOW   **RW**

<u>Listing a Directory on the Default Drive</u>
- Click the Start button, point to Programs, point to Accessories, and then click Command Prompt.
- In the Command Prompt window, type DIR and then press Enter.

If your directory listing contains more directory and file names than the Directory command can list in the window, Windows 2000 adjusts the window view through a process called **scrolling**. By default, the Command Prompt window displays only 25 lines at one time. Once Windows 2000 scrolls through the first part of the directory listing, a partial directory remains in the window. DIR lists the files in **disk order**—the order in which the system keeps track of files.

Listing a Directory on Another Drive

If you want to view the contents of a directory on another drive, you must specify the name of the drive when you use the Directory command. The syntax is as follows:

DIR [*drive name*]

As noted in Tutorial 1, the square brackets indicate that the drive name is an optional parameter. In the next set of steps, you are going to examine the Data Disk you created in Tutorial 1. If you reused that disk and erased its contents, you will need to make another copy of Data Disk #1. If necessary, refer to the instructions in Tutorial 1.

To view a directory listing of the drive that contains your diskette:

1. Insert your copy of Data Disk #1 into drive A.

2. Type **dir**, press **Spacebar**, type **a:** (the name of the drive), and then press **Enter**. Make sure you leave a space between the DIR command and the drive name. Also, remember to type the colon (:) after the drive letter. The Directory command displays a directory listing of your Data Disk. See Figure 2-2.

TROUBLE? If Windows displays "'DIRA:' is not recognized as an internal or external command, operable program or batch file," you did not include a space between **DIR** and **A:**. Retype the command, making sure to include the space.

TROUBLE? If you see the heading "Directory of C:\," and the message "File Not Found," you did not type the colon (**:**) after the drive letter A. In this case, the Directory command assumed you wanted to view information on a file named "A". The Directory command needs the colon to distinguish a drive letter from a file name. Press ↑ to recall the command, and then add the colon to the end of the line.

Figure 2-2	PARTIAL VIEW OF A DIRECTORY LISTING

file times

file dates

file sizes

filenames and extensions

```
Command Prompt
02/27/2002   08:53p        34,304 3 Year Sales Projection.xls
11/20/2003   08:55a        25,088 Projected Growth Memo.doc
08/08/2003   04:12p        20,480 Proposal.doc
03/27/2003   11:19a        22,028 Sales.wk4
10/31/2003   03:33p        14,848 Savings Plan.xls
09/23/2003   01:12p        14,848 Loan Payment Analysis.xls
09/23/2003   01:12p        31,232 Fonts.xls
06/26/2003   10:24a        53,248 Hardware.ppt
06/26/2003   09:30a        52,736 Application Software.ppt
06/26/2003   10:40a        42,496 Software.ppt
06/26/2003   10:55a        41,984 Using the Mouse.ppt
08/08/2003   03:22p        26,624 Formatting Features.xls
07/22/2003   01:32p        20,992 Format Code Colors.xls
07/09/2003   09:42a        49,152 Addressing Cells.xls
10/16/2003   10:31a        84,534 Colors of the Rainbow.bmp
10/16/2003   09:52a        84,446 Color Palette.bmp
10/16/2003   10:15a        17,910 Palette #1.bmp
10/16/2003   10:21a        17,910 Palette #2.bmp
01/24/2003   08:45a        18,944 Balance Sheet.xls
01/02/2003   03:43p        26,624 Sales Projections.xls
04/09/2003   02:12p        21,504 Employees.xls
              41 File(s)    1,248,070 bytes
               0 Dir(s)       207,872 bytes free
C:\>
```

partial directory

number of files on the diskette

available storage

storage space used by files

<u>Listing a Directory on Another Drive</u>
- Open a Command Prompt window, if necessary.
- In the Command Prompt window, type DIR, press the Spacebar, type the drive name, and then press Enter.

When you specify a drive name as part of a command, you are instructing the command to use that drive instead of the default drive. For some commands, such as the Directory command, the drive name is an optional parameter; for other commands, such as the Format command, it is a required parameter.

Changing the Default Drive

If you intend to perform many different operations from the same drive, it is easier to change the default drive to that drive. To change drives, specify the new drive by entering a command that identifies the device name of the drive.

To change the default drive:

1. Type **a:** and then press **Enter**. Windows 2000 updates the command prompt to show you the current drive. Drive A is now the default drive.

2. Type **dir** and then press **Enter**. The DIR command displays a directory listing of your diskette, but you did not need to specify the drive name this time. Instead, DIR uses the current drive specified in the command prompt.

REFERENCE   WINDOW   **RW**

Changing the Default Drive
- Open a Command Prompt window, if necessary.
- In the Command Prompt window, type the name of the drive (with the colon), and then press Enter.

If you need to refer to the current drive in a command, you do not need to type the drive name. This feature simplifies the process of entering commands.

Parts of a Directory Listing

By default, the Directory command's directory listing contains five columns of information. If you're already familiar with MS-DOS, you'll find that Windows 2000 provides a new layout.

- **File date** The first column shows a date for each file. See Figure 2-2. By default, the Directory command displays the date the file was last modified. For example, "Sales Projections.xls", the next to last file, was last saved on 01/02/2003. Each time you save a file to disk, Windows 2000 records the current date with the filename. (*Note*: Data Disk files may display a future date if you are using this book soon after its publication.)

- **File time** The second column shows the time for each file, again set for the time when the file was last modified. For example, "Sales Projections.xls" was last saved at 3:43 p.m. Windows 2000 also records the time with the filename when you save a file to disk. When you create a new file, Windows 2000 separately records the file's creation date and time. It also records the date a file was most recently accessed.

- **Directory marker** The third column identifies subdirectories (or subfolders) within the current directory by displaying the directory marker <DIR>. Earlier, when you viewed a directory of drive C (shown in Figure 2-1), the Directory command identified subdirectories with the use of this directory marker. You'll work with directories in Tutorial 4. If your diskette contains no directories, you'll see an empty column.

- **File size** The fourth column lists the size of each file in bytes (or characters). For example, "Sales Projections.xls" is 26,624 bytes in size. A **byte** is the amount of storage space one character requires on disk. When it displays file sizes, DIR uses commas to offset every three places to the left of the decimal point. DIR does not display the size of directories.

■ **Long filename** The fifth column shows long filenames for files created under windows, or short filenames given to files created under MS-DOS or by the Windows operating system. Like Windows 95, Windows 98, and Windows NT Workstation 4.0, Windows 2000 supports the use and display of long filenames up to 255 characters in length. The Directory command displays file extensions, even if Windows 2000 does not display them in My Computer, Windows Explorer, or in the Open and Save As dialog boxes. A filename typically has two parts—the main part of the filename, and a file extension separated by the last period (.) in the filename (in UNIX, long filenames may contain multiple periods). The **file extension** identifies the type of information in a file. Although file extensions usually are three characters in length, they can be shorter (such as "ra") or longer (such as "html"). Windows programs typically assign extensions to their data files automatically, so you rarely have to include a file extension with a filename. By default, Windows 2000 does not display file extensions in My Computer, Windows Explorer, Open, or Save As, but displays a file type icon determined by the hidden extension. See Figures 2-3 and 2-4 for a list of common extensions used for data and program files. Although it is possible for a directory or folder to have a file extension, the vast majority of directory or folder names do not have a file extension.

Figure 2-3	FILE EXTENSIONS, PART 1		
FILE EXTENSION	**FILE TYPE**	**FILE EXTENSION**	**FILE TYPE**
386	Virtual Device Driver (Windows 3.x)	DER	Security Certificate
ACA & ACF	Microsoft Agent Character File (HTTP)	DIR	Macromedia Director Movie
ACG	Microsoft Agent Preview File	DLL	Dynamic Link Library (Application Extension)
ACS	Microsoft Agent Character File	DOC	Microsoft Word
ACW	Microsoft Accessibility Wizard	DOCHTML	Microsoft Word HTML Document
AIF, AIFC, & AIFF	Audio Interchange File Format	DOS	DOS Configuration File
AIFC	AIF Compressed	DOT	Microsoft Word Template
ANI	Animated Cursor	DOTHTML	Microsoft Word HTML Template
ART	ART Image	DQY	ODBC Query File
ASC	ASCII (DOS, DOS Text, Text, or Print File)	DRV	Device Driver
ASF	Active Streaming Format File	DUN	Dial-Up Networking
ASX	Active Streaming Format Metafile	EML	EMail (Outlook Express Mail Message)
AU	Audio (Sound Clip)	EPS	Encapsulated Postscript
AVI	Audio Video Interleaved	EXE	Executable (Application)
BAK	Backup	FAV	Outlook Bar Shortcuts
BAT	Batch (User-Defined Program)	FMT	Format (Lotus 1-2-3, dBASE)
BKF	Microsoft Backup File	FND	Saved Search
BIN	Binary	FON	Font File

Figure 2-3	FILE EXTENSIONS, PART 1, CONTINUED		
FILE EXTENSION	**FILE TYPE**	**FILE EXTENSION**	**FILE TYPE**
BMP	Windows Bitmap Graphics	GIF	Graphics Interchange Format
CAB	Cabinet (Compressed Program)	GRA	Microsoft Graph 2000 Chart
CAT	Security Catalog	GRP	Group (Microsoft Program Group)
CCC	Microsoft Chat Conversation	HLP	Help
CDA	CD Audio Track	HT	HyperTerminal
CDF	Channel Definition File	HTM & HTML	Hypertext Markup Language
CER	Security Certificate	HTT	HyperText Template
CFG	Configuration	ICO	Icon
CHK	Check Disk & Recovered File Fragments	IDX	Index (Database)
CHM	Compiled HTML	III	Intel IPhone Compatible
CIL	Clip Gallery Download Package	INF	Setup Information
CLP	Clipboard Clip	INI	Initialization (Configuration Settings)
CNF	SpeedDial Conferencing	INS	Internet Communication Settings
CNT	Contents (Help)	IQY	Microsoft Excel Web Query File
COM	Command (DOS Program)	ISP	Internet Communication Settings (Internet Signup)
COV	Fax Coverpage File	ITS	Internet Document Set
CPD & CPE	Cover Page Editor Document (FAX)	IVF	Indeo Video File
CPI	Code Page Information	JPG, JPEG, JPE	Joint Photographic Experts Group
CPL	Control Panel Extension	JFIF	JPEG File Interchange Format
CRL	Certificate Revocation List	JS	JScript Script File
CRT	Security Certificate	JSE	Jscript Encoded Script File
CSS	Cascading Style Sheet	KBD	Keyboard
CSV	Comma Separated Values (Text)	LEX	Lexicon
CUR	Cursor (Static)	LNK	Link (Shortcut)
DAT	Database	LOG	Log
DBF	Database (dBASE)	LSF	Streaming Audio/Video
DCX	DCX Image Document	LSX	Streaming Audio/Video Shortcut
DIB	Windows Device Independent Bitmap	LWV	Microsoft Linguistically Enhanced Sound
DIF	Data Interchange Format		

Figure 2-4	FILE EXTENSIONS, PART 2

FILE EXTENSION	FILE TYPE	FILE EXTENSION	FILE TYPE
M1V	Movie Clip	SND	AU Format Sound
MDA	Microsoft Access Add-In	SPC	PKCS #7 Certificates
MDB	Microsoft Access Database	SST	Microsoft Serialized Certificate Store
MDW	Microsoft Access Workgroup Information	STL	Certificate Trust List
MHT & MHTML	Microsoft MHTML	SYS	System
MID & MIDI	Musical Instrument Device Interface (Sound)	TGA	Targa (Graphics)
MOV	Quick Time Movie	TIF & TIFF	Tagged Image File Format (Graphics)
MP2 & MP2V	Movie Clip	TMP	Temporary File
MPA	Movie Clip	TTC	TrueType Collection Font
MPEG or MPE	Moving Pictures Experts Group	TTF	TrueType Font
MPV2	Movie Clip	TXT	Text
MSC	Microsoft Common Console Document	UDL	Microsoft Data Link
MSG	Message (Outlook Express Item)	ULS	Internet Location Service
MSI	Microsoft Installer (Windows Installer Package)	URL	Uniform Resource Locator (Internet Shortcut)
MSP	Microsoft Patch (Windows Installer Patch)	VBE	VBScript Encoded Script File
NFO	MSInfo.Document (System Information)	VBS	VBScript Script File
NLU	Norton AntiVirus LiveUpdate	VCF	vCard File
NMW	NetMeeting Whiteboard	VIR	Virus Infected File
NWS	Outlook Express News Message	WAB	Address Book File
OFT	Outlook Item Template	VXD	Virtual Device Driver
OQY	Microsoft Excel OLAP Query File	WAV	Wave Sound
OSS	Office Search	WAX	Windows Media Audio Shortcut
OTF	OpenType Font	WB1	Quattro Pro for Windows 5.0
P12	Personal Information Exchange	WBK	Microsoft Word Backup Document
P7B & P7R	PKCS #7 Certificates	WDB	Microsoft Works Database
P7C	Digital ID File	WHT	Microsoft NetMeeting Old Whiteboard
P7S	PKCS #7 Signature	WIF	WIF Image Document
PBK	Dial-Up Phonebook	WIZ	Microsoft Word Wizard
PCD	Photo CD Image	WK1, WK3, WK4	Lotus 1-2-3
PCX	Picture Exchange (PC Paintbrush Graphics)	WKS	Lotus 1-2-3 & MS Works Spreadsheets
PDF	Portable Document Format (Acrobat)	WLG	Dr. Watson Log File

Figure 2-4	FILE EXTENSIONS, PART 2, CONTINUED		
FILE EXTENSION	**FILE TYPE**	**FILE EXTENSION**	**FILE TYPE**
PFM	Type 1 Font	WM	Streaming Audio/Video
PFX	Personal Information Exchange	WMA	Windows Media Audio
PIF	Program Information File (DOS Shortcut)	WMF	Windows Metafiles
PMA, PMC, PML, PMR, & PMW	Performance Monitor File	WMV	Windows Media Audio/Video
PNG	Portable Network Graphics	WPD	WordPerfect Document
PPT	Microsoft PowerPoint Presentation	WPS	Microsoft Works Word Processing
PRF	PICSRules File	WQ1, WQ2	Quattro Pro
PRN	DOS Print File	WRI	Windows 3.x Write
PSS	System Configuration Utility Backup (for System Files)	WSF	Windows Script File
PWL	Password List	WSH	Windows Script Host Settings File
QDS	Directory Query	WVX	Windows Media Audio/Video Shortcut
QIC	Backup File for MS Backup Quarter Inch Cartridge	XBM	X Bitmap
QT	Quick Time (Video Clip)	XLA	Microsoft Excel Add-In
RA, RAM, & RM	Real Audio, or RealMedia File (Sound)	XLB	Microsoft Excel Worksheet
RAT	Rating System File	XLC	Microsoft Excel Chart
REG	Registration	XLD	Microsoft Excel DialogSheet
RLE	Run Length Encoded (Compressed Bitmap)	XLK	Microsoft Excel Backup File
RMI	MIDI Sequence	XLM	Microsoft Excel 4.0 Macro
RQY	Microsoft Excel OLE DB Query	XLS	Microsoft Excel Worksheet
RTF	Rich Text Format (Formatted)	XLSHTML	Microsoft Excel HTML Document
SAM	Ami & AmiPro	XLT	Microsoft Excel Template
SCP	Dial-Up Networking Script	XLTHTML	Microsoft Excel HTML Template
SCR	Screen Saver	XLV	Microsoft Excel VBA Module
SCT	Windows Script Component	XLW	Microsoft Excel Workspace
SET	Settings (File Set for Microsoft Backup)	XNK	Exchange Shortcut
SHB	Shortcut into a Document	XSL	XSL Stylesheet
SHS	Scrap	ZAP	Software Installation Settings
SLK	SLK Data Import Format	ZIP	Zip (Compressed)

Below the directory listing, the Directory command shows the total number of files and the total disk storage space used by those files. This disk has a total of 41 files, which use 1,248,070 bytes of space. A total of 207,872 free bytes of space remain on the diskette. If your diskette has bad, or defective, sectors, the total space left on your disk will be less.

Displaying Help on DIR Command Switches

So you can gain necessary skills for troubleshooting problems within the command line environment, Isabel suggests you become familiar with the different ways in which you can use the Directory command to view information about files on a diskette. Because there are many different switches available for this command, you can use the Help switch to find out which ones meet your needs in a given situation.

To view Help information on the DIR command:

1. At the command prompt, type **dir /?** and then press **Enter**. Windows 2000 displays the first window of Help information on this internal command. See Figure 2-5. At the top of the window, the Help information tells you that this command displays a list of files and subdirectories in a directory. It follows this information with the syntax of the command and then a list of DIR command line switches. You will examine the most commonly used switches in this section of the tutorial, and more advanced switches in the second half of the tutorial.

| Figure 2-5 | DIRECTORY COMMAND HELP DISPLAY, PART I |

directory Help switch

partial Help display

pause prompt

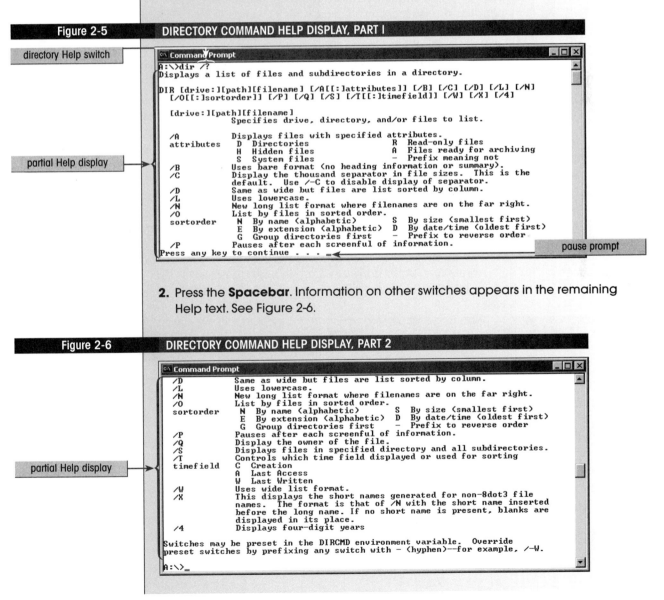

2. Press the **Spacebar**. Information on other switches appears in the remaining Help text. See Figure 2-6.

| Figure 2-6 | DIRECTORY COMMAND HELP DISPLAY, PART 2 |

partial Help display

REFERENCE   WINDOW   **RW**

<u>Displaying Help on Directory Command Switches</u>
- Open a Command Prompt window, if necessary.
- In the Command Prompt window, type DIR /? and then press Enter.
- Press the Spacebar to view the remaining Help text, and then return to the command prompt.

The Help switch provides valuable information about the variety of switches you can use with the DIR command. You'll find it especially useful when you need a quick reminder about how to use particular switches.

Pausing a Directory Listing

If the directory listing you are viewing with the Directory command contains information on more files than the Directory command can display in the window, Windows 2000 will scroll the directory listing. If you want to control this scrolling, you can use one of the Directory command's switches. The **Pause switch (/P)** modifies the Directory command so DIR displays a directory listing one full window or screen at a time, pausing to give you a chance to read the information in the window. The Pause switch is also referred to as the Page switch, because it outputs pages one window or screen at a time.

Let's try the Pause switch.

To view a directory listing one full window at a time:

1. Type **dir /p** and then press **Enter**. DIR displays the first full window, which contains part of the directory listing. See Figure 2-7. At the top of the window, the DIR command displays the volume label. If you did not assign a volume name to the diskette when you formatted it, DIR will tell you that the volume in the drive has no label. In this figure, DIR also shows the serial number assigned to the diskette. On the third line, DIR informs you that you are seeing a directory listing for a specific disk drive. At the bottom of this window, DIR displays a prompt to press any key to continue. Certain keys do not work, such as Caps Lock, Shift, Ctrl, Alt, Scroll Lock, Pause/Break, and Print Screen.

Figure 2-7   **DIR PAUSES AFTER DISPLAYING THE FIRST SCREEN OF THE DIRECTORY LISTING**

```
Command Prompt - dir /p                                     _ □ ×
Volume in drive A has no label.
Volume Serial Number is F065-B557

Directory of A:\

11/05/2003   04:22p              24,064 File0000.chk
11/05/2003   02:35p              10,258 ~WRC0070.tmp
09/05/2003   02:25p              13,824 Commission on Sales.xls
03/21/2003   08:08a              15,872 Client Invoices.xls
11/17/2003   04:41p              15,872 Weekly Worklog.xls
10/29/2003   10:30a              74,024 Invoice Form.wk4
05/07/2003   09:48a              15,872 Software Quotes.xls
05/30/2003   11:22a              22,016 Andre's Employee Payroll.xls
07/01/2003   08:31p              15,360 Daily Sales.xls
01/23/2003   09:21a              78,848 2002 Sales Summary #2.xls
04/18/2003   01:33p              16,896 Advertising Income.xls
01/08/2003   02:06p              24,064 Break Even Analysis.xls
01/23/2003   08:16a              41,472 2002 Sales Summary #1.xls
01/10/2003   10:54a              22,016 Data Systems Budget.xls
01/16/2003   10:46a              20,992 Five Year Growth Plan.xls
01/15/2003   02:21p              17,408 Five Year Plan Template.xls
03/28/2003   04:41p              22,528 Product List.xls
01/03/2003   12:02p              27,648 Product Sales Projection.xls
10/22/2003   01:52p              23,040 Regional Sales Projections.xls
Press any key to continue . . .
```

partial directory

pause prompt

2. Press a key, such as the **Spacebar** or any other key to continue. DIR displays the remainder of the directory listing. See Figure 2-8.

Figure 2-8

DIR DISPLAYS THE NEXT, AND LAST, SCREEN OF THE DIRECTORY LISTING

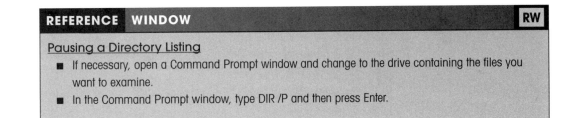

```
Command Prompt                                              _ □ ×
02/27/2002    08:53p          34,304 3 Year Sales Projection.xls
11/20/2003    08:55a          25,088 Projected Growth Memo.doc
08/08/2003    04:12p          20,480 Proposal.doc
03/27/2003    11:19a          22,028 Sales.wk4
10/31/2003    03:33p          14,848 Savings Plan.xls
09/23/2003    01:12p          14,848 Loan Payment Analysis.xls
09/23/2003    01:12p          31,232 Fonts.xls
06/26/2003    10:24a          53,248 Hardware.ppt
06/26/2003    09:30a          52,736 Application Software.ppt
06/26/2003    10:40a          42,496 Software.ppt
06/26/2003    10:55a          41,984 Using the Mouse.ppt
08/08/2003    03:22p          26,624 Formatting Features.xls
07/22/2003    01:32p          20,992 Format Code Colors.xls
07/09/2003    09:42a          49,152 Addressing Cells.xls
10/16/2003    10:31a          84,534 Colors of the Rainbow.bmp
10/16/2003    09:52a          84,446 Color Palette.bmp
10/16/2003    10:15a          17,910 Palette #1.bmp
10/16/2003    10:21a          17,910 Palette #2.bmp
01/24/2003    08:45a          18,944 Balance Sheet.xls
01/02/2003    03:43p          26,624 Sales Projections.xls
04/09/2003    02:12p          21,504 Employees.xls
              41 File(s)   1,248,070 bytes
               0 Dir(s)       207,872 bytes free

A:\>
```

partial directory

REFERENCE   WINDOW   **RW**

Pausing a Directory Listing
- If necessary, open a Command Prompt window and change to the drive containing the files you want to examine.
- In the Command Prompt window, type DIR /P and then press Enter.

The Pause (or Page) switch is the most commonly used switch for the DIR command, because directories often contain more files than will fit in the available window space. You can use this switch for the Directory command in all versions of Windows and DOS.

Viewing a Wide Directory Listing

If you want to view more filenames within the available window, you can use another command line switch. The **Wide switch** (**/W**) displays filenames in columns across the width of the window, and thus enables you to view more filenames at once. Although this switch displays the full filename with a period separating the main part of the filename from the file extension, it does not show the file size, date, and time. The number of columns the Wide switch displays depends on the length of the longest filenames. If the directory folder contains a very long filename, the switch will be unable to display the names side by side and you will still just see them in a single column.

Let's view a directory listing using the Wide switch. Remember that you can recall the last command you entered. Then you can **edit**, or modify, the command so it uses a different switch.

To view a wide directory listing:

1. Type **cls** and then press **Enter** to clear the window of the last directory listing.

2. Press the **↑** until you recall "dir /p." Press **Backspace** until you delete the "p." Then type **w** (the command should read "dir /w"). Now press **Enter**. DIR produces a directory listing that includes all of the files on your diskette in the window. See Figure 2-9.

Figure 2-9 | **DIR DISPLAYS A WIDE DIRECTORY LISTING IN MULTIPLE COLUMNS**

first column / second column

partial wide directory

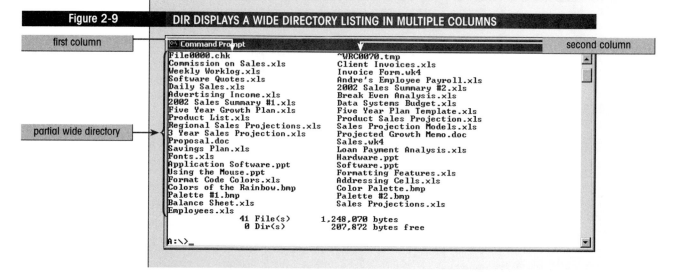

```
File0000.chk                    ~WRC0070.tmp
Commission on Sales.xls         Client Invoices.xls
Weekly Worklog.xls              Invoice Form.wk4
Software Quotes.xls             Andre's Employee Payroll.xls
Daily Sales.xls                 2002 Sales Summary #2.xls
Advertising Income.xls          Break Even Analysis.xls
2002 Sales Summary #1.xls       Data Systems Budget.xls
Five Year Growth Plan.xls       Five Year Plan Template.xls
Product List.xls                Product Sales Projection.xls
Regional Sales Projections.xls  Sales Projection Models.xls
3 Year Sales Projection.xls     Projected Growth Memo.doc
Proposal.doc                    Sales.wk4
Savings Plan.xls                Loan Payment Analysis.xls
Fonts.xls                       Hardware.ppt
Application Software.ppt        Software.ppt
Using the Mouse.ppt             Formatting Features.xls
Format Code Colors.xls          Addressing Cells.xls
Colors of the Rainbow.bmp       Color Palette.bmp
Palette #1.bmp                  Palette #2.bmp
Balance Sheet.xls               Sales Projections.xls
Employees.xls
              41 File(s)     1,248,070 bytes
               0 Dir(s)        207,872 bytes free

A:\>_
```

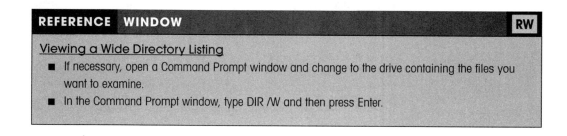

REFERENCE WINDOW   **RW**

Viewing a Wide Directory Listing

■ If necessary, open a Command Prompt window and change to the drive containing the files you want to examine.

■ In the Command Prompt window, type DIR /W and then press Enter.

You can also use the **Down** switch (**/D**) to view filenames in columns. It works just like the /W switch, except that the /D switch arranges filenames vertically instead of horizontally. When the /W switch displays filenames, it displays each filename in sequence "across," meaning on the same line as the previous name (in disk order, unless you specify sorting). When /W reaches the right side of the window, it displays the next name at the beginning of the following line on the left side. The /D switch, on the other hand, displays the next filename "down" instead of "across"—it puts the next name below the previous one in the same column and produces the same number of columns the /W switch would. By default, both /W and /D display filenames in disk order.

You'll find the **/D** switch of DIR in Windows 2000 and Windows NT, but not Windows 98 or Windows 95. You can use the /W switch in all versions of Windows and DOS.

Sorting Directory Listings

Next, you want to verify that the diskette includes a certain file containing a template for a balance sheet. Because DIR does not always display the directory listing in an order that makes it easy to find a file, you can use the **Order switch** (**/O**) to display filenames in alphabetical order. You can also combine this switch with the Pause switch to view one full window at a time.

To display the directory listing in alphabetical order by file-name, one full window at a time:

1. Type **dir /p /o** (making sure you type the letter "o" and not a zero for the Order switch) and then press **Enter**. DIR displays the first full window of filenames in alphabetical order. See Figure 2-10. The ninth file, "**Balance Sheet.xls**," is the one you need. Note that the title bar displays your command during execution, until it finishes and another command prompt appears.

   TROUBLE? If Windows 2000 displays the error message "Invalid switch - "0"," you may have typed the numeral zero (0) instead of the letter o. Recall the command, and change the zero to the letter o.

Figure 2-10	DIR DISPLAYS THE DIRECTORY LISTING IN ALPHABETICAL ORDER BY FILENAME

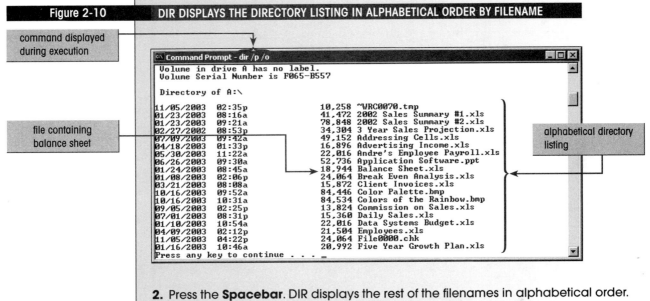

command displayed during execution

file containing balance sheet

alphabetical directory listing

```
Command Prompt - dir /p /o
 Volume in drive A has no label.
 Volume Serial Number is F065-B557

 Directory of A:\

11/05/2003  02:35p            10,258 ~WRC0070.tmp
01/23/2003  08:16a            41,472 2002 Sales Summary #1.xls
01/23/2003  09:21a            78,848 2002 Sales Summary #2.xls
02/27/2002  08:53p            34,304 3 Year Sales Projection.xls
07/09/2003  09:42a            49,152 Addressing Cells.xls
04/18/2003  01:33p            16,896 Advertising Income.xls
05/30/2003  11:22a            22,016 Andre's Employee Payroll.xls
06/26/2003  09:30a            52,736 Application Software.ppt
01/24/2003  08:45a            18,944 Balance Sheet.xls
01/08/2003  02:06p            24,064 Break Even Analysis.xls
03/21/2003  08:08a            15,872 Client Invoices.xls
10/16/2003  09:52a            84,446 Color Palette.bmp
10/16/2003  10:31a            84,534 Colors of the Rainbow.bmp
09/05/2003  02:25p            13,824 Commission on Sales.xls
07/01/2003  08:31p            15,360 Daily Sales.xls
01/10/2003  10:54a            22,016 Data Systems Budget.xls
04/09/2003  02:12p            21,504 Employees.xls
11/05/2003  04:22p            24,064 File0000.chk
01/16/2003  10:46a            20,992 Five Year Growth Plan.xls
Press any key to continue . . . _
```

2. Press the **Spacebar**. DIR displays the rest of the filenames in alphabetical order. Windows 2000 then displays the command prompt.

3. Close the Command Prompt window.

You'll find the Order switch in all versions of Windows and all versions of DOS after DOS 5.0.

REFERENCE WINDOW   **RW**

Displaying a Directory Listing in Alphabetical Order

- If necessary, open a Command Prompt window and change to the drive containing the files you want to examine.
- Type DIR /P /O and then press Enter to display a list of files in alphabetical order by directory and filename, one full window at a time.

The Page, Wide, and Order switches are the most commonly used and handiest switches for the Directory command.

Now that you have used the DIR command and some of its most basic switches, in the next session you will learn additional ways in which to use the DIR command.

Session 2.1 QUICK CHECK

1. Windows 2000 keeps track of the last 50 commands you enter at the command prompt in an area of memory known as the _____.

2. To alternate between inserting and replacing text as you type, use the _____ key.

3. If you do not specify a drive name, the Directory command will refer to the _____ drive shown in the Command Prompt window and display the directory listing for that drive.

4. If your directory listing contains more directory and file names than the Directory command can list in the window, Windows 2000 adjusts the window view through a process called _____.

5. By default, DIR lists the files in _____ —which is the order in which the system keeps track of the files.

6. The _____ identifies the type of information in a file.

7. To modify the Directory command so DIR displays a directory listing one full window at a time, use the _____ switch.

8. To display filenames in columns across the window, and therefore enable you to view more filenames at once, use the _____ switch.

9. What alternative to the above switch can you use, which arranges filenames vertically instead of horizontally?

10. To display filenames in alphabetical order, use the _____ switch.

SESSION 2.2

In this session you will use advanced DIR command line switches, such as adding sort order parameters to the /order switch. You will specify file characteristics normally concealed from view, including five file attributes and short filenames, as well as switches that change the appearance of the DIR display. You will use wildcards with switches, examine the Windows environment, and specify default switches for the Directory command.

Using Advanced Command Line Switches

As you work with the files on the templates disk, Isabel mentions to you that the Directory command has more advanced switches that are helpful in certain situations. Furthermore, some of the switches used with the Directory command have additional parameters that further enhance their usefulness.

Using Sort Order Parameters

You can use sort order parameters with the Order switch to view a directory listing in order by filename, file extension, size, and date and time. The sort order parameters are one-character codes you add to the Order switch, as shown in Figure 2-11. For example, if you want to sort a directory listing by file size, you would use the Size (**S**) sort order parameter in one of two ways:

```
DIR /O:S
DIR /OS
```

Although the syntax for the Directory command indicates that you should use a colon after the Order switch and before the sort order parameter, this command still works properly if you do not include the colon.

Figure 2-11	SORT ORDER PARAMETERS FOR THE ORDER SWITCH
SORT ORDER PARAMETERS	**DISPLAYS FILENAMES IN ORDER BY**
/OE or /O:E	File extension only
/OEN or /O:EN	File extension, then by main part of filename
/OD or /O:D	File date and time
/OS or /O:S	File size
/ON or /O:N	Main part of filename only
/O or /ONE or /O:NE	By main part of filename and then by file extension

You can also reverse the sort order by placing a minus sign (-) in front of the sort order parameter. For example, if you wanted to display filenames in reverse order by file size, you would use the Sort order parameter in one of the following two ways:

DIR /O:-S
DIR /O-S

Isabel recommends you try several of these sort order parameters so you become familiar with their use. So you know what types of files are contained on this templates disk, use the **Extension (E)** sort order parameter with the Order switch. You can also combine this switch with the Page switch to control scrolling in the Command Prompt window.

You can also combine sort order parameters with the Order switch. For example, if you want to display filenames in order by file extension first, then by filename, use the following command:

DIR /OEN

In the above command, /OEN means "in order, by extension, then by name."

To view a directory listing in alphabetical order by file extension:

1. Make sure your copy of Data Disk #1 is in drive A, open a Command Prompt window, change the foreground and background colors if necessary, change to drive A, and then clear the window.

2. Type **dir /p /oe** and then press **Enter**. The Directory command displays filenames in order by file extension, and pauses after the first full window. See Figure 2-12. The first four files have the same file extension, "bmp," which indicates they are bitmap image files produced with a graphics program like Paint. The next file has the file extension "chk," which means it is a Recovered File Fragment created by the Check Disk (CHKDSK) utility program, and then the next two files have the file extension "doc," which stands for "Document." Microsoft Word adds the file extension "doc" to files that you create in it, so these are Word files. Even though the filenames are arranged in order by file extension, note that files with the same file extension are not arranged alphabetically by the main part of the filename. For example, the Directory command lists "Palette #2.bmp" before "Palette #1.bmp."

Figure 2-12 | **DIRECTORY LISTING IN ALPHABETICAL ORDER BY FILE EXTENSION**

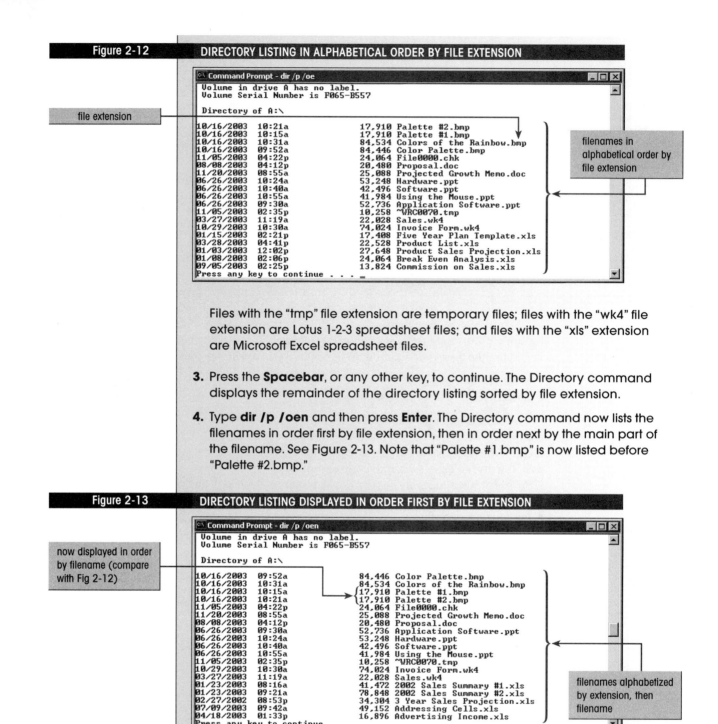

file extension

filenames in alphabetical order by file extension

Files with the "tmp" file extension are temporary files; files with the "wk4" file extension are Lotus 1-2-3 spreadsheet files; and files with the "xls" extension are Microsoft Excel spreadsheet files.

3. Press the **Spacebar**, or any other key, to continue. The Directory command displays the remainder of the directory listing sorted by file extension.

4. Type **dir /p /oen** and then press **Enter**. The Directory command now lists the filenames in order first by file extension, then in order next by the main part of the filename. See Figure 2-13. Note that "Palette #1.bmp" is now listed before "Palette #2.bmp."

Figure 2-13 | **DIRECTORY LISTING DISPLAYED IN ORDER FIRST BY FILE EXTENSION**

now displayed in order by filename (compare with Fig 2-12)

filenames alphabetized by extension, then filename

5. Press the **Spacebar**, or any other key, to continue. The Directory command displays the remainder of the directory listing sorted by file extension and then the main part of the filename.

REFERENCE   WINDOW   RW

Displaying a Directory Listing in Alphabetical Order by File Extension
- If necessary, open a Command Prompt window and change to the drive containing the files you want to examine.
- Type DIR /P /OE and then press Enter to display a list of files in alphabetical order by file extension, one full window at a time.
- Type DIR /P /OEN and then press the Enter key to display a list of files in alphabetical order by file extension first, then by the main part of the filename second, one full window at a time.

If you need to locate important files you created or modified on a certain date, you can do so quickly by using the **Date (D)** sort order parameter. When you use this sort order parameter, the Directory command lists the files in order by date, from the file with the oldest date to the most recently created file. Because you more often than not will need to locate files on which you have recently worked, you can reverse this order by placing a minus sign in front of the Date sort order parameter. DIR then lists the files in reverse order by date, with the most recently created files listed first.

To view a directory listing by file date from the most recent date:

1. Type **dir /p /o-d** and then press **Enter**. Make sure you do not include a blank space between the /o and -d. The Directory command displays filenames in order from the most recent file dates to the oldest file date. See Figure 2-14.

| Figure 2-14 | DIRECTORY LISTING IN REVERSE ORDER BY FILE DATE AND TIME |

```
Command Prompt - dir /p /o-d                                    _ □ X
    Volume in drive A has no label.
    Volume Serial Number is F065-B557

    Directory of A:\

12/10/2003   11:30a          24,064 Sales Projection Models.xls
11/20/2003   08:55a          25,088 Projected Growth Memo.doc
11/17/2003   04:41p          15,872 Weekly Worklog.xls
11/05/2003   04:22p          24,064 File0000.chk
11/05/2003   02:35p          10,258 ~WRC0070.tmp
10/31/2003   03:33p          14,848 Savings Plan.xls
10/29/2003   10:30a          74,024 Invoice Form.wk4
10/22/2003   01:52p          23,040 Regional Sales Projections.xls
10/16/2003   10:31a          84,534 Colors of the Rainbow.bmp
10/16/2003   10:21a          17,910 Palette #2.bmp
10/16/2003   10:15a          17,910 Palette #1.bmp
10/16/2003   09:52a          84,446 Color Palette.bmp
09/23/2003   01:12p          31,232 Fonts.xls
09/23/2003   01:12p          14,848 Loan Payment Analysis.xls
09/05/2003   02:25p          13,824 Commission on Sales.xls
08/08/2003   04:12p          20,480 Proposal.doc
08/08/2003   03:22p          26,624 Formatting Features.xls
07/22/2003   01:32p          20,992 Format Code Colors.xls
07/09/2003   09:42a          49,152 Addressing Cells.xls
Press any key to continue . . .
```

decreasing date order →

← decreasing time order for the same date

2. Press the **Spacebar** to display the remainder of the directory listing. Files with the oldest file dates are listed last in the directory listing.

REFERENCE   WINDOW   **RW**

Displaying a Directory Listing in Order by File Date

- If necessary, open a Command Prompt window and change to the drive containing the files you want to examine.
- Type DIR /P /OD and then press Enter to display files in order by file date (from the oldest file to the most recent file), one full window at a time.
- Type DIR /P /O-D and then press the Enter key to display files in reverse order by file date (from the most recent file to the oldest file), one full window at a time.

You can use the Directory command to check file sizes periodically to determine how efficiently you are using storage space on a disk. If you use the **Size (S)** sort order parameter, the Directory command will list files from the smallest to the largest, or you can use the minus sign to reverse the order and list files from the largest to the smallest. Because large files have the greatest impact on the availability of disk space, you are most likely to list those files first.

To view a directory listing in reverse order by file size:

1. Type **dir /p /o-s** and then press **Enter**. DIR displays the first full window of directory information. The files are listed in reverse order by file size, starting with the largest file on the diskette. See Figure 2-15.

| Figure 2-15 | DIRECTORY LISTING IN REVERSE ORDER BY FILE SIZE |

2. Press the **Spacebar** to display the remainder of the directory listing. The last files in the directory listing are the smallest files on the diskette.

Displaying a Directory Listing in Order by File Size
- If necessary, open a Command Prompt window and change to the drive containing the files you want to examine.
- Type DIR /P /OS and then press Enter to display files in order by file size (from the smallest to the largest file), one full window at a time.
- Type DIR /P /O-S and then press Enter to display files in reverse order by file size (from the largest to the smallest file), one full window at a time.

By using this last option, you can quickly locate the largest files in the first window and decide whether to archive these files. When you **archive** a file, you copy a file you no longer use (but want to keep) from your hard disk to some type of storage medium, such as a recordable CD, DVD, tape, Zip disk or perhaps even a diskette, so you still have a copy of the file, but it is not taking up valuable storage space on your hard disk.

Displaying Short Filenames

As noted earlier, if you use programs designed for Windows 2000, Windows 98, Windows NT Workstation 4.0, or Windows 95, you can use long filenames with up to 255 characters to more clearly identify the contents and purpose of a file. You can also include special symbols or characters, such as the ampersand (&), pound sign (#), dollar sign ($), percent symbol (%), apostrophes (' or '), as well as opening and closing parentheses and spaces. You can also assign long filenames to folders so you can clearly identify the types of files stored within those folders.

If you assign a long filename to a folder or file, all of these versions of Windows also automatically create a short filename for the file to provide compatibility with older programs designed to run under DOS and Windows 3.x (such as Windows 3.1 and 3.11). A **short filename** is an MS-DOS filename (also called an **MS-DOS-Readable filename** or an **alias**) that follows the rules and conventions for 8.3 filenames (that is, names that allow 8 characters and then a 3-character extension). These types of filenames are also referred to as 8dot3 filenames.

When Windows 2000 creates a short filename, it uses the first six characters of the long filename, and then follows this with a tilde (~), a unique number (starting with 1), a period, and the first three (or fewer) characters of the file extension (the characters that follow the last period in the filename). Windows 2000 strips out characters that MS-DOS cannot read as well as spaces and any extra periods, and it displays all short filenames in uppercase (the default for DOS). If you use a filename that follows the 8.3 filenaming convention for DOS and Windows 3.x programs and also use all uppercase characters, then the long filename and alias are the same. Windows 98 and Windows 95 use this same approach.

For example, if you have a directory folder named "Cressler Graphics, Inc.", Windows 2000 will assign this folder the short name CRESSL~1 (assuming there is no other file with the same name) with no file type extension, because the long filename has none (the usual case with directory folder names). Note that mixed case and lowercase (which Windows 2000 recognizes) are converted to uppercase (the default for the DOS operating system). If another file in the same folder had already been assigned the short filename CRESSL~1, Windows 2000 would use an **algorithm**, or formula, to increment the number until a unique filename is found. Windows 2000 would then check to see if another folder (or file if the file has no file extension, such as some Windows 2000 system files) used the short filename CRESSL~2. If not, it would use this short filename for the "Cressler Graphics, Inc." folder.

If there are five or more files that would end up with short filenames where the first six characters are the same, Windows 2000 and Windows NT 4.0 uses a different approach than Windows 98 or Windows 95 for creating a short filename. They use the first two characters of the long filename, and then they mathematically generate the next four characters of the filename. Next, they add a tilde (~) followed by the number 1 (or if necessary, a unique number to avoid a duplicate filename).

In a My Computer or Windows Explorer window, you might see a folder, shortcut, and file with the same name; however, the file extension (if present) differs. Folders usually do not have file extensions. Shortcuts have the file extension "lnk" (for link) or, in the case of shortcuts to DOS programs, "pif" (for Program Information File). Files usually have a file extension that associates the file with a program.

The short filename is important for DOS programs and Windows 3.x programs used under Windows 2000 (as well as Windows 98, Windows NT Workstation 4.0, and Windows 95) because those programs do not recognize long filenames for folders and files. Instead, these programs can recognize only the short filename for folders and files. If you open a program designed for a version of Windows after Windows 3.x, such as Microsoft Word 2000, and then attempt to open a file, you will see only the long filenames in the Open and Save As dialog boxes. If you open a DOS program or a Windows 3.x program (such as an earlier version of Microsoft Word), and then attempt to open a file, you will see only the short filenames in the Open and Save As dialog boxes. This can make it difficult to know which folder or file to open or which file to replace.

To illustrate these two different ways of displaying filenames, examine the next two figures. Figure 2-16 shows an Open dialog box for Microsoft Word 2000—a program that recognizes long filenames. Note that you can see long filenames for folders and files. Also note that the long filenames "2002 Sales Summary #1.xls" and "2002 Sales Summary #2.xls," and the long filenames "Five Year Growth Plan.xls" and "Five Year Plan Template.xls," are similar.

Figure 2-16   OPEN DIALOG BOX FOR MICROSOFT WORD 2000

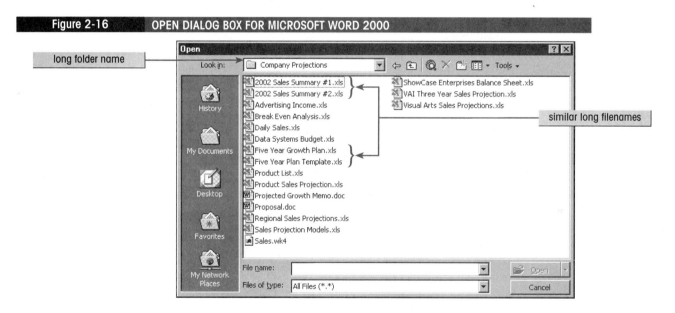

Figure 2-17 shows an Open dialog box for Collage Complete—a Windows 3.1 program used to create the figures in this book. Notice that you can see only the short filenames for folders and files. 2002SA~1.XLS and 2002SA~2.XLS are the short filenames for "2002 Sales Summary #1.xls" and "2002 Sales Summary #2.xls." The "1" and the "2" after the tildes in the short filenames bear no relationship to the "1" and "2" after the pound signs (#) in the original long filenames. If you had created the file "2002 Sales Summary #2.xls" first, its short filename would be 2002SA~1.XLS, and the short filename for "2002 Sales Summary #1.xls" would be 2002SA~2.XLS. Likewise, FIVEYE~1.XLS and FIVEYE~2.XLS are the short filenames for the files "Five Year Growth Plan.xls" and "Five Year Plan Template.xls," but there is no way to tell which is which from these short filenames.

Figure 2-17	**OPEN DIALOG BOX FROM A WINDOWS 3.1 APPLICATION**

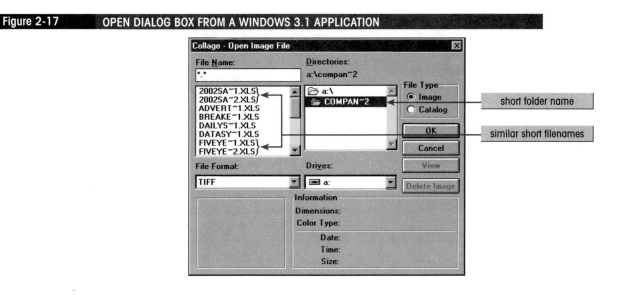

Under Windows 2000 and Windows NT 4.0, you can use the **/X** switch of the Directory command to see short filenames for both files and directories (Tutorial 4 covers directories). This feature might prove useful if you want to know the short filename for a directory or file before you switch to a Windows 3.1 or DOS program and then use the short filename.

To view short filenames in a directory listing:

1. Type **dir /p /o /x** and then press **Enter**. The directory listing now contains the short filename along with each long filename. See Figure 2-18. Note that the short filenames for "2002 Sales Summary #1.xls" and "2002 Sales Summary #2.xls" are similar (2002SA~1.XLS and 2002SA~2.XLS), and note that all short filenames are in uppercase. The operating system assigns the numbers in short filenames without regard to any numbering in the long filenames. For example, "2002 Sales Summary #2.xls" has the short name 2002SA~1.xls because it happened to receive its short filename first during a copy operation, before "2002 Sales Summary #1.xls."

TROUBLE? If your directory listing includes blank lines or lines containing just a few characters, then a long filename on the preceding line was too long to fit on one line, and it wrapped around to the next line.

Figure 2-18   **DIRECTORY LISTING WITH SHORT AND LONG FILENAMES**

short filenames

long filenames

similar short filenames

```
Command Prompt - dir /p /o /x                              _ □ ×
 Volume in drive A has no label.
 Volume Serial Number is F065-B557

 Directory of A:\

11/05/2003  02:35p          10,258 ~WRC0070.TMP     ~WRC0070.tmp
01/23/2003  08:16a          41,472 2002SA~2.XLS     2002 Sales Summary #1.xls

01/23/2003  09:21a          78,848 2002SA~1.XLS     2002 Sales Summary #2.xls

02/27/2002  08:53p          34,304 3YEARS~1.XLS     3 Year Sales Projection.x
ls
07/09/2003  09:42a          49,152 ADDRES~1.XLS     Addressing Cells.xls
04/18/2003  01:33p          16,896 ADVERT~1.XLS     Advertising Income.xls
05/30/2003  11:22a          22,016 ANDRE'~1.XLS     Andre's Employee Payroll.
xls
06/26/2003  09:30a          52,736 APPLIC~1.PPT     Application Software.ppt
01/24/2003  08:45a          18,944 BALANC~1.XLS     Balance Sheet.xls
01/08/2003  02:06p          24,064 BREAKE~1.XLS     Break Even Analysis.xls
03/21/2003  08:08a          15,872 CLIENT~1.XLS     Client Invoices.xls
10/16/2003  09:52a          84,446 COLORP~1.BMP     Color Palette.bmp
10/16/2003  10:31a          84,534 COLORS~1.BMP     Colors of the Rainbow.bmp

09/05/2003  02:25p          13,824 COMMIS~1.XLS     Commission on Sales.xls
Press any key to continue . . . _
```

2. Press the **Spacebar** to display the next part of the directory listing. See Figure 2-19. Note that a long filename—like Fonts.xls, which also meets the guidelines for naming files under MS-DOS (8.3 characters)—has identical long and short filename (except the short filename is in uppercase).

Figure 2-19   **DIRECTORY LISTING WITH SHORT AND LONG FILENAMES**

similar short and long filenames

```
Command Prompt - dir /p /o /x                              _ □ ×
01/10/2003  10:54a          22,016 DATASY~1.XLS     Data Systems Budget.xls
04/09/2003  02:12p          21,504 EMPLOY~1.XLS     Employees.xls
11/05/2003  04:22p          24,064 FILE0000.CHK     File0000.chk
01/16/2003  10:46a          20,992 FIVEYE~1.XLS     Five Year Growth Plan.xls

01/15/2003  02:21p          17,408 FIVEYE~2.XLS     Five Year Plan Template.x
ls
09/23/2003  01:12p          31,232 FONTS.XLS        Fonts.xls
07/22/2003  01:32p          20,992 FORMAT~2.XLS     Format Code Colors.xls
08/08/2003  03:22p          26,624 FORMAT~1.XLS     Formatting Features.xls
06/26/2003  10:24a          53,248 HARDWARE.PPT     Hardware.ppt
10/29/2003  10:30a          74,024 INVOIC~1.WK4     Invoice Form.wk4
09/23/2003  01:12p          14,848 LOANPA~1.XLS     Loan Payment Analysis.xls

10/16/2003  10:15a          17,910 PALETT~1.BMP     Palette #1.bmp
10/16/2003  10:21a          17,910 PALETT~2.BMP     Palette #2.bmp
03/28/2003  04:41p          22,528 PRODUC~1.XLS     Product List.xls
01/03/2003  12:02p          27,648 PRODUC~2.XLS     Product Sales Projection.
xls
11/20/2003  08:55a          25,088 PROJEC~1.DOC     Projected Growth Memo.doc

08/08/2003  04:12p          20,480 PROPOSAL.DOC     Proposal.doc
10/22/2003  01:52p          23,040 REGION~1.XLS     Regional Sales Projection
s.xls
Press any key to continue . . . _
```

3. Press the **Spacebar** as many times as necessary to view the remainder of the directory listing, until you see the command prompt.

REFERENCE   WINDOW   RW

Displaying Short Filenames in a Directory Listing

■ If necessary, open a Command Prompt window and change to the drive containing the files you want to examine.

■ Type DIR /P /O /X and then press Enter to display a list of files in alphabetical order by long and short filenames, one full window at a time.

Understanding how Windows 2000 works with long and short filenames is important if you work with DOS, Windows 3.x, and programs for later versions of Windows on the same or different computer systems. You will need to know how long and short filenames work if you provide support to clients who might have a variety of software configurations on their computers, if you troubleshoot problems, or if you set up, configure, and customize computers for other users. When using DOS and Windows 3.x programs, think carefully about how you name files and adopt a convention or approach that makes it easy to locate files by their short filenames. For example, instead of using long filenames like "Five Year Growth Plan.xls" (with the short filename FIVEYE~1.XLS) and "Five Year Plan Template.xls" (with the short filename FIVEYE~2.XLS), you could use the long filenames "Five Year Growth Plan.xls" (with the short filename FIVEYE~1.XLS) and "Template for a Five Year Plan.xls" (with the short filename TEMPLA~1.XLS). Then you could easily tell these files apart in a Windows 3.x program from their short filenames.

In the Command Prompt window, the DIR command in Windows 98 and Windows 95 uses a different approach from Windows 2000 (and Windows NT 4.0) to display short filenames. The Windows 95/98 DIR command has no /X switch, but always lists the short filename and type extension at the beginning of each line and then displays the long filename at the end of the line, like the DIR command in Windows NT 4.0 and Windows 2000. Again, Windows 95 and 98 do not support long filenames when you boot to "Command prompt only" or "Safe mode command prompt only" from their Startup Menu; the DIR command then shows only short filenames.

Displaying a Directory using File Attributes

The Directory command contains an Attribute (/A) switch for displaying files with specific file attributes. An **attribute** is a setting consisting of a bit turned on or off by the operating system, and defines a particular characteristic of the file. Files with the **System (S)** attribute are operating system files. Files with the **Hidden (H)** attribute on are not displayed in directory listings. System files typically have both the System and Hidden attribute turned on to protect the files. You can open files with the **Read-Only (R)** attribute on, but you cannot save any changes to the file under the same filename (you have to use a different filename). At the command prompt, you cannot delete files with the Read-Only attribute on (although you can in My Computer and Windows Explorer). Each time you create a new file, or open, modify, and save an existing file, Windows 2000 turns on the **Archive (A)** attribute of the file to indicate that it has not been backed up by any standard backup utility. A backup utility can turn off the Archive attribute when it backs up a file. Later, if you make changes to the file, the operating system will turn on its Archive attribute again, so you can back up only newly changed files with your backup utility. Files with their **Directory (D)** attribute turned on are directories. As in UNIX, and other operating systems a directory folder is actually a specialized type of file, which the operating system treats differently from regular files.

If you need to troubleshoot a problem or check certain files to make sure they have a certain attribute turned on, you can use the Attribute switch (/A) with one of the attribute parameters described above.

To view files with a specific attribute turned on:

1. Type **c:** and then press **Enter**. Windows 2000 changes the default drive to drive C—as shown by the command prompt.

2. Type **cls** and then press **Enter** to clear the window.

3. Type **dir /o /p** and then press **Enter**. The Directory command displays the contents of the root directory of drive C in alphabetical order (one full window or screen at a time if there are more directories and files than will fit within the window or screen). On the computer used for Figure 2-20, the directory listing shows that the root directory contains only subdirectories (and no files). On this computer, the figure shows three subdirectories of the root directory.

Figure 2-20	DIR DISPLAYS THE ROOT DIRECTORY OF DRIVE C

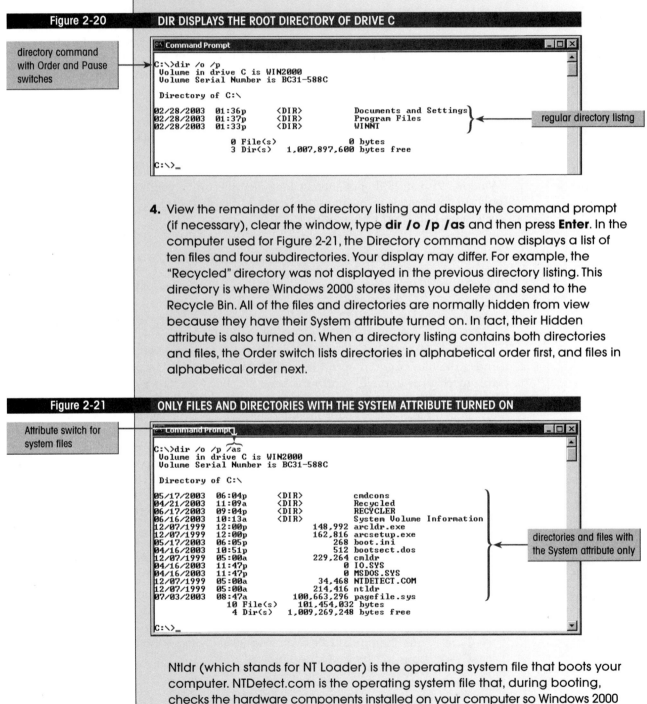

directory command with Order and Pause switches

regular directory listng

4. View the remainder of the directory listing and display the command prompt (if necessary), clear the window, type **dir /o /p /as** and then press **Enter**. In the computer used for Figure 2-21, the Directory command now displays a list of ten files and four subdirectories. Your display may differ. For example, the "Recycled" directory was not displayed in the previous directory listing. This directory is where Windows 2000 stores items you delete and send to the Recycle Bin. All of the files and directories are normally hidden from view because they have their System attribute turned on. In fact, their Hidden attribute is also turned on. When a directory listing contains both directories and files, the Order switch lists directories in alphabetical order first, and files in alphabetical order next.

Figure 2-21	ONLY FILES AND DIRECTORIES WITH THE SYSTEM ATTRIBUTE TURNED ON

Attribute switch for system files

directories and files with the System attribute only

Ntldr (which stands for NT Loader) is the operating system file that boots your computer. NTDetect.com is the operating system file that, during booting, checks the hardware components installed on your computer so Windows 2000 can properly configure your computer system. Boot.ini is an operating system file containing boot settings. Pagefile.sys, the largest of all the files, is an operating system file referred to as a **paging file**, or **swap file**. When Windows 2000 needs more RAM than is installed on your computer in order to support programs, it sets aside storage space on the hard disk as supplemental RAM. That storage space is the paging file. If Windows 2000 needs more memory, it will temporarily write parts of memory you are not currently using to the paging file on disk, so it can load other program code and documents. On the computer in Figure 2-22, Windows 2000 set aside 96 MB of hard disk storage space for the paging file. (Note that there are 1,024 bytes in each kilobyte, and 1,024 kilobytes in each megabyte.) The combination of RAM plus the paging file constitutes what is called **virtual memory**.

5. View the remainder of the directory listing and display the command prompt (if necessary), clear the window, type **dir /o /p /ah** and then press **Enter**. In the computer in Figure 2-22, the Directory command now displays a list of twelve files and four directories with their Hidden attribute on. Your display may differ. The additional two files not shown in the previous directory listing figure are Config.sys and Autoexec.bat—the MS-DOS startup configuration files. You can use the scroll bar to view the output of the previous command.

Figure 2-22	FILES AND SUBDIRECTORIES WITH THE HIDDEN ATTRIBUTE ONLY

Attribute switch for hidden files

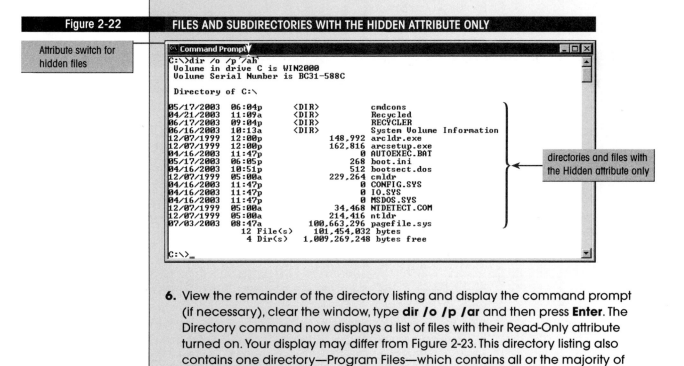

directories and files with the Hidden attribute only

6. View the remainder of the directory listing and display the command prompt (if necessary), clear the window, type **dir /o /p /ar** and then press **Enter**. The Directory command now displays a list of files with their Read-Only attribute turned on. Your display may differ from Figure 2-23. This directory listing also contains one directory—Program Files—which contains all or the majority of the installed software (other than the operating System) on your computer.

Figure 2-23 | FILES AND SUBDIRECTORIES WITH THE READ-ONLY ATTRIBUTE ONLY

Attribute switch for
read-only files

```
C:\>dir /o /p /ar
Volume in drive C is WIN2000
Volume Serial Number is BC31-588C

Directory of C:\

05/17/2003  06:04p    <DIR>          cmdcons
06/16/2003  12:02p    <DIR>          Program Files
12/07/1999  12:00p          148,992 arcldr.exe
12/07/1999  12:00p          162,816 arcsetup.exe
05/17/2003  06:05p              268 boot.ini
12/07/1999  05:00a          229,264 cmldr
04/16/2003  11:47p                0 IO.SYS
04/16/2003  11:47p                0 MSDOS.SYS
12/07/1999  05:00a           34,468 NTDETECT.COM
12/07/1999  05:00a          214,416 ntldr
               8 File(s)        790,224 bytes
               2 Dir(s)   1,009,269,248 bytes free

C:\>
```

directories and files
with the Read-only
attribute only

7. View the remainder of the directory listing and display the command prompt (if necessary), type **dir /o /p /a** and then press **Enter**. If you use the Attribute (/A) switch without attribute parameters, the Directory command displays all files—no matter which attributes are turned on or off. Again, your display may differ from Figure 2-24. You can think of /A as specifying "all files."

Figure 2-24 | ALL FILES AND SUBDIRECTORIES REGARDLESS OF ATTRIBUTES

```
Command Prompt - dir /o /p /a
Volume in drive C is WIN2000
Volume Serial Number is BC31-588C

Directory of C:\

05/17/2003  06:04p    <DIR>          cmdcons
06/19/2003  09:28p    <DIR>          Documents and Settings
06/16/2003  12:02p    <DIR>          Program Files
04/21/2003  11:09a    <DIR>          Recycled
06/17/2003  09:04p    <DIR>          RECYCLER
06/16/2003  10:13a    <DIR>          System Volume Information
06/20/2003  01:50p    <DIR>          WINNT
12/07/1999  12:00p          148,992 arcldr.exe
12/07/1999  12:00p          162,816 arcsetup.exe
04/16/2003  11:47p                0 AUTOEXEC.BAT
05/17/2003  06:05p              268 boot.ini
04/16/2003  10:51p              512 bootsect.dos
12/07/1999  05:00a          229,264 cmldr
04/16/2003  11:47p                0 CONFIG.SYS
04/16/2003  11:47p                0 IO.SYS
04/16/2003  11:47p                0 MSDOS.SYS
12/07/1999  05:00a           34,468 NTDETECT.COM
12/07/1999  05:00a          214,416 ntldr
07/03/2003  08:47a      100,663,296 pagefile.sys
Press any key to continue . . .
```

all directories and files
listed using /A switch

8. View the remainder of the directory listing and display the command prompt (if necessary), type **dir /o /p /ad** and then press **Enter**. The directory listing now contains only directories—no matter what other attributes are on or off for the directories. No files are listed. Again, your display may differ from Figure 2-25. You can use this switch whenever you want to see just the names of subdirectories of a directory quickly.

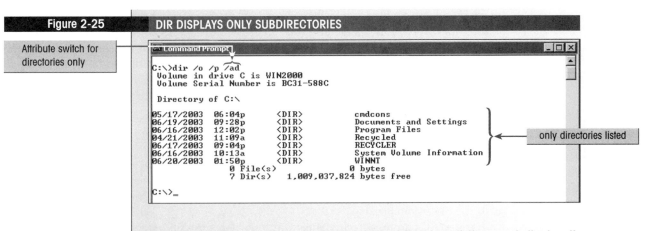

Figure 2-25   **DIR DISPLAYS ONLY SUBDIRECTORIES**

Attribute switch for directories only

only directories listed

```
C:\>dir /o /p /ad
 Volume in drive C is WIN2000
 Volume Serial Number is BC31-588C

 Directory of C:\

05/17/2003  06:04p    <DIR>        cmdcons
06/19/2003  09:28p    <DIR>        Documents and Settings
06/16/2003  12:02p    <DIR>        Program Files
04/21/2003  11:09a    <DIR>        Recycled
06/17/2003  09:04p    <DIR>        RECYCLER
06/16/2003  10:13a    <DIR>        System Volume Information
06/20/2003  01:50p    <DIR>        WINNT
              0 File(s)            0 bytes
              7 Dir(s)   1,009,037,824 bytes free

C:\>_
```

9. If necessary, view the remainder of the directory listing and display the command prompt.

REFERENCE WINDOW   RW

Displaying a Directory Listing by File Attribute

- If necessary, open a Command Prompt window and change to the drive containing the files you want to examine.
- Type DIR /P /O /AS and then press Enter to display a list of files with the System attribute turned on in alphabetical order by filename, one full window at a time.
- Type DIR /P /O /AH and then press Enter to display a list of files with the Hidden attribute turned on in alphabetical order by filename, one full window at a time.
- Type DIR /P /O /AR and then press Enter to display a list of files with the Read-Only attribute turned on in alphabetical order by filename, one full window at a time.
- Type DIR /P /O /A and then press Enter to display a list of all files (no matter which attribute is on or off for each file) in alphabetical order by filename, one full window at a time.
- Type DIR /P /O /AD and then press Enter to display a list of directories with the Directory attribute turned on in alphabetical order by name, one full window at a time.

The Attribute switch and the same attribute parameters are available when working at the command prompt in Windows 98, Windows NT, Windows 95, and MS-DOS, and are invaluable when you need to check attributes of system and configuration files. Although you can select and view files based on their attributes using My Computer or Windows Explorer, the DIR command makes it easier and more straightforward.

Using Wildcards

Isabel informs you that employees will frequently ask about the availability of certain types of files on the templates disk. Until you are more familiar with the disk, Isabel tells you that you can quickly search for files using wildcards with the Directory command. This skill will also improve your proficiency when troubleshooting in a Command Prompt window.

Wildcards simplify the process of selecting files with similar filenames or similar file extensions. A **wildcard** is a symbol that substitutes for one or more characters in a filename. There are two wildcard characters—the question mark and the asterisk. The **question** mark (?) substitutes for a single character in a filename, whereas the **asterisk** (*) typically substitutes for one or more characters. You can use wildcards with any command that operates on files. In the case of the Directory command, you can use wildcards to select and display information on a set of files within a directory, rather than display information about all the files. You can also combine wildcards with switches to improve the results of your selections. The advantage of using wildcards is that you can quickly and efficiently perform operations at the command prompt.

Using the Asterisk Wildcard

Carlos Escobar, SolarWinds' new financial analyst, asks you if there are any Microsoft Excel files on the templates disk containing sales projections, so that he can create financial forecasts for the coming year.

Because files produced with Microsoft Excel have the file extension "xls," you can use the following command with the asterisk wildcard to display a list of spreadsheets:

DIR *.XLS /O /P

The "*.XLS" in the command is called a **file specification**, and it provides information about the type of files you want to select and display in a directory listing. The asterisk instructs the Directory command to display all files regardless of the main part of the filename. The "XLS" instructs the Directory command to display only files with "xls" as the file extension (case does not matter).

To select files with the same file extension:

1. Make sure your Data Disk is in drive A, type **a:** and then press **Enter** to change to drive A.

2. Type **dir *.xls /o /p** and then press **Enter**. The Directory command displays the names of files with the "xls" file extension in alphabetical order by filename, and then pauses after the first full window. See Figure 2-26. As you can see, the asterisk substitutes for any combination of characters in the main part of the filename. The one feature all these files have in common is the "xls" file extension.

| Figure 2-26 | ASTERISK WILDCARD SELECTS FILES WITH THE SAME FILE EXTENSION |

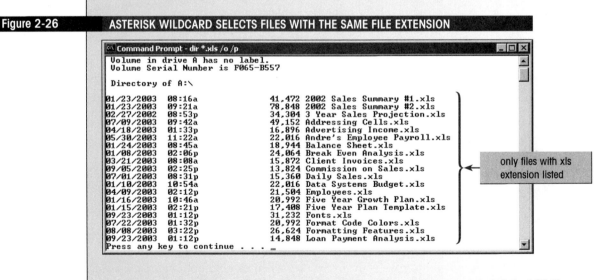

3. Display the next (and last) full window of filenames. There are a total of 27 files out of the 41 files on the disk that contain "xls" as the file extension.

You would like to narrow down the selection even more for Carlos. You notice a file in the directory listing with Projection at the end of the main part of the filename, and decide to list only Excel files with the word "Projection" in their names.

To use a file specification that narrows the selection:

1. Clear the window, type **dir *projection.xls /o /p** and then press **Enter**. The Directory command lists two files that are sales projections. See Figure 2-27. Notice that both filenames have the word "Projection" at the end of the main part of the filename. The asterisk wildcard selected all filenames that had any combination of characters before the word "Projection." Case does not make a difference in the file specification.

| Figure 2-27 | DIRECTORY OF FILENAMES THAT END WITH THE WORD "PROJECTION" |

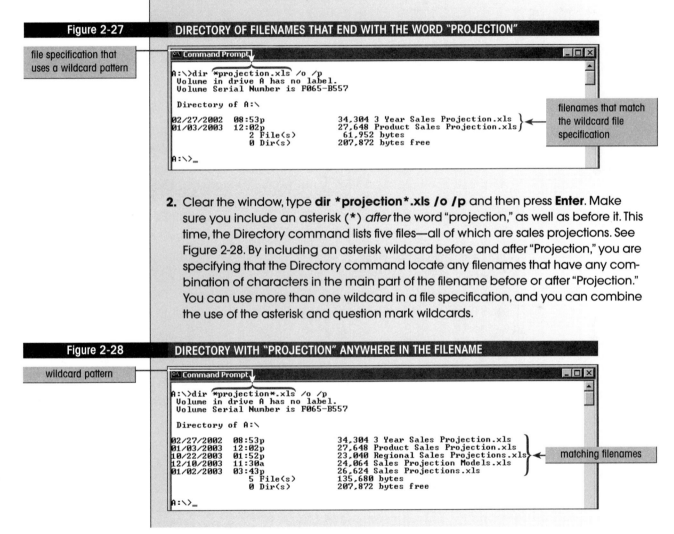

file specification that uses a wildcard pattern

filenames that match the wildcard file specification

2. Clear the window, type **dir *projection*.xls /o /p** and then press **Enter**. Make sure you include an asterisk (*) *after* the word "projection," as well as before it. This time, the Directory command lists five files—all of which are sales projections. See Figure 2-28. By including an asterisk wildcard before and after "Projection," you are specifying that the Directory command locate any filenames that have any combination of characters in the main part of the filename before or after "Projection." You can use more than one wildcard in a file specification, and you can combine the use of the asterisk and question mark wildcards.

| Figure 2-28 | DIRECTORY WITH "PROJECTION" ANYWHERE IN THE FILENAME |

wildcard pattern

matching filenames

Note the flexibility and power in using more than one wildcard character in a file specification. Of the three selections you tested, the last one is the most useful because it includes all the files that might work for Carlos.

Another common use of the asterisk wildcard is to select all filenames that begin with a certain character or combination of characters. You could, for example, look for all files that begin with "Sales" in the main part of the filename, and that contain any file extension.

To select files with "Sales" at the beginning of the filename:

1. Clear the window.

2. Type **dir sales*.*** **/o** and then press **Enter**. The Directory command locates three files that contain "Sales" at the beginning of the filename. See Figure 2-29. Two of the files have the "xls" file extension, while the other has a "wk4" file extension (a Lotus 1-2-3 Release 5 for Windows file). Because you included an asterisk wildcard for the file extension, the Directory command accepted any combination of characters for the file extension.

Figure 2-29	DIRECTORY OF ALL FILENAMES BEGINNING WITH THE WORD "SALES"

wildcard pattern

```
A:\>dir sales*.* /o
 Volume in drive A has no label.
 Volume Serial Number is F065-B557

 Directory of A:\

12/10/2003  11:30a              24,064 Sales Projection Models.xls
01/02/2003  03:43p              26,624 Sales Projections.xls
03/27/2003  11:19a              22,028 Sales.wk4
               3 File(s)         72,716 bytes
               0 Dir(s)         207,872 bytes free

A:\>_
```

matching filenames

The file specification DIR SALES* would have also worked exactly the same way. If you don't specify a file extension, the Directory command includes files with any, or no, file extension.

REFERENCE WINDOW   **RW**

Using the Asterisk Wildcard in a File Specification

- If necessary, open a Command Prompt window and change to the drive containing the files you want to examine.
- Type DIR, press the Spacebar, type * (an asterisk), type . (a period), type a file extension, press the Spacebar, type /P /O, and then press the Enter key to display a list of files with a specific file extension in alphabetical order by filename, one full window at a time.
- Type DIR, press the Spacebar, type the file specification with one or more asterisks to substitute for one or more characters in the filename, press the Spacebar, type /P /O, and then press Enter to display a list of files with filenames that differ by one or more characters in the filename, in alphabetical order one full window at a time.
- Type DIR, press the Spacebar, type the first character or initial characters in the filename, type * (an asterisk), press the Spacebar, type /P /O, and then press Enter to display a list of files that have the same first character or initial characters at the beginning of the filename, in alphabetical order by filename one full window at a time.

Another common use of this wildcard is to display all files starting with a certain letter of the alphabet. For example, if you enter the command DIR S*, the Directory command will list all files that start with the letter "S." This feature is useful if you recall only the first few letters or words of the filename.

Using the Question Mark Wildcard

One of SolarWinds' in-house trainers asks you for a copy of the PowerPoint presentation files on computer hardware and software for an upcoming training session for new staff members.

One common use of the question mark wildcard is to select a group of files with filenames that are identical except for one character. For example, assume you have a set of files containing quarterly sales summaries for 2002 and 2003, as follows:

2002 First Quarter Sales Summary.xls	2003 First Quarter Sales Summary.xls
2002 Second Quarter Sales Summary.xls	2003 Second Quarter Sales Summary.xls
2002 Third Quarter Sales Summary.xls	2003 Third Quarter Sales Summary.xls
2002 Fourth Quarter Sales Summary.xls	2003 Fourth Quarter Sales Summary.xls

You want to locate the sales summaries for the fourth quarter of these two years so you can analyze the company's performance from one year to the next. The only difference between the two filenames is the character at the fourth position of the main part of the filename. To view a directory listing of just these files, substitute the question mark wildcard for the fourth character, as follows:

DIR 200? Fourth Quarterly Sales Summary.xls

The question mark wildcard in this file specification substitutes for the fourth character in the filename, and this file specification would select "2002 Fourth Quarter Sales Summary.xls" and "2003 Fourth Quarter Sales Summary.xls." To save typing, you could also use the following abbreviated file specification where you combine the two types of wildcards: **DIR 200? Fo***

You can use the question mark wildcard and a similar strategy to locate the PowerPoint presentations on computer hardware and software on your disk. The filenames of these files are Hardware.ppt and Software.ppt. Not only is the extension the same, but the last four characters of the main part of the filename are the same. The first four characters are the only ones that vary.

To select the PowerPoint files on computer hardware and software:

1. Clear the window, type **dir ????ware.ppt /o** and then press **Enter**. The Directory command displays the two files you wanted to find. See Figure 2-30. Notice that both files have exactly the same number of characters in the main part of the filename (plus the same file extension). After trying this command, see if "DIR *WARE.PPT /O" also works.

Figure 2-30	USING QUESTION MARK WILDCARDS TO SELECT SIMILAR FILENAMES

wildcard pattern

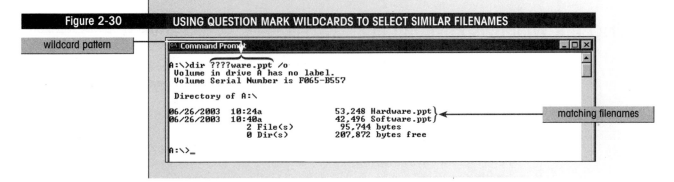

matching filenames

```
A:\>dir ????ware.ppt /o
 Volume in drive A has no label.
 Volume Serial Number is F065-B557

 Directory of A:\

06/26/2003  10:24a             53,248 Hardware.ppt
06/26/2003  10:40a             42,496 Software.ppt
               2 File(s)         95,744 bytes
               0 Dir(s)         207,872 bytes free

A:\>_
```

2. Clear the window, type **dir *ware.ppt /o** and then press **Enter**. The Directory command displays one additional file—one you might or might not need, but note that changing the wildcard specification did produce different results. See Figure 2-31. Note that while the question mark wildcard showed filenames with letters replacing the question marks in a one-for-one substitution, the asterisk wildcard allows any number of letters to substitute for the asterisk.

| Figure 2-31 | USING AN ASTERISK WILDCARD TO SELECT SIMILAR FILENAMES |

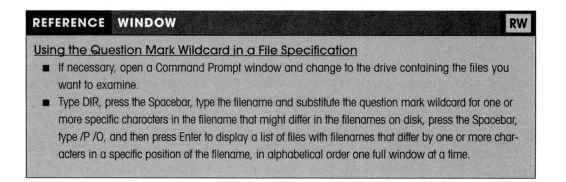

wildcard pattern

matching filenames

This particular use of wildcards with the DIR command is invaluable if you need to locate a small group of files within a directory that contains hundreds of files.

REFERENCE   WINDOW   **RW**

Using the Question Mark Wildcard in a File Specification
- If necessary, open a Command Prompt window and change to the drive containing the files you want to examine.
- Type DIR, press the Spacebar, type the filename and substitute the question mark wildcard for one or more specific characters in the filename that might differ in the filenames on disk, press the Spacebar, type /P /O, and then press Enter to display a list of files with filenames that differ by one or more characters in a specific position of the filename, in alphabetical order one full window at a time.

The use of wildcards provides a powerful tool for selecting groups of files based on their file extensions, or some other set of characters within the filenames that distinguishes them from other files on the disk.

Using the Windows Environment

After working with the Directory command and its switches, you realize that you always use the Sort Order and Page switches. You ask Isabel if there is any way to specify these switches as default switches for the Directory command so you do not need to type them each time. Isabel tells you that you need to create an environment variable for the Directory command and specify these switches as the setting for that variable.

Windows 2000 and other programs store important settings in a small area of memory called the **Windows environment** (formerly known as the DOS environment). Windows 2000, and the other programs you use, will check the Windows environment for specific settings. The settings in the Windows environment are assigned to environment variables. An **environment variable** is a symbolic name associated with a specific setting. For example, you can create an environment variable by the name of DIRCMD, and then assign switches to this environment variable. When you use the Directory command, it will automatically check the Windows environment and use the switches as default settings.

To assign a setting to an environment variable, use the SET command, which is an internal command. Its syntax is as follows:

SET *variable = string*

Variable is the name of the environment variable, and *string* is the setting you want to assign to the environment variable. For example, if you want to store the Pause and Order switches in the Windows environment for use with the Directory command, enter the following command:

SET DIRCMD=/P /O

Now, whenever you enter "DIR" at the command prompt, the Directory command will execute your command as though you had entered "DIR /P /O." Later, if you prefer to use another setting, you can repeat this command and specify new switches.

When you assign a setting to the DIRCMD environment variable, you must not leave a blank space between DIRCMD and the equal sign. If you include a space, Windows 2000 does not use the new setting when you enter the DIR command.

If you want to view the contents of the Windows environment, type SET and then press Enter.

To examine the Windows environment and then specify default switches for the Directory command:

1. Click the **Maximize** button 🗖 to maximize the Command Prompt window, and then clear the window.

2. Type **set** and then press **Enter**. The Setting command displays the environment variables in the Windows environment, and the settings assigned to these variables. See Figure 2-32. Notice that the USERNAME variable identifies the user currently logged on the computer. On the computer in Figure 2-32, there is no DIRCMD environment variable. Your Windows environment will differ.

| Figure 2-32 | SETTINGS IN THE WINDOWS ENVIRONMENT (YOURS MAY DIFFER) |

SET command alone lists entire environment

variable name

```
A:\>set
ALLUSERSPROFILE=C:\Documents and Settings\All Users
APPDATA=C:\Documents and Settings\Isabel\Application Data
CommonProgramFiles=C:\Program Files\Common Files
COMPUTERNAME=THALIA
ComSpec=C:\WINNT\system32\cmd.exe
HOMEDRIVE=C:
HOMEPATH=\
LOGONSERVER=\\THALIA
NUMBER_OF_PROCESSORS=1
OS=Windows_NT
Os2LibPath=C:\WINNT\system32\os2\dll;
Path=C:\WINNT\system32;C:\WINNT;C:\WINNT\System32\Wbem
PATHEXT=.COM;.EXE;.BAT;.CMD;.UBS;.UBE;.JS;.JSE;.WSF;.WSH
PROCESSOR_ARCHITECTURE=x86
PROCESSOR_IDENTIFIER=x86 Family 5 Model 2 Stepping 12, GenuineIntel
PROCESSOR_LEVEL=5
PROCESSOR_REVISION=020c
ProgramFiles=C:\Program Files
PROMPT=$P$G
SystemDrive=C:
SystemRoot=C:\WINNT
TEMP=C:\DOCUME~1\Isabel\LOCALS~1\Temp
TMP=C:\DOCUME~1\Isabel\LOCALS~1\Temp
USERDOMAIN=THALIA
USERNAME=Isabel
USERPROFILE=C:\Documents and Settings\Isabel
windir=C:\WINNT

A:\>_
```

environment variables

variable value

3. Type **set dircmd=/p /o** and then press **Enter**. Make sure you use the letter "o" and not the number zero (0).

4. Clear the window.

5. Type **set** and then press **Enter**. Notice that the DIRCMD environment variable you defined is now stored in the Windows environment along with the settings you assigned for this variable. See Figure 2-33.

Figure 2-33   **DIRCMD ENVIRONMENT VARIABLE IN WINDOWS ENVIRONMENT**

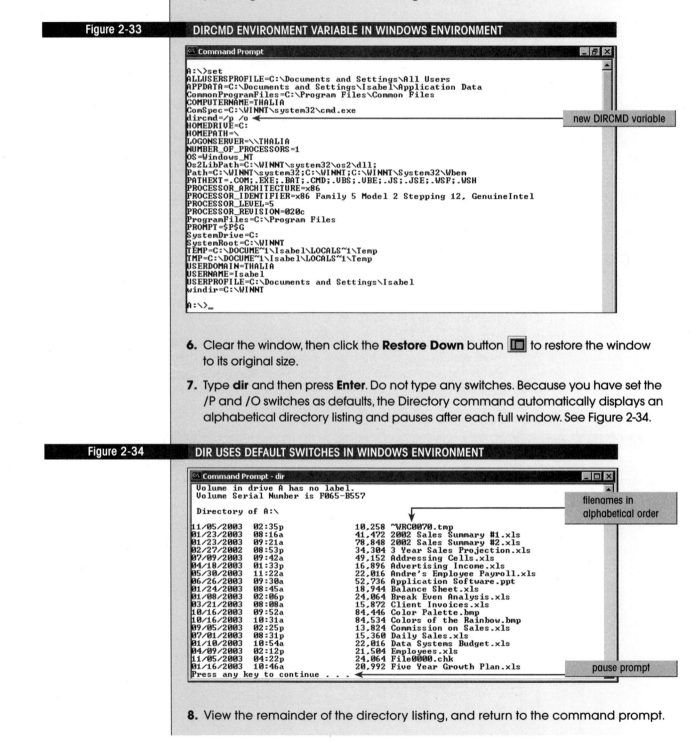

6. Clear the window, then click the **Restore Down** button to restore the window to its original size.

7. Type **dir** and then press **Enter**. Do not type any switches. Because you have set the /P and /O switches as defaults, the Directory command automatically displays an alphabetical directory listing and pauses after each full window. See Figure 2-34.

Figure 2-34   **DIR USES DEFAULT SWITCHES IN WINDOWS ENVIRONMENT**

8. View the remainder of the directory listing, and return to the command prompt.

You can temporarily override these settings by entering the Directory command with a different switch.

To display filenames in order by size, overriding a default setting:

1. Type **dir /o-s** and then press **Enter**. The Directory command displays the file-names in reverse order by file size. See Figure 2-35. Because you changed the parameter associated with the Order switch, the Directory command overrides the default setting for the Order switch in the Windows environment. As you can tell, however, the Directory command still uses the Pause switch.

Figure 2-35	OVERRIDING ONE OF THE SWITCHES IN THE WINDOWS ENVIRONMENT

reverse order by file size

```
Command Prompt - dir /o-s                                    _ □ ×
 Volume in drive A has no label.
 Volume Serial Number is F065-B557

 Directory of A:\

10/16/2003  10:31a              84,534 Colors of the Rainbow.bmp
10/16/2003  09:52a              84,446 Color Palette.bmp
01/23/2003  09:21a              78,848 2002 Sales Summary #2.xls
10/29/2003  10:30a              74,024 Invoice Form.wk4
06/26/2003  10:24a              53,248 Hardware.ppt
06/26/2003  09:30a              52,736 Application Software.ppt
07/09/2003  09:42a              49,152 Addressing Cells.xls
06/26/2003  10:40a              42,496 Software.ppt
06/26/2003  10:55a              41,984 Using the Mouse.ppt
01/23/2003  08:16a              41,472 2002 Sales Summary #1.xls
02/27/2002  08:53p              34,304 3 Year Sales Projection.xls
09/23/2003  01:12p              31,232 Fonts.xls
01/03/2003  12:02p              27,648 Product Sales Projection.xls
08/08/2003  03:22p              26,624 Formatting Features.xls
01/02/2003  03:43p              26,624 Sales Projections.xls
11/20/2003  08:55a              25,088 Projected Growth Memo.doc
01/08/2003  02:06p              24,064 Break Even Analysis.xls
12/10/2003  11:30a              24,064 Sales Projection Models.xls
11/05/2003  04:22p              24,064 File0000.chk
Press any key to continue . . . _
```

2. View the remainder of the directory listing, and return to the command prompt.

3. Close the Command Prompt window.

This setting stays in the Windows environment and remains in effect until you specify a new setting, remove this setting, or exit the Command Prompt window. To specify a new setting, enter "SET DIRCMD=" with a list of the new switches you now want to use. To remove this setting from the temporary Windows environment in your Command Prompt window, type "SET DIRCMD=" without any settings, and then press Enter.

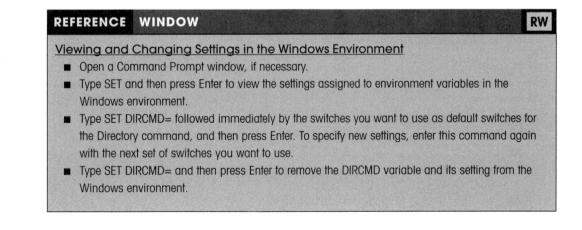

REFERENCE WINDOW RW

<u>Viewing and Changing Settings in the Windows Environment</u>
- Open a Command Prompt window, if necessary.
- Type SET and then press Enter to view the settings assigned to environment variables in the Windows environment.
- Type SET DIRCMD= followed immediately by the switches you want to use as default switches for the Directory command, and then press Enter. To specify new settings, enter this command again with the next set of switches you want to use.
- Type SET DIRCMD= and then press Enter to remove the DIRCMD variable and its setting from the Windows environment.

This timesaving tool streamlines and simplifies the use of the Directory command—the most commonly used command.

Isabel is pleased with the progress you have made in such a short time. When working in a Command Prompt window, you now can quickly provide the information needed by other staff members and also provide copies of the template files employees need to be productive and meet their deadlines.

Session 2.2 QUICK | CHECK

1. A(n) _____ allows only 8 characters and then a 3-character extension.

2. A(n) _____ is a setting consisting of a bit that is turned on or off by the operating system, and defines a particular characteristic of the file.

3. _____, the largest of all the files in the root directory folder, is an operating system file referred to as a paging file, or swap file.

4. A(n) _____ is a symbol that substitutes for one or more characters in a filename.

5. A(n)_____ provides information about the type of files you want to select and display in a directory listing.

6. An environment _____ is a symbolic name associated with a specific setting.

7. What character do you use to reverse a sort order parameter when you use the Order switch?

8. What command would you enter at the command prompt to display filenames in alphabetical order by file extension only?

9. What command would you use to view the contents of the Windows environment?

10. What command would you enter to make DIR default to displaying filenames in order by name, one full window at a time?

For the Tutorial 2 Command Reference table, go to page 93.

REVIEW ASSIGNMENT

To handle the ever-increasing workload during the busiest months of the year, Isabel hires another part-time assistant to help with computer support. She wants all staff members to be comfortable in both Windows 2000 and the command prompt environments, so she asks you to show the techniques and tricks you have learned to the new employee, Langston Ellis.

As you complete each step, write down the commands you use, as well as the answer to any questions so you can submit them to your instructor.

1. Insert your copy of Data Disk #1 into drive A.

2. Open a Command Prompt window.

3. Change to drive A. What command did you use?

4. What is the current default drive now?

5. Display a directory listing of the default drive. What command did you use?

6. Display a directory listing of drive C. What command did you use?

7. Change to drive C. What command did you use?

8. From drive C, display a directory listing of the Data Disk in drive A in alphabetical order by filename, and pause the directory listing after each full window. What command did you use?

9. From drive C, display a wide directory listing of drive A in alphabetical order by filename. What command did you use? Describe how the Directory command lists the files in the Command Prompt window.

10. From drive C, display a directory listing of drive A so files are listed first in alphabetical order by file extension, then by file size (for each type of file extension), pausing the directory listing after each full window. What command did you use? What are the names of the first four files in the directory listing?

11. From drive C, display a directory listing of drive A, and show short filenames for files with the "ppt" file extension in alphabetical order. What command did you use? What are the short and long filenames of the files the Directory command lists?

12. From drive C, display a directory listing of the system files on drive C. What command did you use? What filenames did the Directory command list?

13. From drive C, display a directory listing of all the "doc" files on drive A. What command did you use? What filenames did the Directory command list?

14. Use the SET command to assign to the DIRCMD variable switches that (a) arrange filenames in alphabetical order, (b) display short filenames as well as long filenames, and (c) pause a directory listing after each full window. What command did you use?

15. Display a directory listing of the root directory of drive C, displaying directories only, and with short filenames. What command did you use? What is the short filename for the Program Files directory (or folder)? And for the Documents and Settings directory (or folder)? What is the name of your Windows directory (or folder)? Does it have a short filename? If not, what would be the short filename of this directory (or folder)?

16. Close the Command Prompt window.

CASE PROBLEMS

Case 1. Classifying Files at Steppingstone Development Services Steppingstone Development Services is a non-profit organization that provides in-house training and job development services. The employees at Steppingstone use a combination of DOS, Windows 3.1, and Windows 2000 software. Office manager Angela Pinelli has received a diskette from a branch office. Before her staff makes changes to the files on the disk, she wants to document the entire contents of the disk.

Angela needs to prioritize the order in which her office will work on files, so she asks you to document the long and short filenames on the disk. She also asks you to organize the information on the reports using different switches, and then record the results.

As you complete each step, write down the commands you use so you can submit them to your instructor.

1. Open a Command Prompt window.

2. Insert your copy of Data Disk #1 into drive A, and make it the current default drive. What command did you use to change from drive C to drive A?

3. List the diskette files on screen without using any switches. Did you have to specify the drive? Explain.

4. What type of order did the Directory command use to list the files? Explain.

5. Perform each of the operations below, and indicate the DIR command you used to list both long and short filenames.

- List files by file extension
- List files in date order
- List files in order by file size
- List all filenames containing the word "Employee" in alphabetical order by filename
- List all filenames containing the word "Plan" in alphabetical order by filename

6. Which of these types of directory listings would you find useful in your field of specialty?

Case 2. Creating Files at Fast Track Trainers Samantha Kuehl, Fast Track Trainer's lead training specialist, needs a set of files for an upcoming employee workshop on working with files in a Command Prompt window. She asks you to prepare a set of files that illustrates the advantages and disadvantages of using different types of filenames. She suggests that you examine the files on one of the other training diskettes to see if you can adapt any of them for this new workshop.

As you perform the following steps, record your answers to any questions so you can submit them to your instructor.

1. After examining one of the training diskettes used for an earlier training session, you notice a set of files on the disk named Project1.doc, Project2.doc, Project3.doc, Project4.doc, and Project5.doc. When discussing the Directory command, what feature(s), if any, could Samantha demonstrate with the use of these files? Are there any features that she could not demonstrate? Explain.

2. You notice that the same diskette contains 12 simple text files with the "txt" file extension. What feature(s), if any, could Samantha demonstrate with the use of these files?

3. Another training diskette contains a set of files named "First Quarter Sales Summary.xls," "Second Quarter Sales Summary.xls," "Third Quarter Sales Summary.xls," and "Fourth Quarter Sales Summary.xls." What feature(s), if any, could Samantha demonstrate with the use of these files?

4. You also notice a set of graphics files approximately 10 times larger than the average file size of the remaining files on the same disk. What feature(s), if any, could Samantha demonstrate with the use of these files?

5. An older training diskette contains a set of files named QTR1_INC.WK3, QTR2_INC.WK3, QTR3_INC.WK3, and QTR4_INC.WK3. What feature(s), if any, could Samantha demonstrate with the use of these files?

6. If you need to create files with five different versions of your resume, what types of filenames would you choose for those files? Consider factors such as the advantages and disadvantages of long filenames vs. short filenames, the difficulty or ease of locating all these files, and the difficulty or ease of identifying how one file differs from all the others.

Case 3. Using Wildcards to Locate Files at Northbay Computers Northbay Computers sells and rents computer equipment and supplies for homeowners and businesses. Jonathan Baum, a recent high school graduate, has just been hired to provide training, troubleshooting support, and general assistance to customers. Although Jonathan has a strong background with Windows 2000, he has now discovered that DOS skills are an important part of troubleshooting systems. One common complaint of customers is that they are unable to locate important files they need to complete a project. Although you know how to locate files using the Windows 2000 Search Assistant, he asks you to show him how to improve his skills with the use of wildcards at the command line.

As you complete each step, write down the commands you use, as well as the answer to any questions, so you can submit them to your instructor.

1. Insert your copy of Data Disk #1 into drive A.

2. Open a Command Prompt window.

3. Change the default drive to drive A.

4. Display an alphabetical directory listing of all files with the "bmp" file extension. What command did you use? What files does the Directory command find when you try this command?

5. Display an alphabetical directory listing of all files with "D" as the first character in the filename. What command did you use? What files does the Directory command find when you try this command?

6. Display an alphabetical directory listing of all files with "Software" at the beginning of the filename. What command did you use? What files does the Directory command find when you try this command?

7. Display an alphabetical directory listing of all files with "Plan" anywhere in the main part of the filename. What command did you use? What files does the Directory command find when you try this command?

8. Display an alphabetical directory listing of all files with "Fi" as the first two characters of the filename, any character as the third character of the filename, "e" as the fourth character of the filename, any characters in the remainder of the filename, and any file extension. What command did you use? What files does the Directory command find when you try this command?

9. Display a directory listing of all files with the "xls" file extension in order from the smallest file to the largest file, and pause the directory listing after each full window. What command did you use? What is the first file in the directory listing, and what is the file size for this file? What is the last file in the directory listing, and what is the file size for this file?

10. Display a directory listing of all files with the "xls" file extension in order by file date, and pause the directory listing after each full window. What command did you use? What is the first file in the directory listing, and what is the file date of this file? What is the last file in the directory listing, and what is the file date of this file?

Case 4. Customizing the Windows Environment at Townsend & Sumner Publishing

Townsend & Sumner Publishing is a San Francisco-based firm that contracts with corporate clients to produce employee training manuals on the use of specialized client software. To produce these manuals, Townsend & Sumner's staff must work with many different types of Windows and DOS programs, and compile information, graphics, concept art, and illustrations from many different files. Mike Lyman, who supervises the production of these manuals, keeps track of and provides other staff members with the files they require for these projects. He asks you to help him customize the Windows environment so he can quickly locate files.

As you complete each step, write down the commands you use as well as the answer to any questions so you can submit them to your instructor.

1. Insert your copy of Data Disk #1 into drive A.

2. Open a Command Prompt window, and then maximize the Command Prompt window.

3. Display the variables in the Windows environment. What command did you use? How are the variables organized in the Windows environment? Locate the *SystemDrive* environment variable. What is the setting assigned to this variable?

4. Create a DIRCMD environment variable, and assign switches to the variable that:

    - Pause the directory listing after every full window
    - Display a list of all files—no matter what type of attribute(s) each file is assigned
    - Display filenames in alphabetical order by file extension and then by the main part of the filename

5. What command did you enter to assign these settings to the DIRCMD variable?

6. Check the Windows environment to make sure the setting is assigned to the DIRCMD variable. What command did you use? What setting does the Windows environment show for this variable?

7. Display a directory listing of the files on the Data Disk in drive A. What are the names of the first four files in the directory listing? What do these files have in common?

8. Override the Order switch in the Windows environment and display the directory listing in reverse order by file date so the most recent file is listed first and the oldest file is listed last. What command did you enter? What is the first file in the directory listing, and what is its file date? What is the last file in the directory listing, and what is its file date?

9. Exit the Command Prompt window.

10. Open and maximize the Command Prompt window again, and then display the settings in the Windows environment. Is the DIRCMD variable still listed? Why or why not?

11. Close the Command Prompt window.

QUICK CHECK ANSWERS

Session 2.1

1. command history or command stack
2. Insert
3. default
4. scrolling
5. disk order
6. file extension
7. /P
8. /W
9. /D
10. /O

Session 2.2

1. short filename
2. attribute
3. Pagefile.sys
4. wildcard
5. file specification
6. variable
7. minus sign (-)
8. DIR /OE
9. SET
10. DIR /O /P or DIR /P /O

COMMAND REFERENCE

COMMAND	USE	BASIC SYNTAX	EXAMPLE
drive name	Changes the default drive	*drive name*	A: C:
DIR	Displays a list of files and subdirectories within a directory	DIR [*drive*]	dir dir a:
DIR [*file specification*]	Displays a directory listing of a single file or a group of files	DIR [*file specification*]	dir Sales.wk4 dir "Product List.xls"
DIR /?	Displays Help information on the DIR command	DIR /?	dir /?
DIR /A	Displays a directory listing of files that have the same file attribute. The file attributes include: D Directory H Hidden S System R Read-only A Archive	DIR /A*attribute*	dir /a dir /as
DIR /O	Displays a directory listing in alphabetical order by filename	DIR /O	dir /o

COMMAND REFERENCE (CONTINUED)

COMMAND	USE	BASIC SYNTAX	EXAMPLE
DIR /O<sort order>	Displays a directory listing in order using a sort order parameter. The sort order parameters include: D File date and time S File size E File extension N Main part of filename	DIR O:<sort order parameter> DIR /O<sort order parameter>	dir /o:s dir /os
DIR /O-<sort order>	Displays a directory listing in *reverse* order using a sort order parameter. The sort order parameters include: D File date and time S File size E File extension N Main part of filename	DIR /O:-<sort order parameter> DIR /O-<sort order parameter>	dir /o:-s dir /o-s dir /oen
DIR /P	Pauses the display of a directory listing	DIR /P	dir /p
DIR /W	Displays filenames in a directory listing in columns across the width of the screen	DIR /W	dir /w
DIR /X	Displays a directory listing with short filenames as well as long filenames	DIR /X	dir /x
SET	Displays, sets, or removes environment variables from the Windows environment	SET	set set dircmd=/p /o
SET DIRCMD	Assigns default switches to the DIRCMD environment variable in the Windows environment for use with the DIR command	SET DIRCMD=[*switches*]	set set dircmd=/p /o
SET DIRCMD=	Removes settings for the DIRCMD environment variable from the Windows environment	SET DIRCMD=	set dircmd=

WILDCARDS

*	Used in a file specification to represent one or more characters		dir *.xls dir sales*.* dir *projection*.xls dir *.*
?	Used in a file specification to represent a single character		dir ????ware.ppt

Items shown in italics and *not* enclosed within square brackets are required parameters

Items shown in italics and enclosed within square brackets are optional parameters

In this tutorial you will:

- Understand the importance and features of ASCII text files

- Redirect the output of a command to an ASCII text file

- View the contents of an ASCII text file

- Pipe output to the MORE filter

- Redirect input from an ASCII text file on disk

- Sort and search the content within an ASCII text file

- Append output to an ASCII text file

- Redirect command output to the printer

- Copy, rename, and delete files

WORKING WITH FILES

Using File Commands, Redirection, Piping, and Filters at SolarWinds, Inc.

CASE

SolarWinds Unlimited

As you work with Isabel to provide staff support, you discover that the Command Prompt window supports all of the types of file operations that you typically perform in the Windows 2000 graphical user interface. Not only are these operations faster, but in some cases, you can perform certain types of file operations (such as renaming groups of files) in the Command Prompt window that are not possible from the Windows graphical user interface. Because one of your job responsibilities is to develop and provide the necessary template files needed by the staff, you realize that a better understanding of file operations within the Windows 2000 command line operating environment will improve your productivity and efficiency.

SESSION 3.1

In this session, you will examine the use and importance of ASCII text files, and then you will create and view the contents of ASCII text files. You will use the output redirection operator to store the output of a command in an ASCII text file. You will use the pipe operator to use the output of a command as the input for another command and combine the pipe operator with the MORE filter to page the output of a command. You will use the input redirection operator to write the contents of an ASCII text file to the window, the SORT filter to sort the contents of an ASCII text file, and the FIND filter to locate information within an ASCII text file. Finally, you will use the append output redirection operator to add the output of a command to the end of an existing ASCII text file.

Working with ASCII Text Files

At the weekly meeting of the support staff, Isabel explains to you that most of the configuration and initialization files used by the Windows 2000 operating system are ASCII text files, so it's important that you and other support staff be familiar with these types of files. Furthermore, she notes that ASCII text files are commonly used with other operating systems, such as UNIX.

An **ASCII text file** is a simple file format in which data is stored as text, and therefore it is often referred to as a text file. The name ASCII stands for **A**merican **S**tandard **C**ode for **I**nformation **I**nterchange. This file format is so common and so important that applications like the ones included in Microsoft Office recognize this standard coding format for storing information in a file and adapt their software packages to use, or support, this file format. It is also common practice to refer to ASCII text files as text files, print files, DOS files, or DOS text files.

In contrast, files produced by word processing software and other types of application software store formatting codes for special features (such as fonts, boldface, and underlining), so that you must use that software application when you work on a file created with that application. You can, however, use word processing applications to open and work with ASCII text files. Furthermore, many of these word processing applications can automatically convert ASCII text files into the file format typically used by that application, or vice versa.

The original standard ASCII coding scheme uses 7 bits to represent all uppercase and lowercase letters of the alphabet, the numeric digits 0 through 9, punctuation symbols, and special control codes. Each ASCII character is assigned a numerical code, called the **ASCII code** or **ASCII value**, such as ASCII 65 for the uppercase letter "A," ASCII 97 for the lowercase letter "a," and ASCII 13 for Ctrl+M. By using 7 bits to encode characters and symbols, these values range from 0 (zero) to 127, for a total of 128 codes. **Control codes** are codes for the use of the Ctrl key with another key. For example, when you press the Tab key to indent a line while creating an ASCII text file, you insert a tab code, Ctrl+I (or ASCII 9). At the end of each line in an ASCII text file, there is an ASCII code for a carriage return, Ctrl+M (ASCII 13); a line feed, Ctrl+J (ASCII 10); or both. Some ASCII text files contain a form feed code, Ctrl+L (ASCII 12), to indicate a page break and the start of a new page. In all versions of Windows and DOS, ASCII text files use a special type of code—an **end-of-file (EOF) code**—Ctrl+Z (ASCII 26), as the last character to mark the end of a text-only file (UNIX text files use Ctrl+D or ASCII 4).

The **extended ASCII** code has values that range from 0 (zero) to 255 because it uses 8 bits to encode characters. The 128 additional codes include values for foreign-language characters or symbols, graphics characters, and scientific characters.

You can produce an ASCII control code or character by pressing and holding the Alt key while you type the ASCII value *on the numeric keypad only*. For example, if you press and hold down the Alt key while you type 65 (or 065) using the numeric keypad in a Command Prompt window, the command interpreter will display the character "A." Figure 3-1 contains examples of ASCII characters and codes for both the original and extended ASCII character sets. In some cases, application programs redefine these codes.

Figure 3-1   **EXAMPLES OF ASCII CHARACTERS AND CODES**

ASCII CODE	KEY, OR KEY COMBINATION
009	Ctrl+I (Control code for tab)
010	Ctrl+J (Control code for line feed)
012	Ctrl+L (Control code for page break)
013	Ctrl+M (Control code for carriage return)
026	Ctrl+Z (EOF, or end-of-file, code)
027	Esc key
032	Spacebar
047	/
048	0
049	1
050	2
058	:
059	;
065	A
066	B
067	C
092	\
097	a
098	b
099	c
126	~ (Tilde symbol)
156	£ (British pound sterling)
201	╔ (Box drawing character)
229	σ (Sigma symbol)
246	÷ (Division symbol)

All versions of Windows also support the **ANSI (American National Standards Institute)** character set, which supports characters from different languages. The first 128 characters in the ANSI character set are identical to the first 128 characters in the ASCII character set. The next 128 characters, however, differ for each supported language.

Another important character set, and file format, is **Unicode**. This file format uses 16 bits (or two bytes) to encode characters, so it can represent 65,536 characters and symbols. Unicode can therefore represent all the symbols in all written languages in the world. Unicode has assigned approximately 39,000 of the total possible 65,536 characters, numbers, and symbols (21,000 of these are used to represent Chinese ideographs).

Using Redirection to Create an ASCII Text File

Isabel asks you to produce a list of the files stored on the templates disk so that you have a record of the template files currently used by the staff. She notes that you can create the list by redirecting the output of the Directory command to a file on disk.

When you work in a command line environment, the operating system expects input from the keyboard (called the **standard input device**), and directs or sends output to the screen (the **standard output device**). You can change the destination for the output. For example, you can instruct the operating system to send the output to a printer or a file on diskette. To send output to a device other than the standard output device, you **redirect**, or change the destination of that output with the output redirection operator. The **output redirection operator** is the greater than symbol (>). If you want to redirect output to a file, specify the name of the file you want to create following the output redirection operator. For example, if you want to redirect output to a printer, specify the name of your printer port.

The general syntax for redirecting output to a file on disk is as follows:

[command] **>** *filename*

If *filename* specifies a file that already exists, the above redirection will overwrite the file, and you will lose its previous contents. If you want to add to an existing file instead, see the section "Appending Output to an ASCII Text File" later in this tutorial.

If you want to redirect output to a printer, use the following syntax:

[command] **>** *printer port*

Before you use the output redirection operator, you want to set up your Command Prompt window and make sure the file name you want to assign to the new file is not already in use.

To set up your computer:

1. Open a Command Prompt window.

2. Type **color f0** (an "f" followed by a zero) and then press **Enter**. The COLOR command changes the background color to white, and the foreground color for text to black.

   TROUBLE? If Windows 2000 displays Help information on the use of the COLOR command and does not change the background and foreground colors, then you typed the letter "O" rather than a zero (0). Press the Spacebar to view the next Help screen, and then enter the command again, but use a zero (0) rather than the letter "O."

3. Insert your copy of Data Disk #1 into drive A, and then change the default drive to drive A.

   TROUBLE? If you no longer have your copy of Data Disk #1, make a new copy of this diskette.

4. Clear the window, type **dir /o** and then press **Enter**. This diskette contains 41 files that use 1,248,070 bytes of storage space. See Figure 3-2. Notice the directory listing has no file named "Templates.txt" — the filename you will use for the redirected output of the Directory command in the next set of steps.

TROUBLE? If the operating system informs you that "0" is an invalid switch, then you typed the numeral zero (0) rather than the letter "o" for the Order switch. Repeat the command, and use the letter "o" rather than a zero (0) for the Order switch.

| Figure 3-2 | DISPLAYING A DIRECTORY IN ORDER BY FILENAME |

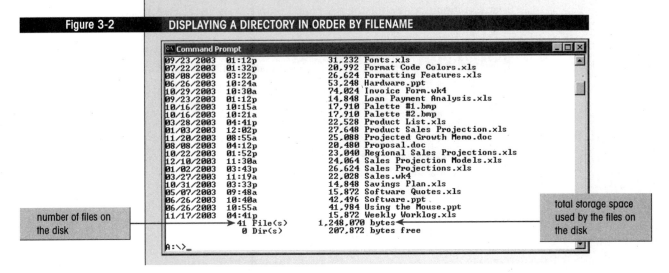

number of files on the disk

total storage space used by the files on the disk

Now you're ready to create an ASCII text file that contains a list of the files on your Data Disk.

To Create an ASCII text File:

1. Type **dir /o > Templates.txt** and then press **Enter**. This command redirects output to a file on your disk. Notice that the Directory command did not display a directory listing in the window.

2. Type (or recall) **dir /o** and then press **Enter**. There is now a new file by the name of Templates.txt. See Figure 3-3. You created this ASCII text file in the last step when you redirected output to a file rather than to the window. Note that the file is 2,736 bytes in size (less than a page in length). Because ASCII text files do not contain formatting or very much text, they are generally small files that require relatively little storage space on disk. The date and time on your Templates.txt file will differ.

| Figure 3-3 | VIEWING AN UPDATED DIRECTORY WITH A NEW ASCII FILE |

ASCII file size

ASCII file created on disk by redirecting output of the Directory command

The output redirection operator is very useful. You have to be careful, however, when redirecting output to a file on disk. As noted earlier, if you specify the filename of an existing file on disk, the operating system will overwrite the existing file without warning you. That's why you should always display a directory listing first to make sure that the filename that you intend to use for the redirected output does not already exist.

REFERENCE WINDOW   **RW**

Redirecting Output of a Directory Listing to a File on Disk
- Open a Command Prompt window.
- Change the default drive to the drive that contains the files you want to examine.
- Type DIR followed by a space and any file specification and switches that you want to use, press the Spacebar, type > (the output redirection operator), press the Spacebar, and type the name of the file that will store the output, and then press Enter.

You can redirect output to a file on disk the same way in other versions of Windows, as well as with different versions of MS-DOS (and UNIX, which introduced redirection). In Windows 95 and later versions of Windows, including Windows 2000, you must put quotation marks around filenames containing spaces.

Viewing the Contents of an ASCII Text File

You can use the TYPE command—another internal command—to display the contents of an ASCII text file in a window or on the screen. The general syntax of the TYPE command is as follows:

TYPE *filename*

The filename is a required parameter.

One advantage of the TYPE command is that you do not need to start a program and then open a file to view its contents. You cannot, however, use the TYPE command to view the contents of a program file or a file produced by an application such as Microsoft Word. If you do, the TYPE command attempts to interpret the file's formatting codes as ASCII characters and therefore will display symbols or blanks in the window or on the screen.

To view the contents of the Templates.txt file:

1. Type **type templates.txt** and then press **Enter**. The TYPE command displays the contents of this ASCII text file in the window, followed by the command prompt. Because the file contains more than 25 lines, Windows 2000 adjusts the view in the window so you only see the end of the file. See Figure 3-4.

Figure 3-4	VIEWING THE CONTENTS OF AN ASCII FILE

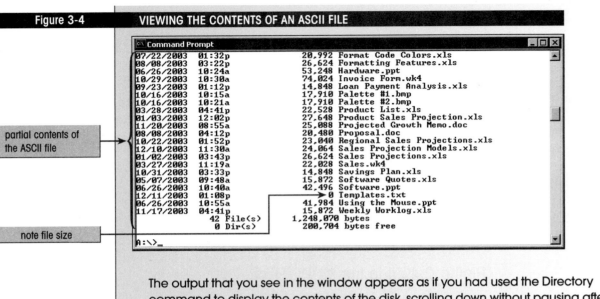

partial contents of the ASCII file

note file size

The output that you see in the window appears as if you had used the Directory command to display the contents of the disk, scrolling down without pausing after the window fills. How can you verify that you used the TYPE command with a text file instead of the DIR command? Note that this directory listing includes an entry for the Templates.txt file at a size of zero (0) bytes. The previous directory listing did not include this entry. When you gave the command to redirect the output of DIR to the Templates.txt file, you immediately created that file on the diskette, and therefore the directory listing included it. However, the file size remained zero while your command was still redirecting its output to the file. If you use the DIR command now, this new filename entry will not show a zero length.

2. Clear the window.

Bear in mind that the directory listing you displayed above is not a current listing of your files. Instead, the TYPE command displayed the contents of the Templates.txt file—the "snapshot" you took of the directory listing at one specific point in time. As you change the contents of a directory—adding, changing, or deleting files—you can create any number of such snapshot files. In sections to come, you will use other commands to rearrange and display parts of this file.

Windows 2000 uses ASCII text files for many purposes, particularly configuration and log files. So that you become familiar with some of these files, Isabel suggests you look at Boot.ini on the hard drive, an important configuration file that displays a menu from which you can pick the operating system or Windows 2000 component you want to use to boot your computer.

To view the contents of the Boot.ini configuration file:

1. If necessary, clear the Command Prompt window.

2. Type **type c:\boot.ini** and then press **Enter**. The TYPE command displays the contents of this configuration file, as shown in Figure 3-5. On the computer used for this figure, there are two options for booting the computer—using Microsoft Windows 2000 Professional or using Microsoft Windows 2000 Recovery Console. Your options might differ.

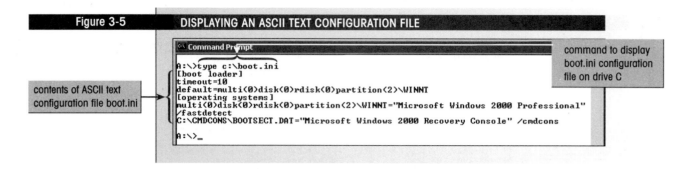

Figure 3-5   **DISPLAYING AN ASCII TEXT CONFIGURATION FILE**

The TYPE command works in the same basic way in other versions of Windows, and different versions of MS-DOS. Again, beginning with Windows 95, you must put quotation marks around filenames containing spaces. Also, under Windows 2000 and Windows NT 4.0, the TYPE command can display the contents of multiple files.

Piping Output to the MORE Filter

After you ask Isabel whether there is a way to control scrolling of the output of a command like the TYPE command that does not have a Pause, or Page switch. Isabel explains that you can pipe the output of the TYPE command to the MORE filter, and thereby control scrolling.

As noted, the TYPE command does not have a Pause switch, and ASCII text files often contain more than 25 lines of text. To display only one screen or window at a time and avoid automatic scrolling, you must send the output of the TYPE command to the MORE filter. A **filter** is a command that can modify the output of another command. The **MORE filter** (or command) is an external command that displays a screen or window of output, pauses, and then displays a "--More--" prompt which permits you to continue when you are ready.

To combine the use of the MORE filter with another command, use the pipe operator, which is usually located on the backslash (\) key and appears as either a solid vertical line or as a vertical line divided into two parts. The **pipe operator** (|) redirects the output produced by one command so that the output then becomes the input for another command. For example, the following command will display the output of an ASCII text file one screen or window at a time:

> **TYPE Templates.txt | MORE**

The first command, TYPE, produces the output, and the operating system redirects the output so that it becomes the input for the MORE filter. The MORE command then displays the output of the TYPE command one screen or window at a time. The redirection of the output of one command so that it becomes the input for another command is called **piping**, and the entire command line is called a **pipeline**. The general syntax for piping output to the MORE filter is as follows:

> [*command*] | **MORE**

To display the contents of the Templates.txt file one screen or window at a time:

1. Type (or recall) **type templates.txt**, press the **Spacebar**, type **| more** and then press **Enter**. The MORE filter displays the first part of this ASCII text file. See Figure 3-6. Notice that the output is identical to what you would expect with the Directory command and Pause switch. The "-- More --" prompt at the end of the directory listing tips you off to the fact that this is not a directory listing produced with the DIR command.

| Figure 3-6 | PIPING OUTPUT WITH THE MORE FILTER |

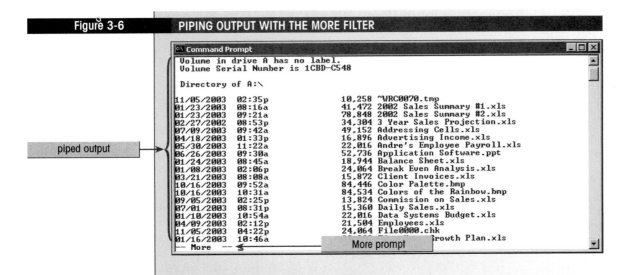

piped output

```
Command Prompt                                                    _□×
 Volume in drive A has no label.
 Volume Serial Number is 1CBD-C548

 Directory of A:\

11/05/2003  02:35p        10,258 ~WRC0070.tmp
01/23/2003  08:16a        41,472 2002 Sales Summary #1.xls
01/23/2003  09:21a        78,848 2002 Sales Summary #2.xls
02/27/2002  08:53p        34,304 3 Year Sales Projection.xls
07/09/2003  09:42a        49,152 Addressing Cells.xls
04/18/2003  01:33p        16,896 Advertising Income.xls
05/30/2003  11:22a        22,016 Andre's Employee Payroll.xls
06/26/2003  09:30a        52,736 Application Software.ppt
01/24/2003  08:45a        18,944 Balance Sheet.xls
01/08/2003  02:06p        24,064 Break Even Analysis.xls
03/21/2003  08:08a        15,872 Client Invoices.xls
10/16/2003  09:52a        84,446 Color Palette.bmp
10/16/2003  10:31a        84,534 Colors of the Rainbow.bmp
09/05/2003  02:25p        13,824 Commission on Sales.xls
07/01/2003  08:31p        15,360 Daily Sales.xls
01/10/2003  10:54a        22,016 Data Systems Budget.xls
04/09/2003  02:12p        21,504 Employees.xls
11/05/2003  04:22p        24,064 File0000.chk
01/16/2003  10:46a                          rowth Plan.xls
-- More  --                     More prompt
```

2. Press the **Spacebar**. The MORE filter displays the next part of this ASCII text file.

3. Press the **Spacebar**. The MORE filter displays the remainder of the file, and then you see the command prompt.

You can use the pipe operator and the MORE filter with any other command that produces more than a full screen or window of output so that you can view all the information generated by the command.

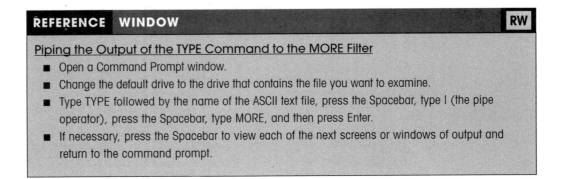

REFERENCE WINDOW   **RW**

Piping the Output of the TYPE Command to the MORE Filter

- Open a Command Prompt window.
- Change the default drive to the drive that contains the file you want to examine.
- Type TYPE followed by the name of the ASCII text file, press the Spacebar, type | (the pipe operator), press the Spacebar, type MORE, and then press Enter.
- If necessary, press the Spacebar to view each of the next screens or windows of output and return to the command prompt.

You can use the TYPE command, the pipe operator, and the MORE filter to view the contents of Readme files included with software packages. When software manufacturers release a software product, they often include Readme files with the latest information on the use of the product—information that is not included in the manual or the software product's Help system. These files are ASCII text files with names such as Readme, Read.me, Readme.doc, or Readme.1st, and they are copied to your hard disk when you install the software. You can then examine these files for important information that you might need to configure the software product so that it works with the hardware components of your computer system. These Readme files might also contain troubleshooting information.

You can pipe output to the MORE filter in the same way in other versions of Windows, as well as in different versions of MS-DOS and UNIX. Remember that when using operating systems that support long filenames, you must put quotation marks around filenames containing spaces.

Redirecting Input Using an ASCII Text File

Isabel explains that you can perform the same type of operation using a different technique. You can redirect the input to the MORE filter directly without using the TYPE command and the pipe operator.

As noted earlier, the operating system assumes that input will come from the standard input device — the keyboard. However, input can come from a file instead. To redirect input from a file, use the **input redirection operator** (<). The general syntax for redirecting input from a file to the MORE filter is as follows:

MORE   <   *filename*

When you perform this type of redirection, the MORE filter pages the output one screen at a time.

> *To redirect input from a file on disk to the MORE filter:*
>
> 1. Clear the window, type **more < templates.txt** and then press **Enter.** The operating system redirects input from the Templates.txt file on disk to the MORE filter, and the MORE filter displays one screen or window at a time. See Figure 3-7. Your view of this file is identical to the one produced by piping output of the TYPE command to the MORE filter. Note, however, that the title bar shows the MORE command name, because, unlike the previous command's display, this screen output is not piped.

Figure 3-7   **REDIRECTING INPUT TO THE MORE FILTER**

redirected page input

-More- prompt

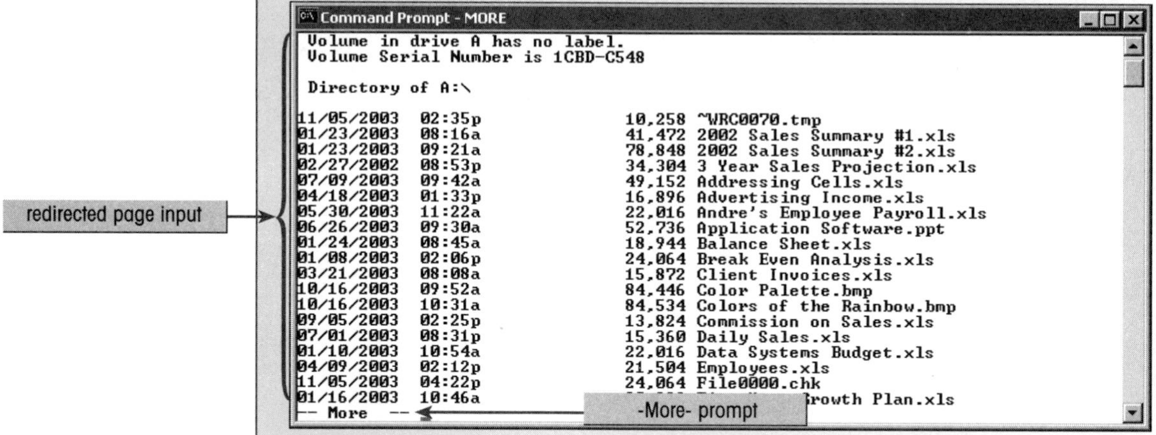

2. Press and hold down the **Ctrl** key, press and release **C**, and then release the **Ctrl** key. Ctrl+C interrupts the command, displays ^C (the Ctrl key is represented by the ^ character) on the next line, and then returns you to the command prompt. See Figure 3-8.

Figure 3-8

CANCELING A COMMAND

```
Command Prompt                                              _ □ ×
    Volume Serial Number is F065-B557

    Directory of A:\

11/05/2003   02:35p           10,258  ~WRC0070.tmp
01/23/2003   08:16a           41,472  2002 Sales Summary #1.xls
01/23/2003   09:21a           78,848  2002 Sales Summary #2.xls
02/27/2002   08:53p           34,304  3 Year Sales Projection.xls
07/09/2003   09:42a           49,152  Addressing Cells.xls
04/18/2003   01:33p           16,896  Advertising Income.xls
05/30/2003   11:22a           22,016  Andre's Employee Payroll.xls
06/26/2003   09:30a           52,736  Application Software.ppt
01/24/2003   08:45a           18,944  Balance Sheet.xls
01/08/2003   02:06p           24,064  Break Even Analysis.xls
03/21/2003   08:08a           15,872  Client Invoices.xls
10/16/2003   09:52a           84,446  Color Palette.bmp
10/16/2003   10:31a           84,534  Colors of the Rainbow.bmp
09/05/2003   02:25p           13,824  Commission on Sales.xls
07/01/2003   08:31p           15,360  Daily Sales.xls
01/10/2003   10:54a           22,016  Data Systems Budget.xls
04/09/2003   02:12p           21,504  Employees.xls
11/05/2003   04:22p           24,064  File0000.chk
01/16/2003   10:46a           20,992  Five Year Growth Plan.xls
^C
A:\>_
```

command output
interrupted and canceled
with Ctrl+C

If a command produces more output than you expected, you can interrupt (and cancel) the command with Ctrl+C.

REFERENCE WINDOW   **RW**

Redirecting Input from an ASCII Text File to the MORE Filter
- Open a Command Prompt window.
- Change the default drive to the drive that contains the file you want to examine.
- Type MORE, press the Spacebar, type < (the input redirection operator), press the Spacebar, type the name of the ASCII text file, and then press Enter.
- Press Spacebar to view each of the next screens or windows of output and return to the command prompt, or if you want to interrupt the output of the command, press and then release Ctrl+C.

You can use this technique of redirecting input to the MORE filter for configuration and initialization files so that you can examine the contents of the files one screen or window at a time. **Initialization files** are files like Boot.ini that contain the file extension "ini," and that contain settings used by the operating system and other programs.

In all versions of Windows, MS-DOS, and UNIX, you can use the MORE filter by redirecting input from a file as above. In general, you redirect input the same way in these operating systems. As noted before, you must put quotation marks around filenames containing spaces for those operating systems that support long filenames.

Viewing Other Kinds of Files

Isabel tells you that in Windows 2000, you can also use the MORE command like the TYPE command, specifying the filename directly without redirecting input. For example, you could have typed "more templates.txt" in the previous section, without the "<" input redirection symbol. This reproduces the way the MORE command works in UNIX. To use the MORE filter this way in Windows NT 4.0, you must use the /E (Extended features) switch.

Although the TYPE and MORE commands are designed for ASCII text files, you can use them with other kinds of files when you need to get an idea of a file's contents, regardless of its format. Files with the "chk" extension provide a good example. The Check Disk utility, creates these files, which contain recovered file fragments resulting from disk errors. They are **binary files**, which can contain any kind of data, rather than just ASCII text, so you will usually see strange characters when you display them with the TYPE command or MORE filter. Isabel suggests you use both commands to examine such a file named File0000.chk on your diskette.

To view a recovered file fragment in File0000.chk:

1. Clear the Command Prompt window, type **type file0000.chk**, and then press **Enter**. In this particular file, you see only a short string of characters as in Figure 3-9, because the TYPE command encounters an End-of-File code (EOF, Ctrl-Z, or ASCII 26) a short way into the file. This code can appear anywhere in binary files, which do not use the EOF code to denote the actual end of the file. However, the TYPE command always stops when it encounters an EOF code.

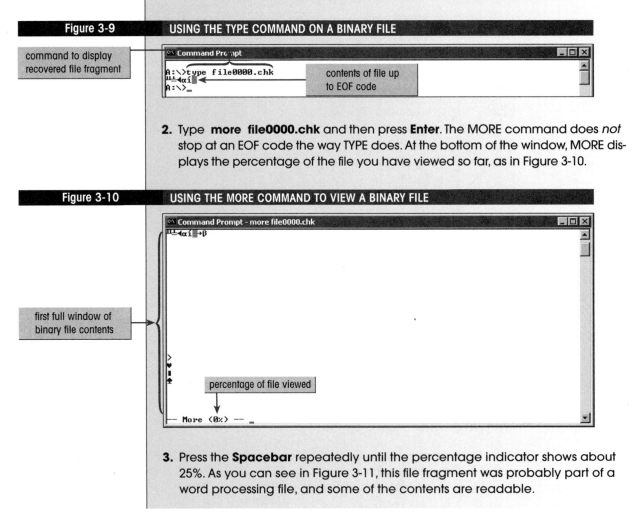

| Figure 3-9 | USING THE TYPE COMMAND ON A BINARY FILE |

command to display recovered file fragment

contents of file up to EOF code

2. Type **more file0000.chk** and then press **Enter**. The MORE command does *not* stop at an EOF code the way TYPE does. At the bottom of the window, MORE displays the percentage of the file you have viewed so far, as in Figure 3-10.

| Figure 3-10 | USING THE MORE COMMAND TO VIEW A BINARY FILE |

first full window of binary file contents

percentage of file viewed

3. Press the **Spacebar** repeatedly until the percentage indicator shows about 25%. As you can see in Figure 3-11, this file fragment was probably part of a word processing file, and some of the contents are readable.

Figure 3-11 **USING MORE TO VIEW READABLE BINARY FILE CONTENTS**

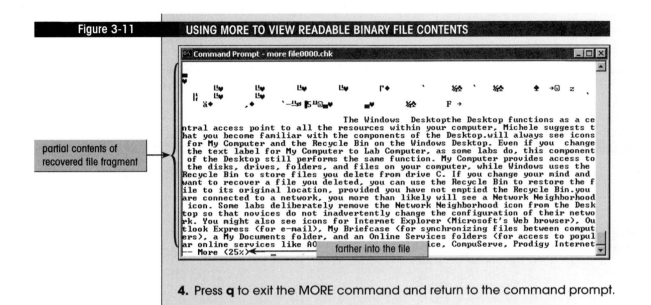

partial contents of
recovered file fragment

The Windows Desktopthe Desktop functions as a central access point to all the resources within your computer. Michele suggests that you become familiar with the components of the Desktop.will always see icons for My Computer and the Recycle Bin on the Windows Desktop. Even if you change the text label for My Computer to Lab Computer, as some labs do, this component of the Desktop still performs the same function. My Computer provides access to the disks, drives, folders, and files on your computer, while Windows uses the Recycle Bin to store files you delete from drive C. If you change your mind and want to recover a file you deleted, you can use the Recycle Bin to restore the file to its original location, provided you have not emptied the Recycle Bin.you are connected to a network, you more than likely will see a Network Neighborhood icon. Some labs deliberately remove the Network Neighborhood icon from the Desktop so that novices do not inadvertently change the configuration of their network. You might also see icons for Internet Explorer (Microsoft's Web browser), Outlook Express (for e-mail), My Briefcase (for synchronizing files between computers), a My Documents folder, and an Online Services folders (for access to popular online services like AO⌐ice, CompuServe, Prodigy Internet

-- More (25%)

farther into the file

4. Press **q** to exit the MORE command and return to the command prompt.

Isabel points out that you can use this technique to determine whether you want to keep the contents of a file like this. In cases where disk errors cause you to lose a valuable file, recovered file fragments may save you some time and effort in restoring your data.

Sorting ASCII Text Files

As Isabel and you talk further about redirection and filters, you learn that there are three other commands that are filters: one for sorting the contents of ASCII text files, and two others for locating information in ASCII text files.

The SORT filter can take input from a command or a file, sort the input, and then display the results. If you want to use an ASCII text file as the source for input, and then sort that input, use the following approach:

> **SORT < *filename***

The SORT filter sorts the contents of the file starting with the first character on each line, comparing that character with the first character on the next line. If the first character on each line is identical, then it compares the second characters, sorting each line with respect to all other lines in a file from left to right. By default, the input is sorted in ascending order (from 0 to 9, and then from A to Z) using the ASCII code of the characters (although it ignores uppercase or lowercase). If you want to sort in descending order (in reverse order), you would use the **Reverse switch** (**/R**), as follows:

> **SORT /R < *filename***

When you produced the Templates.txt file, you used the Order switch to arrange the directory listing in order by filename. You now want to display that same file information in reverse order by date (from the most recent file to the oldest file). Because the date is the first column in this ASCII text file, you can sort the contents of the file by date. If the date is the same for more than one file, then each line is sorted by the time. If the date and time are the same, then each line is next sorted by the file size. If the date, time, and file size are the same, then each line is sorted by the filename. Again, the sort is from left to right.

To redirect input from a file on disk to the SORT filter:

1. Type **sort /r < templates.txt** and then press **Enter**. The operating system redirects input from the Templates.txt file on disk to the SORT filter, and the SORT filter sorts the contents of the file so that file dates are listed in reverse order. See Figure 3-12. However, the output scrolled so fast within the window that you were probably unable to see the first part of the output.

Figure 3-12	SORTING REDIRECTED INPUT

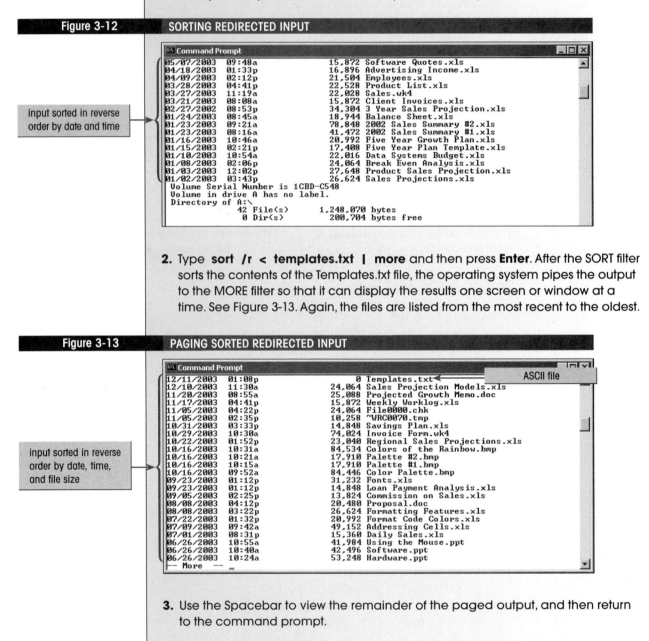

input sorted in reverse order by date and time

2. Type **sort /r < templates.txt | more** and then press **Enter**. After the SORT filter sorts the contents of the Templates.txt file, the operating system pipes the output to the MORE filter so that it can display the results one screen or window at a time. See Figure 3-13. Again, the files are listed from the most recent to the oldest.

Figure 3-13	PAGING SORTED REDIRECTED INPUT

input sorted in reverse order by date, time, and file size

3. Use the Spacebar to view the remainder of the paged output, and then return to the command prompt.

The SORT filter provides a simple and easy mechanism for quickly sorting the contents of an ASCII text file from left to right.

Sorting the Contents of ASCII Text Files with the SORT Filter

- Open a Command Prompt window.
- Change the default drive to the drive that contains the files you want to examine.
- Type SORT, press the Spacebar, type the name of the ASCII text file, press the Spacebar, type | (the pipe operator), press the Spacebar, type MORE, and then press Enter.
- Press the Spacebar to view each of the next screens or windows of sorted output and return to the command prompt.

The SORT filter works in the same basic way in other versions of Windows and different versions of MS-DOS and UNIX. In all these operating systems, you can also use SORT without redirecting input. For example, you could type sort /r templates.txt in the example above, without the "<" input redirection symbol. Again, enclose filenames containing spaces in quotation marks.

You can also use the pipe operator to send the output of another command to the SORT filter as input, as you did previously with the MORE command.

Searching the Contents of an ASCII Text File

After demonstrating the use of the SORT filter, Isabel shows you how to find information in an ASCII text file with the use of the FIND filter. She points out that you can use this filter to quickly search files that contain information about the company's collection of template files. For practice, Isabel suggests you list all the files that contain "Sales" in the filename and store the list of filenames in a new text file called "Sales Templates.txt".

The FIND filter searches one or more ASCII text files for a specific string of text (a set of characters, such as a filename or a setting), and then displays the results by file. The general syntax for this command is as follows:

FIND *"string" filename*

You must enclose the text that you specify as the string within quotation marks. Also, unless you specify otherwise, FIND is case sensitive, and therefore the string must be in the same case as that found in the file (or files).

To search for a text string in an ASCII text file:

1. Clear the window.

2. Type **find "Sales" Templates.txt** and then press **Enter**. The FIND filter searches the contents of the Templates.txt file (an ASCII text file), and lists the lines that contain the word "Sales." See Figure 3-14. The FIND filter has extracted a subset of the information contained in the file.

TROUBLE? If the FIND filter reports that the parameter format is not correct, then you did not include the string within quotation marks. Repeat the command, and use the exact syntax shown.

TROUBLE? If the FIND filter does not list any lines within the Templates.txt file, then you typed "Sales" in all uppercase, all lowercase or you did not capitalize the beginning "S" in "Sales." The FIND filter is case-sensitive. Repeat this step again, but use the exact case shown for the string, or recall the same command and add the Ignore switch (/I) so that the FIND filter ignores the case.

Figure 3-14   **USING THE FIND FILTER TO LOCATE TEXT IN AN ASCII FILE**

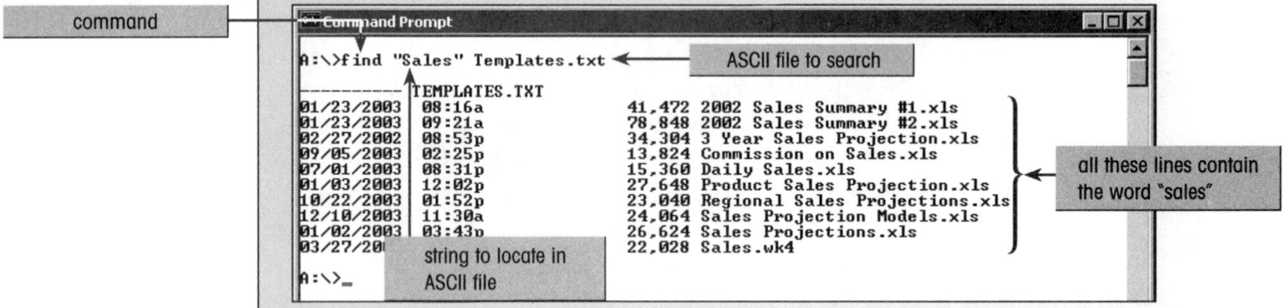

command

3. Clear the window, type **find "Sales" Templates.txt > "Sales Templates.txt"**, and then press **Enter**. You must use quotation marks around the string "Sales" and the filename "Sales Templates.txt" (because the latter contains a space). The operating system records the output of the FIND filter in an ASCII text file on disk.

   TROUBLE? If the FIND filter reports that the parameter format is not correct, then you did not include the string within quotation marks. Repeat the command, and use the exact syntax shown.

4. Type **type "Sales Templates.txt"** and then press **Enter**. TYPE displays the contents of the Sales Templates.txt file. See Figure 3-15. Notice that each of the lines in "Sales Templates.txt" contains the word "Sales."

   TROUBLE? If the command interpreter displays a message indicating that the system cannot find the file you specified, then you did not include quotation marks around the filename. Repeat the step using the exact syntax shown.

Figure 3-15   **REDIRECTING OUTPUT OF THE FIND FILTER TO A FILE**

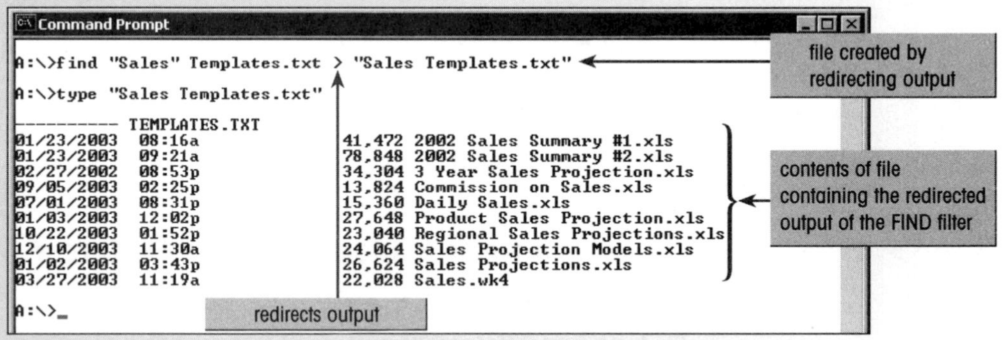

You can use the FIND filter in the same way in other versions of Windows and MS-DOS. For those operating systems that support long filenames, you will need to place quotation marks around filenames with spaces.

Windows 2000 and versions of Windows NT 4.0 also offer the FINDSTR command, a more powerful utility that can locate text strings using a set of specialized wildcards to match patterns, and which also has the ability to examine multiple files in the same pass.

Searching ASCII Text Files with the FIND Filter
- Open a Command Prompt window.
- Change the default drive to the drive that contains the files you want to examine.
- Type FIND, press the Spacebar, type the string (or text) you want to locate within quotation marks (required), press the Spacebar, type the name of the ASCII text file, and then press Enter.
- If you want to redirect output of the FIND filter to a file on disk, type FIND, press the Spacebar, type the string (or text) you want to locate within quotation marks (required), press the Spacebar, type the name of the ASCII text file, type > (the output redirection operator), press the Spacebar, type the name of the file that will store the output, and then press Enter.

Although you will find that you depend on the MORE filter when working in a command line environment, the SORT and FIND filters are also useful tools that you can call on when the need arises.

Appending Output to an ASCII Text File

Now that you are familiar with the use of the output and input redirection operators, Isabel shows you how to append, or add, the output of a command to an existing file by adding a list of all files with "Projection" in the filename to the file you made previously.

If you create an ASCII text file, and then find that you need to append output to the end of that same file, you can use the append redirection operator (>>), as follows:

[*command*] >> *filename*

You need to be careful when you use this redirection operator. If you accidentally type only one greater-than symbol rather than two, the operating system will overwrite the existing file.

If you need to append output to another file, you will probably also want to insert some blank lines between the output that already exists in the file, and the next output you append to that file. You can use the following command to add a blank line to the end of the file:

ECHO. >> *filename*

You can use the ECHO command to display messages or blank lines in a window or on the screen. If you follow the ECHO command with a period (or dot) without any space between ECHO and the period, then the operating system will display a blank line in the window or on the screen. Then, if you use the append redirection operator with this command and specify a filename, the operating system will add a blank line to the bottom of the file, because you are redirecting output from the display device.

To append output in a file on diskette:

1. Clear the window, type **echo. >> "Sales Templates.txt"** and check what you've typed. You must type the period (or dot) right after you type ECHO (no space is allowed). You also have to enclose the long filename within quotation marks because it contains a space. Press **Enter**. The operating system writes a blank line to the bottom of the file "Sales Templates.txt" and then displays the command prompt.

2. Press **F3** to recall the previous command and then press **Enter**. The operating system writes another blank line to the bottom of the same file.

3. Type **find "Projection" Templates.txt** and then press **Enter**. The FIND filter finds five lines in the Templates.txt file that contain the word "Projection". See Figure 3-16. Now that you've tested the command to make sure it works, you can recall the same command and append the output to the Sales Templates.txt file.

   TROUBLE? If the FIND filter reports that the parameter format is not correct, then you did not include the string within quotation marks. Repeat the command, and use the exact syntax shown.

   TROUBLE? If the FIND filter does not list any files, then you might have typed Projection in all uppercase or all lowercase (check the spelling as well). The FIND filter is case-sensitive. Repeat this step, but use the exact case shown for the string, or recall the same command and add the Ignore switch (/I) so the FIND filter ignores the case.

Figure 3-16	USING THE FIND FILTER TO SEARCH FOR TEXT IN AN ASCII FILE

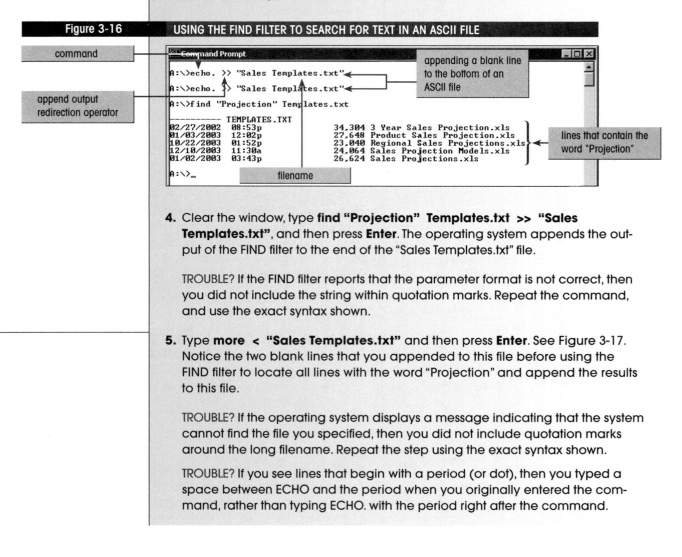

4. Clear the window, type **find "Projection" Templates.txt >> "Sales Templates.txt"**, and then press **Enter**. The operating system appends the output of the FIND filter to the end of the "Sales Templates.txt" file.

   TROUBLE? If the FIND filter reports that the parameter format is not correct, then you did not include the string within quotation marks. Repeat the command, and use the exact syntax shown.

5. Type **more < "Sales Templates.txt"** and then press **Enter**. See Figure 3-17. Notice the two blank lines that you appended to this file before using the FIND filter to locate all lines with the word "Projection" and append the results to this file.

   TROUBLE? If the operating system displays a message indicating that the system cannot find the file you specified, then you did not include quotation marks around the long filename. Repeat the step using the exact syntax shown.

   TROUBLE? If you see lines that begin with a period (or dot), then you typed a space between ECHO and the period when you originally entered the command, rather than typing ECHO. with the period right after the command.

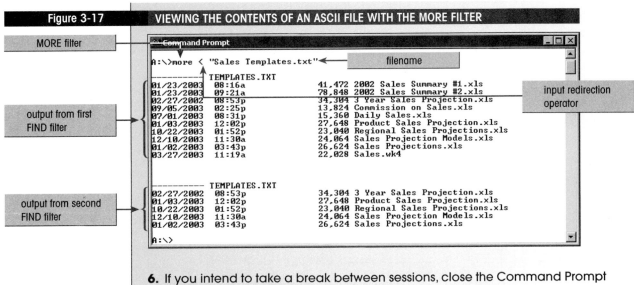

Figure 3-17 · VIEWING THE CONTENTS OF AN ASCII FILE WITH THE MORE FILTER

6. If you intend to take a break between sessions, close the Command Prompt window.

If you use the append output redirection operator and specify a filename that does not already exist, Windows 2000 creates the file first, and then appends the output to the new file.

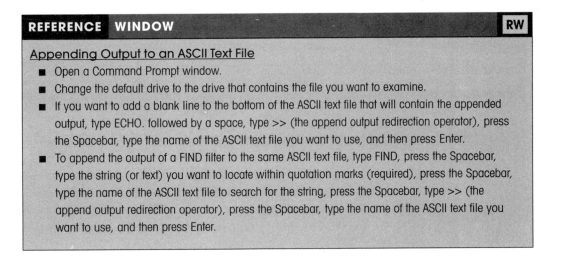

REFERENCE WINDOW · RW

Appending Output to an ASCII Text File

■ Open a Command Prompt window.

■ Change the default drive to the drive that contains the file you want to examine.

■ If you want to add a blank line to the bottom of the ASCII text file that will contain the appended output, type ECHO. followed by a space, type >> (the append output redirection operator), press the Spacebar, type the name of the ASCII text file you want to use, and then press Enter.

■ To append the output of a FIND filter to the same ASCII text file, type FIND, press the Spacebar, type the string (or text) you want to locate within quotation marks (required), press the Spacebar, type the name of the ASCII text file to search for the string, press the Spacebar, type >> (the append output redirection operator), press the Spacebar, type the name of the ASCII text file you want to use, and then press Enter.

You can append output to a file on disk using the output redirection operator the same way in other versions of Windows, MS-DOS, and UNIX. For those operating systems that support long filenames, make sure you place quotation marks around filenames with spaces.

Piping, redirection, and filtering are three powerful tools that are often used in combination with each other to manage input and output in a command line environment.

Session 3.1 QUICK CHECK

1. A(n) _____ file is a simple file format in which data is stored as text.

2. The last character in an ASCII text file is a special type of code—a(n) _____ code.

3. To send output to another device other than the standard output device (the display device), you can _____, or change the destination of, that output and, for example, send the output to a file on disk.

4. You can use the _____ operator to redirect output to a file.

5. To view the contents of an ASCII text file, you use the _____ command.

6. A(n) _____ is a command that can modify the output of another command.

7. The _____ operator redirects the output produced by a command operation so that the output then becomes the input for another command.

8. You can use the _____ operator to redirect input from a file on disk.

9. You can use the _____ operator to redirect output and add it to the end of an existing file.

10. The standard input device is the _____, and the standard output device is the _____.

SESSION 3.2

In this session you will redirect the output of a command to a printer. You will also copy, rename, and delete individual files and groups of files on disk.

Redirecting Output to the Printer

Isabel asks you to print a list of the files on your diskette.

She tells you that besides redirecting the output of a command to a file, you can also send the output directly to the printer. Using this capability with the DIR command allows you to do something that Windows Explorer and My Computer cannot do—print a list of files in a directory.

To send the output of a command, such as DIR, to the printer, redirect the output as you have previously, but instead of typing a filename, specify the device name of your printer port. IBM designated LPT1 (Line Printer #1) as the default printer port on its original PCs. Today, most people still connect their printer to LPT1. If you work on a network, output to LPT1—you can also use the name PRN (for printer)—is more than likely captured and redirected to a network printer. LPT1 and PRN are reserved device names, which you cannot use as folder names or filenames. A **device name** is a name Windows 2000 assigns to one of the devices, or hardware components, in a computer system. Figure 3-18 lists device names used by Windows 2000. The NUL device, sometimes called the "Bit Bucket," is a special device that behaves like a perpetually empty file and discards any data you copy or redirect into it. All versions of Windows and MS-DOS use these device names.

Figure 3-18	RESERVED DEVICE NAMES	

DEVICE NAME	MEANING	ASSIGNED TO
LPT1	Line Printer 1	First parallel port
LPT2	Line Printer 2	Second parallel port
LPT3	Line Printer 3	Third parallel port
PRN	Printer	First parallel port
COM1	Communications port 1	First serial port
COM2	Communications port 2	Second serial port
COM3	Communications port 3	Third serial port
COM4	Communications port 4	Fourth serial port
CON	Console unit	Monitor and keyboard
A:	Drive A	First floppy drive
C:	Drive C	First hard disk drive
NUL	NUL device	"Bit Bucket"

To send the current directory listing to the printer:

1. If necessary, open a Command Prompt window, and then change the foreground and background colors.

2. Make sure your Data Disk is in drive A, change the default drive to drive A, and then clear the window.

3. Make sure your printer is on.

4. Type **dir > prn** and then press **Enter**. The DIR command does not display output in the window, but rather redirects it to your printer port. See Figure 3-19. The print-out contains the directory listing for your Data Disk.

   TROUBLE? If Windows 2000 displays an error message and informs you that the system cannot write to the specified device, enter the command DIR > "Directory Listing.txt" to redirect the output to a file, and then use notepad to print a copy of "Directory Listing.txt".

   TROUBLE? If your printer does not print, check to see if your printer's indicators show that it has received data. You may need to eject the page manually, because the above command does not send a form-feed signal to the printer to eject the page automatically, as a word processor would.

Figure 3-19	REDIRECTING OUTPUT OF A DIRECTORY LISTING TO A PRINTER

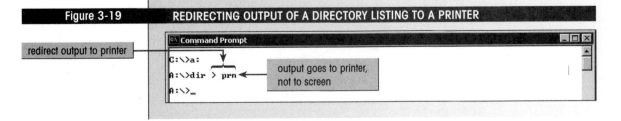

redirect output to printer

output goes to printer, not to screen

```
C:\>a:
A:\>dir > prn
A:\>_
```

Knowing how to redirect output to your printer port is important if you need to troubleshoot a printer problem. In fact, if you are using the Print Troubleshooter in Windows Help, it will recommend that you use this technique as a starting point for troubleshooting the problem and testing the printer connection.

REFERENCE WINDOW **RW**

<u>Redirecting Output to a Printer</u>
- Open a Command Prompt window.
- Change the default drive to the drive that contains the files with which you want to work.
- Type DIR, followed by a space, type **>** PRN, and then press Enter key.
- If necessary, eject the page from your printer manually.

As noted earlier, using redirection to send the output of a command line to the printer allows you to quickly print lists and reports not otherwise available in Windows, such as a list of filenames in a directory.

Other versions of Windows and MS-DOS redirect output to a printer in the same way. If a filename contains one or more spaces, you'll need to enclose it in quotation marks.

Copying Files

Isabel asks you to make a copy of the "Five Year Plan Template.xls" file and to revise it so that you have a new version. She asks you to name the new version "Five Year Plan Draft.xls."

You can use the COPY command to quickly copy the contents of an existing file into a new file on the same disk, and at the same time give the copy a new name. COPY is a versatile, internal command that you can use in a variety of ways. If you want to create a copy of a file from an existing file, the syntax is as follows:

COPY *source* [*destination*]

The original file that you copy is the **source file**—in this case, "Five Year Plan Template.xls." The new file that you produce from the copy operation is the **destination file**, or **target file**—in this case, "Five Year Plan Draft.xls."

If you copy a file and specify a filename that already exists, COPY automatically asks for verification before it overwrites the file. After you make a copy of a file, you should verify that the copy operation produced the file you wanted.

To copy the template file:

1. Type **set dircmd=/p /o** and then press **Enter** to specify default switches for the Directory command.

2. Type **copy "Five Year Plan Template.xls" "Five Year Plan Draft.xls"** and then press **Enter**. Because these filenames each contain spaces, you must place each filename within quotation marks. If the copy is successful, the COPY command displays the message "1 file(s) copied." and then you see the command prompt.

3. Type the command **dir Five*** and then press **Enter**. The file "Five Year Plan Draft.xls" is shown in the directory listing. See Figure 3-20. Note that the new file contains the same number of bytes and date and time of creation as "Five Year Plan Template.xls." Because you have not yet made any changes to "Five Year Plan Draft.xls," it is identical to "Five Year Plan Template.xls."

Figure 3-20 | CREATING A COPY OF A FILE

set default DIR switches

```
A:\>set dircmd=/p /o

A:\>copy "Five Year Plan Template.xls" "Five Year Plan Draft.xls"
        1 file(s) copied.

A:\>dir Five*
 Volume in drive A has no label.
 Volume Serial Number is F065-B557

 Directory of A:\

01/16/2003  10:46a            20,992 Five Year Growth Plan.xls
01/15/2003  02:21p            17,408 Five Year Plan Draft.xls
01/15/2003  02:21p            17,408 Five Year Plan Template.xls
               3 File(s)      55,808 bytes
               0 Dir(s)      185,856 bytes free

A:\>_
```

name of file to copy

check for new file

name of new file

files with the word "Five" at the beginning of the filename

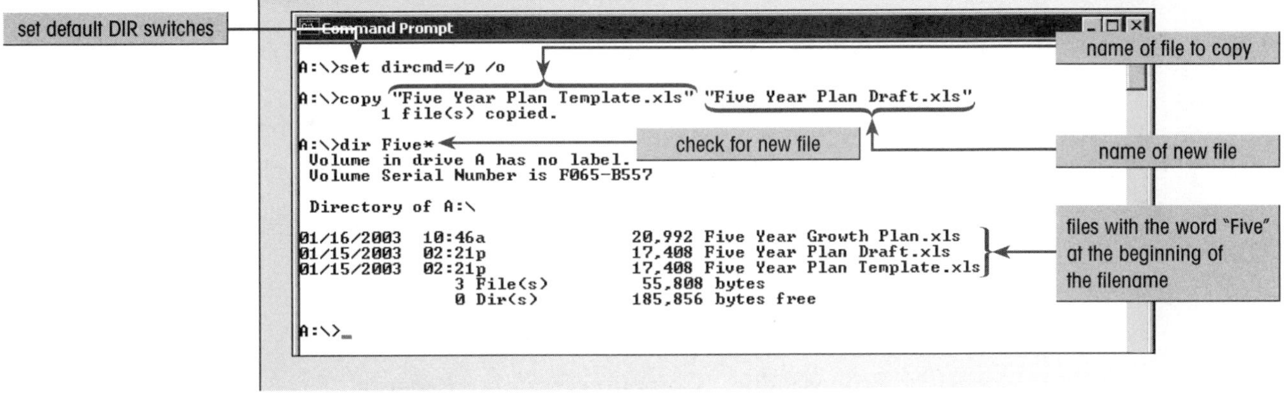

You can also copy files from one drive to another, as well as from one directory to another directory. In Tutorial 4, you will examine some of these techniques for copying files.

REFERENCE WINDOW | **RW**

Creating a Copy of a File
- Open a Command Prompt window.
- Change the default drive to the drive that contains the file you want to copy.
- Type COPY, followed by a space, type the name of the source file, press the Spacebar, and type the name of the destination or target file. If one or both of the filenames contain spaces, you must enclose them within quotation marks.

In other versions of Windows and MS-DOS, you would create a copy of a file in the same way, enclosing filenames in quotation marks when they include spaces.

Renaming Files

Isabel asks you to rename some of the files on your diskette so the filenames more clearly identify the contents of the files. Later, when you are facing deadlines, you will not need to spend valuable time figuring out which file to use.

You can use the RENAME command, or its abbreviated version, REN, to change the name of a file. If you use wildcards with this command, you can change the names of files in a group. By contrast, Windows Explorer and My Computer provide no way to rename a group of files in one step.

The general syntax for these internal commands is as follows:

RENAME *[drive:][path]filename1 filename2*

REN *[drive:][path]filename1 filename2*

When you specify *filename1* (the source filename), you must include the drive and path if the file is on another drive or in another directory. The **path** specifies the name of the directory, or sequence of directories that point to where the file is stored. You *never* specify a drive or path for *filename2* (the destination filename). If you do, the RENAME command displays an error message because it thinks you are attempting to move the file, and this command does not move files. If you use wildcards in *filename2*, the characters represented by the wildcards will be identical to the corresponding characters in *filename1*.

Renaming a Single File

You'd like to make the filename Proposal.doc more descriptive, and because this particular Microsoft Word file is a proposal for computer training, you'd like to rename it to "Computer Training Proposal.doc". You can enter the RENAME command using either of the following approaches:

REN Proposal.doc "Computer Training Proposal.doc"

REN Proposal.doc "Computer Training Proposal.*"
Or, because the disk has no other files named "Proposal," you could also use:

REN Proposal.* "Computer Training Proposal.*"

Again, note that you must use quotation marks when a filename contains spaces. If you substitute an asterisk wildcard for the extension in the destination file, REN assumes you want to use the same extension as the source file. In this case, the asterisk in the source filename substitutes for whatever file extension the first file contains, and the REN command keeps the same extension for the new filename. These features save keystrokes, but more importantly, they preserve the extension, which almost all Windows applications require for their data files.

To rename the Proposal.doc file from the command prompt:

1. Clear the window, type **dir *pro***, and then press **Enter** to verify the file exists. DIR lists all filenames containing the characters "pro," regardless of case. See Figure 3-21.

Figure 3-21	LOCATING THE FILE TO RENAME

```
A:\>dir *pro*            check for file
Volume in drive A has no label.    using wildcards
Volume Serial Number is F065-B557

Directory of A:\

02/27/2002  08:53p          34,304 3 Year Sales Projection.xls
03/28/2003  04:41p          22,528 Product List.xls
01/03/2003  12:02p          27,648 Product Sales Projection.xls
11/20/2003  08:55a          25,088 Projected Growth Memo.doc
08/08/2003  04:12p          20,480 Proposal.doc     file to rename
10/22/2003  01:52p          23,040 Regional Sales Projections.xls
12/10/2003  11:30a          24,064 Sales Projection Models.xls
01/02/2003  03:43p          26,624 Sales Projections.xls
              8 File(s)    203,776 bytes
              0 Dir(s)     185,856 bytes free

A:\>
```

2. Type **ren Proposal.doc "Computer Training Proposal.*"** and then press **Enter**. REN assumes that you want to rename the file on the current drive and that the extension of the new filename is the same. REN will not let you rename a file if there is already a file by the new name that you want to use. You can also use RENAME instead of REN.

3. Type (or recall) **dir *pro*** and then press **Enter** to verify the change. When it renamed the file, REN changed the name, but kept the extension. See Figure 3-22.

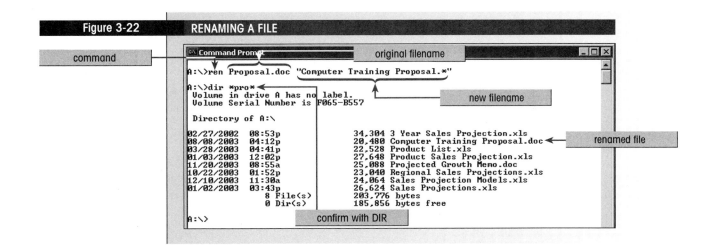

Figure 3-22 RENAMING A FILE

command — original filename

A:\>ren Proposal.doc "Computer Training Proposal.*"

new filename

A:\>dir *pro*
Volume in drive A has no label.
Volume Serial Number is F065-B557

Directory of A:\

02/27/2002	08:53p	34,304	3 Year Sales Projection.xls
08/08/2003	04:12p	20,480	Computer Training Proposal.doc	← renamed file
03/28/2003	04:41p	22,528	Product List.xls
01/03/2003	12:02p	27,648	Product Sales Projection.xls
11/20/2003	08:55a	25,088	Projected Growth Memo.doc
10/22/2003	01:52p	23,040	Regional Sales Projections.xls
12/10/2003	11:30a	24,064	Sales Projection Models.xls
01/02/2003	03:43p	26,624	Sales Projections.xls

8 File(s)   203,776 bytes
0 Dir(s)   185,856 bytes free

confirm with DIR

A:\>

You can also rename a file using the MOVE command, which has a similar syntax to REN, except you can specify a different drive or path in addition to (or instead of) a new name, thus moving the file to a new location. You will learn more about the MOVE command in the next tutorial. Only the REN command, however, allows you to rename multiple files in one command line.

Renaming Multiple Files

Isabel asks you to use the "2002 Sales Summary" files as templates for the upcoming "2003 Sales Summary" files. She notes that you can rename both files in one step.

To rename both "2002 Sales Summary" files:

1. Clear the window, type **dir 2*** and then press **Enter** to verify that the files exist. DIR lists all filenames starting with the numeral "2"—"2002 Sales Summary #1.xls" and "2002 Sales Summary #2.xls."

2. Type **ren 2002* 2003*** and then press **Enter**. REN assumes you want to change only the first four characters of each filename, and preserves the rest of the filename, including the extensions.

3. Type (or recall) **dir 2*** and then press **Enter**. Figure 3-23 shows the change in filenames.

Figure 3-23 RENAMING MULTIPLE FILES

A:\>dir 2*   check original filenames
Volume in drive A has no label.
Volume Serial Number is F065-B557

Directory of A:\

| 01/23/2003 | 08:16a | 41,472 | 2002 Sales Summary #1.xls | ⎫ files to rename |
| 01/23/2003 | 09:21a | 78,848 | 2002 Sales Summary #2.xls | ⎭ |

2 File(s)   120,320 bytes
0 Dir(s)   185,856 bytes free

A:\>ren 2002* 2003*   rename command

A:\>dir 2*
Volume in drive A has no label.
Volume Serial Number is F065-B557

Directory of A:\   confirm rename

| 01/23/2003 | 08:16a | 41,472 | 2003 Sales Summary #1.xls | ⎫ new names |
| 01/23/2003 | 09:21a | 78,848 | 2003 Sales Summary #2.xls | ⎭ |

2 File(s)   120,320 bytes
0 Dir(s)   185,856 bytes free

A:\>

As noted earlier, if you are working in the graphical user interface, you can change the name of only one file at a time. By using REN in a Command Prompt window, you can save yourself a great deal of time and effort when you need to rename many different files.

REFERENCE WINDOW   **RW**

Renaming Files
- Open a Command Prompt window.
- Change the default drive to the drive that contains the file(s) you want to rename.
- Type REN, a space, the name of the original file, another space, and then the new name for the file. If you use wildcards in the new name, REN will keep the characters represented by the wildcards from the original name in the new name.
- To change the names of multiple files at once, type REN, a space, a matching pattern with wildcards to match the existing names, another space, and then a wildcard matching pattern to define which parts of the names you wish to change and which parts you wish to keep.

Other versions of Windows and MS-DOS contain a REN command that works the same way with single or multiple files, requiring quotation marks around filenames with spaces.

Deleting Files

You realize that there are a couple of files you do not need and you want to remove them from your diskette so they do not take up space. You can delete files from the command prompt with the DEL or ERASE commands. The general syntax is as follows:

> **DEL** *filename*

> **ERASE** *filename*

DEL and ERASE are simply two names for the same internal command, so use of either command name will produce the same result.

Deleting files from the command prompt is risky. If you use wildcards, you might inadvertently delete more files than you expect, including important document files you need. The Delete command does not ask if you are sure you want to delete a file or a group of files, except in one case. The only exception is when you enter DEL *.* at the command prompt. Then DEL will automatically ask you if you want to delete all the files in the directory.

Note: DEL and ERASE do *not* store deleted files in the Recycle Bin, and Windows 2000 does not provide any easy or reliable way to recover files deleted with the DEL or ERASE commands.

As a precautionary measure, you should first test your file specification with the DIR command. If the DIR command selects the files you expect, then you can use the DEL or ERASE command with the same file specification. In fact, if you use DEL (the more common choice), you can just recall the DIR command, and change "DIR" to "DEL".

You can also use the **Prompt for Verification switch**, (**/P**). When you use this switch, the Delete command displays a prompt and asks you to verify whether or not you want to delete the file. This switch becomes especially useful when you delete multiple files with wildcard patterns. It verifies that you are deleting the files you want, and allows you to remove selected files out of the matching group.

Because you no longer need the File0000.chk file, you decide to delete it, using the /P switch as a precaution.

To delete the file named File0000.chk:

1. Clear the window, type **dir file*** and then press **Enter** to verify that the file exists. There is only one file (the one you want to delete) that contains the characters "file" at the beginning of the filename. See Figure 3-24.

Figure 3-24 | **LOCATING THE FILE TO DELETE**

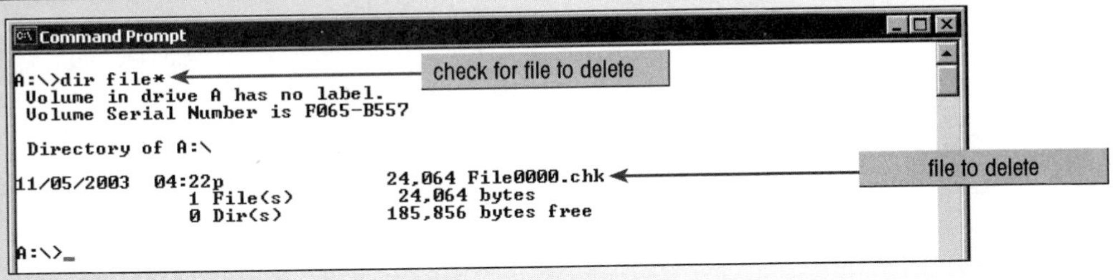

2. Type **del file*** **/p** and then press **Enter**. DEL prompts for verification, displaying the filename and then the message "Delete (Y/N)?". See Figure 3-25.

Figure 3-25 | **DELETING A FILE**

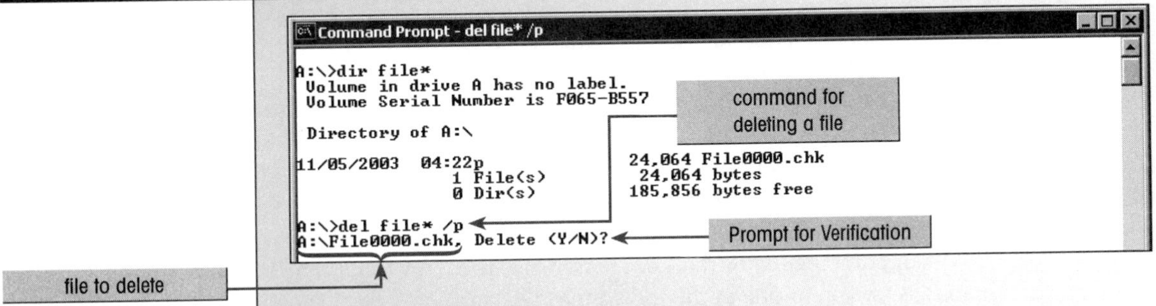

3. Type **y** and then press **Enter**. DEL does not display any further messages.

4. To verify the deletion, type (or recall) **dir file*** and then press **Enter**. The DIR command verifies that the file File0000.chk no longer exists in the directory. See Figure 3-26.

Figure 3-26 | **VERIFYING A DELETED FILE**

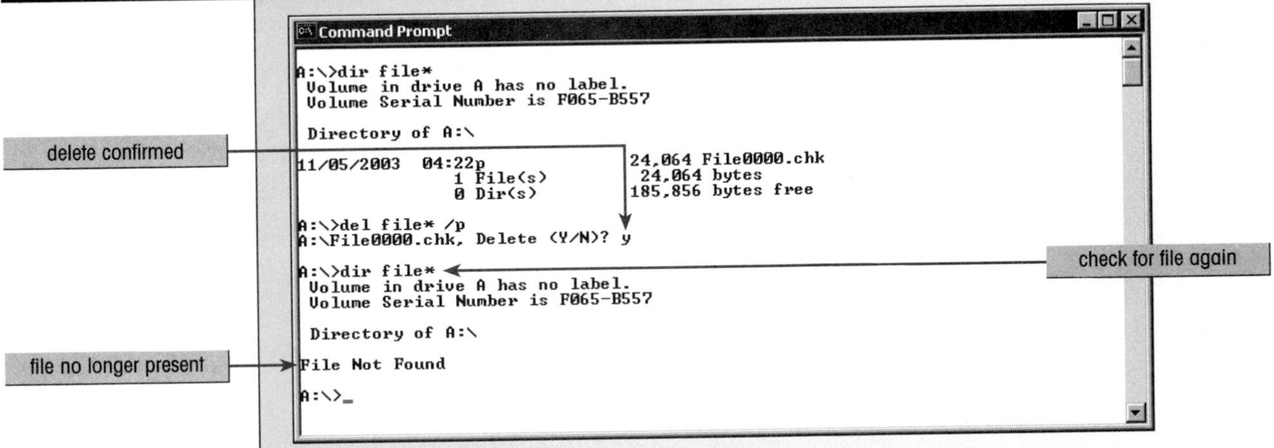

5. Close the Command Prompt window.

You could have also used ERASE to delete the file. Because ERASE is another name for DEL, it uses the same switches, including the Prompt for Verification switch.

REFERENCE WINDOW **RW**

Deleting Files
- Open a Command Prompt window.
- Change the default drive to the drive that contains the files you want to delete.
- Type DEL, press the Spacebar, type the name of the file to delete, press the Spacebar, type /P (the Prompt for Verification switch), and then press Enter. If you use wildcards and do not use the Prompt for Verification switch, DEL will remove all files that match the pattern you give.

If you delete a file from the command prompt and then check the disk that originally contained the file, the directory listing will no longer display the filename. Although you have deleted the file, the file actually still exists on the disk. When the Delete command deletes a file, it does not actually physically remove the file from the disk. Instead, it marks the file as deleted, which prevents the filename entry from appearing in the directory listing. The operating system then knows that it can use the space occupied by this deleted file if it needs that storage space for another file. The deleted file remains on disk until the operating system records the contents of a new file over all or part of that storage space. That means that if you find it necessary, you can acquire a third-party "undelete" utility to restore a file you have deleted. Although Windows 2000 does not include an "undelete" utility, other software products, such as Norton Utilities, include this utility as well as many other disk and file utilities.

Other versions of Windows and MS-DOS have the same Delete command, with the same quotation mark requirements as with other commands.

When combined with the DIR command, the TYPE, COPY, RENAME, and DEL commands assist you in one of the most important tasks you face when using a computer system—managing your files. Furthermore, some of these commands support features that are not available in the Windows 2000 graphical user interface, such as renaming multiple files.

Session 3.2 QUICK CHECK

1. A(n) _____ is a name Windows 2000 assigns to each of the devices, or hardware components, in a computer system.

2. If you want to redirect output to a printer, specify the name of your _____ as the output device.

3. _____ is the device name of the first parallel printer port (also called Line Printer #1).

4. When making a copy of a file, the file you copy is called the _____ file.

5. When making a copy of a file, the file that contains the new copy is called the _____ file.

6. One advantage of the REN command is that you can use wildcards to change the filename of _____ files.

7. When deleting a file, you should use the _____ switch.

8. When redirecting output to a parallel port, you can use _____ instead of LPT1 as the device name.

9. TYPE, COPY, RENAME, REN, DEL, and ERASE all have one feature in common—they are _____ commands.

10. You have to be careful when using _____ with the Delete or Erase commands.

OPERATOR AND COMMAND REFERENCE

OPERATOR	USE	BASIC SYNTAX	EXAMPLE
>	Redirects output to a file on disk, or to a printer	*command* > *filename* *command* > *printer port*	dir /o > templates.txt dir /o > prn
<	Redirects input from a file on disk	*command* < *filename*	more < templates.txt
|	Uses output of one command as the input for another command	*command1* | *command2*	type templates.txt i more
>>	Appends output to the end of an existing file	*command* >> *filename*	find "Projection" Templates.txt >> "Sales Templates.txt"

COMMAND	USE	BASIC SYNTAX	EXAMPLE
TYPE	Displays the contents of a text file (or files)	TYPE *filename*	type config.nt
MORE	Displays output one screen at a time	*command* | MORE MORE < *filename* MORE *filename*	type templates.txt i more more < templates.txt more templates.txt
SORT	Sorts the contents of an ASCII text file	*command* | SORT SORT < *filename* SORT *filename*	type templates.txt i sort sort < templates.txt sort templates.txt
FIND	Displays or changes the system date	FIND "*string*" *filename*	find "Sales" Templates.txt
COPY	Creates new copies of one or more files	COPY *source* [*destination*]	copy "Five Year Plan Template.xls" "Five Year Plan Draft.xls"

OPERATOR	USE	BASIC SYNTAX	EXAMPLE
RENAME	Changes the name of one or more files	RENAME [*drive*:][*path*] *filename1* *filename2*	rename Proposal.doc "Computer Training Proposal.doc"
REN		REN [*drive*:][*path*]*filename1* *filename2*	ren Proposal.doc "Computer Training Proposal.doc"
DEL ERASE	Deletes one or more files	DEL *filename* ERASE *filename*	del *.chk erase *.chk

Items shown in italics and not enclosed within square brackets are required parameters. (See TYPE command.)
Items shown in italics and enclosed within square brackets are optional parameters. (See REN command.)

REVIEW ASSIGNMENTS

Another staff member requests a report that lists the files with templates for spreadsheet solutions. Isabel asks you to create an ASCII text file that contains a list of Excel spreadsheets on the templates disk, verify the contents of the file using the TYPE command as well as the MORE, SORT, and FIND filters, and then append a list of Lotus 1-2-3 spreadsheets on the templates disk. She also asks you to provide the file on a separate disk, and keep a copy of the file for later use.

As you complete each step, write down the commands you use, as well as the answer to each question, so that you can submit them to your instructor.

1. Insert the Data Disk that you used in the tutorial into drive A.

2. Open a Command Prompt window and change the default drive to drive A.

3. Display a directory listing of all the files on your Data Disk that contain the "xls" file extension. What command did you enter to perform this operation?

4. After you have verified that this command selects just files with the "xls" file extension, recall the previous command and redirect the output to a file on disk called "Spreadsheet Solutions.txt." What command did you enter to perform this operation?

5. Use the TYPE command to view the contents of this file, and page the output one screen or window at a time with the MORE filter. What command did you enter to perform this operation? What is the name of the first file listed? View the remainder of the output and return to the command prompt.

6. Redirect input from the "Spreadsheet Solutions.txt" file on disk to the MORE filter. What command did you enter to perform this operation? View the remainder of the output and return to the command prompt.

7. Redirect input from the "Spreadsheet Solutions.txt" file on disk to the SORT filter, and page the output one screen or window at a time with the MORE filter. What command did you enter to perform this operation? What is the name of the first file in the sorted list? How is the information sorted? View the remainder of the output and return to the command prompt.

8. Use the FIND filter to search the "Spreadsheet Solutions.txt" file for files that include the word "Summary" in the filename. What command did you enter to perform this operation? What are the names of the files located by the FIND filter?

9. Use the ECHO command and the append output redirection operator to add two blank lines to the bottom of the "Spreadsheet Solutions.txt" file. What command did you enter to perform this operation?

10. Display a directory listing of all files with the "wk4" file extension in alphabetical order by filename. What command did you enter to perform this operation?

11. Recall the previous command, and append the output to the bottom of the "Spreadsheet Solutions.txt" file. What command did you enter to perform this operation?

12. You decide to give your file a more specific name, so you rename it to "Spreadsheet Solution Files.txt." What command did you enter to perform this operation?

13. Create a copy of the "Spreadsheet Solution Files.txt" file, and name it "Backup of Spreadsheet Solution Files.txt." What command did you enter to perform this operation?

14. Delete the Templates.txt and "Sales Templates.txt" files from your Data Disk, using the Prompt for Verification switch to confirm that you are deleting the right file. What command(s) did you enter to perform this operation?

15. Close the Command Prompt window, and remove the diskette from the drive.

16. Submit a copy of the "Spreadsheet Solutions File.txt" file and your answers to the above questions, either as a printout, on diskette, or by e-mail, as your instructor requests, along with any other requested documentation.

CASE PROBLEMS

Case 1. Preparing a Report Using Redirection at Stratton Graphics   Eve Stratton, owner of Stratton Graphics, and her staff specialize in the design of 3-D images and company presentations for the Web sites of her business clients. So she can develop new proposals, presentations, and graphics for projects with short turnaround times, she relies on an important set of files. She asks you to prepare and print a report that summarizes the types of files on the disk by file type and file size.

As you complete each step, write down the commands you use, as well as the answer to each question so that you can submit them to your instructor.

1. Open a Command Prompt window.

2. Insert your Data Disk into drive A, and then make that drive the default drive.

3. Display a directory listing of your Data Disk *in alphabetical order by file extension*, and redirect the output to a file on your Data Disk with the name "Stratton Graphics.txt." What command did you enter for this operation?

4. Verify that the operating system created the "Stratton Graphics.txt" file on diskette by redirecting input from the file and displaying one screen or window at a time. What command did you enter for this operation? What is the name of the first file listed in this file? View the remainder of the input, and return to the command prompt.

5. Append two blank lines to the bottom of the "Stratton Graphics.txt" file. What two commands did you enter for these operations?

6. Display another directory listing of your Data Disk *in order by file size*, from the largest to the smallest file, and append the output to the "Stratton Graphics.txt" file. What command did you enter for this operation?

7. Verify that the operating system appended the output to the "Stratton Graphics.txt" file by redirecting input from this file on disk and displaying the input one screen or window at a time. What command did you enter for this operation? View the remainder of the input, and return to the command prompt.

8. Display a directory listing of all files with the "xls" file extension in alphabetical order, and redirect the output to your printer port. What command did you use to perform this operation?

9. Submit a copy of the "Stratton Graphics.txt" file, your printed output of all files with the "xls" file extension, and your answers to the above questions, either as printout, on diskette, or by e-mail, as your instructor requests, along with any other requested documentation.

Case 2. Using Filters at Bayview Travel Service   Bayview Travel Service is a small travel agency that arranges personal, group, and escorted tours for its customers, as well as handling worldwide reservations and tickets. Toby Landucci, the financial analyst at Bayview Travel Service, has developed a set of computer files for use in his job over the last fiscal year. For the upcoming year's budget projection, he wants to first make a copy of the diskette containing his budget files and then to prepare and print a list of files he plans to adapt for the new year. He asks you to document the list of files that he currently uses and then prepare and print a report that lists the files he will use for next year's budget analysis.

As you complete each step, write down the commands you use, as well as the answer to each question, so that you can submit them to your instructor.

1. Insert your Data Disk into drive A.

2. Open a Command Prompt window.

3. Change the default drive to the drive containing your Data Disk.

4. Display a directory listing of your Data Disk in alphabetical order by filename, and redirect the output to a file on your Data Disk with the name "Bayview Travel.txt." What command did you enter for this operation?

5. Verify that the operating system created the "Bayview Travel.txt" file on disk by redirecting input from the file and displaying it one screen or window at a time. What command did you enter for this operation? What is the name of the second file listed? View the remainder of the input, and return to the command prompt.

6. Use the FIND filter to search "Bayview Travel.txt" for "xls" in the filename, and page the output one screen by a time. What command did you enter for this operation? What is the first file in this selection?

7. After you test the FIND filter and verify that it is selecting the files you need, use the FIND filter to select the same listings, but this time redirect the output to a file on disk with the name, "Financial Analyses.txt." What command did you enter for this operation?

8. Redirect input using the "Financial Analyses.txt" file on disk to the SORT filter, and display the output one full window at a time. What command did you enter for this operation? What is the name of the first file displayed in the sorted listing? View the remainder of the input, and return to the command prompt.

9. Display a directory listing of all files with the "xls" file extension in alphabetical order, and redirect the output to your printer port.

10. Submit a copy of the "Bayview Travel.txt" and "Financial Analyses.txt" files, your printed output of all files with the "xls" file extension, and your answers to the above questions, either as printout, on diskette, or by e-mail, as your instructor requests, along with any other requested documentation.

Case 3. Copying Presentations at HiPerform Enterprises   After experiencing an unprecedented increase in customers over the last year, James Everett, the owner and manager of HiPerform Enterprises, decides to apply for a business loan to expand his business. He asks you to make a copy of his templates disk, and then assemble copies of the documents that he will need to develop a business plan, which he then can include with his application for a business loan.

As you complete each step, write down the commands you use, as well as the answer to each question, so that you can submit them to your instructor.

1. Insert your Data Disk into drive A.

2. Open a Command Prompt window.

3. Make a copy of your Data Disk. What command did you enter to perform this operation?

4. Change the default drive to the drive containing your Data Disk.

5. On the duplicate of your Data Disk that you just made, free up storage space on your diskette for the new files, by deleting all the files with the file extension "txt," "bmp," "chk," and "tmp." What commands did you enter for these operations?

6. Produce a directory listing of the current drive that displays alphabetically all files whose filenames start with the words "Five Year" and which contain the "xls" file extension. What command did you enter for this operation? What are the names of the files that meet these criteria?

7. Copy the "Five Year Growth Plan.xls" file, and create a new file with the name "Five Year Sales Projection.xls." What command did you enter for this operation?

8. Recall the previous Directory command, and verify that Windows 2000 created a new file by making a copy of an existing file.

9. Using a similar approach, make a new copy of the file "Balance Sheet.xls" with the name "Company Balance Sheet.xls," and a new copy of the file "Loan Payment Analysis.xls" with the name "Loan Analysis.xls". What commands did you enter for these operations?

10. Change the name of the "Loan Analysis.xls" file to "Bank Loan Analysis.xls." What command did you enter for this operation?

11. Display a directory listing of all files on this diskette with the "xls" file extension in alphabetical order by filename, and redirect the output to your printer port. What command did you enter for this operation?

12. Submit your printed output of all files with the "xls" file extension, and your answers to the above questions, either as printout, on diskette, or by e-mail, as your instructor requests, along with any other requested documentation.

Case 4. Managing Files at Turing Enterprises Each year Melissa Turing, owner of Turing Enterprises, creates a copy of the diskette that contains her business files and then updates the files for the upcoming year. She asks you to make a copy of her diskette, remove files she no longer needs, rename files to reflect the current year, and then make copies of files that she can adapt for new ventures this next year.

As you complete each step, write down the commands you use, as well as the answer to each question, so that you can submit them to your instructor.

1. Insert your Data Disk into drive A.

2. Open a Command Prompt window.

3. Make a duplicate copy of your Data Disk.

4. Change the default drive to the drive containing your Data Disk.

5. On the duplicate copy, delete all the files with the "bmp" "chk" "doc" "tmp" "txt" and "wk4" file extensions. What commands did you enter to perform these operations?

6. Change the name of "Balance Sheet.xls" to "Turing Balance Sheet.xls," "Client Invoices.xls" to "Turing Client Invoices.xls," and "Weekly Worklog.xls" to "Turing Weekly Worklog.xls". What commands did you enter for these operations?

7. Change the names of the files "2003 Sales Summary #1.xls" and "2003 Sales Summary #2.xls" to "2003 Trips Summary #1.xls" and "2003 Trips Summary #2.xls" using one command in one step. What command did you enter to perform this operation?

8. Copy "Data Systems Budget.xls" to "Turing Budget Projection.xls," and copy "Software.ppt" to "Mediterranean Excursions.ppt." What commands did you enter for these operations?

9. Display a directory listing of all files on this diskette with the "xls" file extension in alphabetical order by filename, and redirect the output to your printer port. What command did you enter for this operation?

10. Submit your printed output of all files with the "xls" file extension, and your answers to the above questions, either as printout, on diskette, or by e-mail, as your instructor requests, along with any other requested documentation.

QUICK | CHECK ANSWERS

Session 3.1

   1. ASCII

   2. end-of-file (EOF)

   3. redirect

   4. output redirection

   5. TYPE

   6. filter

   7. pipe

   8. input redirection

   9. append output redirection

  10. keyboard, screen (or monitor or video display device)

Session 3.2

   1. device name

   2. printer port

   3. LPT1

   4. source

   5. destination (or target)

   6. multiple (or more than one)

   7. Prompt for Verification (or/P)

   8. PRN

   9. internal

  10. wildcards

In this tutorial you will learn to:

- Examine the concept and use of the full path

- Create and change directories

- Move files to directories

- List and copy files in directories

- Delete files in directories

- Navigate a directory structure

- View, print, and save a directory tree

USING DIRECTORIES AND SUBDIRECTORIES

Organizing Company Files at SolarWinds

CASE

SolarWinds Unlimited

The staff members at SolarWinds depend on the availability of templates for a wide variety of uses—spreadsheet projections, sales summaries, budget analyses, workflow analyses, employee payroll, graphics, presentations, and training. Many different staff members have worked with Isabel to develop the templates that they need and to develop an approach that enables her staff to organize, track, and locate those templates quickly.

In the event you need to navigate, reorganize, and manage the directory structure of a disk in a command-line environment, Isabel wants you to organize the SolarWinds template files using basic directory management commands of the Windows 2000 command line.

SESSION 4.1

In this session, you will examine the importance of using directories to manage files on a hard disk, learn the concept, importance, and use of the full path. You will create and open directories, as well as move and copy files to directories.

Managing Files

Isabel asks you to assist her with the important task of developing a system for organizing and tracking template files needed by her staff. Over the years, the number and types of templates have increased significantly, and managers are increasingly emphasizing the importance of using templates wherever possible to develop complex documents, meet tight deadlines, and provide consistency in the appearance of all company documents. In order to develop your command-line file management skills, Isabel gives you a diskette containing template files used by the SolarWinds staff so that you can practice organizing files as you would on the hard drive.

File management is one of the major tasks faced by any user of a computer system. This task is more complicated on a hard disk because of the enormous storage capacity of the disk and the number of files stored on it. To assist you in this task, Windows 2000 and other operating systems allow you to group related files together in a directory on a disk. You can then work with each group of files as a separate unit, independent of all other files.

A **directory**, also known as a **folder,** acts as a container for files and other directories. Physically, it is actually a special type of file that contains information about the files and other directories it tracks. The term **directory** actually has two meanings. First, it refers to any directory on a disk drive: the root directory or any of its subdirectories. The **root directory** is the first directory created on a disk by an operating system or formatting utility. The operating system refers to it with a backslash (\ ) symbol. Second, as you have already seen in Tutorial 2, the term "directory" also refers to the output of the Directory (DIR) command. In the first three tutorials, you worked in the root directory of either drive C or drive A. When you used the Directory command, you viewed the contents of each of those directories.

The use of directories on a hard disk allows the operating system, software applications, and you to use that storage space effectively. Figure 4-1 shows an example of part of the directory structure of a drive on a hard disk. At the top of a directory structure is the root directory for drive C. Below the root directory, there are directories for installed software as well as directories for documents. A directory contained within, or "below," another directory is called a **subdirectory** of the other directory. (A subdirectory, or subfolder, is subordinate to another directory, or folder.) Conversely, a directory containing, or "above," another directory is called the **parent directory** of the other directory. A parent directory can have many subdirectories, but a subdirectory can have only one parent directory. Just as you can call a person a parent or a child, you can also call a directory a parent directory or a subdirectory, depending on the context.

The Windows 2000 installation program creates directories, such as "Documents and Settings," "Program Files," "Recycled," and "WINNT," for use by the operating system and software applications. The "Documents and Settings" directory contains data files and settings for each user of the computer. The "Program Files" directory contains subdirectories such as "Accessories," "Internet Explorer," "Outlook Express," and "Microsoft Office," for various types of software. The WINNT directory (which stands for "Windows NT," the original name for Windows 2000) contains most of the important Windows 2000 operating system files.

Each of these directories in turn may contain subdirectories. For example, the Microsoft Office directory shown in Figure 4-1 might contain Office and Templates subdirectories. The Recycled directory is a hidden system directory for storing files deleted from the hard disk. The WINNT directory folder contains the Windows 2000 operating system, organized into a myriad of subdirectories, for example, "Fonts," "Help," "History," "System32," "Temporary Internet Files," and "Web" directories, to name a few.

Figure 4-1	PARTIAL DIRECTORY STRUCTURE OF A DISK

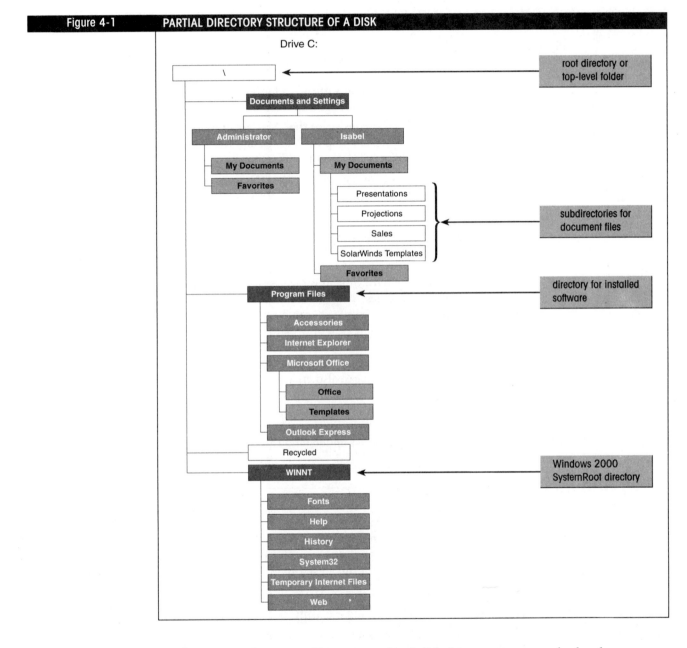

If you store document files on your hard disk drive, as most people do, then you can organize those documents into directories. As shown in Figure 4-1, the "Documents and Settings" directory folder contains a subdirectory for each defined local user of the computer (for example, "Isabel"), which in turn contains subdirectories including "My Documents" and "Favorites." You would store your files in your own "My Documents" directory, and you might create subdirectories such as those named "Presentations," "Projections," and "Sales," where you would store other documents that you create and use in your job.

As you can also tell from this figure, a typical hard disk drive has directories at different levels within the overall directory structure of the disk:

■ The first level is the root directory, represented in the figure by a backslash symbol (\ ).

■ The second level consists of the "Documents and Settings," "Program Files," "Recycled," and "WINNT" directories.

■ The third level consists of the directory folders for the local users of the computer ("Administrator" and "Isabel" in this case), "Accessories," "Internet Explorer," "Microsoft Office," "Outlook Express," "Fonts," "Help," "History," "System32," "Temporary Internet Files," and "Web" directories.

■ The fourth level consists of the "My Documents" and "Favorites" directories for each of the computer's users, and the "Office" and "Templates" subdirectories under "Microsoft Office."

■ The fifth level consists of the "Presentations," "Projections," "Sales," and "SolarWinds Templates" subdirectories under Isabel's "My Documents" directory.

The actual directory structure of a disk is far more complicated than can be illustrated in a figure; however, the important point is that files are organized into directories at different levels within the directory structure of a disk.

If you organize your hard disk into directories, store files in the appropriate directory, and maintain the directories, you can locate files easily and quickly. By approaching file management in an organized way, you can work more productively.

Before you tackle the larger task of organizing the files on a hard disk, Isabel has asked you to start with the files on your templates diskette. She points out that the diskette would correspond to your "My Documents" directory folder on the hard drive. Although you use directories on hard disks, you can also create directories on a diskette and on other types of disks, such as Zip disks and recordable CDs. Once you are familiar with the process of creating directories and moving or copying files to directories, then you are in a better position to evaluate and reorganize how you store document files on a hard disk. Before you can work with directories, you must understand the concept and use of the full path.

The **Importance of the Full Path**

As you start the process of organizing the template files into directories, Isabel emphasizes the importance of understanding the concept and use of the full path so that you can work effectively and efficiently with directories on a disk.

Whether you work from the desktop in the graphical user interface or from the Command Prompt window, Windows 2000 uses the full path to locate and load programs, as well as to locate and open directories and files. The **full path**, originally called the **MS-DOS path**, is a notation that identifies the exact location of a directory or file on a disk. The full path includes the name of the drive that contains the directory or file, the sequence of directory name(s) that identifies the location of a directory or file, and the name of the directory or file. For example, when you open a Command Prompt window, Windows 2000 displays the full path of the current drive and directory in the command prompt itself (C:\>). The current drive and directory is the root directory (or top-level folder) of drive C. If you change the default drive from drive C to drive A, then the full path of the current drive and directory is the root directory of drive A (A:\>). As shown in Figure 4-2, the first backslash symbol identifies the root directory of the drive in each case.

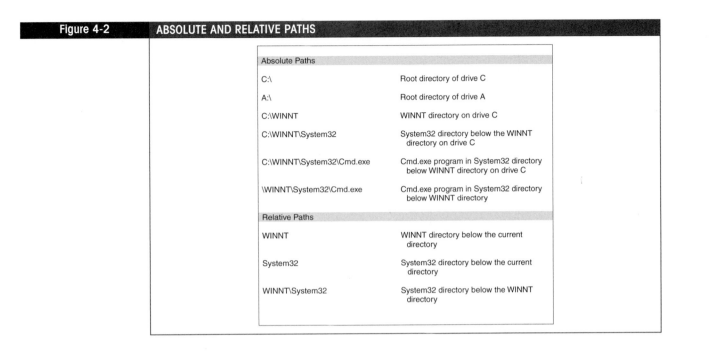

Figure 4-2   **ABSOLUTE AND RELATIVE PATHS**

Absolute Paths

C:\	Root directory of drive C
A:\	Root directory of drive A
C:\WINNT	WINNT directory on drive C
C:\WINNT\System32	System32 directory below the WINNT directory on drive C
C:\WINNT\System32\Cmd.exe	Cmd.exe program in System32 directory below WINNT directory on drive C
\WINNT\System32\Cmd.exe	Cmd.exe program in System32 directory below WINNT directory

Relative Paths

WINNT	WINNT directory below the current directory
System32	System32 directory below the current directory
WINNT\System32	System32 directory below the WINNT directory

Windows 2000 is installed in a directory called the **SystemRoot** folder. In most installations, the *SystemRoot* folder is named WINNT on drive C. In that case, the full path to the WINNT directory is: C:\WINNT. This path identifies the drive name first (C:—drive names always consist of a letter followed by a colon), then a backslash (\ ) identifying the root directory containing the WINNT directory, and finally the actual name of the WINNT directory. If Windows 2000 was installed as an upgrade from a previous version of Windows, it may be installed in the Windows directory on drive C of your computer instead of in WINNT. Then, the full path for the Windows directory would be: C:\Windows.

Within the WINNT (or Windows) directory, program and supporting files are organized into different subdirectories. One of those subdirectories is the System32 directory, which contains important system files and programs. If your Windows SystemRoot directory is named WINNT, then the full path to the System32 directory is: C:\WINNT\System32.

This path indicates that the System32 directory is below the WINNT directory, which is in turn below the root directory of drive C. In a path that specifies a set of connected subdirectories, the subdirectory names are separated from each other by a backslash (\ ). All of the backslashes—other than the one that follows the drive name—are separators between two connected subdirectories. Only the backslash after the drive name refers to the root directory.

As you learned in Tutorial 1, the name of the program that Windows 2000 opens when you choose Command Prompt on the Accessories menu is Cmd.exe. If your Windows SystemRoot directory is named WINNT, then the full path for that program file is: C:\WINNT\System32\Cmd.exe.

This path indicates that the Cmd.exe program file is stored in the System32 directory, which is below the WINNT directory, which is in turn below the root directory of drive C. In this path, all of the backslash symbols except for the first one, are separators. The second backslash separates two subdirectory names, and the third backslash separates a directory name from a filename. As mentioned in Tutorial 1, files like Cmd.exe with the file extension "exe" are **executable** files, or files that contain program code that Windows 2000 can load (or copy) into memory (or RAM) and run.

If a path contains a long filename with spaces for a directory or a file, then you might need to enclose the entire path in quotation marks so Windows 2000 knows it is one specification; otherwise, it might interpret the spaces as separating different parts of a command line. For example, if you have Office 2000 installed on your computer, it is more than likely installed in the Program Files folder. The path to the folder containing Office 2000 would then be: C:\Program Files\Microsoft Office. If you need to reference this path in a command (depending on the command), you might need to enclose the full path within quotation marks so that Windows 2000 correctly interprets the command, as follows: "C:\Program Files\Microsoft Office"

These types of paths are also referred to as **absolute paths**, because they spell out the full path, and there is no ambiguity as to the location of the directory or file. An absolute path always includes a backslash (\ ) before the name of the first directory, meaning that it begins at the root directory. For example, C:\Documents and Settings\Isabel\My Documents\Projections specifies an absolute path. When you work in a command-line environment, you can also use a relative path. A **relative path** makes assumptions about the location of a directory or file, always starting from the current drive and directory. A relative path cannot begin with a backslash. For example, if you use just the path Projections in a command, then the command will assume that the Projections directory is below the current working directory of the current drive (whatever drive that might be). If your current working directory is Isabel's "My Documents" directory on drive C (C:\Documents and Settings\Isabel\My Documents), then the command will assume that the **Projections** directory is located below that directory, and that the full path is: "C:\Documents and Settings\Isabel\My Documents\Projections".

When you enter commands at the command prompt that operate on directories or files (or both), you can use either an absolute or a relative path to specify the directories and files. The advantage of the relative path is that it saves time and keystrokes. As you work with directories in this tutorial, you will try different methods for using absolute and relative paths.

Except where noted, all of the commands you will use in this tutorial are available in all versions of Windows and MS-DOS.

Getting Started

You will need to make a new copy of Data Disk #1 so that you can organize the files into directories. You cannot use the same diskette that you used in the last tutorial, because you deleted files on that disk. Also, you renamed files and created new files using the COPY command. So you can perform all the operations in this tutorial, and so your screen views match those shown in the figures, you will make a new copy of Data Disk #1 in the following steps. When you create your new copy of Data Disk #1, you can reuse your last duplicate of the diskette. (Remember to keep your original version of the Data Disk #1 intact so you can make a copy whenever necessary.)

To make the task of reorganizing the files into directories easier, Isabel recommends that you also print a directory listing in alphabetical order by filename.

To prepare your diskette:

1. Open a Command Prompt window, set colors if necessary, and clear the window.

2. Follow the instructions provided by your instructor for making a copy of Data Disk #1.

3. Change the default drive to A.

4. Print an alphabetical directory listing of drive A using the DIR command with the Order switch and redirecting its output to the printer. If necessary, eject the page manually.

5. Remove your hard copy from the printer.

By using an alphabetical listing of filenames, you can more easily spot similarities in filenames so that you can use wildcards in your file specification and move groups of files at once, rather than having to move them one at a time.

Deleting Files from a Diskette

Before you reorganize the template files, you decide to delete files that you no longer need. Deleting extraneous files will also ensure that you have enough storage space on the diskette for the operations you need to perform.

To delete files you no longer need:

1. Clear the window, type **del *.tmp   /p** and then press **Enter**. The Delete command asks you to verify that you want to delete ~WRC0070.tmp. See Figure 4-3.

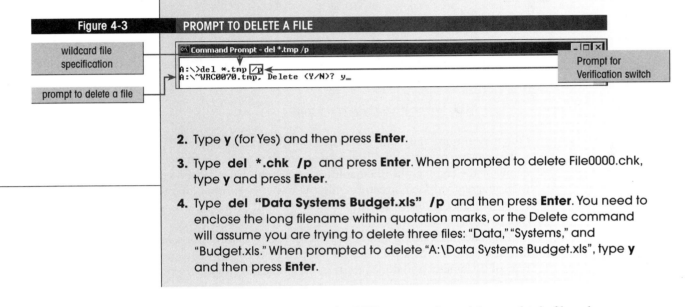

Figure 4-3	PROMPT TO DELETE A FILE

wildcard file specification

prompt to delete a file

Prompt for Verification switch

```
Command Prompt - del *.tmp /p
A:\>del *.tmp /p
A:\~WRC0070.tmp, Delete (Y/N)? y_
```

2. Type **y** (for Yes) and then press **Enter**.

3. Type **del *.chk /p** and press **Enter**. When prompted to delete File0000.chk, type **y** and press **Enter**.

4. Type **del "Data Systems Budget.xls" /p** and then press **Enter**. You need to enclose the long filename within quotation marks, or the Delete command will assume you are trying to delete three files: "Data," "Systems," and "Budget.xls." When prompted to delete "A:\Data Systems Budget.xls", type **y** and then press **Enter**.

As step 4 above points out, the DEL command can delete multiple files whose names are separated by spaces in the command line. Therefore, make sure you place quotation marks around filenames containing spaces. You should develop the habit of using the **Prompt for Verification switch (/P)** whenever you delete files. This switch provides a margin of safety and safeguards against accidentally deleting the wrong file or files.

Creating **Directories**

After discussing with Isabel how best to organize files on your templates disk, you decide to organize your files in groups based on their type of use. For example, you want to store all PowerPoint presentations in a directory called "Presentations". Next, using your printed copy of the directory listing, you prepare a sketch of the directory structure for the types of files contained on the templates diskette, as shown in Figure 4-4. After you reorganize this disk, all the files will be located in five different directories so that you can easily find a file when you need it.

Figure 4-4   **SKETCH OF PROPOSED DIRECTORY STRUCTURE**

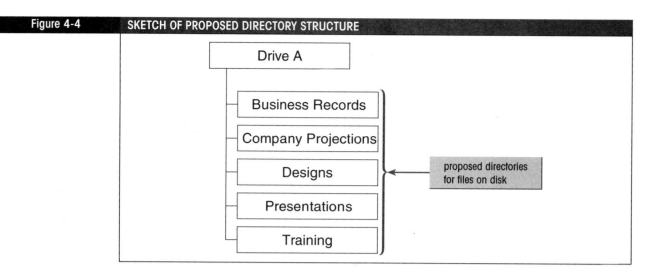

The command for creating a directory is MD (an abbreviation for Make Directory). This internal command has the following syntax:

MD [*drive:*][*path*]*directory name*

(You may also use the name MKDIR for this command, as in UNIX.)

If you want to create the directory on another drive, you must specify the alternate drive name, or the command will default to the current drive. The directory will likewise default to the current working directory unless you specify another directory path. To change locations, identify the directory path, such as the root directory, where you want the new directory to be located.

The rules for naming a directory are the same as those for naming a file, although most directories do not have an extension as part of their name. Just as a filename identifies the type of document stored in the file, a directory's name describes the types of files that you will store in the directory.

Before you create a subdirectory, you should check the current directory shown in the command prompt so that you create a new directory in the right place.

You decide to start by creating the Presentations directory first.

To create a directory:

1. Clear the window, type **md Presentations** and then press **Enter**. The Make Directory command creates a directory below the root directory of the disk drive containing your diskette and displays the command prompt. If you perform this operation from another drive, such as drive C, you would include the drive name and path before the directory name (for example, md A:\ Presentations). Also, if the disk contains a file with the same name as the one you want to use as the directory name, the Make Directory command will display a message and note that a directory or file by that name already exists.

2. Type **dir /ad** and then press **Enter**. The Directory command displays information about the new directory but does not list any files on the disk, because you used the Attribute switch with the parameter for displaying only directories. See Figure 4-5. The <DIR> marker verifies that Presentations is a directory.

| Figure 4-5 | MAKING A DIRECTORY |

Make Directory command

name of directory

switch for displaying
only directories

```
A:\>md Presentations
A:\>dir /ad
 Volume in drive A has no label.
 Volume Serial Number is F065-B557

 Directory of A:\

12/18/2003  07:02p    <DIR>         Presentations
               0 File(s)            0 bytes
               1 Dir(s)       264,192 bytes free
A:\>
```

directory marker

new directory

The Directory command's Attribute switch with the directory parameter (/AD) is useful when you need to screen out all the files in a directory and focus on the subdirectories.

REFERENCE   WINDOW   **RW**

Creating a Directory:
- Open a Command Prompt window, and then change to the drive where you want to create the directory.
- If you want to create a subdirectory below the root directory of the drive, type MD, press the Spacebar, type the name of the new directory, and then press Enter.
- Type DIR /AD and then press Enter to view a list of directories on the disk so you can verify that you created the directory.

Although the MKDIR name for this command works exactly like MD, most people use MD because it saves keystrokes. Because UNIX uses "mkdir," but not "md," those familiar with that operating system might be more comfortable with the longer name.

Changing the Current Working Directory

Isabel notes that another advantage of working within a directory is that you can work with files in that directory without having to type the directory name with each command. That simplifies many types of file operations.

Once you create a directory, you can use the CD (Change Directory) command to switch to that directory, and make it the new current working directory (also known as the current directory). This internal command has the following syntax:

CD [*drive*:][*path*]directory name

(You may also use the name CHDIR for this command. UNIX uses "cd".)

As long as a Command Prompt window remains open, the command interpreter maintains a current working directory for each drive. When you switch drives, you go to whatever directory you most recently set on that drive. If you do not specify a drive name, you remain on the same drive, but you change the current working directory to the one you specify in the Change Directory command. If you haven't used the CD command to change the current directory of a particular drive, you'll switch to the drive's root directory. When you close the Command Prompt window, you lose all the current directory settings.

When you specify the path, you are telling the Directory command the name of the directory to which you want to change, and its location relative to a higher directory, such as the root directory.

After you change to a new directory, you can work more easily with the files stored in it. You will now change to the Presentations directory that you just created and examine its contents.

To change to the Presentations directory:

1. Clear the window, type **cd Presentations** and then press **Enter**. After the Change Directory command changes to the Presentations directory, the command interpreter (Cmd.exe) updates the command prompt to show the full path of what is now the current directory, A:\Presentations. See Figure 4-6. A:\Presentations indicates that Presentations is a subdirectory below the root directory of the diskette in drive A. That subdirectory is now the current directory.

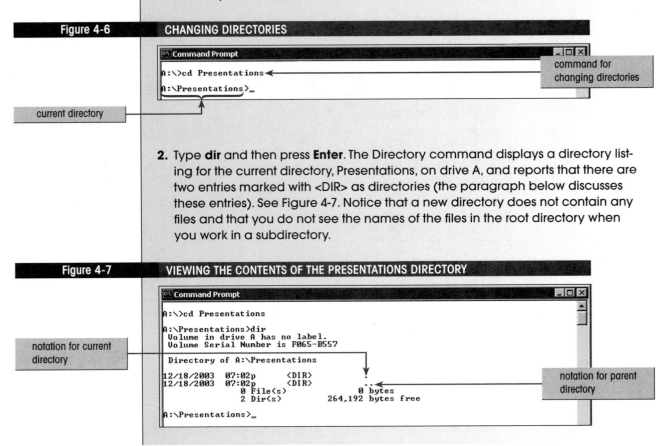

| Figure 4-6 | CHANGING DIRECTORIES |

command for changing directories

current directory

2. Type **dir** and then press **Enter**. The Directory command displays a directory listing for the current directory, Presentations, on drive A, and reports that there are two entries marked with <DIR> as directories (the paragraph below discusses these entries). See Figure 4-7. Notice that a new directory does not contain any files and that you do not see the names of the files in the root directory when you work in a subdirectory.

| Figure 4-7 | VIEWING THE CONTENTS OF THE PRESENTATIONS DIRECTORY |

notation for current directory

notation for parent directory

Whenever the operating system creates a directory, it always creates two entries within the directory. The first entry, named "." (pronounced "dot"), acts as a kind of alias (or alternate name) for the current directory. The second entry, named ". ." (pronounced "dot dot"), refers to the parent directory, which contains the current directory and is located one level higher. On your diskette, for example, the parent directory of Presentations is the root directory. With the exception of the root directory of a drive, every directory has a parent directory. Windows 2000 uses the "." and ". ." entries to keep track of the current directory and the parent directory as you move or navigate from one directory to another. When entering commands at the command prompt, you may use these aliases anywhere in place of the name of the current directory or the parent of the current directory. For example, if you were in "C:\Documents and Settings\Isabel\My Documents\Presentations," and you wanted to switch to the parent directory (My Documents), you could just type cd . . instead of cd \Documents and Settings\Isabel\My Documents.

Now that you have created one of the directories planned for this diskette, you want to move the appropriate files to this directory. To simplify this operation, you decide to return to the root directory where these files are currently stored. Again, you use the CD or CHDIR commands. For the root directory's name, you use the notation that identifies the root directory—the backslash (\ ).

To return to the root directory:

1. Clear the screen, type **cd ** and then press **Enter**. The Directory command updates the command prompt and shows the root directory of drive A as the current directory. See Figure 4-8. If you prefer to reduce keystrokes, you do not have to leave a space between "cd" and the backslash.

   TROUBLE? If the Directory command informs you that the syntax of your command is incorrect, then you may have typed a slash (/) instead of a backslash (\ ). Enter the command again.

Figure 4-8   **CHANGING TO THE ROOT DIRECTORY**

Change Directory command switches to root directory

symbol for root directory

2. Type **dir /o /p** and then press **Enter**. The Directory command lists directories (in this case, there is only one) in alphabetical order, then lists files in alphabetical order. See Figure 4-9.

Figure 4-9   **DISPLAYING THE CURRENT DIRECTORY**

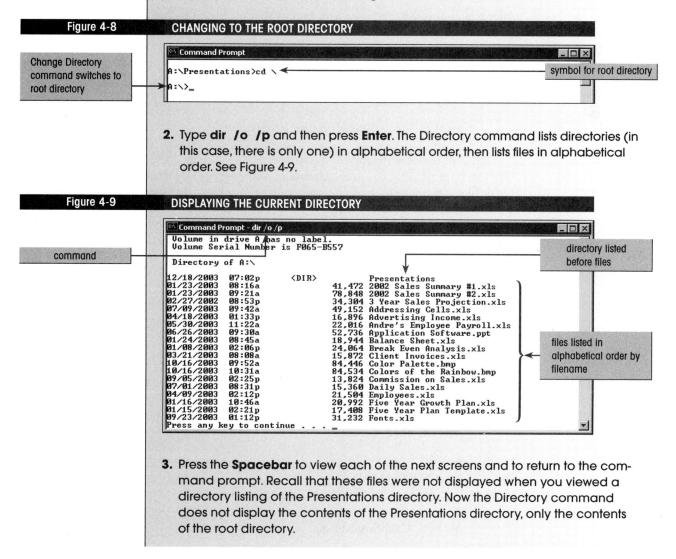

command

directory listed before files

files listed in alphabetical order by filename

3. Press the **Spacebar** to view each of the next screens and to return to the command prompt. Recall that these files were not displayed when you viewed a directory listing of the Presentations directory. Now the Directory command does not display the contents of the Presentations directory, only the contents of the root directory.

This command, CD \, is one of the most useful commands in a command-line environment, because it will switch you to the root directory of the current drive—no matter which directory you start from.

Moving Files to Another Directory

After examining the directory, you realize that all the files that you want to move to the Presentations directory have one feature in common, the same file extension, "ppt" (an abbreviation for PowerPoint Presentation).

You can use the MOVE command (an external command) to move these files in one step. If you want to move one or more files from one directory to another, you use the following syntax:

MOVE [*drive:*][*path*]*filespec destination*

The drive name, path, and filespec (short for file specification) identify the source file or files you want to move to another location. You must specify the drive name for the source file or files if they are located on another drive. You must also specify the path if it is different from that of the current directory. The filespec might be a specific filename or a wildcard pattern. The destination includes the name of the directory where you want to move the files. The destination might also include a drive name and path. If you are moving only one file, you can also specify a new filename for that file. If you are moving a group of files, the destination must be the directory name that will contain the group; you cannot specify new filenames.

For example, to move a file by the name of Cashflow.xls from the root directory of drive A to the Business directory on drive A, you would enter this command:

MOVE Cashflow.xls Business

To move all the files with the "xls" file extension from the root directory of drive A to the Business directory on drive A, you would enter this command:

MOVE *.xls Business

To move a file named Cashflow.xls from the current directory on drive C to the current directory on drive A (that is, whatever directory you most recently made current on drive A with the CD command), you would enter this command:

MOVE Cashflow.xls A:

As you will discover, the MOVE command is quite versatile.

To move all the files with the "ppt" extension to the Presentations directory:

1. Clear the window.

2. Type **move *.ppt Presentations** and then press **Enter**. The MOVE command displays the names of the files that it moves when you use a wildcard in the file specification for the source files. See Figure 4-10. Notice also that all of the files have the same file extension.

Figure 4-10	MOVING FILES TO A DIRECTORY

Move command

```
Command Prompt
A:\>move *.ppt Presentations
A:\Hardware.ppt
A:\Application Software.ppt
A:\Software.ppt
A:\Using the Mouse.ppt

A:\>_
```

wildcard file specification

destination directory for moved files

files with same file extension being moved to a directory

3. Type **dir Presentations** and then press **Enter**. The Directory command displays a directory listing of the files in the Presentations directory (but not the files in the root directory). See Figure 4-11.

Figure 4-11	VIEWING THE FILES IN THE PRESENTATIONS DIRECTORY

```
Command Prompt                                            _ □ ✕
A:\>move *.ppt Presentations
A:\Hardware.ppt
A:\Application Software.ppt
A:\Software.ppt
A:\Using the Mouse.ppt

A:\>dir Presentations
 Volume in drive A has no label.
 Volume Serial Number is F065-B557

 Directory of A:\Presentations

12/18/2003  07:02p    <DIR>          .
12/18/2003  07:02p    <DIR>          ..
06/26/2003  10:24a            53,248 Hardware.ppt
06/26/2003  09:30a            52,736 Application Software.ppt
06/26/2003  10:40a            42,496 Software.ppt
06/26/2003  10:55a            41,984 Using the Mouse.ppt
               4 File(s)        190,464 bytes
               2 Dir(s)         264,192 bytes free

A:\>
```

files moved to the Presentations directory

4. Type **dir *.ppt** and then press **Enter**. The Directory command displays the message "File Not Found," indicating that there are no longer any files in the current directory (the root directory) with the "ppt" file extension.

How did the MOVE command know that Presentations referred to the name of a directory? The MOVE command examines the contents of the root directory and locates the directory named Presentations. It then moves the files you specified to that directory.

Moving a Group of Files to Another Directory
- Open a Command Prompt window.
- Change the default drive to the drive that contains the file or files you want to move.
- If necessary, use the Make Directory (MD) command to create a new directory for the files you want to move.
- Type MOVE, press the Spacebar, type a file specification that uses wildcards to select a group of files (such as all files with the same file extension), press the Spacebar, type the name of the directory where you want to move the files, and then press Enter. You might need to specify the drive name and path for the source or destination.
- To verify the move, type DIR, press the Spacebar, type the name of the directory where you moved the files, and then press Enter.

In this instance, you could have also used \Presentations for the destination, to indicate that it is a subdirectory of the root directory. If you do not specify the backslash (\ ) for the root directory and if the current directory is the root directory (as is the case here), the MOVE command (like other commands) assumes the Presentations subdirectory is located in the current directory (which is the root directory). Likewise, you could have also specified the destination as A:\Presentations. By using a relative path ("Presentations"), the MOVE command assumed that the Presentations subdirectory is located in the current directory on the current drive.

Copying Files to Another Directory

Isabel asks you to use the command line to create a Designs directory folder and place the bitmap graphics files (containing "bmp" file extensions) in it. She informs you that staff members also need one of the files, "Colors of the Rainbow.bmp", in the Presentations directory. She recommends you use the COPY command to put a duplicate of this file into the Presentations directory, and then move the original file, along with the rest of the bitmap files, into the new Designs directory.

To copy a file into one directory, and then move it to another directory as part of a group:

1. Check the command prompt to make sure you are at the root directory of drive A; if not, change the default drive and, if necessary, type **cd ** and then press **Enter** to change to the root directory.

2. Clear the window.

3. Type **dir *.bmp** and then press **Enter** to list the bitmap files. Notice that you can uniquely specify "Colors of the Rainbow.bmp" with just the first six characters, "Colors." See Figure 4-12.

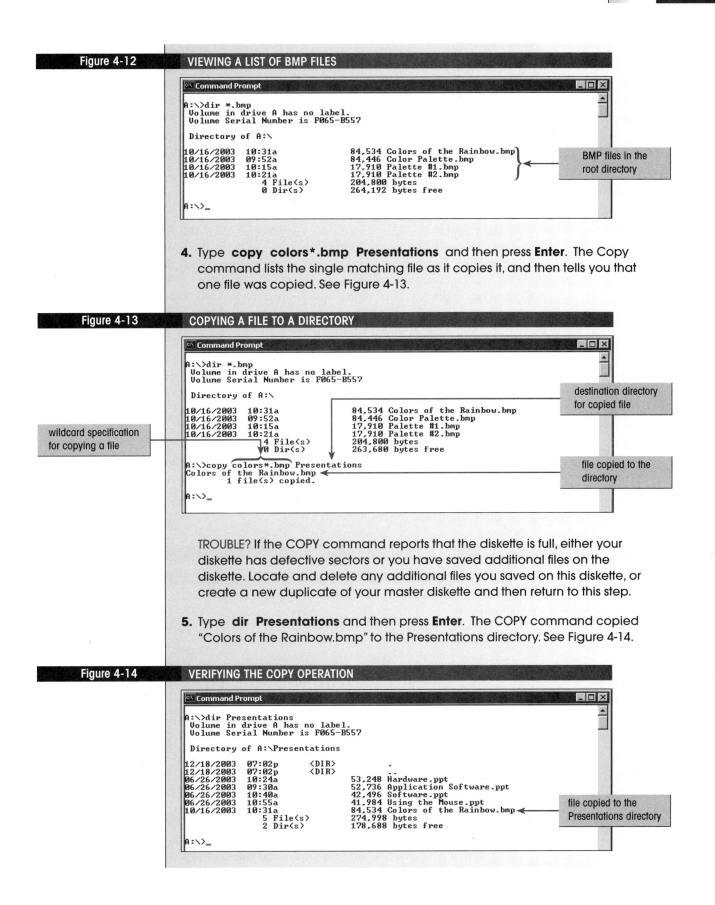

| Figure 4-12 | VIEWING A LIST OF BMP FILES |

```
Command Prompt                                                    _ □ ×
A:\>dir *.bmp
 Volume in drive A has no label.
 Volume Serial Number is F065-B557

 Directory of A:\

10/16/2003  10:31a              84,534 Colors of the Rainbow.bmp
10/16/2003  09:52a              84,446 Color Palette.bmp
10/16/2003  10:15a              17,910 Palette #1.bmp
10/16/2003  10:21a              17,910 Palette #2.bmp
               4 File(s)        204,800 bytes
               0 Dir(s)         264,192 bytes free

A:\>_
```

> BMP files in the root directory

4. Type **copy colors*.bmp Presentations** and then press **Enter**. The Copy command lists the single matching file as it copies it, and then tells you that one file was copied. See Figure 4-13.

| Figure 4-13 | COPYING A FILE TO A DIRECTORY |

```
Command Prompt                                                    _ □ ×
A:\>dir *.bmp
 Volume in drive A has no label.
 Volume Serial Number is F065-B557

 Directory of A:\

10/16/2003  10:31a              84,534 Colors of the Rainbow.bmp
10/16/2003  09:52a              84,446 Color Palette.bmp
10/16/2003  10:15a              17,910 Palette #1.bmp
10/16/2003  10:21a              17,910 Palette #2.bmp
               4 File(s)        204,800 bytes
               0 Dir(s)         263,680 bytes free

A:\>copy colors*.bmp Presentations
Colors of the Rainbow.bmp
               1 file(s) copied.

A:\>_
```

> destination directory for copied file

> wildcard specification for copying a file

> file copied to the directory

TROUBLE? If the COPY command reports that the diskette is full, either your diskette has defective sectors or you have saved additional files on the diskette. Locate and delete any additional files you saved on this diskette, or create a new duplicate of your master diskette and then return to this step.

5. Type **dir Presentations** and then press **Enter**. The COPY command copied "Colors of the Rainbow.bmp" to the Presentations directory. See Figure 4-14.

| Figure 4-14 | VERIFYING THE COPY OPERATION |

```
Command Prompt                                                    _ □ ×
A:\>dir Presentations
 Volume in drive A has no label.
 Volume Serial Number is F065-B557

 Directory of A:\Presentations

12/18/2003  07:02p       <DIR>          .
12/18/2003  07:02p       <DIR>          ..
06/26/2003  10:24a              53,248 Hardware.ppt
06/26/2003  09:30a              52,736 Application Software.ppt
06/26/2003  10:40a              42,496 Software.ppt
06/26/2003  10:55a              41,984 Using the Mouse.ppt
10/16/2003  10:31a              84,534 Colors of the Rainbow.bmp
               5 File(s)        274,998 bytes
               2 Dir(s)         178,688 bytes free

A:\>_
```

> file copied to the Presentations directory

<u>Copying Files to Another Directory</u>
- From the command prompt, change to the directory that contains the file or files you want to copy.
- Type COPY, press the Spacebar, type the name of the file you want to copy or enter a file specification with wildcards to copy a group of files, press the Spacebar, type the path and name of the directory to which you want to copy the file(s), and then press Enter.

Using a similar approach, you can also copy files between disk drives. This option becomes particularly useful if Windows 2000 will not start up normally and you can only work from a command line. For example, if your current drive was C:, your current working directory was your "My Documents" folder, and you wanted to copy a file named "Final Project Report.doc" to the "Reports" directory on a diskette, you could enter the following command:

copy "Final Project Report.doc" a:\Reports

Now you're ready to create the Designs directory and move all the "bmp" files to this directory.

To create the Designs directory and move "bmp" files to this directory:

1. Clear the window, type **md Designs**, and then press **Enter**. The Make Directory command creates this directory.

2. Type (or recall) **dir /ad** and then press **Enter**. Your diskette now contains two directories. See Figure 4-15.

Figure 4-15   ADDING A NEW DIRECTORY

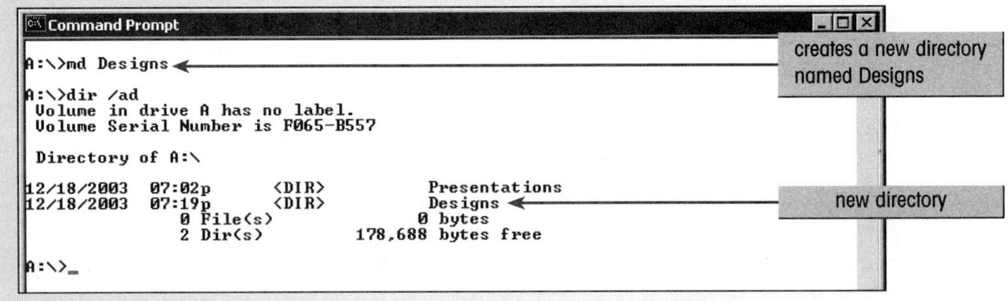

creates a new directory named Designs

new directory

3. Type **dir Designs** and then press **Enter**. Notice that, like the Presentations directory you created earlier, this directory also contains the two standard entries marked as directories ("." and ".."), but no files.

4. Clear the window.

5. Type **move *.bmp Designs** and then press **Enter**. The MOVE command lists the names of the files it copies to the Designs directory when you use a wildcard in the file specification for the source files. See Figure 4-16.

Figure 4-16	MOVING FILES TO A DIRECTORY

wildcard file specification for files to move

destination directory

```
Command Prompt                                            _ □ ×
A:\>move *.bmp Designs
A:\Colors of the Rainbow.bmp
A:\Color Palette.bmp
A:\Palette #1.bmp
A:\Palette #2.bmp

A:\>_
```

files with the bmp file extension being moved to the Designs directory

6. Type (or recall) **dir Designs** and then press **Enter**. The Designs directory contains the four files that the MOVE command moved to this directory. See Figure 4-17.

Figure 4-17	VIEWING THE FILES IN THE DESIGNS DIRECTORY

```
Command Prompt                                            _ □ ×
A:\>move *.bmp Designs
A:\Colors of the Rainbow.bmp
A:\Color Palette.bmp
A:\Palette #1.bmp
A:\Palette #2.bmp

A:\>dir Designs
 Volume in drive A has no label.
 Volume Serial Number is F065-B557

 Directory of A:\Designs

12/18/2003  07:19p      <DIR>          .
12/18/2003  07:19p      <DIR>          ..
10/16/2003  10:31a              84,534 Colors of the Rainbow.bmp
10/16/2003  09:52a              84,446 Color Palette.bmp
10/16/2003  10:15a              17,910 Palette #1.bmp
10/16/2003  10:21a              17,910 Palette #2.bmp
               4 File(s)        204,800 bytes
               2 Dir(s)         178,688 bytes free

A:\>_
```

files moved to the Designs directory

You can use the COPY and MOVE commands to make sure that you have copies of the files you need in the correct directories.

Organizing Training Templates

On your templates disk, you have a set of templates that are used for employee training sessions on the use of Microsoft Excel. You decide to place those files in a Training directory.

To organize templates used for training:

1. Check the command prompt to make sure you are at the root directory of drive A; if not, change the default drive to drive A and, if necessary, type **cd ** and then press **Enter** to change to the root directory.

2. Clear the window, type **md Training** and then press **Enter** to create a Training directory.

3. Type **move "Addressing Cells.xls" Training** and then press **Enter**. (Make sure you place the long filename of the file you are copying within quotation marks; otherwise, the MOVE command will report that you used the incorrect syntax.) The MOVE command moves the file, but unlike moving a group of files, it does not display the name of the file. Also, you could have performed the copy more easily by using the asterisk wildcard. If you had examined your hardcopy of the files on this disk, you would have discovered that there is only one file that starts with the characters "Add"—so you could have used Add* instead of "Addressing Cells.xls" for the file specification of the source file.

4. Type **move fo* Training** and then press **Enter**. This time, the MOVE command moved three files—Fonts.xls, "Format Code Colors.xls", and "Formatting Features.xls". All of these filenames start with the characters "fo".

5. Type **move an* Training** and then press **Enter** (you could do this by recalling the previous command and replacing "fo" with "an"). The MOVE command moves one file—"Andre's Employee Payroll.xls". By using a wildcard, you did not need to type the full filename with quotation marks.

6. Clear the window, type **dir Training** and then press **Enter**. The Directory command lists the five files you moved to this directory. See Figure 4-18.

Figure 4-18   **VIEWING THE FILES IN THE TRAINING DIRECTORY**

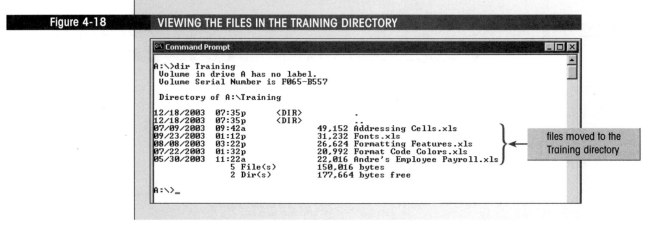

By using wildcards to take advantage of similarities in filenames, you can reduce the time required to move files, and you do not need to remember to put quotation marks around long filenames.

Moving Files from the Parent Directory

Next, you decide to create a Business Records directory and then move templates used for creating files that track business transactions into this directory.

To organize templates into the Business Records directory:

1. Check the command prompt to make sure you are at the root directory of drive A; if not, change the default drive to drive A and, if necessary, type **cd ** and then press **Enter** to change to the root directory.

2. Clear the window, type **md "Business Records"** and then press **Enter**. The Make Directory command creates this directory. You need to enclose the long directory name within quotation marks; otherwise, the Make Directory command will create two directories—one called Business, and the other called Records.

3. Use the DIR command to display a directory listing of your diskette. Your diskette now includes a directory named "Business Records."

TROUBLE? If your directory listing shows two directories, one named Business and the other named Records, and if you do not have a directory named "Business Records," then you did not enclose "Business Records" within quotation marks when you entered the MD command in the previous step. Repeat the previous step, place quotation marks around the directory name, and then display a directory listing to verify that you completed it correctly.

TROUBLE? If you want to remove the directories named Business and Records, type RD Business, then press Enter, and then type RD Records and then press Enter. This use of the Remove Directory (RD) command removes empty directories.

4. Type **move L*** **"Business Records"** and then press **Enter**. The MOVE command moves "Loan Payment Analysis.xls" to the Business Records directory. Because this file is the only one whose filename starts with the letter "L," you can use a wildcard to move the file with a minimal amount of effort.

    TROUBLE? If the MOVE command informs you that the syntax of your command is incorrect, repeat this step, and make sure you enclose the directory name within quotation marks.

5. Type **move i*** **"Business Records"** and then press **Enter** (you may accomplish this by recalling the previous command and changing the "L" to an "i"). The MOVE command moves "Invoice Form.wk4"—the only file that starts with an "i"—to the Business Records folder. Editing the previous command saves time and effort, and results in fewer errors, especially when entering and working with long filenames with spaces.

6. Type **move w*** **"Business Records"** and then press **Enter** (again, you can recall and edit the previous command). The MOVE command moves "Weekly Worklog.xls," the only file that starts with a "w," to the Business Records folder.

7. Type **move d*** **"Business Records"** and then press **Enter**. The MOVE command moves "Daily Sales.xls," the only file that starts with a "d," to the Business Records folder.

8. Type **cd Business Records** and then press **Enter**. The Change Directory command changes to the Business Records directory. See Figure 4-19. Note that you did not need to type the quotation marks around "Business Records" for this command. The CD command doesn't require quotation marks, because it expects just a single target directory name. It therefore assumes that multiple words separated by spaces are all part of the target name.

Figure 4-19	MOVING FILES TO THE BUSINESS RECORDS DIRECTORY

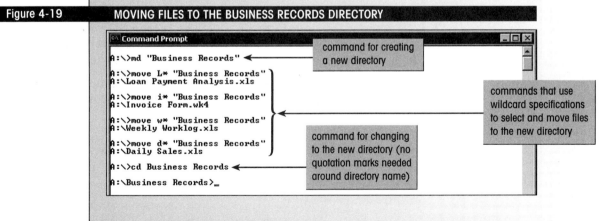

9. Clear the window, type **dir** and then press **Enter**. The Directory command shows the four files that you moved to this folder. See Figure 4-20.

Figure 4-20   **VIEWING THE FILES IN THE BUSINESS RECORDS DIRECTORY**

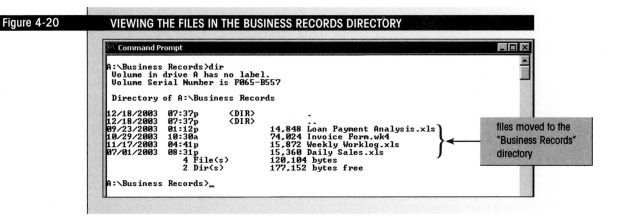

After checking the contents of this directory, you realize that you need to include three other files in it. Since you are already in the directory, you decide to work from there instead of returning to the root directory.

To copy files from the parent directory:

1. Clear the screen, type **move "Savings Plan.xls"** and then press **Enter**. The MOVE command informs you that it cannot find the file you specified. See Figure 4-21. Like other commands, the MOVE command assumes that "Savings Plan.xls" is stored in the current directory (which is now the Business Records directory) because you did not specify the path where the file is stored.

Figure 4-21   **THE IMPORTANCE OF SPECIFYING THE PATH**

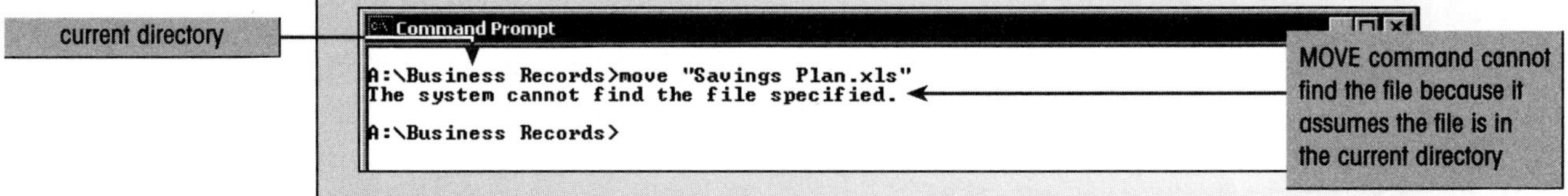

current directory

```
Command Prompt

A:\Business Records>move "Savings Plan.xls"
The system cannot find the file specified.

A:\Business Records>
```

MOVE command cannot find the file because it assumes the file is in the current directory

2. Type **move "\Savings Plan.xls"** and then press **Enter**, making sure you include the backslash (\ )—the name of the root directory—before the "S" in Savings this time. (You can recall and edit the previous command to do this.)

3. Type (or recall) **dir** and then press **Enter**. The MOVE command moved "Savings Plan.xls" from the root directory to the current directory. See Figure 4-22.

Figure 4-22	SPECIFYING THE PATH FOR A FILE

```
Command Prompt                                                    _ □ X

A:\Business Records>move "Savings Plan.xls"
The system cannot find the file specified.

A:\Business Records>move "\Savings Plan.xls"◄

A:\Business Records>dir
 Volume in drive A has no label.
 Volume Serial Number is F065-B557

 Directory of A:\Business Records

12/18/2003  07:37p    <DIR>          .
12/18/2003  07:37p    <DIR>          ..
09/23/2003  01:12p           14,848 Loan Payment Analysis.xls
10/29/2003  10:30a           74,024 Invoice Form.wk4
11/17/2003  04:41p           15,872 Weekly Worklog.xls
07/01/2003  08:31p           15,360 Daily Sales.xls
10/31/2003  03:33p           14,848 Savings Plan.xls◄
               5 File(s)        134,952 bytes
               2 Dir(s)         176,640 bytes free

A:\Business Records>_
```

revised MOVE command now includes the path of the file

MOVE command moved the file using the path

4. Type **move \"Product List.xls"** and then press **Enter**. The MOVE command moves Product List.xls to this directory. Note that you can place the quotation marks around either the entire file specification, or around just the long filename.

5. Type **move *.wk4** and then press **Enter**. The MOVE command moves Sales.wk4, the only file with the "wk4" file extension, to this directory.

6. Type **move *t.xls** and then press **Enter**. The MOVE command moves Balance Sheet.xls, the only file with a "t" before an "xls" file extension, to this directory.

7. Type **move \c*** and then press **Enter**. The MOVE command copies two files from the root directory to the current directory. Again, for the file specification, all you need to type is the minimum amount of information needed to locate the files with the asterisk wildcard, plus the path that indicates where the files are stored. See Figure 4-23 for a summary of these operations.

Figure 4-23	MOVING FILES TO THE CURRENT DIRECTORY

```
Command Prompt                                                    _ □ X
 Directory of A:\Business Records

12/18/2003  07:37p    <DIR>          .
12/18/2003  07:37p    <DIR>          ..
09/23/2003  01:12p           14,848 Loan Payment Analysis.xls
10/29/2003  10:30a           74,024 Invoice Form.wk4
11/17/2003  04:41p           15,872 Weekly Worklog.xls
07/01/2003  08:31p           15,360 Daily Sales.xls
10/31/2003  03:33p           14,848 Savings Plan.xls
               5 File(s)        134,952 bytes
               2 Dir(s)         176,640 bytes free

A:\Business Records>move \"Product List.xls"◄

A:\Business Records>move \*.wk4
A:\Sales.wk4

A:\Business Records>move \*t.xls
A:\Balance Sheet.xls

A:\Business Records>move \c*
A:\Commission on Sales.xls
A:\Client Invoices.xls

A:\Business Records>_
```

quotation marks placed only around the filename rather than the full path

because you did not specify a destination, the MOVE command moves the file to the current directory

file specification for the source files includes the path

8. Type **dir** and then press **Enter**. You have now moved the five additional files you want to store in this directory.

Instead of working from a printed copy of a directory listing, you can use the Directory command to remind you of the names of the files in the current directory so you can use the right wildcard specification to move or copy a specific file or group of files.

If you want to copy a file from the parent directory to the current subdirectory, but leave the original file in the parent directory, you can use the same techniques with the COPY command that you used above with the MOVE command.

REFERENCE WINDOW   **RW**

<u>Moving Files from the Parent Directory</u>
- Open a Command Prompt window.
- If necessary, change the default drive to the drive that contains the files you want to move.
- Type CD, press the Spacebar, type the name of the directory where you want to work, and then press Enter. (You do not need to use quotation marks around long directory names when using this command.)
- Type MOVE, press the Spacebar, type enough of the path as well as the exact name of the file you want to move, or type enough of the path and a file specification that uses a wildcard to select all the files you want to move, and then press Enter. If you specify an exact filename, and if the filename is a long filename with spaces, enclose the filename in quotation marks.

By taking advantage of the fact that commands use the current drive if you do not specify otherwise, you can simplify and streamline file operations in a command-line environment. In contrast, by specifying enough of the path, you can guarantee that commands locate the file you need, without displaying an error and requiring more work on your part to correct the problem and complete the operation.

Completing the Directory Structure

You only have one more directory to create, and then you can move all the remaining files to that directory.

To complete the reorganization of your Data Disk:

1. Clear the window, type **cd ..** (two periods) and then press **Enter**. You return to the root directory. See Figure 4-24. Although you could have referred to the root directory by using the backslash (by entering the command CD \), this command also works. The "dot dot" instructs the Change Directory command to move to the parent directory of the current directory. In this case, the parent directory of the "Business Records" directory is the root directory. Unlike the backslash (\), which can bypass many different levels to get directly to the root directory, "dot dot" only moves up one level.

Figure 4-24	CHANGING TO THE PARENT DIRECTORY

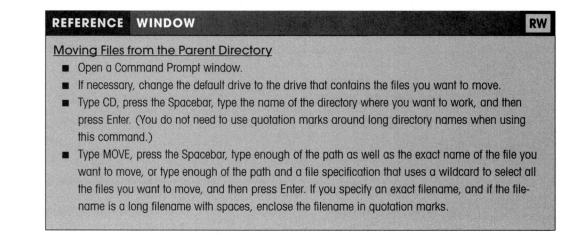

notation for parent directory

Change Directory command changes to the root directory (the parent directory of Business Records)

2. Type **dir /o** and then press **Enter**. You now have four directories, and the remaining files (all ones with the "xls" file extension) are the ones you want to move to the last directory you will now create. See Figure 4-25.

| Figure 4-25 | VIEWING THE CONTENTS OF THE ROOT DIRECTORY |

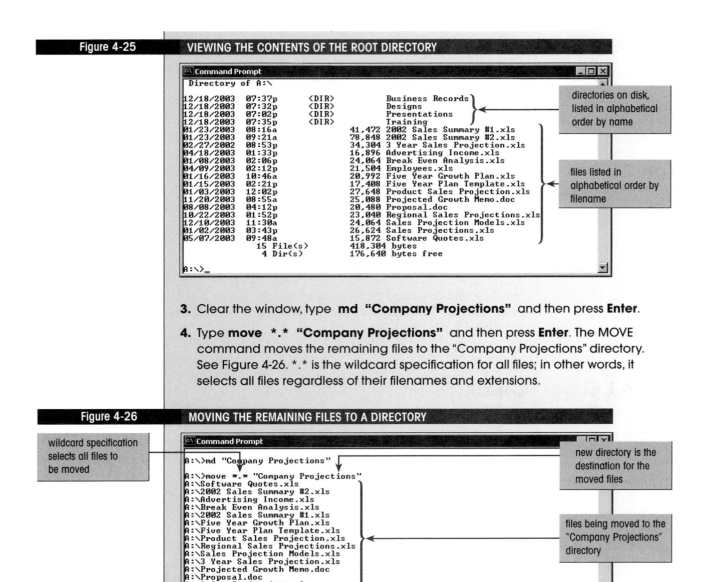

3. Clear the window, type **md "Company Projections"** and then press **Enter**.

4. Type **move *.* "Company Projections"** and then press **Enter**. The MOVE command moves the remaining files to the "Company Projections" directory. See Figure 4-26. *.* is the wildcard specification for all files; in other words, it selects all files regardless of their filenames and extensions.

| Figure 4-26 | MOVING THE REMAINING FILES TO A DIRECTORY |

5. Clear the window, type (or recall) **dir /o** and then press **Enter**. You have organized all the files on your diskette into a set of directories. See Figure 4-27. Notice that the directory listing acts as a "table of contents" for the diskette. Also note that, even though you used *.* as the file specification for the source files in the previous step, the MOVE command did not move your directories, only your files.

Figure 4-27	VIEWING THE CONTENTS OF THE ROOT DIRECTORY

```
Command Prompt                                                      _ □ ✕

A:\>dir /o
 Volume in drive A has no label.
 Volume Serial Number is F065-B557

 Directory of A:\

12/18/2003  07:37p        <DIR>          Business Records
12/18/2003  07:47p        <DIR>          Company Projections
12/18/2003  07:32p        <DIR>          Designs
12/18/2003  07:02p        <DIR>          Presentations
12/18/2003  07:35p        <DIR>          Training
               0 File(s)              0 bytes
               5 Dir(s)         174,592 bytes free

A:\>_
```

all the files on the disk are now organized into directories

6. Close the Command Prompt window.

You have now completed the reorganization of the files on your diskette at the Windows 2000 command line as Isabel requested, creating appropriate new directory folders and copying or moving the data files into them.

Session 4.1 QUICK CHECK

1. The _____ is the first directory created on a disk by an operating system or formatting utility.

2. A(n) _____ is a directory that is subordinate to, and contained within, another directory.

3. The _____ is a notation that identifies the exact location of a directory or file on a disk.

4. Windows 2000 is installed in a directory called the _____ folder.

5. A(n) _____ path spells out the full path, and there is no ambiguity as to the location of the directory or file.

6. A(n) _____ path always starts from the current drive and directory.

7. The command for creating a directory is _____.

8. The _____ command changes the current working directory.

9. The "." entry in a directory listing refers to the _____.

10. You can use the _____ command to move files to another location.

SESSION 4.2

In this session, you will copy files within the same directory. You will display a graphical representation of the directory structure of your disk, explore additional techniques for navigating up and down the directory structure, and save a copy of the directory tree display.

Copying Files within a Directory

Isabel asks you to create sales summary template files for 2003, following the format of the same files for 2002. Your new "Company Projections" directory folder already contains 2002 sales summary files. To save time and effort, you decide to copy these files so you can modify them later. Because you will use these two groups of files in conjunction with each other, you want to keep them in the same directory. When you copy a file within the same directory, you must give it a new name, because a directory cannot contain two files or subdirectories with the same name.

To copy the sales summary files within the "Company Projections" directory:

1. Open a Command Prompt window, set colors if necessary, insert the copy of Data Disk #1 that you used in Session 4.1 in drive A, and make drive A the current drive.

2. Clear the screen, type **cd com*** and then press **Enter**. The Change Directory command changes to the "Company Projections" directory, because only "Company Projections" matched your wildcard specification "com*" (if there had been more than one matching directory, you would have switched to whichever directory came first in the directory listing's arbitrary disk order). The command prompt should now contain the name of the "Company Projections" directory folder.

3. Type **copy 2002* 2003*** and then press **Enter**. The COPY command copies two files and produces two new files with new filenames beginning with "2003".

4. Type **dir 200*** and then press **Enter** to view the new files. See Figure 4-28. Now there are four files that begin with "200" in the "Company Projections" directory folder.

Figure 4-28	COPYING FILES WITHIN A DIRECTORY

change directory with wildcard matches only "Company Projections"

copy matching files, changing the first four characters

wildcard matches both sets of filenames

original files

new files

```
A:\>cd com*

A:\Company Projections>copy 2002* 2003*
2002 Sales Summary #2.xls
2002 Sales Summary #1.xls
        2 file(s) copied.

A:\Company Projections>dir 200*
 Volume in drive A has no label.
 Volume Serial Number is F065-B557

 Directory of A:\Company Projections

01/23/2003  09:21a            78,848 2002 Sales Summary #2.xls
01/23/2003  08:16a            41,472 2002 Sales Summary #1.xls
01/23/2003  09:21a            78,848 2003 Sales Summary #2.xls
01/23/2003  08:16a            41,472 2003 Sales Summary #1.xls
             4 File(s)        240,640 bytes
             0 Dir(s)          54,272 bytes free

A:\Company Projections>
```

5. Type **cd ** and then press **Enter** to return to the root directory to review your work.

Note that copying files within one directory has no effect on files with similar names in any other directories.

REFERENCE WINDOW   **RW**

__Copying Files within a Directory__

- Open a Command Prompt window.
- If necessary, change the default drive to the drive that contains the files you want to copy.
- Type CD, press the Spacebar, type the name of the directory where you want to work, and then press Enter. (You do not need to use quotation marks around long directory names when using this command.)
- Type COPY, press the Spacebar, type the name of the file you want to copy, or type a file specification that uses a wildcard to select all the files you want to copy, type a name or filespec for the name(s) of the new files, and then press Enter. If you specify an exact filename, and if the filename is long, enclose the filename in quotation marks.
- Type DIR and then press Enter to verify that the copy operation worked.

You can perform file operations, such as COPY, within a directory without affecting files in any other directories.

Viewing a Directory Structure

You want to view a graphical representation of the partially completed directory structure of your diskette. You can use the TREE command to display a directory tree from the command prompt. A **directory tree** is a diagrammatic representation of the directory structure of a hard disk or diskette. It shows the current directory and all subdirectories below the current directory. The TREE command is an external command with the following syntax:

TREE [*drive:*][*path*]

If you do not specify a drive or path, the TREE command assumes you want to view the directory structure of the current drive, starting with the current directory. If you want the directory tree to include the root directory and all subdirectories, you must start from the root directory or specify the root directory as the path. If you want to view the directory tree of another drive, or that of a specific directory of a hard disk or diskette, you must specify the other drive name and/or directory path.

To view a directory tree of your Data Disk #1:

1. Check the command prompt to make sure you are at the root directory of drive A; if not, you can get to the root directory by typing **cd /d a:** and pressing **Enter**. The **Drive Switch (/d)** switch changes the current drive in addition to changing the designated current working directory for the drive.

2. Clear the window.

3. Type **tree** and then press **Enter**. TREE displays a diagrammatic representation of the directory structure of your diskette. See Figure 4-29. Next to the name of the drive, TREE displays a dot (.) to indicate that the directory tree starts at the current directory. The directory tree shows the five subdirectories under the root directory.

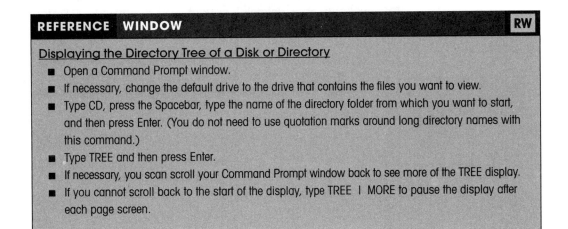

Figure 4-29 DISPLAYING A DIRECTORY TREE

TREE command

dot indicates current directory

In this directory tree, you see the relationship of the subdirectories to the root directory. As you construct or revise the directory structure of your hard disk or diskettes from the command prompt to meet your changing needs, you can quickly view the directory structure to verify directory operations and to refresh your memory of the disk's directory structure.

REFERENCE WINDOW   RW

Displaying the Directory Tree of a Disk or Directory
- Open a Command Prompt window.
- If necessary, change the default drive to the drive that contains the files you want to view.
- Type CD, press the Spacebar, type the name of the directory folder from which you want to start, and then press Enter. (You do not need to use quotation marks around long directory names with this command.)
- Type TREE and then press Enter.
- If necessary, you scan scroll your Command Prompt window back to see more of the TREE display.
- If you cannot scroll back to the start of the display, type TREE | MORE to pause the display after each page screen.

The TREE command gives you a quick overview of a directory folder structure. Later, you'll save a copy of a TREE display to a file, but first you'll practice moving between directories on your hard drive.

Navigating a Directory Tree

Now you want to learn how to navigate within a directory folder tree at the command prompt. There are two techniques you can use; you can change to a directory in one step by specifying its full path, or you can traverse the directory tree one subdirectory at a time by specifying the directory's name.

You want to examine directories of your hard drive. First, because you want to make sure that your computer contains some new fonts that you've installed on your hard disk, you are going to change to the Windows 2000 Fonts directory by specifying its full path and then check the contents of this directory.

To change to the Fonts directory in one step:

1. Type **cd /d c:\win*\fonts** and then press **Enter**. The "/d" changes your default drive to C as well as changing your current directory folder. See Figure 4-30. Again, each drive maintains its own current default directory in a Command Prompt

window. "Win*" will match your Windows 2000 SystemRoot directory name as long as it begins with the letters "win," such as Windows or WinNT. The command prompt shows that the current directory is the Windows 2000 Fonts directory.

| Figure 4-30 | CHANGING TO THE FONTS DIRECTORY |

```
Command Prompt                                                      _ □ ☒
A:\>tree
Folder PATH listing
Volume serial number is 0006FE80 F065:B557
A:.
    ├──Presentations
    ├──Designs
    ├──Training
    ├──Business Records
    └──Company Projections

A:\>cd /d c:\win*\fonts  ◄
C:\WINNT\Fonts>
```

new current directory

CD command changes to the Fonts directory on drive C

TROUBLE? If you get an error message saying, "The filename, directory name, or volume label syntax is incorrect," your Windows 2000 SystemRoot directory name may not begin with the letters "win" (or it might be on another volume with a different drive letter). List your root directory's subdirectories by typing **dir c:\ /ad** and pressing **Enter**. Look for the name of your SystemRoot directory folder and substitute its name for "win*" in the step above. If you have trouble identifying your Windows 2000 SystemRoot folder name, ask a lab assistant or instructor.

2. Type **dir /o /p** and then press **Enter** to view the files in this directory. When prompted, use the Spacebar to view the remainder of the directory listing.

3. Type **cd ** and then press **Enter**. As you can tell from the command prompt, the CD command moved the current working directory up two directories to the root directory.

REFERENCE WINDOW   **RW**

Changing to Another Drive and Directory
- Open a Command Prompt window.
- If necessary, change the default drive to the drive that contains the files you want to copy.
- Type CD, press the Spacebar, type the /D switch, press the Spacebar, type the full path (with or without wildcards) of the drive and directory where you want to work, and then press Enter.

The enhanced features of the Change Directory command in Windows 2000 now allow you to not only change directories, but also change drives.

Stepping Down a Directory Tree

You next want to examine the Windows 2000 SystemRoot and the System32 directories. Again, the SystemRoot directory is typically C:\WINNT or, if you have an upgraded system, C:\Windows. The System32 directory folder contains most of the command prompt utility programs you use. You can step down the directory tree one directory at a time.

To change to the Windows 2000 SystemRoot directory and then to the System32 subdirectory:

1. Clear the window, type **cd win*** and then press **Enter** (substitute your Windows 2000 SystemRoot directory name for "win*" if necessary; if your SystemRoot is on another drive, add /d and the drive letter as well). The command prompt shows that the current directory is the Windows 2000 directory.

2. Recall (or type) **dir /o /p** and then press **Enter**. DIR displays a list of the subdirectories below your Windows 2000 SystemRoot directory folder. See Figure 4-31. As you can tell from this directory listing, the Windows SystemRoot directory contains many different subdirectories for the Windows 2000 program and supporting files.

Figure 4-31	DISPLAYING THE CONTENTS OF THE SYSTEMROOT DIRECTORY

```
Command Prompt - dir /o /p                          _ □ ×
 Uolume in drive C is DRIVE
 Uolume Serial Number is E461-9D1C

 Directory of C:\WINNT ◄                              SystemRoot directory
                                                      name
02/28/2000  01:33p    <DIR>          .
02/28/2000  01:33p    <DIR>          ..
02/28/2000  01:33p    <DIR>          addins
02/28/2000  01:33p    <DIR>          AppPatch
02/28/2000  01:33p    <DIR>          Config
02/28/2000  01:33p    <DIR>          Connection Wizard
02/28/2000  01:33p    <DIR>          Cursors
02/28/2000  01:33p    <DIR>          Debug
02/28/2000  01:33p    <DIR>          Driver Cache
12/14/2003  01:19p    <DIR>          DrWatson
02/28/2000  01:33p    <DIR>          Help               subdirectories
02/28/2000  01:33p    <DIR>          java
02/28/2000  01:33p    <DIR>          Media
12/15/2003  12:00p    <DIR>          Minidump
02/28/2000  01:33p    <DIR>          msagent
02/28/2000  01:33p    <DIR>          msapps
02/28/2000  01:49p    <DIR>          mww32
02/28/2000  01:47p    <DIR>          Offline Web Pages
02/28/2000  01:45p    <DIR>          Registration
Press any key to continue . . . _
```

3. Use the Spacebar to view the remainder of the directory listing. The Windows directory also contains important operating system files as well as directories.

4. Type **cd system32** and then press **Enter**. The command prompt shows that the current directory is the System32 directory, which is positioned below the Windows 2000 directory.

5. Recall (or type) **dir /o /p** and then press **Enter** to view the files in this directory.

6. Use the Spacebar to view the next screen of the directory listing, and then use **Ctrl+C** to interrupt the Directory command and return to the command prompt. If you examined the entire directory listing for the directory used on the computer in Figure 4-31, you would find that it contains 26 directories and over 1,400 files. The number of directories and files on your computer system might differ.

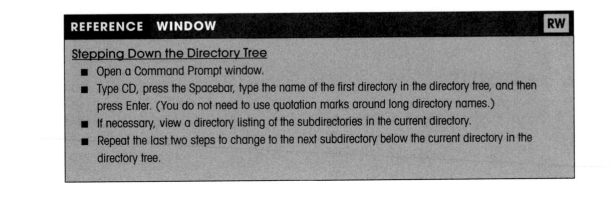

REFERENCE WINDOW **RW**

<u>Stepping Down the Directory Tree</u>
- Open a Command Prompt window.
- Type CD, press the Spacebar, type the name of the first directory in the directory tree, and then press Enter. (You do not need to use quotation marks around long directory names.)
- If necessary, view a directory listing of the subdirectories in the current directory.
- Repeat the last two steps to change to the next subdirectory below the current directory in the directory tree.

To change to a directory, you can step down the directory tree one directory at a time, or if you know the full path to a directory, you can switch to that directory in one step.

Stepping Up the Directory

You first want to return to the Windows 2000 SystemRoot folder and then to the root directory. If you change to a subdirectory and then want to move one level higher in the directory tree to its parent directory, you can use this variation of the Change Directory command:

CD ..

Because ". ." (dot dot) refers to the parent directory of the current directory, you can change to a parent directory without specifying its full path. In the following steps you will return to the root directory, one directory level at a time.

To change to the parent directory of System32:

1. Clear the screen, type **cd ..** and then press **Enter**. The command prompt shows that the current directory is the Windows 2000 SystemRoot directory (probably C:\WINNT). See Figure 4-32. You can now use this same command to move to the parent directory of the SystemRoot directory.

Figure 4-32	STEPPING UP THE DIRECTORY TREE

parent directory of system32

root is the parent of the WINNT directory

```
C:\WINNT\system32>cd ..
C:\WINNT>_
```

two dots indicate the parent directory

2. Type **cd ..** and then press **Enter**. The command prompt shows that you are at the root directory. See Figure 4-33.

Figure 4-33	CHANGING TO THE ROOT DIRECTORY

parent directory of the current directory

root directory

```
C:\WINNT\system32>cd ..
C:\WINNT>cd ..
C:\>
```

REFERENCE   WINDOW   **RW**

Stepping Up a Directory Tree
- Open the Command Prompt window.
- Type CD, press the Spacebar, type .. and then press Enter.
- If necessary, view a directory listing of the subdirectories in the current directory.
- Repeat the last two steps to change to the next subdirectory in the directory tree above the current directory.

Next, you want to change to the Media subdirectory folder (containing sound files), examine the files included with Windows 2000 for use as sound events, and switch to the Fonts subdirectory to check for additional fonts before returning to the root directory. Later, you can install the additional sound files and fonts that you need on your computer for your next project.

To traverse the subdirectories of the Windows 2000 directory folder:

1. Type **cd c:\win*\media** and then press **Enter**. The command prompt shows that the current directory folder is Media.

2. Recall (or type) **dir   /o /p** and then press **Enter** to view the files in this directory. When prompted, press the Spacebar to view the remainder of the directory listing.

3. Clear the screen, type **cd ..\fonts** and then press **Enter**. This command changes to the Fonts directory, which is below the parent directory of your current working directory. See Figure 4-34. Because the Fonts directory is under the same parent directory, you can reference the parent directory by using "dot dot." Directories that are located in the same level of the directory tree are called **parallel directories**. You could also enter "cd \win*\fonts" to achieve the same result.

| Figure 4-34 | CHANGING TO A PARALLEL DIRECTORY |

```
Command Prompt

C:\WINNT\Media>cd ..\fonts
C:\WINNT\Fonts>
```

new directory on the same level as the previous directory

move up to the parent directory

move down to another subdirectory of the parent

4. Type **cd ** and then press **Enter** to return to the root directory.

You can use the same techniques to navigate a more complex directory structure elsewhere on your hard disk in order to locate client or business files.

Saving a Directory Tree Display

You want to save a copy of the directory tree that includes the files contained in each of the directories of your new templates diskette. If you reorganize your templates diskette later, you can use this documentation to help you in planning the changes you intend to make. Likewise, if you reorganize a disk and then change your mind later, you can quickly reconstruct the directory structure and restore your business files to the original directories.

Earlier, you used the TREE command to view a directory tree at the command prompt. You can use a variation of the same command to view filenames by directory. You can then save a copy of the directory tree display by redirecting that output to a file. The **Filename switch (/F)** displays the directory tree and lists the filenames in each directory. When you save this information, you can also include the **ASCII switch (/A)**, so that any program or printer can reproduce it, even if the program cannot display the graphics lines in TREE's regular directory display. If you use the ASCII switch, TREE substitutes other symbols for the graphics lines. Let's try it.

To display and save a directory tree of your Data Disk:

1. Be sure drive A contains your Data Disk. Check the command prompt to make sure you are at the root directory of drive A; if not, move there in one step by typing **cd /d a:** and pressing **Enter**.

2. Clear the window, type **tree /f | more** and then press **Enter**. The MORE filter displays the first page of output from the TREE command. See Figure 4-35. The directory tree displays and lists the filenames in each directory.

Figure 4-35 **VIEWING A DIRECTORY TREE WITH FILENAMES**

```
Command Prompt
Folder PATH listing
Volume serial number is 0006FE80 F065:B557
A:.
    Presentations
        Hardware.ppt
        Application Software.ppt
        Software.ppt
        Using the Mouse.ppt
        Colors of the Rainbow.bmp
    Designs
        Colors of the Rainbow.bmp
        Color Palette.bmp
        Palette #1.bmp
        Palette #2.bmp
    Training
        Addressing Cells.xls
        Fonts.xls
        Formatting Features.xls
        Format Code Colors.xls
        Andre's Employee Payroll.xls
    Business Records
-- More --
```

directory

names of files in the Presentations directory

3. Use the Spacebar to view the remainder of the directory tree and return to the command prompt.

4. Type **tree /f /a > treefile.txt** and then press **Enter**. As you've seen earlier, you can redirect the output of any command to a file or device by using the output redirection operator (>) and the name of the file or device.

5. Type **treefile.txt** and then press **Enter**. If necessary, maximize the Notepad window. Because you typed the data file name (treefile.txt) without specifying a command, and because Windows 2000 associates the "txt" extension with the Notepad program, Windows opens Notepad and opens treefile.txt. See Figure 4-36. Notice that ASCII symbols are used instead of graphical lines to show the directory tree and the relationship of directories to each other.

Figure 4-36	VIEWING A SAVED DIRECTORY TREE USING NOTEPAD

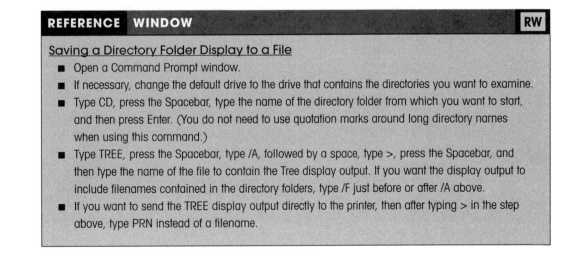

6. In Notepad, scroll up and down to view the tree display of your diskette.

7. If requested by your instructor, print this directory tree file from Notepad.

8. Exit Notepad after you examine the directory tree.

9. Note that you can also provide another person with treefile.txt by delivering the diskette, or by sending the file by e-mail.

For a quick overview of the directory structure of a hard disk or diskette, use the TREE command at the command prompt. You can then locate specific directories and periodically evaluate the organization of directories on diskettes or hard disks.

REFERENCE WINDOW   **RW**

<u>Saving a Directory Folder Display to a File</u>

- Open a Command Prompt window.
- If necessary, change the default drive to the drive that contains the directories you want to examine.
- Type CD, press the Spacebar, type the name of the directory folder from which you want to start, and then press Enter. (You do not need to use quotation marks around long directory names when using this command.)
- Type TREE, press the Spacebar, type /A, followed by a space, type >, press the Spacebar, and then type the name of the file to contain the Tree display output. If you want the display output to include filenames contained in the directory folders, type /F just before or after /A above.
- If you want to send the TREE display output directly to the printer, then after typing > in the step above, type PRN instead of a filename.

The TREE command is a useful tool for providing an overview of the directory structure of a disk and for use before, during, and after the process of reorganizing it. You also can rely on it as a navigational aide as you step up and down the directory tree.

Isabel compliments you on your use of directory commands to organize the template files and says that the new directory folder layout makes it much easier to locate and work with related files.

Session 4.2 QUICK CHECK

1. When you copy a file within the same directory, you must give it a(n) _____.

2. A(n) _____ is a diagrammatic representation of the directory structure of a hard disk or diskette.

3. Next to the name of the drive, TREE may display a dot (.) to indicate that the directory tree starts at the _____ directory.

4. The _____ option of the CD command changes your current default drive as well as changing your current working directory folder.

5. If you change to a subdirectory and then want to move one level higher in the directory tree to its parent directory, you can use the command _____.

6. The _____ switch of the TREE command displays the directory tree and lists the filenames in each directory.

7. If you use the _____ switch, the TREE command substitutes other symbols for the graphics lines.

COMMAND REFERENCE

COMMAND	USE	BASIC SYNTAX	EXAMPLE
CD	Changes the current working directory	CD [drive:][path]directory name CHDIR [drive:][path]directory name	cd \Documents and Settings cd Projections cd \
CD ..	Changes to the parent directory above the current directory	CD ..	cd ..
MD	Creates (or makes) a new directory	MD [drive:][path]directory name MKDIR [drive:][path]directory name	md Presentations
MOVE	Moves one or more files to another drive and/or directory	MOVE [drive:][path]filespec destination	move *.bmp Designs
TREE	Displays a diagram of the directory tree; the /F switch adds filenames to the display; the /A switch displays with ASCII characters only	TREE [drive:][path] [/F] [/A]	tree a:\ /f /a

Items shown in italics and not enclosed within square brackets are required parameters
Items shown in italics and enclosed within square brackets are optional parameters

REVIEW ASSIGNMENTS

One of your co-workers at SolarWinds, Judith, wants to organize her document template files into directories by document type so she can quickly locate templates for a specific type of application. She asks you to help her create the directories and move the files to the directories on that disk.

As you perform the following steps, record your answers to any questions so you can submit them to your instructor.

1. Open a Command Prompt window.

2. Make a copy of the original Data Disk #1(do not use the Data Disk you used in the tutorial). You can use DISKCOPY to copy over the diskette that you used in the tutorial.

3. Change the default drive to drive A.

4. Specify default switches for the Directory command in the Windows environment so that this command displays filenames in alphabetical order first by file extension, then by the main part of the filename, one screen at a time. What command did you enter for this operation?

5. Display a directory listing of your new Data Disk, and verify that filenames are arranged alphabetically, first by file extension, then by the main part of the filename. If necessary, change the default switches for the Directory command in the Windows environment.

6. Delete the files named File0000.chk and ~WRC0070.tmp using the Prompt for Verification switch. What commands did you enter to perform these operations?

7. Create a directory named Images, and move bitmapped image files with the "bmp" file extension to this directory. What commands did you enter for these two operations? How did you verify this operation?

8. Create a directory named "Word Templates"; copy the files with the "doc" file extension to this directory; verify that the copy operation worked; and then delete the document files with the "doc" file extension from the root directory. What commands did you enter for these four operations?

9. Create a directory named Presentations; change to the Presentations directory; and then move files with the "ppt" file extension from the root directory to this directory. What commands did you enter for these three operations?

10. Change to the root directory; create a directory named "Lotus Templates"; and then move files with the "wk4" file extension to this directory. What commands did you enter for these three operations?

11. Create a directory named "Excel Templates"; change to the "Excel Templates" directory; and then move files with the "xls" file extension to this directory. What commands did you enter for these three operations?

12. Change to the root directory, and display the directory structure of your diskette on screen. What commands did you enter for these two operations?

13. Change to the "Excel Templates" directory, and display the directory contents. Now, using one command, change to the "Word Templates" directory. Display the "Word Templates" directory contents. What commands did you enter for these four operations?

14. Change to the root directory. Create a text file that contains the directory structure of the diskette, with no line-drawing characters, and includes all filenames in each directory. Display the resulting text file with Notepad. What commands did you enter for these three operations?

CASE PROBLEMS

Case 1. Organizing Client Files at The Perfect Match   The Perfect Match, an employment agency, hires temporary employees to assist their clients in the preparation of documents. Corey Tanner, the Office Manager, asks you to organize the spreadsheet documents on one of their clients' disks, and to prepare documentation for that client so her employees can easily find the files on the disk.

As you perform the following steps, record your answers to any questions so you can submit them to your instructor.

1. Open a Command Prompt window.

2. Make a copy of the original Data Disk #1 (do not use the Data Disk you used in the tutorial). You can use DISKCOPY to copy over the diskette that you used in the tutorial.

3. Change the default drive to drive A.

4. Specify default switches for the Directory command in the Windows environment so this command displays filenames in alphabetical order first by file extension, then by the main part of the filename, one screen at a time. What command did you enter for this operation?

5. Display a directory listing of your new Data Disk, and verify that filenames are arranged alphabetically first by file extension, then by the main part of the filename. If necessary, change the default switches for the Directory command in the Windows environment.

6. Delete the files named File0000.chk and ~WRC0070.tmp using the Prompt for Verification switch. What commands did you enter to perform these operations?

7. Display all the files with the file extension "bmp." What command did you enter for this operation? Recall that command, and change the DIR command to DEL, and then delete all these files.

8. Repeat this same process to view, then delete, all the files with the "doc," "ppt," and "wk4" file extensions. What commands did you use to view and then delete these three types of files?

9. Display a directory of your disk. The only files that remain are those with the "xls" file extension.

10. Using Figure 4-37 as a guideline, create a subdirectory named "Spreadsheet Templates" in the root directory of the disk. What command did you enter for this operation?

11. Move all the files with the "xls" file extension from the root directory to the "Spreadsheet Templates" subdirectory. What command did you enter for this operation?

12. Change to the "Spreadsheets Templates" subdirectory. What command did you enter for this operation?

13. Create a directory named "Business Records", and then move the files shown under it in Figure 4-37 to that directory. List the commands you used to move the files. *Note*: Use wildcards wherever possible to reduce the number of steps and commands that you need to enter.

14. Create the remaining directories shown in Figure 4-37, and move the remaining files to the directories shown in Figure 4-37.

15. Change to the "Sales Summaries" directory and then, using a wildcard, copy the two files that begin with "2002" to produce two new files that begin with "2003" in the filenames. Repeat the process to produce two other new files that begin with "2004" in the filenames. What command did you enter to change to this directory? What commands did you enter to create copies of the two files that begin with "2002?"

16. In the root directory of your diskette, create an ASCII file containing a directory tree, which shows the final directory structure of your Data Disk with a list of the files in each directory. What command did you enter for this operation? If your instructor requests a printed copy of this file, then open the file in Notepad and print it, or redirect the contents of this file to your printer port.

Figure 4-37	ORGANIZING CLIENT FILES AT THE PERFECT MATCH

Spreadsheet Templates

- Business Records

  Balance Sheet.xls
  Client Invoices.xls
  Commissions on Sales.xls
  Daily Sales.xls
  Data Systems Budget.xls
  Employees.xls
  Loan Payment Analysis.xls
  Product List.xls
  Software Quotes.xls
  Weekly Worklog.xls

- Projections

  3 Year Sales Projection.xls
  Advertising Income.xls
  Break Even Analysis.xls
  Five Year Growth Plan.xls
  Five Year Plan Template.xls
  Product Sales Projection.xls
  Regional Sales Projections.xls
  Sales Projection Models.xls
  Sales Projections.xls

- Sales Summaries

  2002 Sales Summary #1.xls
  2002 Sales Summary #2.xls

- Training

  Addressing Cells.xls
  Andre's Employee Payroll.xls
  Fonts.xls
  Format Code Colors.xls
  Formatting Features.xls
  Savings Plan.xls

Case 2. Preparing Projections at Fast Track Trainers   The end of Fast Track Trainers' fiscal year is quickly approaching, and Samantha Kuehl wants to create a diskette with sales projections and summaries for the next five years. She asks you to make a copy of her working disk and then create directories for FY 2002 and FY 2003 (FY stands for Fiscal Year). After copying the files with the current years' sales summaries and sales projections to the FY 2002 directory, she asks you to make duplicate copies of these same files and copy them to the FY 2003 directory. She also asks that you update the filenames so that the fiscal year is clear from the filename.

As you perform the following steps, record your answers to any questions so you can submit them to your instructor.

1. Open a Command Prompt window.

2. Make a copy of the original Data Disk #1 (do not use the Data Disk you used in the tutorial). You can use DISKCOPY to copy over the diskette that you used in the tutorial.

3. Change the default drive to drive A.

4. Specify default switches for the Directory command in the Windows environment so that this command displays filenames in alphabetical order first by file extension, then by the main part of the filename, one screen at a time. What command did you enter for this operation?

5. Display a directory listing of your new Data Disk, and verify that filenames are arranged alphabetically first by file extension, then by the main part of the filename. If necessary, change the default switches for the Directory command in the Windows environment.

6. Display all the files with the file extension "bmp." What command did you enter for this operation? Recall the command, change the DIR command to DEL, and then delete all these files. What is the final revised command that you used to delete these files?

7. Repeat this same process to view and then delete all the files with the "chk," "doc," "ppt," "tmp," and "wk4" file extensions.

8. Display a directory of your disk. The only files that remain are those with the "xls" file extension.

9. Create a subdirectory named "FY 2002" in the root directory of the disk. What command did you enter for this operation?

10. Copy "2002 Sales Summary #1.xls" and "2002 Sales Summary #2.xls" to the "FY 2002" directory. What command did you enter for this operation?

11. Copy "Sales Projections.xls" to the "FY 2002" directory and, in the process, change the filename to "2002 Sales Projections.xls". What command did you enter for this operation?

12. Create a subdirectory named "FY 2003" in the root directory of the disk.

13. From the root directory, copy the files in the "FY 2002" directory to the "FY 2003" directory, and during the copy operation, change the first part of the filename from "2002" to "2003". What command did you enter for this operation?

14. Delete the remaining files in the root directory of drive A. What command did you enter for this operation?

15. In the root directory of your diskette, create an ASCII file containing a directory tree that shows the final directory structure of your Data Disk with a list of the files in each directory. What command did you enter for this operation? If your instructor requests a printed copy of this file, then open the file in Notepad and print it, or redirect the contents of this file to your printer port.

Case 3. *Preparing for Computer Training Workshops at HiPerform Systems* HiPerform Systems is a small business in Ipswich, Massachusetts, that sells and services computer systems and hard disk drives. James Everett, owner of HiPerform Systems, would like to offer introductory computer courses to customers who buy HiPerform computers. James gives you a copy of a work diskette and asks you to reorganize it, creating and using different folders for the PowerPoint presentation files, bitmap images, and selected spreadsheets he plans to use in his courses.

As you perform the following steps, record your answers to any questions so that you can submit them to your instructor.

1. Open a Command Prompt window.

2. Make a copy of the original Data Disk #1 (do not use the Data Disk you used in the tutorial). You can use DISKCOPY to copy over the diskette that you used in the tutorial.

3. Change the default drive to drive A.

4. Specify default switches for the Directory command in the Windows environment so that this command displays filenames in alphabetical order first by file extension, then by the main part of the filename, one screen at a time. What command did you enter for this operation?

5. Display a directory listing of your new Data Disk, and verify that filenames are arranged alphabetically first by file extension, then by the main part of the filename. If necessary, change the default switches for the Directory command in the Windows environment.

6. Display all the files with the file extension "doc." What command did you enter for this operation? Recall the command, change the DIR command to DEL, and then delete these files. What is the final revised command that you used to delete these files?

7. Repeat this same process to view, then delete, all the files with the "chk," "tmp," and "wk4" file extensions.

8. Display a directory of your disk. The only files that should remain are those with the "xls," "bmp," and "ppt" file extensions.

9. Create a directory named "Computer Courses" in the root directory of the disk. What command did you enter for this operation?

10. Move all the files with the "ppt" file extension from the root directory to the "Computer Courses" directory. What command did you enter for this operation?

11. Move "Fonts.xls" and "Software Quotes.xls" from the root directory to the "Computer Courses" directory. What command did you enter for this operation?

12. Create a subdirectory named Images in the root directory of the disk. What command did you enter for this operation?

13. Move all the files with the "bmp" file extension from the root directory to the Images directory. What command did you enter for this operation?

14. Delete the remaining files in the root directory of drive A. What command did you enter for this operation?

15. In the root directory of your diskette, create an ASCII file containing a directory tree that shows the final directory structure of your Data Disk with a list of the files in each directory. What command did you enter for this operation? If your instructor requests a printed copy of this file, then open the file in Notepad and print it, or redirect the contents of this file to your printer port.

Case 4. *Investigating Advertising Images at Turing Enterprises*   Melissa Turing, owner of Turing Enterprises, plans to prepare a Web site advertising the company's tour packages for women, and she wants to use and enhance the outdoor images in the Windows 2000 Wallpaper directory folder in her advertising. But before she uses these images, she wants to get permission from Microsoft so that she can avoid copyright infringement. Melissa asks you to copy the image files to a folder on a diskette and prepare a file listing the filenames so she can refer to them when she contacts Microsoft.

As you perform the following steps, record your answers to any questions so that you can submit them to your instructor.

1. Open a Command Prompt window.

2. Place a blank diskette in drive A. If you have completed the tutorial thus far, you can reformat your duplicate of Data Disk #1.

3. Change the default drive to drive A.

4. Display a directory listing of your Data Disk, and verify that your diskette is blank.

5. Create a subdirectory named "Windows Images" in the root directory of the disk. What command did you enter for this operation?

6. Change to your new "Windows Images" directory folder. What command did you enter for this operation?

7. Change to the root directory of drive C in one step. What command did you enter for this operation?

8. Change to your Windows directory folder. What command did you enter for this operation?

9. From your Windows directory, change to the Wallpaper subdirectory under the Web directory using one command. What command did you enter for this operation?

10. Copy all the files in the Wallpaper directory to the "Windows Images" directory on drive A. What command did you enter for this operation?

11. Change the default drive to drive A.

12. In the root directory of your diskette, create an ASCII file containing a directory tree, which shows the final directory structure of your Data Disk with a list of the files in each directory. What command did you enter for this operation? If your instructor requests a printed copy of this file, then open the file in Notepad and print it, or redirect the contents of this file to your printer port.

13. Display a directory of the Web Wallpaper folder on drive C, and verify that you have all of the images that you copied to your diskette. What command did you enter for this operation?

14. Delete all the files in the "Windows Images" folder. What command did you enter for this operation?

QUICK | **C**HECK ANSWERS

Session 4.1

1. root directory
2. subdirectory
3. full path
4. SystemRoot
5. absolute
6. relative
7. MD
8. CD
9. parent directory
10. MOVE

Session 4.2

1. new name
2. directory tree
3. current
4. /D
5. CD . .
6. /F or the Filename switch
7. /A or the ASCII switch

OBJECTIVES

In this tutorial you will:

- Examine the importance of organizing files on a hard disk

- Evaluate and reorganize a data directory structure

- Move, rename, and remove directories

- Locate files within a directory structure

- Examine commonly used backup strategies

- Examine how backup utilities use the Archive bit for backups

- Perform normal and incremental backups

- Restore files from normal and incremental backups

MANAGING AND BACKING UP A HARD DISK

Organizing Files at SolarWinds Unlimited

CASE

SolarWinds Unlimited

Isabel asks you to reevaluate the directory structure of your hard disk and decide on a strategy for organizing your document files more efficiently in the "My Documents" directory on your computer. She recommends that you copy the directories and folders from the "My Documents" directory to a diskette, and, after you have decided on how best to organize your document files, change the directory structure on that diskette before you implement the same changes on your hard disk. After you develop a new directory structure that works, you can then copy the directory structure and files back to the "My Documents" directory on your hard disk.

Isabel also recommends that you develop a backup strategy that will enable you to restore the most recent copies of your document files in the event you experience a problem with your computer or the files stored on your computer. As part of your backup strategy, you have to decide what type of media to use for backups, how frequently you need to back up your document files, and what types of backups will provide the best protection.

SESSION 5.1

In this session, you will examine, evaluate, and reorganize the directory structure of a disk. As you reorganize the directory structure of this disk, you will create, rename, and remove directories, and you will move files from directory to directory. You will also use the DIR command to search for and locate files within that directory structure.

Organizing Files on a Hard Disk

Isabel emphasizes that, whether you work on a desktop computer, a computer connected to a network, or a laptop, one of the most important tasks you face is the management of disks, drives, directories, and files. The software for the operating system, as well as the software for the programs, utilities, and games that you use on your computer, is all stored on your hard disk. Because most people's computers contain a single volume (drive C), the operating system software is stored within directories on that drive. If the hard disk on your computer is partitioned or divided into two volumes, C and another drive such as D, you might have software installed on both volumes. If your computer is connected to a network, the network file server may contain some or all of your software. When you first install an operating system, program, utility, or game on your computer, a setup or install program automatically creates directories on the hard disk and then copies the files for that software product to those directories. This organization of software into directories is important for several reasons:

- **Installation.** First, most of the files for a software product are stored in the same location. For example, the software for the Windows 2000 operating system is installed primarily in one directory. That directory, as you know, is usually named WINNT, or it might have another name, such as Windows, depending on how Windows 2000 was originally installed. Within the WINNT directory, you will find not only program and supporting files, but also approximately 36 subdirectories that contain groups of related subdirectories and files. The Help directory contains Help files for the Windows Help system. The Fonts directory contains all the installed fonts used by Windows 2000 and other Windows programs. The Windows 2000 Setup program also creates a separate Program Files directory (in the root directory) that includes subdirectories for installed software, such as Internet Explorer, Outlook Express, and Microsoft Office. Although most of the files for an installed program are located in the directory for that program, "dll" (dynamic link library) files for programs are commonly stored in the Windows System32 or System subdirectories. A **dynamic link library** is a file with executable program code that provides support to one or more software programs and that has the file extension "dll."

- **Updating software.** A second reason that software organization is important is that, by installing software into specific directories, it is easier to update the installed software or remove or uninstall the software. If a software program contains its own install and uninstall programs, use them to install, update, and remove software for that program. Never remove software by simply deleting its directory. Because Windows software adds and changes files and settings throughout the system, your system will probably begin to malfunction if you delete a software directory without first running its Uninstall program.

- **Locating files.** Finally, because of the massive storage capacities of hard disks, it is important to impose a filing system similar to a manual filing system to simplify the process of organizing and locating files. By organizing software into subdirectories, it is easier for you to locate the subdirectories and files that you might need to examine, modify, document, or troubleshoot.

Likewise, you can benefit by organizing your business and personal files into directories. For instance, if you operate a small business where you perform contract work for various clients, then you will want to organize the directories on your hard disk so you can reliably, quickly, and easily find client information. Under your "My Documents" directory, you might create a directory named "Clients" to track all client information, as shown in Figure 5-1. Within that directory, you might create a subdirectory for each client for whom you do contract work. Because you will more than likely perform the same type of work for each client, you probably will have the same types of subdirectories for each client so that you can track similar information. For example, within each client directory, you might have subdirectories for contracts, correspondence, invoices, and project information. You probably will also have a directory for your business records so you can track information such as assets, cash flow, and taxes.

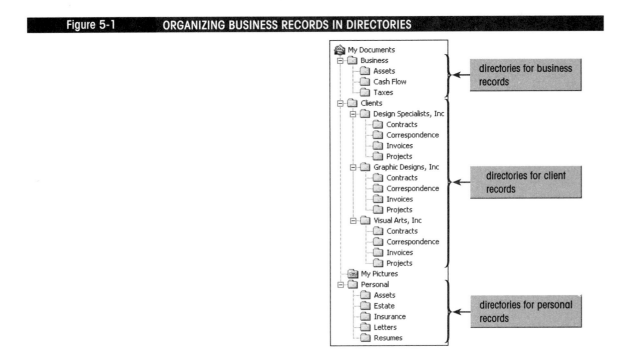

You might also have your own directory for tracking important personal information, such as your portfolio, personal assets (useful for bank loans and insurance), investments, estate information (such as a will), insurance information, correspondence, and résumés.

By organizing files into logical directories, you know exactly where to find a contract for a specific client. If you need to print a monthly cash flow report for your business, you know which directory contains that business report. If you need to update your database of personal assets, you know which directory contains that file.

The directory structure shown in Figure 5-1 obviously represents only a small part of the entire directory structure of a hard disk. The hard disk would also include all the directories with installed software, largely under the Program Files directory. Your "My Documents" directory could also contain any additional directories you need for organizing and tracking business and personal documents.

Periodically, you will **back up**, or make duplicate copies of, the files on your hard disk. Windows 2000 facilitates this process by centralizing all users' data in the "Documents and Settings" directory, including each user's "My Documents" directory. If all of your computer's software stores files in each user's "My Documents" directory, then you could save everyone's data by opening up your backup software, selecting the "Documents and Settings" directory, and indicating that you want to back up all the subdirectories and files within the "Documents and Settings" directory. You could also back up just a particular user's data by selecting that person's user name directory under "Documents and Settings," or you could select just that person's "My Documents" directory. Within your "My Documents" directory, you can make more specific backups quickly and easily if you have planned the directory structure in advance. For example, if you need to back up just your client information, you could select only your Clients directory in your backup program. You can take exactly the same approach to the directories that contain your business records and your personal records. If you work for just a single client or employer, you might prefer to organize the information on your hard disk by project rather than by client.

As noted earlier, when you install software on your computer, the setup or install program assigns names to the directories for storing the files that constitute that software product (although oftentimes you have a choice as to what name or names to use). For the directories that contain your business and personal files, assign directory names that clearly identify the purpose of each directory.

As you plan the organization of subdirectories and files on your hard disk, follow these guidelines:

- **Use the root directory folder for directories and system files.** When you, or the dealer or company from which you purchased your computer, format a disk (including a hard disk), the operating system creates a **top-level folder**, or **root directory**, on the disk at the end of the formatting process. The top-level root directory folder constitutes the first part of the file system for that disk and it tracks information on the directories and files that you subsequently place on the disk. On a hard disk, you should reserve the root directory folder for the first level of subdirectories, which include directories for your installed software, as well as for specific system files. When you view the directories in the root directory of your hard disk, you want that view to look like a table of contents for your computer system. You should not store your document files in the root directory, but rather store them in a directory under "My Documents" with other similar files. Also, if the operating system uses the FAT16 filing system (which you will examine in more detail later), there is a limit to the number of subdirectories and files allowed in the root directory of a disk, so you must organize files under directories. The operating system, and other software that you install on your computer, will store or create files in the root directory for their use. You should leave those files there. If you move or delete those files, then the operating system might not be able to boot your computer.

- **Store software and document files in different directories.** In the past, it was common practice to create a subdirectory for document files below the directory of the program used to produce those files. This approach implies that documents are subordinate to programs—a situation which is no longer the case with document-oriented operating systems like Windows 2000. Also, this approach posed problems. If you removed the directory with the installed software, you ran the risk of removing the subdirectory or subdirectories that contained your files as well. If you backed up your files on the hard disk, you might have overlooked certain subdirectories that contained important files because they were located in a software directory. Furthermore, you might find that you use several programs to produce different types of files for the same general purpose, and it makes sense to store those files together in a directory separate from the directories for the programs you used to create the documents. For example, if you use Microsoft Word to produce a project summary for your clients, you might then use Microsoft Excel to create a spreadsheet projection or forecast for that same project, and then produce a three-dimensional bar chart that visually illustrates the projection or forecast. You might then want to copy the chart into the project summary report that you produce with Microsoft Word. Even though you produce these files with two different programs, you should store the two files together in the same directory. When you are working on one file, then you can quickly find and open the other files if they are in the same directory.

■ **Limit the directory structure to the minimum number of levels you need to organize and locate the contents of those directories efficiently.** If you create a complex directory structure that extends six or seven levels deep, then you will waste time navigating from one directory to another in an attempt to locate the files you want to work with. This is true whether you are working in the graphical user interface, and opening directories and files from an Open dialog box, or working in a Command Prompt window, and attempting to locate a set of files in a specific directory. When you create a new directory, evaluate if it would be better to create it under the "My Documents" directory, or if it would be better to create it below the root directory or another directory. The advantage of using the "My Documents" directory for the subdirectories that contain your document files is that you can step down four directory levels with a double-click (or a single-click in Web view) by opening the "My Documents" folder on the desktop. Furthermore, the Windows 2000 "My Documents" folder now contains a "My Pictures" folder for organizing graphics images. The directory organization shown in Figure 5-1 illustrates how to organize subdirectories within the "My Documents" directory.

■ **Subdivide directories that contain your document files when the number of files exceeds a manageable level**. As the number of files in a directory increases, you should periodically examine the files and determine whether the files actually fall into two or more logical groups. If so, then create new directories for those files and move the files to the new directories. You might also accidentally discover files that you thought you had lost because you did not store those files in the correct directory in the first place. If you subdivide a directory, also think about whether it makes sense to create the new subdirectories within this same directory, or if it would be better to move all the new subdirectories up one level in the directory structure and delete the original directory, which may now be empty. *This guideline applies only to subdirectories that contain your own files, not to subdirectories with software. Do not reorganize the structure of subdirectories that contain installed software; otherwise, the software will not work.*

■ **Select directory folder names carefully**. Windows 2000, Windows 98, Windows NT Workstation 4.0, and Windows 95, as well as programs designed for these operating systems, support the use of long filenames. That means that you can now pick a filename for a directory that clearly identifies the contents of that directory. Directory and file names can be up to 255 characters in length. You are not limited to the 8 character directory and file names that were required by the DOS operating system. Avoid creating directories or files with long filenames in the root directory; instead, create them under your "My Documents" directory. Microsoft recommends that you limit the use of long directory and file names in the root directory of the hard disk if you are using the FAT16 filing system (which you will examine later), because those long filenames will quickly use up the available **directory space**—the storage space available for tracking filenames and information about directories and files.

If you are working on a network, find out if that network's operating system supports the use of long directory and file names. *If it doesn't support long filenames, then that network operating system might truncate (chop off) or modify a long filename.* There is one other important limitation on the use of long filenames. The full path cannot exceed 260 characters. For example, assume you are working in a Windows Explorer or My Computer window, and assume the current folder has a long filename and is located several levels down in the folder structure of the disk. Also assume that all the folders above this one have long filenames. If you now attempt to create a new folder (or a file) within the current folder, and assign it a long filename, you might find that the keyboard appears to have jammed. The real problem is that you have reached the maximum limit on the number of characters for the path, and Windows will not accept any more.

- **Do not move or rename directories that contain installed software**. As noted earlier, if you move or rename a directory that contains software (for example, the WINNT directory or the Microsoft Office directory), Windows 2000 will not be able to locate and load any of the programs stored in that directory. *Do not modify directories containing software unless you are sure that your modifications will not affect the use of that software.*

- **Periodically evaluate your current document directory folder structure**. After you have used your computer for a while, you should reevaluate its directory folder structure. You might find a more efficient approach to organizing the directories that contain your files. If you do move or rename folders, then you will also have to update your software programs so they default to these new subfolders and they do not inadvertently store files somewhere other than where you expect. For example, if you work with Microsoft Word 2000, you open the Tools menu, select Options, and, after the Options dialog box opens, select the File Locations tab. On the File Locations sheet, Word displays a list of file types (such as Documents) and the default location (the path to the folder where Word stores these types of files), as shown in Figure 5-2. You can then use the Modify button to update this path to point to a new folder or to a folder that you just moved or renamed.

Figure 5-2 **SPECIFYING THE DEFAULT DIRECTORY FOR WORD DOCUMENTS**

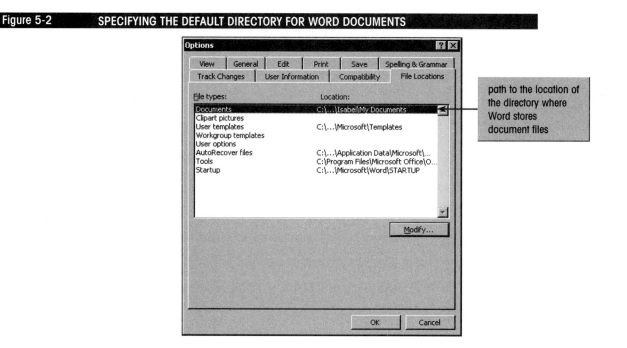

With the ever-increasing storage capacities of hard disk drives and the ever-increasing storage space required to install software, it is important for computer owners to manage the use of storage space on their hard disk effectively. For example, a standard installation of just Windows 2000 might require 800 MB or more of storage space and include over 15,700 files in 2,333 subdirectories. Because most people use multiple programs and create a wide variety of files, the management of the computer's drives, subdirectories, and files becomes of paramount importance and is an ongoing process. As you work with Windows 2000, you will discover that it offers a powerful set of features that help you manage, organize, navigate, and view the drives, subdirectories, and files on your computer.

Viewing the Directory Structure of a Hard Drive

Before you begin the reorganization, Isabel recommends that you familiarize yourself with the directory structure on your hard disk. Because Windows 2000 has a complex, multi-tiered directory structure, you can use Windows Explorer or the TREE command at the command prompt, to display directories. You decide to redirect the output of the TREE command to a file on your diskette so you can view the directory tree with Notepad.

Getting Started

To simplify the task of examining the organization of files in subdirectories, you decide to specify default window colors and switches for the DIR command. You also decide to make a copy of the diskette Isabel provided you and work on the copy, in case you need the original diskette again.

You will need to make a copy of Data Disk #2 so you can organize the files into subdirectories. You can copy over the same diskette that you used in previous tutorials. Also, this tutorial and subsequent tutorials use a different format than the previous tutorials for those steps where you enter commands. Instead of instructing you to type a specific command and then press the Enter key, the step will just tell you to enter a specific command. You will have to remember to press the Enter key after you enter that command.

To set up your computer and copy Data Disk #2:

1. Open a **Command Prompt** window, set the background and foreground colors, and specify default settings for the DIR command to display directory listings in alphabetical order by filename one page at a time.

2. Enter: `set`

   to verify that you correctly entered the switches for the DIRCMD environment variable. If not, correct this setting before you continue.

3. Use the **DISKCOPY** command to make a copy of Data Disk #2.

4. Change the default drive to drive A.

Viewing the Directory Structure of the Hard Disk

You can use the TREE command to view the directory structure of a hard disk and, if you want to document this information, you can redirect the output to a file on disk, and then store that file with the other documentation you maintain on your computer.

The steps in this tutorial describe how to perform operations using drive C. If you are using another local drive, such as drive D or drive E, replace C: with the name of your local drive, such as D: or E:.

To display a directory tree of a hard disk drive:

1. Clear the **Command Prompt** window

2. Enter: `tree c:\ /a > hdtree.txt`

    (Use the name of your local drive, if different.)

    The TREE command then creates a directory tree for your local drive, starting at the root directory. As noted in Tutorial 4, the ASCII switch (/A) instructs the TREE command to use ASCII characters to represent the graphical lines that would otherwise be shown in the graphical representation of the directory tree. The results of the TREE command are not displayed in the window, but rather are redirected to a file on disk called "hdtree.txt" so that you have a permanent record of the directory structure of your local drive. Because you did not specify where you want to store the new file created by redirecting the output, the command interpreter stores it on the current drive (drive A).

3. Enter: `hdtree.txt`

    Windows opens hdtree.txt in Notepad. Figure 5-3 shows the first Notepad screen of a directory tree of a hard disk drive. Your directory structure will be different.

Figure 5-3	DIRECTORY TREE OF A HARD DISK

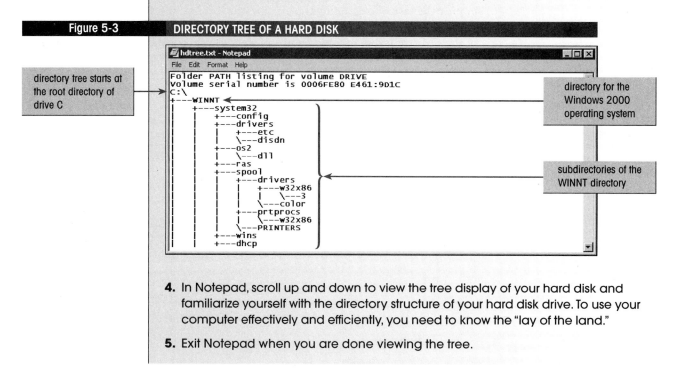

directory tree starts at the root directory of drive C

directory for the Windows 2000 operating system

subdirectories of the WINNT directory

4. In Notepad, scroll up and down to view the tree display of your hard disk and familiarize yourself with the directory structure of your hard disk drive. To use your computer effectively and efficiently, you need to know the "lay of the land."

5. Exit Notepad when you are done viewing the tree.

Now that you have a better idea of how information is organized on a hard disk, you are ready to modify the directory structure of a disk.

Saving the Directory Folder Structure

Before you begin, you want a printed copy of the directory tree on your diskette. You can then prepare a sketch of a new directory structure for this disk.

To display and save a directory tree of your Data Disk:

1. Clear the window, and then enter: `tree /f /a > beforetree.txt`

As noted in Tutorial 4, the Filename switch (/F) displays the names of the files in each directory. (When you complete the reorganization, you'll create a file called "aftertree.txt".)

2. Enter: `beforetree.txt`

Windows 2000 opens Notepad and beforetree.txt. See Figure 5-4.

Figure 5-4	DIRECTORY STRUCTURE [SKK1] OF DATA [SKK2] DISK

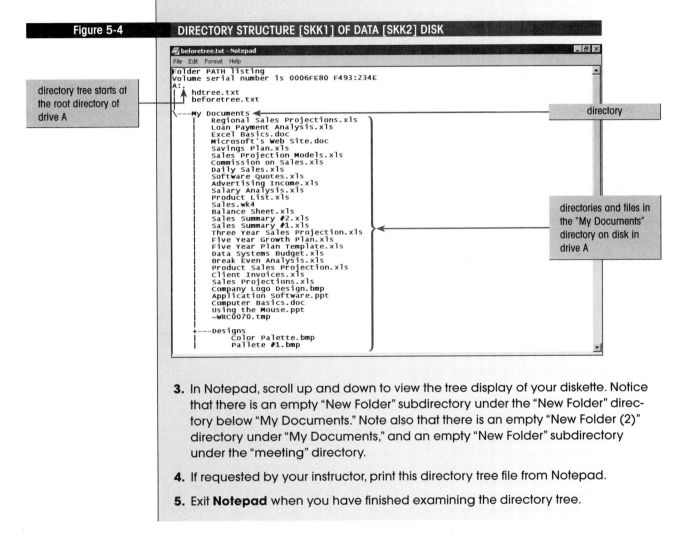

directory tree starts at the root directory of drive A

directory

directories and files in the "My Documents" directory on disk in drive A

3. In Notepad, scroll up and down to view the tree display of your diskette. Notice that there is an empty "New Folder" subdirectory under the "New Folder" directory below "My Documents." Note also that there is an empty "New Folder (2)" directory under "My Documents," and an empty "New Folder" subdirectory under the "meeting" directory.

4. If requested by your instructor, print this directory tree file from Notepad.

5. Exit **Notepad** when you have finished examining the directory tree.

After a quick glance at the directory structure, you realize that you could improve this directory structure and make it easier to locate your files. You can also clean up the disk's directory structure by removing the empty directories.

Removing Directories

Now you are ready to reorganize the directory structure of your diskette. First, you notice that this "My Documents" directory folder contains, at different levels, three directories named "New Folder" and one named "New Folder (2)," none of which contain any files.

Novice Windows users commonly create these directories when they attempt to make a new directory folder in My Computer or Windows Explorer. The command for creating a folder initially names it "New Folder" and places it in Rename mode, waiting for the user to give it a real name. If the user presses the Enter key, or clicks somewhere else with the mouse, the folder's name remains "New Folder", or, if a folder by that name exists already in the current directory, the folder's name becomes "New Folder (2)". You decide to remove these directory folders as a first step in reorganizing the structure of your disk.

To remove a directory, you use the RD (Remove Directory) command. The directory that you remove *must* be empty; by default, RD will not remove a directory folder that contains any files or subdirectories. Also, you *cannot* remove the root directory with this command. The syntax for this internal command is as follows:

RD [*drive:*][*path*]*directory name*

(You can also use the RMDIR command, as in UNIX.)

You specify the path and name of the directory. If the directory is located on another drive, you also must specify the drive name.

Because "New Folder (2)" contains no files or subdirectories, you decide to remove it first.

To remove the "New Folder (2)" directory:

1. Be sure you are at the root directory of drive A.

2. Clear the **Command Prompt** window.

3. To change to the "My Documents" directory, enter: `cd my*`

4. To display the subdirectories under "My Documents", enter: `tree`

Note that the diskette has a directory named "New Folder (2)". See Figure 5-5.

| Figure 5-5 | VIEWING THE DIRECTORY STRUCTURE OF A DISKETTE |

```
A:\>cd my*

A:\My Documents>tree
Folder PATH listing
Volume serial number is 0006FE80 F493:234E
A:.
├───Designs
├──New Folder ◄
│  └──New Folder ◄
├──New Folder (2) ◄
└──meeting
   ├───Training
   └──New Folder ◄

A:\My Documents>
```

empty directories in directory structure

5. Enter: `rd "new folder (2)"`

Because the directory name contains spaces, you need to enclose the name in quotation marks; however, case does not make a difference.

6. Display a directory tree. "My Documents" no longer contains a directory named "New Folder (2)". See Figure 5-6.

Figure 5-6	REMOVING AN EMPTY DIRECTORY

```
Command Prompt                                            _ □ ✕

A:\My Documents>rd "new folder (2)"

A:\My Documents>tree
Folder PATH listing
Volume serial number is 0006FE80 F493:234E
A:.
├───Designs
├───New Folder
│   └───New Folder
└───meeting
    ├───Training
    └───New Folder

A:\My Documents>
```

remove this directory

command for removing a directory

directory structure no longer includes the "New Folder (2)" directory

Next, you want to remove the "New Folder" directory. Because "New Folder" contains another subdirectory, also named "New Folder," RD by itself can't remove it. You either have to remove the lower subdirectory first, or remove the entire branch in one step using the Subdirectory switch (/S). You decide on this quicker approach.

To remove the "New Folder" branch in one step:

1. Clear the **window**, and then enter: `rd /s "new folder"`

2. When RD responds with "new folder, Are you sure (Y/N)?" type **y** and then press **Enter**.

3. Display a **directory tree.** "New Folder" and its subdirectory are gone. See Figure 5-7.

Figure 5-7	REMOVING A DIRECTORY AND ITS CONTENTS

```
Command Prompt

A:\My Documents>rd /s "new folder"
new folder, Are you sure (Y/N)? y

A:\My Documents>tree
Folder PATH listing
Volume serial number is 0006FE80 F493:234E
A:.
├───Designs
└───meeting
    ├───Training
    └───New Folder

A:\My Documents>
```

command for removing a directory and its subdirectories and files

updated directory structure

The Subdirectory switch (/S) displays a prompt that gives you only a small margin of safety when you remove directory branches. As a rule, make sure that you know exactly what you are deleting before using the /S switch.

REFERENCE WINDOW **RW**

<u>Removing a Directory</u>
- Open a Command Prompt window.
- Change to the drive and directory containing the subdirectory you wish to remove.
- Type RD, press the Spacebar, type the name of the directory to remove, and then press Enter. If the directory name contains spaces, enclose the name in quotation marks.
- If the directory you want to remove contains files or subdirectories, and you wish to remove the entire branch, type /S after the RD command. When RD responds with a confirmation request, type Y to remove the directory and all of its files and subdirectories.
- Type DIR /AD or TREE to confirm that you removed the directory.

The RD command is similar under different versions of Windows and MS-DOS; however, under Windows 2000, you also have the option of removing all directories and files within the directory you want to delete by using the Subdirectory switch (/S). As with the DELTREE command, which performed a similar function in other Windows and MS-DOS versions, use RD /S with extreme caution. This command makes it very easy to inflict massive destruction on your files and directories.

Moving a Directory

The "meeting" directory actually contains files set aside for making overhead transparencies, and the Training directory currently under "meeting" contains files that are not used for producing overhead transparencies. You decide first to move the Training directory so that it is located directly under "My Documents," and is at the same level as the "meeting" and Designs directories. Isabel reminds you that you can use the MOVE command to move a directory in one step—files and all.

To move the Training directory folder up one level to the "My Documents" directory:

1. Make sure your current drive and directory is A:\My Documents.

2. Clear the **window**, and then display a **directory tree** to view the current directory structure under "My Documents."

3. To change to the "meeting" directory, enter: cd me*

4. View a directory listing of this directory. The "meeting" directory contains two subdirectories—one named "New Folder" and the other named Training. See Figure 5-8.

Figure 5-8	VIEWNG A DIRECTORY LISTING OF THE MEETING DIRECTORY

```
Command Prompt                                                    _ □ ×

A:\My Documents>cd me*

A:\My Documents\meeting>dir
 Volume in drive A has no label.
 Volume Serial Number is F493-234E

 Directory of A:\My Documents\meeting

12/12/2003  09:01a       <DIR>          .
12/12/2003  09:01a       <DIR>          ..
12/12/2003  09:01a       <DIR>          New Folder
12/12/2003  09:01a       <DIR>          Training
09/10/2003  09:22a               6,080 Cycle.wk4
01/16/2003  10:46a              20,992 Five Year Growth Plan.xls
09/26/2003  11:40a              74,024 Invoice Form.wk4
03/27/2003  11:19a              22,028 Sales.wk4
05/05/2003  03:33p               9,646 Thank You Letter.doc
05/05/2003  03:33p               9,662 Thank You Letter.wpd
              6 File(s)        142,432 bytes
              4 Dir(s)         197,120 bytes free

A:\My Documents\meeting>_
```

> empty directory
>
> move this directory

5. Clear the **window**, and then enter: move Training "\My Documents"

   As noted in Tutorial 4, you have to enclose the path within quotation marks if the path includes long folder or file names that contain spaces.

6. To change back to "My Documents," enter: cd ..

7. Display a **directory tree**. The Training directory is now located under the current directory. See Figure 5-9.

Figure 5-9	MOVING A DIRECTORY

```
Command Prompt                                                    _ □ ×

A:\My Documents\meeting>move Training "\My Documents"

A:\My Documents\meeting>cd ..

A:\My Documents>tree
Folder PATH listing
Volume serial number is 0006FE80 F493:234E
A:.
    ├───Designs
    ├───meeting
    │   └───New Folder
    └───Training

A:\My Documents>_
```

> command for moving a directory
>
> move this directory
>
> destination of the Training directory
>
> Training directory moved to a new level in the directory structure

The MOVE command simplifies the process of rearranging a directory structure when you are working in a Command Prompt window.

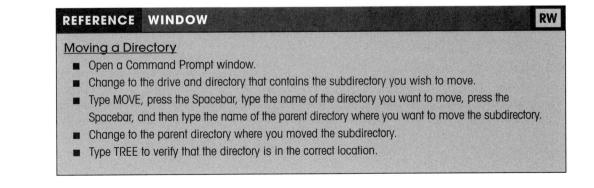

REFERENCE   WINDOW   RW

<u>Moving a Directory</u>
- Open a Command Prompt window.
- Change to the drive and directory that contains the subdirectory you wish to move.
- Type MOVE, press the Spacebar, type the name of the directory you want to move, press the Spacebar, and then type the name of the parent directory where you want to move the subdirectory.
- Change to the parent directory where you moved the subdirectory.
- Type TREE to verify that the directory is in the correct location.

Now that you have moved the Training folder so it is directly under the "My Documents" directory, you want to rename the "meeting" directory to something more descriptive.

Renaming a Directory

The contents of the "meeting" directory have changed considerably since the directory was first created, and this directory now contains files used to produce overhead transparencies. You decide that a more appropriate name for this directory would be "Overhead Transparencies".

> ### To rename the "meeting" directory to "Overhead Transparencies":
>
> 1. Make sure your current drive and directory is A:\My Documents.
>
> 2. Clear the **window**, and then display a **directory tree**. Note that the "meeting" directory has a subdirectory named "New Folder".
>
> 3. Enter: `ren meeting "Overhead Transparencies"`
>
> 4. Display a **directory tree**. You no longer have a "meeting" directory; instead it is now named "Overhead Transparencies". This directory still contains the "New Folder" subdirectory. See Figure 5-10.

Figure 5-10	RENAMING A DIRECTORY

```
Command Prompt                                          _ □ ✕
A:\My Documents>tree
Folder PATH listing
Volume serial number is 0006FE80 F493:234E
A:.
    ├───Designs
    ├───meeting          ◄────────────────   rename this directory
    │   └───New Folder
    └───Training

A:\My Documents>ren meeting "Overhead Transparencies"  ◄──  command for renaming
                                                             a directory
A:\My Documents>tree
Folder PATH listing
Volume serial number is 0006FE80 F493:234E
A:.
    ├───Designs
    ├───Training
    └───Overhead Transparencies   ◄──────────   renamed directory
        └───New Folder

A:\My Documents>
```

The REN command can rename directories under other versions of Windows, including Windows 95, 98, and NT 4.0. REN will not rename directories in MS-DOS 6.22 or earlier versions. You can also use the MOVE command to rename directories. The MOVE command was first introduced in MS-DOS 6.0, and it was your only option for renaming directories under this and later versions of MS-DOS.

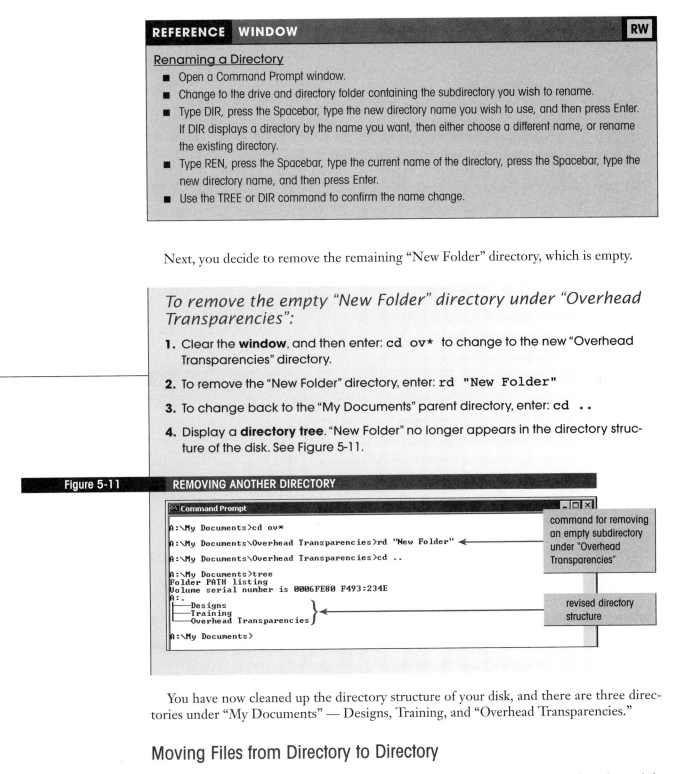

Renaming a Directory
- Open a Command Prompt window.
- Change to the drive and directory folder containing the subdirectory you wish to rename.
- Type DIR, press the Spacebar, type the new directory name you wish to use, and then press Enter. If DIR displays a directory by the name you want, then either choose a different name, or rename the existing directory.
- Type REN, press the Spacebar, type the current name of the directory, press the Spacebar, type the new directory name, and then press Enter.
- Use the TREE or DIR command to confirm the name change.

Next, you decide to remove the remaining "New Folder" directory, which is empty.

To remove the empty "New Folder" directory under "Overhead Transparencies":

1. Clear the **window**, and then enter: **cd ov*** to change to the new "Overhead Transparencies" directory.

2. To remove the "New Folder" directory, enter: **rd "New Folder"**

3. To change back to the "My Documents" parent directory, enter: **cd ..**

4. Display a **directory tree**. "New Folder" no longer appears in the directory structure of the disk. See Figure 5-11.

Figure 5-11   **REMOVING ANOTHER DIRECTORY**

```
Command Prompt                                                      _ □ ×

A:\My Documents>cd ov*

A:\My Documents\Overhead Transparencies>rd "New Folder"  ◄────  command for removing
                                                                an empty subdirectory
A:\My Documents\Overhead Transparencies>cd ..                   under "Overhead
                                                                Transparencies"
A:\My Documents>tree
Folder PATH listing
Volume serial number is 0006FE80 F493:234E
A:.
   ─Designs
   ─Training                                            ◄────  revised directory
   ─Overhead Transparencies                                    structure

A:\My Documents>
```

You have now cleaned up the directory structure of your disk, and there are three directories under "My Documents" — Designs, Training, and "Overhead Transparencies."

Moving Files from Directory to Directory

After examining the files in the "My Documents" directory folder, you realize that, while most of the files are company templates, some of the files belong in the Training and Designs folders. There is also one file that contains a memorandum that you want to place in a new folder that will hold just memos.

Before you move any files using wildcards, verify that the wildcard specifications you want to use will select the specific files you want to move.

To move selected files to the Training and Designs directories:

1. Make sure your current drive and directory is A:\My Documents.

2. Clear the **window**, and then enter: `dir app* *basics* *mouse* *logo*`

   The DIR command displays the files "Application Software.ppt," "Company Logo Design.bmp," "Computer Basics.doc," "Excel Basics.doc," and "Using the Mouse.ppt." These are the exact files you want to move.

3. Clear the **window**, and then enter: `move app* Training`

   to move "Application Software.ppt" to the Training directory.

4. Enter: `move *basics* Training`

   to move "Excel Basics.doc" and "Computer Basics.doc" to the Training directory.

5. Enter: `move *mouse* Training`

   to move "Using the Mouse.ppt" to the Training directory.

6. Enter: `move *logo* Designs`

   to move "Company Logo Design.bmp" to the Designs directory. See Figure 5-12 for a summary of these steps.

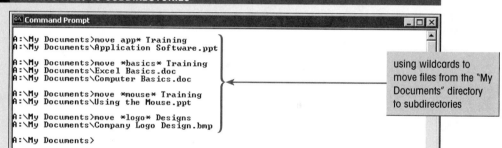

Figure 5-12   MOVING FILES TO SUBDIRECTORIES

```
Command Prompt                                                        _ | □ | ×

A:\My Documents>move app* Training
A:\My Documents\Application Software.ppt

A:\My Documents>move *basics* Training
A:\My Documents\Excel Basics.doc
A:\My Documents\Computer Basics.doc

A:\My Documents>move *mouse* Training
A:\My Documents\Using the Mouse.ppt

A:\My Documents>move *logo* Designs
A:\My Documents\Company Logo Design.bmp

A:\My Documents>
```

using wildcards to move files from the "My Documents" directory to subdirectories

7. Clear the **window**, and then enter: `dir Training Designs`

   to display the listings for both the Training and the Designs directories, and confirm that you have moved the files to the right places. See Figure 5-13.

Figure 5-13   VIEWING THE CONTENTS OF TWO DIRECTORIES

command for viewing the contents of two directories

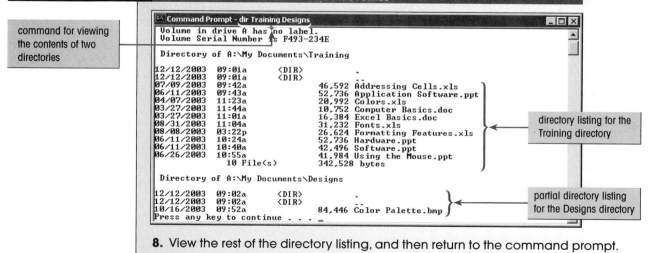

```
Command Prompt - dir Training Designs                                _ | □ | ×
 Volume in drive A has no label.
 Volume Serial Number is F493-234E

 Directory of A:\My Documents\Training

12/12/2003  09:01a    <DIR>          .
12/12/2003  09:01a    <DIR>          ..
07/09/2003  09:42a           46,592 Addressing Cells.xls
06/11/2003  09:43a           52,736 Application Software.ppt
04/07/2003  11:23a           20,992 Colors.xls
03/27/2003  11:44a           10,752 Computer Basics.doc
03/27/2003  11:01a           16,384 Excel Basics.doc
08/31/2003  11:04a           31,232 Fonts.xls
08/08/2003  03:22p           26,624 Formatting Features.xls
06/11/2003  10:24a           52,736 Hardware.ppt
06/11/2003  10:40a           42,496 Software.ppt
06/26/2003  10:55a           41,984 Using the Mouse.ppt
              10 File(s)         342,528 bytes

 Directory of A:\My Documents\Designs

12/12/2003  09:02a    <DIR>          .
12/12/2003  09:02a    <DIR>          ..
10/16/2003  09:52a           84,446 Color Palette.bmp
Press any key to continue . . .
```

directory listing for the Training directory

partial directory listing for the Designs directory

8. View the rest of the directory listing, and then return to the command prompt.

The ability to specify more than one directory or more than one file specification with the DIR command is a new feature of Windows 2000, not found in earlier versions of Windows or MS-DOS.

Now you want to create directories for the company templates and the single memorandum file, and move files into them. You decide to start by putting the memo into a Memos folder, and then by moving the remaining spreadsheet template files into a "Company Templates" directory.

To move files into the new directory folders "Memos" and "Company Templates":

1. Clear the **window**, and then create a directory named "Memos".

2. Enter: `dir *web*`

   to make sure the documents you will select are the ones you want. There is only one file—"Microsoft's Web Site.doc"—and that's the one you want to move.

3. Clear the window, and then enter: `move *web* Memos`

   to move "Microsoft's Web Site.doc" into the new Memos directory.

4. Enter: `dir Memos`

   to confirm your result. See Figure 5-14.

| Figure 5-14 | MOVING A FILE INTO A NEW DIRECTORY |

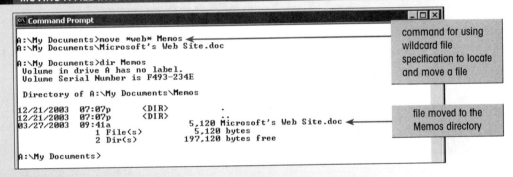

5. Make a directory called "Company Templates", and then display the remaining contents of the "My Documents" directory folder. Notice that the directory contains the temporary file "~WRC0070.tmp", which you no longer need.

6. Use the **Spacebar** to view the rest of the directory listing.

7. Delete the file named **~WRC0070.tmp**

8. Enter: `move *.* "Company Templates"`

   to move the remaining 22 files from "My Documents" to "Company Templates."

9. Clear the window, and then view a directory listing to confirm that you have moved all the files from the "My Documents" directory, leaving only five subdirectories. See Figure 5-15.

| Figure 5-15 | COMPLETING THE [SKK4] REORGANIZATION OF DIRECTORIES |

```
Command Prompt                                                    _ □ ×

A:\My Documents>dir
 Volume in drive A has no label.
 Volume Serial Number is F493-234E

 Directory of A:\My Documents

12/12/2003  09:01a    <DIR>          .
12/12/2003  09:01a    <DIR>          ..
12/21/2003  07:08p    <DIR>          Company Templates
12/12/2003  09:01a    <DIR>          Designs
12/21/2003  07:07p    <DIR>          Memos
12/12/2003  09:01a    <DIR>          Overhead Transparencies
12/12/2003  09:01a    <DIR>          Training
               0 File(s)              0 bytes
               7 Dir(s)        205,312 bytes free

A:\My Documents>_
```

final directory structure

You have now reorganized the files and directory folders in your copy of the "My Documents" directory.

Documenting the Directory Structure

To complete this process, Isabel asks you to document the new directory structure.

To display and save a directory tree of your Data Disk:

1. Change to the **root directory** of drive A, and then clear the **window**.

2. Enter: `tree /f /a > aftertree.txt`

3. Enter: `aftertree.txt`

   Windows 2000 opens "aftertree.txt" in Notepad. See Figure 5-16.

| Figure 5-16 | VIEWING THE FILES IN THE REORGANIZED DIRECTORY STRUCTURE |

```
aftertree.txt - Notepad                                          _ ⯑ ×
File  Edit  Format  Help
Folder PATH listing
Volume serial number is 0006FE80 F493:234E
A:.
|    hdtree.txt
|    beforetree.txt
|    aftertree.txt
|
\---My Documents
    +---Designs
    |       Company Logo Design.bmp
    |       Color Palette.bmp
    |       Pallete #1.bmp
    |       Pallete #2.bmp
    |
    +---Memos
    |       Microsoft's Web Site.doc
    |
    +---Company Templates
    |       Regional Sales Projections.xls
    |       Loan Payment Analysis.xls
    |       Savings Plan.xls
    |       Sales Projection Models.xls
    |       Commission on Sales.xls
    |       Daily Sales.xls
    |       Software Quotes.xls
    |       Advertising Income.xls
    |       Salary Analysis.xls
    |       Product List.xls
    |       Sales.wk4
    |       Balance Sheet.xls
    |       Sales Summary #2.xls
    |       Sales Summary #1.xls
    |       Three Year Sales Projection.xls
    |       Five Year Growth Plan.xls
    |       Five Year Plan Template.xls
    |       Data Systems Budget.xls
    |       Break Even Analysis.xls
    |       Product Sales Projection.xls
    |       Client Invoices.xls
    |       Sales Projections.xls
```

documentation on the directory tree of the hard disk and diskette

files organized by subdirectory

4. In Notepad, scroll up and down to view the directory tree of your copy of the "My Documents" folder.

5. If requested by your instructor, print this directory tree from Notepad.

6. Exit **Notepad** when you have finishing examining the directory tree.

You can now add this documentation to the other documentation for your computer.

Locating Files in Directories

Next, Isabel offers to show you a quick and easy way for locating a file in the directory structure of a disk if you are working in a Command Prompt window.

You can quickly search for files by using the Subdirectory switch (/S) of the DIR command to search through directories for one or more files. You can look for a single file by name, or you can use wildcards to expand the scope of a search and look for a group of files.

Before you use this switch, you must decide where in the directory tree you want to start the search. DIR will then search through that directory and all its subdirectories. If it locates a file or files using the file specification that you provide, it shows the full path of the directory and the filename, size, date, and time. If DIR locates files with the same name but in different directories, it lists each occurrence of the file.

Isabel decides to show you how to display all the filenames on the diskette that begin with "Sales".

To locate files starting with "Sales" from the command prompt:

1. Make sure you are in the **root directory** of drive A, and then clear the window.

2. Enter: `dir sales*`

(without the /S switch)

DIR reports that it found no file by that name. You did not include the /S switch, so DIR limited its search to the current directory. Because you were already at the root directory of drive A, the DIR command did not search the directories below the root directory.

3. Recall the `dir sales*` command, press **Spacebar**, type `/s` and then press **Enter**. DIR locates filenames beginning with "Sales" in the "Company Templates" and "Overhead Transparencies" subdirectories. See Figure 5-17. Notice that duplicates of the file Sales.wk4 appear in both the "Company Templates" and "Overhead Transparencies" subdirectories. You might have accidentally saved or copied the file to two different directories or deliberately made a duplicate of the same file so you could use it as the basis for creating another file.

4. Save your reorganized diskette for the next session on backing up and for the Review Assignments.

Figure 5-17   SEARCHING FOR A FILE BY SUBDIRECTORY

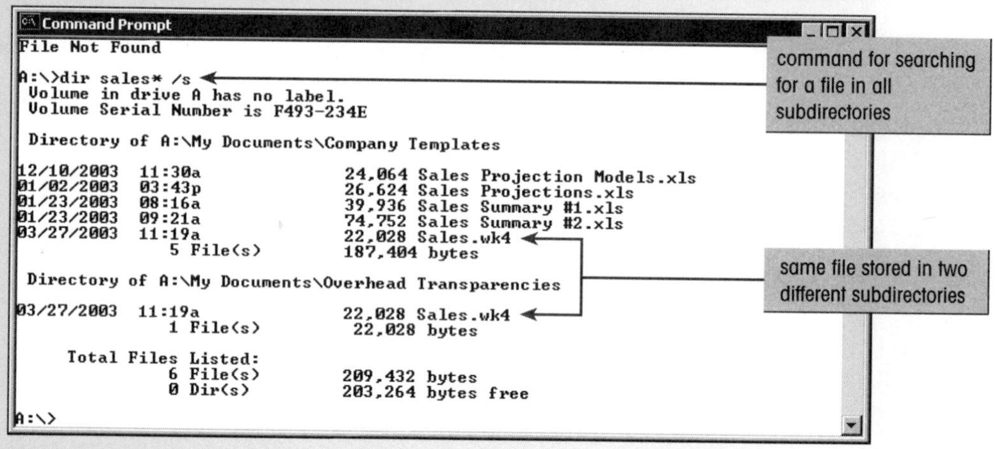

```
Command Prompt                                                    _ | □ | ×
File Not Found

A:\>dir sales* /s  ←                                              command for searching
 Volume in drive A has no label.                                  for a file in all
 Volume Serial Number is F493-234E                                subdirectories

 Directory of A:\My Documents\Company Templates

12/10/2003  11:30a              24,064 Sales Projection Models.xls
01/02/2003  03:43p              26,624 Sales Projections.xls
01/23/2003  08:16a              39,936 Sales Summary #1.xls
01/23/2003  09:21a              74,752 Sales Summary #2.xls
03/27/2003  11:19a              22,028 Sales.wk4  ←
          5 File(s)            187,404 bytes                      same file stored in two
                                                                 different subdirectories
 Directory of A:\My Documents\Overhead Transparencies

03/27/2003  11:19a              22,028 Sales.wk4  ←
          1 File(s)             22,028 bytes

   Total Files Listed:
          6 File(s)            209,432 bytes
          0 Dir(s)             203,264 bytes free

A:\>
```

Isabel points out that you can use this feature to locate duplicate copies of files stored in various directories quickly, or to locate different versions of the same file stored in different directories on a hard disk. This feature also simplifies the process of reorganizing files into new directories, and it enables you to locate the most recent version of a file, no matter where it's stored.

This use of the Subdirectory switch (/S) with the DIR command is common to all versions of Windows and the later versions of MS-DOS.

REFERENCE   WINDOW   RW

Locating Files
- Open a Command Prompt window.
- Change to the directory where you want to start your search.
- Type DIR, press the Spacebar, type the name of a file (or a file specification that uses wildcards), press the Spacebar, type /S, and then press Enter. If you want to control scrolling, also include the /P switch.

Isabel congratulates you on the reorganization of your "My Documents" directory. She looks forward to using your skills and ideas to assist other employees in improving the organization of their hard disks.

Session 5.1 QUICK CHECK

1. True or False? You can remove the root directory with the Remove Directory command.

2. True or False? You should not remove or rename directories that contain installed software.

3. To limit a directory listing to just the names of subdirectories, you use the _____ command and the _____ switch.

4. To remove an empty directory, you use the _____ command without any switches.

5. If you want to remove a directory and its contents, you use the _____ command and its _____ switch.

6. To rename a directory, you can use the _____ or _____ commands.

7. True or False? You can use the DIR command to view the contents of only one directory at the same time.

8. If you want to specify that a command operate on all files in a directory (irrespective of their filenames), you would use the _____ wildcard for the file specification.

9. To document the directory structure of a disk, you can _____ the output of the TREE command to a file on disk.

10. To locate a file within the directory structure of a disk, you would use the _____ command and its _____ switch.

SESSION 5.2

In this session, you will use the XCOPY command to back up and restore a directory structure with all its subdirectories and files. You will perform both full and incremental backups using XCOPY, and you will use XCOPY to restore directories and files. You will use the ATTRIB command to examine the Archive attribute before and after backups. You will also examine different backup strategies.

The Importance of Backing Up Files

Like many others who depend on computers for their jobs, Isabel understands the importance of regular backups. When Isabel first started at SolarWinds, she worked as a client representative. While rushing to meet a deadline, she accidentally deleted some important client contract files. Fortunately, she had developed the habit of performing regular backups and was able to quickly restore those client contract files from her backups so she and her staff could complete negotiations on a new contract. If she had not made backup copies of those clients' files, then she and her staff would have had to reconstruct all her contract documents using printed copies of previous versions of those files.

Common causes for loss of data are:

- User errors (such as accidentally deleting or overwriting folders and files)
- Hardware failure (such as the failure of the hard disk)
- Software problems (such as a failed installation of a new software product or a software upgrade)
- Damage caused to a computer by a hacker
- Loss of a computer system (and even backups) from theft or vandalism
- Loss from some type of natural disaster (such as a fire, flood, or earthquake)
- Damage caused by a computer virus

In 1994, when hard disk storage capacities commonly ranged from 340-540 MB, Microsoft estimated it would take an average of 2,000 hours to replace lost files on a typical hard disk. Assuming you worked eight hours a day Monday through Friday, and did not work on the weekends or evenings, it would take you 50 weeks—or close to one year—to re-enter 2,000 hours of lost files from scratch. Today, hard disks store gigabytes of data, and not only is the potential loss greater, but without backups, the time for restoring business documents could increase substantially. If you operate a business and do not routinely back up important business and client records, and if a hard disk failure resulted in the loss of all your business and client records, then you could easily be out of business.

Even though the reliability of hard disks has improved considerably, they are still susceptible to damage. Furthermore, the average lifetime of a hard disk is estimated at five years, so the chances that it will fail during the useful life of a computer is high. All hard disks will fail at some time–it's just a matter of when. As noted, restoring the contents of a hard disk from scratch would be a formidable task—one that could cost you a lot of time and money. That's why it's important to regularly back up your hard disk. Think of a backup as a kind of insurance policy that will help you protect your business assets.

Approaches Used in Backing Up Files

The method you use to back up files on your computer depends on how you work, how much data you store on your hard disk, and how important that data is. Three common approaches that individuals use are as follows:

- **Backing up files on a diskette.** If you work with a small set of files that you prefer to save on diskettes, then you can use the Windows 2000 disk copy feature to back up the diskette that you work with daily. When you get ready to make your next backup copy of your working diskette, you should use a brand new diskette rather than copy over your first backup. If this next disk copy fails, then you still have your first backup. When you are ready to make the next backup copy of that same working diskette, you should again use a brand new diskette and keep your first two backups in reserve. After the backup is complete, you will have a total of three backups. When you are ready to perform your next backup, you can reuse the diskette with the oldest backup. By using this strategy, you will always have your two most recent backups.

  After you make a backup, you should write-protect the diskette or diskettes that contains the backup and keep them in a safe area away from your computer. You might even want to consider keeping a set off site. If your original diskette fails, you can make a new copy from your most recent backup. Likewise, if you lose an important file on your working disk, you can make a copy of that file from one of your backups. Write-protection serves two purposes. First, you will not accidentally copy over a diskette that has backup copies of your important files. Second, if your computer is infected with a computer virus, that virus cannot infect your backup copy if it is write-protected.

  One obvious advantage of working with diskettes is portability. You can take them with you wherever you go, and work on whatever computer is available to you. However, there are some disadvantages. First, the lifetime of diskettes is much shorter than that of a hard disk. Second, because it takes much longer for your computer to access files stored on a diskette as compared to a hard disk, you will spend more time waiting for disk reads and writes. Third, file sizes are limited to the size of the diskette (1.44 MB)—a size that is not practical for documents produced with certain programs, such as desktop publishing and graphics software. That's why computer users now rely on CD-R (recordable CDs), CD-RW (rewritable CDs), DVD-RAM (rewritable DVDs) and removable types of media, such as Zip and Jaz disks, for storing working copies of their documents.

- **Copying files from a hard disk.** If you work with a small set of files that are stored in one or more folders on your hard disk, you can copy the entire folder with all its files to one or more diskettes, a removable disk, a network drive, or a second hard disk drive. This backup approach is useful if you need to make a quick backup at the end of a busy day before you leave the office. It's important to remember that you cannot copy a file to a diskette if the file size exceeds the diskette's storage capacity; however, you might be able to use a file compression utility like PKZIP or WinZip to compress it so it will fit on the disk. Figure 5-18 shows a 17 MB PowerPoint Presentation that was backed up with Microsoft Backup in Windows 98 and that was also compressed with WinZip. Although Microsoft Backup compresses files during a backup, notice that WinZip is far more effective. Also, although the Microsoft Backup file would fit on one diskette, notice that you could fit four of these WinZip files on a diskette. If you were compressing four such PowerPoint files, you might be able to fit close to 69 MB on one 1.44 MB diskette.

| Figure 5-18 | COMPARING MICROSOFT BACKUP WITH WINZIP |

original PowerPoint presentation file is approximately 17 MB in size

Microsoft Backup compresses the file to a size that just fits a diskette

WinZip compresses the file to a much smaller file size

- **Using a backup utility.** If you work with a large number of files stored in many different folders on your hard disk, then your best bet is to use a backup utility like HP Colorado Tape Backup or Microsoft Windows Backup to back up those files onto some type of permanent storage medium such as tape. Backup utilities use storage space more efficiently than copying files to a disk because they store all the backed up files in one larger file and therefore do not leave any space unused. These utilities also let you back up to a variety of media, including diskettes, removable disks or tape, network drives, and other hard disk drives. In the case of diskettes, if you want to back up a file that's larger than the capacity of the disk, the backup utility can split the file over two or more diskettes. If you need to restore a file or files from a backup that you made with a backup utility, you must use the restore features in the *same* backup utility. You cannot open one of your files directly from the backup set, and generally you cannot restore the files using another backup utility.

Also keep in mind that sometimes a combination of these approaches will serve your purpose best.

Organizing Folders and Files for Backups

When Isabel worked as a client representative for SolarWinds, she quickly discovered that her computer contained client contract files that were stored in many different document folders, including folders that were located below the folders of the software product that produced the file. When she was ready to perform her first backup of client files on her hard disk, she was faced with the time-consuming task of trying to locate all the files for the backup. Furthermore, she could not be sure that she had even found all of the files she needed to include in the backup. Rather than run the risk of not backing up important client contract files, she immediately set aside time from her busy schedule to evaluate the folder structure of her computer's hard disk and to reorganize the files so backups were not only easier, but would also include everything she needed.

If you store all or most of your files on your hard disk and work primarily from that disk, then you should pay close attention to how the files are organized. You can streamline your backup process if files and folders are organized logically. As noted earlier, you might want to make sure that your software programs store all your document files in the "My Documents" directory folder. If you work with a large number of files, then you can organize them into subfolders within the "My Documents" directory folder. When you are ready to back up your files, all you have to do is select the "My Documents" directory folder, and then start the backup. Or, you can set up your computer so the hard disk is divided into two logical volumes—a drive C and a drive D, or you might install a second hard disk drive. You could then use drive C just for installed software, and store all your document files on drive D. When you are ready to back up your document files, open your backup utility, select drive D, and then start the backup.

You do not need to back up installed software as frequently as you back up folders that contain your document files. Your document files change more frequently and, if lost, require the most time to reconstruct. If your computer crashes, you can always reinstall software from the original CDs or diskettes, or download software obtained from Web sites. However, you might want to back up certain installed software, especially if it takes less time to restore it from backups than to reinstall it. Another advantage of this approach is that the backup will contain settings that you specified and changed after originally installing the software. By installing from a backup, you do not have to spend time checking and changing settings so the software program is set up the way in which you prefer to use it. However, in the case of an office suite like Microsoft Office, which installs many different files in many different folders, including the Windows folder, it is easier to reinstall it from the original CD.

You should also back up your existing software before installing new software programs or upgrades. If a problem occurs while you are installing a new software product or upgrade, then you can restore a working version of your previously installed software from the backup. It is important to note that because the Setup program for software programs typically installs files to the Windows folder, you should also back up the Windows folder and the top-level folder, as well as the existing software. Before installing software or an upgrade to the operating system or its Web browser, you might want to make a full system backup. A **full system backup** includes everything stored on your hard disk. Your hard disk might be partitioned into only one drive, or it might contain several drives, all of which you want to back up.

Although reorganizing your document folders can streamline the backup process, as noted earlier, you should not reorganize folders containing installed software. When you first install a software product, it is copied to the folder or folders proposed by the Setup or installation program, or to a folder or folders you specify. That information is stored in the Windows 2000 Registry so it can locate the program files needed to start and run a software program. As noted previously, the Windows 2000 Registry is a database that contains information about a computer's configuration, and includes hardware, software, and user settings. If you reorganize your software folders or change the names of these folders, the software will not work.

Selecting the Appropriate Backup Media

The most common types of media used for backups are tapes, recordable or rewriteable CD-ROM discs, removable high-capacity disks, hard disk drives, "Super floppy" disks (high capacity), and diskettes. Diskettes are inexpensive and are useful in situations where you only need to back up a small folder, a group of files, or a single file quickly and easily. However, if you want to back up a major portion of your hard disk, or the entire hard disk, diskettes are not a viable backup medium. Not only would you need to purchase and format many diskettes, you would also have to constantly insert and remove the diskettes. This approach is time-consuming and tedious. Furthermore, if one diskette out of the 20 or 30 diskettes that you use is bad, then you will not be able to retrieve information from the disks that follow the bad disk.

If you need to back up a large amount of data, you might want to purchase a tape drive and use tapes as your backup media. A **tape drive** is a unit in which you insert magnetic tapes that are similar in appearance and use to cassette tapes. Although you do have to pay for and install the tape drive unit, tape drives support large storage capacities and cost the least per megabyte of backed-up data. Depending on the size of your hard disk and the storage capacity of the tapes you use in your tape drive, you might be able to store the entire contents of a hard disk on one tape. Tape drives typically come with backup software designed to work with those units, so you would most likely use that backup utility rather than the Windows 2000 Backup utility. Businesses commonly rely on tape backup units for backing up hard disks on PCs because they are the most cost effective.

There are different types of tape technologies from which you can choose:

- **QIC (Quarter-Inch Cartridge) and Travan.** QIC (pronounced "quick") is a standard type of tape cartridge technology commonly used for backing up data on PCs. Manufacturers that belong to the Quarter-Inch Cartridge Drive Standards, Inc. consortium define the standards for this technology. You can purchase tape drives that use either minicartridges or full-size cartridges and that support different storage capacities. QIC-40 and QIC-80 tape drives do not require a special controller, but rather use your computer's diskette drive controller. Storage capacities range from 40 MB (for QIC-40) to 13 GB or more.

  Travan tape drives support high-capacity Travan tapes, as well as QIC tapes. Storage capacities of Travan tapes range from 400 MB to 8 GB. The 3M Corporation originally developed this technology.

- **DAT (Digital Audio Tape).** Like videotapes, DAT tapes use a **helical scan recording** technology to increase the storage capacity of the tapes. The drive records data in diagonal stripes across the tape and, as a result, storage capacities range from 2 GB to 40 GB. Different companies use this technology in their tape drives.

- **DLT (Digital Linear Tape).** DLT tapes have storage capacities of 15 GB to 70 GB and are faster than most other types of tape drives. DEC (Digital Equipment Corporation) originally developed this technology, but now other manufacturers also use this technology in their tape drives.

Increasingly, CD-R (for recordable) and CD-RW (for rewriteable) drives are becoming popular for backing up data by both businesses and home computer users. The CD-R drives allow you to record to the CD only once, whereas the CD-RW drives allow you to record repeatedly to the same CD. You can record and store large quantities of data on CDs (650 MB), as well as quickly backing up a large portion of your hard disk with a simple drag-and-drop operation. CDs are inexpensive compared to other types of removable media like Zip disks (100 MB or 250 MB) or Jaz disks (1 GB or 2 GB); however, if you want to archive and store data for longer than six years, you should use the high-quality CDs that are rated by the manufacturer to have useful lifetimes of up to 100 or 200 years. Like any other type of storage media, the actual lifetime varies with the conditions and environment in which you store the CDs. Another advantage of CDs is that almost any computer can read them. In the near future, DVD-RAM (rewritable) drives are anticipated to become a viable option for backups because of their increased storage capacities. DVD is an acronym for "Digital Video Disc" or "Digital Versatile Disc." DVD-RAM drives can store 2.6 GB of data on each side of a disc.

You can even use a second hard disk drive for backups. This approach provides one of the fastest methods for backing up and recovering data and can also provide you with many gigabytes of storage. The cost of a second hard disk drive is approximately the same as other types of backup options (when you take into account the cost of the tape or removable disk drive unit), plus you do not have to continue to purchase backup media. One disadvantage of using a second hard disk drive is that you cannot store that drive off site, and problems that arise, such as a computer virus infection, might affect all the drives in the computer.

Because backup technology, like all other types of technology, changes rapidly, you should check industry magazines, such as *PC World* and *PC Magazine*, or their Web sites, to help you figure out the best backup approach to use. These magazines test and evaluate the performance, reliability, and costs of backup drive units and strategies, and publish information on the newest developments in backup technologies. As you compare different backup media, calculate the cost per megabyte of storage space, and then you will have a common denominator for evaluating the most cost-effective solution that meets your needs.

Media Maintenance, Care, and Storage

Because you rely on backups in the event of an emergency or disaster, you should take proper care of your backup devices and media. If you are using a tape backup unit, check the manual for that device and follow the instructions for periodically cleaning the media heads and properly maintaining the unit. You might need to clean the unit after every eight hours of use so the tape unit performs reliably on subsequent backups.

No matter what type of backup device or media you use, you should protect it from magnetic fields, dust, smoke, humidity, water, solvents, light (especially UV), and extreme temperatures. You might also want to consider other options for protecting backups, such as contracting with businesses that specialize in off-site storage in facilities where the environment is carefully regulated and backups are protected from natural disasters. Today, with the rapid growth of the Internet and with the increased availability and improvement in high-speed communication links, you can back up your documents to an Internet site that provides an array of services for storing and protecting your backups.

Always label your backup tapes or disks with the name and software version number of the utility used to produce the backup; then you can properly restore files from any of your backup sets if the need should arise (and, of course, if Windows 2000 supports those backup utilities). If your backup set includes two or more backup media, then you should label each one with a sequential numbering scheme, such as #1 of n, #2 of n, etc., where "n" is the total number of backup media.

Developing **an Effective Backup Strategy**

As Isabel discovered, another important part of backing up your computer is to develop an effective backup strategy. This strategy should guarantee that you have copies of important document files so you can restore them at any time. An effective backup strategy also reduces the amount of time, effort, and media required for each backup you perform.

Your backup strategy should always include a full backup at regular intervals, such as every week, month, or quarter. This interval of time is called the **backup cycle**, and it begins by backing up your whole system, or an integral part of your system, then continues with backups of important files at shorter intervals of time within the backup cycle, and ends with the next full backup. The first backup, a **normal backup** (or **full backup**) marks the start of a backup cycle and might include the entire contents of your hard disk (a full system backup). Or, to save time and effort, you might limit your full backups to folders that contain just your document files (a partial backup). Because full backups can become time consuming, you can perform shorter intermediate backups between full backups. Intermediate backups back up only new or recently changed files. Most backup programs provide two types of intermediate backups: differential and incremental backups.

Combining Differential Backups with a Normal Backup

If you perform a normal backup each month, you might then perform either a differential or an incremental backup weekly; on the other hand, if you perform a normal backup each week, then you would perform a differential or incremental backup every day. A **differential backup** includes all new and modified files since your last normal or full backup. Therefore, each additional differential backup that you perform during a backup cycle includes not only the files you created or modified since the previous backup, but also any new or modified files you backed up during previous differential backups. For example, after you perform a normal backup, you might perform your first differential backup at the end of the first week. This backup would include all files that you created or modified during the first week, since the previous normal backup. Any file that did not change is not included in the differential backup. At the end of the second week, perform your second differential backup. This backup includes all files that you created or modified during the first *and* second weeks, since the normal backup. At the end of the third week, you perform your third and last differential backup. This backup will include all files that you created and modified during the first, second, *and* third weeks, since the normal backup at the start of the backup cycle. At the end of the month, you perform a new normal backup that includes all files, and then you start a new backup cycle with a new set of tapes or disks.

Figure 5-19 illustrates an example of this use of differential backups. Assume you regularly back up two folders on your hard disk: a "Clients" folder and a "Business Records" folder. At the beginning of the backup cycle, you back up all your client and business records, including your business portfolios. During the first week, assume you change two of your business portfolios—"Portfolio 1.doc" and "Portfolio 2.doc". When you do your first differential backup, the backup will include these two files. During the second week, you change "Portfolio 3.doc" and "Portfolio 4.doc". Your second differential backup will include these two files plus the two you worked on during the first week ("Portfolio 1.doc" and "Portfolio 2.doc"). During the third week, you change "Portfolio 2.doc", create a new portfolio called "Portfolio 5.doc", and revise your Portfolio Cover Letter. These three files, plus the others you worked on during the previous two weeks, are backed up when you perform your third differential backup. During the last week of the backup cycle, you revise "Portfolio 1.doc" again. At the end of the fourth week, you start a new backup cycle with a new normal backup that includes all the files in your Clients and Business Records folders, plus any files that you've recently created or revised, like "Portfolio 1.doc". After the first differential backup, you can think of each new differential backup as a cumulative backup because each one includes all files backed up in previous differential backups.

Figure 5-19	COMBINING A NORMAL BACKUP WITH DIFFERENTIAL BACKUPS		
	NEW OR MODIFIED FILES	**TYPE OF BACKUP**	**FILES BACKED UP**
Beginning of Backup Cycle:		Normal Backup #1	Folders & Files in Clients Folder
			Folders & Files in Business Records Folder
By the End of Week 1:	Portfolio 1.doc	Differential Backup #1	Portfolio 1.doc
	Portfolio 2.doc		Portfolio 2.doc
By the End of Week 2:		Differential Backup #2	Portfolio 1.doc
			Portfolio 2.doc
	Portfolio 3.doc		Portfolio 3.doc
	Portfolio 4.doc		Portfolio 4.doc
By the End of Week 3:		Differential Backup #3	Portfolio 1.doc
	Portfolio 2.doc		Portfolio 2.doc
			Portfolio 3.doc
			Portfolio 4.doc
	Portfolio 5.doc		Portfolio 5.doc
	Portfolio Cover Letter.doc		Portfolio Cover Letter.doc
By the End of Week 4: Start of a New Backup Cycle	Portfolio 1.doc	Normal Backup #2	All Folders & Files in Clients Folder
			All Folders & Files in Business Records folder

After the first differential backup, subsequent differential backups take longer because you are backing up more and more files. Once you complete a differential backup, you do not need to keep the backup media with the previous differential backups in that same backup cycle (unless you want to play it safe and take additional precautions). Therefore, differential backups keep only the most recent version of files that you have worked on during the current backup cycle. However, if you keep each of your differential backup sets, you might be able to find previous versions of some files on a differential backup set. Another advantage of differential backups is that they are easy to restore. For example, if you need to restore all the files in your Clients and Business Records folders, first restore all the files from your last normal backup, and then restore all the files in the last differential backup for that backup cycle.

Combining Incremental Backups with a Normal Backup

Instead of using a differential backup strategy, you can combine a normal backup with incremental backups. An **incremental backup** includes only those files that you created or changed since your previous backup—whether your previous backup was a normal backup or an incremental backup. Assume that you've just started a new backup cycle, and that you've performed a normal backup. At the end of the first week, you perform your first incremental backup. This first incremental backup will include all files that you created or modified during the first week (and would therefore be identical to a differential backup). At the end of the second week, you perform your second incremental backup. This backup includes all files that you created or modified during the second week *only*. Unlike a differential backup, this next incremental backup would not include files that you created or modified and backed up during the first incremental backup. At the end of the third week, you perform your third and last incremental backup. This backup includes all files you created or modified during the third week *only*. It does not include files you created or modified during the first week and the second week. At the end of the month, you perform a new normal backup that includes all files, and start a new backup cycle.

Figure 5-20 illustrates the use of incremental backups. Again, assume you regularly back up two folders on your hard disk—a "Clients" folder and a "Business Records" folder. At the beginning of the backup cycle, you back up all files in the "Clients" and "Business Records" folders. During the first week, you modify "Portfolio 1.doc" and "Portfolio 2.doc". Your first incremental backup at the end of the first week includes those two files. During the second week, you modify "Portfolio 3.doc" and create "Portfolio 4.doc". Your second incremental backup at the end of that week includes *only* "Portfolio 3.doc" and "Portfolio 4.doc". It does not include "Portfolio 1.doc" and "Portfolio 2.doc", which you worked on during the first week. During the third week, you modify "Portfolio Cover Letter.doc" and "Portfolio 2.doc", and you create "Portfolio 5.doc". Your third incremental backup at the end of that week includes *only* those three files. It does not include "Portfolio 1.doc", "Portfolio 3.doc", and "Portfolio 4.doc" from the first two weeks. The copy of "Portfolio 2.doc" in your third incremental backup is a more recent version of the copy of "Portfolio 2.doc" in your first incremental backup. So you now have two versions of this file in your incremental backups (allowing you to return to an earlier version of the same file). In contrast, with a differential backup strategy, you would have only the most recent version of this file. During the last week of this backup cycle, you revise "Portfolio 1.doc". At the end of the fourth week, you start a new backup cycle with a new normal backup that includes all the files in your "Clients" and "Business Records" folders, including files that you've recently created or revised, such as "Portfolio 1.doc".

Figure 5-20	COMBINING A NORMAL BACKUP WITH INCREMENTAL BACKUPS		
	NEW OR MODIFIED FILES	**TYPE OF BACKUP**	**FILES BACKED UP**
Beginning of Backup Cycle:		Normal Backup #1	All Folders & Files in Clients Folder
			All Folders & Files in Business Records Folder
By the End of Week 1:	Portfolio 1.doc	Incremental Backup #1	Portfolio 1.doc
	Portfolio 2.doc		Portfolio 2.doc
By the End of Week 2:	Portfolio 3.doc	Incremental Backup #2	Portfolio 3.doc
	Portfolio 4.doc		Portfolio 4.doc
By the End of Week 3:	Portfolio Cover Letter.doc	Incremental Backup #3	Portfolio Cover Letter.doc
	Portfolio 2.doc		Portfolio 2.doc
	Portfolio 5.doc		Portfolio 5.doc
By the End of Week 4:	Portfolio 1.doc	Normal Backup #2	All Folders & Files in Clients Folder
Start of a New Backup Cycle			All Folders & Files in Business Records folder

Incremental backups are faster than differential backups because your backup includes fewer files. Because they do not include files backed up during previous incremental backups, you do not need to use as much backup media. Unlike a differential backup strategy, however, you need to keep each incremental backup, and therefore incremental backups take longer to restore. For example, if you need to restore all the files in your "Clients" and "Business Records" folders, first restore all the files from your previous normal backup, and then restore all the files in each of your incremental backup sets in the order in which you produced them during that backup cycle.

Why do you need to restore all the incremental backups? You might have created a new file during the second week of the backup cycle but not worked on it during the remainder of the backup cycle. The only copy of that file is in the second incremental backup. If you restore just the normal backup and the last incremental backup, you will not have that file, because it's not included in either the full or last incremental backups.

If you had used differential backups, then that file would automatically be included in the last differential backup, so you would only need to restore the normal backup and the last differential backup.

Why not, then, use a differential background strategy rather than an incremental one? If you've worked on a document every day during a backup cycle, each incremental backup will have a different version of the file that contains that document. Unlike a differential backup strategy, where you typically do not save previous differential backups, you can restore earlier versions of a file if you use an incremental backup strategy. You just choose the incremental backup that contains the version of the file you want to restore. Incremental backups are the most common types of backups that people make because they permit you to more easily restore previous versions of files.

The Windows 2000 Backup utility supports two other types of backups—a copy backup and a daily backup. A **copy backup** copies all the files you select without affecting the other types of backups that you create in a backup cycle. For example, if you combine a normal backup with an incremental backup strategy, you can use a copy backup at any point during the backup cycle to back up files that you select. Any new or modified files included in the copy backup are also backed up in the next incremental backup. A **daily backup** copies all selected files that have been created or modified on the day you perform the daily backup. Like the copy backup, a daily backup does not interfere with an incremental backup strategy because it does not change a file's Archive bit (which you will examine in the next section). Copy backups and daily backups both allow you to make additional backups of very important files on the spot—files that you will back up later as part of your regular backup cycle.

As noted earlier, it is a good habit to always save the three most recent backup sets. After you have completed three backup cycles, you should use a new set of tapes or disks for your next backup cycle. Once you've completed that backup, you can reuse the backup media from your oldest backup for the next backup cycle. By using this approach, you will always have backup sets for the three most recent backup cycles. If you have only one normal backup and decide to perform your next normal backup over it, and if the backup, drive, or computer fails in the process, you lose your only backup.

You should not rely on just one backup or even one backup strategy. You might, for example, want to back up important files on your computer to some type of removable storage (such as disk or tape), and also perform the same backup to a network drive or second hard disk drive so that you can restore the same set of files in one of two different ways should the need arise.

As part of your backup process, keep a log of what backups you have made—including the date of the backup, the backup utility (and version) you used, what's included in the backups, and where the backups are stored. Also, as noted earlier, it is also a good idea to store one set of backups off site, even for your personal computer. In fact, you should find out if the company which insures your business also requires you to store backups off site before they will insure your data. Like insurance policies, backups are invaluable when you need them.

The Importance **of the Archive Attribute**

When you start a new backup cycle, you open your backup utility and instruct it to perform a normal backup. You then select the drive(s), directory folder(s), and file(s) you want to include in the backup. If you select a drive, the backup utility automatically includes all the files in all the directory folders on that drive in the backup. If you instead select just a directory folder, the backup utility automatically selects all the files in that directory folder. If that directory has subdirectory folders, the files in those subdirectory folders are also included. When you are ready to perform a differential or an incremental backup, you open the backup utility and select either differential or incremental for the type of backup. The backup utility then automatically selects all new files as well as all files that you modified.

The obvious question is, "How does the backup utility know which files to select for those types of backups?" When you create a new file, Windows 2000 turns on the Archive attribute of that file. The **Archive attribute** is actually a bit, called the Archive bit, that is turned on and off. Likewise, if you modify a file, Windows 2000 also turns on the Archive bit. When you perform a normal backup, a backup utility will back up all the files—no matter whether the Archive bit is on or off. Once all the files are backed up, most backup utilities turn off the Archive bit of any file that previously had the Archive bit turned on.

After a normal backup, the Archive bit of all the backed-up files has been reset to off. If you then open a file and make a change to it, or create a new file, Windows 2000 turns the Archive bit on again when you save the file. Then, if you perform a differential backup, the backup utility selects all those files (either new or modified) that have the Archive bit turned on and backs them up. The backup utility does not include files that have the Archive bit turned off (they have already been backed up). Unlike a normal backup, a differential backup does not turn off the Archive bit of the files that it backed up during your first differential backup. See Figure 5-21. During the next differential backup, the backup utility selects and backs up all files with the Archive bit turned on – new files, modified files, and files previously backed up only with a differential backup. When you perform your next normal backup of those files, the backup utility turns off the Archive bits of all the files. Notice in Figure 5-21 that, under the differential backup strategy, Archive bits are turned off after the normal backup but are not turned off after each differential backup.

Figure 5-21   **HOW DIFFERENTIAL BACKUPS AFFECT THE ARCHIVE BIT**

	NEW OR MODIFIED FILES	ARCHIVE BIT (BEFORE BACKUP)	TYPE OF BACKUP	FILES BACKED UP	ARCHIVE BIT (AFTER BACKUP)
Beginning of Backup Cycle:			Normal Backup #1	All Folders & Files in Clients Folder	Off
				All Folders & Files in Business Records Folder	Off
By the End of Week 1:	Portfolio 1.doc / Portfolio 2.doc	On / On	Differential Backup #1	Portfolio 1.doc / Portfolio 2.doc	On / On
By the End of Week 2:	Portfolio 3.doc / Portfolio 4.doc	On / On	Differential Backup #2	Portfolio 1.doc / Portfolio 2.doc / Portfolio 3.doc / Portfolio 4.doc	On / On / On / On
By the End of Week 3:	Portfolio 2.doc / Portfolio 5.doc / Portfolio Cover Letter.doc	On / On / On	Differential Backup #3	Portfolio 1.doc / Portfolio 2.doc / Portfolio 3.doc / Portfolio 4.doc / Portfolio 5.doc / Portfolio Cover Letter.doc	On / On / On / On / On / On
By the End of Week 4: Start of a New Backup Cycle	Portfolio 1.doc	On	Normal Backup #2	All Folders & Files in Clients Folder / All Folders & Files in Business Records Folder	Off / Off

What happens to the Archive bit during an incremental backup? After the normal backup, all Archive bits are turned off. If you open a file and make a change to it, Windows 2000 turns the Archive bit back on when you save the file. And, if you create and save a new file, Windows 2000 turns the Archive bit on. If you then perform an incremental backup, the backup utility selects all those files that have the Archive bit turned on and backs them up—just like what happens during a differential backup. After an incremental backup, however, the backup utility turns off the Archive bits of all the files that it backed up. See Figure 5-22. When you perform your next incremental backup, you back up any newly created or newly modified files because their Archive bit is turned on. Previously backed up files are not included in the next incremental backup because their Archive bits were turned off. When you perform your next normal backup of all of those files, the backup utility turns off the Archive bits of all the files. Notice in Figure 5-22 that, under this backup strategy, Archive bits are turned off after the normal backup *and* after each incremental backup.

Figure 5-22	HOW INCREMENTAL BACKUPS AFFECT THE ARCHIVE BIT				
	NEW OR MODIFIED FILES	ARCHIVE BIT (BEFORE BACKUP)	TYPE OF BACKUP	FILES BACKED UP	ARCHIVE BIT (AFTER BACKUP)
Beginning of Backup Cycle:			Normal Backup #1	All Folders & Files in Clients Folder	Off
				All Folders & Files in Business Records Folder	Off
By the End of Week 1:	Portfolio 1.doc	On	Incremental Backup #1	Portfolio 1.doc	Off
	Portfolio 2.doc	On		Portfolio 2.doc	Off
By the End of Week 2:	Portfolio 3.doc	On	Incremental Backup #2	Portfolio 3.doc	Off
	Portfolio 4.doc	On		Portfolio 4.doc	Off
By the End of Week 3:	Portfolio Cover Letter.doc	On	Incremental Backup #3	Portfolio Cover Letter.doc	Off
	Portfolio 2.doc	On		Portfolio 2.doc	Off
	Portfolio 5.doc	On		Portfolio 5.doc	Off
By the End of Week 4: Start of a New Backup Cycle	Portfolio 1.doc	On	Normal Backup #2	All Folders & Files in Clients Folder	Off
				All Folders & Files in Business Records Folder	Off

The copy backup and daily backup do not modify the Archive bit of files selected for the backup.

As you can tell, the Archive bit provides a simple, but powerful, technique for determining the status of a file for backup operations.

Creating a Directory for Backups

Isabel recommends that you adopt her one-week backup cycle. On Friday afternoons, she performs a normal backup and starts a new backup cycle. On Monday, Tuesday, Wednesday, and Thursday afternoons, she performs incremental backups. She chose incremental backups over differential backups because she can easily restore earlier versions of important files.

Although the most common way to back up files is to use a backup utility like Microsoft Windows Backup, which operates in the graphical user interface, you can also perform backups from the command-line environment. These backups are faster than backups that you perform in the graphical user interface, and one of these approaches might prove useful if you are experiencing problems with your computer and need to do a backup before you start to troubleshoot a problem.

So you are familiar with how to perform backups from a command-line environment, you are going to copy the contents of your Data Disk to a new directory (called SolarWinds) within the "My Documents" directory. Because individuals and businesses upgrade their computers to Windows 2000 from different operating systems, computer systems are invariably configured in different ways. So you can locate the "My Documents" directory in the command-line environment, you will use the full path for the "My Documents" folder on the desktop. Then, you will create a SolarWinds directory within the "My Documents" directory, and copy the directory structure and files from your data disk to the SolarWinds directory folder.

To complete this part of the tutorial, you will need a copy of your Data Disk with the reorganized directory structure from the first part of the tutorial, and one or two additional formatted diskettes to restore your backups.

If you plan on completing this tutorial in a computer lab at your college, it is strongly recommended that you complete the remainder of this tutorial in one sitting, rather than stop and restart, because another student working on the same tutorial or the technical support personnel in your computer lab might delete the SolarWinds directory, along with the changes you have made to this directory folder. Then you would have to start over.

To complete the remainder of the tutorial, you will also need permission from your instructor or technical support staff to copy the contents of your Data Disk to the "My Documents" directory on drive C or to another local drive.

In the next set of steps, you will set up your computer. You will also need to change the properties of the Command Prompt window so you can see long path names, long directory names, and long filenames.

To set up your computer:

1. If necessary, open a **Command Prompt** window, set the background and foreground colors, specify default switches for the DIR command so directories and filenames are listed in alphabetical order one page at a time, and then clear the **window**.

2. Right-click the blue **title bar**, click **Properties**, and then after Windows 2000 displays the "Command Prompt" Properties dialog box, click the **Layout** tab. If you increase the Screen Buffer Size Width setting on this property sheet, then the long path names and filenames will not wrap around from line to line in the Command Prompt window. See Figure 5-23.

Figure 5-23   **CHANGING THE SCREEN BUFFER SIZE**

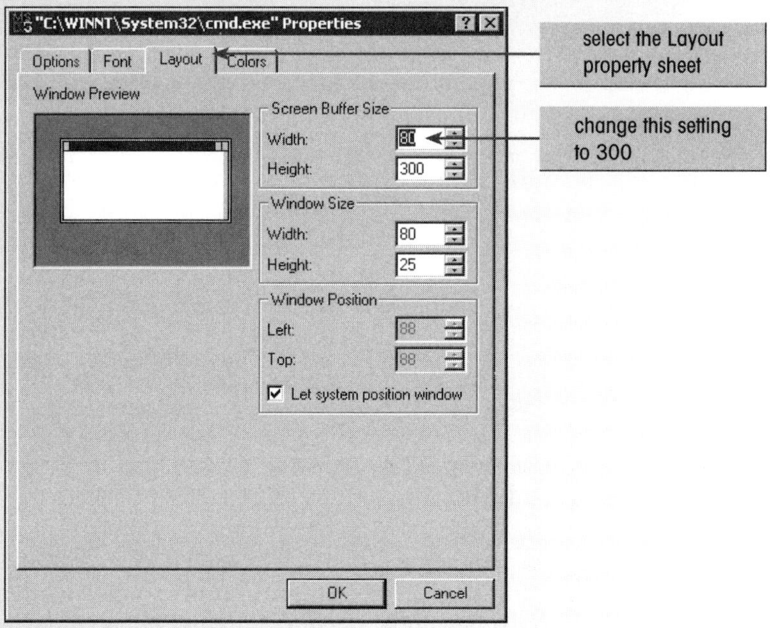

3. Under the Screen Buffer Size section, select **80** in the Width box (if it is not already selected), type **300**, and then click **OK**. Windows displays an "Apply Properties To Shortcuts" dialog box.

4. If it is not already selected, click the "Apply properties to current window only" option button, and then click **OK**. Windows 2000 closes the Command Prompt Properties dialog box and applies the new setting to the Command Prompt window.

5. Click the **Maximize** button [ ] on the right side of the title bar.

TROUBLE? If the Command Prompt window does not fill the entire screen after you click the Maximize button [ ], click the Restore Down button [ ], and then click [ ] again.

6. If necessary, format two additional diskettes. Do not format your Data Disk, which contains the reorganized directory structure from the first part of this tutorial.

In the next few steps, you are going to copy the path to the "My Documents" folder from the "My Documents" desktop shortcut to a command line so that you can switch to that directory.

To copy the path to the "My Documents" folder:

1. Click the **Show Desktop** button [ ] on the taskbar, right-click the **"My Documents"** folder icon on the desktop, and then click **Properties**. On the Target property sheet of the "My Documents" Properties dialog box, Windows 2000 shows the full path to the "My Documents" folder for your logon. See Figure 5-24.

Figure 5-24 COPYING THE PATH FOR THE "MY DOCUMENTS" DIRECTORY

path to "My Documents" directory on a computer

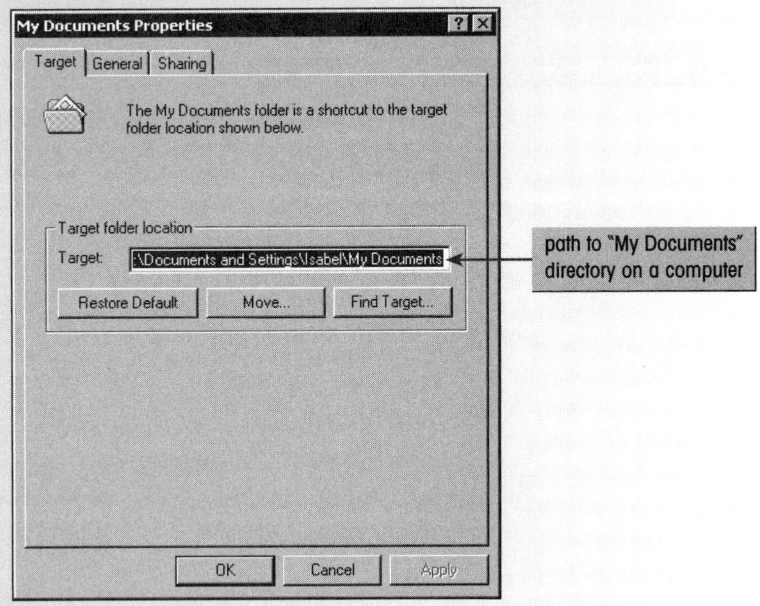

2. While pressing and holding down the **Ctrl** key, press and release **C**, and then release the **Ctrl** key. Although nothing appears to have happened, you have just copied the path to the Windows 2000 Clipboard. The **Clipboard** is an area of memory where an item or items are temporarily stored for copy and move operations.

3. Click **Cancel** to close the "My Documents" Properties dialog box without making any changes to your computer.

4. Click the **Command Prompt** button on the taskbar to restore the Command Prompt window.

5. Check the command prompt and make sure you are at the root directory of drive C.

6. Type **cd** and then press the **Spacebar**, click the **Application** icon on the left side of the title bar, point to **Edit**, and then click **Paste**. Windows 2000 pastes the full path from the Clipboard to the command line. See Figure 5-25. Your path will differ. You can not only copy text from the graphical user interface or from a document in an application window to the Command Prompt window, but you can also copy text from the Command Prompt window to a document in an application window.

Figure 5-25 PASTING THE PATH TO THE MY DOCUMENTS DIRECTORY

path to "My Documents" directory pasted into a command line

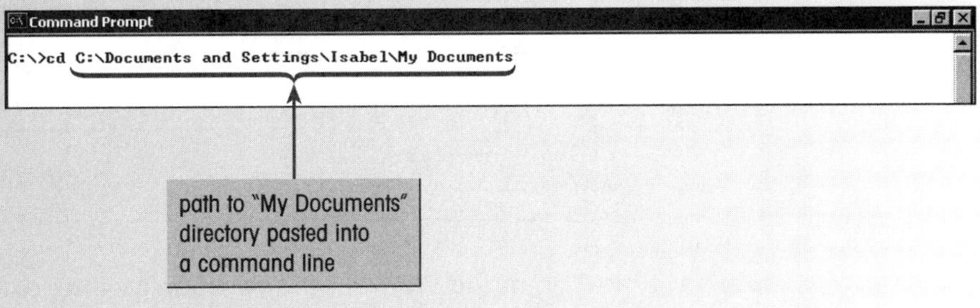

7. Press **Enter**. The CD command changes to the "My Documents" directory for your user account. See Figure 5-26.

Figure 5-26

CHANGING TO THE "MY DOCUMENTS" DIRECTORY

```
Command Prompt                                                    _ □ ×

C:\>cd C:\Documents and Settings\Isabel\My Documents

C:\Documents and Settings\Isabel\My Documents>
```

Isabel's "My Documents" directory

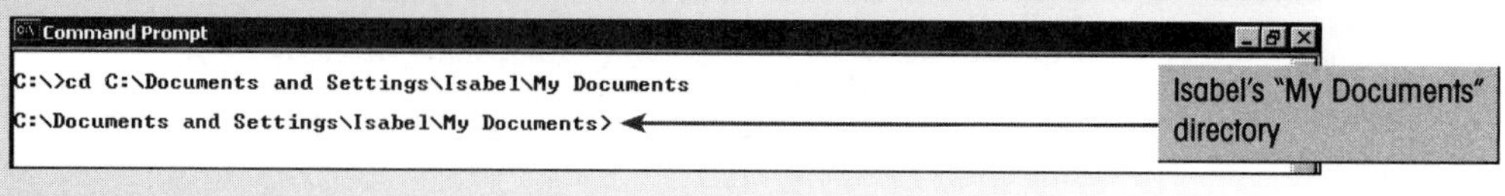

Now you're ready to create the SolarWinds folder. But first, you need to make sure a folder by that name does not already exist.

To create the SolarWinds directory folder:

1. Display a **directory listing** of the current directory. The DIR command displays the contents of the "My Documents" directory. If a SolarWinds subdirectory already exists in the "My Documents" directory, and if you are working in a computer lab, then another student probably stopped in the middle of the tutorial and left the SolarWinds subdirectory in the "My Documents" directory. If this is the case, you will need to remove that directory and all the subdirectories and files contained within it. If you are working on your own computer and if you have a directory named SolarWinds that you want to keep, then you can skip the next step, continue with Step 3, and create a directory with a different name.

2. If a SolarWinds subdirectory already exists in the "My Documents" directory, and if you want to remove it, type **rd SolarWinds /s** and then press **Enter**. When prompted as to whether or not you are sure you want to remove SolarWinds, type **y** (for Yes) and then press **Enter**. Display a **directory listing** to verify that the SolarWinds folder no longer exists.

3. Clear the **Command Prompt** window.

4. Enter: **md SolarWinds**

If you are working on your own computer and already have a folder named SolarWinds that you want to keep, use a different name for the directory folder—such as Solar Winds (with a space) or SolarWind (with no "s" at the end of the directory name), and use that name for the rest of the tutorial.

5. Display a **directory listing**. You now have a SolarWinds directory in the "My Documents" folder. See Figure 5-27.

Figure 5-27

CREATING A DIRECTORY UNDER "MY DOCUMENTS"

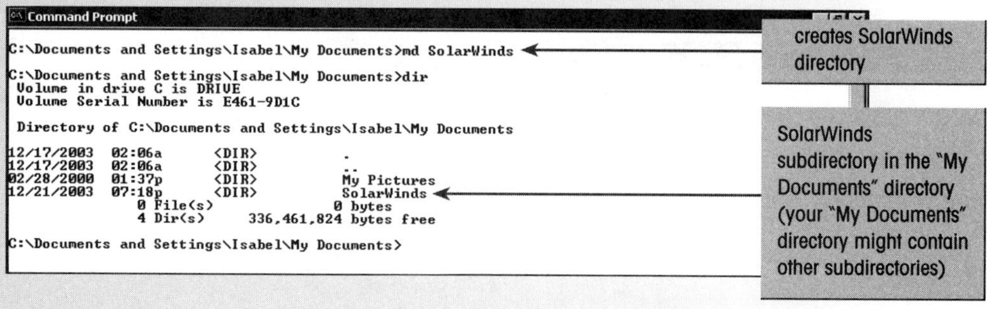

```
Command Prompt                                                    _ □ ×

C:\Documents and Settings\Isabel\My Documents>md SolarWinds

C:\Documents and Settings\Isabel\My Documents>dir
 Volume in drive C is DRIVE
 Volume Serial Number is E461-9D1C

 Directory of C:\Documents and Settings\Isabel\My Documents

12/17/2003  02:06a    <DIR>          .
12/17/2003  02:06a    <DIR>          ..
02/28/2000  01:37p    <DIR>          My Pictures
12/21/2003  07:18p    <DIR>          SolarWinds
               0 File(s)              0 bytes
               4 Dir(s)     336,461,824 bytes free

C:\Documents and Settings\Isabel\My Documents>
```

creates SolarWinds directory

SolarWinds subdirectory in the "My Documents" directory (your "My Documents" directory might contain other subdirectories)

6. Leave the Command Prompt window open for the next section.

The ability to copy a path from the Windows 2000 graphical user interface and use it as part of a command that you're entering in the Command Prompt window simplifies the process for specifying and locating subdirectories.

Using XCOPY to Copy Directories and Files

Your next step is to copy the subdirectories and files from your Data Disk to the SolarWinds directory. You can use the XCOPY (Extended Copy) command to copy the directory structure and contents of a disk or another directory. The XCOPY command is similar to the COPY command, except it can copy the contents of more than one directory at a time. The general syntax of this external command is:

XCOPY *source* **[***destination***] /S**

The *source* is a disk, a subdirectory, a group of files, or a single file, and it is a required parameter. The *destination* is the name of the drive *or* directory to which you want to copy the files. For example, if you want to copy all the files in a directory named SolarWinds to a diskette in drive A, you might use this command:

```
XCOPY SolarWinds A:
```

If you want to include all the subdirectories and files located below a directory, you include the Subdirectory switch (/S). For example, if the SolarWinds directory contained subdirectories, and if you want to copy the SolarWinds directory, and all its subdirectories and files, using the same directory structure, to a diskette in drive A, you might use this command:

```
XCOPY SolarWinds A: /S
```

You can omit the destination if you want to copy to the current drive and directory. For example, if you are already in the "My Documents" directory, and if you want to copy the SolarWinds directory and all its subdirectories and files from drive A to the current directory, you could use either of the following commands:

```
XCOPY A:\SolarWinds /S
XCOPY A:\SolarWinds . /S
```

If you include a "dot" as the destination (as shown in the second of the two previous commands), then you are specifying that the current directory is the destination.

In the next steps, you are going to use XCOPY to copy the contents of your Data Disk to the SolarWinds directory. Again, make sure you have permission to perform this operation if you are working in a computer lab.

To copy subdirectories and files to the SolarWinds directory:

1. Make sure your Data Disk (the one with the reorganized directory structure from the first part of the tutorial) is in drive A.

2. Clear the **Command Prompt** window.

3. Enter: `xcopy "a:\My Documents" SolarWinds /s`

   XCOPY shows the full path of each file that it copies, and after the operation is complete, it reports that it copied 43 files. See Figure 5-28. "A:\My Documents" is the source for this copy operation, and SolarWinds is the destination.

Figure 5-28   **COPYING FILES TO A SUBDIRECTORY**

```
Command Prompt - xcopy "a:\My Documents" SolarWinds /s
C:\Documents and Settings\Isabel\My Documents>xcopy "a:\My Documents" SolarWinds /s
A:\My Documents\Designs\Company Logo Design.bmp
A:\My Documents\Designs\Color Palette.bmp
A:\My Documents\Designs\Pallete #1.bmp
A:\My Documents\Designs\Pallete #2.bmp
A:\My Documents\Memos\Microsoft's Web Site.doc
A:\My Documents\Company Templates\Regional Sales Projections.xls
A:\My Documents\Company Templates\Loan Payment Analysis.xls
A:\My Documents\Company Templates\Savings Plan.xls
A:\My Documents\Company Templates\Sales Projection Models.xls
A:\My Documents\Company Templates\Commission on Sales.xls
A:\My Documents\Company Templates\Daily Sales.xls
A:\My Documents\Company Templates\Software Quotes.xls
A:\My Documents\Company Templates\Advertising Income.xls
A:\My Documents\Company Templates\Salary Analysis.xls
A:\My Documents\Company Templates\Product List.xls
A:\My Documents\Company Templates\Sales.wk4
A:\My Documents\Company Templates\Balance Sheet.xls
A:\My Documents\Company Templates\Sales Summary #2.xls
A:\My Documents\Company Templates\Sales Summary #1.xls
A:\My Documents\Company Templates\Three Year Sales Projection.xls
A:\My Documents\Company Templates\Five Year Growth Plan.xls
A:\My Documents\Company Templates\Five Year Plan Template.xls
A:\My Documents\Company Templates\Data Systems Budget.xls
A:\My Documents\Company Templates\Break Even Analysis.xls
A:\My Documents\Company Templates\Product Sales Projection.xls
A:\My Documents\Company Templates\Client Invoices.xls
A:\My Documents\Company Templates\Sales Projections.xls
A:\My Documents\Training\Addressing Cells.xls
A:\My Documents\Training\Excel Basics.doc
A:\My Documents\Training\Colors.xls
A:\My Documents\Training\Computer Basics.doc
A:\My Documents\Training\Using the Mouse.ppt
A:\My Documents\Training\Fonts.xls
A:\My Documents\Training\Formatting Features.xls
A:\My Documents\Training\Hardware.ppt
A:\My Documents\Training\Software.ppt
A:\My Documents\Training\Application Software.ppt
A:\My Documents\Overhead Transparencies\Sales.wk4
A:\My Documents\Overhead Transparencies\Five Year Growth Plan.xls
A:\My Documents\Overhead Transparencies\Cycle.wk4
A:\My Documents\Overhead Transparencies\Thank You Letter.wpd
A:\My Documents\Overhead Transparencies\Invoice Form.wk4
```

command for copying all files in all directories

files being copied from drive A to a directory on drive C

4. Change to the **SolarWinds directory**, and then clear the **Command Prompt** window.

5. Enter: `tree "a:\My Documents"`

The TREE command displays the directory structure of the "My Documents" directory on your Data Disk in drive A.

6. Enter: `tree`

The TREE command now shows the directory structure within the SolarWinds directory folder. Your directory structure might differ. See Figure 5-29. Notice that XCOPY reproduced the directory structure with the "My Documents" directory on drive A exactly. In contrast, the COPY command cannot copy a directory structure; it can copy only files.

Figure 5-29   **VIEWING THE SOURCE AND DESTINATION DIRECTORY TREES**

```
Command Prompt
C:\Documents and Settings\Isabel\My Documents\SolarWinds>tree "a:\My Documents"
Folder PATH listing
Volume serial number is 0006FE80 F493:234E
A:\MY DOCUMENTS
├───Designs
├───Memos
├───Company Templates
├───Training
└───Overhead Transparencies

C:\Documents and Settings\Isabel\My Documents\SolarWinds>tree
Folder PATH listing for volume DRIVE
Volume serial number is 0006FE80 E461:9D1C
C:.
├───Designs
├───Memos
├───Company Templates
├───Training
└───Overhead Transparencies

C:\Documents and Settings\Isabel\My Documents\SolarWinds>
```

directory tree on source disk

directory tree copied to drive C

7. Clear the **Command Prompt** window, and then enter:

```
dir "a:\my documents\training"
```

The DIR command reports that there are 10 files, which require 342,528 bytes of storage space in this directory on drive A.

8. Enter: `dir training`

The DIR command reports that there are 10 files, which require 342,528 bytes of storage space in the corresponding subdirectory below the SolarWinds directory. XCOPY copied all the files on the diskette in drive A to the correct subdirectories on your local drive. See Figure 5-30.

Figure 5-30	VIEWING FILES ON THE SOURCE DISK AND IN THE DESTINATION DIRECTORY

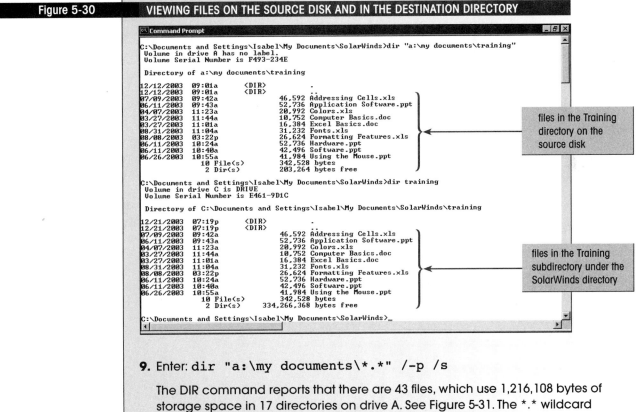

files in the Training directory on the source disk

files in the Training subdirectory under the SolarWinds directory

9. Enter: `dir "a:\my documents\*.*" /-p /s`

The DIR command reports that there are 43 files, which use 1,216,108 bytes of storage space in 17 directories on drive A. See Figure 5-31. The *.* wildcard specification instructs the DIR command to display all files. The /-p switch overrides the default /p switch in the Windows environment.

Figure 5-31   VIEWING ALL THE FILES ON THE SOURCE DISK

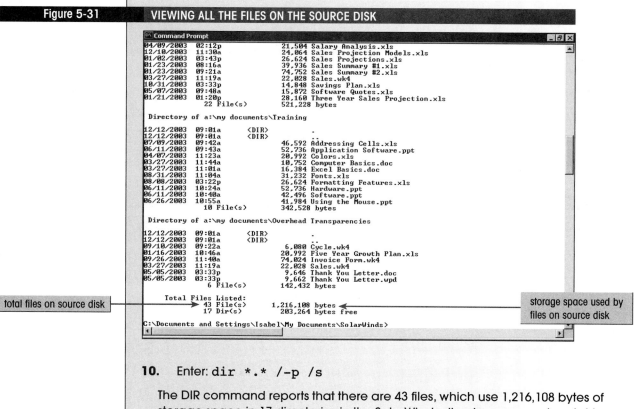

10.   Enter: `dir *.* /-p /s`

The DIR command reports that there are 43 files, which use 1,216,108 bytes of storage space in 17 directories in the SolarWinds directory on your local drive. The XCOPY command copied all the files from your Data Disk.

After you use the XCOPY command, it's a good habit to check the results of the copy operation and verify that this program copied subdirectories and files to the correct location and that it also produced the same directory structure.

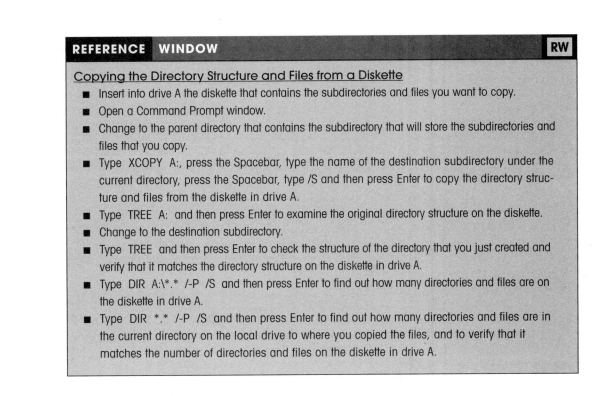

XCOPY is a powerful command for duplicating the directory structure and file organization on another disk, or within another subdirectory. XCOPY works in a similar way under different versions of Windows and MS-DOS; however, the switches that are available for use with this command vary.

Examining File Attributes

So you can follow the progress of a normal backup, and then a subsequent incremental backup, Isabel recommends that you view file attributes before and after backing up.

You can use the ATTRIB (Attribute) command to display or change attributes of files. When you view file attributes, this program shows whether the System, Hidden, Read-Only, and Archive attributes of each file are turned on or turned off.

If you want to view the attributes of all files in all subdirectories, you can use the Subdirectory switch (/S) with the ATTRIB command. To control scrolling, you can also pipe the output to the MORE filter.

To view file attributes:

1. Check the command prompt, and make sure you are in the SolarWinds subdirectory under the "My Documents" directory.

2. Enter: `attrib /s | more`

   The ATTRIB command displays the full path for all the files in each directory, and, on the left side of the screen, it displays attributes for each file. See Figure 5-32. Notice that all the files shown on the first screen have their Archive attribute turned on—represented by the letter "A." If you want to view the remainder of the filenames, you can scroll to the right.

Figure 5-32   **VIEWING FILE ATTRIBUTES**

Archive attribute assigned to all files

3. Press the **Spacebar** to view each of the next screens, if necessary. Notice that the Archive attribute of all the files displayed on the next screen are turned on.

The Archive attribute of all the files in all the subdirectories below the SolarWinds directory are turned on because you copied the files from a different location and you will eventually need to back them up from their new location.

REFERENCE WINDOW   **RW**

Viewing Attributes of Files
- Open a Command Prompt window.
- Change to the directory that contains the files whose attributes you want to examine.
- Type ATTRIB and press Enter to view attributes of all files. If you want to control scrolling, type ATTRIB I MORE and press Enter to view one page at a time of filenames and file attributes.
- If you want to view file attributes in the current directory and all subordinate directories, type ATTRIB /S I MORE and press Enter.

The ATTRIB command and its switches have remained the same under different versions of Windows and MS-DOS.

Performing a Normal Backup with XCOPY

Although you routinely use a backup utility to back up the entire system, Isabel suggests that you use the XCOPY command when you are working in a Command Prompt window so you can perform a quick backup of selected directories to a diskette in drive A.

As noted earlier, although most people use a backup utility to back up files on their hard disk to some type of permanent storage medium, such as a tape or CD, you can also use the XCOPY command in a command-line environment to make backups of specific directories on a volume. By using different switches with the XCOPY command, you can perform normal backups combined with either incremental or differential backups.

To complete this section of the tutorial, you will need an additional, formatted (but empty), high-density diskette.

To back up the SolarWinds directory folder:

1. Remove your Data Disk from drive A, and then insert a formatted, but empty, high-density diskette.

2. Clear the **Command Prompt** window.

3. Enter: `xcopy . "a:\SolarWinds Normal Backup" /m /s`

The screen will scroll to the right as you enter this command. XCOPY displays a prompt, and asks if "A:\SolarWinds Normal Backup" specifies a filename or directory name on the target disk. See Figure 5-33. The period ("dot") following the XCOPY command is the notation for the current directory. The Modify switch (/M) removes the Archive attribute after XCOPY copies the file. The Subdirectory switch (/S) instructs the XCOPY command to copy all subdirectories and their files.

Figure 5-33	PERFORMING A NORMAL BACKUP

```
Command Prompt - xcopy . "a:\SolarWinds Normal Backup" /m /s                    _ □ ×

C:\Documents and Settings\Isabel\My Documents\SolarWinds>xcopy . "a:\SolarWinds Normal Backup" /m
Does A:\SolarWinds Normal Backup specify a file name
or directory name on the target
(F = file, D = directory)?
```

is the destination a file or directory?   source directory   destination directory

4. When prompted, enter: **d** (for Directory)

After creating a "SolarWinds Normal Backup" directory on the diskette in drive A, XCOPY copies each file to that directory. See Figure 5-34. Notice that, as it copies, it uses "dot" at the beginning of the path name to represent the current directory. After the backup copy is complete, XCOPY reports that it copied 43 files.

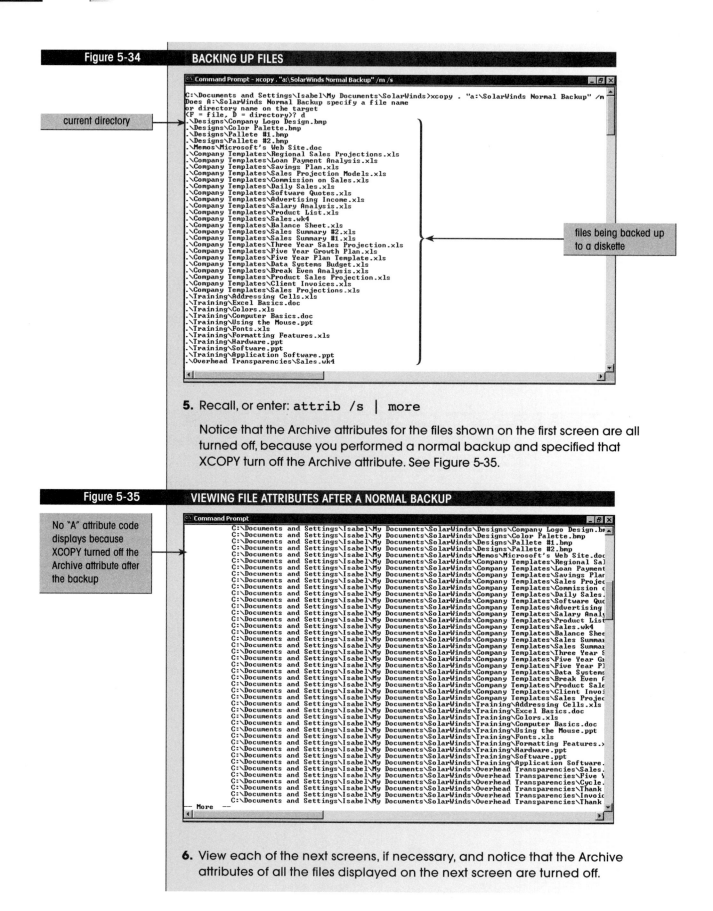

Figure 5-34   BACKING UP FILES

current directory

files being backed up
to a diskette

5. Recall, or enter: attrib /s | more

Notice that the Archive attributes for the files shown on the first screen are all
turned off, because you performed a normal backup and specified that
XCOPY turn off the Archive attribute. See Figure 5-35.

Figure 5-35   VIEWING FILE ATTRIBUTES AFTER A NORMAL BACKUP

No "A" attribute code
displays because
XCOPY turned off the
Archive attribute after
the backup

6. View each of the next screens, if necessary, and notice that the Archive
attributes of all the files displayed on the next screen are turned off.

7. Clear the **Command Prompt** window, and then enter: tree a:

XCOPY copied the same directory structure to the diskette in drive A. See Figure 5-36.

Figure 5-36	VIEWING THE DIRECTORY STRUCTURE OF A BACKUP

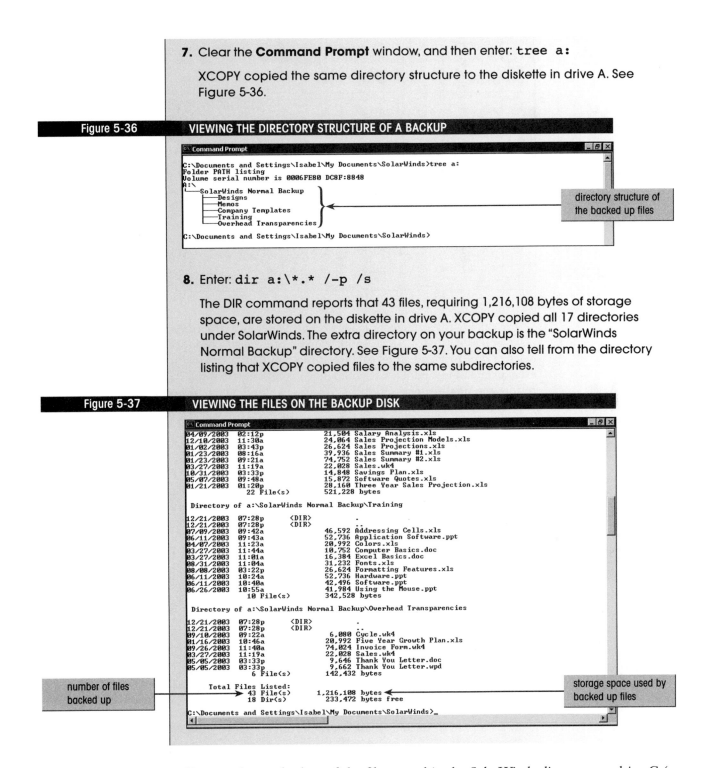

8. Enter: dir a:*.* /-p /s

The DIR command reports that 43 files, requiring 1,216,108 bytes of storage space, are stored on the diskette in drive A. XCOPY copied all 17 directories under SolarWinds. The extra directory on your backup is the "SolarWinds Normal Backup" directory. See Figure 5-37. You can also tell from the directory listing that XCOPY copied files to the same subdirectories.

Figure 5-37	VIEWING THE FILES ON THE BACKUP DISK

You now have a backup of the files stored in the SolarWinds directory on drive C (or another local drive). You also now know a commonly used strategy for copying files from one diskette to another using only one drive: you copy files from a diskette to a local drive, and then you copy the files from a local drive to another diskette.

You should also label your diskette to include the name of the backup utility (in this case, XCOPY), the type of backup (in this case, Normal Backup), and the date that you made the backup.

REFERENCE WINDOW ⬛ **RW**

Performing a Normal Backup with XCOPY

- Insert a formatted, but empty, high-density diskette into drive A.
- Open a Command Prompt window.
- Change to the directory that contains the files you want to copy to drive A.
- Type XCOPY . A:\ followed by the name of the directory you want to use for the files on the diskette in drive A, press the Spacebar, type /M /S and then press Enter. *Note:* The period (or "dot") refers to the current directory.
- If XCOPY displays a prompt, and asks if the directory name you entered is for a file or directory on the target disk, type D (for Directory) and then press Enter. XCOPY will list all the files it copies to the disk and report on the total number of files copied.
- Type TREE A: and then press Enter to verify the directory structure on the diskette that contains the copied files.

You can use the same techniques to copy a directory structure and files to another type of disk, such as a Zip disk, or to another drive, or even to a network drive. If you accidentally delete a directory and all its subdirectories and files, a single directory, a group of files, or even a single file, and if what you deleted is no longer stored in the Recycle Bin, you can restore the subdirectories and files (or file) by using XCOPY to copy what you need from your backup disk to the appropriate level in the directory structure of your hard disk.

Modifying Files After a Backup

After you make changes to some of the files stored in the SolarWinds directory, you decide to update your backup copy of these files.

After you make a normal backup of selected files, the backup utility turns off the Archive bit on all the files. As you may recall, once you modify and save changes to a file, Windows 2000 turns the Archive bit back on. If you create a new file, Windows 2000 also turns on its Archive bit. The next time you perform an incremental or differential backup, the backup utility knows which files to back up. All you have to specify is that you want an incremental or differential backup instead of a normal backup.

In the next set of steps, you are going to make changes to a couple of files so you can then perform an incremental backup.

To edit the contents of two files:

1. Clear the **Command Prompt** window, and then enter: `cd memos`

The CD command changes to the Memos directory.

2. Enter: `"Microsoft's Web Site.doc"`

If Microsoft Word is installed on your computer, Windows 2000 will automatically open the file in Microsoft Word because it associates the "doc" file extension with this software product. If Microsoft Word is not installed on your computer, and if the "doc" file extension is not associated with any other word-processing application on your computer, then Windows 2000 will open the file in WordPad. See Figure 5-38.

TROUBLE? If Windows 2000 informs you that the filename you typed is not recognized as an internal or external command, operable program or batch file, then you mistyped the filename or did not enclose the filename in quotation marks, or both. Repeat the step, paying close attention to what you type.

Figure 5-38	OPENING A FILE FROM THE COMMAND LINE

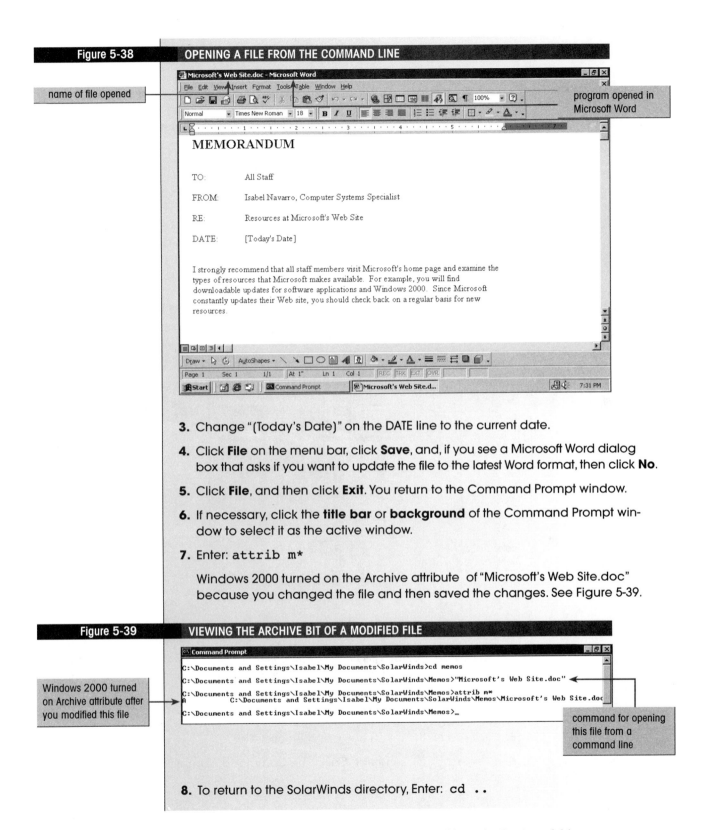

name of file opened

program opened in Microsoft Word

3. Change "(Today's Date)" on the DATE line to the current date.

4. Click **File** on the menu bar, click **Save**, and, if you see a Microsoft Word dialog box that asks if you want to update the file to the latest Word format, then click **No**.

5. Click **File**, and then click **Exit**. You return to the Command Prompt window.

6. If necessary, click the **title bar** or **background** of the Command Prompt window to select it as the active window.

7. Enter: `attrib m*`

   Windows 2000 turned on the Archive attribute of "Microsoft's Web Site.doc" because you changed the file and then saved the changes. See Figure 5-39.

Figure 5-39	VIEWING THE ARCHIVE BIT OF A MODIFIED FILE

Windows 2000 turned on Archive attribute after you modified this file

command for opening this file from a command line

8. To return to the SolarWinds directory, Enter: `cd ..`

Now you're ready to make changes to another file in the Designs folder.

To modify a file with a graphics image:

1. Enter: **cd Designs**

2. Enter: **"Color Palette.bmp"**

   Windows 2000 opens the file in Paint because it associates the "bmp" file with Paint. See Figure 5-40.

   TROUBLE? If Windows 2000 opens "Color Palette.bmp" in an application other than Paint, you still can use that program to make some small change to the file, so that once saved, Windows 2000 will turn the Archive attribute back on.

   TROUBLE? If Windows 2000 informs you that the filename you typed is not recognized as an internal or external command, operable program or batch file, then you mistyped the filename or did not enclose the filename in quotation marks, or both. Repeat the step, paying close attention to what you type.

Figure 5-40   **MODIFYING A GRAPHIC IMAGE**

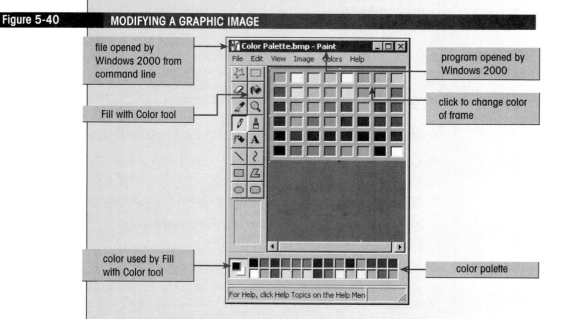

file opened by Windows 2000 from command line

program opened by Windows 2000

Fill with Color tool

click to change color of frame

color used by Fill with Color tool

color palette

3. Click the **Fill With Color** button in the toolbox, and then position the tip of the mouse pointer (the end showing paint flowing from the bucket) on the dark gray frame (not the gray background) that outlines the color blocks in the graphic image, and then click the **dark gray frame**. Paint changes the color of the frame from a dark gray to black.

4. Click **File** on the menu bar, and then click **Save**.

5. Click **File** on the menu bar, and then click **Exit**.

6. If necessary, click the **title bar** of the Command Prompt window to select it as the active window.

7. Enter: **attrib**

   Windows 2000 turned on the Archive attribute of "Color Palette.bmp" because you changed the file and then saved the changes. See Figure 5-41. Notice that the Archive attributes of all the other files are turned off.

Figure 5-41	VIEWING FILE ATTRIBUTES AFTER CHANGING A FILE

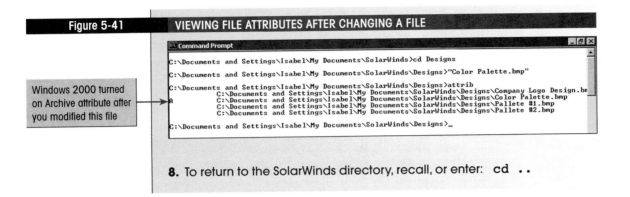

Windows 2000 turned on Archive attribute after you modified this file

8. To return to the SolarWinds directory, recall, or enter: **cd . .**

You made changes to two files in two different directories. In each case, Windows 2000 turned on the Archive bit, and the files are now marked for inclusion in the next backup.

Performing an Incremental Backup

Because you might need to restore a previous version of a file, Isabel recommends that you use an incremental backup strategy rather than a differential backup strategy.

There are two options for backing up these files. You can use XCOPY to copy these files to the appropriate subdirectories on the disk that contains your normal backup. The advantage of this approach is that your backup is automatically updated. The disadvantage is that you will have only the most recent version of files that you changed or created. Or, as is typical of an incremental backup strategy, another option is to keep different versions of a file in case you need to return to an earlier version. If the latter is the case, then you can copy the files to a different disk, or to a different directory on the same disk (assuming space is available).

Let's assume Isabel wants you to keep both versions of the two files you changed in the last section.

If you do not have enough storage space for another backup on the diskette that contains your normal backup, then you will need to use another empty, but formatted, diskette.

To perform an incremental backup:

1. Display a **directory listing** of the diskette that contains your normal backup of the SolarWinds directory. If the DIR command reports that you have more than 100,000 bytes of storage space free on the disk, then you can copy your incremental backup to this disk; otherwise, you will need to insert a new formatted, but empty, high-density diskette. It is always a good idea to check your backup medium to make sure it contains enough space for the backup you intend to perform.

2. Clear the **Command Prompt** window.

3. Enter: **xcopy . "a:\SolarWinds Incremental Backup #1" /m /s**

XCOPY displays a prompt, and asks if "A:\SolarWinds Incremental Backup #1" is a file or directory on the target disk. Recall that the period ("dot") following the XCOPY command is the notation for the current directory. With the Modify switch (/M), the XCOPY command copies only files with the Archive bit on, and then turns off the Archive attribute after it copies the file. The Subdirectory switch (/S) instructs the XCOPY command to copy all subdirectories and their files under this directory.

4. When prompted, type **d** (for Directory)

After creating a "SolarWinds Incremental Backup #1" directory on the diskette in drive A, XCOPY copies each file to that directory. See Figure 5-42. Notice that, as it copies, it uses "dot" at the beginning of the path name to represent the current directory. After the copy is complete, it reports that it copied 2 files—the same two files that you changed.

Figure 5-42	PERFORMING AN INCREMENTAL BACKUP

```
C:\Documents and Settings\Isabel\My Documents\SolarWinds>xcopy . "a:\SolarWinds Incremental Backup
Does A:\SolarWinds Incremental Backup #1 specify a file name
or directory name on the target
(F = file, D = directory)? d
.\Designs\Color Palette.bmp
.\Memos\Microsoft's Web Site.doc
2 File(s) copied

C:\Documents and Settings\Isabel\My Documents\SolarWinds>_
```

XCOPY backs up only those files that changed

6. Clear the **Command Prompt** window, and then enter: `tree a:`

The TREE command shows the directory structure of the disk. See Figure 5-43. The directory that contains the incremental backup contains only two subdirectories—Memos and Designs — the two folders that contained the files you changed.

Figure 5-43	VIEWING THE DIRECTORY STRUCTURE OF THE BACKUP DISK

```
C:\Documents and Settings\Isabel\My Documents\SolarWinds>tree a:
Folder PATH listing
Volume serial number is 0006FE80 DC8F:8848
A:\
    ┌──SolarWinds Normal Backup
    │     ├──Designs
    │     ├──Memos
    │     ├──Company Templates
    │     ├──Training
    │     └──Overhead Transparencies
    └──SolarWinds Incremental Backup #1
          ├──Designs
          └──Memos

C:\Documents and Settings\Isabel\My Documents\SolarWinds>
```

incremental backup includes only those subdirectories that contain modified files

You have successfully made an incremental backup using the XCOPY utility.

REFERENCE	WINDOW	RW

Performing an Incremental Backup

- Open a Command Prompt window.
- Change to the directory that contains the files you want to back up.
- Use the DIR command with the Subdirectory switch (/S) to determine how much storage space you will need for the backup.
- Insert a diskette that contains enough storage space for this backup.
- Type XCOPY . A:\ followed by the name of the directory you want to use for the files on the diskette in drive A, press the Spacebar, type /M /S and then press Enter. *Note:* The period (or "dot") refers to the current directory.
- If XCOPY displays a prompt and asks if the directory name you entered is for a file or directory on the target disk, type D (for Directory). The XCOPY utility will list all the files it copies to the disk and report on the total number of files copied.
- Type TREE A: and then press Enter to verify the directory structure on your disk.

You can add incremental or differential backups to the same media that contains the normal backup, assuming there is still space on the backup media. However, you must make sure that you specify a new directory on the backup disk for each incremental or differential backup; otherwise, you might overwrite some or all of the files for a previous backup because the names of the files you back up will be the same as those you backed up previously. Because incremental and differential backups take less space, and assuming you are backing up to a medium other than diskettes, you might be able to store all the backups for a backup cycle together on the same medium.

Restoring Files from a Normal and Incremental Backup

The next day, you discover that some of the files in your SolarWinds directory have become corrupted. Because you are unable to use these files, you need to restore these files from your backup. A **corrupted file** is a program or document file whose contents have been altered as the result of hardware, software, or power problems, or a computer virus infection.

If you discover corrupted files, if you accidentally delete a folder or files within a folder, or if your hard disk drive fails, you can restore files from your backup (once you have resolved any problems that occurred with your computer). If your hard disk drive fails, you have to replace the drive and install Windows 2000 first. Then you can restore all the files that you lost. If you used a backup utility to back up your hard disk, you will need to use that same backup utility to restore the files. If you used the XCOPY utility to create a backup of a directory folder, you can use XCOPY to restore copies of those files to their original locations.

To delete a directory and its files:

1. Check the command prompt, and make sure you are in the SolarWinds subdirectory under the "My Documents" directory.

2. Clear the **Command Prompt** window, and then enter:
   rd "Company Templates" /s

   The RD command displays a prompt and asks if you are sure you want to delete the "Company Templates" directory and all the files contained in it.

3. Type y (for Yes) and then press **Enter**.

4. View a **directory listing** to verify that the RD command deleted the "Company Templates" directory. The SolarWinds directory no longer contains a "Company Templates" subdirectory. See Figure 5-44.

| Figure 5-44 | DIRECTORY ACCIDENTALLY DELETED |

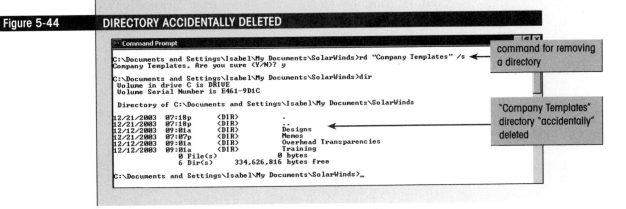

Suddenly you realize that you accidentally deleted one of your own directories. Windows 2000 does not store subdirectories and files that you delete from the Command Prompt in the Recycle Bin, so you cannot restore them with Windows 2000. Fortunately, you can use your previous backup to restore this directory.

5. Clear the **window,** and then enter:

`xcopy "a:\SolarWinds Normal Backup\Company Templates" "Company Templates"`

The XCOPY command asks if the name "Company Templates" (the destination) refers to a file or directory. The source is the "Company Templates" directory on your backup disk, and the destination is a new "Company Templates" directory under the current directory (in this case, SolarWinds).

If you do not specify a target or destination, the XCOPY command copies *just* the files in the directory you specify to the current directory, without re-creating the directory structure. If the "Company Templates" directory contained subdirectories, then you would also need to use the Subdirectory switch (/S) to create subdirectories for the files you're copying.

6. When prompted, type **d** (for Directory). The XCOPY command copies 22 files in the "Company Templates" directory on drive A to the current directory.

7. Clear the **Command Prompt** window, and then display a **directory listing** of the current directory. You have now restored the "Company Templates" directory. See Figure 5-45.

Figure 5-45	DIRECTORY RESTORED FROM A BACKUP

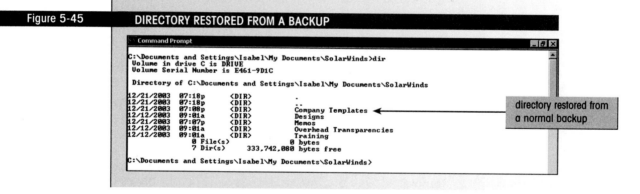

Next, thinking that you no longer need the "Microsoft's Web Site.doc" in the Memos folder, you decide to delete it.

To delete a file:

1. Clear the **Command Prompt** window, and then enter: **cd m***

The CD command changes to the Memos directory. The Memos directory is the only directory whose name starts with "m".

2. Enter: **del *.***

The DEL command asks if you are sure. (*Note:* You might need to scroll to the right to see this prompt.)

3. Type y (for Yes) and then press **Enter.** The DEL command deletes all the files in this directory.

4. View a **directory listing** of the current directory. The Memos directory no longer contains "Microsoft's Web Site.doc". See Figure 5-46.

| Figure 5-46 | ACCIDENTALLY DELETING A FILE |

command for deleting all files in a directory

all files "accidentally" deleted from a directory

Shortly after you deleted this file, Isabel hands you a revised copy of the "Microsoft's Web Site" memo, and asks you to update your copy of this file, and then print a new copy for distribution to the staff. Right after the immediate shock wears off, you recall that you have two copies of this file on your backup disk. You have the original copy in the "SolarWinds Normal Backup" directory. The most recent version, however, is in the "SolarWinds Incremental Backup #1" directory. You decide to restore the most recent version.

5. Clear the **Command Prompt** window.

6. Enter:

   xcopy "a:\SolarWinds Incremental Backup #1\Memos\Microsoft's Web Site.doc"

   The XCOPY command copies the file you specified. Because you did not specify a destination for the copy operation, XCOPY copied the file to the current directory (which, in this case, is the Memos directory). If you want to specify a destination for the copy, you can use a "dot" in the command to represent the current directory.

7. Display a **directory listing**. You have now restored the "Microsoft's Web Site.doc" file to this directory. See Figure 5-47.

| Figure 5-47 | FILE RESTORED FROM A BACKUP |

file restored from an incremental backup

8. Enter: cd ..

   The CD command moves you up one directory level to the SolarWinds directory.

You have to make sure you specify enough of the path for both the source and the target for the XCOPY command to distinguish the proper source and destination. You can also use wildcards if you want to restore a group of files.

REFERENCE WINDOW   RW

Using XCOPY to Restore a Directory or File

- Insert the disk that contains the directory or file you want to restore.
- Open a Command Prompt window.
- Change to the directory where you want to restore a subdirectory or a file to set the default destination directory.
- Type XCOPY, press the Spacebar, type the name of the source directory or file (specifying enough of the path to identify the proper source), press the Spacebar, type the name of the destination folder or file (specifying enough of the path to identify the destination), press the Spacebar, type /S for the Subdirectory switch (if needed), and then press Enter. If you are copying a file, you do not need to specify the destination if it is the current folder.
- If XCOPY asks whether the destination is a file or directory, type D (for Directory) if you want to copy files to a directory.
- Type DIR and then press Enter to verify that you have restored the directory or file.

If you accidentally delete an entire directory and all its subdirectories and files, or if all the files in a directory become corrupted, you will need to first restore your normal backup, and then restore each of the incremental backups in the order in which you made them. This process restores the entire directory from your backups.

If you prefer to perform differential backups instead of incremental backups, use the XCOPY command with the Modify switch (/M) when you perform each normal backup at the beginning of a backup cycle. When you perform differential backups, use the XCOPY command with the Archive switch (/A) so that the XCOPY command copies only files with the Archive bit turned on. This switch also instructs XCOPY not to change the Archive attribute. When you are ready to do the next differential backup, use XCOPY to back up the same files as well as any newly modified or newly created files with the Archive attributes turned on. At the beginning of the next backup cycle, you again use the Modify switch with XCOPY to turn off all Archive attributes. If you need to restore all the files from a backup set, you would first restore the normal backup and then restore the last differential backup.

You have successfully stepped through the process for performing a normal backup, restoring a normal backup, performing an incremental backup of modified files, and restoring a file from a normal backup and an incremental backup.

Note: XCOPY does not preserve the original short (i.e., DOS) filenames of files and directories with long names. Instead, it generates new short names in the destination directory that may be different from the original short names in the source directory. Because many Windows program configurations store file and directory references with short names, using XCOPY to duplicate program directories may lead to program malfunctions if the short names change. Therefore, avoid using XCOPY to replicate program directories or entire drives. If you need to replicate an entire drive, use a utility specifically designed for that purpose.

Restoring Your Computer

To restore your computer, you will need to remove the SolarWinds subdirectory from the "My Documents" directory.

> *To restore your computer:*
>
> **1.** If necessary, change to the "My Documents" directory for your logon.
>
> **2.** Enter: `rd SolarWinds /s`
>
> **3.** When the RD command prompts you as to whether you are sure you want to remove the SolarWinds directory, type **y** (for Yes) and then press **Enter**.

Restoring Other Types of Backups

If you have upgraded your computer from MS-DOS to Windows 3.1 (or Windows 3.11), and then to Windows 95, Windows 98, or Windows NT Workstation 4.0, before upgrading to Windows 2000, then you might have backups of files made with backup utilities designed for one or more of those operating systems. If you find that you need to restore files from those backups, then you need to use the same backup utility. You should, therefore, keep copies of those backup and restore utilities in the event that you need them later. You will also have to find out if you can install and use that backup utility under Windows 2000. Consider using dual or multiple boot configurations that provide access to different operating systems and that use different partitions on your hard disk to support different file systems.

After reviewing and reevaluating your backup strategies and options with Isabel, you decide to implement a combination of backup strategies so you can restore important business files no matter what type of problem might arise. The skills and techniques you've learned for managing a hard disk are ones that are invaluable not only to the company or business where you work, but also for more efficiently managing and protecting your own computer system and the important files you work with every day.

Session 5.2 QUICK CHECK

1. The first backup performed during a backup cycle is called a(n) _____ backup.

2. A(n) _____ backup includes only those files that you created or changed since your previous backup–whether your previous backup was a normal backup or an incremental backup.

3. _____ backups always include all new and modified files since the last normal backup or last full backup.

4. Most backup utilities use the _____ attribute to determine which files to back up.

5. If you use the _____ switch with the _____ command, you can copy all the subdirectories and files within a directory to another disk and retain the same directory structure.

6. You can use the _____ command to view attributes of files.

7. If you use the _____ switch, the XCOPY command will copy only files with their Archive bit turned on, and then it will turn off the Archive attributes after the copy is complete.

8. A(n) _____ file is a program or document file whose contents have been altered as the result of hardware, software, or power problems.

9. A(n) _____ backup is a special type of Windows 2000 backup that copies all the files you select without affecting other types of backups that you perform during a backup cycle.

10. A(n) _____ backup is a special type of Windows 2000 backup that copies all selected files that have been created or modified on the day you perform the backup, without affecting other types of backups that you perform during a backup cycle.

COMMAND REFERENCE

COMMAND	USE	BASIC SYNTAX	EXAMPLE
ATTRIB	Displays, or changes, file attributes in a directory; when used with the Subdirectory switch (/S), displays or changes file attributes in all directories under the current directory	ATTRIB [/S]	attrib /s | more
DIR	Locates files in the directory structure of a disk	DIR filespec /S	dir sales* /s
DIR	Displays multiple files in the same directory	DIR filespec1 filespec2 etc.	dir *logo* *web* *basics*
DIR	Displays the contents of multiple directories	DIR directory1 directory2 etc.	dir Designs Training
MOVE	Renames a directory	MOVE directory new-directory-name	move Designs Templates
RD	Removes an empty directory when used without the /S switch; removes a directory and all its contents when used with the /S switch	RD [drive:][path]directory name [/S] RMDIR [drive:][path]directory name [/S]	rd Projections rd Projections /S
REN	Renames a directory	REN directory new-directory-name	ren Designs Templates
XCOPY	Copies a directory and all its subdirectories and files as well as the directory structure	XCOPY source destination /S	XCOPY SolarWinds a: /s
XCOPY	Copies all files with the Archive bit on, and then turns the Archive bit off	XCOPY source destination /M	XCOPY SolarWinds a: /m

Items shown in italics and *not* enclosed within square brackets are required parameters
Items shown in italics and enclosed within square brackets are optional parameters

REVIEW ASSIGNMENTS

Because you will be adding more files to the "Company Templates" directory, Isabel suggests you organize the files in this directory into subdirectories.

To complete the Review Assignments, you will need the reorganized diskette that you created in the first part of the tutorial, and you will need an additional diskette for backups. If you have completed the tutorial, you can reformat the diskette that you used for backups and reuse it in this assignment.

If you are working in a computer lab, you will also need to make sure you have permission to create a "SolarWinds Templates" subdirectory under the "My Documents" directory.

As you complete each step, record your answers to any questions so you can submit them with your lab assignment.

1. If necessary, open a Command Prompt window, set the default background color to white and the foreground color to black, and specify default switches for the DIRCMD variable.

2. Use DISKCOPY to make a duplicate copy of your reorganized Data Disk in case you need to start over.

3. Change the default drive to drive A, change to the "My Documents" directory, and then change to the "Company Templates" directory. What commands did you enter for these operations?

4. Create a "Cash Flow" directory. What command did you use?

5. Move "Client Invoices.xls" to the "Cash Flow" directory. What command did you use?

6. Move "Data Systems Budget.xls" to the "Cash Flow" directory and change its name to "Company Budget.xls". What command did you use for this operation?

7. Move "Savings Plan.xls" to the "Cash Flow" directory. What command did you use?

8. Using Figure 5-48 as a guideline, organize the remainder of the files in the "Company Templates" directory into the subdirectories shown in the figure.

9. Change the name of the Personnel directory to "Accounting". What command did you use?

10. Move the Accounting directory up one level to the "My Documents" directory. What command did you use?

11. Switch to the "My Documents" directory. What command did you use?

12. Remove the Training directory. What command did you use?

13. Display a directory tree of your disk. What command did you use?

14. Redirect the output of the directory tree to a file named "Reorganized Disk.txt" in the "My Documents" directory. What command did you use?

15. Change to the "My Documents" directory on your hard disk drive. What command did you use?

16. Create a directory named "SolarWinds Templates". What command did you use?

17. Copy the directory structure of the My Documents directory on your Data Disk and its files to the "SolarWinds Templates" directory. What command did you use?

18. Make a normal backup of the "SolarWinds Templates" directory, and all the files within this directory, to a directory named "SWT Normal Backup" on a formatted, but empty, diskette in drive A. Remember to turn off the Archive attribute during the copy operation. What command did you use?

19. Search the directory structure for the file named "Product Sales Projection.xls". What command did you use?

20. Copy "Product Sales Projection.xls" to the Projections directory. What command did you use?

21. Copy "Sales Summary #2.xls" in the Sales directory to "Sales Summary #3.xls" (in the same directory). What command did you use?

22. Make a differential backup of the "SolarWinds Templates" directory and all the files within this directory to a directory named "SWT Differential #1" on the same backup disk. What command did you use?

23. Display the directory tree of the "SolarWinds Templates" directory and redirect the output to a file named "SolarWinds Templates.txt" in the root directory of the backup disk. What commands did you use?

24. Submit your answers and copies of any requested files in the format requested by your instructor, either as a printout, on diskette, or by e-mail, along with any other requested documentation.

Figure 5-48	PROPOSED STRUCTURE FOR COMPANY TEMPLATES

```
Company Templates
    Cash Flow
        Client Invoices.xls
        Company Budget.xls
        Savings Plan.xls
    Personnel
        Commission on Sales.xls
        Salary Analysis.xls
    Portfolio
        Balance Sheet.xls
        Break Even Analysis.xls
        Loan Payment Analysis.xls
    Products
        Product List.xls
        Product Sales Projection.xls
        Software Quotes.xls
    Projections
        Advertising Income.xls
        Five Year Growth Plan.xls
        Five Year Plan Template.xls
        Regional Sales Projection.xls
        Sales Projection Models.xls
        Sales Projections.xls
        Three Year Sales Projection.xls
    Sales
        Daily Sales.xls
        Sales Summary #1.xls
        Sales Summary #2.xls
        Sales.wk4
```

CASE PROBLEMS

Case 1. *Organizing Client Record Files at Steppingstone Development Services* Office manager Angela Pinelli at Steppingstone Development Services asks you to arrange a set of data files for different staff members who specialize in particular software programs. She needs the files organized by the type of program appropriate for each file.

1. Make a new duplicate copy of Data Disk #2. If you have completed the tutorial, you can reuse the same diskette.

2. Starting with the file arrangement on Data Disk #2, produce a new directory folder arrangement on the diskette to organize the files by program. Explain why you selected your directory names and structure.

3. Specify which files and/or directories you removed, and explain why you removed them.

4. When you have completed the reorganization, create a file in the diskette's root directory containing the complete directory tree of the diskette.

5. Submit your answers and copies of any requested files in the format requested by your instructor, either as a printout, on diskette, or by e-mail, along with any other requested documentation.

Case 2. *Developing a Backup Strategy at Fast Track Trainers* Samantha Kuehl, Fast Track Trainer's corporate training specialist, wants to develop a backup strategy for quickly restoring her computer system and the files she develops for on-site training should she experience problems with her computer. She asks you to analyze the following factors, and develop a comprehensive backup strategy for her business.

- Samantha wants to restore her entire system in the event her drive C fails.

- On her drive C, she has created a directory called Training in which she stores all the information and files she needs to develop custom training for her company's clients.

- Within the Training directory, she organizes documents used for specific types of training sessions (such as Windows 2000, Office 2000, Word 2000, Excel 2000, PowerPoint 2000, and Access 2000) by subdirectory. Within each of these directories, she organizes files in separate subdirectories by the level of training ("Beginning Level", "Intermediate Level", and "Advanced Level").

- As she prepares for an upcoming training session, she works with the same set of files each day.

- Because technology is constantly changing, and because she updates these files for each training session, Samantha does not need to restore earlier versions of these files. Instead, she wants to keep backup copies of only the most recent versions of the files she develops for training.

Using the factors listed above, answer the following questions.

1. What type of backup strategy should Samantha use to ensure that she could restore her entire system and the most recent versions of her files in the Training folder?

2. Outline a backup strategy for Samantha in a table using the format shown in Figure 5-49.

3. Submit your answers and copies of any requested files in the format requested by your instructor, either as a printout, on diskette, or by e-mail, along with any other requested documentation.

BACKUP SCHEDULE	TYPE OF BACKUP	FILES INCLUDED IN THE BACKUP
Figure 5-49 — **BACKUP SCHEDULE FOR FAST TRACK TRAINERS**		
Start of Backup Cycle: Friday		
End of Day 1: Monday		
End of Day 2: Tuesday		
End of Day 3: Wednesday		
End of Day 4: Thursday		
Start of Next Backup Cycle: Friday		

Case 3. Developing a Backup Strategy for Turing Enterprises Melissa Turing, the proprietor of Turing Enterprises, wants to develop a backup strategy for reconstructing her business records should she experience problems with her computer. She asks you to analyze the following factors, and develop a comprehensive backup strategy for her business.

- Melissa wants to restore her entire system in the event her drive C fails.

- On her drive C, she has a directory for all her business records, and within that directory, she has organized her files by subdirectory. For example, she has subdirectories with her schedules for upcoming travel tours, outings, and other events; her business advertising; her customer mailing list; the vendors that provide equipment for outings; and the financial records for her business.

- Although Melissa is constantly updating her financial records, she needs to be able to restore earlier versions of other files, such as graphic designs and tour schedules, so that she can adapt them for use with new tour packages and outing events.

Using the factors listed above, answer the following questions.

1. What type of backup strategy should Melissa use so she can restore her computer system in the event of a problem and also be able to restore earlier versions of files?

2. Outline a backup strategy for Melissa in a table using the format shown in Figure 5-50.

3. Submit your answers and copies of any requested files in the format requested by your instructor, either as a printout, on diskette, or by e-mail, along with any other requested documentation.

BACKUP SCHEDULE	TYPE OF BACKUP	FILES INCLUDED IN THE BACKUP
Figure 5-50 — **BACKUP SCHEDULE FOR TURING ENTERPRISES**		
Start of Backup Cycle: Friday		
End of Day 1: Monday		
End of Day 2: Tuesday		
End of Day 3: Wednesday		
End of Day 4: Thursday		
Start of Next Backup Cycle: Friday		

Case 4. Evaluating the Organization of Directories on Your Computer's Hard Disk After completing a Windows 2000 course at your college, you decide that it's time to implement a new directory structure on your hard disk. Before taking this course, you stored new subdirectories below whatever directory you felt was appropriate at the time. You have taken this same approach with your document files and stored them in whatever directory seemed easiest at the time. Using the approach taken during the tutorial, you will first document and evaluate your existing directory structure, then you will develop a new directory structure for your document files only.

To complete this exercise, you will need to work on a computer that contains directories for document files.

1. Is the computer you are using one that contains only one volume (drive C), or is there more than one volume (such as drive C and drive D)? If your computer has multiple volumes, or if you use another computer's shared directories on a network, where do you store the directories with your document files?

2. Produce a directory tree of the first-level directory folder that contains your document files, and redirect the output to a file named "Directory Organization.txt".

3. Using the directory tree in the "Directory Organization.txt" file, or the screen output of the directory tree piped to the MORE filter, describe the organization of the directories for your document files. For example, are these directories under the root directory of drive C (or another drive), are they under one central directory such as the "My Documents" directory, are they under another computer's shared network directory, or do you use a combination of these approaches?

4. What factors led you to implement that directory structure for your document files? For example, do you group document files by project, file type, client, some other factor, or a combination of factors?

5. Based on what the tutorial covers, what changes would you make to the directory structure for your document files, and why?

6. If you implemented these changes, in what other ways would they affect your use of your computer? For example, what default settings would you have to change for the applications you use, or how would you change the way in which you perform your backups?

7. Submit your answers and copies of any requested files in the format requested by your instructor, either as a printout, on diskette, or by e-mail, along with any other requested documentation.

Quick | Check answers

Session 5.1

1. F or FALSE
2. T or TRUE
3. DIR, /AD
4. RD
5. RD, /S
6. REN, MOVE, or RENAME
7. F or FALSE
8. *.*
9. redirect
10. DIR, /S

Session 5.2

1. normal or full
2. incremental
3. differential
4. Archive
5. Subdirectory (or /S), XCOPY
6. ATTRIB
7. Modify (or /M)
8. corrupted
9. copy
10. daily

USING

TROUBLESHOOTING TOOLS

Troubleshooting Computer Systems at SolarWinds

In this tutorial you will:

- Develop a strategy for troubleshooting problems

- Examine the booting process and the importance of CMOS

- Use the Windows 2000 Advanced Options Menu to boot to a command prompt

- Create Windows 2000 Setup Disks

- Make an Emergency Repair Disk

- Examine the file systems supported by Windows 2000

- Use the Check Disk utility for analyzing and repairing disks

- Examine the installation and use of the Recovery Console

SolarWinds Unlimited

Now that the support staff at SolarWinds is more familiar with Windows 2000 and the use of commands in a Command Prompt window, Isabel Navarro Torres decides to present a workshop in the company training facility on how to troubleshoot computer problems. Isabel asks you to attend the workshop as part of your training to be an assistant network administrator.

In this session, you'll examine a strategy for troubleshooting computer problems, and examine the booting process and the importance of CMOS. You will restart your computer, open CMOS, check system settings, and then change your boot drive. After you save your changes, you will examine different options for booting your computer, and then boot your computer using the Safe Mode with Command Prompt boot option on the Windows 2000 Advanced Options menu. Then you will produce Windows 2000 Setup Disks and an Emergency Repair Disk.

Developing a Troubleshooting Strategy

At the beginning of her presentation, Isabel points out that you can troubleshoot problems by utilizing not only the tools and features in Windows 2000, but also by using your prior experience with previous versions of Windows and DOS. Isabel emphasizes that the ability to work within a command-line environment is especially important when you encounter problems with your computer. Although you may be able to troubleshoot many problems within the Windows 2000 graphical user interface, you will have to use a command-line interface if Windows 2000 does not boot properly or if your hard disk fails.

She suggests to the staff that they use the following strategy for troubleshooting problems:

- **Define the problem**. First, make sure you know the exact nature of the problem, so you can effectively focus your efforts and use your time wisely in troubleshooting and resolving the problem. For example, if a printer does not work properly, ask yourself and your coworkers questions that will provide the information you need to troubleshoot the problem. Can you print at all? If so, are there problems with the quality of the printed document? Did Windows 2000 display any error messages, and did these messages provide any useful information? When were you last able to print a document without any problems? Did you or someone else make changes to the configuration of the computer since then? Is this the first time you or anyone else in your office has encountered this particular problem?

- **Analyze the problem**. Next, analyze the problem by evaluating your answers to the previous questions. For example, if you change the configuration on your computer and find you are then unable to print, could the problem be caused by the change in configuration? Or is there a possibility of some other type of error, such as a loose cable, a hardware problem, or a change in a software setting?

- **Devise ways to test the possible cause of the problem**. To obtain more information about the nature of a problem, devise other tests to help you identify its cause. For example, if you are unable to print a document created in Microsoft Word 2000, open another program and try printing a document produced with that program. If you are now able to print, you can deduce that the problem is probably not with the printer, but rather with the print settings for the first program. If you cannot print in either program, then check Windows 2000's configuration settings for your printer. As a simple test, you could also redirect the output of a DIR command to the printer, as you did in Tutorial 2.

- **Check hardware and software settings**. If any hardware or software settings have been changed, restore them to their original values. To restore these settings, you will need to periodically document the hardware and software settings on your computer, especially before you install new hardware or software, or change settings to existing hardware and software. You can use Device Manager to print a summary of all the hardware settings on your computer. Print this information when your computer is functioning properly—don't wait until you have a problem. Bear in mind that this printed summary can take many pages.

- **Draw on all the resources you have to resolve the problem.** Check the Help information provided with your operating system and programs. This Help information might provide you with some ideas and direction, or it might even have special troubleshooting tools. Check Readme files provided with software and hardware that you install on your computer. A Readme file is a text file (often named Readme.txt or Readme.1st) that contains troubleshooting information or more up-to-date information on software and hardware than that found in the documentation provided with the software. Check any reference manuals provided with your hardware or software. If the manufacturer of the hardware or software you purchased has a technical support line, call and talk to a technical support person about the problem. That person might know the answer immediately, or might be able to replicate the problem and then determine how to resolve it. Many companies have their own Web sites where they provide assistance, publish answers to frequently asked questions (FAQs), and post updates (such as device drivers) that users can download. Microsoft's Support Online Web site (http://support.microsoft.com) is another valuable source for information on the Windows 2000 operating system.

- **Consider other alternatives.** If you attempt to troubleshoot a problem and cannot resolve it, consider other possible causes. For example, if you cannot print a document that you printed a few days ago, it's possible a computer virus might have infected your computer. Have you scanned your computer recently for viruses? Have you updated the virus definitions for your antivirus software recently? Did you disable, and then forget to enable, your antivirus software? Have you tried another antivirus software package, which might catch a virus the first one did not?

If your field of specialty is technical support and troubleshooting, you should implement a system for reporting problems that includes the following:

- **A database of problems and solutions to those problems.** You can create a database of problems that users already have encountered or are likely to encounter, identify the operating systems and programs to which the problems and solutions apply, include specific steps for resolving the problems, and also include precautions. You can design the database for yourself and other technical support staff, and prepare an online version for users so they can search for, and resolve, common problems that do not require major changes to the configuration of a computer.

- **Using the Registry:** If in your attempts to troubleshoot a problem you find that the Windows 2000 Registry requires modification, you will need to bring the situation to the attention of the network administrator. The **Registry** is a system database that consists of a set of files where Windows 2000 stores your computer's hardware, software, and security settings, as well as user settings or profiles, and property settings for folders and programs. Changing the Registry successfully requires experience, care, and skill. Windows 2000 allows you to modify the Registry only if you are a member of the Power Users or Administrators group. You will examine the Registry in more detail in Tutorial 9.

- **Online form for reporting problems.** Rather than relying on recording information via the telephone, you could create an online form for reporting problems, gathering all of the necessary information and detail you need on a problem, and standardizing the reporting process.

- **Remote control of user's screen.** You might also want to use a software tool, such as PC Anywhere or Microsoft's NetMeeting (which can be downloaded for free) to control the user's screen from a remote location, and troubleshoot the problem that the user is experiencing.

Isabel concludes her discussion of troubleshooting strategies by noting that operating systems are more complicated than ever, and because of this, users have to know more than ever and be more savvy than in the past to use and troubleshoot their operating system effectively.

The Booting Process

Isabel explains to the workshop participants that it's important to understand what happens when you boot your computer. If Windows 2000 detects a problem with a hardware device during the booting process, it might boot in a different operating mode, and you should know what to expect and what to do. Booting, she explains, is a complex process that proceeds in many different phases and involves many different components built into the Windows Operating system.

When you turn on an Intel-based computer system, the microprocessor locates and executes startup **routines**, or programs, stored in the **BIOS** (Basic Input/Output System) on a computer chip (called the ROM-BIOS) on the system board. These startup routines identify and enable devices, perform a Power-On Self-Test, and then locate and load the operating system. The BIOS also contains instructions for communicating with hardware devices.

The **Power-On Self-Test** (**POST**) checks for hardware errors, including memory errors, during booting. Although the way that some computers alert you to errors may vary, the standard approach is to emit a particular number of audible beeps. If you hear a single beep after the boot process, then the hardware components passed the POST. If the POST detects a problem or failure with a hardware component needed to boot the computer, your computer will emit a series of beeps to identify the nature of the first problem that the POST discovered. For example, if you hear one long and one short beep, then there is a problem with the system board, video display adapter, or power supply. The use of beeps is important, because the problem might reside with the video display adapter, and the POST may be unable to display a message on the screen, indicating the nature of the problem. If the video display adapter is functioning, the POST reports subsequent problems with an error code on the screen, and perhaps a brief message. For example, an error code of 100 through 199 would indicate a problem with the system board. Consult a reference manual to determine the problems identified by the series of beeps and the POST error codes. If POST reports a memory error, you might have a malfunctioning RAM chip and may need to replace it. If POST reports problems for other hardware components, such as the keyboard, first check the obvious—make sure all cables are properly attached—then boot the computer again.

After the POST, another startup routine checks the first boot device for the operating system software (the next section discusses this topic in detail). If drive A is set as the first boot device in CMOS (a computer chip that stores system settings and is pronounced "Sea Moss"), and if drive A contains a boot disk with operating system files, then the computer boots from that diskette and starts the process of loading the operating system software into memory. A **boot disk** is just a diskette that contains the core operating system files needed to start a computer from drive A. If drive A does not contain a diskette, the routine examines the next boot device specified in CMOS. If that boot device is the hard disk, this routine locates the operating system files on that drive, and then loads them into memory so the operating system can then manage the operation of the computer system. If you leave a diskette with document files (but no operating system files) in drive A by mistake (a common problem), and if drive A is the first boot device, you will see an error message as your system tries to boot from this diskette. If this occurs, you should remove that diskette from the drive, boot your computer to the desktop, and then check your computer for computer viruses, in case the diskette was infected.

Many computer systems are configured by the dealer so they attempt to boot first from the hard disk, rather than from drive A. When booting from the hard disk drive, the BIOS locates the **Master Boot Record** (**MBR**)—the first sector on the hard disk—and reads the MBR into memory. A **boot loader** program in the Master Boot Record locates the boot partition and then starts the process of loading the operating system. It loads NTLdr ("NT Loader," a hidden system file in the root directory of the boot drive), then NTLdr switches the microprocessor from real mode (DOS mode) to protected mode, which uses extended memory, and loads drivers for reading NTFS and FAT volumes. **Real mode** is an operating mode in which the microprocessor can address only 1 MB of memory. This mode was the native operating mode for the first PCs with 8088 and 8086 microprocessors. Because the DOS operating system operates within the first megabyte of memory, this mode is often called DOS mode. In contrast, **protected mode** is an operating mode in which the microprocessor can:

- Address more than 1 MB of memory
- Support the use of **virtual memory** (a technique for supplementing RAM by using unused storage space on a hard disk as memory)
- Provide memory protection features for programs (so one program does not attempt to use the memory space allocated to another program)
- Use 32-bit (rather than 16-bit) processing
- Support **multitasking** (the ability to open and use two or more programs at once)

If you search for NTLdr and other Windows 2000 system files, you will not find them, because they are hidden system files. Even if you choose the option for showing hidden files and folders in My Computer or Windows Explorer, Windows 2000 does not display NTLdr and certain other system files, unless you turn off the option to hide protected system files. As you've seen, however, if you open a Command Prompt window, and use the Directory command (DIR) with the Attribute switch (/AS) to display system files in the root directory (C:\), as shown in Figure 6-1, Windows 2000 will list those hidden system files.

| Figure 6-1 | VIEWING SYSTEM FILES IN THE ROOT DIRECTORY OF DRIVE C |

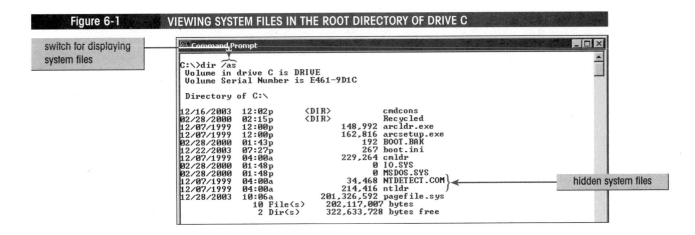

switch for displaying system files

hidden system files

NTLdr uses settings in Boot.ini (another hidden system file), shown in Figure 6-2, to boot your computer. The [boot loader] section of this file identifies the location of the default operating system to load, and the [operating systems] section identifies which operating systems are installed on the computer and available during the booting process. If Windows 2000 is the only operating system installed on your computer, the [operating systems] section will only list Windows 2000. On the computer used for Figure 6-2, two operating systems—Windows 2000 and the Recovery Console—are installed. You will examine the Recovery Console in more detail at the end of the tutorial. The pathname multi(0)disk(0)rdisk(0)partition(1)\WINNT identifies the location of the Windows 2000 system partition—the partition from which Windows 2000 boots—on an IDE disk. An **IDE (Integrated Drive Electronics)** disk is a commonly used PC hard disk interface that integrates controller electronics into the drive itself. A **controller** is a circuit board or card that controls a peripheral device. On the computer used for Figure 6-2, rdisk(0) refers to the first IDE controller on the hard disk drive, and partition(1) refers to the first partition number of the disk.

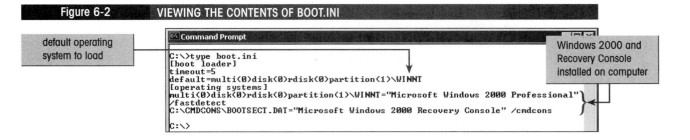

Figure 6-2   VIEWING THE CONTENTS OF BOOT.INI

default operating system to load

Windows 2000 and Recovery Console installed on computer

```
C:\>type boot.ini
[boot loader]
timeout=5
default=multi(0)disk(0)rdisk(0)partition(1)\WINNT
[operating systems]
multi(0)disk(0)rdisk(0)partition(1)\WINNT="Microsoft Windows 2000 Professional"
/fastdetect
C:\CMDCONS\BOOTSECT.DAT="Microsoft Windows 2000 Recovery Console" /cmdcons

C:\>
```

NTLdr loads and runs NTDetect.com (another hidden system file), which checks the hardware in the computer so Windows 2000 can configure the computer properly. Then, core components of the Windows 2000 operating system, such as the Windows 2000 kernel (ntoskrnl.exe) and Hardware Abstraction Layer (HAL.dll), are loaded into memory along with the device drivers for the hardware on the computer. A **device driver** is a file with program code that the operating system uses to communicate with, manage, and control the operation of a hardware or software component. These two system files are located in the System32 directory, which is within the WINNT directory (or whatever the SystemRoot directory is called, such as Windows). The **kernel** is the portion of the Windows 2000 operating system that resides in memory and provides services for programs. The **Hardware Abstraction Layer** (**HAL**) contains the machine-specific program code for a particular type of microprocessor. If you boot your computer and enable boot logging (covered later in the tutorial), Windows 2000 will produce a boot log, called NTBtLog.txt in the WINNT directory folder, which lists the boot operations. See Figure 6-3.

Figure 6-3   VIEWING THE CONTENTS OF NTBTLOG.TXT

loads Windows 2000 kernel and Hardware Abstraction Layer (HAL)

```
Microsoft (R) Windows 2000 (R) Version 5.0 (Build 2195)
12 14 2003 09:07:35.500
Loaded driver \WINNT\System32\ntoskrnl.exe
Loaded driver \WINNT\System32\hal.dll
Loaded driver \WINNT\System32\BOOTVID.DLL
Loaded driver ACPI.sys
Loaded driver \WINNT\System32\DRIVERS\WMILIB.SYS
Loaded driver pci.sys
Loaded driver isapnp.sys
Loaded driver intelide.sys
Loaded driver \WINNT\System32\DRIVERS\PCIIDEX.SYS
Loaded driver MountMgr.sys
Loaded driver ftdisk.sys
Loaded driver Diskperf.sys
Loaded driver dmload.sys
Loaded driver dmio.sys
Loaded driver PartMgr.sys
Loaded driver atapi.sys
Loaded driver disk.sys
Loaded driver \WINNT\System32\DRIVERS\CLASSPNP.SYS
Loaded driver Fastfat.sys
Loaded driver KSecDD.sys
Loaded driver NDIS.sys
Loaded driver Mup.sys
-- More
```

Now that you have a better understanding of the boot process, Isabel introduces a Key component you will use to control booting: CMOS.

The Importance of CMOS

Isabel and her staff have already configured the computers at SolarWinds so they automatically boot first from drive C. This change guarantees that an employee's computer system does not attempt to boot from a diskette that is accidentally left in drive A—a diskette that might contain a computer virus, which then could infect a computer system. If a problem develops and Windows 2000 does not start, you will need to know how to change this boot drive setting so you can then boot the computer from drive A. Then, if necessary, you can reinstall or repair Windows 2000. At the next workshop, Isabel shows you how to open CMOS and change this setting.

CMOS, which stands for **Complementary Metal Oxide Semiconductor**, refers to a special type of computer chip, or integrated circuit, that requires less power and, with the use of a battery backup, retains important computer settings after you turn off the power to your computer. CMOS contains settings that identify the types and specifications of your disk drives, the system date and time, password options, the boot sequence or boot order, power management settings, and a number of other settings. These settings are needed by the operating system whenever you power on your computer.

A rechargeable battery provides power to CMOS so it can retain settings. This battery usually loses its ability to hold a charge in five to seven years. When it does fail, your computer loses all of its CMOS settings, and you may not be able to boot your computer. Since the CMOS settings are very important, it's a good idea to know how to open and use CMOS and also how to print a copy of the settings on your computer.

To view and change the settings in CMOS, you must launch a built-in setup utility program during booting by pressing a specified key within the first few seconds after startup, such as Delete (or Del), F1, F2, or F10, or perhaps even a combination of keys, such as Ctrl+Alt+S. This CMOS setup program is not part of Windows 2000 or any other operating system; it is built in to your computer's circuitry. During booting, most systems will identify the key or keys to press for Setup on the initial startup screen. Some computers do not display the name of the key that starts the CMOS utility program, and you will have to check the computer's documentation. For example, many Compaq computers use the F10 function key, but do not display its name during startup. Other computers may require you to insert a special startup diskette into drive A before you restart in order to launch the CMOS utility program.

When you reboot your computer, pay attention to the information displayed on the monitor. Some computers display a full-screen graphic image on startup that hides the information on how to open CMOS; you may be able to clear the image by pressing the Esc key. See if you can locate and identify the key(s) you need to press to launch the Setup utility for CMOS. Most computers will display the name of the key (such as <DEL>) for just a few seconds before proceeding with the rest of the startup process, and you must press the key(s) at that point, before booting continues. Otherwise, you have to let Windows 2000 boot to the desktop, then restart Windows 2000 and try again.

When you open CMOS, you have to be extremely cautious. You do not want to change a setting accidentally that, in turn, might affect the performance of your computer system and, for instance, prevent your computer from even booting.

If you are working in a computer lab, your lab staff might password-protect CMOS so no one (including instructors) can access and change these settings. If you are working in a computer lab and CMOS is not password-protected, *do not perform the following steps without the permission of your instructor or technical support staff*. If you cannot open CMOS, or prefer not to until you are more familiar with how it is organized and what settings it contains, read (but do not keystroke) the following steps.

Read these three steps before you actually perform them, because you might not have enough time to read them and then check the screen at the same time. This information is displayed on the initial screen for only a moment.

To check the boot order in CMOS:

1. Close all open programs and windows.

2. From the Start menu, click **Shut Down**, select the **Restart** option button in the "What do you want the computer to do?" list box within the Shut Down Windows dialog box, and then click **OK**.

3. During rebooting, watch the screen for information on which key(s) to press, and then press the key(s) required to enter CMOS or BIOS Setup. For example, you might see the message, "Press <DEL> to enter Setup."

TROUBLE? If you see the Windows 2000 logo, wait for Windows 2000 to boot to the desktop. Restart your computer and try again. If you do not see a message on how to open the Setup utility, check your computer documentation for this information, or if that is not available or does not contain this information, try tapping Delete, F1, F2, or F10 in the first few seconds of the boot process.

Your view of CMOS will vary depending on the type of computer you use. Even computers with the same microprocessor might present a different view of CMOS because there are different companies that manufacture different types of CMOS chips. The opening, or first screen, that you see might contain a category of settings, or you might see a menu from which you can choose a category of settings. Figure 6-4 shows CMOS settings from a high-performance Pentium III computer, while Figure 6-5 shows CMOS settings from an older Pentium II MMX computer. Even though your system might display some of the same settings, the screen layout, menu options, and help information might vary.

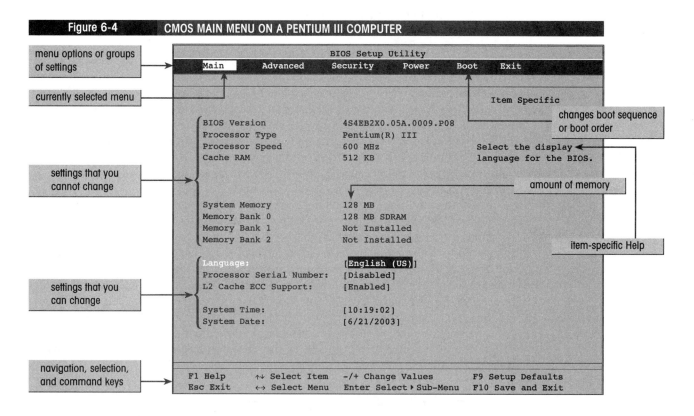

Figure 6-4   CMOS MAIN MENU ON A PENTIUM III COMPUTER

| **Figure 6-5** | **CMOS MAIN MENU ON A PENTIUM II COMPUTER** |

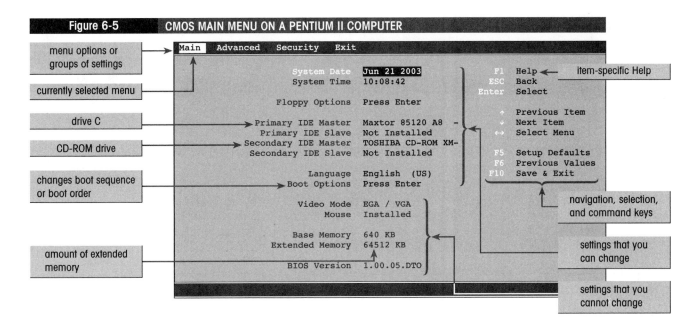

On the computer shown in Figure 6-4, the opening screen shows the BIOS version, processor type, processor speed, cache RAM, total system memory (128 MB of RAM), amount and type of system memory installed in each memory bank (or slot on the motherboard), the BIOS display language, processor serial time disabled, L2 Cache ECC support (an error-checking feature) enabled, the system time, and the system date. At the bottom of the opening screen, you will see information on how to get help, exit, select items and menus, change values, restore Setup defaults, and how to save and exit. Your options might vary from those shown in the figure. For example, your opening screen might show the format capacity and size of the diskette drive A as well as information about drive C, the CD-ROM disc drive, and the video system (EGA/VGA).

On the computer used for Figure 6-4, an area on the right displays item-specific Help. When you select an item from one of the BIOS Setup Utility Screens, the item-specific Help briefly describes that option. In this example, the Language option was automatically selected when CMOS was opened, so the Item Specific Help area explains that this option is used to "Select the display language for the BIOS." Settings shown within square brackets are ones you can select and change. Settings shown without square brackets, such as the processor type and speed in this figure, are ones you cannot change.

On the computer shown in Figure 6-5, CMOS displays information about drive C (usually identified as Primary IDE Master), the CD-ROM drive (usually identified as Secondary IDE Master), the amount of base (or system) memory (640 KB), and the amount of extended memory. All memory (or RAM) above 1 MB is **extended memory**. If your BIOS reports the amount of system memory (640 KB) and the amount of extended memory, then extended memory will be 1 MB less than you would expect because part of the first megabyte of RAM, which includes the 640KB base or system memory, is identified as a separate component of the total amount of memory. Early microprocessors were designed to access only one megabyte of memory (in real mode), and DOS worked only within the first 640KB of memory. This first 640KB of memory was known as **conventional memory**.

If you select the Boot menu on the computer in Figure 6-4, Setup will display the current boot order. As shown in Figure 6-6, there are five boot devices on the computer used for this figure and it can boot from one of these devices, in the order listed. In this example, the computer would first attempt to boot from a diskette in the diskette drive (drive A). If there is no boot disk in drive A, the computer would attempt to boot from the hard disk drive. If that failed, the computer would then attempt to boot from a CD disc in the CD-ROM drive. The number of boot devices available to you varies and depends on the type of computer.

Figure 6-6   **VIEWING THE BOOT ORDER**

currently selected menu

order of devices
checked during booting

```
                              BIOS Setup Utility
        Main      Advanced     Security     Power      Boot      Exit

                                                    Item Specific Help

        Boot-time Diagnostic Screen:   [Disabled]
        Quick Boot Mode:               [Enabled]
        Scan User Flash Area:          [Disabled]       Display the diagnostic
                                                        screen during boot

        AfterPowerFailure:             [Last State]
        On Modem Ring:                 [Power On]
        On LAN:                        [Power On]
        On PME:                        [Stay Off]

        First Boot Device              [Removable Devices]
        Second Boot Device             [Hard Drive]
        Third Boot Device              [ATAPI CD-ROM Driv]
        Fourth Boot Device             [Nework Boot]
        Fifth Boot Device              [MBA UNDI]

        System Time:                   [10:19:02]
        System Date:                   [6/21/2003]

        ▶ HardDrive
        ▶ RemovableDevices


      F1 Help          ↑↓ Select Item   -/+ Change Values    F9 Setup Defaults
      Esc Exit         ↔  Select Menu    Enter Select ▶ Sub-Menu  F10 Save and Exit
```

In the past, PCs were typically configured so the system would first check drive A, and then drive C. If drive A did not contain a diskette, the computer checked drive C for the operating system and booted from drive C. If drive A contained a boot disk, the computer booted from that diskette, and drive C was not checked. If drive A contained a diskette that was not a boot disk (such as a data diskette), then the bootstrap loader program in the boot record displayed an error message, such as "Non-system disk or disk error" or "Invalid system disk."

Today, computers are typically configured so they check drive C first, and then drive A. If there are no problems with drive C, the computer boots from that drive and loads the operating system. If the computer cannot boot from drive C, it will check drive A. If drive A contains a boot disk, the computer boots from that diskette. If drive A contains a diskette that is not a boot disk (such as a data diskette), the bootstrap loader program in the boot record displays an error message.

If you encounter problems starting Windows 2000, you can use a set of diskettes called Windows 2000 Setup Disks (which you will examine later in the tutorial) that allows your computer to boot from drive A so you can reinstall Windows 2000 from your Windows 2000 CD, or repair your installed version of Windows 2000. Before you can test and use these diskettes, you have to change the boot order on your computer.

To change the order of the boot devices, select the option for the first boot device, and use the minus sign (–) or positive sign (+) keys on the numeric keypad to alternate through all possible options. In the case of the computer shown in Figure 6-6, pressing these keys moves an option up or down in the list of boot devices.

After you check and, if necessary, change the settings for the boot order, exit CMOS. You also will have the option of saving your changes before you exit CMOS. How you exit varies. You might see an Exit option, as shown in Figure 6-7 (yours may differ), where you can choose from a variety of options for exiting—such as "Exit Saving Changes" and "Exit Discarding Changes." Or, you can press the Esc key until you see a dialog box that asks you to confirm that you want to discard any configuration changes you might have made and then exit. If you intentionally change the boot order, you need to save the new settings and exit so your system uses them as it continues to boot.

Figure 6-7   **OPTIONS FOR EXITING CMOS**

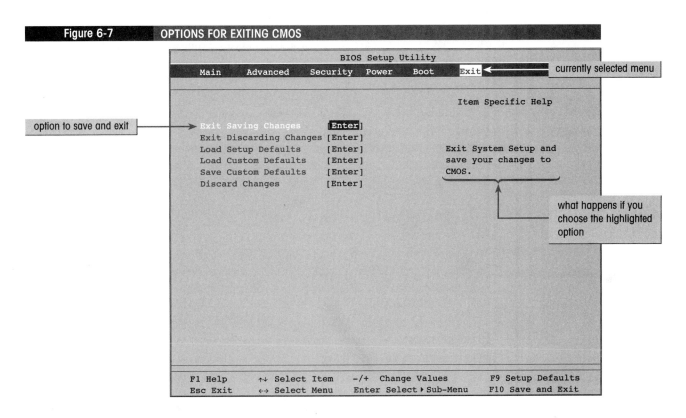

CMOS will also have an option for loading default Setup settings in case you want to restore the original settings in CMOS.

To view and change the boot sequence:

1. Locate the CMOS menu, category, or screen that contains information on the boot sequence on the computer you are using.

2. If you are connected directly to a local printer (not a network printer), press the **Print Scrn** key to dump the image of the screen with your boot settings and send it to the printer. You might also need to use the Form Feed button on the printer to advance the sheet of paper through the printer. If you are not directly connected to a printer, or did not print a copy of your boot settings in CMOS in the previous step, manually record the boot sequence on paper so you can restore it at the end of the tutorial. It is a good idea to save a hard copy for your permanent records as well.

3. If you want to change the boot order, change the boot options in CMOS so your computer boots first from drive A and then from drive C. If necessary, ask your instructor or the technical support staff for assistance.

4. If you did not make any changes to CMOS, or want to exit without saving changes, choose the option to exit without saving or the option to exit and discard changes. If you changed CMOS setting, and want to use those settings, choose the option to exit and save your changes. If necessary, ask your instructor or the technical support staff for assistance.

Because CMOS settings are so important and because they affect the performance of your computer, you should check the materials that came with your computer to see if they contain any information on the options available in CMOS on your computer. You can also search the Web for sites that contain information on CMOS settings and on troubleshooting problems using CMOS.

REFERENCE WINDOW   RW

Changing the Boot Sequence in CMOS

■ If you have already started Windows 2000 and booted to the desktop, close all open programs and windows and then restart Windows 2000.

■ During booting, watch the screen for information on which key(s) to press to enter Setup or BIOS Setup (which goes by different names), and then press the key or keys shown on the screen. For example, you might see the message, "Press F2 to enter Setup."

■ Select the Boot menu (not necessarily the same as Boot Options), and change the boot sequence to the order you want to use.

■ If you are connected directly to a local printer (not a network printer) and want to print a copy of your CMOS settings, press the Print Scrn key, and then use the Form Feed button on your printer to advance the sheet of paper through the printer. If you are connected to a network printer, or decide not to print the CMOS boot settings, manually record the boot sequence on paper so you can restore it later as needed.

■ Select the Exit option, and then choose the option that allows you to save your changes and exit CMOS.

Familiarity with your CMOS settings and how they affect your computer's operation will prove useful when you need to check or change settings, troubleshoot problems, or reconfigure your computer for new hardware.

Windows 2000 Booting Options

Isabel emphasizes that Windows 2000, like its Windows NT predecessors, is a stable operating system and you are not likely to experience problems booting your computer. However, if Windows 2000 cannot boot to the desktop, or if Windows 2000 reports a problem during the boot process, then you can try to boot the computer by using the Windows 2000 Advanced Options Menu.

This menu, shown in Figure 6-8, contains a list of booting options, and provides alternate approaches for booting your computer. To display the Windows 2000 Advanced Options Menu, press the F8 function key when you see the Starting Windows screen as your computer boots. The options available on this menu depend on the configuration of your computer.

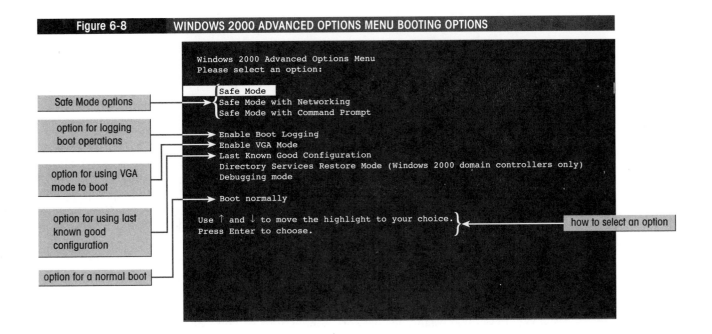

Figure 6-8 | **WINDOWS 2000 ADVANCED OPTIONS MENU BOOTING OPTIONS**

Boot Normally, Enable Boot Logging, and Last Known Good Configuration Options

The **Boot Normally** option on the Windows 2000 Advanced Options Menu is the default boot option. If you choose this option, Windows 2000 performs a full boot. The **Enable Boot Logging** option is identical to the Boot Normally option, except that Windows 2000 creates or updates a special startup log called NTBtLog.txt in the WINNT directory during booting (shown in Figure 6-3), and records all the device drivers and services that it loads (or fails to load). A **service** is a program, routine, or process that provides support to other programs. By examining the drivers and services that failed to load, you might be able to identify the exact cause of a problem and also eliminate possible causes of the problem you're experiencing. The **Last Known Good Configuration** booting option starts Windows 2000 using the configuration saved by the operating system from the last successful boot. Since this booting option restores the Registry to the last set of configuration settings saved during the last shutdown, you could lose any recent changes you made to the configuration of your computer. You would use the Last Known Good Configuration option only if you discover that your computer is not properly configured. This booting option, however, does not resolve problems caused by missing or damaged drivers or system files.

Using Safe Mode

The Safe Mode option starts Windows 2000 but loads only the minimum set of files and drivers—those for the mouse, monitor, keyboard, mass storage, and video as well as default system services. This basic set of drivers will often get your computer up and running, so you can then attempt to troubleshoot the source of the problem or problems you were experiencing. For example, you might use Safe Mode to troubleshoot an upgrade to Windows 2000 or change settings for newly installed software (or remove the software); then restart your computer to see if it boots in Normal mode. If the problem that caused you to choose the Safe Mode booting option does not appear in Safe Mode, then the basic device drivers and settings loaded by Windows 2000 during Safe Mode are not the source of the problem. Rather, the problem is more likely to lie with a new device that you've added to your computer or with a change in device drivers for a hardware component.

Microsoft recommends that you boot your computer using Safe Mode if:

- You installed new software or device drivers, and your computer will not boot in Boot Normally mode
- Hardware components, such as the video display, do not work properly
- Windows 2000 stalls for an extended period of time during the booting process
- Windows 2000 does not perform reliably and predictably

After rebooting in Safe Mode, first try restarting Windows 2000 in Normal Mode, to determine if the operating system can rebuild damaged files and reconfigure itself. If your computer will not start in Safe Mode, you might need to use an Emergency Repair Disk (ERD), which you will make later in this tutorial, to repair Windows 2000. If the ERD does not resolve the problem, you will need to reinstall Windows 2000 with the Windows 2000 Setup Disks.

When you boot your computer in Safe Mode, you might not have access to all of the hardware devices on your computer. Also, if your computer is on a network, you do not have access to the network and cannot browse the network.

The Safe Mode with Networking option is similar to the Safe Mode option, except that Windows 2000 establishes network connections so you can troubleshoot a problem that requires network access. The Safe Mode with Command Prompt option is similar to Safe Mode, but Windows 2000 boots to a command prompt (C:\>), instead of booting to the desktop, so you can use a command-line operating environment to troubleshoot system problems. If you are connected to a network, this option will not load network drivers. The Safe Mode with Command Prompt option is useful when the Safe Mode option does not work, or if you prefer to work from a command prompt.

The Enable VGA Mode starts Windows 2000 with the basic VGA device driver. All of the Safe Mode options use the same basic VGA video driver but change other drivers as well. If you install a new device driver for your video card, or if a problem develops with your current video display driver, and you discover that Windows 2000 will not start properly, then you can start your computer with the Enable VGA Mode booting option, to troubleshoot the problem. The currently installed video driver might be corrupt or incompatible. If Windows 2000 then works properly in Enable VGA Mode, you have isolated the video driver as the source of the problem, and you might need to change or update the video device driver.

So you can become familiar with how to work in Safe Mode with Command Prompt, you will now restart your computer and boot in that mode. When you reboot your computer, you will need to press the F8 key when you see the Starting Windows screen with the progress indicator. If you miss this step, Windows 2000 will boot to the desktop. Also, when you switch from one operating mode to another, Windows 2000 boots more slowly, so be patient.

To boot in Safe Mode with Command Prompt:

1. Open the Start menu and choose the option to restart your computer.

2. When you see a menu that asks you to select an operating system, choose "Windows 2000 Professional."

3. Wait until you see the Starting Windows screen (the one with the progress indicator moving along the bottom of the screen), then press the **F8** key. You will then see the Windows 2000 Advanced Options Menu. Safe Mode, the first option, will be highlighted.

   TROUBLE? If you miss the Starting Windows screen, let Windows 2000 boot to the desktop, then repeat Steps 1 and 2.

4. Press ↓ twice to highlight the "Safe Mode with Command Prompt" option, press **Enter**, and be patient as Windows 2000 boots in this mode because it's very slow. You will see a Please Wait dialog box informing you that Windows 2000 is starting up. At each corner of the screen, you will also see the label "Safe Mode." Your computer will boot more slowly when you select Safe Mode with Command Prompt (or just Safe Mode). Even though you may think something is wrong, be patient. After a much longer interval of time than seems reasonable, Windows 2000 displays a Log On to Windows dialog box.

TROUBLE? If you are unable to boot successfully to Safe Mode with Command Prompt, boot to the desktop, log on to your computer, open a Command Prompt window, and then keystroke the steps in the remainder of this session in a Command Prompt window.

5. If necessary, log on to your computer. Windows 2000 then displays a Command Prompt window similar to the one you can access from the desktop. See Figure 6-9. Notice that the title bar informs you that the program cmd.exe is currently open and running.

Figure 6-9	SAFE MODE WITH COMMAND PROMPT WINDOW

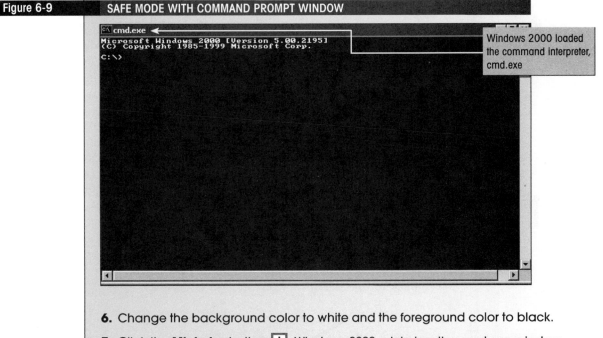

```
cmd.exe
Microsoft Windows 2000 [Version 5.00.2195]
(C) Copyright 1985-1999 Microsoft Corp.
C:\>
```

Windows 2000 loaded the command interpreter, cmd.exe

6. Change the background color to white and the foreground color to black.

7. Click the **Minimize** button ⊞. Windows 2000 minimizes the cmd.exe window, and now you can see "Safe Mode" displayed in three corners of the screen. See Figure 6-10.

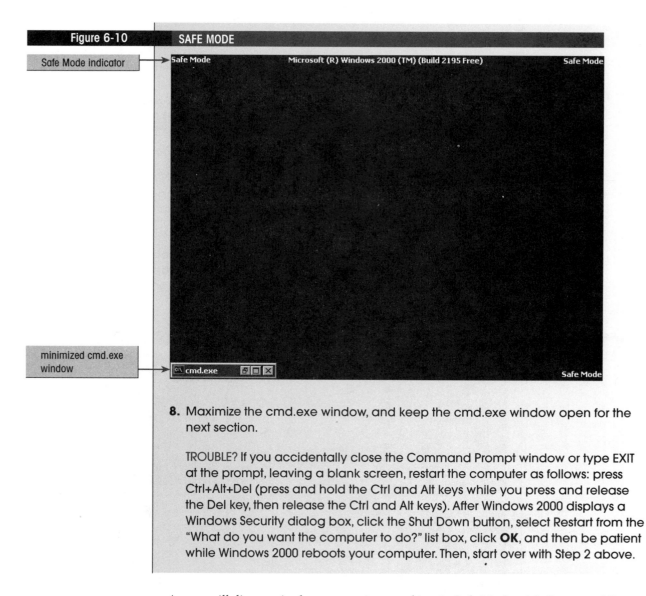

Figure 6-10   SAFE MODE

Safe Mode indicator

minimized cmd.exe window

8. Maximize the cmd.exe window, and keep the cmd.exe window open for the next section.

TROUBLE? If you accidentally close the Command Prompt window or type EXIT at the prompt, leaving a blank screen, restart the computer as follows: press Ctrl+Alt+Del (press and hold the Ctrl and Alt keys while you press and release the Del key, then release the Ctrl and Alt keys). After Windows 2000 displays a Windows Security dialog box, click the Shut Down button, select Restart from the "What do you want the computer to do?" list box, click **OK**, and then be patient while Windows 2000 reboots your computer. Then, start over with Step 2 above.

As you will discover in the next section, working in Safe Mode with Command Prompt is very similar to working in a Command Prompt window.

REFERENCE   WINDOW   **RW**

Booting in Safe Mode with Command Prompt
- If you want to troubleshoot a problem with your computer, close all open dialog boxes, programs, and windows, and try a simple reboot first.
- If a simple boot does not resolve the problem, then choose the option for restarting your computer again.
- When you see the Starting Windows screen during booting, press the F8 key.
- From the Windows 2000 Advanced Options Menu, choose the Safe Mode, or Safe Mode with Command Prompt option, and then press **Enter**.
- If necessary, log on to the computer under your user name.
- In Safe Mode with Command Prompt, you can enter commands in the cmd.exe window, or open programs and files in the graphical user interface from the command prompt, and then troubleshoot problems. Once you correct the problem, press Ctrl+Alt+Del (press and hold the Ctrl and Alt keys while you press and release the Del key, then release the Ctrl and Alt keys). After Windows 2000 displays a Windows Security dialog box, click the Shut Down button, select Restart from the "What do you want the computer to do?" list box, click **OK**, and then be patient while Windows 2000 reboots your computer.
- If necessary, log on to your computer.

If you boot your computer using the Safe Mode with Command Prompt option, you can then use internal and external commands to perform all operations you are able to perform in a Command Prompt window from the normal desktop. You can even open programs and files in the graphical user interface by starting the programs from the command prompt. For instance, you can type "NOTEPAD" to use the Windows Notepad editor, or type "NTBACKUP" to launch the Microsoft Windows Backup program. You can also launch other programs after changing to the program file's directory. For example, if you had WinZip installed, you could launch it by changing to the C:\Program Files\WinZip directory and then entering "WINZIP32".

Making Windows 2000 Setup Disks from the Command Prompt

Next, Isabel emphasizes that the support staff should make sure they have at least one set of the Windows 2000 Setup Disks so they can reinstall or repair Windows 2000 on any computer if the need should arise.

To make the Windows 2000 Setup Disks, you run a program called MakeBoot.exe in the BootDisk folder on your Windows 2000 CD. This program prepares four Setup diskettes that allow you to boot your computer from drive A and install Windows 2000 or repair your computer by restoring Windows 2000 settings. If your computer has more than one diskette drive, you must make the Setup diskettes using drive A. You cannot use drive B because the BIOS (Basic Input/Output) routine that looks for the operating system files during the booting process checks drive A and drive C—not drive B—for a boot disk.

After performing a full, or normal boot, you can make the Windows 2000 Setup Disks from the desktop either by using the Run option from the Start menu and entering the full path to MakeBoot.exe, or by double-clicking on the program file from a Windows Explorer or My Computer window. You can also make them in a standard Command Prompt window, or after booting with the Safe Mode with Command Prompt option. If Windows 2000 will not start properly, and you do not already have these diskettes, you will need to know how to make them from a command-line environment.

To create Windows 2000 Setup Disks, you will need your Windows 2000 CD disk, and four blank, formatted diskettes. The Windows 2000 CD contains a directory called BOOTDISK that contains the MAKEBOOT.EXE program used to prepare the Windows 2000 Setup Disks. Obviously, you will also need to know the name of the CD-ROM drive on the computer you are using. If you do not have access to a Windows 2000 CD disk, read, but do not keystroke, the following steps and examine the figures.

To make Windows 2000 Setup Disks:

1. Format each of the four diskettes. If a diskette contains defective sectors, do not use it as a Windows 2000 Setup Disk. A diskette with defective sectors could prove unreliable, and you need a reliable set of diskettes. After Windows 2000 formats the diskettes, you can display a directory of each diskette. If the Directory command reports that there is used space on a diskette, then that diskette contains defective sectors. You can also use the Check Disk utility (which you will examine later in the tutorial) to check for defective sectors on a newly formatted diskette.

2. Label the diskettes Windows 2000 Setup Disk #1, Windows 2000 Setup Disk #2, Windows 2000 Setup Disk #3, and Windows 2000 Setup Disk #4, and add the current date to each label.

3. Insert the Windows 2000 Setup Disk #1 in drive A, and then insert the Windows 2000 CD into the CD drive.

   TROUBLE? If an "Install Program As Other User" dialog box appears, accept the first selection, "Run the program as *computername/username* (where *computername* is the name of your computer and *username* is your user logon name) and click OK.

   TROUBLE? If a "Microsoft Windows 2000 CD" dialog box appears, close it and proceed to the next step.

4. To change to your CD-ROM drive, enter: **d:** (make sure you use the correct drive name for your CD drive –"D" in this case).

5. Enter: **cd bootdisk**

   The Change Directory command changes to the BOOTDISK directory.

6. Enter: **makeboot a:**

   The MakeBoot program explains that this program creates the Setup boot diskettes for Windows 2000, informs you that you will need four blank, formatted, high-density diskettes, and then prompts you to insert the first of these diskettes into drive A. See Figure 6-11.

| Figure 6-11 | STARTING THE PROGRAM FOR MAKING WINDOWS 2000 SETUP DISKS |

change to
CD-ROM drive

command for making
Windows 2000 Setup
Disks using drive A

change to bootdisk
subdirectory

what you need

what to do

```
cmd.exe - makeboot a:                                        _ □ X

C:\>d:

D:\>cd bootdisk

D:\BOOTDISK>makeboot a:

***********************************************************
This program creates the Setup boot disks
for Microsoft Windows 2000.
To create these disks, you need to provide 4 blank,
formatted, high-density disks.

Insert one of these disks into drive a:.  This disk
will become the Windows 2000 Setup Boot Disk.
Press any key when you are ready.
```

> TROUBLE? If you forget to specify drive A, the program for making these Setup Disks will prompt you for the drive in the Command Prompt window. Type A and then press Enter.

> TROUBLE? If Windows 2000 reports that "d:\bootdisk is not accessible," and that the folder was moved or renamed, you did not use the correct drive name for your CD drive. Repeat this step again using the correct drive name.

7. Press the **Spacebar**. The MakeBoot program will show the percentage complete and, after it prepares the first Setup diskette, it will prompt you to insert the next diskette into drive A.

8. When you see the prompt for the next diskette, as a precaution you should check the drive A light indicator (if you have one; some laptop computers have their drive A light somewhere other than on or near the drive), and when the indicator shows that Windows 2000 is no longer accessing the diskette, remove the Windows 2000 Setup Disk #1 and insert the Windows 2000 Setup Disk #2, and then press the **Spacebar** to continue.

9. Repeat this process for the Windows 2000 Setup Disk #3 and Windows 2000 Setup Disk #4. After preparing the last setup diskette, the MakeBoot program informs you that it successfully created the setup boot diskettes. See Figure 6-12.

Figure 6-12	MAKING WINDOWS 2000 SETUP DISKS

Windows 2000 Setup Disks successfully created

```
cmd.exe
D:\>cd bootdisk

D:\BOOTDISK>makeboot a:

**********************************************************
This program creates the Setup boot disks
for Microsoft Windows 2000.
To create these disks, you need to provide 4 blank,
formatted, high-density disks.

Insert one of these disks into drive a:.  This disk
will become the Windows 2000 Setup Boot Disk.
Press any key when you are ready.
   100% complete.

Insert another disk into drive a:.  This disk will
become the Windows 2000 Setup Disk #2.
Press any key when you are ready.
   100% complete.

Insert another disk into drive a:.  This disk will
become the Windows 2000 Setup Disk #3.
Press any key when you are ready.
   100% complete.

Insert another disk into drive a:.  This disk will
become the Windows 2000 Setup Disk #4.
Press any key when you are ready.
   100% complete.

The setup boot disks have been created successfully.
**********************************************************

D:\BOOTDISK> _
```

You can create these Windows 2000 Setup Disks from the Windows 2000 CD on any other computer that runs any version of DOS or Windows.

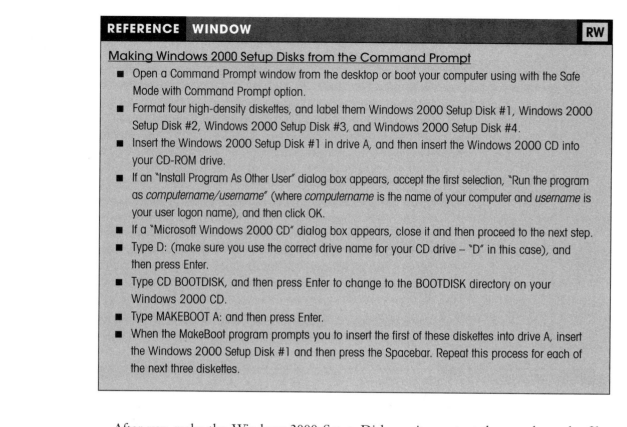

REFERENCE WINDOW [RW]

<u>Making Windows 2000 Setup Disks from the Command Prompt</u>

- Open a Command Prompt window from the desktop or boot your computer using with the Safe Mode with Command Prompt option.
- Format four high-density diskettes, and label them Windows 2000 Setup Disk #1, Windows 2000 Setup Disk #2, Windows 2000 Setup Disk #3, and Windows 2000 Setup Disk #4.
- Insert the Windows 2000 Setup Disk #1 in drive A, and then insert the Windows 2000 CD into your CD-ROM drive.
- If an "Install Program As Other User" dialog box appears, accept the first selection, "Run the program as *computername/username*" (where *computername* is the name of your computer and *username* is your user logon name), and then click OK.
- If a "Microsoft Windows 2000 CD" dialog box appears, close it and then proceed to the next step.
- Type D: (make sure you use the correct drive name for your CD drive – "D" in this case), and then press Enter.
- Type CD BOOTDISK, and then press Enter to change to the BOOTDISK directory on your Windows 2000 CD.
- Type MAKEBOOT A: and then press Enter.
- When the MakeBoot program prompts you to insert the first of these diskettes into drive A, insert the Windows 2000 Setup Disk #1 and then press the Spacebar. Repeat this process for each of the next three diskettes.

After you make the Windows 2000 Setup Disks, write-protect them to keep the files from being overwritten and to guard against a computer virus infecting any of the diskettes.

To view the contents of the first setup diskette:

1. Insert the Windows 2000 Setup Disk #1 into drive A.

2. Clear the window, and then enter: `dir a: /o /a`

The dates in the directory listing are the original dates assigned to the operating system files in your release of Windows 2000.

Figure 6-13 | **VIEWING THE CONTENTS OF WINDOWS SETUP DISK #1**

```
cmd.exe                                                                    _ 回 ×
D:\BOOTDISK>dir a: /o /a
 Volume in drive A is W2PEUB1_EN
 Volume Serial Number is 27B4-1985

 Directory of A:\
                                                                   disk ID file
12/07/1999  12:00p            20,949 BIOSINFO.INF
12/07/1999  12:00p                 3 DISK101
12/07/1999  12:00p            34,468 NTDETECT.COM              hardware detection
12/07/1999  12:00p           717,749 NTKRNLMP.EX_              program
12/07/1999  12:00p           229,264 SETUPLDR.BIN
12/07/1999  12:00p           356,925 TXTSETUP.SIF
               6 File(s)    1,359,358 bytes
               0 Dir(s)        96,768 bytes free
```

As shown in Figure 6-13, the Windows 2000 Setup Disk #1 contains the following files:

- **BIOSINFO.INF** is a setup information file that contains information about using Setup for this version of Windows 2000 with different BIOSs. **Setup information files** with the "inf" file extension contain information for configuring hardware devices or software.

- **DISK101** is a file that identifies the diskette number in the current set.

- **NTDETECT.COM** is a system program file that checks your computer's hardware during booting so that Windows 2000 can configure and manage that hardware. The "com" file extension stands for "command" and indicates a small executable program.

- **NTKRNLMP.EX_** is a compressed program file that provides support for (multiprocessors) or computers with more than one microprocessor. The extension "ex_" signifies a compressed executable program.

- **SETUPLDR.BIN** is the operating system file that loads Windows 2000 Setup. "Bin" means a binary file, usually containing additional program instructions.

- **TXTSETUP.SIF** contains detailed information on installing Windows 2000 and providing support for hardware devices, such as the keyboard and mouse. It is used during device detection and has information on the power management capabilities of devices, that is, the extent to which the computer can turn devices on and off to conserve electricity. The extension "sif" stands for Setup Information File.

If you examine the other three setup diskettes, you will find that they contain primarily compressed files in which the last letter of the filename extension is replaced with an underscore (_). A **compressed file** is a copy of a file whose size has been reduced using an algorithm, or special formula. When you use a utility program to uncompress this file, you create a new copy of the original file. You can use the EXTRACT utility to uncompress compressed files whose extension ends with an underscore. When you use the setup disks, the setup program uncompresses the files automatically. These compressed files include dynamic link libraries (with the "dl_" extension, which becomes "dll" when uncompressed), compressed device drivers (with the "sy_" extension, which is then changed to become "sys"), and compressed language support files (with the "nl_" extension, which is then changed to "nls"). As noted earlier, a dynamic link library is a file with executable program code that provides support to one or more software programs and has the file extension "dll."

Should the occasion arise when you need to use these setup diskettes, insert the Windows 2000 Setup Disk #1 in drive A, and then choose the option to restart Windows 2000. If your computer is set up to boot from drive A rather than drive C, you will first see a message informing you that Setup is inspecting your computer's configuration. Then, you will see a Windows 2000 Setup screen similar to the one shown in Figure 6-14. On the status bar at the bottom of the screen, Setup displays information on which Windows 2000 components are being loaded. After loading components from the first setup diskette, the Setup program prompts you for each of the next diskettes and loads device drivers and other Windows 2000 components, including support for FAT, NTFS, and CDFS (the CD file system). Then, you can install Windows 2000 or repair your computer.

If, on the other hand, your computer is set up to boot from drive C first, you'll need to change the CMOS setting so that it boots first from drive A or from the CD-ROM drive.

Figure 6-14   BOOTING WITH THE WINDOWS 2000 SETUP DISK #1

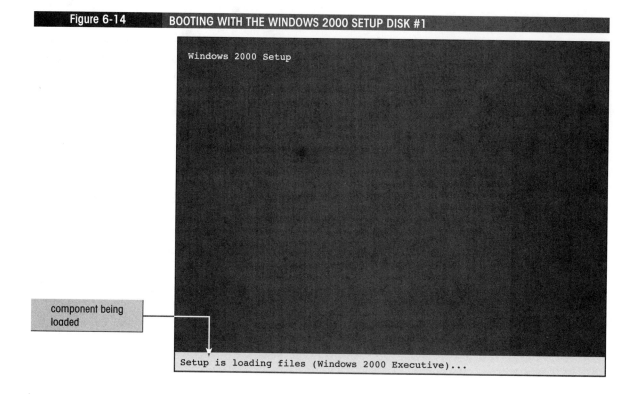

component being
loaded

You might want to make a second set of the Windows 2000 Setup Disks in case you experience a problem with one of the diskettes in the other copy. If you upgrade Windows 2000, you should make new copies of the Windows 2000 Setup Disks.

Making an Emergency Repair Disk

In addition to having a copy of the Windows 2000 Setup Disks, Isabel also emphasizes the importance of having an Emergency Repair Disk to restore system settings and repair a computer should the need arise.

The Emergency Repair Disk (ERD) is a diskette you create with the Backup utility to store information about your Windows 2000 system settings and system files. You can use this diskette to repair problems with system files (such as damaged or missing files), your startup environment for dual-boot or multiple-boot systems, and the partition boot sector on your boot volume. **System files** are files that Windows 2000 uses to load, configure, and run the operating system. The **startup environment** consists of configuration settings that specify which operating systems to start and how to start each one. A **dual-boot system** is a computer configuration for starting two different operating systems (such as Windows 2000 or MS-DOS), while a **multiple-boot system** is a computer configuration with more than two operating systems. Windows 2000 supports multiple booting with Windows NT 4.0, Windows NT 3.51, Windows 98, Windows 95, Windows 3.1, and MS-DOS. The **partition boot sector** contains information about a partition's file system structure and a program for loading the Windows 2000 system files.

It is also important to note that the ERD program in Windows 2000 is different from the Emergency Repair Disk and Emergency Recovery Disk programs found in earlier versions of Windows, although each process produces a troubleshooting diskette. The original version of Windows 95 and Windows 95a included a program called Erd.exe for making an Emergency Recovery Disk (ERD), (note that the second word here is "recovery" rather than "repair"); however, Windows 95b, Windows 95c, and Windows 98 do not include that same program and do not support its use. All versions of Windows 95 and Windows 98 provide an option for making a boot disk called Startup Disk that contains troubleshooting components, which allows you to boot your computer from drive A and, in the case of the Windows 98 Startup Disk, also to access the CD-ROM drive. Windows NT 4.0 and earlier versions of Windows NT included a program called Rdisk.exe for making an Emergency Repair Disk (ERD). That program is not included in Windows 2000.

To complete the following steps, you will need another formatted, but empty, diskette.

To create an Emergency Repair Disk:

1. If necessary, format another diskette in drive A. If the diskette contains defective sectors, do not use the diskette as an Emergency Repair Disk, because you need a reliable diskette, and a diskette with defective sectors is less reliable than one without any.

2. Enter: `ntbackup`

   NTBackup displays a "Removable Storage Not Running" dialog box, and explains that it cannot connect to the Removable Storage service (which is required for using tape drives and other backup devices).

3. Press **Enter**. On the Welcome sheet of the Backup window, there is an option for creating an Emergency Repair Disk. See Figure 6-15. Note that this option is used to repair and restart Windows if it is damaged. It does not back up your files or programs, and is not a replacement for regular backups of your computer system.

Figure 6-15	MAKING AN EMERGENCY REPAIR DISK

click this button to make an Emergency Repair Disk

explanation of the Emergency Repair Disk option

4. Click the **Emergency Repair Disk** button. Backup displays an Emergency Repair Diskette dialog box, prompting for a formatted diskette in drive A. See Figure 6-16. You also have the option of backing up the Windows 2000 Registry to the Repair directory. This option is not automatically selected, because it restores the original version of the Windows 2000 Registry, or, if you have backed up the Registry, it restores the previous copy rather than repairing the current version of the Registry. It is a good idea, however, to make a new backup copy of the Registry periodically in case you ever need it.

Figure 6-16	OPTION FOR BACKING UP THE WINDOWS 2000 REGISTRY

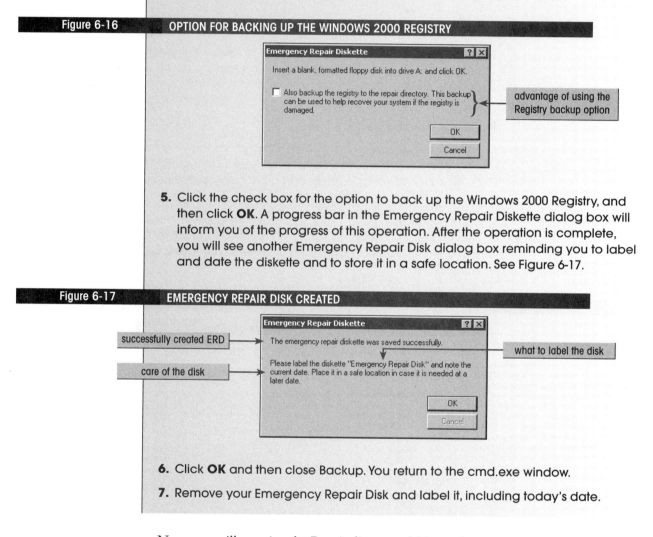

5. Click the check box for the option to back up the Windows 2000 Registry, and then click **OK**. A progress bar in the Emergency Repair Diskette dialog box will inform you of the progress of this operation. After the operation is complete, you will see another Emergency Repair Disk dialog box reminding you to label and date the diskette and to store it in a safe location. See Figure 6-17.

Figure 6-17	EMERGENCY REPAIR DISK CREATED

6. Click **OK** and then close Backup. You return to the cmd.exe window.

7. Remove your Emergency Repair Disk and label it, including today's date.

Next, you will examine the Repair directory folder and its contents.

To view the contents of the ERD and Repair directory:

1. Change the default drive to drive C.

2. Insert the Emergency Repair Disk into Drive A.

3. Clear the window and then enter: `dir a: /o /a`

There are three files on the Emergency Repair Disk. See Figure 6-18. Autoexec.nt and config.nt are Windows 2000 configuration files for configuring and customizing your computer during the booting process. Setup.log contains information on the location of Windows 2000 system files and settings. The size of your setup.log file may differ.

Figure 6-18	VIEWING THE CONTENTS OF THE EMERGENCY REPAIR DISK

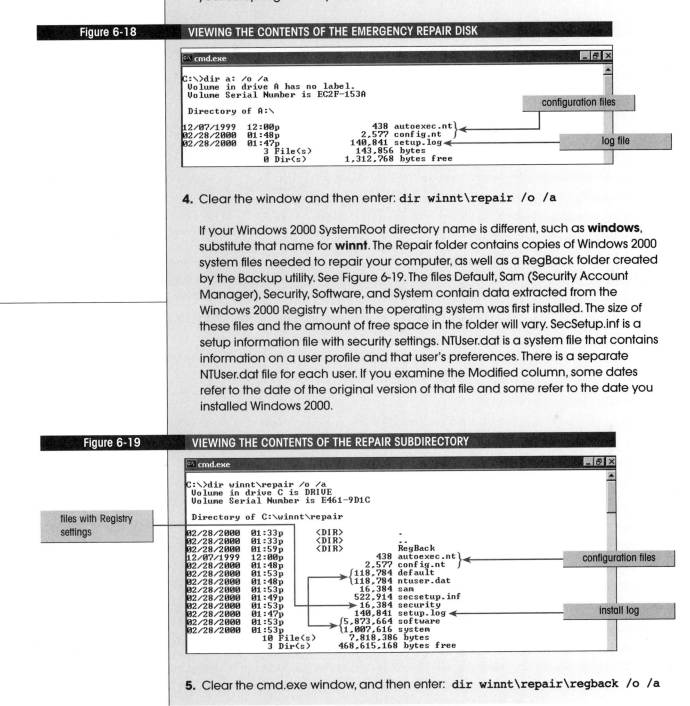

4. Clear the window and then enter: `dir winnt\repair /o /a`

If your Windows 2000 SystemRoot directory name is different, such as **windows**, substitute that name for **winnt**. The Repair folder contains copies of Windows 2000 system files needed to repair your computer, as well as a RegBack folder created by the Backup utility. See Figure 6-19. The files Default, Sam (Security Account Manager), Security, Software, and System contain data extracted from the Windows 2000 Registry when the operating system was first installed. The size of these files and the amount of free space in the folder will vary. SecSetup.inf is a setup information file with security settings. NTUser.dat is a system file that contains information on a user profile and that user's preferences. There is a separate NTUser.dat file for each user. If you examine the Modified column, some dates refer to the date of the original version of that file and some refer to the date you installed Windows 2000.

Figure 6-19	VIEWING THE CONTENTS OF THE REPAIR SUBDIRECTORY

5. Clear the cmd.exe window, and then enter: `dir winnt\repair\regback /o /a`

The RegBack directory contains files with recent backups of Windows 2000 Registry settings as well as user preferences. See Figure 6-20. Because these files are the most recent Registry backups, their sizes will differ from the parent directory's files with the same names in the previous step, which Windows 2000 created during installation.

Figure 6-20   **VIEWING THE CONTENTS OF THE REGBACK SUBDIRECTORY**

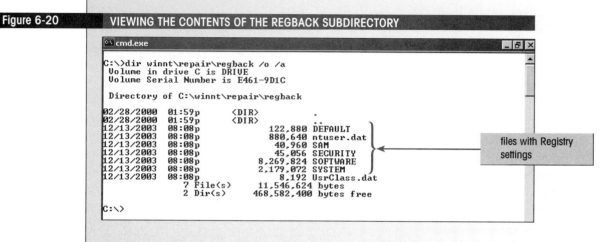

6. Restart the computer by pressing Ctrl+Alt+Del (press and hold the **Ctrl** and **Alt** keys, press and release the **Del** key, then release the Ctrl and Alt keys). Windows 2000 displays a Windows Security dialog box.

7. If your CD drive is a bootable drive, remove your Windows CD from the CD drive.

8. Click the **Shut Down** button, select **Restart** from the "What do you want the computer to do?" list box, click **OK**, and then wait while Windows 2000 reboots your computer.

As with the Windows 2000 Setup Disks, label the diskette with the operating system and the name of the computer on which you prepared this diskette so you know which diskette to use on your computer when you need it.

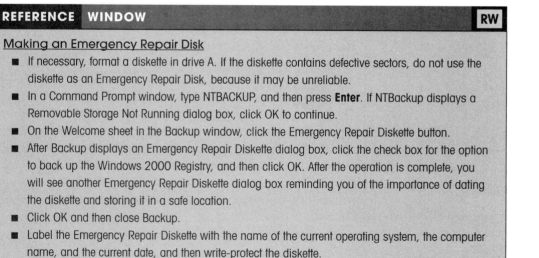

REFERENCE WINDOW   **RW**

Making an Emergency Repair Disk

■ If necessary, format a diskette in drive A. If the diskette contains defective sectors, do not use the diskette as an Emergency Repair Disk, because it may be unreliable.

■ In a Command Prompt window, type NTBACKUP, and then press **Enter**. If NTBackup displays a Removable Storage Not Running dialog box, click OK to continue.

■ On the Welcome sheet in the Backup window, click the Emergency Repair Diskette button.

■ After Backup displays an Emergency Repair Diskette dialog box, click the check box for the option to back up the Windows 2000 Registry, and then click OK. After the operation is complete, you will see another Emergency Repair Diskette dialog box reminding you of the importance of dating the diskette and storing it in a safe location.

■ Click OK and then close Backup.

■ Label the Emergency Repair Diskette with the name of the current operating system, the computer name, and the current date, and then write-protect the diskette.

Using the Emergency Repair Disk

Isabel points out that if your computer will not start, or if your system files are damaged or missing, you would use the Emergency Repair Disk with the following approach to restore your system to a working state.

Note: Do not keystroke the following bulleted items; instead, use them as a reference if you encounter a problem with starting Windows 2000 and need to repair Windows 2000 with the Emergency Repair Disk.

- Boot your computer from your Windows 2000 Setup Disks (starting with the Windows 2000 Setup Disk #1). On newer computer systems, you can boot your computer directly from the Windows 2000 CD.

- After the Setup program starts from your Windows 2000 Setup Disks or from the Windows 2000 CD, Setup will ask you if you want to set up and install Windows 2000, repair an existing installation, or quit Setup without installing Windows 2000. See Figure 6-21. Choose the option for repairing your system.

Figure 6-21	STARTING WINDOWS SETUP FROM THE SETUP DISKS

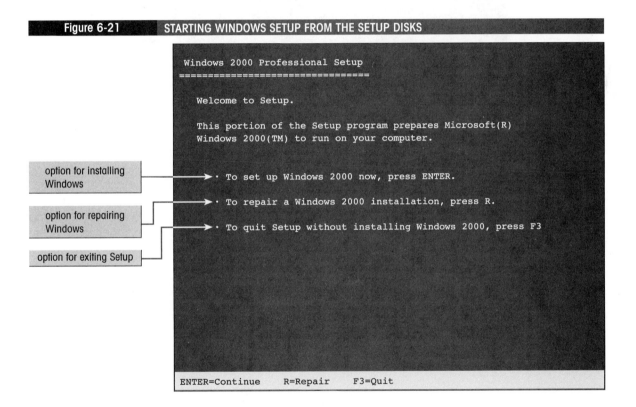

- After you choose the repair option, Setup will ask if you want to use the Recovery Console or the emergency repair process to repair your system. See Figure 6-22. Setup also notes that if the repair operation is not successful, you should run Windows Setup again. You may have to reinstall Windows 2000. Later in the tutorial, you will examine the use of the Recovery Console—an alternate option for working in a command-line environment and troubleshooting computer problems.

Figure 6-22 **REPAIR OPTIONS**

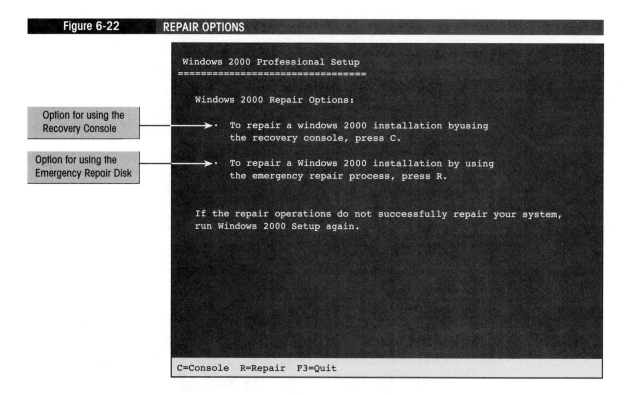

Option for using the
Recovery Console

Option for using the
Emergency Repair Disk

```
Windows 2000 Professional Setup
====================================

    Windows 2000 Repair Options:

    · To repair a windows 2000 installation byusing
      the recovery console, press C.

    · To repair a Windows 2000 installation by using
      the emergency repair process, press R.


    If the repair operations do not successfully repair your system,
    run Windows 2000 Setup again.




C=Console   R=Repair   F3=Quit
```

- Choose the type of repair you want Setup to use. If you choose the option for using your Emergency Repair Disk, you will have two repair options: a Manual Repair or a Fast Repair. See Figure 6-23. The Fast Repair is quicker because it does not require any user interaction. If you choose this option, Setup will restore the original copy of the Registry, and the Registry will no longer contain the settings for any changes made to your system since you made the backup copy of the Registry. The Manual Repair option allows you to choose whether you want to repair system files, troubleshoot partition boot sector problems, or diagnose startup environment problems. The Manual Repair option does not repair the Registry.

Figure 6-23	CHOOSING A REPAIR OPTION

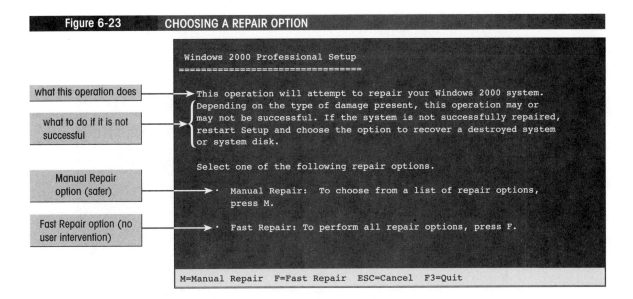

what this operation does

what to do if it is not successful

Manual Repair option (safer)

Fast Repair option (no user intervention)

- If you choose the Manual Repair option, you will see a list of the tasks that Setup can perform, as shown in Figure 6-24.

Figure 6-24	VERIFY, OR CHOOSE, TASKS FOR THE REPAIR

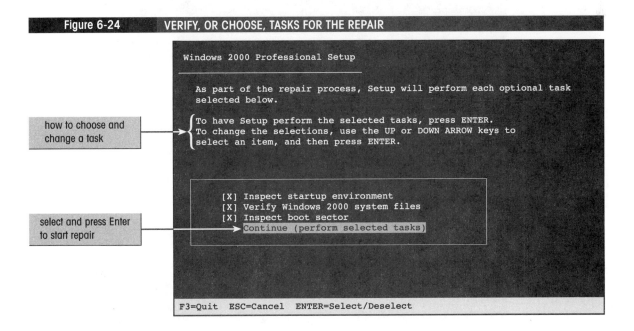

how to choose and change a task

select and press Enter to start repair

■ Start the repair. Setup will use your Emergency Repair Disk (if available) and the original Windows 2000 installation CD to repair Windows 2000 on your hard disk. See Figure 6-25. If you do not have an Emergency Repair Disk, Setup will attempt to locate the Windows 2000 directory for you.

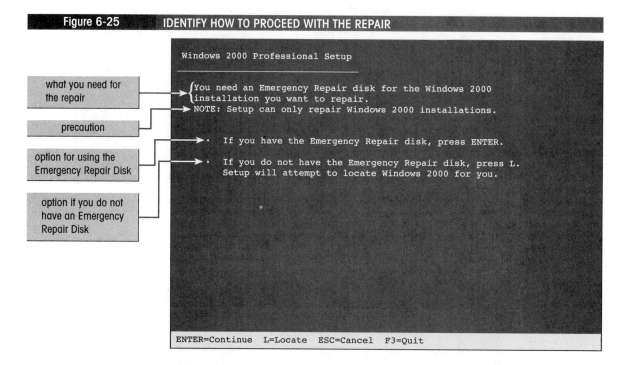

Figure 6-25   IDENTIFY HOW TO PROCEED WITH THE REPAIR

```
Windows 2000 Professional Setup
_____

You need an Emergency Repair disk for the Windows 2000
installation you want to repair.
NOTE: Setup can only repair Windows 2000 installations.

    .   If you have the Emergency Repair disk, press ENTER.

    .   If you do not have the Emergency Repair disk, press L.
        Setup will attempt to locate Windows 2000 for you.

            o




ENTER=Continue   L=Locate   ESC=Cancel   F3=Quit
```

what you need for the repair

precaution

option for using the Emergency Repair Disk

option if you do not have an Emergency Repair Disk

■ If you previously chose the emergency repair option, you will be prompted to insert the Emergency Repair Disk into drive A. At the next screen, Setup informs you that it will examine your computer's drives to see if your hard disk has the original installation files. See Figure 6-26.

Figure 6-26   FIRST STEP IN THE REPAIR PROCESS

```
Windows 2000 Professional Setup
=================================

Setup will now examine your computer's drives.

Setup needs the original installation files. If you do not have
them, you may skip the drive examination.

    .   If you have the Emergency Repair disk, press ENTER.

    .   If you do not have the Emergency Repair disk, press L.
        Set up will attempt to locate Windows 2000 for you.




F3=Quit   ENTER=Continue   ESC=Cancel
```

what Setup will do

what Setup needs for this step

option for using the Emergency Repair Disk

option for skipping this step

■ If Setup determines that a system file on your computer is not the original file that Setup copied to your hard disk when you installed Windows 2000, it will ask you if you want to skip the file and not repair it, repair this file only, repair all such files, or exit Setup. See Figure 6-27. Chances are you will see a number of screens like this one, identifying different files which actually might be newer versions of specific program files that you updated using Windows Update. Unless you know exactly which file you need to restore and are familiar with all the system files, you will not know what to do. Your best bet would be to skip all such files, and see if the rest of the repair process resolves the problem you encountered.

Figure 6-27	VERSION CONFLICT PROBLEM

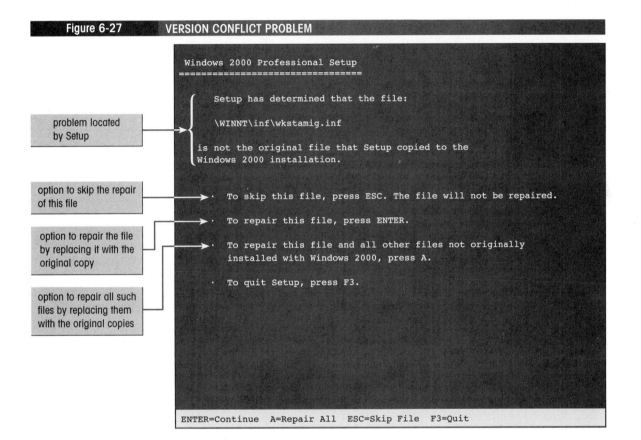

problem located by Setup

option to skip the repair of this file

option to repair the file by replacing it with the original copy

option to repair all such files by replacing them with the original copies

```
Windows 2000 Professional Setup
==================================

     Setup has determined that the file:

     \WINNT\inf\wkstamig.inf

  is not the original file that Setup copied to the
  Windows 2000 installation.


   ·  To skip this file, press ESC. The file will not be repaired.

   ·  To repair this file, press ENTER.

   ·  To repair this file and all other files not originally
      installed with Windows 2000, press A.

   ·  To quit Setup, press F3.




  ENTER=Continue   A=Repair All   ESC=Skip File   F3=Quit
```

■ At the end of the repair process, Setup will prompt you to remove the Emergency Repair Disk from drive A, and it then reboots the computer.

The Emergency Repair Disk is a snapshot of the user, disk, and Registry configurations at a particular point in time. Whenever you change the configuration of your computer, you should create a new Emergency Repair Disk so that it reflects the changes you have made.

Repairing a Windows 2000 installation with the Emergency Repair Disk is much faster than reinstalling Windows 2000 from scratch, so if you are experiencing problems starting Windows 2000, you should try your Emergency Repair Disk first. Also, the Emergency Repair Disk is not a boot disk. You must first boot with the Windows 2000 Setup Disks, or from your Windows 2000 CD, and then you have the option of using the Emergency Repair Disk.

If there is a problem with the partition boot sector—a portion of a hard disk partition that contains information about the file system used on that partition and a program for loading Windows 2000—you can use your Windows 2000 Setup Disks and the Emergency

Repair Disk together to fix the problem. Boot your computer with the Windows 2000 Setup Disks, choose the option for repairing Windows 2000, and then Setup will use your Emergency Repair Disk to repair system files, the partition boot sector, and the startup environment (and the Registry, if you so choose).

If the emergency repair process outlined above does not fix the problem, you can try the Recovery Console (covered later in the tutorial), reinstall Windows 2000, or consult someone experienced in troubleshooting Windows 2000.

Session 6.1 QUICK CHECK

1. The _____ is a system database that consists of a set of files where Windows 2000 stores your computer's hardware, software, and security settings as well as user settings or profiles, and property settings for folders and programs.

2. A(n) _____ is a diskette that contains the core operating system files needed to start a computer from drive A.

3. When booting from the hard disk drive, the BIOS locates the _____ (the first sector on the hard disk), and reads it into memory.

4. _____ mode uses extended memory and loads drivers for reading NTFS and FAT volumes

5. _____ is a technique for supplementing RAM by using available storage space on a hard disk as memory.

6. A(n) _____ disk is a commonly used PC hard disk interface that integrates controller electronics into the drive itself.

7. A(n) _____ is a file with program code that enables the operating system to communicate with, manage, and control the operation of a hardware or software component.

8. _____ refers to a special type of computer chip, or integrated circuit, that requires less power and, with the use of a battery backup, retains important computer settings after you turn off the power to your computer.

9. A(n) _____ is a program, routine, or process that provides support to other programs.

10. The _____ booting option starts Windows 2000 using the configuration saved by the operating system from the last successful boot.

11. The _____ option starts Windows 2000, but loads only the minimum set of files and drivers for the mouse, monitor, keyboard, mass storage, and video as well as default system services.

12. You should make sure you have at least one set of the Windows 2000 _____ for your own computer system so you (or someone else) can reinstall or repair Windows 2000 on that computer if the need should arise.

13. When you make Windows 2000 Setup Disks, you must use drive _____.

14. _____ files have the "inf" file extension and contain information for configuring hardware devices or software.

15. The Emergency Repair Disk (ERD) is a diskette that you create with the _____ utility to store information about your Windows 2000 system settings and system files.

SESSION 6.2

In this session, you will examine the types of file systems supported by Windows 2000 and the advantages and disadvantages of each file system. You will use the Check Disk utility to inspect the integrity of a disk and its file system. As part of this process, you will examine different types of problems that might arise in the file system of a disk.

The Windows 2000 File Systems

At the beginning of the second half of the workshop, Isabel introduces the file systems supported by Windows 2000. During the installation of Windows 2000 on a computer, you must specify which file system to use on the hard disk, choosing the one that best suits your needs. Windows 2000 supports three file systems: FAT16, FAT32, and NTFS.

A **file system** refers to the data structures that an operating system uses to track information on files stored on a disk. When you install Windows 2000, you must choose which file system you will use on the hard disk volume containing the operating system. When you format an additional hard disk volume, you must also choose that volume's file system.

The FAT16 File System

The original versions of Windows 95 and Windows 95a used the FAT16 file system (also known simply as FAT) for hard disk drives to provide backward compatibility with DOS, which also used the FAT16 file system. The FAT16 file system uses a set of data structures referred to as **File Allocation Tables**. To illustrate how this file system works, let's look at what happens when you format a diskette.

Operating systems that use the FAT file system perform three basic operations when you format a diskette:

- **Subdivides the disk into tracks and sectors**. As noted in Tutorial 1, the operating system creates concentric tracks around the inner circumference of the diskette, and then subdivides each track into **sectors**.
- **Checks the surface of the disk for defective sectors**. As noted in Tutorial 1, the operating system performs a surface scan and checks the integrity of the disk's surface. Although the sector is the basic unit of storage on a disk, operating systems that rely on the FAT file system allocate storage space on a cluster-by-cluster basis rather than a sector-by-sector basis. A cluster, also called an allocation unit, consists of one or more sectors of storage space, and represents the minimum amount of space that an operating system allocates when saving the contents of a file to disk. As shown in Figure 6-28, an allocation unit or cluster on a high-density diskette consists of one sector. On a hard disk drive, the number of sectors in an allocation unit or cluster varies, depending on the size of the hard disk and also the file system, but might consist of 8, 16, 32, or 64 sectors. If you create a small file, such as a short note or memo that is no larger than a sector in size, then it is assigned one cluster of storage space whether you store it on a diskette or a hard disk. Because the number of sectors per cluster varies on different types of disk, however, this file would use one sector of storage space on a high-density diskette, and up to 64 sectors of storage space on a hard disk. Any space allocated to a file, but not used to store the contents of the file, is wasted space and is referred to as **slack**. No other file uses that wasted space.

Figure 6-28   CLUSTER SIZES ON DIFFERENT TYPES OF DISKS USING DIFFERENT FILE SYSTEMS

TYPE OF DISK	TYPE OF FILE SYSTEM	CLUSTER SIZE	
		SECTORS	BYTES
High-Density Diskette (HD or DS/HD)	FAT12	1 sector	512 bytes
Double-Density Diskette (DS/DD)	FAT12	2 sectors	1024 (1 KB)
2 GB Hard Disk	FAT16	64 sectors	32 KB
2 GB Hard Disk	FAT32	8 sectors	4 KB
2 GB Hard Disk	NTFS	8 sectors	4 KB
32 GB Hard Disk	FAT32	32 sectors	16 KB
32 GB Hard Disk	NTFS	8 sectors	4 KB
(HD-High Density, DS-Double=Sided, DD-Double=Density)			

- **Creates four system tables.** The operating system creates four tables at the outer edge of the disk in an area called the **system area**. Right after the system area is the **files area** where you store your document files. The four tables for the FAT file system are the following:
  - Boot record
  - File Allocation Table #1
  - File Allocation Table #2
  - Directory table

Each of these tables, or data structures, plays an important role in the FAT file system.

The Boot Record

The **boot record** (sometimes called the **boot sector**) is a table that contains the name and the version number of the operating system used to format the diskette, as well as information on the physical characteristics of the disk, such as:

- number of bytes per sector
- number of sectors per cluster or allocation unit
- number of FATs (File Allocation Tables)
- maximum number of files allowed in the top-level folder (the root directory)
- total number of sectors
- **media descriptor byte**, which identifies the type of disk
- number of sectors for the FAT
- number of sectors per track
- number of sides formatted
- drive number
- volume serial number (calculated from the date and time on the computer)
- volume label (an electronic label)
- type of file system
- number of hidden, reserved, and unused sectors

A **volume** is a physical storage device, such as a diskette, or a logical storage device, such as a partition of a hard drive, and which the operating system designates with a drive letter, such as C or D. The boot sector also contains the names of the operating system files and a bootstrap loader program whose sole function is to locate and load the operating system if the diskette is a boot disk and contains those operating system files. If the diskette is not a boot disk, but rather stores document files, the bootstrap/loader program displays an error message if you leave the diskette in drive A and if your computer attempts to boot from that drive.

When the operating system accesses a drive that contains a diskette, it reads the boot record so it knows how to work with the allocation of storage space on that disk drive. The boot sector, therefore, is important because different types of disks (including hard disks) have different storage capacities and allocate storage space differently.

The File Allocation Tables

After creating the boot sector, the operating system creates a table called the **File Allocation Table** (**FAT**) to keep track of which allocation units (or clusters) are available or unused, which ones store the contents of files, which are defective and unusable, and which are reserved for use by the operating system. Familiarity with the File Allocation Table will help you understand information you receive from system troubleshooting tools such as CHKDSK, covered later in this tutorial. Also, it is the one file system recognized by many different operating systems.

Figure 6-29 shows a diagrammatic representation of a portion of the File Allocation Table. This figure shows two files, which use clusters 1500-1505 and 1506-1508 respectively. Each files directory entry contains the filename and first cluster number (in this example, 1500 and 1506). Each cluster entry contains the number of the next cluster for that same file (shown in the column labeled "FAT"); the final cluster entry of a file contains an end-of-file (EOF) code or marker. Since the operating system can determine the cluster number shown in the figure by counting the entries in the table, the File Allocation Table only contains the information shown in the FAT column.

Figure 6-29	PARTIAL VIEW OF CLUSTER USAGE IN THE FILE ALLOCATION TABLE

	CLUSTER	FAT
pointer to next cluster in file	1500	1501
	1501	1502
	1502	1503
	1503	1504
	1504	1505
end of file code	1505	EOF
	1506	1507
	1507	1508
	1508	EOF
unused cluster	1509	Available
	1510	Available
	1511	Available
defective cluster	1512	Defective

Because the File Allocation Table is so important to the operating system's ability to locate files, the operating system places two copies of this table onto a disk. One copy is called FAT1, the other, FAT2. Each time the operating system saves a new or modified file to a disk, it updates both copies of the FAT, so FAT2 is a backup of FAT1. If the area of the disk where FAT1 is stored fails, the operating system uses FAT2 to locate the clusters that belong to a file. However, if you receive an error message that this has occurred, you should immediately back up your hard disk (if possible), because it may indicate that the drive is failing. Then you can try to reformat the drive to determine if it is still functional. If so, reinstall the operating system, the program software, and any utilities, and then restore your document files from backups.

The Directory Table

The **directory table** keeps track of information on the directories (or folders) and files stored in the root directory. This table contains the names of directories and files, as well as information on their sizes, dates, and times of creation or modification, and any special attributes, or characteristics, turned on for each directory or file by the operating system. In Figure 6-30, you see a diagrammatic representation of some of the contents of a diskette's root directory table and one of its subdirectories, Presentations. The root directory table keeps track of only the subdirectories and files located in the root directory. This table does not keep track of the folders and files contained within subdirectories *below* the root directory. Each subdirectory below the root directory has its own directory table, like the one for the root directory, and each directory table keeps track of the subdirectories and files contained within that subdirectory. As Figure 6-30 shows, each subdirectory table also contains the "." and ". ." entries, pointing to the subdirectory itself and to its parent directory, respectively. In essence, there is a division of labor with respect to tracking directories and files on a hard disk.

Figure 6-30	DIRECTORY TABLES

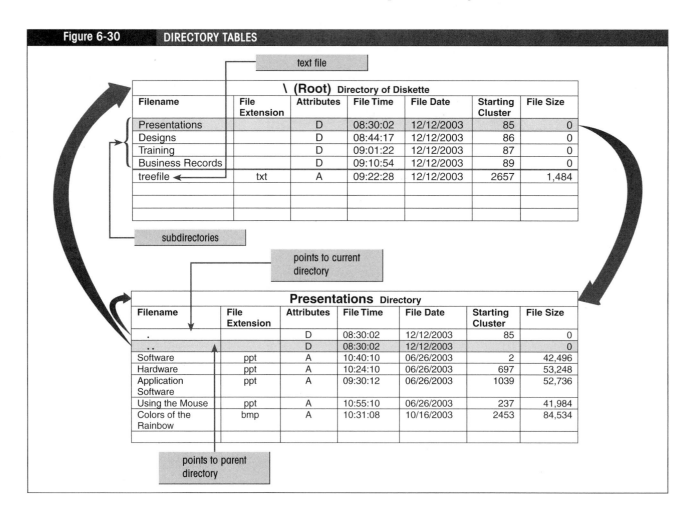

text file

\ (Root) Directory of Diskette

Filename	File Extension	Attributes	File Time	File Date	Starting Cluster	File Size
Presentations		D	08:30:02	12/12/2003	85	0
Designs		D	08:44:17	12/12/2003	86	0
Training		D	09:01:22	12/12/2003	87	0
Business Records		D	09:10:54	12/12/2003	89	0
treefile	txt	A	09:22:28	12/12/2003	2657	1,484

subdirectories

points to current directory

Presentations Directory

Filename	File Extension	Attributes	File Time	File Date	Starting Cluster	File Size
.		D	08:30:02	12/12/2003	85	0
. .		D	08:30:02	12/12/2003		0
Software	ppt	A	10:40:10	06/26/2003	2	42,496
Hardware	ppt	A	10:24:10	06/26/2003	697	53,248
Application Software	ppt	A	09:30:12	06/26/2003	1039	52,736
Using the Mouse	ppt	A	10:55:10	06/26/2003	237	41,984
Colors of the Rainbow	bmp	A	10:31:08	10/16/2003	2453	84,534

points to parent directory

In the FAT file system, the directory table keeps track of the Read-Only, Hidden, System, Archive, and Directory attributes. Files with the Read-Only attributes turned on, such as Msdos.sys (a Windows 98 and Windows 95 startup file with boot settings) can be read, but not modified or deleted. Files with the Hidden attribute turned on, such as System.dat and User.dat (the Windows 98 and Windows 95 Registry files), are not displayed in file listings unless you choose the option to display all files. Files with the System attribute turned on, such as Io.sys and Msdos.sys (Windows 98 or Windows 95 startup files), are operating system files that play a role in the booting process. Windows turns on the Archive attribute of newly created or modified files so a backup utility can identify which files should be backed up. Directory folders are listed as file entries that have the Directory attribute turned on.

Another important feature of the directory table is that it contains the number of the starting cluster for each subdirectory and file on a disk. By using the directory table and the File Allocation Table, the operating system can locate all the clusters used by a file on the disk and assemble the file in memory so you can work with the data in that file.

The MS-DOS file system for hard disks uses FAT16, but the MS-DOS file system for diskettes uses FAT12 because of the limited storage capacities of diskettes. FAT12 supports a maximum of 4,096 clusters (2^{12}) on a diskette.

In contrast, FAT16 supports a maximum of 65,536 clusters (2^{16}) clusters on a hard disk and the boot record, File Allocation Table #1, File Allocation Table #2, and directory table are fixed in size. Hard disk File Allocation Tables cannot exceed 128 KB, which affects the availability of storage space on hard disk drives. As hard disk drive storage capacities increase, the number of sectors per cluster must increase because the number of clusters cannot increase. Figure 6-31 shows cluster sizes on different-sized hard disk drives that use FAT16. For hard disk drives that range in capacity from 1 GB up to 2 GB, each cluster is 64 sectors in size. Most operating systems using the FAT16 file system do not normally support hard disks over 2 GB. Although you can format a FAT16 disk volume up to 4 GB in Windows 2000, Microsoft recommends against it, in order for the disk volume to maintain compatibility with other operating systems that can access only 2 GB FAT16 volumes.

Figure 6-31	CLUSTER SIZES FOR FAT16 VOLUMES	
HARD DISK DRIVE	**FAT16 CLUSTER SIZE**	
	SECTORS	**BYTES**
7 MB—16 MB (FAT12)	4 sectors	2 KB
17 MB—32 MB	1 sector	512 bytes
33 MB—64 MB	2 sectors	1 KB
65 MB—128 MB	4 sectors	2 KB
129 MB—256 MB	8 sectors	4 KB
257 MB—512 MB	16 sectors	8 KB
513 MB—1 GB	32 sectors	16 KB
1 GB—2 GB	64 sectors	32 KB

The directory table for the root directory of a hard disk that uses FAT16 is also fixed in size, so it can track a maximum of 512 subdirectories and files. Therefore, organize files into directories so that the root directory does not become full and limit your use of long filenames for directories and files in the root directory, because long filenames take more than one directory entry. Each directory below the root directory can track as many other subdirectories and files as you want or need, because there is no limit on the size of the directory table for each subdirectory, and you can use long filenames freely.

The Master Boot Record and Hard Disk Partition Table

Each drive on a hard disk that uses the FAT file system has a boot record, two copies of the File Allocation Table, and a directory table. The very first sector on a hard disk is not the boot sector for drive C, but rather the Master Boot Record. The boot sector for drive C is the next sector after the Master Boot Record. The **Master Boot Record** (**MBR**) contains information on the disk's partitions. A **partition** is all or part of the physical hard disk that is set aside for a drive or set of logical drives. A **primary partition** is a bootable partition that contains an operating system (drive C in Windows). An **extended partition** does not contain operating system files, but can be divided into additional logical drives, such as drive D and drive E. You can have as many as 23 logical drives (drive D through drive Z). Within the Master Boot Record is a table called the **Hard Disk Partition Table** that contains information about the partitions on the hard disk. Figure 6-32 shows the Hard Disk Partition Table for a computer that contains two partitions. The primary partition, labeled HUGE, is the boot drive (drive C) with 2 GB of storage space; the extended partition, labeled EXTEND, is drive D with 23.5 GB of storage space. On this computer, drive C uses the FAT16 file system, while drive D uses the NTFS file system.

Figure 6-32   HARD DISK PARTITION TABLE

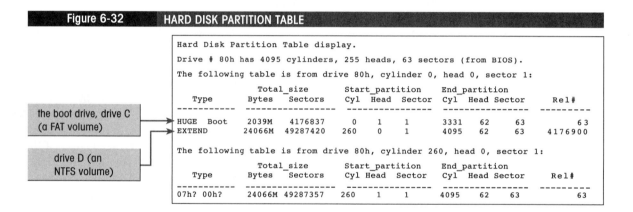

```
Hard Disk Partition Table display.

Drive # 80h has 4095 cylinders, 255 heads, 63 sectors (from BIOS).

The following table is from drive 80h, cylinder 0, head 0, sector 1:

              Total_size       Start_partition    End_partition
    Type     Bytes    Sectors  Cyl  Head  Sector  Cyl   Head  Sector     Rel#
----------- ------------------ ----------------   ---------------   ---------
HUGE  Boot  2039M    4176837     0    1     1     3331   62    63          63
EXTEND      24066M  49287420   260    0     1     4095   62    63     4176900

The following table is from drive 80h, cylinder 260, head 0, sector 1:

              Total_size       Start_partition    End_partition
    Type     Bytes    Sectors  Cyl  Head  Sector  Cyl   Head  Sector     Rel#
----------- ------------------ ----------------   ---------------   ---------
07h? 00h?   24066M  49287357   260    1     1     4095   62    63          63
```

the boot drive, drive C (a FAT volume)

drive D (an NTFS volume)

As you can see in the figure, the first table is from cylinder 0, head 0, sector 1 of drive 80h (a boot indicator value that identifies the partition used to boot the computer). A **head** refers to a side of one of the disks, or platters, within the hard disk. Head 0 is the first side of the platter.

A **platter** is similar to the disk within a diskette jacket, except that it is made of aluminum or glass, and provides all or part of the storage capacity of the entire hard disk drive. See Figure 6-33.

Figure 6-33   PLATTERS IN A HARD DISK DRIVE UNIT

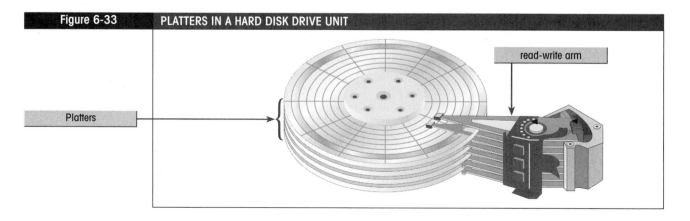

read-write arm

Platters

On a hard disk, a combination of tracks is referred to as a **cylinder**. Each cylinder consists of tracks located at the same position on different sides of each of the platters that constitute the hard disk. See Figure 6-34.

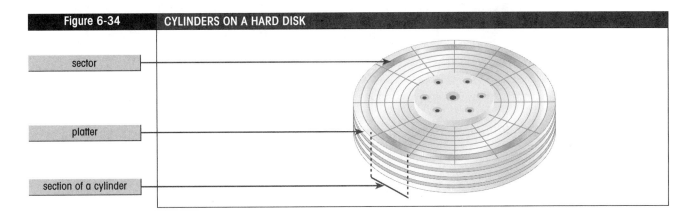

Figure 6-34	CYLINDERS ON A HARD DISK

sector

platter

section of a cylinder

When your computer finds your hard drive, it reads the Master Boot Record, finds the location of the boot partition (drive C), and then reads the boot record on drive C. Then, from the drive C boot record, the bootstrap loader locates and loads the operating system from the hard disk.

The FAT32 File System

Windows 2000, Windows 98, Windows 95b, and Windows 95c support another type of file system called FAT32. FAT32 improves the efficiency with which the operating system uses storage space. FAT32 supports a maximum of 4,177,918 clusters on a hard disk, so cluster sizes can be smaller and storage space on the disk can be used more efficiently than was possible with FAT16. For example, as shown in Figure 6-35, on a 2 GB hard disk that uses FAT32, a cluster consists of only 8 sectors (as compared to 64 sectors for FAT16). Under FAT32, hard disk drives with storage capacities less than 8 GB have cluster sizes of 8 sectors, or 4 KB. Another important feature of FAT32 is that it can support larger hard disk drives, up to 32 GB.

Figure 6-35	CLUSTER SIZES FOR FAT32 VOLUMES	

| HARD DISK DRIVE | FAT32 CLUSTER SIZE | |
	SECTORS	BYTES
257 MB—8 GB	8 sectors	4 KB
8 GB—16 GB	16 sectors	8 KB
16 GB—32 GB	32 sectors	16 KB

Although large files take a lot of storage space on disk, numerous small files waste a lot of storage space relative to their size and create more slack. For example, on a 2 GB hard drive volume that uses FAT16, a shortcut that is 399 bytes in size and requires less than one sector of storage space (512 bytes), but actually uses 32 KB of storage space because the operating system allocates an entire 32KB cluster (64 sectors) to the shortcut. That shortcut wastes over 31.5 KB (63 sectors), which now becomes slack. If that same file were stored on a volume that used FAT32, the operating system would still allocate one cluster to that shortcut; but since a FAT32 cluster comprises only 4 KB (8 sectors), only about 3.5 KB (7 sectors) of storage space would be wasted and end up as slack. Figure 6-36 shows the property sheets of two identical shortcuts on different hard drive volumes, one using FAT16 and the other using FAT32.

Figure 6-36   SHORTCUTS ON FAT16 AND FAT32 VOLUMES

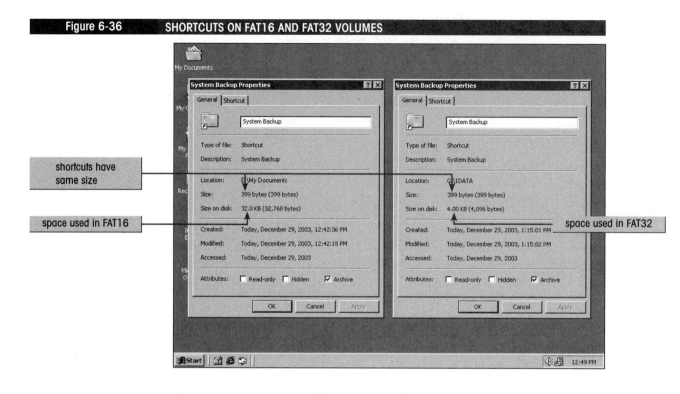

The boot record on a FAT32 drive is different from that of a FAT16 drive, in that it is larger—up to 2 MB in size—and it also contains a backup of critical data structures. Unlike FAT16, the File Allocation Tables in the FAT32 file system are not fixed in size, they spill over from the system area to the files area of the disk where they are stored on disk like directories and files. An added advantage is that there is no limitation on the number of sub-directories and files in the root directory.

The larger size of each copy of the File Allocation Tables in the FAT32 file system does pose a problem though, because the FAT is read into RAM. If you have a computer with a limited amount of RAM, only part of the FAT will be loaded into memory. Windows 2000 will have to go back to the hard disk to locate information on the location of directories and files, and disk access is far slower than accessing RAM. For example, a computer might have a hard disk with an access time of 6 milliseconds (6 thousands of a second or 0.006 seconds) and RAM with an access time of 50 nanoseconds (50 billionths of a second or 0.00000005 seconds). The RAM access time in this example is 120,000 times faster than the hard disk access time. **Access time** is the amount of time it takes a device to locate an item of data and make it available to the rest of the computer system.

Microsoft states that FAT32 is 10 to 15% more efficient in using disk space than FAT16, and that it improves the use of storage space on large drives—drives that range in size from 512 MB to 2 TB (terabytes). If you have a 2 GB drive that uses FAT16, you can gain from 200 to 300 MB of additional storage space on the disk by switching to FAT32. Although the gain in storage space might not seem as much as you would expect, the combined features of the FAT32 file system offer a significant improvement over FAT16.

The Virtual File Allocation Table

The File Allocation Table formed the basis of the file system used by MS-DOS to keep track of the location of files stored on disk. To maintain backward compatibility with MS-DOS and Windows 3.x, Windows 98 and Windows 95 use the MS-DOS File Allocation Table as the foundation for their own file systems, but expand the capabilities of that file system with the use of a virtual device driver. Under MS-DOS, a device driver managed the use of a system resource for a single program. Under Windows 98 and Windows 95, on the other hand, a virtual device driver manages a hardware or software resource so more than one program can use that resource at the same time. Virtual device drivers therefore allowed Windows 98 and Windows 95 to support **multitasking** (the concurrent use of more than one program). A **virtual device driver**, also referred to as a VxD, is a special type of device driver that Windows 98 or Windows 95 uses when it operates in protected mode. A VxD can take advantage of the full capabilities of 80386 and later microprocessors to address memory above 1 MB and also provide memory protection features.

Windows 98 and Windows 95 automatically use a virtual device driver called **VFAT** (**Virtual File Allocation Table**) with the FAT file system . VFAT provides faster disk access and supports the use of long filenames (up to 255 characters for each directory and filename). Windows 2000 also supports the use of VFAT for FAT volumes.

The NTFS File System

Windows 2000 supports the use of the FAT16 and FAT32 file system, and also has its own native file system, called **NTFS** (the **NT File System**). When you install Windows 2000, you can specify a file system, and you can also specify a file system if you format a volume. Windows 2000 can convert a FAT16 or FAT32 volume to an NTFS volume without formatting the volume.

The NTFS file system does not use a File Allocation Table with pointers, but instead relies on a **Master File Table** (**MFT**), a special file that keeps information about the files on disk. Some of the information in the MFT is stored in the boot sector, and a duplicate copy of the boot sector is stored at the midpoint of the volume or drive. The MFT contains a transaction log of disk activities so Windows 2000 can recover files if disk problems occur, and even repair itself, if necessary. Under the NTFS file system (and unlike FAT16 and FAT32), each file stores information about its own filename, file size, date and time of modification, and attributes. Like Windows 98 and Windows 95, NTFS supports long filenames and object-oriented programs that treat files as objects with user-defined and system-defined properties. NTFS also supports very large-capacity storage media.

In addition to the System, Hidden, Read-Only, and Archive attribute, NTFS supports three other attributes—Compress, Encrypt, and Index.

- The **Compress attribute**, when enabled, compresses a directory or file so it uses less disk space; you also have the option of uncompressing a directory or file. (You can compress or uncompress an NTFS directory or file with the COMPACT command.)

- The **Encrypt attribute** prevents access to a directory or file by any person other than the Administrator and the user who encrypted the directory or file, you also have the option of decrypting a directory or file. You can encrypt or decrypt an NTFS directory or file with the CIPHER command.

- The **Index attribute** indexes the content of a directory or file and its properties so you can search for text within a file or directory, as well as search for properties.

You can also set security permissions for files and folders on NTFS volumes. A **permission** is a rule associated with an object to regulate which users can gain access to the object and in what manner. When you set permissions for a file or folder, you specify what access a group or user has to the directory or file. File permissions include Full Control, Modify, Read & Execute, Read, and Write; folder permissions include all these as well as List Folder Contents.

If you want to find out what file system your computer currently uses, you can use the Check Disk utility (CHKDSK), which is covered in the next section of the tutorial.

Dual-Boot Configurations

If you want to create a dual-boot configuration, you must install each operating system on a separate volume, and each volume must be formatted with a file system which that operating system supports. As a rule, you cannot install more than one operating system on the same volume. The following guidelines identify which file system(s) you can use for various dual-boot configurations with Windows 2000:

- If you want to use a dual-boot configuration with the original version of Windows 95 or Windows 95a, you must use the FAT16 file system since these versions do not support FAT32 or NTFS.

- If you want to use a dual-boot configuration with Windows 95B, Windows 95c, or Windows 98, you can use either FAT16 or FAT32 (preferably the latter as it uses disk storage space more efficiently and does not limit the volume size to 2 GB). Like Windows 95 and 95a, these versions do not support the NTFS file system.

- If you want to use a dual-boot configuration with Windows NT 4.0, you could use either FAT16 or NTFS; Windows NT 4.0 does not support FAT32.

NTFS is currently considered the optimal file system for use with Windows 2000. If your hard disk is partitioned into two drives, with Windows 98 or Windows 95 on drive C and Windows 2000 on drive D, Windows 98 or Windows 95 will not be able to access and read the contents of drive D if that drive uses NTFS; however, Windows 2000 will be able to access and work with both drives, because it can work with both FAT16 and FAT32.

The Check Disk Utility

Another tool Isabel feels you will find useful is the Check Disk utility—the Windows 2000 Error-checking tool for both FAT and NTFS volumes.

The Check Disk utility is a disk analysis and repair utility that examines disks for errors and, where possible, repairs them. It checks the **logical structure** (the file system) of a disk, and it can also check the physical integrity of a disk's surface. The Check Disk utility examines different data structures, including filenames, important to tracking folders and files on both FAT volumes and NTFS volumes. When examining the integrity of a disk on either type of volume, the Check Disk utility will check for bad sectors, and, if it finds data stored in a bad sector, it will attempt to move the data to another location and recover the data.

Using Check Disk on FAT Volumes

Even though the native file system for the Windows NT product line (including Windows 2000) is NTFS, the FAT file system is still important for Windows 2000 users. All of the PC operating systems support the FAT file system. If you want to use a dual-boot configuration between Windows 2000 and Windows 98, Windows 95, or and Windows 3.1, you must have a FAT partition where you can install those other operating systems. Windows 2000 can access the FAT volume, but the other operating systems will not be able to recognize or access the Windows 2000 NTFS volume.

When it examines the file system on a FAT volume, the Check Disk utility checks the File Allocation Tables (FAT1 and FAT2), the directory table for the root directory, the directory structure, the integrity of files, and the validity of long filenames. Recall that the File Allocation Table contains information on cluster usage and that the operating system keeps and updates two copies of that File Allocation Table (FAT1 and FAT2). When Check Disk examines the File Allocation Tables, it traces out the chain for each file and accounts for all clusters in use by each file. The directory table for the root directory tracks information on the subdirectories and files that are stored in the root directory of a disk, including the starting cluster for each file and its size. Check Disk verifies that the size of each file matches the total amount of storage space assigned to clusters for each file in the File Allocation Table.

The integrity of the directory structure is also quite important because Windows 2000 must be able to navigate it to locate and store files on a disk. The Check Disk utility navigates up and down the entire directory structure of a disk to ensure that it is functional and intact.

Checking for Lost Clusters

When Check Disk checks the integrity of files, it looks for the presence of lost clusters and cross-linked files. A **lost cluster** is a cluster on a disk that contains data that once belonged to a program, document, or some other type of file, such as a temporary file. A **temporary file** is a file that Windows 2000 or another program creates while it is performing some function or processing data in a file. In the File Allocation Table, there is no pointer to the lost cluster. Lost clusters might develop when a power failure occurs, when you reboot a computer system after it locks up, when a brownout (a diminished supply of power) or a power surge occurs, or when you turn off the power to your computer without first closing all the open programs and properly shutting down Windows 2000.

In these cases, Windows 2000 might not be able to record any remaining information it has on the location of all clusters of a file in the File Allocation Table or the starting cluster in the directory file and, therefore, lost clusters develop. Figure 6-37 illustrates this common problem.

Figure 6-37	AN EXAMPLE OF HOW A LOST CLUSTER MAY OCCUR

CLUSTER	STATUS		CLUSTER	STATUS
1500	1501		1500	1501
1501	1502		1501	1502
1502	1503		1502	1503
1503	1504		1503	1504
1504	1505		1504	1505
1505	EOF		1505	EOF
1506	1507		1506	1507
1507	1508		1507	1508
1508	1509		1508	1509
1509	1510		1509	1510 EOF
1510	1511		1510	1511
1511	1512		1511	1512
1512	EOF		1512	EOF

a "power failure" modifies the FAT entry for cluster 1509

one chain of lost clusters

Assume you are looking at a portion of the File Allocation Table where Windows 2000 tracks the usage of clusters 1500 through 1512. In this example, assume clusters 1500 through 1505 are used by one file, and clusters 1506 through 1512 are used by another file. Also assume that, as a result of a power failure, the pointer for cluster 1509 for the second file changes to an end-of-file code (EOF). If you open the second file, using the program that produced it, Windows 2000 will read clusters 1506 through 1509 and then stop, because it finds an end-of-file code for cluster 1509. If you examine the end of this file (assuming you can open it), you will not only discover that part of the file is missing, but you more than likely will see uninterpretable characters. Clusters 1510 through 1512, which once belonged to the second file, are now lost clusters. In fact, they constitute one **chain** of lost clusters because they were derived from a single file. The File Allocation Table shows those clusters in use; however, those clusters are not associated with any file on disk because there is no pointer to cluster 1510. The operating system cannot use the storage space occupied by these lost clusters, and since you cannot access these lost clusters, they just end up wasting valuable storage space on disk. Lost clusters are the most common type of problem encountered on FAT16 and FAT32 hard disk volumes.

You should always shut down Windows 2000 by using the Shut Down option on the Start menu to prevent the creation of lost clusters or other types of disk problems. If you turn off the power near the end of a file save operation, you might end up with lost clusters on a disk. For example, Figure 6-38 shows a DIR listing of a diskette that contains a file that is approximately 250 KB in size. Note that there are no other files on the disk, and that there are 1,202,176 bytes of free space.

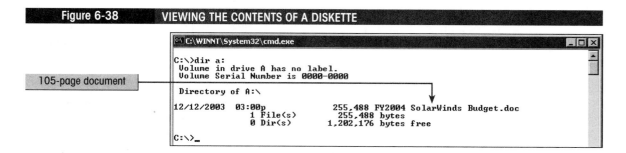

Figure 6-38 VIEWING THE CONTENTS OF A DISKETTE

C:\WINNT\System32\cmd.exe

```
C:\>dir a:
 Volume in drive A has no label.
 Volume Serial Number is 0000-0000

 Directory of A:\

12/12/2003  03:00p             255,488 FY2004 SolarWinds Budget.doc
               1 File(s)        255,488 bytes
               0 Dir(s)       1,202,176 bytes free

C:\>_
```

105-page document

If a power failure occurs while you are saving this file to the disk, you might end up with a situation similar to that shown in Figure 6-39, where DIR reports the file size to be 0 (zero). All of the clusters originally assigned to the file are now lost clusters. Note that DIR shows one file in drive A, and it takes up 0 (zero) bytes of storage space.

Figure 6-39 FILE LOST DURING A "POWER FAILURE"

C:\WINNT\System32\cmd.exe

```
C:\>dir a:
 Volume in drive A has no label.
 Volume Serial Number is 0000-0000

 Directory of A:\

12/12/2003  03:00p                   0 FY2004 SolarWinds Budget.doc
               1 File(s)              0 bytes
               0 Dir(s)       1,202,176 bytes free

C:\>_
```

file size now zero after "power failure"

not all the storage space on the disk is available (used by lost clusters)

In a situation like this, how would you know that there were lost clusters on the disk? The clue in this DIR display is in the number of bytes free. An empty diskette normally has 1.44 MB, or 1,457,664 bytes, free. But Figure 6-39 shows only 1,202,176 bytes free. The remaining 255,488 bytes (the size of the original file) constitute the space used by lost clusters.

If you use Check Disk with the Fix switch (/F), it will report that it found errors on the disk and ask you if you want to convert the lost chains to files. See Figure 6-40. Check Disk also reports that the disk uses the FAT file system.

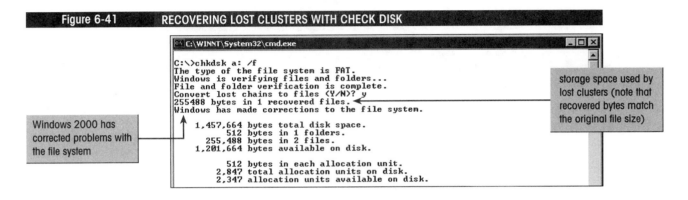

Figure 6-40 USING CHECK DISK'S FIX SWITCH TO REPAIR FILE SYSTEM ERRORS

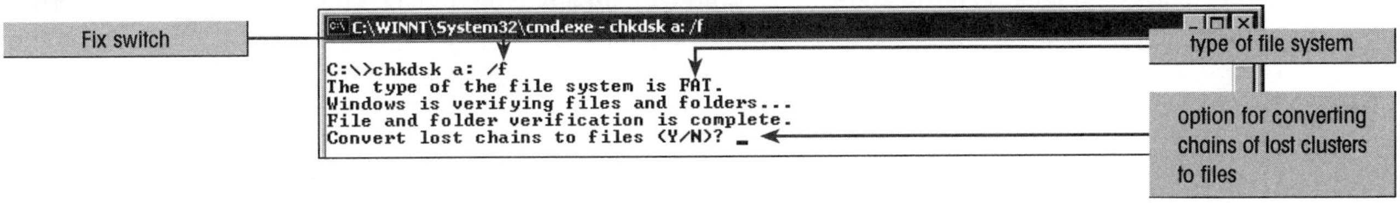

Fix switch

type of file system

option for converting chains of lost clusters to files

Once you choose the option of converting lost chains to files, Check Disk recovers one file with 255,488 bytes of data. A **lost chain** is a sequence of lost clusters that once belonged to a single file. See Figure 6-41.

Figure 6-41 RECOVERING LOST CLUSTERS WITH CHECK DISK

storage space used by lost clusters (note that recovered bytes match the original file size)

Windows 2000 has corrected problems with the file system

If you use Check Disk to correct the problem, it will create a directory named FOUND.000 in the root directory of the disk, recover the lost clusters, and then store them in a file named FILE0000.CHK within that directory, as shown in Figure 6-42. If there had been more than one chain of lost clusters, the second chain would be named FILE0001.CHK, the third FILE0002.CHK, and so on. (The file extension "chk" stands for "Check Disk.")

Figure 6-42 IDENTIFYING THE FILE WITH RECOVERED LOST CLUSTERS

subdirectory for storing file(s) with recovered lost clusters

recovered lost clusters are stored in this file

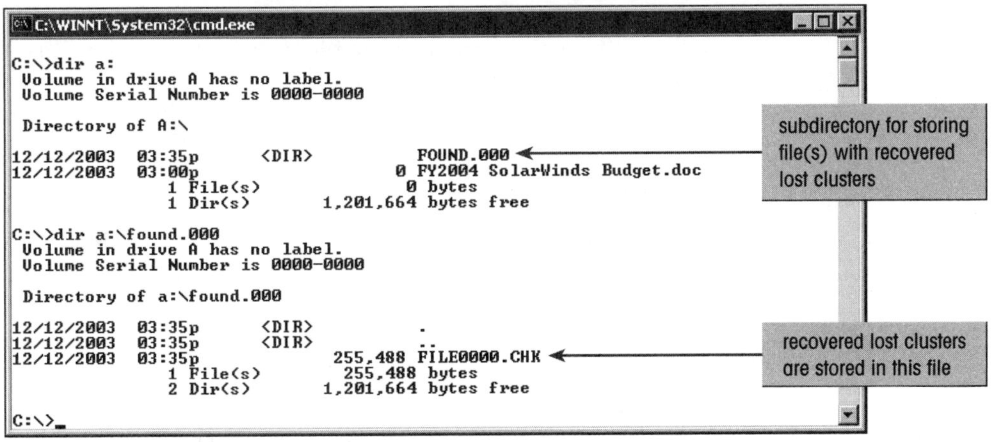

At this point, open FILE0000.CHK, and attempt to determine if it has anything you might need. A "CHK" file could contain any type of data, and you can't tell what program originally produced it. Therefore, your best bet is to open it with a readily available program, such as Notepad or Wordpad, that can produce some kind of display out of any file's data. For example, if you opened FILE0000.CHK in WordPad, you would see something similar to what is shown in Figure 6-43. The document in this file, which is 105 pages long, contains text as well as uninterpretable characters that represent formatting codes inserted by the original program. Although you might have assumed that the file is a Microsoft Word document because of the "doc" file extension and the file icon, the "WPC" code at the beginning of this file indicates that this file was produced in WordPerfect. The next step would be to close WordPad without saving, then open the file in WordPerfect so it can interpret the formatting codes.

Figure 6-43   **EXAMINING A FILE THAT CONTAINS RECOVERED LOST CLUSTERS**

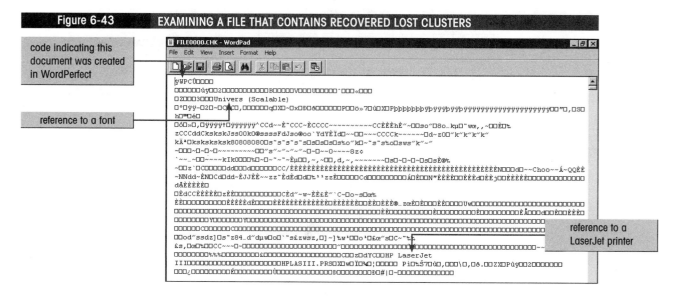

If the file contains useful information, you can insert the contents into another file, or use copy-and-paste to copy what you need from the file to another file. You could also rename the file and edit it. If the file does not contain anything of value to you, or if you still cannot tell what program produced the file or what type of information was contained in the file, delete the file to recover the disk space used by the file. Later, if you discover that a program fails to operate properly or not at all, then reinstall that program on your hard disk or restore it from a backup set. If you are missing part of a data file, you would restore it from a backup set.

Over time, lost clusters can increase in number, waste additional valuable disk space, lead to further disk errors, and affect the proper functioning of your computer. In most cases, you will delete the files that contain lost clusters and reclaim the storage space on your hard disk drive.

Checking for Cross-Linked Files

Another important, but less common, problem is cross-linked files. A **cross-linked file** is a file that contains at least one cluster that belongs to, or is shared by, two or more files. In most cases, you will find that one file is cross-linked with only one other file through just one shared cluster. In the File Allocation Table, Windows 2000 has recorded the cross-linked cluster as the next available cluster for two different files. Figure 6-44 illustrates how cross-linked clusters might occur.

Figure 6-44	AN EXAMPLE OF HOW CROSS-LINKING MAY OCCUR

CLUSTER	STATUS		CLUSTER	STATUS
1500	1501		1500	1501
1501	1502		1501	1502
1502	1503		1502	1503
1503	1504		1503	1504
1504	1505		1504	1505
1505	EOF		1505	~~EOF~~ 1510
1506	1507		1506	1507
1507	1508		1507	1508
1508	1509		1508	1509
1509	1510		1509	1510
1510	1511		**1510**	**1511**
1511	1512		**1511**	**1512**
1512	EOF		**1512**	**EOF**

shared clusters

Assume you are using a utility program to look at cluster usage in the File Allocation Table for the same two files you examined earlier. As a result of a power problem, the end-of-file (EOF) code for the last cluster in the first file changes so there is a pointer to a cluster used by another file. In this example, the end-of-file code for cluster 1505 changes to a pointer that points to cluster 1510. If you open the first file in the program that produced it, Windows 2000 would read clusters 1500 through 1505, and then, because there is a pointer to another cluster and not an EOF code, Windows 2000 would read clusters 1510 through 1512 (which are part of the second file). Windows 2000 stops when it encounters the EOF code for cluster 1512. If you examine this file (assuming you can open it at all), you will discover uninterpretable characters in the file where the cross-link occurs, and perhaps in other parts of the file as well. If you open the second file in the program that produced it, Windows 2000 would read clusters 1506 through 1512, the clusters originally assigned to this file before the cross-link occurred. Again, if you examine this file, you will discover uninterpretable characters and perhaps lost data where the cross-link occurs.

You can repair cross-linked files by copying each file to a new location and remove the original files so that the files are no longer cross-linked. You then open both files (if possible), examine them, and edit the files to remove the uninterpretable characters and add any data that might have been lost.

Using Check Disk on an NTFS Volume

The NTFS file system uses a Master File Table (MFT) to keep track of every file on an NTFS volume, including the Master File Table itself. As noted earlier, the MFT contains entries on all the information that Windows 2000 tracks on a file, including its size, date and time stamps, permissions, and data content.

When you use the Check Disk utility on an NTFS volume, it makes three passes of the volume and examines all the tracking information for all of the files on the volume. This data also includes information on the allocation units assigned to the file for storing data, the available (or free) allocation units, and the allocation units that contain bad sectors.

- **During the first pass, the Check Disk utility verifies files**. The Check Disk utility examines each file record segment in the volume's Master File Table for internal consistency, and identifies which file record segments and clusters are in use. The **file record segment** (FRS) refers to a unique ID assigned to each folder and file in the MFT. At the completion of this phase, the utility compares the information it compiled against the same type of information that NTFS maintains on disk in an effort to find discrepancies or problems such as corrupted file record segments.

- **During the second pass, the Check Disk utility verifies indexes, or NTFS directories, on the volume**. The utility examines each directory on the volume for internal consistency. It makes sure that every directory and file belongs to at least one directory, and that the reference to the file record segment in the master file table is valid. This utility also checks and verifies time stamps and file sizes. From the information garnered during this phase, Check Disk can determine if there are any orphaned files. An **orphaned file** is a file that has a valid file record segment in the master file table, but which is not listed in any directory. An orphaned file is comparable to a lost cluster. Check Disk can restore an orphaned file to its original directory if that directory still exists. If that directory does not exist, the utility creates a directory in the root directory for that file. If Check Disk finds a file record segment which is no longer in use or which does not correspond to the file in the directory, it removes the directory entry. This phase takes the most time.

- **In the third pass, Check Disk checks and verifies security descriptors for each directory and file**. A **security descriptor** contains information about the owner of the directory or file, permissions granted to users and groups for that directory or file, and information on security events to be audited for that directory or file.

If Check Disk detects a problem on an NTFS or a FAT volume, it will try to fix the problem, but this utility is not a substitute for backups.

Using the Check Disk Utility

Isabel emphasizes the importance of using the Check Disk utility on a regular basis to check and maintain the integrity of hard disks that contain important company documents. She points out that it is easier to repair problems while they are relatively minor, rather than wait until the problems become more serious and perhaps impossible to repair.

Before you run the Check Disk utility, you must close all other programs that you are using, including applications and other utilities. For example, you might need to disable your antivirus software and turn off your screen saver. If the Check Disk utility finds a defective cluster on the hard disk, it will attempt to move the data in that bad cluster to another location on the same disk. If an open program is also using that same cluster, it will interfere with the Check Disk utility. In order to operate, Check Disk will attempt to **lock**, or prevent access to, the drive. If it cannot lock the drive, it will offer to check the drive the next time you start the computer.

If you want to use Check Disk to examine your hard disk drive, and you have never used Check Disk before, you should back up the hard disk drive before you run Check Disk. If Check Disk detects and then repairs errors in the file system or the surface of the disk, you might lose important information. In fact, it is a good idea to back up on a regular basis in any case.

You should not use a Check Disk utility designed for DOS, Windows 3.1, or another version of Windows with Windows 2000 because it could corrupt long filenames. If that occurs, you might discover that your programs do not work properly if at all. Furthermore, because the Check Disk utilities in different versions of Windows are designed for different file systems (FAT16, FAT32, or NTFS), you should use only the Check Disk utility included with your version of Windows 2000.

Although Windows 2000 contains a graphical interface version of Check Disk, the CHKDSK utility provides a quicker way to use the same function, and it displays more information.

By default, the Check Disk utility operates in **read-only mode**, a diagnostic mode in which Check Disk checks the drive and, if it finds errors, reports the presence of these errors and simulates how it would correct the problem. After you see how Check Disk would correct the problem, you can decide what course of action you want to take. As noted earlier, you can use the Check Disk utility's **Fix switch** (**/F**) to repair certain types of problems, such as lost clusters. The Check Disk utility can also check the physical structure of a disk if you use the **Repair switch** (**/R**). When you use this switch, the Check Disk utility attempts to recover data stored in bad sectors before marking those sectors as unusable. Any recovered data is recorded in other unused good sectors on the disk. However, both the /F and /R switches greatly lengthen the Check Disk process; with very large hard disks it can even take days, during which the hard disk will be inaccessible to you, so use these switches carefully with hard drive volumes.

In the next set of steps, you are going to run the Check Disk utility and check one of your diskettes. Although it is a more common practice to use Check Disk on your hard disk drive, you can also use it to check diskettes. To check drive C (or another drive on your hard disk), you must log on as Administrator or under an account with Administrator privileges.

In previous tutorials, you opened a Command Prompt window by choosing Command Prompt from the Accessories menu. You can also open a Command Prompt window using the Run command on the Start menu. This approach is faster and displays the full path on the title bar of the Command Prompt window.

To run the Check Disk utility on drive A:

1. Select **Run** form the Start menu. Windows 2000 displays a Run dialog box, in which you can enter commands (like working in a limited command-line environment). See Figure 6-45. The Open list box will either be empty, or it will display the last command that you or someone else entered. If you have previously entered a command, you can click the Open drop-down list arrow, and then select the command from a list box instead of typing the command.

| Figure 6-45 | USING RUN TO OPEN A COMMAND PROMPT WINDOW |

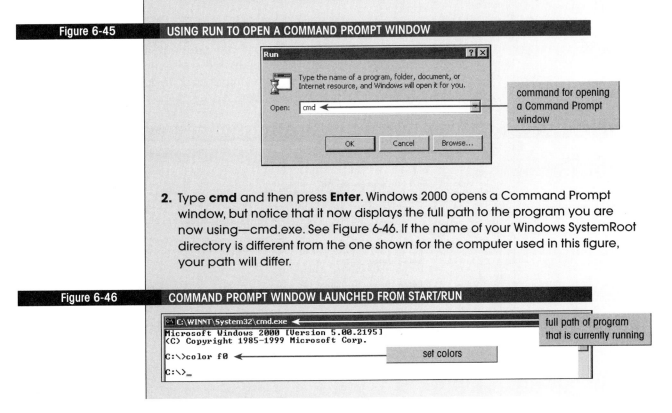

command for opening a Command Prompt window

2. Type **cmd** and then press **Enter**. Windows 2000 opens a Command Prompt window, but notice that it now displays the full path to the program you are now using—cmd.exe. See Figure 6-46. If the name of your Windows SystemRoot directory is different from the one shown for the computer used in this figure, your path will differ.

| Figure 6-46 | COMMAND PROMPT WINDOW LAUNCHED FROM START/RUN |

`C:\WINNT\System32\cmd.exe`

```
Microsoft Windows 2000 [Version 5.00.2195]
(C) Copyright 1985-1999 Microsoft Corp.

C:\>color f0

C:\>_
```

full path of program that is currently running

set colors

3. Set the Command Prompt window colors to black characters on a white background.

4. Make a duplicate of Data Disk #2. Leave your duplicate diskette in drive A.

5. Enter: `chkdsk a:`

The Check Disk utility checks drive A.

6. Read the three-section report that shows the results of the check, storage space usage on the diskette, and storage space allocation on the diskette. If there are errors on the diskette, it will first report on those errors, as shown in Figure 6-47. Some information in your Check Disk report will probably differ from that in the figure.

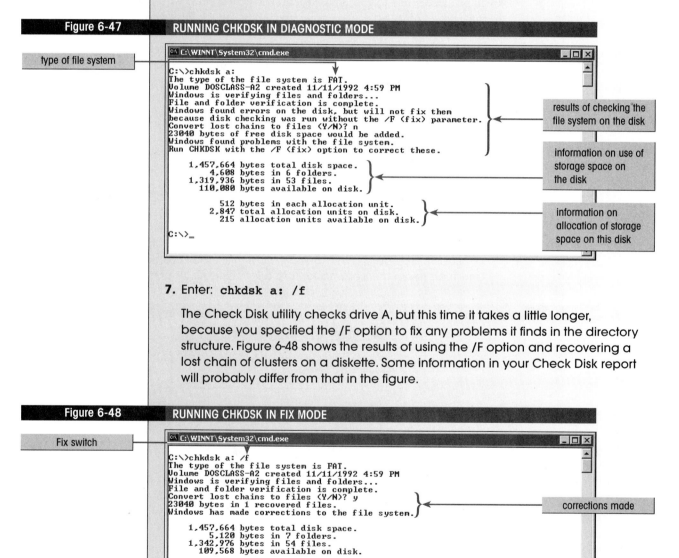

Figure 6-47   RUNNING CHKDSK IN DIAGNOSTIC MODE

type of file system

results of checking the file system on the disk

information on use of storage space on the disk

information on allocation of storage space on this disk

7. Enter: `chkdsk a: /f`

The Check Disk utility checks drive A, but this time it takes a little longer, because you specified the /F option to fix any problems it finds in the directory structure. Figure 6-48 shows the results of using the /F option and recovering a lost chain of clusters on a diskette. Some information in your Check Disk report will probably differ from that in the figure.

Figure 6-48   RUNNING CHKDSK IN FIX MODE

Fix switch

corrections made

8. Enter: `chkdsk a: /r`

The Check Disk utility checks drive A, but this time it takes even longer, because the /R option checks the entire surface of the diskette, locating any bad sectors and recovering readable information. Like /F, the /R option the repairs directory structure problems and checks the free space on the diskette for errors. Figure 6-49 shows the /R option finding a bad sector on a diskette, as well as recovering lost clusters the /F option would have also found. Again, your display may look different, depending on the type of disk you use.

| Figure 6-49 | RUNNING CHKDSK IN REPAIR MODE |

Repair switch

```
C:\WINNT\System32\cmd.exe

C:\>chkdsk a: /r
The type of the file system is FAT.
Volume DOSCLASS-A2 created 11/11/1992 4:59 PM
Windows is verifying files and folders...
Windows replaced bad clusters in file \8WK\84-1\D1FINAL.TST
of name (null).
File and folder verification is complete.
Convert lost chains to files (Y/N)? y
23040 bytes in 1 recovered files.
Windows is verifying free space...
Free space verification is complete.
Windows has made corrections to the file system.

    1,457,664 bytes total disk space.
        5,120 bytes in 7 folders.
    1,342,976 bytes in 54 files.
          512 bytes in bad sectors.
      109,056 bytes available on disk.

          512 bytes in each allocation unit.
        2,847 total allocation units on disk.
          213 allocation units available on disk.

C:\>_
```

results of the disk check

9. Close the Command Prompt window.

During this process, the Check Disk utility identifies the file system used on drive A (FAT), and then shows the volume name for the drive and the date and time the volume name was assigned, as well as its serial number. Then it verifies the integrity of the file system.

If you archive valuable data to removable media, such as diskettes, be sure to copy the data to fresh media at least once a year to avoid loss due to deterioration of both the magnetic signals and the physical media itself. Otherwise, you are liable to see errors such as those illustrated above.

If the drive uses FAT16, you can determine the size of a cluster by dividing the number of bytes in each allocation unit (or cluster) by 512 bytes/sector. In the case of the diskette shown in the figures above, each cluster has 512 bytes, so it consists of just one sector (512 bytes divided by 512 bytes per sector). As the drive size increases, FAT16 must increase the cluster size. On a 2 GB FAT16 hard drive volume, there are 64 sectors, or 32 KBs, per cluster—not a very efficient use of disk storage space.

If you use Check Disk on an NTFS volume, as shown in Figure 6-50, it runs in a read-only mode — like it did for the FAT volume. First, it identifies the file system as NTFS (this information might scroll off the screen), and then it shows the three phases of its check: file verification, index verification, and security descriptor verification. Notice that Check Disk found problems on this drive. Your next step would be to backup your computer. Then, you would use the CHKDSK command with the Fix switch (/F), and see if it reports and corrects the problem. You might also need to use the Recover switch (/R) for a more thorough (and more time-consuming) check of your hard disk.

On this NTFS drive, which is 23.5 GB in size, there are 4,096 bytes in each allocation unit (or cluster). That translates to 8 sectors/cluster (4,096 divided by 512)—a much more efficient use of storage space than what you would find on a disk that used the FAT16 file system.

It also is important to note that if you use CHKDSK /F on very large hard drive volumes, such as 70 GB, or on volumes with millions of files, it can take *days* to complete. You will be unable to access the hard drive volume until CHKDSK is done with it.

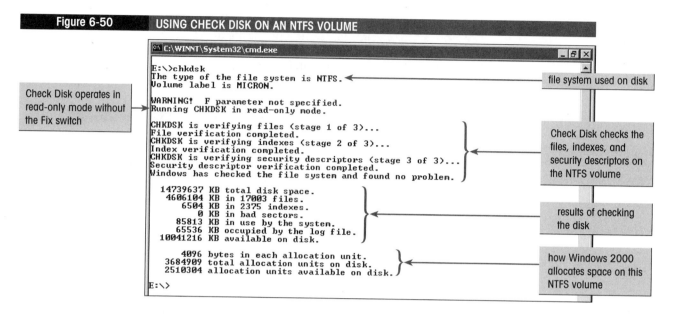

Figure 6-50 | **USING CHECK DISK ON AN NTFS VOLUME**

The average useful lifetime of a hard disk drive is estimated at 3 to 5 years. After this point, the chance of a hard disk failure from a worn-out component increases. The actual lifetime, however, depends on how well you take care of your hard disk drive and the demands placed on it. If you monitor your hard disk drive frequently with Check Disk and eliminate errors that might cause serious problems if left unresolved, you can expect to extend the longevity of your hard disk drive. Even with care, all hard disks will eventually fail. The various diagnostic and repair utilities cannot substitute for performing regular backups—as discussed in the previous tutorial.

Session 6.2 Quick Check

1. Windows 2000 supports three file systems: _____, _____, and _____.

2. The _____ file system provides backward compatibility with DOS.

3. Formatting a disk subdivides the disk into _____ and _____

4. A(n) _____ represents the minimum amount of space that an operating system allocates when saving the contents of a file to disk.

5. The _____ is a table that contains the name and the version number of the operating system used to format the diskette, as well as information on the physical characteristics of the disk.

6. The _____ keeps track of space on a disk that is unused, defective, occupied by files, or reserved for use by the operating system

7. Most operating systems using the FAT16 file system do not normally support hard disks over _____ in size.

8. A(n) _____ is all or part of the physical hard disk that is set aside for a drive or set of logical drives.

9. In the NTFS file system, the _____ is a special file that keeps information about the files on disk.

10. A(n) _____ is a rule associated with an object to regulate which users can gain access to the object and in what manner.

11. The _____ utility is the Windows 2000 Error-checking tool for both FAT and NTFS volumes.

SESSION 6.3

In this session, you will install and use the Recovery Console, a troubleshooting tool. You will launch the Recovery Console from Windows 2000 Setup Disks or CD. You will also install the Recovery Console on your hard drive, launch it from the OS Choices menu, and practice some basic Recovery Console commands.

Using the Recovery Console

Isabel reminds the SolarWinds support staff of the value of the Emergency Repair Disk system. She points out, however, that the standard start-up options available for using the Emergency Repair Disk are sometimes not adequate to fix a Windows 2000 system that will not start or work properly. The Recovery Console is designed to give you a more flexible repair environment in such situations.

The Recovery Console is a command-line interface for advanced users, separate from the Windows 2000 command prompt, which provides access to a set of commands for repairing a computer. You choose the Recovery Console during booting, instead of choosing Windows 2000.

In the Recovery Console, you can start and stop services, read and write to any local disk even if it uses a different file system, format drives, and copy files from a diskette or CD-ROM to the hard disk. A **service** is a program, routine, or process that provides support to other programs. You can also repair the Registry by using Recovery Console's COPY command to replace individual Registry files with backup copies.

You can launch Recovery Console either from your Windows 2000 Setup Disks, from the Windows 2000 installation CD, or by installing Recovery Console on your hard drive and adding it to your OS Choices menu. To use the Recovery Console, you must log on as Administrator.

The next section covers the most convenient way to make the Recovery Console available.

Installing Recovery Console

You can use a fast and convenient method of launching the Recovery Console utility by installing it to the Windows 2000 hard drive volume. It requires about 7 MB of storage space and will work as long as you can restart your computer and reach the OS Choices menu.

Removing the Recovery Console is a complex and detailed process that requires changing system files, and may affect your ability to restart your computer, if done incorrectly.

Note: If you are working on someone else's computer (such as a computer in your college lab) and you do not have permission to install Recovery Console, then read, but do not perform, this section and the following section, Launching Recovery Console from the OS Choices menu. Instead, you may be able to perform the subsequent section, Launching Recovery Console from Setup Disks or CD.

To install Recovery Console to the hard drive:

1. To log on as Administrator, click **Start** and then click **Shutdown**. In the "Shut Down Windows" dialog box, click the drop-down list and select "**Log off username**", and then click **OK**. When the "Log On to Windows" dialog box appears, type **Administrator** in the "User Name" text box and the Administrator's password in the "Password" text box, and then click **OK**.

2. Open a Command Prompt window, set colors if necessary, and then clear the window.

3. Insert the Windows 2000 installation CD.

   TROUBLE? If a Windows 2000 Setup CD window automatically opens, close it and proceed to the next step.

4. Type the drive letter for your CD-ROM drive, followed by a colon, and then press **Enter** to make the CD-ROM the default drive. For example, if your CD-ROM is drive D, type **d:** and then press **Enter**.

5. Enter: **\i386\winnt32 /cmdcons** (as shown in Figure 6-51).

   Cmdcons stands for Command Console.

| Figure 6-51 | INSTALLING THE RECOVERY CONSOLE |

change to CD-ROM drive

```
Command Prompt                                    _ □ ×
C:\>d:
D:\>\i386\winnt32 /cmdcons
D:\>_
```

command for installing the Recovery Console

6. When you see the Windows 2000 Setup Recovery Console installation dialog box, as shown in Figure 6-52, click **Yes** to install.

Figure 6-52	INFORMATION ON USING AND INSTALLING THE RECOVERY CONSOLE

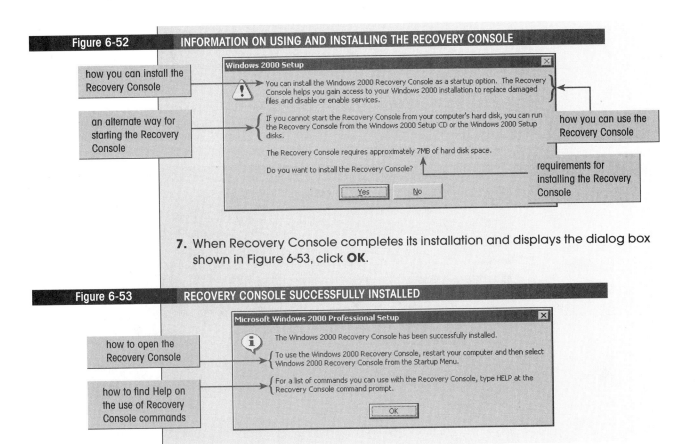

how you can install the Recovery Console

an alternate way for starting the Recovery Console

how you can use the Recovery Console

requirements for installing the Recovery Console

7. When Recovery Console completes its installation and displays the dialog box shown in Figure 6-53, click **OK**.

Figure 6-53	RECOVERY CONSOLE SUCCESSFULLY INSTALLED

how to open the Recovery Console

how to find Help on the use of Recovery Console commands

Installing Recovery Console to the hard drive provides you with a handy way to run it when needed or access it for practice.

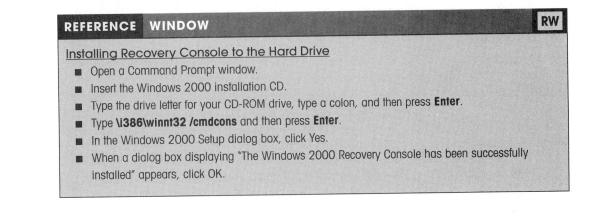

REFERENCE WINDOW   RW

Installing Recovery Console to the Hard Drive
- Open a Command Prompt window.
- Insert the Windows 2000 installation CD.
- Type the drive letter for your CD-ROM drive, type a colon, and then press **Enter**.
- Type **\i386\winnt32 /cmdcons** and then press **Enter**.
- In the Windows 2000 Setup dialog box, click Yes.
- When a dialog box displaying "The Windows 2000 Recovery Console has been successfully installed" appears, click OK.

Now that you have installed Recovery Console to the hard drive, you are ready to launch it.

Launching Recovery Console from the OS Choices Menu

Launching Recovery Console from the hard drive's OS Choices startup menu is much faster than using Windows 2000 Setup Disks or the Windows 2000 CD.

To launch Recovery Console from the hard drive:

1. Remove any diskettes or CDs from your drives, and restart your computer. The computer reboots, then you see the OS Choices startup menu,

2. Press the ↓, select Microsoft Windows 2000 Recovery Console, if necessary, and then press **Enter**. See Figure 6-54. The Recovery Console opening screen appears.

Figure 6-54   MICROSOFT WINDOWS 2000 OS CHOICES MENU

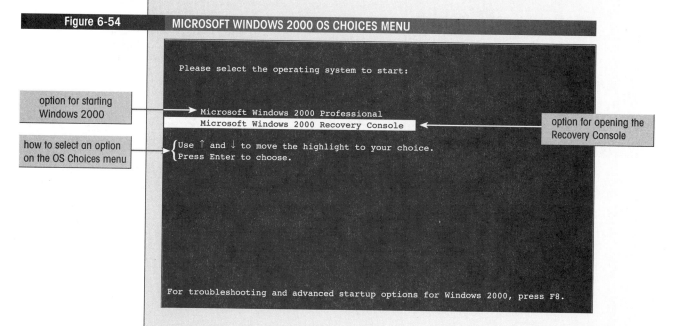

option for starting Windows 2000

how to select an option on the OS Choices menu

option for opening the Recovery Console

```
     Please select the operating system to start:


        Microsoft Windows 2000 Professional
        Microsoft Windows 2000 Recovery Console

  ⎰ Use ↑ and ↓ to move the highlight to your choice.
  ⎱ Press Enter to choose.








  For troubleshooting and advanced startup options for Windows 2000, press F8.
```

REFERENCE WINDOW   **RW**

<u>Launching Recovery Console from the OS Choices Menu</u>
- Restart your computer.
- When you see the OS Choices menu, press the ↓, select Microsoft Windows 2000 Recovery Console, if necessary, and then press Enter.
- Select the Windows 2000 installation directory folder.
- Type the Administrator password and then press Enter.

Microsoft recommends that you install Recovery Console to your hard drive so you can launch it from the OS Choices Menu when needed. However, if your computer will not start at all, you need an alternative approach.

Now you are ready to log into Recovery Console. Read, but do not perform, the following section, Launching Recovery Console from Setup Disks or CD, and proceed with the subsequent section, Logging into Recovery Console.

Launching Recovery Console from Setup Disks or CD

The simplest way to launch Recovery Console (although not the fastest) is to boot your computer from your Windows 2000 Setup Disks or installation CD. If your computer will not otherwise start, this will be your only available method.

Note: If you have already installed Recovery Console to your hard drive and launched it—or if you do not have permission to run Recovery Console on your computer—then read, but do not perform, the following steps.

To start Recovery Console from your Windows 2000 Setup Disks or installation CD:

1. If necessary, restart your computer, open CMOS, and then change your BIOS settings so your computer will first boot from a diskette in drive A, or from the CD-ROM drive if you are booting from the Windows 2000 CD.

2. Depending on the boot method you have chosen in Step 1, either put your Windows 2000 Setup Boot Disk #1 in drive A, or put your Windows 2000 installation CD in the CD-ROM drive, and then restart your computer.

3. Starting the Windows 2000 Setup program is a time-consuming process. If you are booting from diskettes, insert each Windows 2000 Setup Disk when prompted.

   TROUBLE? If the Windows 2000 Setup program doesn't launch, be sure you have set your CMOS to boot from the media you are using: either drive A or your CD-ROM drive. You may need to turn your computer off completely and then turn it on again. Some computers will pause briefly, prompting you to boot from the CD if desired.

4. When you see the screen titled Welcome to Setup, type **r** to select the option to repair a Windows 2000 installation.

   TROUBLE? If you have an evaluation version of the Windows 2000 CD, you will see a message informing you of this situation, and prompts you to press Enter to continue, or F3 to quit. Press Enter and proceed with the Welcome to Setup in Step 4 above.

5. At the screen titled Windows 2000 Repair Options, type **c** to launch the Recovery Console.

Starting from Windows 2000 Setup Disks or the Windows 2000 CD is a straightforward, but time-consuming way, to launch Recovery Console. However, if Windows 2000 will not boot at all, it may be the only way you can access this utility.

Logging into Recovery Console

Once you launch the Recovery Console from the OS Choices Menu, Setup Disks, or CD, you will see the opening screen of Recovery Console. Recovery Console displays the available Windows 2000 SystemRoot directory folders. Normally you will see just one, named C:\WINNT.

Note: This section requires that you log in as the Administrator of your computer. If you are working on someone else's computer (such as a computer in your college lab) and you do not have permission to log in as Administrator, then read, but do not perform, this section and the following one, Using Recovery Console Commands.

To log into Recovery Console:

1. Type the number of the SystemRoot folder (usually **1**) and then press **Enter.**

2. Type the Administrator password when prompted and then press **Enter**. The password characters will appear on the screen as asterisks. Recovery Console then displays a command prompt showing the Windows 2000 SystemRoot directory as the current default. See Figure 6-55.

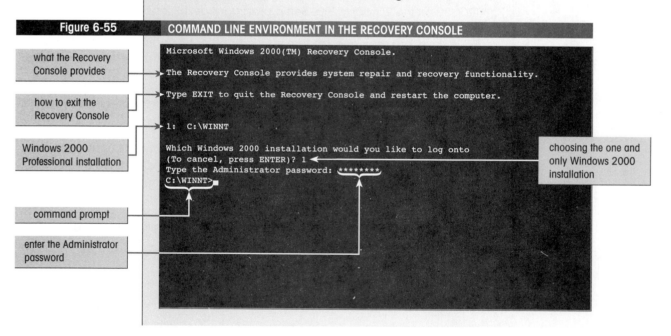

| Figure 6-55 | COMMAND LINE ENVIRONMENT IN THE RECOVERY CONSOLE |

what the Recovery Console provides

how to exit the Recovery Console

Windows 2000 Professional installation

command prompt

enter the Administrator password

```
Microsoft Windows 2000(TM) Recovery Console.

The Recovery Console provides system repair and recovery functionality.

Type EXIT to quit the Recovery Console and restart the computer.


1:  C:\WINNT

Which Windows 2000 installation would you like to log onto
(To cancel, press ENTER)? 1
Type the Administrator password: ********
C:\WINNT>
```

choosing the one and only Windows 2000 installation

From this point, you can enter Recovery Console commands.

Logging into Recovery Console

- Launch Recovery Console from the OS Choices startup menu, Windows 2000 Setup Disks, or Windows 2000 CD.
- Type the number of the desired Windows 2000 SystemRoot directory folder (usually 1 for C:\WINNT) and then press Enter.
- Type the Administrator password when prompted, and then press Enter. Recovery Console displays a Windows 2000 system directory command prompt.

Using Recovery Console Commands

You learn from Isabel that Recovery Console provides a limited set of commands that you can use to repair a Windows 2000 system that will not start or run properly, due to a variety of causes from a corrupted Registry to a damaged hard drive volume. Although Recovery Console looks like a regular command line environment, you can use only 26 commands, and you cannot run any other programs or utilities. Most Recovery Console commands look like commands you use at the normal command prompt, but they have important differences and limitations. A complete list of Recovery Console commands with brief descriptions is shown in Figure 6-56.

Figure 6-56	RECOVERY CONSOLE COMMANDS

COMMAND	DESCRIPTION
attrib	Changes limited attributes of one file or folder. No switches; no wildcards.
batch	Executes commands specified in a text file.
cd *or* chdir	Changes to a specified directory folder. No switches; no wildcards; limited target directories.
chkdsk	Checks a disk and, if needed, repairs or recovers the volume. Limited switches.
cls	Clears the screen.
copy	Copies one file; no switches; no wildcards.
del *or* delete	Deletes one file; no switches; no wildcards.
dir	Displays files and directory folders within a directory folder. Displays attributes. Wildcards okay; no switches.
disable	Disables a Windows 2000 system service or driver. (Use **listsvc** to list services and drivers.)
diskpart	Manages hard drive partitions.
enable	Enables a Windows 2000 system service or driver. (Use **listsvc** to list services and drivers.)
exit	Quits Recovery Console and reboots.
expand	Expands compressed files; extracts from, or lists files in, a CAB (cabinet) file on the Windows 2000 CD.
fixboot	Rewrites a hard drive boot sector.
fixmbr	Rewrites the hard drive's Master Boot Record (MBR).
format	Formats a specified volume to a specified file system. Limited switches.
help	Displays command help text.

Figure 6-56 | **RECOVERY CONSOLE COMMANDS (CONTINUED)**

COMMAND	DESCRIPTION
listsvc	Lists all available services, drivers, and their start types.
logon	Restarts Recovery Console at the installation directory and password prompts.
map	Lists drive letters, file system types, volume sizes, and mappings to currently active physical devices.
md *or* mkdir	Creates one directory.
more *or* type	Displays a text file, pausing at each full screen.
rd *or* rmdir	Deletes a directory. No switches; no wildcards.
ren *or* rename	Renames a file or directory. No wildcards.
set	Displays limited Recovery Console environment variables; variable assignment capability limited.
systemroot	Changes to the System Root directory (usually **c:\winnt**).

Recovery Console is designed primarily for getting a failed Windows 2000 system to work again; therefore, by default, it only allows you access to a few directory folders, most importantly the Windows 2000 System Root directory (usually C:\WINNT) and its subdirectories.

You decide to explore the available directory structure from Recovery Console's starting point, the System Root directory folder.

To explore the Recovery Console directories:

1. Make sure you are at the Recovery Console command prompt in the Windows 2000 System Root directory.

2. Enter: `dir`

Note that the DIR command in the Recovery Console displays the attributes of each file and directory, including the "d" attribute for directories. Notice also that directory entries show a file size of zero (0). In addition, this DIR command automatically pauses at each full screen. See Figure 6-57.

| Figure 6-57 | DISPLAYING A DIRECTORY OF THE WINDOWS FOLDER |

attributes

subdirectory files

files

```
The volume in drive C is DRIVE
The volume Serial Number is e461-9d1c

 Directory of C:\WINNT

02/28/00  01:33p  d-------         0 .
02/28/00  01:33p  d-------         0 ..
02/28/00  01:33p  d-------         0 system32
02/28/00  01:33p  d-------         0 system
02/28/00  01:33p  d-------         0 repair
02/28/00  01:33p  d--h----         0 inf
02/28/00  01:33p  d-------         0 Help
02/28/00  01:33p  d-r-s---         0 Fonts
02/28/00  01:33p  d-------         0 Config
02/28/00  01:33p  d-------         0 msagent
02/28/00  01:33p  d-------         0 Cursors
02/28/00  01:33p  d-------         0 Media
02/28/00  01:33p  d-------         0 java
02/28/00  01:33p  d---s---         0 Web
02/28/00  01:33p  d-------         0 addins
02/28/00  01:33p  d-------         0 Connection Wizard
02/28/00  01:33p  d-------         0 Driver Cache
02/28/00  01:33p  d-------         0 security
02/28/00  01:33p  d-------         0 twain_32
02/28/00  01:33p  d-------         0 msapps
02/28/00  01:33p  d-------         0 AppPatch
02/28/00  01:33p  d-------         0 Debug
12/07/99  12:00p  -a------       707 _default.pif
12/07/99  12:00p  -a------     41744 discover.exe
12/07/99  12:00p  -a------    238352 explorer.exe
12/07/99  12:00p  -a------        80 explorer.scf
12/07/99  12:00p  -a------     26896 hh.exe
 More:    ENTER=Scroll (Line)    SPACE=Scroll (Page)    ESC=Stop
```

3. Press the **Spacebar** as many times as is necessary to view the rest of the directory listing.

4. Enter: `type ntbtlog.txt`

Note that in Recovery Console, "type" and "more" are two names for the same command. They both display a text file and pause at each full screen. See Figure 6-58.

Figure 6-58

kernel

USING TYPE TO VIEW THE CONTENTS OF THE NBTLOG.TXT

```
Microsoft (R) Windows 2000 (R) Version 5.0 (Build 2195)
 4 20 2003 09:07:35.500
Loaded driver \WINNT\System32\ntoskrnl.exe
Loaded driver \WINNT\System32\hal.dll
Loaded driver \WINNT\System32\BOOTVID.DLL
Loaded driver pci.sys
Loaded driver isapnp.sys
Loaded driver intelide.sys
Loaded driver \WINNT\System32\DRIVERS\PCIIDEX.SYS
Loaded driver MountMgr.sys
Loaded driver ftdisk.sys
Loaded driver Diskperf.sys
Loaded driver \WINNT\System32\Drivers\WMILIB.SYS
Loaded driver dmload.sys
Loaded driver dmio.sys
Loaded driver PartMgr.sys
Loaded driver atapi.sys
Loaded driver disk.sys
Loaded driver \WINNT\System32\DRIVERS\CLASSPNP.SYS
Loaded driver Fastfat.sys
Loaded driver KSecDD.sys
Loaded driver NDIS.sys
Loaded driver ppa3.sys
Loaded driver Mup.sys
Did not load driver Audio Codecs
Did not load driver Legacy Audio Drivers
Did not load driver Media Control Devices
Did not load driver Legacy Video Capture Devices
Did not load driver Video Codecs
Did not load driver WAN Miniport (L2TP)
Did not load driver WAN Miniport (IP)
Did not load driver WAN Miniport (NetBEUI, Dial In)
  More:   ENTER=Scroll (Line)    SPACE=Scroll (Page)     ESC=Stop
```

Hardware Abstration Layer

5. Press the **Spacebar** as many times as is necessary to view the rest of the text file. You can press **Esc** to stop in the middle and return to the command prompt.

6. To change to the root directory folder, enter: `cd \`

7. To display a directory listing; enter: `dir`

   Note the differences in attributes of the various files and directories in the listing. See Figure 6-59. Your display may be different.

8. Press the **Spacebar** as many times as is necessary to view the rest of the directory listing.

Figure 6-59	VIEWING THE CONTENTS OF THE SYSTEM ROOT DIRECTORY

change to System Root directory

attributes

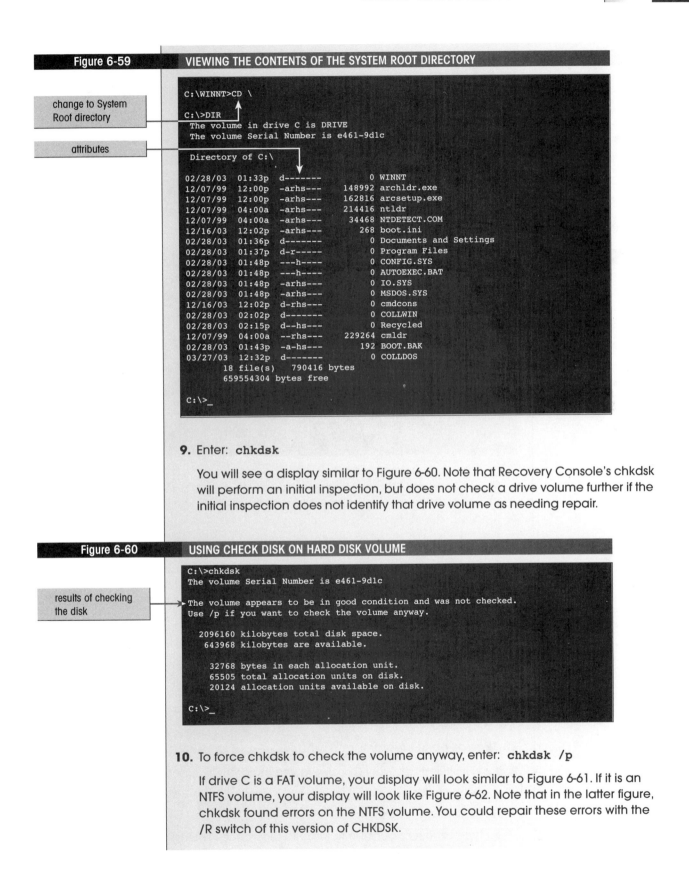

```
C:\WINNT>CD \

C:\>DIR
 The volume in drive C is DRIVE
 The volume Serial Number is e461-9d1c

 Directory of C:\

02/28/03  01:33p  d-------          0 WINNT
12/07/99  12:00p  -arhs---     148992 archldr.exe
12/07/99  12:00p  -arhs---     162816 arcsetup.exe
12/07/99  04:00a  -arhs---     214416 ntldr
12/07/99  04:00a  -arhs---      34468 NTDETECT.COM
12/16/03  12:02p  -arhs---        268 boot.ini
02/28/03  01:36p  d-------          0 Documents and Settings
02/28/03  01:37p  d-r-----          0 Program Files
02/28/03  01:48p  ---h----          0 CONFIG.SYS
02/28/03  01:48p  ---h----          0 AUTOEXEC.BAT
02/28/03  01:48p  -arhs---          0 IO.SYS
02/28/03  01:48p  -arhs---          0 MSDOS.SYS
12/16/03  12:02p  d-rhs---          0 cmdcons
02/28/03  02:02p  d-------          0 COLLWIN
02/28/03  02:15p  d--hs---          0 Recycled
12/07/99  04:00a  --rhs---     229264 cmldr
02/28/03  01:43p  -a-hs---        192 BOOT.BAK
03/27/03  12:32p  d-------          0 COLLDOS
        18 file(s)    790416 bytes
        659554304 bytes free

C:\>_
```

9. Enter: `chkdsk`

You will see a display similar to Figure 6-60. Note that Recovery Console's chkdsk will perform an initial inspection, but does not check a drive volume further if the initial inspection does not identify that drive volume as needing repair.

Figure 6-60	USING CHECK DISK ON HARD DISK VOLUME

results of checking the disk

```
C:\>chkdsk
The volume Serial Number is e461-9d1c

The volume appears to be in good condition and was not checked.
Use /p if you want to check the volume anyway.

 2096160 kilobytes total disk space.
  643968 kilobytes are available.

   32768 bytes in each allocation unit.
   65505 total allocation units on disk.
   20124 allocation units available on disk.

C:\>_
```

10. To force chkdsk to check the volume anyway, enter: `chkdsk /p`

If drive C is a FAT volume, your display will look similar to Figure 6-61. If it is an NTFS volume, your display will look like Figure 6-62. Note that in the latter figure, chkdsk found errors on the NTFS volume. You could repair these errors with the /R switch of this version of CHKDSK.

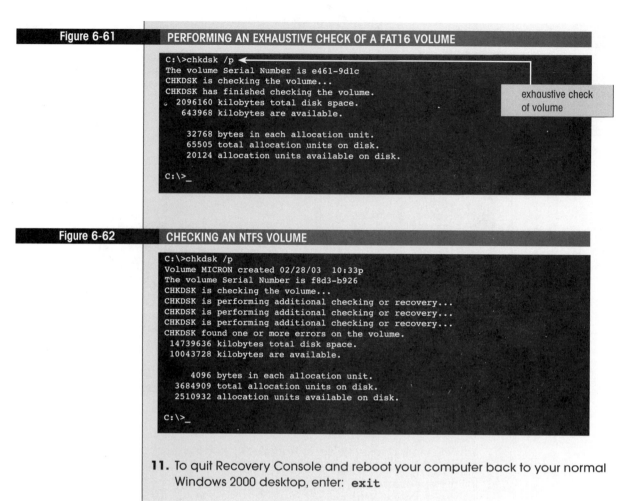

Figure 6-61   **PERFORMING AN EXHAUSTIVE CHECK OF A FAT16 VOLUME**

```
C:\>chkdsk /p
The volume Serial Number is e461-9d1c
CHKDSK is checking the volume...
CHKDSK has finished checking the volume.
   2096160 kilobytes total disk space.
    643968 kilobytes are available.

     32768 bytes in each allocation unit.
     65505 total allocation units on disk.
     20124 allocation units available on disk.

C:\>_
```

exhaustive check
of volume

Figure 6-62   **CHECKING AN NTFS VOLUME**

```
C:\>chkdsk /p
Volume MICRON created 02/28/03  10:33p
The volume Serial Number is f8d3-b926
CHKDSK is checking the volume...
CHKDSK is performing additional checking or recovery...
CHKDSK is performing additional checking or recovery...
CHKDSK is performing additional checking or recovery...
CHKDSK found one or more errors on the volume.
 14739636 kilobytes total disk space.
 10043728 kilobytes are available.

      4096 bytes in each allocation unit.
   3684909 total allocation units on disk.
   2510932 allocation units available on disk.

C:\>_
```

11. To quit Recovery Console and reboot your computer back to your normal Windows 2000 desktop, enter: **exit**

Now that you have learned about file systems, basic repairs with chkdsk, and the use of Recovery Console, Isabel feels confident that you have the basic knowledge to approach troubleshooting a Windows 2000 system.

Restoring **Your Computer**

If you want to restore your computer to its original state before you started the tutorial, complete the following steps.

To restore your computer:

1. Close all open programs and windows.

2. If you installed Recovery Console to your hard drive, you can remove it as follows:

   a. Open the Windows Help system.

   b. Click the Index tab.

   c. Type **recovery console** to jump to the corresponding index entry.

   d. Double-click on the sub-entry removing.

   e. Follow the instructions shown to delete Recovery Console and remove it from the OS Choices Menu.

3. Click the **Start** button, click **Shut Down**, select the **Restart** option button in the Shut Down Windows dialog box, and then click OK.

4. Press the key, or combinations of keys, you need to use to open the CMOS Setup utility.

5. If you changed the boot order, use the documentation you printed or recorded by hand to restore the original boot sequence using the instructions in CMOS. If necessary, ask your instructor or lab staff person for assistance.

6. Using the instructions in CMOS, save your changes and exit CMOS. If necessary, ask your instructor or lab staff person for assistance.

Session 6.3 QUICK CHECK

1. A(n) _____ is a program, routine, or process that provides support to other programs.

2. To use the Recovery Console, you must log on as _____.

3. The simplest way to launch the Recovery Console (although not the fastest) is to boot your computer from your _____ or _____.

4. The DIR command in the Recovery Console displays the _____ of each file and directory.

5. In the Recovery Console, "type" and _____ are two names for the same command.

6. In the Recovery Console, type CHKDSK with the _____ option to force CHKDSK to check the volume even if its initial inspection does not identify it as needing repair.

7. Type _____ to quit Recovery Console and reboot your computer.

COMMAND REFERENCE

COMMAND	USE	BASIC SYNTAX	EXAMPLE
[F8]	Keyboard command for displaying the Windows 2000 Advanced Options Menu during booting	[F8]	[F8]
Ctrl+Alt+Del	Keyboard command for shutting down Windows 2000 after booting into Safe Mode with command prompt	Ctrl+Alt+Del	Ctrl+Alt+Del
MAKEBOOT	Creates Windows 2000 Setup Disks using the Windows 2000 CD	MAKEBOOT [*drive*]	makeboot a:
NTBACKUP	Creates an Emergency Repair Disk from the Backup utility	NTBACKUP	ntbackup
CHKDSK	Checks a disk for errors, corrects certain types of disk errors (with /F switch), locates bad sectors and recovers readable data (with /R switch) and displays a status report	CHKDSK [*drive*] [/F]	chkdsk a: chkdsk c: chkdsk c: /f chkdsk c: /r
\i386\winnt32 /cmdcons	Installs the Recovery Console from the Windows 2000 CD	\i386\winnt32 /cmdcons	\i386\winnt32 /cmdcons
CHKDSK /P	In the Recovery Console, forces Check Disk to check a volume	CHKDSK [*drive*] [/P]	chkdsk /p
EXIT	Exits the Recovery Console and reboots computer	EXIT	exit

Items shown in italics and not enclosed within square brackets are required parameters
Items shown in italics and enclosed within square brackets are optional parameters

REVIEW ASSIGNMENTS

Isabel asks you to show a new intern how to set the boot sequence in CMOS, boot to Safe Mode with Command Prompt, make Windows 2000 Setup Disks, and create an Emergency Repair Disk.

If you are working in a computer lab and if the lab restricts access to CMOS, you might not be able to complete all the steps. For those steps that include questions about CMOS, note whether the lab restricts access to CMOS.

In these Review Assignments, you will step through the process of making an extra copy of the Windows 2000 Setup Disks and the Emergency Repair Disk, so you will need a Windows 2000 CD and five diskettes. If you want to reuse the five diskettes that you used in the tutorial, reformat them first.

As you complete each step, record your answers to any questions so you can submit them to your instructor.

1. Restart your computer, display the Windows 2000 Advanced Options menu, and choose the option for booting in Safe Mode with Command Prompt. What program does Windows 2000 start after you log on your computer?

2. Format five high-density diskettes and make sure the diskettes do not contain defective sectors. *Note*: If you are using the same diskettes as you used in the tutorial, and if you recently formatted those diskettes, you can use the Quick switch (/Q) with the FORMAT command to reformat the diskettes quickly.

3. Insert the Windows 2000 CD into your CD-ROM drive.

4. Use the MakeBoot program to make a set of Windows 2000 Setup Disks. How did you launch, or start, this program? What command did you enter, and what path did you specify for the location of this program? Can you create these diskettes on a computer that uses Windows 98 or DOS?

5. Make an Emergency Repair Disk. Describe how you performed this operation. Why would it be important to update your copy of the Emergency Repair Disk periodically?

6. Remove any diskette you have in drive A.

7. Restart your computer, and as it boots, open CMOS. What key(s) did you press to access CMOS?

8. Some computers contain an option in CMOS for write-protecting the fixed disk boot sector to protect it from computer viruses. Examine the Security settings in CMOS. Is there an option for write-protecting the fixed disk boot sector? What is that setting?

9. If necessary, set the boot order so your computer will boot from drive A first, and enable the option for write-protecting the fixed disk boot sector. What boot sequence does your computer now use?

10. Examine the other settings in CMOS. Are there any other settings that you might want to change? If so, what are they and why would you want to change them? Do not make these changes unless you are sure you want to implement them now.

11. Exit CMOS, save your changes, and reboot your computer.

12. Make a duplicate copy of Data Disk #1.

13. Execute the Check Disk program with the Fix option on your duplicate diskette. What information does Check Disk report?

14. Execute the Check Disk program with the Repair option on your duplicate diskette. What information does Check Disk report?

    Note: The following steps require you to use the Recovery Console, and therefore are optional. Skip them if you do not have Administrator privileges on your computer.

15. Install Recovery Console on your hard drive.

16. Launch Recovery Console, either from the hard drive, from your Setup Disks, or from your Windows 2000 installation CD.

17. In Recovery Console, change to the config directory folder under the System Root directory.

18. Execute the DIR command. How many files does dir list, and what are their attributes?

19. Execute the Check Disk command on your hard drive. What information does Check Disk report?

20. Quit Recovery Console and reboot.

21. If you are working in a computer lab, restore any changes that you made to CMOS.

CASE PROBLEMS

Case 1. Comparing NT File Systems at The Perfect Match Zhou Qiao, President of Perfect Match, and his department managers discussed the status of the company's computer systems at their recent monthly meeting. Managers reported that the storage space on the hard disk drives in their departments was not being used efficiently. Some employees were encountering problems with limited storage space, and had to stop their regular work in order to check their computers and free up storage space. Zhou asks you to prepare a recommendation on what the company might do to reduce these problems so employees can work more productively. After examining the company's computers, you discover all of the computers currently use the FAT16 file system, storage space on the hard disk drives is in fact limited, and some of the computers use a dual-boot configuration with Windows 98 and Windows 2000.

1. Prepare and print a 1½- to two-page, double-spaced paper in which you discuss the advantages and disadvantages of upgrading to FAT32 and NTFS versus retaining the FAT16 file system. In particular, focus on whether this upgrade would improve the availability and use of storage space on the hard disks of the company's computers.

2. Include a short section at the end of your paper on the value of retaining a dual-boot configuration on some of the computers in the company's offices versus switching all of the computers over to just Windows 2000.

Case 2. Sleuthing at Computer Troubleshooters Unlimited   Employees at Computer Troubleshooters Unlimited tackle a wide array of problems encountered by its corporate and home user customers. Miles Biehler, a specialist at rebuilding and repairing computer systems and at troubleshooting computer virus infections, works with customers either at the customer's site or over the telephone to identify and resolve problems.

As you complete each step, record your answers to any questions so you can submit them to your instructor.

1. The first customer of the day tells Miles that she picked up a computer virus from a diskette that she accidentally left in drive A. She wants to know if there is any way to avoid this type of problem. What should Miles recommend that she do to keep this from happening in the future?

2. A customer who recently bought a computer system explains to Miles that his computer stalls for an extended period of time whenever he powers on the computer. What should Miles recommend the customer try before that customer brings the computer into their service center?

3. Another customer drops buy Computer Troubleshooters Unlimited and asks Miles how she can reinstall the original version of a Windows 2000 system file. What questions should Miles ask this customer? What should he recommend that this customer do to restore the file in question?

4. A new user wants to know what he should do if he needs to reinstall Windows 2000. What questions should Miles ask this customer? What should Miles recommend this customer do?

5. Yet another customer wants to know how to repair a damaged Registry on her computer. What questions should Miles ask this customer? What should he recommend that this customer do? What potential problems should Miles warn the customer about?

Case 3. Checking a Disk at Steppingstone Development Services   At the non-profit organization Steppingstone Development Services, Office Manager Angela Pinelli has a diskette from a branch office upon which her staff has made file changes. Before she sends then diskette back, she would like you to check it for errors, repair any problems and report the results to her.

1. Open a Command Prompt window, and then make a duplicate of Data Disk #1.

2. With your duplicate of Data Disk #1 in drive A, run the Check Disk utility in diagnostic mode only (do not use the option to fix any problems). What information does Check Disk report?

3. Now run Check Disk with the Fix option. How is the display different this time?

4. If Check Disk had reported that it fixed errors on your diskette after the above command, what would you do next? What kind of errors would Check Disk report and fix?

5. Run Check Disk again, this time with the option to find bad sectors on your diskette. What information does Check Disk report this time?

6. If Check Disk reported that it repaired bad sector errors on a diskette, what would you do next?

Case 4. Evaluating the Recovery Console at Centaur Graphics   Marcee Zimmerman works as a Web design artist at Centaur Graphics, and keeps an updated copy of the Windows 2000 Setup Disks and the Emergency Repair Disk. She also wants to research the use of the Recovery Console to determine whether she should install it on her computer.

As you complete each step, record your answers to any questions so you can submit them to your instructor.

1. Open Windows 2000 Help and Windows 2000 Professional Getting Started Help (which you can access via Windows 2000 Help), and search for information on the Windows 2000 Recovery Console.

2. What is the Recovery Console? What two ways can you start the Recovery Console?

3. What types of operations can you perform with the Recovery Console?

4. Are there any requirements for using the Recovery Console? Explain.

5. Can you use the Recovery Console on a dual-boot or multiple-boot computer, and if so, are there any requirements? Explain.

6. How do you install the Recovery Console so it appears on the boot menu?

7. One of the commands you can use in the Recovery Console is the command for the Check Disk utility. Describe three ways in which you can use this utility once you start the Recovery Console.

8. Can you remove the Recovery Console once you've installed it? If so, explain how you would perform this operation.

QUICK | CHECK ANSWERS

Session 6.1

1. Registry
2. boot disk
3. MBR or Master Boot Record
4. Protected
5. virtual memory
6. IDE or Integrated Drive Electronics
7. device driver
8. CMOS or Complementary Metal Oxide Semiconductor
9. service
10. Last Known Good Configuration
11. Safe Mode
12. Setup Disks
13. A
14. Setup information
15. Backup

Session 6.2

1. FAT16, FAT32, and NTFS
2. FAT16
3. tracks, sectors
4. cluster or allocation unit
5. boot or boot sector
6. FAT or File Allocation Table
7. 2 GB
8. partition
9. MFT or Master File Table
10. permission
11. Check Disk or CHKDSK

Session 6.3

1. service
2. Administrator
3. Windows 2000 Setup Disks, or installation CD
4. attributes
5. "more"
6. /P
7. exit

In this tutorial you will:

- Examine the importance of batch programs

- Create a batch program for automating a routine command operation

- Change the path in the Windows environment

- Use replaceable parameters in a batch program

- Create a batch program to load applications from a Command Prompt window

- Control the display of batch program commands

- Display user messages from a batch program

- Temporarily pause batch program execution

- Document batch program operations

- Create a desktop shortcut to a batch program.

- Expand the capabilities of Recovery Console

- Create and execute a batch program for Recovery Console

USING BATCH PROGRAMS

Automating Routine Operations at SolarWinds

CASE

Isabel Navarro uses batch programs to automate and simplify routine operations that she performs daily on her computer, so she can effectively and efficiently use her time to focus on her most important tasks. Furthermore, she has integrated the coverage of batch programs in staff training workshops so others can benefit from time-saving measures that batch programs offer. Her support staff prepares batch programs not only for use with their own computer systems, but also for use on computers of other staff members. A **batch program**, or **batch file**, is an ASCII file that contains one or more commands for performing an operation or a set of operations.

SESSION 7.1

In this session, you will examine the importance of batch programs, as well as the features and advantages they offer users. You will create a batch program using the MS-DOS Editor and store it in a batch program directory under the directory for your user account. You will then test the batch program under different conditions and examine the importance of the search path in batch program execution. You will store the search path in a batch program so you can restore the path setting in the Windows environment, then you will modify the search path to include your batch program directory. You will further enhance your batch program with the use of a replaceable parameter so you can provide the batch program with variable information when you run it.

The Importance of Batch Programs

Over the years, Isabel and her staff have relied on the use of a variety of batch programs to simplify and automate the most common types of operations as well as complex procedures that they perform daily on their computers.

If you find that you perform the same operation or same types of operations repeatedly in a Command Prompt window, you can store the command or commands in a special type of file called a batch program, and execute the batch program as you would any other program file. A **batch program** is a user-defined program that contains commands that Windows 2000 executes when you run the batch program. The words user-defined program indicate that you are the one who creates the batch program. Batch programs do not require that a user be a programmer in order to benefit from their use. Under MS-DOS and previous versions of Windows, a batch program was referred to as a batch file.

In order for Windows 2000 to recognize a batch program as a program file, you *must* add the "bat" (batch) or "cmd" (command) extension to the filename for the batch program when you create it. In contrast, under Windows 98, Windows 95, and MS-DOS, you must use only the "bat" file extension.

You can create and use batch programs either from the Command Prompt window or from the Windows 2000 desktop by using text editors such as the MS-DOS Editor and Notepad. In either operating environment, batch programs automate frequently performed operations and save time and effort, including keystroking in the command line environment, and clicking and double-clicking in the graphical user operating environment.

Batch programs represent one important and valuable way in which you can optimize the performance of your computer system. Not only can you use batch programs to automate routine operations, such as formatting a disk or customizing the Command Prompt environment, you can also create batch programs that perform more complex sets of procedures. For example, you might use batch programs to collect and document information about your computer, back up the contents of multiple drives and directories, open a set of other programs, and install other programs.

Creating a Batch Program

As part of their preparation for in-house workshops, Isabel and her staff routinely format a diskette for each participant, and copy specific files that the participants will use to the newly formatted disks. To reduce the amount of time involved in preparing these diskettes and to simplify the overall process, Isabel and her staff decide to prepare a set of batch programs that will allow them to prepare these diskettes in different ways for different types of training sessions.

Isabel asks you to first prepare a batch program that will format a diskette and assign a volume label to the disk. Before you create this batch program, set up your computer.

To set up your computer:

1. Open a Command Prompt window.

2. Change the background and foreground colors (if necessary).

3. Create the DIRCMD environment variable, and then assign default settings to this variable so the DIR command lists directories and files in order by filename, one window at a time.

4. Right-click the Command Prompt window **title bar**, click **Properties**, and then, after Windows 2000 displays the "Command Prompt" Properties dialog box, click the **Layout** tab. As you saw in Tutorial 5, if you change the Screen Buffer Size Width on this property sheet, then long pathnames and filenames will not wrap in the Command Prompt window.

5. Under the Screen Buffer Size section, select **80** in the Width box (if it is not already selected), type **300**, and then click **OK**. Windows displays an "Apply Properties To Shortcuts" dialog box.

6. If it is not already selected, click the **Apply properties to current window only** option button, and click **OK**. Windows 2000 closes the Command Prompt Properties dialog box and applies the new setting to the Command Prompt window.

7. Maximize the **Command Prompt** window.

   TROUBLE? If the Command Prompt window does not fill the entire screen after you click the Maximize button ⬜, click the Restore Down button ⬜, and then click ⬜ again to determine whether you can increase the size of the window.

Your next step is to create a directory for your batch programs.

Creating a Directory for Batch Programs

Isabel notes that, in the past, most users created a directory called BAT in the root directory of drive C for their batch programs. However, since network Administrators and technicians typically store batch programs for customizing a networked computer in this directory, she recommends that you create your batch program directory under your own user account. That way, you can keep your batch programs separate from those of other users, and you can easily locate and update your batch programs.

If you are working in a computer lab, you will need permission under your user account to create a batch program directory on the hard disk to complete this tutorial.

To set up your batch program directory:

1. Clear the window, and then enter the command: `cd %userprofile%`
   The command interpreter changes to the directory for your user account by using the path to your account directory stored in the Windows environment. Your path may differ from the one shown for Isabel in Figure 7-1. The USERPROFILE, an environment variable like DIRCMD, stores the path to the directory for your user account in the Windows environment. For example, when Isabel logs onto her computer, she enters Isabel for her user name. When she first created this

account as the network Administrator, Windows 2000 created a directory named Isabel under the "Documents and Settings" directory. Each time she logs on, Windows 2000 stores the path to her user account directory in the Windows environment under the USERPROFILE environment variable. The % symbols around the name of the environment variable instruct the CD command to pull this information from the Windows environment and substitute it for USERPROFILE. So, in Isabel's case, the command interpreter translates %USERPROFILE% into "C:\Documents and Settings\Isabel".

Figure 7-1   CHANGING TO YOUR USER LOGON DIRECTORY

current directory changed to the directory for Isabel's user logon

```
Command Prompt                                                    _ □ x
C:\>cd %userprofile%  ◄
C:\Documents and Settings\Isabel>
```

environment variable with path to directory for your user logon

2. Enter the command: `dir /ad`

DIR displays the subdirectories below the current directory. All of the directories shown in Figure 7-2 are created by Windows 2000 for each user account. You can create new subdirectories within the directory for your user account, or you can open the "My Documents" directory and create subdirectories under that directory (as you did in Tutorial 5). The Attribute switch with the Directory parameter (/ad) lists all directories; however, if you display a directory without this switch, DIR displays only the "Start Menu," "My Documents," "Favorites," and "Desktop" directories because the other directories are hidden system directories.

Figure 7-2   SUBDIRECTORIES FOR A USER LOGON DIRECTORY

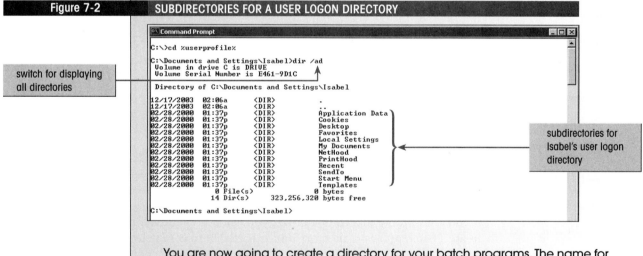

switch for displaying all directories

```
Command Prompt                                                    _ □ x
C:\>cd %userprofile%

C:\Documents and Settings\Isabel>dir /ad
 Volume in drive C is DRIVE
 Volume Serial Number is E461-9D1C

 Directory of C:\Documents and Settings\Isabel

12/17/2003  02:06a    <DIR>          .
12/17/2003  02:06a    <DIR>          ..
02/28/2000  01:37p    <DIR>          Application Data
02/28/2000  01:37p    <DIR>          Cookies
02/28/2000  01:37p    <DIR>          Desktop
02/28/2000  01:37p    <DIR>          Favorites
02/28/2000  01:37p    <DIR>          Local Settings
02/28/2000  01:37p    <DIR>          My Documents
02/28/2000  01:37p    <DIR>          NetHood
02/28/2000  01:37p    <DIR>          PrintHood
02/28/2000  01:37p    <DIR>          Recent
02/28/2000  01:37p    <DIR>          SendTo
02/28/2000  01:37p    <DIR>          Start Menu
02/28/2000  01:37p    <DIR>          Templates
               0 File(s)              0 bytes
              14 Dir(s)     323,256,320 bytes free

C:\Documents and Settings\Isabel>
```

subdirectories for Isabel's user logon directory

You are now going to create a directory for your batch programs. The name for this directory will include the words "Batch Programs for" followed by a space and your name, so that you can distinguish your batch programs from those of other users on the same computer who might use the same user name. For example, if all the individuals in your course log on a computer in your computer lab under the user name CIS (to indicate the Computer and Information Sciences department), then the user account directory for each person would be CIS. Under that directory, you would then make a batch program directory with your name (for example, "Batch Programs for Isabel Navarro").

3. Check the directory listing and make sure you do not already have a directory named "Batch Programs for *(Your Name)*", where *(Your Name)* is your actual name. If there is no directory by this name, create a directory for your batch programs by entering the command:

   md   **"Batch Programs for** *[Your Name]***"**

   Remember to replace *(Your Name)* with your first and last names. If there is a directory by this name belonging to someone else, then use another name for your batch program directory, and then substitute that name in the remaining steps in this tutorial. On the other hand, if you have your own user logon name on your computer that no one else can use, you may choose a shorter name for your batch program directory and then substitute that name henceforth.

4. Display a directory listing, and make sure you successfully created this batch program directory. Figure 7-3 shows the directory that Isabel created for her batch programs.

Figure 7-3	CREATING A BATCH PROGRAM DIRECTORY

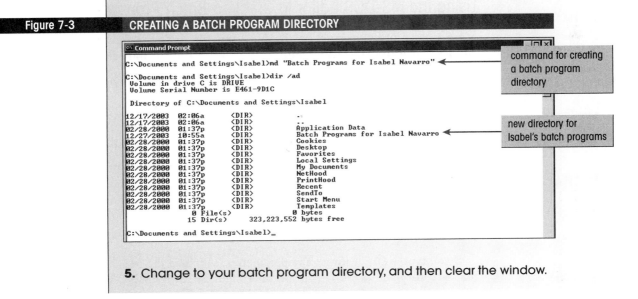

5. Change to your batch program directory, and then clear the window.

If you already have batch programs in your batch program directory, it is good practice to check the names of your existing batch program files so you do not create a new batch program file with the name of an existing one, thereby accidentally overwriting it.

Although it's possible to create and store batch programs in several different directories, you might want to store all your batch programs in the same directory for ease of access.

Using the MS-DOS Editor to Create a Batch Program

Since a batch program must be an ASCII text file, Isabel recommends that you use a text editor, such as the MS-DOS Editor or Notepad, to create and edit the batch program.

The MS-DOS Editor is a separate utility that was first introduced in MS-DOS 5.0 and is available in subsequent versions of MS-DOS, as well as in Windows 95, Windows 98, Windows NT Workstation 4.0, and Windows 2000. If you prefer to create batch programs from the graphical user interface, you can use Notepad instead. You should, however, know how to use both utilities. If you are unable to boot a version of Windows to the desktop, you will need to use the MS-DOS Editor (or a comparable command line utility) in a command line environment. Whichever utility you use, it is important to remember that the file must be an ASCII text file and that the file extension of the batch program file must be "bat" or "cmd".

To start the MS-DOS Editor, use the EDIT command. The **EDIT** command is an external command with the following general syntax:

EDIT [[*drive*:][*path*]*filename*]

If you type EDIT without any parameters, you load the MS-DOS Editor from the current directory and drive. If you specify a filename, the MS-DOS Editor retrieves that file after the command interpreter loads the MS-DOS Editor into memory, or if there is no file by that name, the MS-DOS Editor creates a new file using that filename. If the file is stored on another drive or in another directory, you must specify the drive name and path of the file; otherwise, the MS-DOS Editor will create a new file in the current drive and directory with that same name.

In the next set of steps, you are going to open the MS-DOS Editor and assign the name FormatDisk.bat to the batch program at the same time. If your batch program directory already contains a batch program named FormatDisk.bat, then use another name, such as FD.BAT, to refer to that batch program file. In the past, it was common practice to use one, two, or perhaps three characters (as in FD.BAT) for the batch program's filename; however, if you use abbreviated filenames, you might find that you do not remember what the batch program does, or you might execute a batch program other than the one you intended to use.

To create a batch program:

1. Enter the command: **edit FormatDisk.bat**
   The Command Prompt window's title bar shows the command you just entered. See Figure 7-4. Within the Command Prompt window, you see the MS-DOS Editor application window and document window. Like other application windows, the MS-DOS application window has a menu bar and a status bar. The status bar indicates that you can use the F1 Help key to access the MS-DOS Editor Help. On the right side of the status bar, the MS-DOS Editor displays the line and column position of the cursor. When you first start, the cursor is on line 1 and in column 1. At the top of the document window, the MS-DOS Editor displays the full or partial path as well as the filename of the batch program. If you had not included a filename with the EDIT command, then you would see "UNTITLED1" instead.

Figure 7-4	CREATING A BATCH PROGRAM WITH THE MS-DOS EDITOR

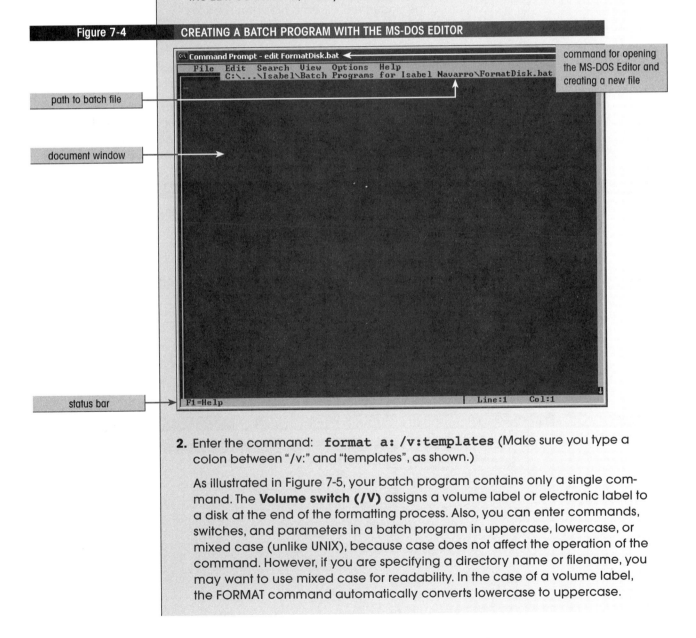

path to batch file

document window

status bar

command for opening the MS-DOS Editor and creating a new file

2. Enter the command: **format a: /v:templates** (Make sure you type a colon between "/v:" and "templates", as shown.)

   As illustrated in Figure 7-5, your batch program contains only a single command. The **Volume switch (/V)** assigns a volume label or electronic label to a disk at the end of the formatting process. Also, you can enter commands, switches, and parameters in a batch program in uppercase, lowercase, or mixed case (unlike UNIX), because case does not affect the operation of the command. However, if you are specifying a directory name or filename, you may want to use mixed case for readability. In the case of a volume label, the FORMAT command automatically converts lowercase to uppercase.

Figure 7-5   **BATCH PROGRAM FOR FORMATTING A DISK**

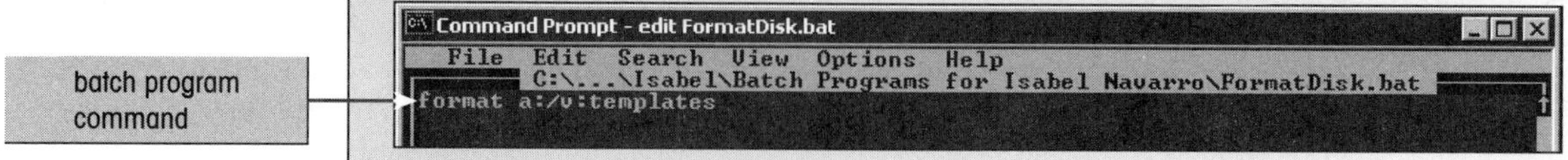

batch program command

Command Prompt - edit FormatDisk.bat

File   Edit   Search   View   Options   Help
C:\...\Isabel\Batch Programs for Isabel Navarro\FormatDisk.bat
format a:/v:templates

3. Press the **Alt** key. The MS-DOS Editor highlights File on the menu bar. Note that the first letter of each menu name is shown in white. As in other programs, to select a menu, you can press an arrow key to highlight the menu name and then press Enter to select that menu, or you can type the letter shown in white for the menu name. If you want to select the currently highlighted menu, just press Enter. If you activate the menu bar and then change your mind and want to return to the document window, press the Esc key.

4. Press **Enter**, type **x** to select the Exit option on the File menu, and then, in the Save File dialog box, press **Enter** (or type **y**) to save your work and exit at the same time. Notice that the command prompt now shows the short filenames for the "Documents and Settings" directory and your batch program directory.

5. Display a directory listing of your batch program directory. As is typical of most batch programs, this batch program is very small in size. On the computer shown in the figure, the batch program is only 23 bytes. See Figure 7-6. Your file size may differ.

Figure 7-6   **VIEWING THE BATCH PROGRAM FILE IN THE BATCH PROGRAM DIRECTORY**

Command Prompt

C:\Documents and Settings\Isabel\Batch Programs for Isabel Navarro>edit FormatDi

C:\DOCUME~1\Isabel\BATCHP~1>dir
 Volume in drive C is DRIVE
 Volume Serial Number is E461-9D1C

 Directory of C:\DOCUME~1\Isabel\BATCHP~1

12/27/2003 10:55a   <DIR>   .
12/27/2003 10:55a   <DIR>   ..
12/27/2003 11:00a   23 FormatDisk.bat
               1 File(s)   23 bytes
               2 Dir(s)   323,518,464 bytes free

C:\DOCUME~1\Isabel\BATCHP~1>_

the command interpreter uses short filenames in the path for the command prompt

batch program file (note small size)

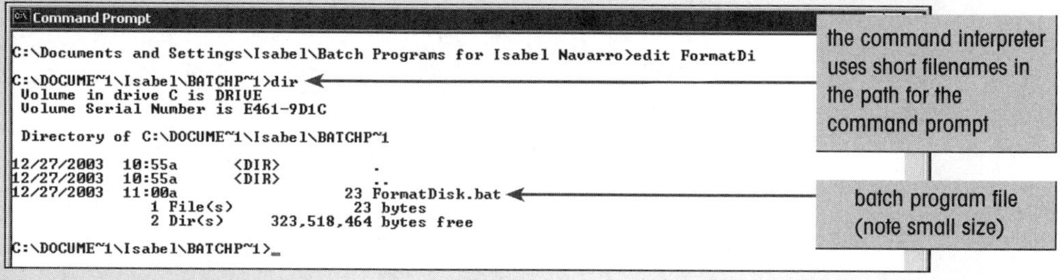

6. Clear the window, and then enter the command: **type FormatDisk.bat**

The TYPE command displays the contents of this ASCII text file. See Figure 7-7.

Figure 7-7   **VIEWING THE CONTENTS OF THE BATCH PROGRAM FILE**

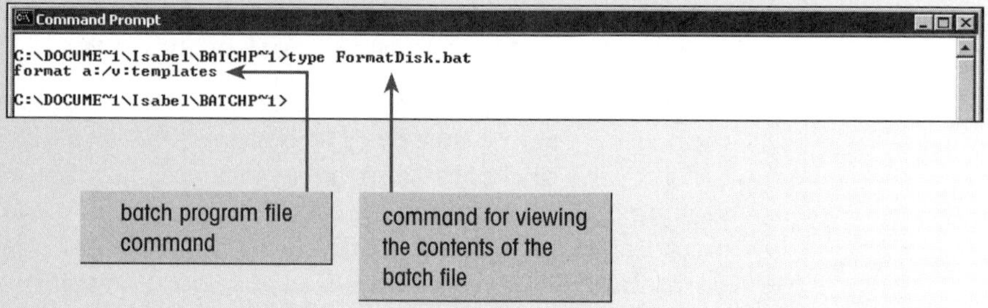

Command Prompt

C:\DOCUME~1\Isabel\BATCHP~1>type FormatDisk.bat
format a:/v:templates

C:\DOCUME~1\Isabel\BATCHP~1>

batch program file command

command for viewing the contents of the batch file

You can use the **TYPE** command to remind you of the contents of a batch program file before you use it.

Using the MS-DOS Editor to Create a Batch Program
- Open a Command Prompt window, and change to the batch program directory.
- Type EDIT, a space, the name of the batch program (remember to include the "bat" or "cmd" file extension), and then press Enter.
- After the command interpreter opens the MS-DOS Editor, type each command on a separate line.
- To save your batch program and exit, press the Alt key, press Enter to select the File menu, type X to exit, and in the Save File dialog box, press Enter (or type Y).

After you create a batch program, you are then ready to test it and, if necessary, modify it further so it performs the operation (or operations) in the way that you want.

Executing a Batch Program

Isabel recommends that you test the batch program to make sure it works properly.

To execute the contents of a batch program, type the main part of the filename of the batch program file at the command prompt. You do not need to specify the file extension, although if you do, the batch program will still work. As with any other command, after you enter the name of the batch program file, the command interpreter checks memory to determine if the command that you entered is an internal command. If the command that you enter is not an internal command, the command interpreter checks the current directory for a program file with the filename that you entered with one of the following file extensions: com, exe, bat, cmd, vbs, vbe, js, jse, wsf, or wsh. Figure 7-8 lists each of these file extensions and their meanings.

Assume you have created a batch program named FormatDisk.bat. If you type FormatDisk at the command prompt and then press Enter, the command interpreter will look in the current directory for a file by the name of FormatDisk.com. If there is no file by this name, it then looks for one by the name of FormatDisk.exe. If there is no file by this name, it then looks for FormatDisk.bat. When it locates FormatDisk.bat, it executes the commands stored in the batch program file. If there is no file by the name of FormatDisk.bat, then the command interpreter will continue to look for files based on the other file extensions listed in Figure 7-8, in the order shown in the figure.

| Figure 7-8 | PROGRAM FILE EXTENSIONS USED IN THE SEARCH PATH |

PROGRAM FILE EXTENSION	MEANING
com	Command (or MS-DOS Application) File
exe	Executable (or Application) File
bat	MS-DOS Batch Program File
cmd	Windows NT Command Script File
vbs	VBScript Script File
vbe	VBScript Encoded Script File
js	JScript Script File

Figure 7-8   **PROGRAM FILE EXTENSIONS USED IN THE SEARCH PATH, CONTINUED**

PROGRAM FILE EXTENSION	MEANING
jse	JScript Encoded Script File
wsf	Windows Script File
wsh	Windows Script Host Settings File
Where VB = Visual Basic	

If the command interpreter does not find a file in the current directory by the name you entered with one of the file extensions shown in this figure, then it will check in each of the directories listed in the search path in the Windows environment in an attempt to locate the program file. As you've seen earlier, the PATH environment variable in the Windows environment lists a sequence of directories, each of which is separated from the previous directory by a semicolon (;). The command interpreter searches each directory in the search path for a file with the name you entered and with one of the file extensions mentioned previously. If the command interpreter does not locate any file with your batch program filename and one of the previously mentioned file extensions, it displays an error message that the command "is not recognized as an internal or external command, operable program, or batch file."

Because you are currently working in the directory that contains the batch program file, you can execute the batch program from this directory. To test this batch program, you will need to use a diskette that is either unformatted or that does not contain information you want to keep.

To execute the batch program:

1. Clear the window, and then insert a blank or empty diskette into drive A.

2. Enter the command: **FormatDisk**

   Next to the command prompt, the command interpreter **echoes**, or displays, the command stored in the batch program. See Figure 7-9. The FORMAT utility then prompts you to insert a disk in drive A.

   TROUBLE? If you need to stop a batch program, or if you accidentally invoke another batch program, you can press Ctrl+C to cancel or Ctrl+Break to interrupt the program. The command interpreter will then display the message "Terminate batch job (Y/N)?". Type Y and press Enter.

   TROUBLE? If a batch program does not perform as you expect, then open the batch program file in the MS-DOS Editor or Notepad, carefully check the order and syntax of each command, make any corrections, and then test the batch program again.

Figure 7-9   **EXECUTING A BATCH PROGRAM**

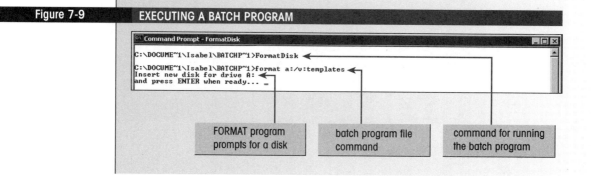

FORMAT program prompts for a disk

batch program file command

command for running the batch program

3. Press **Enter**. The batch program runs the FORMAT utility, which identifies the file system used on the disk, formats the disk, assigns the volume label "Templates" to the disk, initializes the File Allocation Table (FAT), displays information about the storage space and allocation of space on the disk, and then asks you if you want to format another disk. See Figure 7-10.

| Figure 7-10 | FORMATTING A DISKETTE |

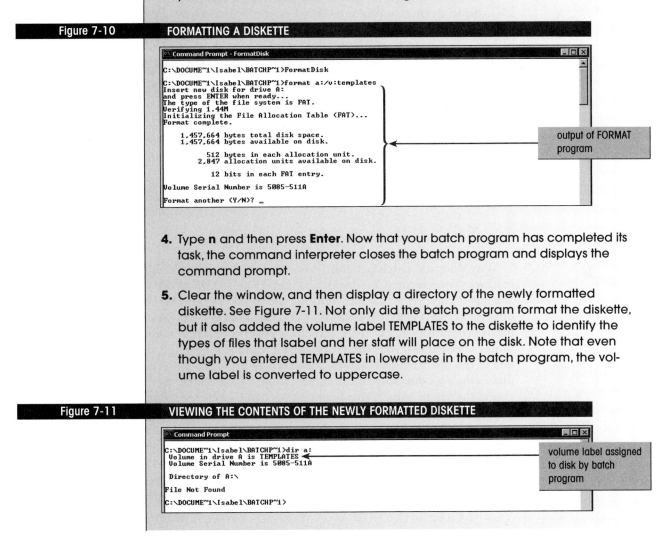

output of FORMAT program

4. Type **n** and then press **Enter**. Now that your batch program has completed its task, the command interpreter closes the batch program and displays the command prompt.

5. Clear the window, and then display a directory of the newly formatted diskette. See Figure 7-11. Not only did the batch program format the diskette, but it also added the volume label TEMPLATES to the diskette to identify the types of files that Isabel and her staff will place on the disk. Note that even though you entered TEMPLATES in lowercase in the batch program, the volume label is converted to uppercase.

| Figure 7-11 | VIEWING THE CONTENTS OF THE NEWLY FORMATTED DISKETTE |

volume label assigned to disk by batch program

You just successfully created and tested a batch program. Once you know that the syntax for the command (or commands) in a batch program works properly, you can use the batch program whenever you want, just by typing the name of the batch program. You do not need to type the entire command contained within the batch program. Also, when you enter a command at the command prompt, you can easily make a typo, and then have to correct or re-enter the command. Once a batch program works, then you can expect it to perform the same way every time.

Executing a Batch Program from Another Directory

Isabel recommends that you also test your batch program under different conditions so you can make sure it operates as you expect.

Whenever you open a Command Prompt window, you are placed in the root directory of drive C. If you then decide to format a diskette with your batch program, you would enter the command from the root directory, and you would expect the batch program to work. So the next logical step is to test the batch program from the root directory.

To test the batch program from the root directory:

1. If necessary, return to the root directory by entering the command: **cd **

2. Clear the window, and then enter the command: **FormatDisk**
   The command interpreter displays the message "'FormatDisk' is not recognized as an internal or external command, operable program or batch file."
   See Figure 7-12.

Figure 7-12	EXECUTING THE BATCH PROGRAM FROM ANOTHER DIRECTORY

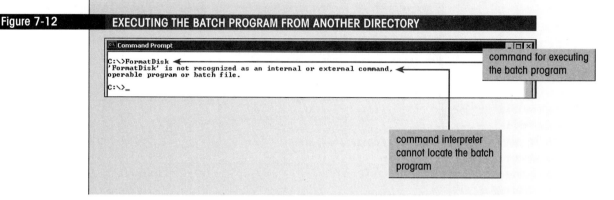

command for executing the batch program

command interpreter cannot locate the batch program

Why does the batch program work in one instance and not the other? In the first instance, you executed the batch program from the directory where you stored it. The command interpreter was able to locate the batch program because it checked the current directory after it checked memory. In the second instance, you attempted to execute the batch program from the root directory. After checking memory, the command interpreter checked the root directory for a program file by the name "FormatDisk" with one of the file extensions shown previously in Figure 7-8. Because there are no program files in the root directory of the current drive by this name, the command interpreter then checks the search path. If there are no program files by the name "FormatDisk" with one of the file extensions shown in Figure 7-8, the command interpreter displays the error message shown in Figure 7-12. From this result, you can conclude that the command interpreter does not check the batch program directory because it is not included in the list of directories in the search path. You could switch back to your batch program directory and then execute the batch program, but then you would always have to remember to perform this one extra step. To be able to execute a batch program from any drive or directory, you will need to modify the search path.

The Importance of the Search Path

Isabel recommends that you check, and then modify, the search path so your batch program will work properly.

Although you can use the SET command to display all the variables and their settings in the Windows environment, you would have to locate the variable whose setting you want to check from a long list of environment variables. Instead of using the SET command, you can use the PATH command to display the list of directories assigned to the PATH environment variable. You can also use this command to change the search path (also called the path, or the Windows path). If you want to view only the search path setting, you enter the PATH command without any parameters. If you want to change the search path, you use the following syntax:

PATH=[*drive:*]*path1*;[*drive:*]*path2*;[*drive:*]*path3*;...

After entering the PATH command, you list the paths of all the directories that you want Windows 2000 to search for a program file. You separate the various directory paths with a semicolon. No spaces are allowed between the paths to different directories, or before or after the semicolon. You must use a semicolon between directories; you cannot use a colon. It is a good idea to specify an absolute path and include the drive name with each directory path so that Windows 2000 knows the exact location of each directory. For example, to change the current search path setting to include the name of Isabel's batch program directory, enter the following command:

PATH="C:\Documents and Settings\Batch Programs for Isabel Navarro"; %PATH%

Once executed, the PATH command adds "C:\Documents and Settings\Batch Programs for Isabel Navarro" to the beginning of the search path. This directory is now the first directory in the search path's list. The %PATH% after the semicolon instructs the PATH command to append the current setting for the search path (which includes all the other directories listed in the search path when you open a Command Prompt window) to the new search path. The advantages of this approach are :

- You can quickly update the search path to include a new directory (or directories).
- You do not have to retype the remainder of the search path, because it's extracted from the PATH environment variable in the Windows environment.
- The directory path for your batch program directory is now listed first in the search path.

Because the PATH command is an internal command, you can execute it from any drive or directory.

Viewing the Search Path

Isabel suggests that you examine the search path on your computer system and update it to include the name of your batch program directory.

To view the search path:

1. Clear the Command Prompt window.

2. Enter the command: **path**

The PATH command displays the current search path. See Figure 7-13. On the computer used for this figure, the search path includes the System32 directory (C:\WINNT\system32), the WINNT directory (C:\WINNT), and the Wbem directory (C:\WINNT\System32\Wbem). WBEM is an abbreviation for Web-Based Enterprise Management. WBEM is an initiative designed to establish standards for accessing and sharing information over an enterprise network. The search path on your computer system may be different.

Figure 7-13   **VIEWING THE SEARCH PATH**

setting assigned to PATH environment variable

command for displaying the Windows search path

```
C:\>path
PATH=C:\WINNT\system32;C:\WINNT;C:\WINNT\System32\Wbem

C:\>
```

As noted earlier, the search path lists a series of directories for Windows 2000 and other programs to search to locate a program file not stored in the current directory in which you are working. Although the search path may vary from one computer to another, you would expect the search path to include the WinNT and System32 directories, where most of the Windows 2000 operating systems files are stored. If you are using a computer network, you will more than likely also see the names of network drives, such as G:, H:, U:, X:, Y:, and Z:.

Storing the Search Path in a Batch Program

Before you make a change to the search path, Isabel recommends that you store the current search path in a batch program so you can later restore it if the need arises.

As with any other command, you can redirect the output of the PATH command to a file—but in this case, it will be a batch program file.

To store the search path in a batch program file:

1. Enter the command (substituting your own name in the path, and remembering to include quotation marks around the path and filename):

   `path > "%userprofile%\Batch Programs for [Your Name]\Reset.bat"`

   Windows 2000 records the current setting for the search path in a file named Reset.bat in your batch program directory.

2. Enter the command (substituting your own name in the path):

   `type "%userprofile%\Batch Programs for [Your Name]\Reset.bat"`

   The TYPE command displays the contents of this new batch program file. See Figure 7-14. As with the batch program for formatting a diskette, this one contains one command—the PATH command with the current search path.

   TROUBLE? If the path shown in Reset.bat does not match the path shown for the first "path" command, then repeat the last two steps, checking your work as you go.

Figure 7-14   **STORING THE SEARCH PATH IN A BATCH PROGRAM FILE**

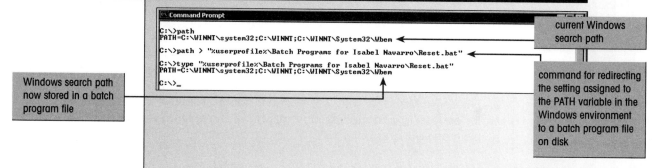

current Windows search path

Windows search path now stored in a batch program file

command for redirecting the setting assigned to the PATH variable in the Windows environment to a batch program file on disk

```
C:\>path
PATH=C:\WINNT\system32;C:\WINNT;C:\WINNT\System32\Wbem

C:\>path > "%userprofile%\Batch Programs for Isabel Navarro\Reset.bat"

C:\>type "%userprofile%\Batch Programs for Isabel Navarro\Reset.bat"
PATH=C:\WINNT\system32;C:\WINNT;C:\WINNT\System32\Wbem

C:\>_
```

If you close the Command Prompt window and then open it later, you will discover that Windows 2000 automatically uses the original search path. The advantage of storing the search path in a batch program file is that you not only document an important system setting, but you can also restore the search path at any time before you close the Command Prompt window.

Changing the Search Path

After further discussion with Isabel, you discover that you can change the search path in one of two ways. You can specify a brand new search path that includes only the directories you specify, or you can add the path for the batch program directory to the current search path. The obvious advantage of the latter approach is that you retain access to all other programs available through the search path.

As noted earlier, you can use the following strategy to add the path of another directory to the current search path:

PATH=[*drive:*]*path;%path%*

The **[*drive:*]*path*** parameter is the path for the new directory you want to add to the current search path (for example, the path to your batch program directory). The **%path%** parameter pulls the current setting stored in the PATH environment variable from the Windows environment and inserts it into the new search path you are defining. The percent symbols before and after "path" identify it as an environment variable, so Windows 2000 uses the current setting for the search path.

Next, you will update the search path using this power user's technique.

To change the search path:

1. Enter the command:
   `path="%userprofile%\Batch Programs for [Your Name]"; %path%`

2. Enter the command: `path`
   The search path now contains your batch program directory plus the original search path. See Figure 7-15. However, because of the length of the new search path, you may not be able to see the end of the search path.

   TROUBLE? If the search path on your computer does not include the name of the batch program directory, or if the search path does not include your original search path, type "%userprofile%\Batch Programs for *(Your Name)*\Reset" (substituting your own name in the path) to restore the original search path, and then repeat these two steps, checking your work as you go.

Figure 7-15	CHANGING THE SEARCH PATH

environment variable to include the current Windows search path in the new Windows search path

path for batch program directory

path now includes the batch program directory plus the original Windows search path

```
C:\>path
PATH=C:\WINNT\system32;C:\WINNT;C:\WINNT\System32\Wbem

C:\>path > "%userprofile%\Batch Programs for Isabel Navarro\Reset.bat"

C:\>type "%userprofile%\Batch Programs for Isabel Navarro\Reset.bat"
PATH=C:\WINNT\system32;C:\WINNT;C:\WINNT\System32\Wbem

C:\>path="%userprofile%\Batch Programs for Isabel Navarro";%path%

C:\>path
PATH="C:\Documents and Settings\Isabel\Batch Programs for Isabel Navarro";C:\WINNT\system32;C:\W

C:\>_
```

Viewing, Saving, and Changing the Search Path

- Type PATH and then press Enter to view the search path in the Windows environment.
- Type PATH, press the Spacebar, type >, press the Spacebar, type the full path and name of your batch program directory, followed immediately by a backslash and the name of the batch program file where you want to store the current search path, and then press Enter.
- Type PATH=[drive:[path]];%PATH% (substituting the absolute path of the directory you want to list at the beginning of the search path) and then press Enter.
- Type PATH and press Enter to view the updated search path and verify that it's correct.

Now that you have changed the search path setting, you are ready to test your batch program again from the root directory.

To test your batch program with the updated search path:

1. Make sure you insert a blank or empty diskette in drive A (you can use the same one you used earlier).

2. Clear the window, and then enter the command: **FormatDisk**

   The command interpreter locates the batch program (now that the batch program directory is listed in the search path) and displays the command stored in the batch program. See Figure 7-16. The FORMAT command then prompts you to insert a disk into drive A.

   TROUBLE? If Windows 2000 informs you that the command you entered "is not recognized as an internal or external command, operable program or batch file," then you either mistyped the command for the batch program, or you made a mistake in updating the search path. First check to make sure you entered the command correctly; if not, enter the command again with the proper spelling. If you typed the command correctly, and if Windows displays the error message described above, you will need to update the search path by repeating the steps in the "To change the search path" section.

| Figure 7-16 | EXECUTING THE BATCH PROGRAM |

batch program executes because the batch program directory is included in the search path

3. Press **Enter**, and when the FORMAT command asks you if you want to format another diskette, type **n** and then press **Enter**.

Having learned the importance of the search path, you now know how to update the setting for the search path in the Windows environment.

If, at any point during the remainder of this tutorial, Windows 2000 informs you that the command you entered "is not recognized as an internal or external command, operable program or batch file," first check the spelling of the command you typed. If you did not incorrectly enter the command, return to this section and update the search path using the steps in this section.

Using **Replaceable Parameters in a Batch Program**

Isabel recommends that you revise the batch program so it prompts you to specify the volume label when you execute the batch program. Then the person who prepares diskettes for any training session can use the batch program to assign a specify volume label.

To pass an item of information (such as a volume name, drive name, directory name, or filename) back to a batch program, you include a replaceable parameter in the command within the batch program file. A **replaceable parameter** is a placeholder in the batch program file for an item of information that you provide when you execute the batch program. If you want to reserve a place for one item of information in the batch program file, you mark the place for inserting that item by typing %1 (a percent symbol followed by the number 1). When you type the name of the batch program file at the command prompt, you also type the item of information after the batch program filename. The command interpreter then uses that item of information in the batch program file in every line containing the %1 replaceable parameter.

For example, you can replace the "templates" volume label with the %1 replaceable parameter so that the command in the batch program file now reads as follows:

FORMAT A: /V:%1

When you execute the batch program, you type its filename, followed by a space, and then the volume label you want to use, for example:

FormatDisk SolarWinds

The command interpreter uses the word SolarWinds wherever the %1 replaceable parameter occurs in the batch program. The "FORMAT A: /V:%1" command in the batch program is then executed as if you had typed "FORMAT A: /V:SolarWinds" in the batch program file itself.

The obvious advantage of using this replaceable parameter is that you can specify different volume labels when you format a disk with the batch program. You could, for example, enter the following command:

FormatDisk TRAINING

The batch program would then use "TRAINING" as the volume name.

What happens if you do not provide a value for the replaceable parameter? If you type only the batch program filename and do not provide a volume label for the replaceable parameter, the command interpreter removes the replaceable parameter from the command line without substituting any value. The batch program still works; the command interpreter loads the FORMAT program, and the FORMAT utility formats a disk, but it does not add a volume label to the disk (even with the Volume switch present in the command).

In the next set of steps, you are going to make a copy of the batch program and then modify the copy so that you have both the original and a revised batch program. Your original batch program will still format a disk and automatically add a volume label; the revised one will provide the option for specifying a different volume label.

To copy and then revise the batch program:

1. Clear the window, and then change to the directory for your user account by entering the command:

   cd %userprofile%

2. Change to your batch program directory.

3. Enter the command: **copy FormatDisk.bat VolumeLabel.bat**
   The COPY command displays the message "1 file(s) copied."

4. Enter the command: **notepad VolumeLabel.bat**
   Once Notepad opens, you see the copy of your original batch program file.

5. Position the insertion point before "t" in "templates," and then, while pressing and holding down the **Shift** key, press the **End** key to select the remainder of the line, and then type **%1** to replace the word "templates." Figure 7-17 shows the revised command.

Figure 7-17	ADDING A REPLACEABLE PARAMETER TO THE BATCH PROGRAM

batch program command includes a replaceable parameter

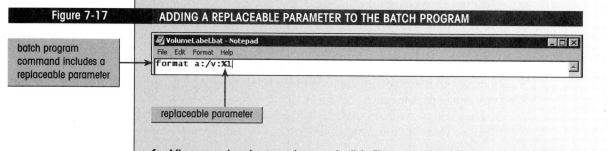

replaceable parameter

6. After you check your change to this file, press the **Alt** key, press **Enter**, type **x** and then, in the Notepad dialog box, press **Enter** again to save your changes and exit Notepad. Note that the sequence of steps for saving and exiting Notepad are identical to those for saving and exiting from the MS-DOS Editor. However, note that the command prompt still shows long filenames after you exit.

7. Check your batch program file one final time by entering the command:
   type VolumeLabel.bat

   The contents of your batch program file should match what's shown in Figure 7-17.

You can test the batch program from this directory.

To test the replaceable parameter:

1. Make sure you insert a blank or empty diskette in drive A (you can use the same one as you used earlier).

2. Clear the window, and then enter the command: **VolumeLabel SolarWinds**
   The command interpreter echoes, or displays, the command on the next line, and substitutes the word SolarWinds for the %1 replaceable parameter. See Figure 7-18.

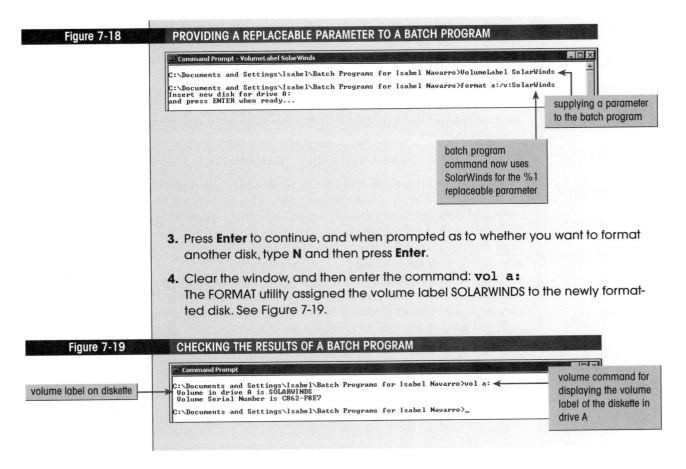

Figure 7-18   PROVIDING A REPLACEABLE PARAMETER TO A BATCH PROGRAM

supplying a parameter to the batch program

batch program command now uses SolarWinds for the %1 replaceable parameter

3. Press **Enter** to continue, and when prompted as to whether you want to format another disk, type **N** and then press **Enter**.

4. Clear the window, and then enter the command: **vol a:**
The FORMAT utility assigned the volume label SOLARWINDS to the newly formatted disk. See Figure 7-19.

Figure 7-19   CHECKING THE RESULTS OF A BATCH PROGRAM

volume label on diskette

volume command for displaying the volume label of the diskette in drive A

As you can see, the use of replaceable parameters provides more flexibility of use to a batch program.

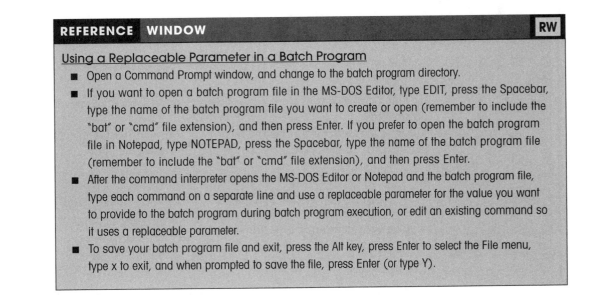

REFERENCE WINDOW   RW

Using a Replaceable Parameter in a Batch Program
- Open a Command Prompt window, and change to the batch program directory.
- If you want to open a batch program file in the MS-DOS Editor, type EDIT, press the Spacebar, type the name of the batch program file you want to create or open (remember to include the "bat" or "cmd" file extension), and then press Enter. If you prefer to open the batch program file in Notepad, type NOTEPAD, press the Spacebar, type the name of the batch program file (remember to include the "bat" or "cmd" file extension), and then press Enter.
- After the command interpreter opens the MS-DOS Editor or Notepad and the batch program file, type each command on a separate line and use a replaceable parameter for the value you want to provide to the batch program during batch program execution, or edit an existing command so it uses a replaceable parameter.
- To save your batch program file and exit, press the Alt key, press Enter to select the File menu, type x to exit, and when prompted to save the file, press Enter (or type Y).

You can also provide a batch program with more than one item of information by using the replaceable parameters %1 through %9. For example, you might want to provide a single command with more than one item of information, provide several commands with several values, or do both in a batch program.

When you enter a command to use a batch program at the command prompt, the command interpreter uses the position of the item of information on the command line to assign the parameter to the appropriate replaceable parameter in the batch program, as follows:

%0	%1	%2	%3	...
COMMAND	PARAMETER 1	PARAMETER 2	PARAMETER 3	...

Each part of a command is assigned a replaceable parameter (even if that part of the command is not used in the batch program file). This is also true for the command itself. The command interpreter automatically assigns %0 as the replaceable parameter for the command (the name of the batch program file), which you can use if, for example, you want to display an error message that includes the name of the batch program file itself. The first item of information following the command is %1, the second item is %2, and so on. You can use any of these replaceable parameters in the batch program, even the 0% replaceable parameter for the batch program file command itself. The parameters you provide a batch program can be any parameter used with a command, including the names of directories and files.

If you want to provide two replaceable parameters for a command, you would use the following syntax:

command %1 %2

For example, you might want to create a batch program that copies files and allows you to change the source and destination filenames each time you use the batch program, as follows:

COPY %1 %2

Since you can enter multiple commands in a batch program, you could also use the same replaceable parameter with more than one command, as follows:

command %1
command %1

For example, if you wanted the batch program to create a directory, and then to change to that directory, you could use the following approach:

MD %1
CD %1

The name you provide for the directory is then used whenever %1 occurs in the batch program file.

Or, a batch program might have two commands that use two different replaceable parameters. In this case, you would use the following syntax:

command %1
command %2

For example, you might have a simple batch program for changing both the date and time on your computer, as follows:

DATE %1
TIME %2

Whenever you use this batch program, you can pass whatever date and time you want to use to the batch program, entering the command, a space, the date (in date format), a space, and the time (in time format). Remember, though, that the batch program does not prompt you for the data used by replaceable parameters; it is your responsibility to provide that data when you enter the name of the batch program.

As you can tell, replaceable parameters provide flexibility in the way in which you can use batch programs.

Restoring the Search Path

Before you start Session 2, reset the path on your computer system. Earlier, you created a batch program named Reset.bat, which contains the original search path setting stored in the Windows environment. If you execute this batch program now, the command interpreter will replace the current search path setting you specified with the original one stored in this file.

To check, reset, and verify the search path:

1. Clear the window, and then enter the command: **path**

   The command interpreter shows the current setting for the path.

2. Enter the command: **reset**

   The command interpreter displays and executes the command in the batch program named Reset.bat.

3. Enter the command: **path**

   The batch program restored the original search path. See Figure 7-20.

4. Close the Command Prompt window.

Figure 7-20	RESTORING THE SEARCH PATH

batch program restores the Windows search path

search path restored in Windows environment

batch program command

```
Command Prompt

C:\Documents and Settings\Isabel\Batch Programs for Isabel Navarro>path
PATH="C:\Documents and Settings\Isabel\Batch Programs for Isabel Navarro";C:\WINNT\syst

C:\Documents and Settings\Isabel\Batch Programs for Isabel Navarro>reset ◄

C:\Documents and Settings\Isabel\Batch Programs for Isabel Navarro>PATH=C:\WINNT\system32;C:\WIN

C:\Documents and Settings\Isabel\Batch Programs for Isabel Navarro>path
PATH=C:\WINNT\system32;C:\WINNT;C:\WINNT\System32\Wbem

C:\Documents and Settings\Isabel\Batch Programs for Isabel Navarro>
```

You can also use a batch program to change the path, perform an operation, and then reset the path in one step by including the commands needed for each operation in the batch program file.

Session 7.1 QUICK CHECK

1. In order for Windows 2000 to recognize a batch program as a program file, you must add the _____ extension to the filename for the batch program.

2. The _____ environment variable contains the full path to the directory for your user account.

3. To execute a batch program, type the _____ at the command prompt.

4. After you enter a command to execute a batch program, the command interpreter searches for the batch program file using the _____.

5. If the command interpreter displays the message, "[*name of batch program file*] is not recognized as an internal or external command, operable program or batch file.", then the _____ that contains the batch program file is not in the search path.

6. To view the current search path, use the _____ command.

7. The current search path is assigned to the _____ environment variable in the Windows environment.

8. A(n) _____ is a placeholder in a batch program file for an item of information that you provide when you execute the batch program.

9. When assigning parts of a command line to replaceable parameters, the command interpreter assigns %0 to the _____.

10. %1 is assigned to the _____ item of data that you provide, or pass to, a batch program file when you enter the command for that program at the command prompt.

SESSION 7.2

In this session, you will create a batch program that starts multiple programs. From the command prompt, you will test the commands that you intend to use in the batch program. After creating the batch program with Notepad, you will test the batch program, and then revise it so it includes commands to control the batch program's display, to display messages and pause, and to add comments that document the batch program's operations. Finally, you will create a shortcut to start the batch program from the desktop.

Creating a Batch Program to Open Multiple Applications

In your job at SolarWinds, you frequently open and use the same combination of programs to complete projects that Isabel assigns you. To ensure that others in the company—all of whom use Windows 2000—can read and edit the documents you produce, you have been preparing them in WordPad, a simple and fast word processor that comes as an accessory with recent versions of Windows. At the same time, you also run the Calculator and Address Book accessories, and switch between the three programs. Although you could customize Windows 2000 so that it automatically opens these three programs after you boot your computer, you prefer to create a batch program that opens these three applications from the desktop only when you need them, and without having to restart your computer or log in again.

Defining the Steps for a Batch Program

Because this batch program must perform more than one operation, Isabel recommends that you go through the operations manually so you know the types and order of steps needed for the batch program.

After checking the properties of the shortcuts in the Accessories menu, you learn the full paths of each of the three programs, and find that each resides in a different directory folder with the following paths:

- WordPad's path is "C:\Program Files\Windows NT\Accessories\wordpad.exe"
- Address Book's path is "C:\Program Files\Outlook Express\wab.exe"
- Calculator's path is "%SystemRoot%\System32\calc.exe"

Calculator's path uses the environment variable SystemRoot. As noted earlier, Windows 2000 stores the full path to your Windows 2000 directory in this environment variable when your computer boots.

If the full path to your Windows 2000 directory is "C:\WINNT", then Windows 2000 stores "C:\WINNT" in the SystemRoot environment variable. When you instruct Windows 2000 to open Calculator, it substitutes "C:\WINNT" for "%SystemRoot%" in the full path noted above, so the full path for Calculator translates to "C:\WINNT\System32\calc.exe".

Likewise, if the full path to your Windows 2000 directory is "C:\Windows", then Windows 2000 stores "C:\Windows" in the SystemRoot environment variable during booting. When you instruct Windows 2000 to open Calculator, it substitutes "C:\Windows" for "%SystemRoot%" in the full path noted above, so the full path for Calculator translates to "C:\Windows\System32\calc.exe". Also as noted earlier, the % symbols around the "%SystemRoot%" environment variable in the full path for Calculator instructs Windows to substitute the actual directory path assigned to SystemRoot into the full path for Calculator.

Now that you know this information, you are ready to test each of the steps to make sure it does what you want it to do before you enter it into the batch program. As you complete these steps, make a note of the paths to the directories for WordPad, Address Book, and Calculator on your computer. You will need this information later for your new batch program.

To get started:

1. Open a Command Prompt window, set the colors (if necessary), update the search path to include the name of your batch program directory (if necessary, refer to the information in the first session for updating the search path), and then clear the window.

2. Enter the command:

   `cd /d C:\Program Files\Windows NT\Accessories`

   You are now in the Accessories directory on drive C, where the WordPad program file resides. The batch program must perform this step first, because the path to this directory is not in the search path. As you may recall, the /D switch (not available in Windows 98 or Windows 95) allows you to change drives in addition to changing the current directory. As noted previously, you can use uppercase, lowercase, or mixed case when entering commands, switches, directory names, and filenames.

   TROUBLE? If the CD command in Step 2 fails, the directory folder may not reside on drive C. Use the DIR command and the /S switch to search for and locate the Accessories directory. Then repeat this step using the current path for that directory.

3. Enter the command: `wordpad.exe`

   The WordPad program launches in a separate window, which is the second step required in the batch program.

4. Click the **Command Prompt** taskbar button to switch back to the Command Prompt window and continue with the next step in the batch program.

5. Enter the command: `cd /d C:\Program Files\Outlook Express`
   This performs the third step—switching to the directory folder containing the Address Book program.

6. Enter the command: `wab.exe`

In the fourth step, the Address Book program launches in a separate window.

TROUBLE? If Address Book displays a dialog box with the message "Address Book is currently not your default vCard viewer. Would you like to make it your default vCard viewer?" and displays a check box with the message, "Do not perform this check when starting the Address Book," leave the check box blank, and answer No, to leave the setup unchanged for now.

7. Switch back to the Command Prompt window to continue.

8. For the fifth step—moving to Calculator's directory—enter the command: `cd /d %SystemRoot%\System32`

9. For the sixth and last step—launching the Calculator program in a separate window—enter the command: `calc.exe`

10. Close **WordPad**, **Address Book**, and **Calculator**.

By stepping through the operations manually, you've identified which steps you need to include in the batch program and the correct order of the steps. See Figure 7-21. In turn, the batch program changes to each program's directory and launches the respective program.

Figure 7-21   MANUALLY TESTING THE STEPS FOR A BATCH PROGRAM

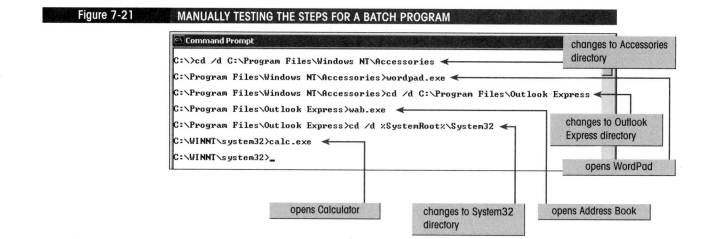

Now you are ready to write the batch program and to see if it works as planned.

Creating the Batch Program with the Notepad Editor

You can use the Windows 2000 Notepad Editor to create this batch program.

To create the batch program with Notepad:

1. Change to the batch program directory folder that you created and used in the first session. If the computer you are using for this session has no such batch program directory, re-create the batch program directory first.

2. Launch the **Notepad Editor** by entering the command: `notepad`

Now you can enter the steps required for this batch program. The steps include the commands that you executed manually from the command prompt. When you create a batch program that performs more than one operation, you list each command on a separate line in the batch program. When you test the batch program, it executes each command in the order in which each command appears in the batch program (unless you specify otherwise).

In each of the steps below, substitute the correct drive letters or directory paths if WordPad or Address Book reside in different locations.

To enter the batch program commands:

1. After Notepad opens, enter the following command lines in your batch program:

```
cd /d C:\Program Files\Windows NT\Accessories
wordpad.exe
cd /d C:\Program Files\Outlook Express
wab.exe
cd /d %SystemRoot%\System32
calc.exe
```

2. Check your batch program against the command lines above and, if necessary, make any corrections. You can also check the contents of your Notepad window against Figure 7-22.

| Figure 7-22 | ENTERING COMMANDS IN A BATCH PROGRAM FILE |

3. To save your work, click **File**, and then click **Save As**. Notepad displays a Save As dialog box.

4. Make sure the "Save in" text box at the top of the dialog box displays the name of the directory folder that you are using for your batch programs; if not, click the **Save in** list arrow, and switch to the correct directory.

5. In the "File name:" text box, replace *.txt with **3app.bat** and then click the **Save** button. Notepad saves this batch program as 3app.bat in the batch program directory.

6. Exit Notepad and return to the **Command Prompt** window.

Testing the Batch Program

You are ready to test your batch program.

To execute this batch program:

1. In the Command Prompt window, change back to your batch program directory (if necessary), and then clear the window.

2. Enter the command: **3app**

   3app.bat displays and executes its first command: it switches to the "C:\Program Files\Windows NT\Accessories" directory (or whatever directory contains WordPad). 3app then displays and executes the second command: it loads WordPad.

   Notice that the batch program stopped. Switch back to the Command Prompt window and observe that 3app.bat has not continued beyond the "wordpad.exe" command line. This problem occurs because a batch program waits for each command line to complete before proceeding to the next line. Therefore, 3app.bat will not continue until you exit and close WordPad. You will see how to resolve this problem below.

3. Switch back to the **WordPad** window, and exit WordPad. 3app.bat now displays and executes its next two command lines: it changes to the "C:\Program Files\Outlook Express" directory, launches Address Book, and then stops again.

4. Exit the Address Book. 3app.bat executes its last two commands, first changing to the System32 directory for your Windows 2000 SystemRoot, launching Calculator, and then stopping again.

5. Exit Calculator. 3app.bat terminates and returns you to the command prompt. Figure 7-23 shows the commands the batch program executed.

Figure 7-23	EXECUTING A BATCH PROGRAM FOR LOADING APPLICATIONS

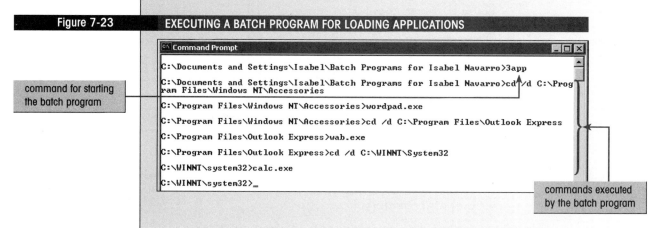

command for starting the batch program

commands executed by the batch program

Why didn't the batch program proceed through all of the commands? This batch program moved to the correct directory folders and launched its programs, but it stopped after launching each one and would not proceed until you exited that program. Therefore, it could open only one program at a time. This problem didn't happen when you tested the same command lines one at a time in the Command Prompt window. After you launched each program, you didn't have to close that program before launching the next one. The command interpreter displayed another command prompt immediately, ready to process your next command line. A batch program, however, will run another program differently than the command interpreter would by itself, and will wait for the other program to terminate before processing the next command line.

Because you want all three programs to open at the same time, you need to instruct the batch program to continue after launching each program. Isabel shows you the START command, which is designed for this purpose. In a batch program, if you precede a program (or data file) name with "start" and then a space, **START** will launch the program and immediately return to the batch program to process the next command. The START command has the following general syntax:

> **START** [*"title"*] [*filename* | *command*]

The *filename* parameter, if used, is the name of a program file or data file you want to launch in a separate window. If the *filename* is a data file, START opens it with the program associated with the file's extension. If the *filename* contains spaces, you must precede it with a window *title* in quotes, and also surround the *filename* in quotes. START doesn't display the *title*, so you may include anything between the quotes, even a blank space, just so you account for this parameter. If you specify a *command* instead of a *filename*, such as the command for opening a program like WordPad, START opens just the program. Recall that a vertical bar (|) separating two parameters means that they are mutually exclusive—you can use one or the other, but not both at the same time.

Windows 98 and Windows 95 also have a START command; however, its syntax does not use the *title* parameter.

Revising the Batch Program

Now that Isabel has familiarized you with the START command, you can modify the batch program to include it at the beginning of each line that launches a program, and then test the modifications to the batch program.

To revise the batch program:

1. In the Command Prompt window, change back to your batch program directory (if necessary), and clear the window.

2. Enter the command: `notepad 3app.bat`

   Like the MS-DOS Editor, if you specify a filename after the Notepad command, Notepad automatically opens the file.

3. Press ↓ to position the insertion point at the beginning of the line containing the "wordpad.exe" command.

4. Type `start` and press the **Spacebar**, but do *not* press Enter. The command line should now read, "start wordpad.exe".

5. Place a START command and space before the "wab.exe" and "calc.exe" commands, and type Start as you did in the previous step. Your 3app.bat file should now look like that shown in Figure 7-24.

Figure 7-24   ADDING START COMMANDS TO THE BATCH PROGRAM

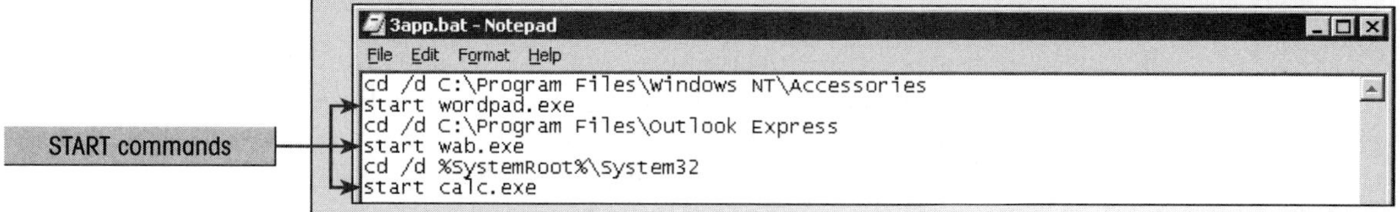

START commands

```
3app.bat - Notepad
File   Edit   Format   Help
cd /d C:\Program Files\Windows NT\Accessories
start wordpad.exe
cd /d C:\Program Files\Outlook Express
start wab.exe
cd /d %SystemRoot%\System32
start calc.exe
```

6. Exit Notepad, and when Notepad asks if you want to save the changes in 3app.bat, click **Yes**.

You have now revised your batch program with the necessary commands to make it run continuously, instead of stopping after launching each program.

Testing the Revised Batch Program

You are now ready to test the modified batch program.

To test the batch program:

1. Clear the Command Prompt window.

2. Enter the command: **3app**

This time, 3app.bat launches all three programs in separate windows and terminates itself in the Command Prompt window, leaving the three program windows open. The program windows may not open in the order you specified in the batch program, but all three program windows will open.

3. Switch back to the **Command Prompt** window. Notice that the batch program has completed all of its steps, as shown in Figure 7-25.

Figure 7-25   EXECUTING A BATCH PROGRAM CONTAINING START COMMANDS

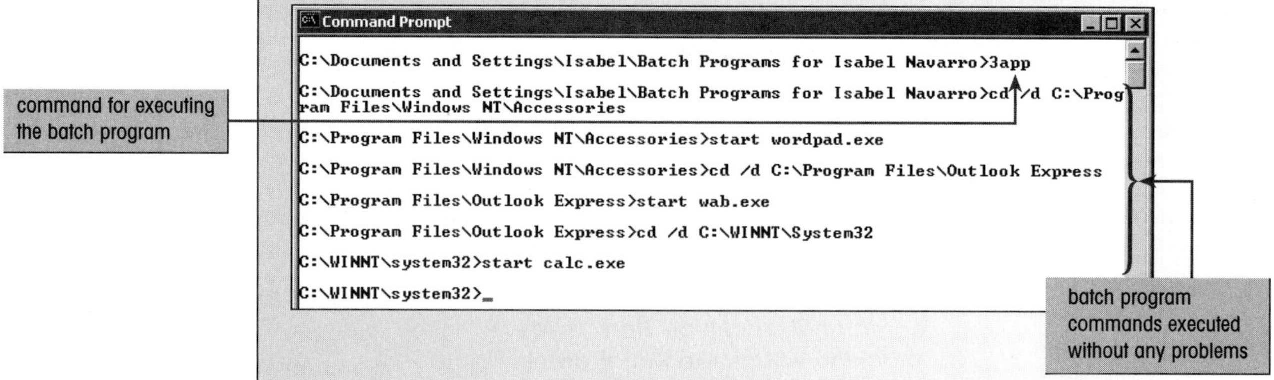

command for executing the batch program

```
Command Prompt
C:\Documents and Settings\Isabel\Batch Programs for Isabel Navarro>3app

C:\Documents and Settings\Isabel\Batch Programs for Isabel Navarro>cd /d C:\Program Files\Windows NT\Accessories

C:\Program Files\Windows NT\Accessories>start wordpad.exe

C:\Program Files\Windows NT\Accessories>cd /d C:\Program Files\Outlook Express

C:\Program Files\Outlook Express>start wab.exe

C:\Program Files\Outlook Express>cd /d C:\WINNT\System32

C:\WINNT\system32>start calc.exe

C:\WINNT\system32>_
```

batch program commands executed without any problems

4. Close each of the three programs—**WordPad**, **Address Book**, and **Calculator**.

In addition to testing your proposed command lines at the command prompt, when you are constructing batch programs you should consider ways in which your batch program will execute commands differently from the way the command prompt executes them when you enter them one at a time. In this example, the command lines in your batch program work differently from the same command lines entered at the Command Prompt. When a command line in your batch program launched an application without the START command, the batch program waited until that application exited before it processed the next command line. The Command Prompt window, on the other hand, launched the application and immediately displayed another command prompt. It did not need to wait for the application to finish before it allowed you to enter the next command line, so you did not need the START command.

Controlling the Display of Batch Program Commands

Isabel notes that when a batch program executes its commands, it displays each command next to a command prompt. This feature is useful because you can verify that the batch program is performing all of the operations without producing any error messages. However, after you test and verify that a batch program is working properly, Isabel suggests that you use the ECHO command to turn off the display of the commands that the batch program executes.

The **ECHO** command controls what the batch program echoes, or displays, on the monitor during execution. By default, the command interpreter sets ECHO to ON, and displays each batch program command during batch program execution. If you add ECHO OFF to the beginning of a batch program file, then the command interpreter does not display any commands that come after the ECHO OFF command. However, it does display the ECHO OFF command. To turn off the display of this command and any single command line, you can place an @ ("at" symbol) at the beginning of the command line. This approach works for the ECHO OFF command as well. If you add @ECHO OFF at the beginning of a batch program, the command interpreter turns off the display of all commands, including ECHO OFF.

ECHO OFF does not suppress the display of prompts produced by a command, such as the FORMAT command, because these commands are needed for the proper execution of the command. You still see the prompt, but you do not see the command that produces the prompt. Also, ECHO OFF does not suppress the display of error messages. If you inadvertently enter an incorrect command in a batch program and then execute the batch program, the command interpreter will display an error message when it attempts to execute the incorrect command.

The syntax for the internal command ECHO is:

ECHO [ON | OFF]

This notation for the ECHO command indicates that you can use the ON parameter or the OFF parameter with the command, but not both. ECHO ON turns on the display of commands, and ECHO OFF turns off, or suppresses, the display of commands. If you type ECHO without either of these parameters, the command interpreter displays the current setting for ECHO (either ON or OFF).

It is also common practice to include a CLS command after @ECHO OFF (or ECHO OFF). The CLS command clears the window (or screen) before the command interpreter executes the remainder of the commands in the batch program. Therefore, any commands or messages already present on the screen are cleared from the screen before the batch program performs its operations, and they do not distract the user or interfere with messages displayed by the batch program.

You now modify the batch program to include these two options.

To revise the batch program:

1. Change to your batch program directory.

2. Enter the command: `notepad 3app.bat`
   Notepad launches and opens the batch program file.

3. Press **Enter** to insert a blank line at the beginning of the file, and then press ▲ to position the insertion point at the beginning of the blank line.

4. Type **@echo off** and then press **Enter**.

5. Type **cls** but do *not* press Enter (otherwise, you'll insert an extra blank line). Figure 7-26 shows these additions to your batch program. Check your batch program against this figure.

Figure 7-26   **USING ECHO TO SUPPRESS THE DISPLAY OF COMMANDS**

option for clearing the window or screen of any previous output

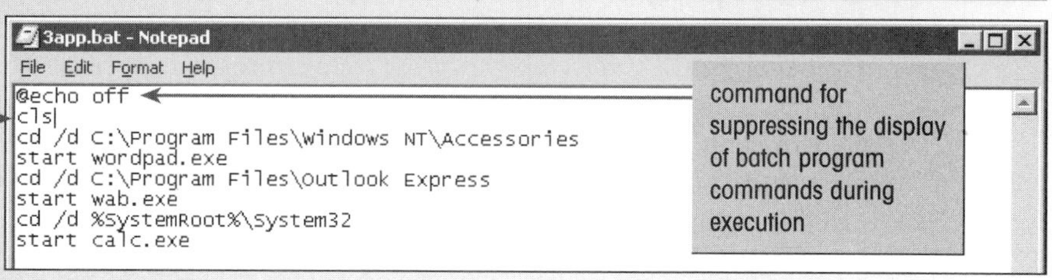

command for suppressing the display of batch program commands during execution

```
3app.bat - Notepad
File  Edit  Format  Help
@echo off
cls
cd /d C:\Program Files\Windows NT\Accessories
start wordpad.exe
cd /d C:\Program Files\Outlook Express
start wab.exe
cd /d %SystemRoot%\System32
start calc.exe
```

REFERENCE WINDOW   **RW**

Controlling the Display of Batch Program Commands
■ If necessary, open a Command Prompt window.
■ Use Notepad or MS-DOS Editor to open your batch program.
■ If necessary, press Enter to insert an additional blank line at the beginning of the batch program file.
■ Type @ECHO OFF and then press Enter.
■ Type CLS but do not press Enter.
■ Save your changes to the batch program, and then close Notepad or the MS-DOS Editor.

You have now added the necessary commands to suppress the output of your batch program's commands and to clear the window during the execution of your batch program.

Displaying Messages from a Batch Program

While you are making changes to the batch program, you decide to add some additional steps. Whenever you revise one of your documents with WordPad, you print a copy for your records. You want the batch program to display a message that reminds you to turn on your printer before it loads WordPad and the other programs.

You can use the ECHO command to display such messages. If you type ECHO followed by a space and then the text of a message, the batch program displays the message on the monitor during execution, *even if ECHO is OFF*. The general syntax is:

ECHO [*message***]**

If you want blank lines before and after a message that the batch program displays on the screen, you can use a special variation of the ECHO command. If you type ECHO followed *immediately* by a period, the batch program produces a blank line on the monitor when it executes the ECHO command.

You are now ready to incorporate these two features of the ECHO command in your batch program.

To include steps for displaying blank lines around a message:

1. Position the insertion point at the end of the line with the "cls" command. (*Note*: You can press the End key to quickly move the insertion point to the end of a line.)

2. Press **Enter** to insert a blank line.

3. Type **echo.** (include the period) and then press **Enter**. *Do not leave a blank space between ECHO and the period; if you do, ECHO will display a period on the screen rather than a blank line.*

4. Type **echo.** again (include the period) and then press **Enter**.

5. Type **echo** (do not include a period this time), press the **Tab** key twice, type *****Be sure the printer is on and operational***** and then press **Enter**. The Tab key inserts tab codes before the message so the message appears centered when the batch program executes this command.

6. Enter two more lines of **echo.** (include the period) as you did above. Figure 7-27 shows the message block with ECHO commands in the batch program. Check your batch program against this figure.

Figure 7-27   **USING ECHO TO DISPLAY BLANK LINES AND A MESSAGE**

displays a blank line in the window (or on the screen)

displays a message in the window (or on the screen) during batch file execution

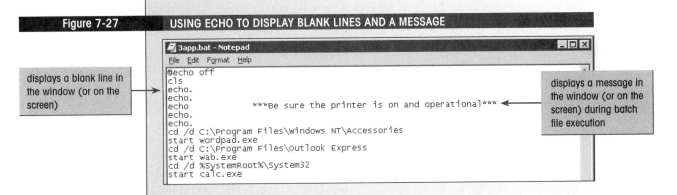

```
3app.bat - Notepad
File  Edit  Format  Help
@echo off
cls
echo.
echo.
echo                  ***Be sure the printer is on and operational***
echo.
echo.
echo.
cd /d C:\Program Files\windows NT\Accessories
start wordpad.exe
cd /d C:\Program Files\outlook Express
start wab.exe
cd /d %SystemRoot%\System32
start calc.exe
```

REFERENCE   WINDOW   **RW**

Displaying Messages from a Batch Program

- If necessary, open a Command Prompt window.
- Use Notepad or MS-DOS Editor to open your batch program.
- Position the insertion point at the beginning of the line in the batch program where you want to insert a message block.
- If you want to display one or more blank lines on the monitor during batch program execution, but before the message, type ECHO. (the period must immediately follow the ECHO command) for each blank line you need, and then press Enter.
- If you want to display a message on the monitor during batch program execution, type ECHO, press the Spacebar, type the text of the message you want to display, and then press Enter. (*Note*: You can use the Tab key to center the message on the monitor.)
- If you want to display one or more blank lines on the monitor after the message, type ECHO. (the period must immediately follow the ECHO command) for each blank line you need, and then press Enter.
- Save your changes to the batch program, and then close Notepad or the MS-DOS Editor.

Now that you have added commands to display a message, you need to include some provision to ensure you see this message.

Pausing Batch Program Execution

Isabel explains that, whenever you display a message from a batch program, you should temporarily stop batch program execution so you can see the message and have the chance to act on it. For example, before a batch program changes to your diskette drive, you might want to display a message to remind you to insert a diskette into that drive. And you also want the batch program to wait until you check the drive and, if necessary, insert a diskette.

You can use the PAUSE command to temporarily stop execution of a batch program. The **PAUSE** command displays a message that tells you to press a key when ready to continue. When you press a key, the batch program executes its remaining steps. The syntax for the PAUSE command is:

PAUSE

After a PAUSE command, you can use a CLS command to erase the message displayed by one or more ECHO commands, as well as the prompt displayed by the PAUSE command.

Add these additional steps to the batch program so it is more useful.

To insert an option for pausing batch program execution and then clearing the window:

1. Make sure the insertion point is positioned at the beginning of the line that follows the last ECHO command in your message block.

2. Type **pause** and then press **Enter**.

3. Type **cls** but do *not* press **Enter**. Figure 7-28 shows these modifications to the batch program. Check your batch program against this figure.

| Figure 7-28 | INCLUDING AN OPTION FOR PAUSING BATCH PROGRAM EXECUTION |

```
@echo off
cls
echo.
echo.
echo                ***Be sure the printer is on and operational***
echo.
echo.
pause
cls
cd /d C:\Program Files\Windows NT\Accessories
start wordpad.exe
cd /d C:\Program Files\Outlook Express
start wab.exe
cd /d %SystemRoot%\System32
start calc.exe
```

pauses batch program execution so you can see the message displayed in the window

clears the window after you continue batch program execution

Pausing Batch Program Execution
- If necessary, open a Command Prompt window.
- Use Notepad or MS-DOS Editor to open your batch program.
- Position the insertion point at the beginning of the line that follows a message block with ECHO commands.
- Type PAUSE and then press Enter.
- Type CLS and then press Enter.
- Save your changes to the batch program, and then close Notepad or the MS-DOS Editor.

Your batch program is now complete. But what if someone else needs to examine your batch program file? Will they understand how it works right away? Will you remember what you did, and why, six months from now? For these reasons, good programming always needs to include documentation.

Documenting Batch Program Operations

The batch program now has a number of steps, each of which serves a different purpose. So you and others can understand and follow the batch program's logic when you examine it at a later date, Isabel recommends that you document the batch program's operations.

When you create a batch program, document the purpose and features of the batch program for your use later, and for others as well. To document batch program operations, you use the **REM** (an abbreviation for "Remark") command, as follows:

REM [*comments*]

When a batch program executes, it ignores any lines that start with the REM command and any text or comments that follow REM. You can also use REM by itself to create blank space in the text of the batch program to make the batch program easier to read.

In the next step, you will add documentation to the batch program. Here are some guidelines for moving the insertion point and making changes to the batch program as you work in Notepad:

- To move to the beginning of a line, click anywhere on that line, and then press the Home key.
- To move to the end of a line, click anywhere on that line, and then press the End key.
- To insert a blank line below the current line, move the insertion point to the end of the line, and then press Enter.
- To insert a blank line above the current line, move the insertion point to the beginning of the line, press Enter, and then press ↑.
- To delete a line, move the insertion point to the beginning of the line, hold down the Shift key while you press ↓, and then press the Delete key.
- To indent lines, move the insertion point to the beginning of the line, and then press the Tab key.

Now you're ready to add documentation to your batch program.

To document and then test batch program operations:

1. Use Figure 7-29 as a guideline to add documentation to your batch program, adjust the spacing in your batch program, and check the accuracy of your batch program commands. You will be entering REM commands to include lines with a title for the batch program, the batch program's filename, your name, the current date, and comments that describe the next step or set of steps in the batch program. To improve the spacing in a batch program, you can leave blank lines. The command interpreter ignores any blank lines and any blank spaces before or after commands.

Figure 7-29   DOCUMENTING BATCH PROGRAM OPERATORS

```
3app.bat - Notepad
File  Edit  Format  Help
        @echo off
        cls

rem        Batch program for Launching WordPad, Address Book, and Calculator
rem
rem        Filename:  3app.bat
rem
rem        Name:  [Your Name]                    Date:  [Today's Date]

rem     Check Status of Printer:
rem

        echo.
        echo.
        echo                 ***Be sure the printer is on and operational***
        echo.
        echo.
        pause
        cls

rem     Change to WordPad's Directory and Launch WordPad:
rem

        cd /d C:\Program Files\Windows NT\Accessories
        start wordpad.exe

rem     Change to Address Book's Directory and Launch Address Book:
rem

        cd /d C:\Program Files\Outlook Express
        start wab.exe

rem     Change to Calculator's Directory and Launch Calculator:
rem

        cd /d %SystemRoot%\System32
        start calc.exe
```

documentation identifying the purpose of each section in the batch program

documentation on the purpose of the batch program

2. Save your changes, and then exit Notepad.

3. Make sure your batch program directory is the current directory.

4. Enter the command: **3app**

The batch program clears the screen, displays a message prompting you to check the printer's status, temporarily pauses batch program execution, and displays another message that informs you how to continue. See Figure 7-30.

TROUBLE? If the command interpreter displays any error messages, or if your batch program does not work properly, or at all, check the contents of your batch program with that shown in Figure 7-29. Make any needed changes and repeat Step 4 again.

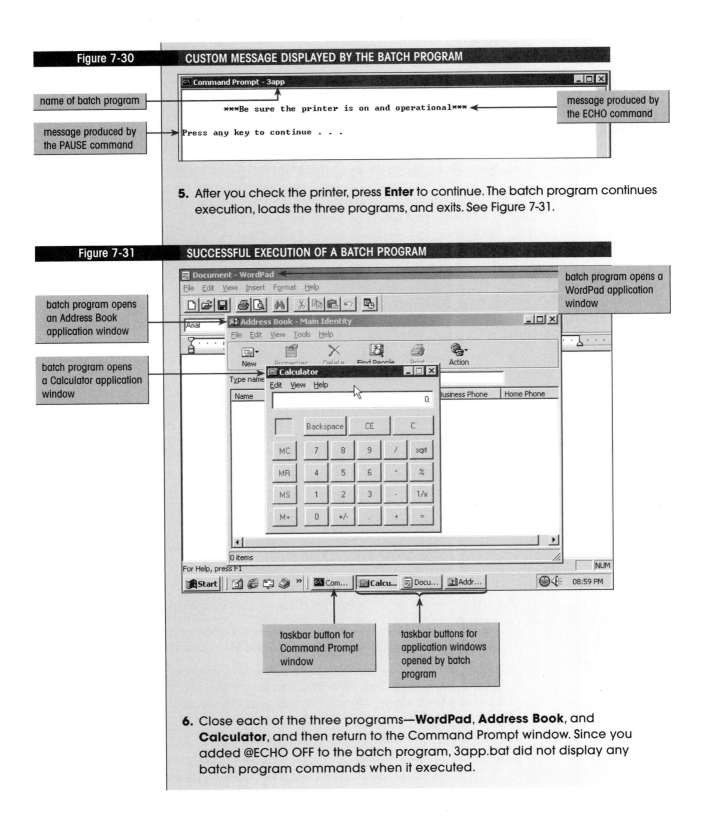

Figure 7-30   CUSTOM MESSAGE DISPLAYED BY THE BATCH PROGRAM

name of batch program

Command Prompt - 3app

message produced by the ECHO command

Be sure the printer is on and operational

message produced by the PAUSE command

Press any key to continue . . .

5. After you check the printer, press **Enter** to continue. The batch program continues execution, loads the three programs, and exits. See Figure 7-31.

Figure 7-31   SUCCESSFUL EXECUTION OF A BATCH PROGRAM

batch program opens an Address Book application window

batch program opens a Calculator application window

batch program opens a WordPad application window

Document - WordPad

File   Edit   View   Insert   Format   Help

Arial

Address Book - Main Identity

File   Edit   View   Tools   Help

New   Properties   Delete   Find People   Print   Action

Calculator

Edit   View   Help

0.

Type name

Name   Business Phone   Home Phone

Backspace   CE   C

MC   7   8   9   /   sqrt

MR   4   5   6   *   %

MS   1   2   3   -   1/x

M+   0   +/-   .   +   =

0 items

For Help, press F1   NUM

Start   Com...   Calcu...   Docu...   Addr...   08:59 PM

taskbar button for Command Prompt window

taskbar buttons for application windows opened by batch program

6. Close each of the three programs—**WordPad**, **Address Book**, and **Calculator**, and then return to the Command Prompt window. Since you added @ECHO OFF to the batch program, 3app.bat did not display any batch program commands when it executed.

Documenting a Batch Program

- If necessary, open a Command Prompt window.
- Use Notepad or MS-DOS Editor to open your batch program.
- Create a title block that documents the purpose of the batch program, as follows: At the beginning of the batch program, type REM, press Tab, and then type a title. If you want to insert a blank line to separate the title from the next comment, type REM and then press Enter, or just press Enter to leave a blank line (without REM), whichever you prefer. Use the REM command to enter any additional comments, such as a short paragraph that explains the purpose of the batch program in more detail than would be possible on the title line, and that mentions any unusual feature of the batch program that you or someone else might need to know later. Also use the REM command to enter the name of the author of the batch program, the date the batch program was created or modified, the version of the batch program, the batch program's filename, and any other documentation important to you. If you need to enter a long line of text, you can break it into multiple lines, each with its own REM command.
- Before each set of related operations in a batch program, including message blocks, insert a REM command followed by text that explains the purpose of that section of the batch program.
- Save your changes to the batch program, and then close Notepad or the MS-DOS Editor.

You have now successfully created a batch program to launch your three programs, added documentation, and tested the batch program. However, you decide to further automate the process of using this batch program by making a shortcut on the desktop to your batch program.

Making a Shortcut to a Batch Program

You can simplify the launching of your three programs further by making a desktop shortcut to your new batch program. You can then double-click that desktop shortcut to start your batch program.

To create a desktop shortcut to your batch program:

1. Make sure you are in the Command Prompt window and that your batch program directory is your current directory, and then clear the window.

2. Type **start** and then press the **Spacebar**. Type **.** (a period), and then press **Enter**. If you include the name of a directory folder after the START command, it opens a My Computer window into that directory. Because you use a period (**.**) after the START command, it will open a My Computer window into the current directory you are using for your batch programs.

3. If necessary, resize the My Computer window so you can see part of the desktop, and then locate the icon for 3app.bat in the window (you may not see the "bat" file extension in the filename).

4. Right-drag the **3app.bat** icon to a visible area of the desktop. To right-drag, hold down the right mouse button over the file icon, and then move the mouse pointer to the target area on the desktop. When you release the right mouse button over the desktop area, a shortcut menu appears. See Figure 7-32.

Figure 7-32 | CREATING A DESKTOP SHORTCUT FOR A BATCH PROGRAM

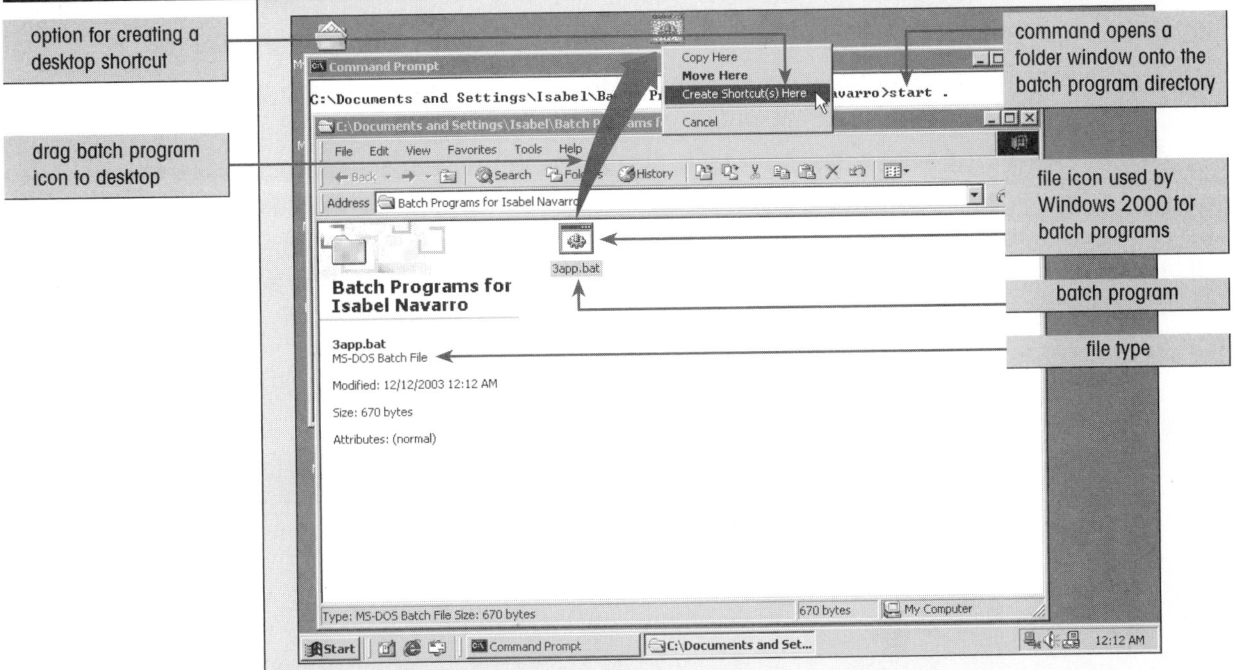

option for creating a
desktop shortcut

command opens a
folder window onto the
batch program directory

drag batch program
icon to desktop

file icon used by
Windows 2000 for
batch programs

batch program

file type

5. Click **Create Shortcut(s) Here**. Windows 2000 creates a desktop shortcut to your batch program.

6. Close the My Computer window and the Command Prompt window. Notice the new shortcut on your desktop, as shown in Figure 7-33.

Figure 7-33 | DESKTOP SHORTCUT FOR BATCH PROGRAM

desktop shortcut for
batch program

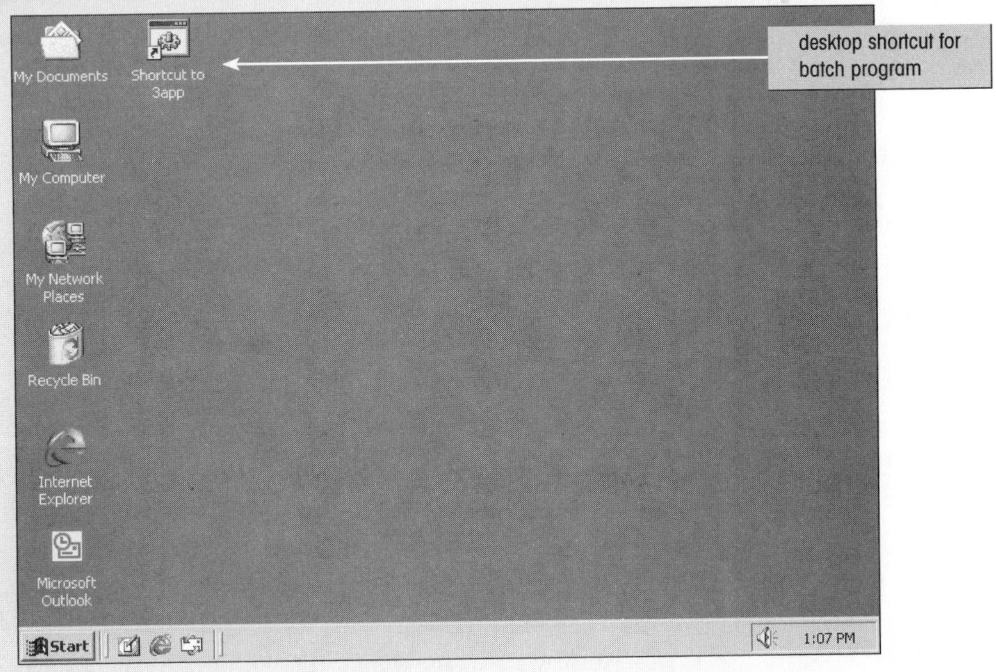

7. If necessary, change the name of your desktop shortcut from "Shortcut to 3app" or "Shortcut to 3app.bat" to "3app" by selecting the desktop shortcut, pressing the F2 Rename key, and then retyping or editing the name.

8. Double-click the **3app** desktop shortcut. You should see a check printer status message in a window similar to that in Figure 7-30.

9. Press **Enter** to continue. The batch program continues execution and loads the three programs, as in Figure 7-31, and then terminates. Notice that Windows 2000 closed the window containing the printer status message.

10. Close each of the three programs—**WordPad**, **Address Book**, and **Calculator**.

You have successfully tested, written, and modified a batch program for opening programs.

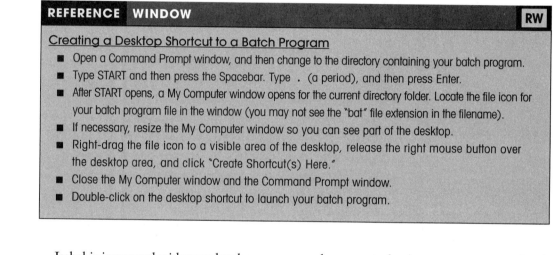

REFERENCE WINDOW   RW

Creating a Desktop Shortcut to a Batch Program
- Open a Command Prompt window, and then change to the directory containing your batch program.
- Type START and then press the Spacebar. Type . (a period), and then press Enter.
- After START opens, a My Computer window opens for the current directory folder. Locate the file icon for your batch program file in the window (you may not see the "bat" file extension in the filename).
- If necessary, resize the My Computer window so you can see part of the desktop.
- Right-drag the file icon to a visible area of the desktop, release the right mouse button over the desktop area, and click "Create Shortcut(s) Here."
- Close the My Computer window and the Command Prompt window.
- Double-click on the desktop shortcut to launch your batch program.

Isabel is impressed with your batch programs and your use of a shortcut to execute a batch program. She is particularly pleased to see that you've used batch programs to automate routine operations you perform in your job.

Session 7.2 QUICK CHECK

1. After you create a batch program, you should test the batch program from different _____ and _____ to make sure it operates under different conditions.

2. Windows 2000 stores the full path to your Windows 2000 directory in the _____ environment variable when your computer boots.

3. You can use the Windows 2000 _____ command to launch a program from a batch program, and then immediately return to the batch program to process the next command.

4. To suppress the display of all commands in a batch program during execution, you must insert a(n) _____ command at the beginning of the batch program.

5. To display a message during batch program execution, you include a(n) _____ command followed by the text of the message.

6. To display blank lines on the monitor before or after messages during batch program execution, you use the _____ command.

7. To pause batch program execution so you can view messages displayed on the monitor by a batch program, you use the _____ command after the message block in the batch program.

8. To clear the window or screen of previously displayed output, or to clear the window or screen of messages displayed by a batch program, you use the _____ command in the batch program.

9. To document the purpose of a batch program, and the operations within a batch program, you use the _____ command in the batch program.

10. If your batch program does not work from a different directory, you might want to include a(n) _____ command at the beginning of the batch program to add the path of your batch program directory to the beginning of the search path.

SESSION 7.3

In this session, you will create and execute a batch program from the Recovery Console after using Administrator privileges to extend Recovery Console's capabilities.

Recovery Console Batch Programs

After updating Isabel on the progress that you've made in creating batch programs, she asks you to create a batch program for enhancing the capabilities of the Recovery Console. She reminds you that the Recovery Console has restrictions on its use for security reasons, and therefore the approach for creating and using batch programs is different from the approach you use in a Command Prompt window.

Expanding the Recovery Console's Capabilities

The Recovery Console contains a version of the SET command that can work with only four environment variables, three of which each control a particular default rule. During a discussion with Isabel, you learn the defaults of the Recovery Console and which variable can change each of them:

- You can change only to the root directory folder, the SystemRoot directory (usually C:\WINNT), and, if it is installed, the CMDCONS directory containing the Recovery Console system. You do not have access to any other directory folders on your hard drive. The AllowAllPaths variable controls this default.

- You can copy from removable media such as floppy drive A to the hard drive, but you cannot copy any files from the hard drive to drive A. The AllowRemoveableMedia variable controls this default.

- You cannot use wildcards. Therefore, for example, you can copy or delete only one file at a time, and you must specify the entire filename. The AllowWildCards variable controls this default.

The fourth environment variable, NoCopyPrompt, determines whether the COPY command asks for confirmation to overwrite a file. All four environment variables can have only the values TRUE or FALSE, and they are always set to FALSE when you start the Recovery Console. By default, however, SET cannot change these variables—it can only display them.

Using an account with Administrator privileges, you can enable the Recovery Console's SET command to change these environment variables, reducing security but enhancing the capabilities of the Recovery Console.

To complete the steps in this section of the tutorial, the Recovery Console must be installed on the computer you are using, or you must be able to run the Recovery Console from the Windows 2000 CD or Windows 2000 Setup Disks. Also, you will need to log on to your computer using an account that has Administrator privileges. If the Recovery Console is not installed on the computer you are using, or if you cannot log on under an account with Administrator privileges, read, but do not keystroke, this section of the tutorial.

If you are working in a computer lab, your instructor will inform you in advance whether or not you can access and use the Recovery Console on the computers in your lab, and, if so, how to log on to a computer with an account that has Administrator privileges.

To change the use of the SET command in the Recovery Console:

1. If necessary, log on to your computer under an account with Administrator privileges.

2. From the **Start** menu, point to **Programs**, point to **Administrative Tools**, click **Local Security Policy**, and, if necessary, maximize the Local Security Settings window.

   TROUBLE? If you do not see an Administrative Tools option on the Programs menu, right-click an empty area of the taskbar, click Properties, click the Advanced tab in the Taskbar and Start Menu Properties dialog box, add a check mark to the Display Administrative Tools option in the Start Menu Settings box, click OK, and then try Step 2 again.

3. In the Console pane on the left, click the **expand view** box ⊞ next to the Local Policies folder node, and then click the **Security Options** folder subnode under Local Policies. Windows 2000 displays security policies and their settings in the details pane on the right. See Figure 7-34.

Figure 7-34	VIEWING LOCAL SECURITY SETTINGS

expand Local Policies
open Security Options

Policy	Local Setting	Effective Setting
Additional restrictions for anonymous connections	None. Rely on defa...	None. Rely on defa...
Allow server operators to schedule tasks (domain controllers only)	Not defined	Not defined
Allow system to be shut down without having to log on	Enabled	Enabled
Allowed to eject removable NTFS media	Administrators	Administrators
Amount of idle time required before disconnecting session	15 minutes	15 minutes
Audit the access of global system objects	Disabled	Disabled
Audit use of Backup and Restore privilege	Disabled	Disabled
Automatically log off users when logon time expires (local)	Enabled	Enabled
Clear virtual memory pagefile when system shuts down	Disabled	Disabled
Digitally sign client communication (always)	Disabled	Disabled
Digitally sign client communication (when possible)	Enabled	Enabled
Digitally sign server communication (always)	Disabled	Disabled
Digitally sign server communication (when possible)	Disabled	Disabled
Disable CTRL+ALT+DEL requirement for logon	Not defined	Not defined
Do not display last user name in logon screen	Disabled	Disabled
LAN Manager Authentication Level	Send LM & NTLM re...	Send LM & NTLM re...
Message text for users attempting to log on		
Message title for users attempting to log on		
Number of previous logons to cache (in case domain controller is not available)	10 logons	10 logons
Prevent system maintenance of computer account password	Disabled	Disabled
Prevent users from installing printer drivers	Disabled	Disabled
Prompt user to change password before expiration	14 days	14 days
Recovery Console: Allow automatic administrative logon	Disabled	Disabled
Recovery Console: Allow floppy copy and access to all drives and all folders	Disabled	Disabled
Rename administrator account	Not defined	Not defined
Rename guest account	Not defined	Not defined
Restrict CD-ROM access to locally logged-on user only	Disabled	Disabled

4. In the details pane, locate and double-click "**Recovery Console: Allow floppy copy and access to all drives and all folders**," as shown in Figure 7-35.

| Figure 7-35 | SELECTING A RECOVERY CONSOLE POLICY |

choose this Recovery
Console policy

5. After Windows 2000 displays the Local Security Policy Setting dialog box, click **Enabled**, as shown in Figure 7-36.

| Figure 7-36 | ENABLING A LOCAL POLICY SETTING |

local security policy

security policy setting

choose option for
enabling this security
policy setting

6. Click **OK** to close the Local Security Policy Setting dialog box, and then close the Local Security Settings window.

Now when you launch the Recovery Console, you will be able to use the SET command in the next section to change the environment variables that allow you greater access to the contents of your hard drive.

Writing a Recovery Console Batch Program

After you start the Recovery Console, the first task you want to perform is to change the setting for three environment variables to allow you access to multiple files in any directory folder on the hard drive. Because these environment variables have long names, Isabel recommends that you use a batch program to automatically change these settings.

Recovery Console does not have a text editor like Notepad or the MS-DOS Editor, and it cannot run external programs. Therefore, you must write and save your batch program outside the Recovery Console, and then launch the Recovery Console to execute your batch program. As noted previously, the Recovery Console allows access to only two system directories on drive C— the root directory folder and the SystemRoot directory—and to a diskette in drive A. Therefore, you must save your batch program to a diskette on drive A, and run it from that diskette.

To prepare a batch program for changing the settings of environment variables in the Recovery Console:

1. Open a **Command Prompt** window.

2. Insert a diskette into drive A, and change your default drive to **A**. (*Note:* Since the batch program only requires a small amount of storage space, you do not need to use a new diskette.)

   You can use any file extension for your batch program because the Recovery Console ignores the file extension. For example, you can use "txt" as the file extension, or no file extension at all. One advantage of not using a "bat" or "cmd" file extension is that you cannot accidentally execute the batch program from the Windows 2000 command line operating environment.

3. Enter: `notepad setrc.txt`

   Click **Yes** when Notepad asks if you want to create a new file.

4. Enter the following batch program. Make sure you include spaces on either side of the equal signs (=). Be very careful to type this batch program exactly as shown (case does not matter); if you make a typo or leave out any spaces, the batch program will not work, and you will have to restart your computer so that you can change it. Note also that because the Recovery Console does not include the REM or ECHO commands, you cannot include comments or documentation in this batch program.

   ```
   set AllowWildCards = TRUE
   set AllowAllPaths = TRUE
   set AllowRemovableMedia = TRUE
   ```

5. Close **Notepad**, and click **Yes** when Notepad asks if you want to save your batch program file.

6. Close the **Command Prompt** window, and then remove your diskette from drive A.

Now that you have completed your Recovery Console batch program, you are ready to run it under the Recovery Console.

To run your Recovery Console batch program:

1. Restart your computer, and launch the **Recovery Console** either from your Windows 2000 Setup Disks or CD, or from the Windows 2000 Startup Menu during booting.

2. When Windows 2000 prompts you for the Windows 2000 installation you would like to log on to, as shown in Figure 7-37, type the number for your installed version of Windows 2000, press the **Enter** key, and then enter your Administrator password.

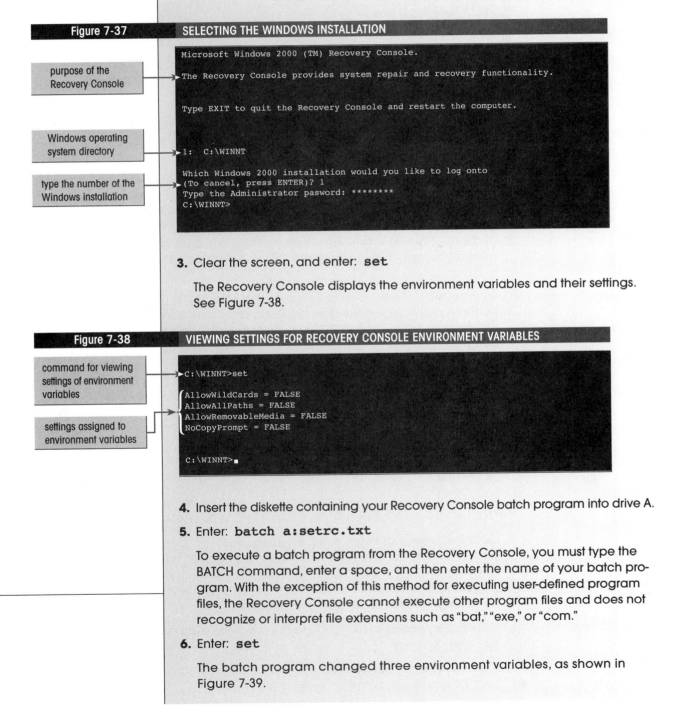

Figure 7-37   SELECTING THE WINDOWS INSTALLATION

purpose of the Recovery Console

Windows operating system directory

type the number of the Windows installation

```
Microsoft Windows 2000 (TM) Recovery Console.

The Recovery Console provides system repair and recovery functionality.


Type EXIT to quit the Recovery Console and restart the computer.



1:  C:\WINNT

Which Windows 2000 installation would you like to log onto
(To cancel, press ENTER)? 1
Type the Administrator pasword: ********
C:\WINNT>
```

3. Clear the screen, and enter: **set**

    The Recovery Console displays the environment variables and their settings. See Figure 7-38.

Figure 7-38   VIEWING SETTINGS FOR RECOVERY CONSOLE ENVIRONMENT VARIABLES

command for viewing settings of environment variables

settings assigned to environment variables

```
C:\WINNT>set

AllowWildCards = FALSE
AllowAllPaths = FALSE
AllowRemovableMedia = FALSE
NoCopyPrompt = FALSE


C:\WINNT>
```

4. Insert the diskette containing your Recovery Console batch program into drive A.

5. Enter: **batch a:setrc.txt**

    To execute a batch program from the Recovery Console, you must type the BATCH command, enter a space, and then enter the name of your batch program. With the exception of this method for executing user-defined program files, the Recovery Console cannot execute other program files and does not recognize or interpret file extensions such as "bat," "exe," or "com."

6. Enter: **set**

    The batch program changed three environment variables, as shown in Figure 7-39.

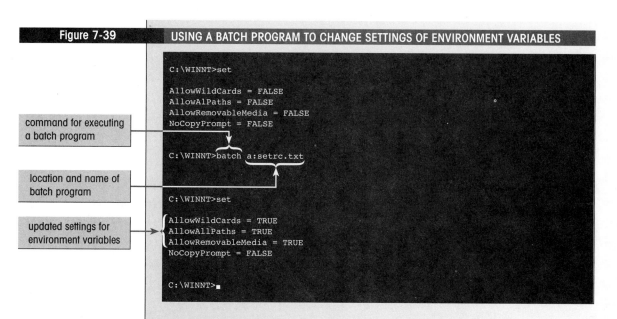

Figure 7-39   USING A BATCH PROGRAM TO CHANGE SETTINGS OF ENVIRONMENT VARIABLES

command for executing a batch program

location and name of batch program

updated settings for environment variables

```
C:\WINNT>set

AllowWildCards = FALSE
AllowAlPaths = FALSE
AllowRemovableMedia = FALSE
NoCopyPrompt = FALSE


C:\WINNT>batch a:setrc.txt


C:\WINNT>set

AllowWildCards = TRUE
AllowAllPaths = TRUE
AllowRemovableMedia = TRUE
NoCopyPrompt = FALSE


C:\WINNT>_
```

TROUBLE? If your batch program does not change the settings for the AllowWildCards, AllowAllPaths, or AllowRemovableMedia environment variables to TRUE, type SET followed by a space, type the environment variable name, press the Spacebar (required), type an equals sign, press the Spacebar (required), type TRUE, and then press the Enter key. Type SET and then press the Enter key to verify that the Recovery Console changed the setting.

TROUBLE? If you see any error messages, your batch program may contain a typing mistake. Type EXIT and then press the Enter key to restart your computer, perform a full boot with Windows 2000, log on to your computer, and make any needed corrections to A:SETRC.TXT by comparing it against Step 5 with the batch program code. Then, repeat Step 1 through Step 6.

To test the enhanced abilities of the Recovery Console, you decide to try a task you might perform as part of system maintenance: Update CONFIG.NT on an Emergency Recovery Disk by copying the file from the hard drive to the diskette. Normally, you would not be able to copy any file from the hard drive to a diskette in the Recovery Console. However, you can do so now that you have set the AllowRemovableMedia environment variable to TRUE.

For testing purposes, you decide to use a regular diskette.

To test expanded Recovery Console features:

1. Clear the screen, and then enter: **systemroot**
In the Recovery Console, SYSTEMROOT is a command (not an environment variable) that changes to the SystemRoot directory (usually C:\WINNT). It is a built-in internal command, like all Recovery Console commands. Make sure you are in the Windows 2000 SystemRoot directory.

2. Enter: **cd system32** to change to the System32 subdirectory under your Windows directory.

3. Enter: **copy config.nt a:**
The COPY command copies Config.nt to drive A.

TROUBLE? If you get an error message saying, "Access is denied," your AllowRemovableMedia environment variable may be set to FALSE. Try setting it to TRUE by typing SET AllowRemovableMedia = TRUE. If you can't change this setting and get the error message "The SET command is currently disabled. The SET command is an optional Recovery Console command that can only be enabled by using the Security Configuration and Analysis snap-in," you will need to remove your diskette, type EXIT, restart your computer, allow it to boot into the regular Windows 2000 system, and start this session over again, beginning with changing the settings in Local Security Policy.

4. Display a directory listing of drive A to further verify that the Recovery Console copied the file successfully.

5. Remove your diskette from drive A.

6. Enter: **exit** to restart your computer.

The Recovery Console is an important tool for troubleshooting your computer; however, for security reasons, you are restricted in what you can do. As you've seen, you can increase its functionality by changing the settings for specific environment variables. Also, you can execute simple batch programs from the Recovery Console and automate routine operations, such as copying files.

Restoring **Your Computer**

If you are working in a computer lab, then you will need to remove the batch programs that you created in this tutorial. If you created a batch program directory, you will also need to remove that directory. Before you remove the programs and directory, copy them to your Data Disk in case you need them later. If your instructor assigns the extra case problem, you will need your copy of 3app.bat.

If you are working on your own computer and want to keep the batch program directory and the batch programs you created, then skip the remaining steps.

So you will have a backup copy of the batch programs you created in this tutorial, you will copy them to a diskette before you remove them from the hard disk.

To restore your computer:

1. Insert a diskette into drive A that contains enough storage space for your batch program directory.

2. Create a directory on this diskette for your batch program files.

3. Switch to the batch program directory on drive C, and copy your batch program files to the batch program directory you just created on the diskette in drive A.

4. Use the **Remove Directory** command with the **/S** switch to remove the batch program directory on drive C for your user account (the one you used in this tutorial).

5. Close the **Command Prompt** window.

Session 7.3 QUICK CHECK

1. The four environment variables that control the Recovery Console's abilities are _____, _____, _____, and _____.

2. To change the use of the SET command in the Recovery Console, your account must have _____ privileges.

3. Under the Administrative Tools menu, the _____ program changes the use of the Recovery Console's SET command.

4. To execute a batch program from the Recovery Console, you must type the _____ command, and then enter the name of your batch program.

5. The _____ Recovery Console command changes to the SystemRoot directory (usually C:\WINNT).

6. To restart your computer from the Recovery Console, use the _____ command.

COMMAND REFERENCE

COMMAND	USE	BASIC SYNTAX	EXAMPLE
Ctrl+C	Keyboard shortcut for canceling batch program execution	Ctrl+C	Ctrl+C
Ctrl+Break	Keyboard shortcut for interrupting batch program execution	Ctrl+Break	Ctrl+Break
batch program filename	Executes a batch program and, if provided, passes data to a batch program for use with replaceable parameters	*batch program filename[data-item1] [date-item2]* ...	FormatDisk VolumeLabel Training
CD %USERPROFILE%	Changes to the directory for your user account	CD %USERPROFILE%	cd %userprofile%
EDIT	Opens the MS-DOS Editor, and creates or opens a file if a filename is provided	EDIT [[drive][path] [filename] edit FormatDisk.bat	edit
PATH	Specifies a new setting for the PATH environment variable (changes the search path)	PATH=[drive]path1; [drive]path2;[drive] path3;...	path=c:\winnt;c:\winnt\system32;c:\winnt\system32\wbem
PATH	Displays the setting for the PATH PATH environment variable (displays the search path)	PATH	path
PATH	Updates the setting for the PATH environment variable by appending the existing path to the new search path	PATH=[drive]path; %PATH%	path=c:\bat;%path%
START *command*	Starts an application from a batch program, and then immediately returns to the batch program to process the next command	START *command*	start wordpad.exe

COMMAND REFERENCE (CONTINUED)

COMMAND	USE	BASIC SYNTAX	EXAMPLE
START *filename*	In a batch program, opens a file with the application associated with the file's extension	START *filename*	start Cashflow.xls
ECHO OFF	Turns off the display of all batch program commands, including this command	@ECHO OFF	@echo off
ECHO OFF	Turns off the display of all batch program commands after this command	ECHO OFF	echo off
ECHO ON	Turns on the display of all batch program commands after this command	ECHO ON	echo on
ECHO.	Displays a blank line on the monitor	ECHO.	echo.
ECHO *message*	Displays a message on the monitor during batch program execution, even if ECHO is set to OFF	ECHO *message*	echo Processing data...
PAUSE	Temporarily stops batch program execution, and displays a message to press a key when ready to continue	PAUSE	pause
REM	Documents batch program operations	REM *[comments]*	REM Format a Disk

RECOVERY CONSOLE COMMANDS

COMMAND	USE	BASIC SYNTAX	EXAMPLE
SET	Displays the values of all four environment variables	SET	set
SET *variable* = *value*	Assigns TRUE or FALSE to one of four environment variables	SET *variable* = value	set AllowAllPaths = TRUE
BATCH	Excecutes commands in a Recovery Console batch program file	BATCH filename	batch setrc.txt
SYSTEMROOT	Changes to the Windows 2000 SystemRoot directory (usually C:\WINNT)	SYSTEMROOT	systemroot
CD	Displays the current working directory	CD	cd
CD *directory*	Changes the current working directory to another directory	CD *directory*	cd system32
COPY	Copies a file from one directory to another on the same drive or a different drive	COPY *filename target*	copy config.nt a:
EXIT	Restarts the computer	EXIT	exit

Items shown in italics and *not* enclosed within square brackets are required parameters.

Items shown in italics and enclosed within square brackets are optional parameters.

REVIEW ASSIGNMENTS

So that you will have a backup of your batch programs, Isabel asks you to create a batch program that will copy the batch programs in your batch program directory to a diskette. At the request of a co-worker, she also asks you to make an icon on the Windows desktop that launches the Wordpad and Character Map Accessories simultaneously.

As you complete each step, record your answers to any questions so you can submit them with your lab assignment.

1. Open a Command Prompt window.

2. Change to the directory for your user account, and if necessary, create a directory for your batch programs.

3. Change to the batch program directory.

4. Use Notepad or the MS-DOS Editor to create a batch program that performs the following operations:
   a. Turns off the echo of all commands in the batch program.
   b. Clears the window (or screen).
   c. Displays three blank lines.
   d. Displays the following message near the center of the screen:
        *** Insert a diskette in drive A ***
   e. Displays three more blank lines.
   f. Temporarily halts batch program processing.
   g. Clears the screen after resuming batch program execution.
   h. Uses the XCOPY command to copy the batch program directory and the batch programs within the directory to a diskette in drive A.

5. Before you test the batch program, store the current search path in a batch program file and then change the search path so the name of your batch program directory is listed first in the search path. What commands did you use to perform these operations?

6. Test the batch program from two different directories on drive C. What directories did you use?

7. Once you are satisfied that the batch program is operating properly, document batch program operations within the batch program file. Also include documentation in the batch program file that identifies the purpose, filename, author, and date of the batch program.

8. Reset the path on your computer system. How did you perform this operation?

9. If you wanted to modify this batch program so you can specify the name of the directory you want to copy each time you use the batch program, what would you do?

10. Using Notepad or the MS-DOS Editor, create a batch program that launches the Wordpad and Character Map accessory programs, so they are both running at the same time. (*Note*: You can locate the directories containing WORDPAD.EXE and CHARMAP.EXE by using DIR /S.)

11. Once you are satisfied that the batch program is operating properly, document batch program operations within the batch program. Also include documentation in the batch program that identifies the purpose, filename, author, and date of the batch program.

12. Create a shortcut on the Windows 2000 desktop to the batch program.

13. Use Notepad or the MS-DOS Editor to print copies of your batch program files.

14. Submit your answers to the questions in this Review Assignment and your printed copies of the batch program files.

CASE PROBLEMS

Case 1. Documenting the Directory Tree of the My Document Folder at The Perfect Match
In an ongoing effort to improve the organization of files on each employee's computer, your department manager at The Perfect Match, a temp-placement agency, asks you to create a batch program that prints a directory tree of your My Documents directory so you can evaluate your current directory structure. Once you develop this batch program, you can give each of your co-workers a copy so they can adapt it for use on their computers.

1. Use Notepad or the MS-DOS Editor to construct a batch program that performs the following operations in the following order:
   a. Turns off the echo of all commands in the batch program.
   b. Clears the window.
   c. Produces three blank lines.
   d. Displays the following message near the center of the screen:
      `*** Be sure the printer is operational ***`
   e. Produces three more blank lines.
   f. Temporarily halts batch program processing.
   g. Clears the window after resuming batch program execution.
   h. Displays a directory tree of the My Documents directory for your account using the path to that directory, and then redirects the output to the PRN printer port.

2. Before you test the batch program, store the current search path in a batch program and then change the search path so the name of your batch program directory is listed first in the search path.

3. Test the batch program from two different directories on drive C. What directories did you use?

4. Once you are satisfied that the batch program is operating properly, document batch program operations within the batch program. Also include documentation in the batch program that identifies the purpose, filename, author, and date of the batch program.

5. Print a copy of your batch program file.

6. Reset the path on your computer system.

7. Submit your printed copy of the directory tree for the My Documents directory and your printed copy of the batch program.

Case 2. Customizing the Command Prompt Window at Computer Troubleshooters Unlimited Miles Biehler, a technician at Computer Troubleshooters Unlimited, asks you to set up your computer so you can open a customized Command Prompt window using a desktop shortcut. Then, you'll be ready to provide technical support to customers.

1. Use Notepad or the MS-DOS Editor to construct a batch program that performs the following operations in the following order:
   a. Turns off the echo of all commands in the batch program.
   b. Sets the background color to bright white, and the foreground color to black.
   c. Specifies a setting in the Windows environment for the DIR command so it displays directories and files one screen at a time, in order by filename.
   d. Clears the window.

2. Before you test the batch program, store the current search path in a batch program file and then change the search path so the name of your batch program directory is listed first in the search path.

3. Test the batch program from two different directories on drive C.

4. Once you are satisfied that the batch program is operating properly, document batch program operations within the batch program file. Also include documentation in the batch program file that identifies the purpose, filename, author, and date of the batch program.

5. On the Windows 2000 desktop, create a shortcut to your new batch program.

6. Test your shortcut by double-clicking on the shortcut icon.

7. Print a copy of your batch program file.

8. Reset the path on your computer system.

9. Submit your printed copy of the batch program file.

Case 3. Running Dual Graphics Programs at Stratton Graphics   Because Stratton Graphics sometimes receives graphic image files that they can process quickly with standard Windows Accessories, owner Eve Stratton asks you to create a quick way to launch Windows Paint and Imaging for Windows simultaneously from the Windows 2000 Desktop. You decide to create a shortcut to a batch program to complete your assignment.

1. Use Notepad to construct a batch program that performs the following operations in the following order:

    a. Turns off the echo of all commands in the batch program.
    b. Change to the drive and directory folder containing Windows Paint. You can use the following technique to copy and paste the path to Paint into Notepad:

       ■ Click Start, Programs, Accessories, right-click Paint, and then click Properties.

       ■ The selection highlight should already highlight the entry in the Target text box. If necessary, drag the cursor across the Target text box to select the entry in this box.

       ■ Press Ctrl+C to copy the contents of the Target text box.

       ■ Switch to the Notepad window.

       ■ Press Ctrl+V to paste the full path of the Windows Paint program into Notepad.

       ■ Edit the line so it contains a command to change to the directory with the Paint program.

    c. Launch the Windows Paint program so the batch program will continue executing without stopping.
    d. Using the same approach as above, change to the drive and directory folder containing Imaging for Windows, and launch the Imaging program.
    e. Change back to your batch program directory folder.

2. In a Command Prompt window, test your batch program to make sure it works properly. Windows 2000 should open two program windows: Paint and Imaging. Close the Paint and Imaging windows after each test.

3. If your batch program does not work properly, make the necessary changes to your batch program, and then test the batch program again.

4. Once you are satisfied that the batch program is operating properly, document batch program operations within the batch program. Also include documentation in the batch program that identifies the purpose, filename, author, and date of the batch program.

5. Test your batch program again to make sure it works correctly with your documentation changes.

6. On the Windows 2000 desktop, create a shortcut to your new batch program.

7. Test your shortcut by double-clicking the shortcut icon. Close the two program windows when you are finished.

8. Submit a copy of your batch program, either as a printout, on a diskette, or by e-mail, as your instructor requests, along with any other requested documentation.

Case 4. Launching Applications at Townsend & Sumner Publishing Supervisor Mike Lyman of Townsend & Sumner Publishing in San Francisco has asked you to create a batch program that enables employees to launch three Microsoft Office programs—Word, Excel, and Outlook—at once from a single shortcut on the desktop.

This case problem requires that you use a computer with Microsoft Office. If you do not have access to such a computer, your instructor may select or recommend other applications.

1. Use Notepad or the MS-DOS Editor to construct a batch program that performs the following operations in the following order:

   a. Turns off the echo of all commands in the batch program.
   b. Clears the window.
   c. Displays three blank lines in the window.
   d. Displays the following message near the center of the screen:
      ```
      *** Be sure the printer is operational ***
      ```
   e. Displays three more blank lines.
   f. Temporarily halts batch program processing.
   g. Changes to the drive and directory folder containing Microsoft Office. Usually, the path to the directory with Microsoft Office is "C:\Program Files\Microsoft Office\Office." If necessary, use DIR /S to locate the program filenames described in the next three steps.
   h. Launch the Microsoft Word program, WINWORD.EXE, so the batch program will continue executing without stopping.
   i. Launch Microsoft Excel, EXCEL.EXE, in the same way as above.
   j. Launch Microsoft Outlook, OUTLOOK.EXE, as above.
   k. Change back to your batch program directory folder.

2. In a Command Prompt window, test your batch program to make sure it works properly. You should see a window with a printer status prompt. When you press a key, Windows 2000 should open Word, Excel, and Outlook application windows. The batch program window then closes. Close the Word, Excel, and Outlook windows after each test.

3. If your batch program does not work properly, make any necessary changes to the batch program, and then test the batch program again.

4. Once you are satisfied that the batch program is operating properly, document batch program operations within the batch program. Also include documentation in the batch program that identifies the purpose, filename, author, and date of the batch program.

5. Test your batch program again to make sure it works correctly with your documentation.

6. On the Windows desktop, create a shortcut to your new batch program.

7. Test your shortcut by double-clicking the desktop shortcut.

8. After testing the batch program, close the three program windows.

9. Submit a copy of your batch program, either as a printout, on a diskette, or by e-mail, as your instructor requests, along with any other requested documentation.

QUICK | CHECK ANSWERS

Session 7.1

1. BAT (or CMD)
2. USERPROFILE
3. filename
4. search path
5. directory
6. PATH
7. PATH
8. replaceable parameter
9. command
10. first

Session 7.2

1. drives, directories
2. SystemRoot (or WINDIR)
3. START
4. @ECHO OFF
5. ECHO
6. ECHO.
7. PAUSE
8. CLS
9. REM
10. PATH

Session 7.3

1. AllowAllPaths, AllowRemoveableMedia, AllowWildCards, and NoCopyPrompt
2. Administrator
3. Local Security Policy
4. BATCH
5. SYSTEMROOT
6. EXIT

OBJECTIVES

OBJECTIVES

In this tutorial you will:

- Use the console to create a batch program that customizes the Command Prompt window

- Use an environment variable to switch to your "My Documents" directory

- Use the & operator to execute two commands on the same command line

- Use IF to check for the presence of files and directories before performing a command

- Pass variable values to a batch program for use with replaceable parameters in the batch program

- Use the IF command to compare text strings before performing a command

- Add error handling to a batch program using the IF command and target labels

- Process multiple parameters using the IF and the SHIFT commands

- Use GOTO and target labels to process a specific set of commands in a batch program

- Use FOR to process simple text strings, a set of files, environment variables with multiple parts, files in all subdirectories of a directory tree branch, and lines of text within a text file

- Examine the Windows Script Host and the use of scripts

ENHANCING THE POWER OF BATCH PROGRAMS

Improving Productivity with Batch Programs at SolarWinds

CASE

SolarWinds Unlimited

Company employees at SolarWinds increasingly rely on document templates that Isabel and her staff prepare because the templates provide a consistent look to company documents, and employees can use them to produce more sophisticated and complex documents. Furthermore, many of these templates save the employees hours of work and, in the case of Excel templates, provide formulas that would otherwise require expertise in many different areas, such as financial management. Isabel's staff constantly updates the existing templates, creates new templates with the assistance of company employees, and downloads templates from Web sites. To meet changing needs, improve the productivity of her own staff, and provide company employees with templates in a more timely manner, Isabel wants to further automate the process for providing templates by using more advanced batch programs.

SESSION 8.1

In this session, you will first create an assortment of small batch programs that will assist in the process of developing and testing subsequent batch programs. You will create a batch program that uses the IF command to check for the presence of a directory, a group of files, or a single file, and, if the directory or files exist, the batch program will then back up the directory and files. Then you will learn to use replaceable parameters in a batch program so you can pass wildcard file specifications to this same batch program. Finally, you will modify that batch program so it uses the & operator to combine two separate commands on the same line.

Creating a Toolkit of Batch Programs

Isabel wants you to create a batch program that you can use to copy a document template from any of the subdirectories under the SolarWinds directory to a diskette, either as a backup or for distribution to company employees. Before you create this batch program, Isabel recommends that you create a toolkit of simple batch programs that you can use to simplify the process of designing and testing new batch programs. As a starting point, she recommends that you create one batch program to save the current search path, a second batch program to change the search path so it includes the path to your batch program directory, and a third batch program to customize the Command Prompt environment, change to the SolarWinds directory, and display a tree of the directory where you work.

The first batch program will contain a copy of the current search path so that you can quickly and easily restore the search path after you test your batch programs. If you change the search path in a Command Prompt window, that change is only temporary. When you close the Command Prompt window, and then open a new one later, Windows 2000 automatically restores the search path using the permanent setting stored in the Windows environment. If you needed to restore the search path as you were testing a batch program, you could close the Command Prompt window and then open a new one; however, this approach wastes time and effort. Instead, you can just use your batch program to restore the setting for the search path in the Windows environment without having to exit the Command Prompt window.

Creating a Batch Program Directory

Because you are going to create and store your batch programs in a batch program directory on drive C, if one does not already exist, you will first need to create a batch program directory on the computer you are using. As in the previous tutorial, you will create the batch program directory under your user account directory.

To set up your batch program directory:

1. Open a **Command Prompt** window, but do *not* change the foreground and background colors. Later, you will create a batch program that will change colors for you automatically.

2. Right-click the **Command Prompt title bar**, click **Properties**, click the **Layout** tab (if necessary), change the **Width** in the Screen Buffer Size section from 80 to **300**, click **OK**, make sure "Apply properties to current window only" is selected in the "Apply Properties to Shortcut" dialog box, and then click **OK**.

3. Maximize the **Command Prompt** window so that you can see long path names.

4. Enter: `cd %userprofile%`

   As you may recall from the previous tutorial, the command interpreter changes to the directory for your user account by using the path to your account directory stored in the USERPROFILE environment variable in the Windows environment.

5. Enter: `dir /ad`

   As you may recall from the previous tutorial, the DIR command displays directory names only when you use the Attribute switch with the Directory parameter (/AD). As in the previous tutorial, you are also going to create a directory for your batch programs that consists of the words "Batch Programs for", followed by a space and your name, so that you can distinguish your batch programs from those of other users on the same computer who might use the same user account.

6. Check the directory listing, and make sure you do not already have a directory named "Batch Programs for *(Your Name)*", where *(Your Name)* is your actual name. If there is no directory by this name, enter:

   `md "Batch Programs for [Your Name]"`

   Remember to replace *(Your Name)* with your first and last name. If there is a directory by this name belonging to someone else, use another name for your batch program directory and substitute that name in the remaining steps in this tutorial. If you have your own user logon name on your computer that no one else can use, you may choose a shorter name for your batch program directory and then substitute that name throughout this tutorial.

7. Display a **directory listing**, and make sure you have successfully created this batch program directory.

8. Change to your **batch program** directory, and then clear the **window**.

   As noted in Tutorial 7, if you already have batch programs in your batch program directory, it is a good practice to check the names of your existing batch program files before you name a new one so that you do not accidentally overwrite an existing batch program with the same name.

Storing the Current Search Path in a Batch Program

Now you're ready to create the first batch program for your toolkit—a batch program that will store the current search path so you can restore it when needed. To create this batch program, you will use the same approach you used in the last tutorial, redirecting the output of the PATH command to a batch program file.

To store the search path in a batch program file:

1. Check the batch program directory to see if there is already a batch program named Reset.bat (case does not matter). You will use this name for your first batch program, so make sure that your computer system does not already have a batch program with this name. If your computer has a batch program named Reset.bat, use a different name, such as ResetPath.Bat. If you use a name without spaces, such as ResetPath.bat, rather than Reset Path.bat, you do not have to enclose the filename within quotation marks. Whatever name you decide to use, make sure that your batch program directory does not

already contain a batch program by that name. If you choose a different name, you will have to substitute that name in the steps that follow.

2. Enter: `path > reset.bat` (or the filename that you want to use).

Windows 2000 records the current path setting in a file named Reset.bat in the batch program directory. If the path in the command prompt is long, your command line will wrap around to the next line, but the command will still work.

3. To view the contents of your batch program file, enter: `type reset.bat`

This batch program contains one command—the PATH command with the current search path. In Figure 8-1, the search path includes the full path for the system32 directory (C:\WINNT\system32), the full path for the Windows directory (C:\WINNT), and the full path for the Web-Based Enterprise Management (WBEM) directory (C:\WINNT\System32\Wbem). As noted in the last tutorial, WBEM is an initiative that establishes standards for accessing and sharing management information over an enterprise network. Your path may differ. Also note that the Command Prompt window in Figure 8-1 has the default black background with white text because you have not yet created and executed the batch program that will change the colors.

Figure 8-1   **STORING THE CURRENT WINDOWS SEARCH PATH IN A BATCH PROGRAM FILE**

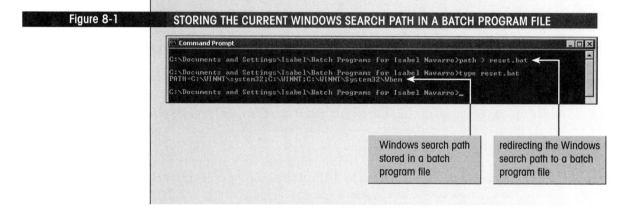

Windows search path stored in a batch program file

redirecting the Windows search path to a batch program file

Your batch program file now stores the search path setting that Windows 2000 uses when you open a Command Prompt window. As you discovered in the previous tutorial, if you change the search path setting while testing batch programs, you can restore the original search path by using this batch program.

Updating the Search Path

You will now create a batch program, which you will name UpdatePath.bat, to add the name of your batch program directory to the beginning of the current search path. Whenever you use this batch program, it will change the search path and guarantee that the command interpreter (or Windows 2000) will search your batch program directory immediately after examining the current directory, before searching other directories in the search path.

To create a batch program that updates the search path:

1. Enter: `notepad UpdatePath.bat`

When Notepad asks whether you want to create a new file, click **Yes**.

2. After Notepad opens, enter the following commands and documentation in your batch program:

```
@echo off
cls

rem    Batch Program for Updating the Search Path

rem    Name:  [Your Name]  Date:  [Today's Date]
rem    Filename:  UpdatePath.bat

rem    This batch program updates the search path by adding the
rem    full path of the batch program directory to the beginning
rem    of the search path.

rem    Add Batch Program Directory to Search Path:
       path="%userprofile%\Batch Programs for [Your Name]";%path%
```

3. Check your batch program and make sure you enclosed the path to your batch program directory within quotation marks, that you substituted your own name for *(Your Name)*, and that you enclosed the reference to the current path within % symbols.

4. Save your **batch program**, and then exit **Notepad**.

Now that you have this batch program, you can use it immediately to update the search path as you develop and test your other batch programs.

To update the search path with your batch program:

1. Enter: `UpdatePath`

2. Enter: `path`

Your batch program updated the search path. The search path assigned to the PATH environment variable in the Windows environment now includes your batch program directory. See Figure 8-2.

TROUBLE? If your search path is long, you will not see the entire path displayed within the width of the window; however, you should be able to see the path to your batch program directory at the beginning of the search path.

Figure 8-2	CHECKING THE WINDOWS SEARCH PATH

Windows search path updated by batch program to include batch file directory

```
Command Prompt                                                    _ | □ | X
C:\Documents and Settings\Isabel\Batch Programs for Isabel Navarro>path
PATH="C:\Documents and Settings\Isabel\Batch Programs for Isabel Navarro";C:\WINNT\system32;C:\W

C:\Documents and Settings\Isabel\Batch Programs for Isabel Navarro>
```

By using %path% in your batch program, you guarantee that the command interpreter has access to program files stored in specific directories used by the Windows 2000 operating system. By placing the path to your batch program directory before the remainder of that path, you allow the command interpreter to locate your batch programs quickly.

Creating a SolarWinds Directory

Before you create your next batch program, you need to create a SolarWinds directory, and then copy the contents of Data Disk #3 to that directory. Because you want to place the SolarWinds directory under the "My Documents" directory for your user account, you first need to change to that directory.

To create, and then copy files to the SolarWinds directory:

1. Clear the **window**, and then enter: `cd %userprofile%\My Documents`

   The Change Directory command changes to the "My Documents" directory for your user account by using the full path to your account directory stored in the Windows environment. See Figure 8-3. Before you create a SolarWinds directory here, and then copy files to that directory, check to make sure you do not already have a directory by that name on the computer you are using.

Figure 8-3   USING AN ENVIRONMENT VARIABLE TO CHANGE DIRECTORIES

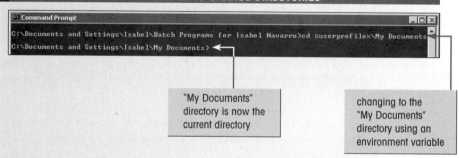

```
Command Prompt                                                                    _ □ ×
C:\Documents and Settings\Isabel\Batch Programs for Isabel Navarro>cd %userprofile%\My Documents
C:\Documents and Settings\Isabel\My Documents>
```

"My Documents" directory is now the current directory

changing to the "My Documents" directory using an environment variable

2. Enter: `dir SolarWinds`

3. If your computer does not have a SolarWinds directory under your "My Documents" directory, skip this step and continue with the next step. If your computer already has a SolarWinds directory, enter: `tree`

   If the directory tree shows that the SolarWinds directory contains subdirectories named Designs, Memos, Overhead Transparencies, Training, and Company Templates, then you or someone else previously created this directory when working on this or the previous tutorial, and you can safely remove the existing SolarWinds directory so that you can complete the entire tutorial. If this is the case, enter: `rd /s SolarWinds`

   Verify that you want to delete this directory, as well as all of its subdirectories and files.

4. To create a SolarWinds directory, and then change to that directory, clear the **window**, and then enter: `md SolarWinds & cd SolarWinds`

   Notice that you entered and executed two commands in one step. See Figure 8-4. In Windows NT and Windows 2000, the & operator is used to combine two different commands on one command line. Once the command interpreter has executed the first command, it then executes the second command. This operator is very useful, and you might be able to think of other ways in which you can benefit from its use. For example, you can use this operator to change to a directory and then copy or back up files in that directory to another diskette. (The & operator corresponds to the ; (semicolon) operator in UNIX for executing multiple commands in a single command line.)

Figure 8-4	USING THE & OPERATOR

```
Command Prompt                                                          _ □ ×
C:\Documents and Settings\Isabel\My Documents>md SolarWinds & cd SolarWinds  ◄
C:\Documents and Settings\Isabel\My Documents\SolarWinds>
```

& operator

using the & operator to execute two commands on a single command line

Now you're ready to copy the contents of Data Disk #3 to the SolarWinds directory.

5. Make a copy of Data Disk #3, and then insert your Data Disk into drive A.

6. Enter: `xcopy a:\SolarWinds /s`

   XCOPY copies the directory structure and files from Data Disk #3 into the SolarWinds directory.

7. Clear the **window**, and then display a **directory tree** that starts from this directory. The SolarWinds directory now contains four subdirectories: "Presentations," "Memos," "Graphic Designs," and "Templates," as shown in Figure 8-5.

Figure 8-5	CHECKING THE STRUCTURE OF SOLARWINDS

```
Command Prompt                                                          _ □ ×
C:\Documents and Settings\Isabel\My Documents\SolarWinds>tree
Folder PATH listing for volume DRIVE
Volume serial number is 0006FE80 E461:9D1C
C:.
    ├───Presentations
    ├───Memos
    ├───Graphic Designs
    └───Templates
C:\Documents and Settings\Isabel\My Documents\SolarWinds>
```

structure of "SolarWinds" directory

8. To return to your batch program directory, enter:
   `cd "%userprofile%\Batch Programs for [Your Name]"`

The final batch program in your toolkit will also simplify the process for working in the Command Prompt window.

Customizing the Command Prompt Window

The final batch program in your startup toolkit, which you will name Home.bat, will customize the Command Prompt window by changing the title on the title bar, setting the background and foreground colors, setting the screen buffer size width and height, shortening the prompt, changing to the SolarWinds directory on drive C, and displaying the directory structure of the SolarWinds directory. Although you have learned to change the screen buffer size manually, in the future you can let the batch program perform this operation for you.

To create a batch program for customizing the Command Prompt window:

1. Enter: `notepad Home.bat`

When Notepad asks you whether you want to create a new file, click **Yes**.

2. After Notepad opens, enter the following commands and documentation in your batch program:

```
@echo off
cls


rem     Batch Program for Customizing the Command Prompt Window

rem     Name:  [Your Name]           Date:  [Today's Date]
rem     Filename:  Home.bat

rem     This batch program assigns a custom title to the Command
rem     Prompt window, changes background and foreground colors,
rem     sets the screen buffer width and height, shortens the
rem     command prompt, changes to the SolarWinds directory, and
rem     displays the structure of the SolarWinds directory.

rem     Assign a New Title to the Window:
        title SolarWinds Templates

rem     Change Background and Foreground Colors:
        color f0

rem     Set Screen Buffer Width and Height:
        mode con: cols=300 lines=40

rem     Change to Short Prompt:
        prompt $n$g

rem     Change to the SolarWinds Directory:
        cd %userprofile%\My Documents\SolarWinds

rem     Display Structure of the SolarWinds Directory:
        tree
```

3. Check your typing for accuracy. (You will test the batch program shortly.)

4. Save your **batch program**, and then exit **Notepad**.

The TITLE command changes the title bar of the Command Prompt window to display a more descriptive name for the work you're doing for Isabel. The external MODE command sets the screen buffer width and height by specifying the number of columns (300) to show within the width of the window and the number of lines (40) within the height of the window. With this increased width, long command lines do not wrap from the end of one line to the beginning of the next, so you can scroll to the right to view long command lines. **Con:** is the device name for the console (you can also use "con" without the colon). As noted in Tutorial 1, the console refers to the display on the video monitor.

The MODE command is a multipurpose command used to configure, or specify the characteristics of, various system devices such as the console (as is the case here), keyboard, printer, parallel ports, and serial ports.

The PROMPT command in the above batch program command further alleviates the problem of long command lines by shortening the command prompt. Normally, the command prompt displays the current drive letter and the full path of the current working directory. When the full path is long, the prompt can take up much of the width of the Command Prompt window, leaving less room for viewing the command line you type.

The syntax for this internal command is:

```
PROMPT [text]
```

The text can consist of characters that you want to display as part of the prompt. You can also include special codes that customize the appearance of the DOS prompt. You can display a list of these codes by entering PROMPT /? or by reading the Windows Help entry for the PROMPT command. All of these codes consist of a dollar sign ($) followed by another character. In the command PROMPT NG, the $N code displays the current drive letter only, without a colon or the current working directory path. The $G displays a greater than symbol (>) after the drive letter, marking the end of the prompt.

Now you're ready to test your batch program.

To test the Home batch program:

1. Enter: home

The batch program displays "SolarWinds Templates" on the title bar, sets the background color to white, sets the foreground color to black, sets the screen buffer width to 300 columns, sets the screen buffer height to 40 lines, changes to a short prompt, changes to the SolarWinds directory under "My Documents," and then displays a directory tree showing the subdirectory structure under the SolarWinds directory. See Figure 8-6.

TROUBLE? If your batch program did not perform all these operations, or if it reported one or more error messages, change to the batch program directory, open the batch program file in Notepad, and then check to see that you have typed the instructions exactly. If not, make any necessary modifications to the batch program and save those changes, exit Notepad, and test your batch program again. Repeat this process until the batch program works properly.

| Figure 8-6 | USING THE BATCH PROGRAM FOR CUSTOMIZING THE COMMAND PROMPT WINDOW |

new title displayed on title bar by batch program

new short prompt

directory tree displayed by batch program

batch program expanded window size and height

2. Enter: **cd**

If you do not specify a directory name with the CD command, the command displays the full path to the current directory. See Figure 8-7. Since you can no longer see the full path in the command prompt, you can periodically use this variation of the CD command to verify that you are in the correct directory. (This form of CD corresponds to the pwd command in UNIX.)

| Figure 8-7 | DISPLAYING THE CURRENT DIRECTORY PATH NAME |

command to display current directory name

batch program has changed to the "SolarWinds" directory

This last batch program automates many of the steps that you performed manually in this and previous tutorials when you had to type each individual command. This example also illustrates how you can use batch programs to set up your computer quickly so you are ready to work.

Using Conditional Processing Commands and Operators

Earlier, Isabel asked you to create a batch program that would copy a template file from a directory to a diskette for use by other company employees. She asks you to design the batch program so that you can specify the template file to copy when you run the batch program. Therefore, you must include a replaceable parameter that can pass any template filename to the batch program. Because it's also possible a staff member might request a template file that no longer exists, Isabel suggests that you design your batch program so that it first checks for one of two different conditions—the presence or absence of that particular file.

Using the IF Conditional Processing Command

When you're designing certain batch programs like the one you will create next, you will want the batch program to perform a **conditional test**, that is, to examine a condition and then perform an operation if the condition is true, meeting a criterion that you specify. If the condition is false, then the batch program does not perform the operation—or it might perform some other type of operation instead. To prevent these situations, include the IF command in your batch program. The syntax of the IF command varies depending on the way in which you want to use it. If you want to check for the presence of a file, you would use this general syntax:

IF EXIST *filename command*

When the command interpreter executes this command, it checks for the existence of a file and, if the file exists, performs a command operation that you specify. If the file does not exist, it does not perform the operation. Assume, for example, that your batch program contained the following IF command:

```
IF EXIST "Five Year Growth Plan.xls" COPY "Five Year Growth Plan.xls" A:
```

If the file named "Five Year Growth Plan.xls" exists in the current directory, the IF command uses the COPY command to copy the file to a diskette in drive A. If the file does not exist in the current directory, nothing happens. Notice that in this instance you have to include the filename within quotation marks because it includes spaces.

The disadvantage of the command used for this last example is that it can only copy one file—"Five Year Growth Plan.xls." Suppose you want to copy different files at different times. The easiest way would be to replace every instance of the filename in the command with a replaceable parameter, as follows:

```
IF EXIST %1 COPY %1 A:
```

You do not need the quotation marks around the first instance of the %1 replaceable parameter because you specify the filename when you run the batch program. In the steps below, you will create a batch program named CopyCheck.bat, which will use the IF command with the EXIST conditional parameter to check for the presence of a file before copying it to drive A. If you want the batch program to check for the presence of the "Five Year Growth Plan.xls" file and copy it to a diskette in drive A, then you would enter this command at the command prompt (the name of the batch program is not case sensitive):

```
CopyCheck "Five Year Growth Plan.xls"
```

Then the filename "Five Year Growth Plan.xls" is assigned to the %1 replaceable parameter, and substituted wherever the %1 replaceable parameter occurs in the file. The batch program would then execute the IF command as if you had typed the following command in the batch program:

```
IF EXIST "Five Year Growth Plan.xls" COPY "Five Year Growth Plan.xls" A:
```

If you then needed to check for a file named Invoices.xls, you would invoke the batch program with this command:

```
CopyCheck Invoices.xls
```

You don't need quotation marks for this filename because it does not contain any spaces. The command interpreter assigns the filename "Invoices.xls" to the %1 replaceable parameter and substitutes that filename wherever the %1 replaceable parameter occurs in the file. The batch program would then execute the IF command as if you had typed the following in the batch program:

```
IF EXIST Invoices.xls COPY Invoices.xls A:
```

In the next set of steps, you are going to create and test the CopyCheck batch program. So that you can see how the IF command works, you will deliberately leave out the @ECHO OFF and CLS commands that you typically place at the beginning of a batch program to suppress the display of commands and clear the window of any previous output. Then you will be able to see the command interpreter process each command in the batch program as if the command had been entered manually at the command prompt. You will also see the command interpreter substitute filenames for the replaceable parameter. After you modify and test the batch program, you can add the @ECHO OFF and CLS commands.

To create a batch program that performs conditional processing:

1. Use the **CD command** to return to your batch program directory, and then clear the **window**.

2. Enter: `notepad CopyCheck.bat`

   When Notepad asks you if you want to create a new file, click **Yes**.

3. After Notepad opens, enter the following commands and documentation in your batch program:

   ```
   rem    Batch Program to Copy a File

   rem    Name:  [Your Name]          Date:  [Today's Date]
   rem    Filename:  CopyCheck.bat

   rem    This batch program receives a filename as a replaceable
   rem    parameter and copies the file to drive A if it exists
   rem    in the current directory.

   rem    Copy file to drive A if it exists:
          if exist %1 copy %1 a:
   ```

4. Save your changes, exit **Notepad**, and then clear the **window**.

5. To check your batch program's operation when you do not provide a filename, enter: `CopyCheck`

   The command interpreter echoes each command in your batch program file, including REM commands, and then displays the IF command. See Figure 8-8.

Figure 8-8	CHECKING YOUR BATCH PROGRAM'S OPERATION WHEN YOU OMIT A FILENAME

command line to execute the CopyCheck batch program with no filename

does not copy without a filename

commands within batch program displayed as they execute

```
C>CopyCheck
C>rem    Batch Program to Copy a File
C>rem    Name:  Isabel Navarro Torres     Date:  12/12/2003
C>rem    Filename:  CopyCheck.bat
C>rem    This batch program receives a filename as a replaceable
C>rem    parameter and copies the file to drive A if it exists
C>rem    in the current directory.
C>rem    Copy file to drive A if it exists:
C>if exist copy a:
C>
```

Now that you have created the CopyCheck batch program, you can use it to copy files from one of the SolarWinds directories. You will need a formatted empty diskette to complete the rest of the tutorial.

To copy files from one of the "SolarWinds" directories:

1. Remove your copy of Data Disk #3 from drive A, and then insert a formatted empty diskette into drive A.

2. Return to the SolarWinds directory by entering: `home`

3. Change to the **Templates** directory, and then clear the **window**.

4. Enter: `CopyCheck "Five Year Growth Plan.xls"`

   After the batch program completes the copy operation, the COPY command within the CopyCheck batch program displays the message "1 file(s) copied." Notice how the command interpreter inserted the filename into the command that the command executed. See Figure 8-9.

   TROUBLE? If the command interpreter does not display the message "1 file(s) copied," make sure you changed to the Templates directory, check the command that you just entered for errors, and, if necessary, correct those errors. If the batch program still does not work, then change back to the batch program directory, open the batch program, and check what you entered using the previous set of steps. Correct any errors, save your batch program, change back to the Templates directory, and then try this step again.

| Figure 8-9 | USING A BATCH PROGRAM TO COPY A FILE |

```
SolarWinds Templates
C>CopyCheck "Five Year Growth Plan.xls"
C>rem   Batch Program to Copy a File
C>rem   Name:  Isabel Navarro Torres      Date:  12/12/2003
C>rem   Filename:  CopyCheck.bat
C>rem   This batch program receives a filename as a replaceable
C>rem   parameter and copies the file to drive A if it exists
C>rem   in the current directory.
C>rem   Copy file to drive A if it exists:
C>if exist "Five Year Growth Plan.xls" copy "Five Year Growth Plan.xls" a:
        1 file(s) copied.
C>_
```

command for invoking batch program

filename passed as variable value to batch program

filename replaces the %1 replaceable parameters

5. Clear the **window**, and then enter: `dir a:`

   The batch program copied the "Five Year Growth Plan.xls" file from the Templates directory to the diskette in drive A. See Figure 8-10.

| Figure 8-10 | VERIFYING A BATCH PROGRAM'S OPERATION |

```
SolarWinds Templates
C>dir a:
 Volume in drive A has no label.
 Volume Serial Number is 0B1F-15DD

 Directory of A:\

01/16/2003  10:46a            20,992 Five Year Growth Plan.xls
               1 File(s)        20,992 bytes
               0 Dir(s)      1,436,672 bytes free
C>_
```

file copied to disk by batch program

6. Clear the **window**, and then enter: `CopyCheck invoices.xls`

The command interpreter again inserted this filename into the command before it copied the file to drive A. See Figure 8-11.

| Figure 8-11 | USING THE BATCH PROGRAM TO COPY ANOTHER FILE |

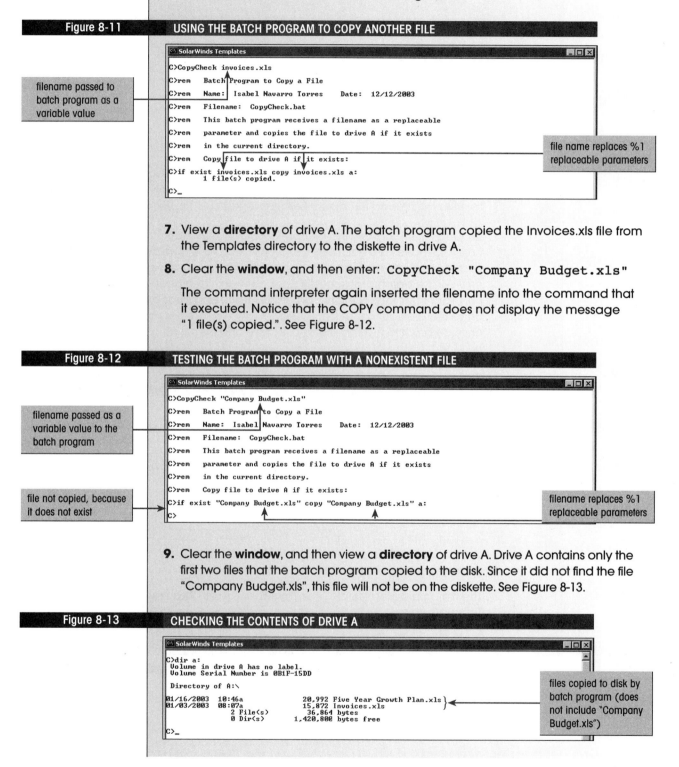

filename passed to batch program as a variable value

file name replaces %1 replaceable parameters

```
C>CopyCheck invoices.xls
C>rem    Batch Program to Copy a File
C>rem    Name:  Isabel Navarro Torres      Date:  12/12/2003
C>rem    Filename:  CopyCheck.bat
C>rem    This batch program receives a filename as a replaceable
C>rem    parameter and copies the file to drive A if it exists
C>rem    in the current directory.
C>rem    Copy file to drive A if it exists:
C>if exist invoices.xls copy invoices.xls a:
        1 file(s) copied.
C>_
```

7. View a **directory** of drive A. The batch program copied the Invoices.xls file from the Templates directory to the diskette in drive A.

8. Clear the **window**, and then enter: `CopyCheck "Company Budget.xls"`

The command interpreter again inserted the filename into the command that it executed. Notice that the COPY command does not display the message "1 file(s) copied.". See Figure 8-12.

| Figure 8-12 | TESTING THE BATCH PROGRAM WITH A NONEXISTENT FILE |

filename passed as a variable value to the batch program

file not copied, because it does not exist

filename replaces %1 replaceable parameters

```
C>CopyCheck "Company Budget.xls"
C>rem    Batch Program to Copy a File
C>rem    Name:  Isabel Navarro Torres      Date:  12/12/2003
C>rem    Filename:  CopyCheck.bat
C>rem    This batch program receives a filename as a replaceable
C>rem    parameter and copies the file to drive A if it exists
C>rem    in the current directory.
C>rem    Copy file to drive A if it exists:
C>if exist "Company Budget.xls" copy "Company Budget.xls" a:
C>
```

9. Clear the **window**, and then view a **directory** of drive A. Drive A contains only the first two files that the batch program copied to the disk. Since it did not find the file "Company Budget.xls", this file will not be on the diskette. See Figure 8-13.

| Figure 8-13 | CHECKING THE CONTENTS OF DRIVE A |

files copied to disk by batch program (does not include "Company Budget.xls")

```
C>dir a:
 Volume in drive A has no label.
 Volume Serial Number is 0B1F-15DD

 Directory of A:\

01/16/2003  10:46a              20,992 Five Year Growth Plan.xls
01/03/2003  08:07a              15,872 Invoices.xls
               2 File(s)        36,864 bytes
               0 Dir(s)      1,420,800 bytes free

C>_
```

Conditional processing with the IF command provides you with a powerful tool for your batch programs. You will use additional features of the IF command later in this tutorial.

Using Wildcard Specifications as Variable Values

Another company employee asks for a copy of your Word document templates for producing memos, reports, and letters. All of these files are stored in the Memos directory. You wonder whether or not you can use this same batch program to copy a set of files using wildcard specifications.

To test your batch program using wildcard specifications:

1. Clear the **window**, then enter: `cd ..\Memos`

   The Change Directory command looks for the Memos subdirectory under the parent directory of the current directory (Templates), as instructed by the "dot dot" (..) notation, then changes to the Memos subdirectory.

2. Enter: `CopyCheck *.doc`

   Notice that the command interpreter substituted "*.doc" for the %1 replaceable parameters and that the batch program has copied four files to the disk in drive A. The order of the displayed filenames may differ from that shown in Figure 8-14.

| Figure 8-14 | PASSING A WILDCARD SPECIFICATION TO THE BATCH PROGRAM |

wildcard specification

wildcard specification replaces %1 replaceable parameters

batch program copies files with the ".doc" file extension to drive A

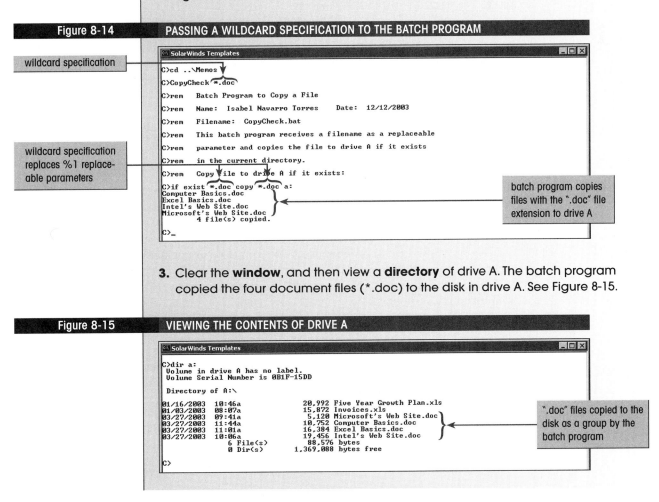

3. Clear the **window**, and then view a **directory** of drive A. The batch program copied the four document files (*.doc) to the disk in drive A. See Figure 8-15.

| Figure 8-15 | VIEWING THE CONTENTS OF DRIVE A |

".doc" files copied to the disk as a group by the batch program

Isabel appreciates the extra effort you took to modify your batch program so it provides more power and flexibility than you had originally anticipated.

Checking for the Presence of a Directory

Your last batch program copied all the document template files in the Memos directory. You realize that it may be useful to create a variation of your batch program so you can copy an entire directory and all its files to a diskette. All you need to add is a provision for making a new directory on the diskette at the same time. Therefore, you must build into the IF command an option for first making a directory, and then include a command for copying the files in that directory. You also want to make sure the batch program checks only for directories, not for files.

If you want to test for the presence of a directory, include in your IF command a provision for testing for the null device with the device name NUL. The **null device** is a special device that behaves like a perpetually empty file and has several useful features. First, the operating system treats every directory as though it contains a hidden NUL entry. Second, the operating system discards any data you copy or redirect into the null device. If you want to prevent unwanted messages or other displayed output of a command from appearing on the screen, you can redirect the output to NUL. Also, because it is *not* a file, you can use the null device with the IF command to distinguish a directory from a file. If a name refers to a directory, IF will find a NUL entry, but if the name refers to a file, IF will not find a NUL entry and will take no action. The syntax for this command is:

```
IF EXIST %1\NUL COPY %1 A:
```

When you execute the batch program, you give the batch program a directory name as a variable value for the %1 replaceable parameter. Below, you will create a variation of your batch program named DirCopy.bat. Assume that you want to copy a directory named Presentations. You would invoke the DirCopy batch program as follows:

```
DirCopy Presentations
```

The command interpreter assigns "Presentations" as the variable value for %1, and the command in your batch program translates into the following:

```
IF EXIST Presentations\NUL COPY Presentations A:
```

If Presentations contains the NUL entry, it is a directory and the batch program will copy it to drive A. If the directory does not exist, the IF command will find no NUL entry for it, and the batch program takes no action. Remember, a file cannot contain a NUL entry, so the batch program takes no action if you have specified a filename instead of a directory name.

The DirCopy batch program also needs to create a new directory before it copies the contents of that directory to the diskette in drive A. Earlier, you used the & operator to combine two commands on one command line. You can use that same technique in an IF command line, as follows:

```
IF EXIST %1\NUL MD A:\%1 & COPY %1 A:\%1
```

If the directory exists, then the Make Directory command creates a new directory on drive A with the same name, and the COPY command copies the files within the original directory to that new directory on drive A. Again, you would invoke the batch program as follows:

```
DirCopy Presentations
```

The command interpreter would assign Presentations as the variable value for %1, and the command in your batch program would translate to the following:

```
IF EXIST Presentations\NUL MD A:\Presentations & COPY Presentations A:\Presentations
```

In other words, if the Presentations directory exists (that is, it contains a NUL entry and is therefore a directory rather than a file), then the DirCopy batch command will make a new directory, also called Presentations, on drive A, and will copy the contents of the original directory to it. If the original Presentations directory does not exist (and, consequently, contains no NUL entry) the batch program will take no action. If you specify a filename instead of a directory name, then it will contain no NUL entry, and the batch program will likewise take no action. Figure 8-16 lists conditional processing symbols that you can use in a batch program. (Strictly speaking, & is an operator rather than a conditional processing symbol, but if you are examining Windows 2000 Help for more information on this operator, you will discover that Microsoft lists it as a conditional processing symbol.)

Figure 8-16

CONDITIONAL PROCESSING SYMBOL (OR OPERATOR)	USE	EXAMPLE
&	Separates multiple commands on one command line	MD SolarWinds & CD SolarWinds Creates a subdirectory named "SolarWinds" first, and then switches to the "SolarWinds" directory next.

( )	Groups multiple commands	IF EXIST Presentations\NUL (
		  MD A:\Presentations
		  COPY Presentations A:\Presentations)
		If a subdirectory named "Presentations" exists, creates a "Presentations" directory on drive A, and copies the contents of the directory to the new directory on drive A.

^	Cancels the special meaning of the command processing operator that follows it	CD Memos, Reports, ^& Correspondence Switches to a subdirectory named "Memos, Reports, & Correspondence".
&&	The batch program executes the command following this operator only if the command preceding this operator is successful	MD SolarWinds && CD SolarWinds Switches to the "SolarWinds" subdirectory only if the Make Directory command successfully creates a directory named "SolarWinds".
||	The batch program executes the command following this operator only if the command preceding this operator fails	CD SolarWinds || ECHO No such directory Attempts to switch to a subdirectory named "SolarWinds", or if that fails, displays an error message.

In the next set of steps, you will create a batch program that only copies directories.

To create a batch program for copying a directory:

1. Change back to your **batch program directory** and then clear the **window**.

2. Enter: `notepad DirCopy.bat`

   When Notepad asks you whether you want to create a new file, click **Yes**.

3. After Notepad opens, enter the following commands and documentation in your batch program:

```
rem    Batch Program to Copy an Entire Directory

rem    Name:  [Your Name]          Date:  [Today's Date]
rem    Filename:  DirCopy.bat

rem    This batch program receives a directory name as a replaceable
rem    parameter and, if it locates a directory by that name under
rem    the current directory, copies the directory and its files
rem    to drive A.

rem    If directory exists, create it on drive A and copy its files:
       if exist %1\nul md a:\%1 & copy %1 a:\%1
```

4. Save your changes, and then close **Notepad**.

5. Use your HOME batch program to return to the **SolarWinds directory**.

Now, you're ready to test your batch program.

To test the batch program:

1. Clear the **window**, and then enter: `DirCopy Presentations`

   Your batch program copies 10 files from the old Presentations directory on drive C to a new Presentations directory on drive A. The order of the filenames displayed may differ from that shown in Figure 8-17. Notice that the IF command includes the path Presentations\nul as the directory to check, creates a directory on drive A named Presentations, and then copies the contents of the original Presentations directory on drive C (the current drive) to the new Presentations directory on drive A.

| Figure 8-17 | COPYING A DIRECTORY WITH A BATCH PROGRAM |

does the Null device in the "Presentations" directory exist?

if so, create a directory named "Presentations" on drive A

& operator joins two commands in one line

& operator copies the files in the "Presentations" directory on drive C to the Presentations directory on drive A

files in "Presentations" directory copied to drive A

2. Clear the **window**, and then view a **directory listing** of drive A. Note that your diskette now has a Presentations directory. See Figure 8-18.

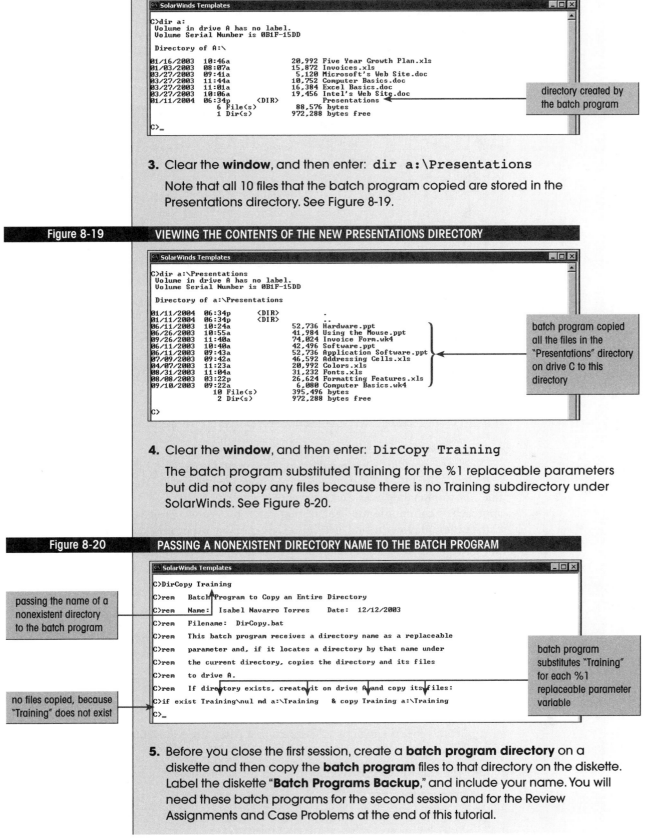

Figure 8-18 CHECKING THE BATCH PROGRAM'S COPY OPERATION

```
C>dir a:
Volume in drive A has no label.
Volume Serial Number is 0B1F-15DD

Directory of A:\

01/16/2003  10:46a           20,992 Five Year Growth Plan.xls
01/03/2003  08:07a           15,872 Invoices.xls
03/27/2003  09:41a            5,120 Microsoft's Web Site.doc
03/27/2003  11:44a           10,752 Computer Basics.doc
03/27/2003  11:01a           16,384 Excel Basics.doc
03/27/2003  10:06a           19,456 Intel's Web Site.doc
01/11/2004  06:34p    <DIR>         Presentations
               6 File(s)        88,576 bytes
               1 Dir(s)        972,288 bytes free

C>_
```

directory created by
the batch program

3. Clear the **window**, and then enter: `dir a:\Presentations`

   Note that all 10 files that the batch program copied are stored in the Presentations directory. See Figure 8-19.

Figure 8-19 VIEWING THE CONTENTS OF THE NEW PRESENTATIONS DIRECTORY

```
C>dir a:\Presentations
Volume in drive A has no label.
Volume Serial Number is 0B1F-15DD

Directory of a:\Presentations

01/11/2004  06:34p    <DIR>          .
01/11/2004  06:34p    <DIR>          ..
06/11/2003  10:24a           52,736 Hardware.ppt
06/26/2003  10:55a           41,984 Using the Mouse.ppt
09/26/2003  11:40a           74,024 Invoice Form.wk4
06/11/2003  10:40a           42,496 Software.ppt
06/11/2003  09:43a           52,736 Application Software.ppt
07/09/2003  09:42a           46,592 Addressing Cells.xls
04/07/2003  11:23a           20,992 Colors.xls
08/31/2003  11:04a           31,232 Fonts.xls
08/08/2003  03:22p           26,624 Formatting Features.xls
09/10/2003  09:22a            6,080 Computer Basics.wk4
              10 File(s)       395,496 bytes
               2 Dir(s)        972,288 bytes free

C>
```

batch program copied
all the files in the
"Presentations" directory
on drive C to this
directory

4. Clear the **window**, and then enter: `DirCopy Training`

   The batch program substituted Training for the %1 replaceable parameters but did not copy any files because there is no Training subdirectory under SolarWinds. See Figure 8-20.

Figure 8-20 PASSING A NONEXISTENT DIRECTORY NAME TO THE BATCH PROGRAM

passing the name of a
nonexistent directory
to the batch program

```
C>DirCopy Training

C>rem    Batch Program to Copy an Entire Directory

C>rem    Name:  Isabel Navarro Torres    Date:  12/12/2003

C>rem    Filename:  DirCopy.bat

C>rem    This batch program receives a directory name as a replaceable

C>rem    parameter and, if it locates a directory by that name under

C>rem    the current directory, copies the directory and its files

C>rem    to drive A.

C>rem    If directory exists, create it on drive A and copy its files:

C>if exist Training\nul md a:\Training    & copy Training a:\Training

C>_
```

batch program
substitutes "Training"
for each %1
replaceable parameter
variable

no files copied, because
"Training" does not exist

5. Before you close the first session, create a **batch program directory** on a diskette and then copy the **batch program** files to that directory on the diskette. Label the diskette "**Batch Programs Backup**," and include your name. You will need these batch programs for the second session and for the Review Assignments and Case Problems at the end of this tutorial.

There are two other variations of these IF commands that you might find useful:

```
IF NOT EXIST filename command
IF NOT EXIST directory\NUL command
```

Both of these variations perform the designated command (or commands) if the filename or directory does not exist. For example, you may want a batch program to create a new subdirectory if it does not already exist and then copy files to that subdirectory.

REFERENCE WINDOW **RW**

<u>Using the IF Conditional Processing Command and the & Operator in a Batch Program</u>
- Open a Command Prompt window, change to the batch program directory, and then create a new batch program. Or, open an existing batch program that you want to modify.
- To use the IF command to check for the presence of a file or a set of files, type IF EXIST followed by a space and the actual filename, or a replaceable parameter that permits you to pass a filename or file specification to the batch program when you invoke it. Then, after including another space, type the command you want the batch program to perform if the condition is true. If you want to include multiple commands, separate each command by the & operator.
- To use an IF command to check for the presence of a directory, type IF EXIST followed by a space, and then the reference to the NUL device in a directory. You can either include a specific directory by name (such as Templates\nul), or use a replaceable parameter for the directory (such as %1\nul). Then, after another space, type the command you want the batch program to perform if the condition is true. If you want to include multiple commands, separate each command by the & operator.
- Save your changes to this batch program, and then test the batch program.
- After testing the batch program, add any finishing touches you want to include, such as @ECHO OFF, CLS, and documentation.

Neither CopyCheck.bat nor DirCopy.bat contain the @ECHO OFF command. By not including @ECHO OFF in these batch programs, you were able to view each command that the command interpreter executed when you invoked the batch program. This approach is commonly used for testing batch programs. After you have finished testing a batch program, you can add @ECHO OFF and any other final commands, as well as whatever additional documentation you want to include in the batch program file.

Session 8.1 QUICK CHECK

1. You can use the _____ command to change the appearance of the command prompt, such as not displaying the path of the current directory.

2. If you want a batch program to examine a condition, and then perform an operation if the condition is true, use the _____ command in the batch program.

3. If you want a batch program to test for the presence of a directory and distinguish it from a file, then you would design that batch program so it checks for the presence of _____.

4. You can combine two commands on the same command line by using the _____ operator.

5. If you want a batch program to check for the presence of a file or a directory, then you would use the following general syntax: _____.

> In this session, you will use the **IF** command to compare text strings and handle errors by combining the **IF** command with the **GOTO** command and target labels. Then you'll add the **SHIFT** command to a batch program so it can process any number of command line parameters.

Using **IF** to Test Parameters

Isabel recommends that you further develop your CopyCheck batch program for copying files—first, by adding a conditional test to check whether or not you have specified a filename in the command line for the batch program to copy. You can design the batch program so that if you don't provide a filename, it will not perform a copy operation.

Using **IF** to Compare Text Strings

Isabel recommends that you include a second IF command at the beginning of your batch program to see if you typed a filename in the command line or if you inadvertently left it out.

To check for the presence or absence of a filename, another form of the IF command will perform a **string comparison**, that is, it will test whether two pieces of text are identical. The syntax for this use of the IF command is:

```
IF string1 == string2 command
```

Notice that this syntax uses *two* equals signs (==) for the string comparison. The IF command will execute the target *command* above only if *string1* and *string2* are identical. As a purely illustrative example, consider this command line:

```
IF ABC == ABC DIR A:
```

This command line would always execute the command DIR A:, because the literal string ABC on the left of the equal signs is identical to ABC on the right. The condition ABC == ABC is always true. Conversely, consider the line:

```
IF ABC == XYZ DIR A:
```

This command line would *never* execute DIR A:, because ABC on the left is not the same as XYZ on the right. The condition ABC == XYZ is always false.

Notice that the literal strings above (ABC and XYZ) are not surrounded by quotation marks (""). Each string is simply a sequence of characters. Unlike most programming languages, the IF command does not use any special characters to designate a string. The quotation mark has no special status; the IF command considers it just another character. You don't need to include quotation marks around each string, but each string on both sides of the equals signs must consist of at least one character.

In practice, you would not use IF statements like the examples above, because they always produce the same result: ABC == ABC is always true, and ABC == XYZ is always false. The IF command with the text string comparison operator (==) is most commonly used with a replaceable parameter variable, instead of with literal strings as shown above.

Recall that when you run a batch program from the command line by entering its name, replaceable parameter variables carry whatever words you type after the name of a batch program: %1 would carry the first word; %2 would carry the second word, and so on to %9. You would separate these words with spaces on the command line you type, and they could represent anything: a filename, your own name, or some other data. You just need to make sure that your batch program deals with the data in a way that fits.

For example, say you run a batch program by entering the command line:

```
Sysbackup CurrentCashFlow AugustCashFlow
```

The command line above consists of three words, separated by spaces: Sysbackup (the name of the batch program) and two parameter words, CurrentCashFlow and AugustCashFlow. The SysBackup batch program assigns the word CurrentCashFlow (the name of a directory) to the replaceable parameter variable %1. It then assigns the word AugustCashFlow (the name of a new directory that stores the cashflow files for the previous month; in this case, August) to %2, and it assigns nothing to %3 through %9, because you did not type any more words in the command line. If the SysBackup batch program contained the command:

```
ECHO Backing up %1 to %2
```

then you would see the following message displayed on the monitor as the batch program performed a backup:

```
Backing up CurrentCashFlow to AugustCashFlow
```

Assume you want to design your batch program so it determines whether you typed data for the %1 replaceable parameter when you entered the batch program filename. One way to test for an empty %1 replaceable parameter variable would be to enter the following command:

```
IF test%1 == test command
```

where the word "test" is an arbitrary string placed on both sides of the equals signs. You could use almost any character or string of characters instead. If you launched the batch program from the command prompt and didn't type anything after the name of the batch program, the batch program would replace the %1 variable name in the line above with nothing. This result occurs because the %1 variable stands for the first word you typed on your command line right after the batch program name. Then the resulting command line would be changed to:

```
IF test == test command
```

Consider a batch program named BATCHNAME containing a line like the one above. If you just type BATCHNAME at the command prompt, with nothing after the batch program name, then the %1 variable would be blank. Therefore, the line above would become "IF test == test *command*." Because the word "test" on the left of "==" is identical to "test" on the right, the condition tests as true. Therefore, the target *command* would execute.

If you *did* type a word after the batch program name in your command line, the %1 variable would contain that word. If you type BATCHNAME ABC, then the %1 variable would contain the character string ABC. Then, the line above would become "IF testABC == test *command*." Because "testABC" on the left is not the same as "test" on the right, the condition would test false and prevent the target *command* from executing.

The above example uses the arbitrary word test to help make it clear that you do not need any particular special characters to designate a literal string in an IF command line—unlike most programming languages, which require you to enclose literal strings in quotation marks.

Your CopyCheck batch program must also include an instruction to bypass the COPY operation in the event that you fail to provide a filename. One way to bypass lines in a batch program, called **branching**, is to use the GOTO ("go to") command. The syntax of GOTO is as follows:

```
GOTO label
```

In the GOTO command, the *label* is a word—which may optionally start with a colon (:)— that marks a specific position within the batch program. When the batch program executes the GOTO command, it searches for another line which must consist of a colon (:) followed by the *label* you specify, and then the batch program executes the command(s) after the line containing the label. For example, if you use the command:

```
GOTO LOOP
```

then the batch program will look for the line:

```
:LOOP
```

and proceed to execute any commands after that line. The label can be anywhere in the batch program, either before or after the GOTO command.

Normally, the GOTO command requires you to put a corresponding target label elsewhere in the batch program, so GOTO can jump to it. A special case of GOTO (in Windows NT and Windows 2000 only) does not require a separate target label in the batch program:

```
GOTO :EOF
```

Instead of looking for a separate :EOF (end of file) label line, this form of GOTO always jumps to the end of the batch program, thereby terminating it. You must include the colon in **:EOF** above.

You can adapt the CopyCheck batch program that you created earlier, checking for a missing filename by adding an IF command that tests for a blank replaceable parameter, and then bypasses the command for copying a file if you inadvertently did not provide a filename for the batch program to process.

To modify CopyCheck.bat to test for a blank replaceable parameter:

1. Open a **Command Prompt** window, and then change to your **batch program directory** on drive C. If you do not have a batch program directory on the computer you are using, create one, using the instructions in the first session of this tutorial, and then copy your files from the batch program directory on your "Batch Programs Backup" diskette (which you made at the end of the previous session) into the batch program directory on drive C.

2. If necessary, remove your "Batch Programs Backup" diskette, and then insert a formatted empty diskette so you can test the batch programs you create in this session. (You can reformat the diskette you used in the first session.)

3. If you closed the Command Prompt window after the first session, execute your **UpdatePath.bat batch program** to add your batch program directory to the Windows path.

4. Execute your **Home.bat batch program** to set the background and foreground colors and size of the Command Prompt window. Home.bat also changes to the SolarWinds directory folder and displays a directory tree.

5. Change back to your **batch program directory**.

6. Use Notepad to edit **CopyCheck.bat**, which you created in the previous session.

7. Add the lines shown in boldface:

```
rem   Batch Program to Copy a File

rem   Name:  [Your Name]        Date:  [Today's Date]
rem   Filename:  CopyCheck.bat

rem   This batch program receives a filename as a replaceable
rem   parameter and copies the file to drive A if it exists
rem   in the current directory.
```

```
rem    End program without copying if you typed no filename
       if test%1 == test goto :EOF

rem    Copy file to drive A if it exists:
       if exist %1 copy %1 a:
```

8. Save your changes and exit **Notepad**.

The new IF command you entered determines whether the batch program will attempt the COPY operation, depending on whether you entered a filename after CopyCheck at the command prompt. You can now test your revised version of this batch program.

To test the revised CopyCheck.bat:

1. Enter: **home** to return to the SolarWinds directory, then enter: **cd pres*** to change to the Presentations subdirectory.

2. Clear the window, and then enter: **CopyCheck Hardware.ppt**

Notice where the command interpreter inserted this filename in place of %1 in the commands. See Figure 8-21. Because you typed the filename "Hardware.ppt" after the batch program name, the operating system assigned it to %1. Inside CopyCheck.bat, the batch program replaced %1 with "Hardware.ppt" before executing the first IF command. Because "testHardware.ppt" did not match "test", the IF command did not terminate by jumping to the end of the file, but rather executed the next IF command, which copied the file to your diskette in drive A.

Figure 8-21	TESTING A STRING COMPARISON WITH A FILENAME

command for invoking the batch program

filename passed as a parameter to the batch program

filename substituted for %1 replaceable parameter

string comparison

copies file to disk in drive A

3. Clear the **window**, then test how your batch program behaves when you do not provide a filename by entering: **CopyCheck**

Because you did not type a filename after CopyCheck, the operating system assigned nothing to %1. Inside CopyCheck.bat, the batch program replaced %1 with nothing (thus removing it) before executing the first IF command. Notice that you see only the word "test" on both sides of the equals signs, because nothing was assigned to %1. See Figure 8-22. Therefore, the condition is true (the two strings matched), and the first IF command executed the GOTO command and jumped to the end of the file as specified, ending the batch program. The second IF command never executed, so the batch program did not attempt a copy operation—which is just how you wanted it to perform.

| Figure 8-22 | TESTING A STRING COMPARISON BY NOT PROVIDING A FILENAME |

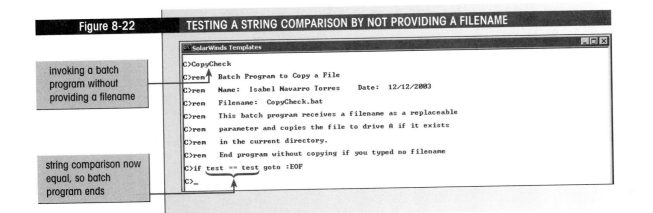

invoking a batch
program without
providing a filename

string comparison now
equal, so batch
program ends

```
C>CopyCheck
C>rem    Batch Program to Copy a File
C>rem    Name:  Isabel Navarro Torres     Date:  12/12/2003
C>rem    Filename:  CopyCheck.bat
C>rem    This batch program receives a filename as a replaceable
C>rem    parameter and copies the file to drive A if it exists
C>rem    in the current directory.
C>rem    End program without copying if you typed no filename
C>if test == test goto :EOF
C>_
```

By including an IF command that compares two strings in a batch program, you can determine whether the command interpreter executes other commands in the batch program.

If you have a background in programming languages, you may expect to be able to use a line like IF %1 == "" *command* in batch programs. This syntax will not work here for two reasons:

- The two quotation marks ("") do not signify an empty string, as is typical of other programming languages; instead, you would be comparing %1 with a string of two quotation mark characters.

- Before executing one of the batch program's command lines containing a replaceable parameter variable like %1, a batch program always removes the variable name and replaces it with its contents—if any. If you ran the batch program and didn't type anything after the batch program name, making %1 empty, the above line would become: IF == "" *command*. This would produce an error, because the comparison operator (==) would have nothing to compare on its left side.

Always type one or more additional characters next to the replaceable parameter variable on either side, and type the same character or characters on the other side of the equals signs. You can use a command line like IF "%1" == "" *command*, but bear in mind that quotation marks are not string delimiters in batch programs.

| REFERENCE | WINDOW | RW |

Performing String Comparisons and Branching in a Batch Program

- Open a Command Prompt window, change to your batch program directory, and then either open an existing batch program, or create a new batch program.
- To determine if a replaceable parameter is empty and then branch to another line in the batch program if the condition is true, include or insert an IF command that contains a replaceable parameter variable name with one or more characters added, compared with the same characters on the other side of a pair of equals signs (for example, IF test%1 == test GOTO :EOF). Then include a GOTO command with a label (for example, :EOF) if the condition is true so the batch program branches to another line in the batch program, and executes whatever commands follow that line.

Adding Error Handling to a Batch Program

Now that you have added a test for a blank replaceable parameter to the batch program, you would like the batch program to handle the error by alerting or reminding you of the correct syntax if you forget to specify a filename when invoking the batch program. You can revise your IF command so, instead of jumping to the end of the file, the command branches to a line that displays an error message before the batch program ends.

To add error handling to your batch program:

1. Change to your **batch program directory**.

2. Use Notepad to edit CopyCheck.bat by changing or adding the lines shown in boldface:

```
@echo off

rem     Batch Program to Copy a File

rem     Name:   [Your Name]        Date:   [Today's Date]
rem     Filename:  CopyCheck.bat


rem     This batch program receives a filename as a replaceable
rem     parameter and, if the file exists in the current directory,
rem     copies it to drive A.


rem     Jump to error message if you typed no filename:
        if test%1 == test goto :ERR

rem     Copy file to drive A if it exists:
        if exist %1 copy %1 a: > nul

rem     Copy complete, so bypass error message and end:
        goto :EOF

:ERR
rem     Error message if you typed no filename:
        echo Please include a filename, like this:
        echo CopyCheck filename
```

3. Save your changes and then exit **Notepad**.

In this version of your batch program:

- You added @ECHO OFF to prevent the batch program from displaying every command.
- You changed the target label of the first IF command so the batch file program branches to the error-handling section :ERR if the replaceable parameter %1 tests as empty (instead of just ending the program by jumping to :EOF).

- To avoid executing the error section when you pass a filename to the batch program, you added GOTO :EOF after the line that performs the copy operation, so the batch program completes the operation, jumps to the end of the file, and exits.

- By adding "> nul" after the COPY command for the second IF statement, you redirected the screen output of the COPY command to the NUL device (also known in computer parlance as the bit bucket) so the batch program does not display the message "1 File(s) copied."

- You added a new error-handling section labeled :ERR, which uses ECHO commands to display a message explaining what the user should do if no filename is entered after CopyCheck when the batch program is invoked at the command prompt.

Now test the error handling.

To test the error handling features:

1. Enter: **home** to return to the "SolarWinds" directory, then enter: **cd pres***
   to change to the "Presentations" subdirectory.

2. Clear the window, then enter: **CopyCheck Software.ppt**

   This command tests the intended use of your batch program (to copy a file that exists). Notice that you do not see the message "1 File(s) copied" because you redirected the screen output of the COPY command to the NUL device.

3. Check the contents of drive A to make sure the batch program copied "Software.ppt" to your Data Disk. Make sure your default drive is C when you are done.

4. Clear the **window**, and then enter: **CopyCheck**

   This will test your batch program's behavior when you inadvertently leave out the filename. This time you should see a usage message because you didn't enter a filename to copy. See Figure 8-23.

| Figure 8-23 | TESTING THE ERROR-HANDLING CAPABILITY OF THE BATCH PROGRAM |

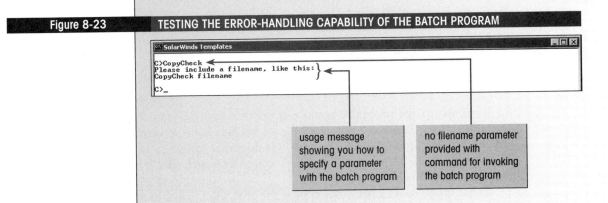

This error-handling technique relies on the use of GOTO, first to bypass commands that require parameters in order to function properly, and then to display a message on the proper use of the batch program if you did not provide the parameters the batch program needed. This batch program also relies on the use of a second GOTO to bypass the error-handling section of the batch program if no error occurred.

Error-handling messages improve the usefulness of batch programs by identifying what the user must do to use the batch programs properly. Without error-handling messages in a batch program, you might have to view and reinterpret the contents of the program if you have not used it recently, so you know how the batch program works and what information you must provide when you execute it.

Processing Multiple Files and Parameters

You decide you would like your batch program to copy a list of files, instead of just one file. You would like the option of providing multiple filenames to the batch program, for example:

```
CopyCheck firstfile.txt secondfile.doc thirdfile.xls
```

The above example uses three file specifications. Because you have nine replaceable parameter variables, %1 through %9, available for use in batch programs, you could repeat the commands in the batch program up to nine times, each time using a different variable.

The example above would assign parameters to variables this way:

	%1	%2	%3
CopyCheck	firstfile.txt	secondfile.doc	thirdfile.xls

Then, inside the batch program, you could have a series of three IF commands on separate lines, as follows:

```
if exist %1 copy %1 a: > nul
if exist %2 copy %2 a: > nul
if exist %3 copy %3 a: > nul
```

This sample batch program would require exactly three replaceable parameters. If you typed just two filenames, you would have no %3, and the third command above would translate into "if exist copy a: > nul" which would fail with an error. If you typed four filenames, the batch program wouldn't copy the fourth file, because the batch program contains no command that uses %4.

What if you could write a batch program that would copy as many or as few files as you wanted, without having to determine the number of files in advance? By using an IF command with GOTO to repeatedly execute the first line, "if exist %1 copy %1 a: > nul", you can then use the SHIFT command to place each filename in turn into %1.

Each time a batch program executes the SHIFT command, it moves the next item on the command line into the %1 replaceable parameter variable, as follows:

Before SHIFT:
Variable: %1
Parameter: firstfile.txt   secondfile.doc   thirdfile.xls

When the batch program begins, the first variable value, *firstfile.txt*, is assigned to %1, and the other two variable values are held in reserve. Then, after processing the first variable value, SHIFT drops *firstfile.txt* and then moves *secondfile.doc* into %1, like the next baseball player up to bat :

Variable: %1
Parameter: secondfile.doc   thirdfile.xls

After processing the second variable value, the batch program drops *secondfile.doc*, and then moves *thirdfile.xls* to %1. After processing the third variable value, the batch program ends.

You are going to revise your batch program so that it uses SHIFT and an IF command with GOTO commands to repeat the same operations until all the filenames you type on the command line are processed. You can also type wildcard specifications, such as *.wk4, instead of specific filenames. Your IF command will contain an ELSE clause, with which you can specify an alternate command to execute when the condition is false.

To add multiple file processing to your batch program:

1. Change to your **batch program directory**.

2. Use Notepad to edit CopyCheck.bat, changing or adding the lines (including documentation) shown in boldface. Make sure you remove the "Copy complete, so bypass error message and end:" and "goto :EOF" lines.

```
@echo off

rem   Batch Program to Copy a File

rem   Name:  [Your Name]        Date:  [Today's Date]
rem   Filename:  CopyCheck.bat


rem   This batch program takes a series of filenames as
rem   replaceable parameters and, if the files exist
rem   in the current directory, copies them to drive A.


rem   Jump to error message if you typed no filename
     if test%1 == test goto :ERR

:LOOP
rem   Start of loop, repeated for each parameter:

rem   Copy file to drive A if it exists:
     if exist %1 copy %1 a: > nul

rem   Move next filename parameter into %1:
     shift

rem   If no filename is provided, quit; otherwise repeat loop:
     if test%1 == test (goto :EOF) else goto LOOP
```

```
:ERR
rem   Error message if you typed no filename:
      echo Please include at least one filename, like this:
      echo CopyCheck filename1 filename2 ...
```

3. Save your changes and then exit **Notepad**.

In this version of your batch program:

- You changed the descriptive paragraph to reflect the batch program's new behavior.
- You inserted a :LOOP label as a target for a subsequent GOTO command. By placing the :LOOP label before the IF command that performs the copy operation, the batch program repeats commands between the LOOP label and the GOTO command.
- You inserted a SHIFT command to pull the next filename from the command line into the %1 variable. If there is no filename left on the command line, %1 becomes empty.
- You changed the old GOTO :EOF line to an IF command that checks the new %1 to see if it is empty. If so, the IF command executes the GOTO :EOF command, bypassing the :ERR error-handling section and ending the batch program. Otherwise, the IF command executes the command after the word ELSE, which is GOTO :LOOP, and jumps back to the :LOOP label to perform the copy operation again (for the next variable value assigned to the %1 parameter).
- You included an ELSE clause for the IF command so you can specify what the batch program should do if the condition is false (loop again).
- You put parentheses around the previous command (GOTO :EOF), which this ELSE clause requires. Parentheses ( ) group one or more command lines together to operate as a single command and provide a way to indicate the end of a command without requiring you to go to the next line. Here, they separate GOTO :EOF from the ELSE clause.
- You changed the ECHO usage messages in the :ERR error-handling section to remind you that you can use more than one parameter.

Now you are ready to test your enhanced batch program.

To test multiple file processing in your batch program:

1. Enter: **home**

This will return you to the "SolarWinds" directory.

2. Change to the "Presentations" subdirectory.

3. Clear the **window**, and then enter: **CopyCheck**
This will test CopyCheck's operation when you neglect to provide any file-names. Because you didn't enter anything after CopyCheck, you should see only the new usage message, "Please include at least one filename."

4. Enter: **CopyCheck fonts.xls colors.xls *.wk4**

These three parameters (two filenames and one wildcard specification) test the operation of your enhanced batch program, which should now copy four files to drive A.

5. Check the contents of drive A to verify that the batch program copied Fonts.xls, Colors.xls, "Invoice Form.wk4", and "Computer Basics.wk4". The order of the file-names displayed may differ from that shown in Figure 8-24.

Figure 8-24	PASSING MULTIPLE PARAMETERS TO A BATCH PROGRAM

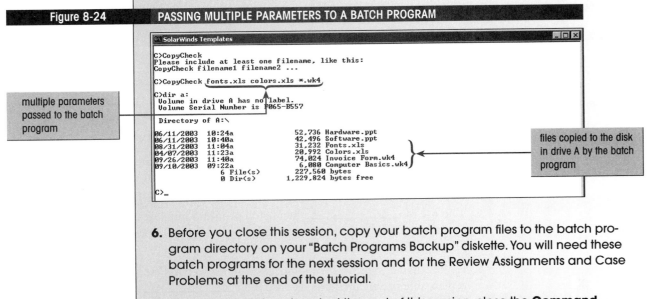

multiple parameters passed to the batch program

files copied to the disk in drive A by the batch program

```
SolarWinds Templates

C>CopyCheck
Please include at least one filename, like this:
CopyCheck filename1 filename2 ...

C>CopyCheck fonts.xls colors.xls *.wk4

C>dir a:
 Volume in drive A has no label.
 Volume Serial Number is F065-B557

 Directory of A:\

06/11/2003  10:24a            52,736 Hardware.ppt
06/11/2003  10:40a            42,496 Software.ppt
08/31/2003  11:04a            31,232 Fonts.xls
04/07/2003  11:23a            20,992 Colors.xls
09/26/2003  11:40a            74,024 Invoice Form.wk4
09/10/2003  09:22a             6,080 Computer Basics.wk4
               6 File(s)        227,560 bytes
               0 Dir(s)      1,229,824 bytes free

C>_
```

6. Before you close this session, copy your batch program files to the batch pro-gram directory on your "Batch Programs Backup" diskette. You will need these batch programs for the next session and for the Review Assignments and Case Problems at the end of the tutorial.

7. If you plan to take a break at the end of this session, close the **Command Prompt** window.

By using IF and GOTO to make a loop that includes the SHIFT command, you can run your batch program with any number of parameters on the command line, increasing the power and flexibility of your batch program and saving yourself the time and tedium of per-forming each operation separately.

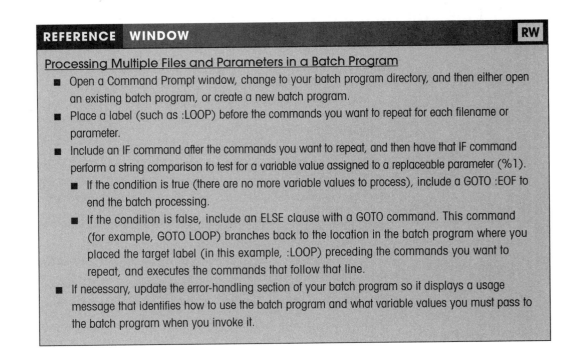

REFERENCE WINDOW   RW

Processing Multiple Files and Parameters in a Batch Program

- Open a Command Prompt window, change to your batch program directory, and then either open an existing batch program, or create a new batch program.
- Place a label (such as :LOOP) before the commands you want to repeat for each filename or parameter.
- Include an IF command after the commands you want to repeat, and then have that IF command perform a string comparison to test for a variable value assigned to a replaceable parameter (%1).
  - If the condition is true (there are no more variable values to process), include a GOTO :EOF to end the batch processing.
  - If the condition is false, include an ELSE clause with a GOTO command. This command (for example, GOTO LOOP) branches back to the location in the batch program where you placed the target label (in this example, :LOOP) preceding the commands you want to repeat, and executes the commands that follow that line.
- If necessary, update the error-handling section of your batch program so it displays a usage message that identifies how to use the batch program and what variable values you must pass to the batch program when you invoke it.

As you've discovered in this and preceding sections, not only can you use batch programs to customize the command-line operating environment, but you can also use the IF command in batch programs to perform conditional processing.

Session 8.2 QUICK CHECK

1. If you need to determine whether you passed a filename as a variable value to a batch program, you would use the IF command to perform a _____ comparison.

2. In a batch program, if you want to branch to another line within the batch program, or loop back to an earlier line in the batch program after performing a conditional test, then you would use the _____ command and a _____.

3. If you want a batch program to branch to the end of the batch program and terminate after performing a conditional test, then you would use the following command: _____.

4. The use of _____ in a batch program improves the usefulness of a batch program by displaying a message and explaining how to use the batch program properly.

5. Rather than designing a batch program so it can handle only a fixed number of replaceable parameters, you can use the _____ command to provide a series of values to the same replaceable parameter.

SESSION 8.3

In this session, you'll work with a variety of forms of the FOR command to process simple text strings, a set of files, environment variables with multiple parts, files in all subdirectories of a directory tree branch, and lines of text within a text file.

Using the FOR Command

Isabel recommends that you examine and experiment with the FOR command so you can enhance the capability of your batch programs. Since the syntax of the FOR command is more complex than that of other batch program commands, and since you can use it in different ways, Isabel suggests that you first examine how to use the FOR command to process a set of variable values. Then you can create a batch program that uses the same features to process a set of files.

The FOR command takes a list of items and repeats the same operation or operations with each item in turn until it processes all the items in the list. Each item can be any string of characters, such as a person's name, a filename or a directory name, or it can be a wildcard specification for similar filenames. In your next batch program, you will use a FOR command to repeat the COLOR command with different color codes in a list.

Although you typically use the FOR command in a batch program, you can enter the FOR command directly from the command prompt to test the command and verify that it works properly. When entered at the command prompt, rather than in a batch program, the syntax of the FOR command is:

```
FOR %A IN (item1 item2 item3 ...) DO command %A
```

For each item in the list (starting with whatever data will be substituted for *item1*), the FOR command temporarily stores the item in a one-letter **index variable** (represented by %*A* above), executes the *command* after the keyword DO, and then starts over with the next item in the list and repeats the same operations on the next item. You include the list of items in parentheses, represented above by (*item1 item2 item3 ...*), where the three dots (...) indicate that the list may contain any number of items. You can separate the items with spaces, commas, or semicolons. When you enter the FOR command directly from the command prompt (rather than in a batch program), the index variable always consists of a percent sign (%) followed by a single letter of the alphabet from uppercase A to uppercase Z and lowercase a to lowercase z, for a total of 52 possible variables. The term **index variable** distinguishes the one-letter variables used by the FOR command (for example, **%A**) from replaceable parameter variables (such as **%1**) and from environment variables (such as **%PATH%**).

Using FOR With a List of Simple Text Strings

To familiarize you with the mechanics of the FOR command, Isabel illustrates its simplest form by showing you how to process a list or set of literal text strings. A **literal text string** consists of a word or sequence of characters that is processed without treating any of the characters as a variable. You can test the FOR command with literal text strings at the command prompt to see how it works, before you use it in a batch program.

To test FOR with a simple set of text strings:

1. Open a **Command Prompt** window, and then change to your **batch program directory** on drive C. If you do not have a batch program directory on the computer you are using, create one, and then copy your batch program files from the batch program directory on your "Batch Programs Backup" diskette into the batch program directory on drive C.

2. If necessary, remove your "Batch Programs Backup" diskette, and then insert a formatted empty diskette so you can test the batch programs you create in this session.

3. If you closed the Command Prompt window after the previous session, switch to your **batch program directory**, and then execute your **UpdatePath.bat batch program** to add your batch program directory to the Windows path.

4. Execute your **Home.bat batch program** to set the background and foreground colors and size of the Command Prompt window, change to the **SolarWinds directory folder**, and then display a **directory tree**.

5. Clear the **window**, and then enter:
   `for %a in (alpha beta gamma) do echo %a`

   FOR cycles through each of the words in parentheses, each time assigning one of the words—literally "alpha," "beta," then "gamma"—to %a, and using ECHO to display each value assigned to %a. In each case, you also see a new command prompt, reflecting the fact that the batch program processes the same FOR command repeatedly, but with a different index variable value. In turn, FOR repeatedly displays the ECHO command for each variable value. As with a batch program, you can suppress this display with the @ sign.

6. Recall the previous command and add an @ sign before the ECHO command, so it reads: `for %a in (alpha beta gamma) do @echo %a`

   This time, the FOR command line displays only the output of the repeated ECHO commands, but not the commands themselves. See Figure 8-25.

Figure 8-25 — TESTING FOR WITH SIMPLE TEXT STRINGS

variable placeholder for text string currently being processed

```
C>for %a in (alpha beta gamma) do echo %a

C>echo alpha
alpha
C>echo beta
beta
C>echo gamma
gamma

C>for %a in (alpha beta gamma) do @echo %a
alpha
beta
gamma

C>_
```

text strings processed by FOR command

ECHO command displays each text string processed by the FOR command

text strings processed by FOR command

"@" suppresses display of each ECHO command

Isabel asks you to devise a FOR command line, using the technique she just illustrated, that will cycle through the Command Prompt window colors so you can look for combinations that work well with the company's overhead display panel and that will make it easy for participants in a workshop to see the techniques illustrated by the workshop trainer. After using the Help switch (/?) to examine the codes for the COLOR command (available in Windows NT and Windows 2000), you decide to test your command line with six background colors.

To cycle through color combinations:

1. Clear the **window**, and enter:
```
for %a in (a0,b0,c0,d0,e0,f0) do color %a
```

Note that you separated the items in this list with commas instead of spaces; semicolons (;) or equals signs (=) can also be used as separators. Without stopping between commands, the FOR command line repeats the COLOR command for each code in the list. Depending on your computer's speed, you may see colors flash briefly on the screen. See Figure 8-26.

Figure 8-26 — CYCLING THROUGH COLOR CODES WITH THE FOR COMMAND

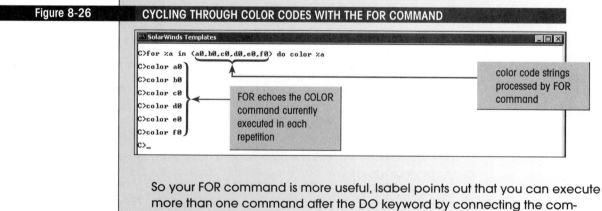

```
C>for %a in (a0,b0,c0,d0,e0,f0) do color %a
C>color a0
C>color b0
C>color c0
C>color d0
C>color e0
C>color f0
C>_
```

color code strings processed by FOR command

FOR echoes the COLOR command currently executed in each repetition

So your FOR command is more useful, Isabel points out that you can execute more than one command after the DO keyword by connecting the commands with the & operator. She suggests you add a PAUSE command so you can see the results one at a time.

2. Clear the **window**, and enter:
```
for %a in (a0,b0,c0,d0,e0,f0) do color %a & pause
```

3. After viewing each color, press the **Spacebar** until you cycle through the entire list of color codes. See Figure 8-27.

Figure 8-27	PAUSING AT EACH COLOR CODE

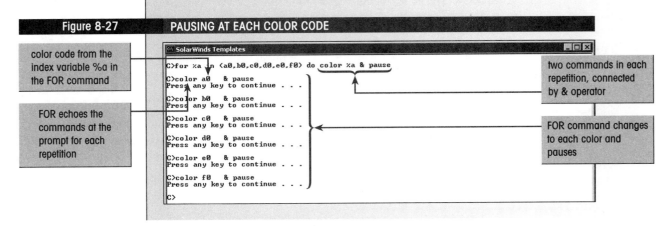

color code from the index variable %a in the FOR command

FOR echoes the commands at the prompt for each repetition

two commands in each repetition, connected by & operator

FOR command changes to each color and pauses

To illustrate the difference in syntax, Isabel asks you to try the same command in a batch program. Because this batch program is just for testing the capabilities of the FOR command, she tells you that you can dispense with the REM statement documentation you normally would include.

In a batch program, you must use two percent signs in the index variable, like this:

FOR %%A IN (*item1 item2 item3* ...) DO *command* %%A

The command interpreter strips off each initial percent sign inside a batch program in preparation for substituting the value of a replaceable parameter or environment variable, so you must add an additional percent sign. The second percent sign remains and allows the FOR command to use its index variable properly, as though it was executed at the regular command prompt outside the batch program.

To execute your color tester in a batch program:

1. Change to your **batch program directory**.

2. Enter: `notepad ColorTest.bat`

Click **Yes** when Notepad asks you if you want to create a new file.

3. Enter: `for %%a in (a0,b0,c0,d0,e0,f0) do color %%a & pause`

Be sure to use two percent signs (%%) in your batch program.

4. Save the **batch program** and exit **Notepad**, then return to the **Command Prompt** window.

5. Clear the **window**, and then test your batch program by entering: `ColorTest`

Press the **Spacebar** to view each color combination in the Command Prompt window. Notice that your batch program works just like the FOR command you entered earlier at the command prompt.

This simple batch program illustrates the basic way in which the FOR command works: it repeatedly uses the same command or set of commands to process a set of values that you provide.

REFERENCE WINDOW   **RW**

<u>Using FOR With a List of Simple Text Strings</u>

- Open a Command Prompt window.
- If you want to use the FOR command directly at the command prompt, type FOR, a space, an index variable name consisting of a single percent sign and a single letter of the alphabet (for example, %a), a space, IN, a space, a pair of parentheses containing a list of text strings (separated by spaces, tabs, commas, semicolons, or equals signs), a space, DO, a space, and then a command repeating the index variable name.
- If you want to use this same FOR command in a batch program, change to your batch program directory, either open an existing batch program or create a new batch program, and then include or insert a line containing a FOR command as described above, but use two percent signs in the index variable name (for example, %%a) instead of one.

You can now build on this knowledge of the FOR command to further enhance your batch programs.

Using FOR to Divide a List in an Environment Variable

Isabel notes that you can also use the FOR command at the command prompt and in a batch program to work with a list of items stored in an environment variable. For example, the PATH environment variable contains the search path—a list of full directory paths through which the operating system searches to locate programs you launch at the command prompt. Since each directory path is separated from the previous and next directory path by a semicolon, it can be difficult to pick out the beginning and end of each directory path. Because the semicolon is one of the delimiters used by the FOR command to separate items in a list, however, FOR can assign each item in the search path to an index variable, such as %a, and execute a command with each directory path. Therefore, you can use the FOR command to break up the search path into each of its component parts and list each of the directory paths on a separate line.

To display the component parts of the PATH environment variable on separate lines:

1. Clear the **Command Prompt** window, and then enter: `path`

Examine the contents of the PATH environment variable. For example, the default search path stored by Windows 2000 in the PATH environment variable displays as: `PATH=C:\WINNT\system32;C:\WINNT;C:\WINNT\System32\Wbem`

Your path will also include the name of your batch program directory.

2. Enter: `for %a in (%path%) do @echo %a`

Because the semicolon is a delimiter, similar to the space or comma when specifying a list of items, the FOR statement splits the list of directory paths in the PATH environment variable at the semicolons (;), assigns each directory path in turn to %a, and then displays each directory path on a separate line. Your listed directories may differ from those shown in Figure 8-28.

Figure 8-28 | **PROCESSING THE CONTENTS OF THE PATH ENVIRONMENT VARIABLE**

current contents of the PATH environment variable used as a list of strings for processing by the FOR command

```
SolarWinds Templates                                                    _ □ ✕
C>path
PATH="C:\Documents and Settings\Isabel\Batch Programs for Isabel Navarro";C:\WINNT\system32;C:\WIN

C>for %a in (%path%) do @echo %a
"C:\Documents and Settings\Isabel\Batch Programs for Isabel Navarro"
C:\WINNT\system32
C:\WINNT
C:\WINNT\System32\Wbem

C>
```

FOR command displays the path to each subdirectory listed in the Windows path

current setting for the Windows search path

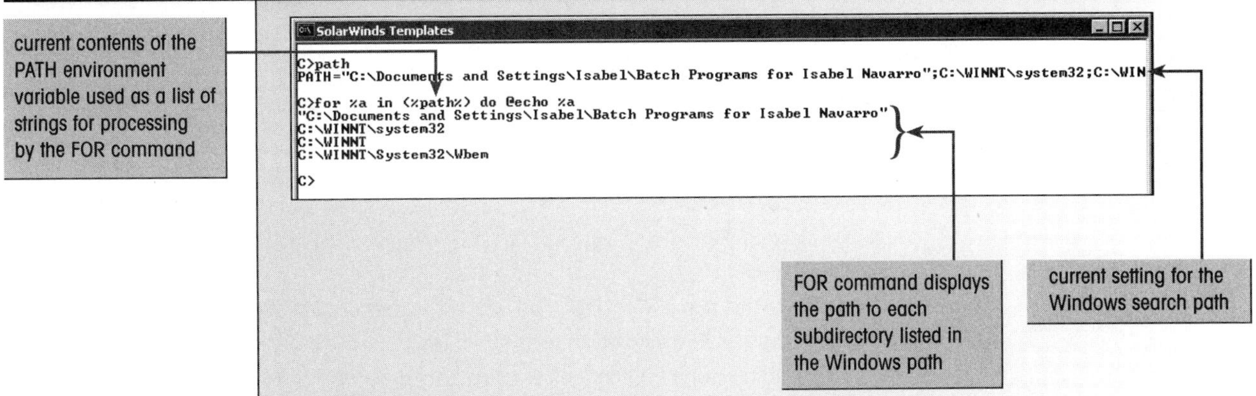

3. Clear the **window**, and enter: `set pathext`

The SET command displays the name and contents of the PATHEXT environment variable, which is a list of file extensions separated by semicolons. Windows 2000 identifies these extensions as belonging to executable program files, as described in Tutorial 7. The contents of your PATHEXT variable may differ from Figure 8-29.

Figure 8-29 | **VIEWING THE SETTING FOR THE PATHEXT ENVIRONMENT VARIABLE**

environment variable

```
SolarWinds Templates                                                    _ □ ✕
C>set pathext
PATHEXT=.COM;.EXE;.BAT;.CMD;.VBS;.VBE;.JS;.JSE;.WSF;.WSH

C>_
```

list of executable extensions in PATHEXT environment variable

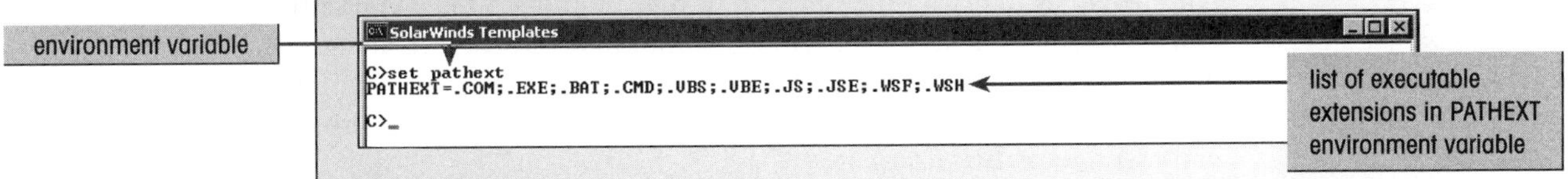

4. Recall the previous FOR command, and then edit the command so it reads:
`for %a in (%pathext%) do @echo %a`

The FOR statement splits PATHEXT into separate lines in the same way as it split the PATH environment variable earlier. See Figure 8-30.

Figure 8-30 | **PROCESSING THE CONTENTS OF THE PATHEXT ENVIRONMENT VARIABLE**

```
SolarWinds Templates                                                    _ □ ✕
C>set pathext
PATHEXT=.COM;.EXE;.BAT;.CMD;.VBS;.VBE;.JS;.JSE;.WSF;.WSH

C>for %a in (%pathext%) do @echo %a
.COM
.EXE
.BAT
.CMD
.VBS
.VBE
.JS
.JSE
.WSF
.WSH

C>_
```

FOR command displays each program file extension stored in the PATHEXT environment variable

current contents of the PATHEXT environment variable used as a list of strings for processing by the FOR command

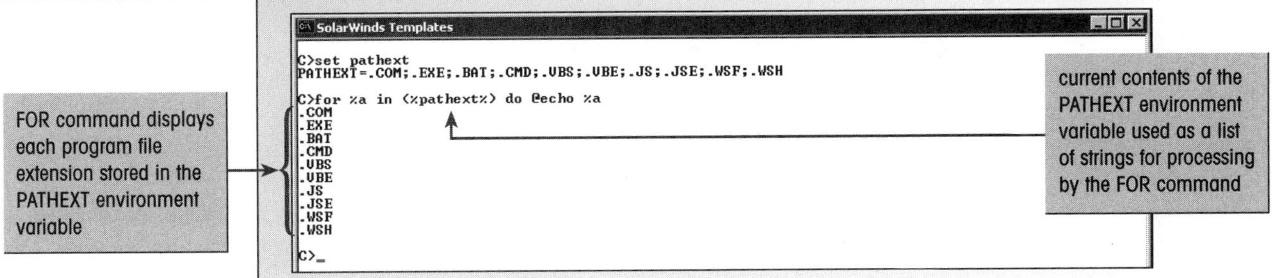

This use of the FOR command subdivides the component parts of a list assigned to an environment variable so you easily can work with those parts. Isabel points out that you can use this approach with any environment variable you create yourself, containing a list of any type of items, such as personal names.

REFERENCE WINDOW **RW**

Using FOR to Divide a List in an Environment Variable
- Open a Command Prompt window.
- If you want to use the FOR command directly at the command prompt, type FOR, a space, an index variable name consisting of a single percent sign and a single letter of the alphabet (for example, %a), a space, IN, a space, a pair of parentheses containing one or more environment variables (separated by spaces, tabs, commas, semicolons or equal signs) surrounded by percent signs (for example, (%path%)), a space, DO, a space, and then a command repeating the index variable name.
- If you want to use this same FOR command in a batch program, change to your batch program directory, either open an existing batch program or create a new batch program, and then include or insert a line containing a FOR command as described above, but use two percent signs in the index variable name (for example, %%a) instead of one.

Using FOR to Process a List of Files

Isabel asks you to apply the features and principles of the FOR command to create a batch program that will first locate a file or files matching a wildcard specification, and then rename those files by adding a prefix (a word or character string) to the beginning of each matching filename. For example, she suggests that you add the word "Model" at the beginning of certain filenames to clarify the purpose of those template files. While the REN (Rename) command is used to change the names of multiple files by replacing specific characters in the names (see Tutorial 3), it cannot add words or characters to a set of names.

First, you'll test a strategy you intend to use in your batch program, discover a common error, and learn how to fix it.

To determine whether your initial command syntax will add a prefix to multiple filenames:

1. Use your HOME batch program to change to the **SolarWinds** directory.

2. Change to the **Templates** directory.

   In the next step, you will enter a command line to test whether it will successfully rename two files.

3. Clear the **window** and then enter:

   ```
   for %a in ("Daily Sales.xls",Invoices.xls) do ren %a "Model %a"
   ```

   You enclose "Daily Sales.xls" in quotation marks because it contains a space; likewise, you enclose "Model %a" within quotation marks because you are adding the word "Model" followed by a space to the beginning of each filename. You didn't put quotation marks around Invoices.xls because the filename does not contain any spaces.

4. Observe the screen output. As shown in Figure 8-31, although the command successfully renames Invoices.xls to "Model Invoices.xls," it fails to rename "Daily Sales.xls" to "Model Daily Sales.xls." Instead, the REN command line generated by your FOR command produces too many quotation marks and displays a syntax error.

Figure 8-31   **TESTING A COMMAND LINE TO ADD A PREFIX TO MULTIPLE FILENAMES**

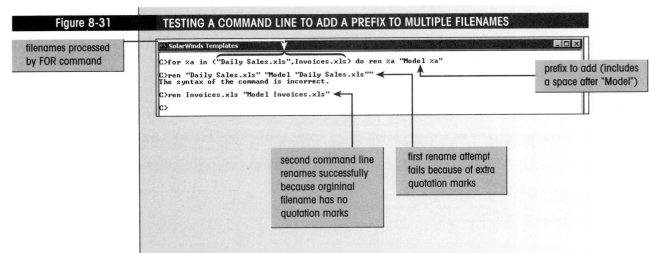

filenames processed
by FOR command

```
C>for %a in ("Daily Sales.xls",Invoices.xls) do ren %a "Model %a"

C>ren "Daily Sales.xls" "Model "Daily Sales.xls""
The syntax of the command is incorrect.

C>ren Invoices.xls "Model Invoices.xls"

C>
```

prefix to add (includes
a space after "Model")

second command line
renames successfully
because orgininal
filename has no
quotation marks

first rename attempt
fails because of extra
quotation marks

5. Rename "Model Invoices.xls" back to **Invoices.xls** in preparation for another try.

Why didn't your FOR command produce a REN command line to properly rename "Daily Sales.xls" to "Model Daily Sales.xls"? Isabel tells you that the FOR command stored the filename "Daily Sales.xls" in the %a variable, quotation marks and all, as it would with any list item surrounded by quotation marks. Because you surrounded the REN command's target filename "Model %a" with quotation marks, and "Daily Sales.xls" already had quotation marks around it, you ended up with an extra set of quotation marks in the resulting REN target filename when FOR replaced %a with "Daily Sales.xls":

```
ren "Daily Sales.xls" "Model "Daily Sales.xls""
```

To illustrate the FOR command's behavior with quoted names such as "Daily Sales.xls," Isabel asks you to revise your command line with an ECHO command to simply display the contents of %a in each repetition, so you can see the quotation marks.

To test the FOR command with quoted names:

1. Clear the **window** and then enter:

```
for %a in ("Daily Sales.xls",Invoices.xls) do @echo %a
```

This will test the appearance of filenames in the list. Notice that the @ECHO command displays the first filename, "Daily Sales.xls," with quotation marks. The @ sign prevents the display of the ECHO command itself and shows just the results. See Figure 8-32.

Figure 8-32   **VIEWING QUOTED FILENAMES IN A FOR COMMAND**

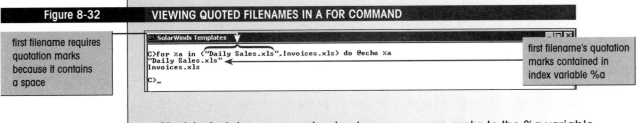

first filename requires
quotation marks
because it contains
a space

```
C>for %a in ("Daily Sales.xls",Invoices.xls) do @echo %a
"Daily Sales.xls"
Invoices.xls
C>
```

first filename's quotation
marks contained in
index variable %a

Next, Isabel shows you a simple change you can make to the %a variable name to remove the quotation marks.

2. Enter:

```
for %a in ("Daily Sales.xls",Invoices.xls) do @echo %~a
```

You may recall the previous command and revise it. The tilde (~) removes quotation marks from a filename stored in the variable %a. See Figure 8-33. (The use of the tilde modifier to remove quotation marks is not available in Windows or MS-DOS versions prior to Windows 2000.)

Figure 8-33   **REMOVING QUOTATION MARKS WITH THE TILDE MODIFIER**

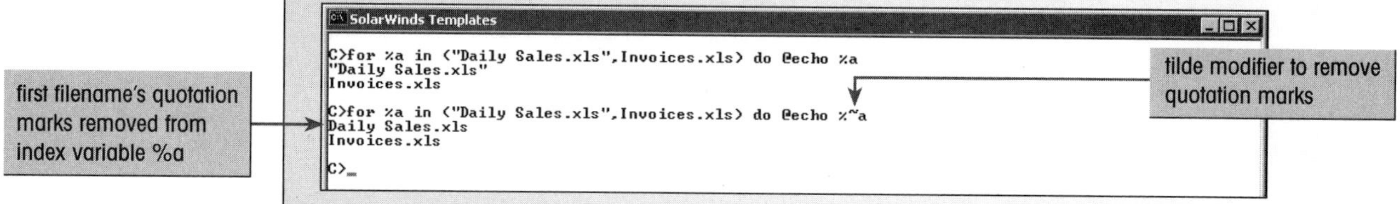

first filename's quotation marks removed from index variable %a

tilde modifier to remove quotation marks

Isabel now asks you to re-enter your original command line, adding the tilde modifier.

3. Clear the **window** and then enter:

```
for %a in ("Daily Sales.xls",Invoices.xls) do ren %a "Model %~a"
```

By using %~a to remove any quotation marks already stored as part of the variable before enclosing it in new quotation marks, the REN command successfully renamed "Daily Sales.xls" to "Model Daily Sales.xls." See Figure 8-34.

Figure 8-34   **REVISING A COMMAND LINE TO ADD A PREFIX TO MULTIPLE FILENAMES**

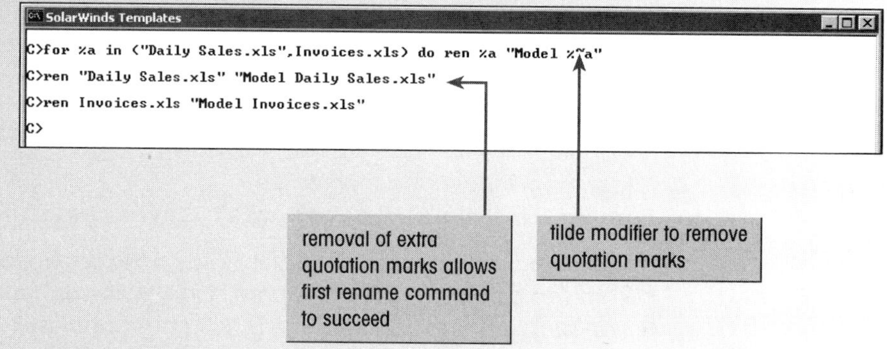

removal of extra quotation marks allows first rename command to succeed

tilde modifier to remove quotation marks

Now Isabel asks you to create your batch program, using the techniques you have learned.

To create a batch program to rename files by adding a prefix to the filename:

1. Change to your **batch program** directory.

2. Enter: `notepad AddPrefix.bat`

Click **Yes** to create a new file.

3. After Notepad opens, enter the following commands and documentation in your batch program:

```
@echo off

rem    Batch Program to Add a Prefix to Filenames

rem    Name: [Your Name]          Date:  [Today's Date]
rem    Filename:  AddPrefix.bat

rem    This batch program receives a prefix and a file
rem    specification as replaceable parameters,
rem    and for each matching file, renames it,
rem    adding the prefix to the beginning of the filename.

rem    Jump to error message if you did not type both
rem    a word and a filespec as parameters:
       if test%2 == test GOTO :ERR

rem    Rename each matching file, adding the prefix:
       for %%a in (%2) do ren "%%~a" "%1 %%~a"

rem    End the program:
       GOTO :EOF

:ERR
rem    Error message if you left out the prefix and filespec:
       echo Please include one prefix and one filespec,
       echo like this:
       echo AddPrefix prefix filespec
```

Again, you use two percent signs (%%) for your index variable %%a in a batch program, and then add the tilde in %%~a to remove any quotation marks around filenames enclosed within quotation marks.

4. Save your changes and then exit **Notepad**.

In this batch program, you included:

- The same type of error handling as in previous batch programs, starting with a test for the second replaceable parameter %2. When you execute AddPrefix, you must type two parameters, represented by %1 and %2, on the command line after the batch program name AddPrefix. %1 is a prefix, such as the word "Model." %2 is a file specification, such as "Five*". By testing the content of %2, you don't need to test %1, because a blank %2 means you didn't type enough parameters.

■ A FOR command line which repeats the REN command for every filename that matches the file specification you typed as the second parameter, %2. In the REN command, %%~a removes any quotation marks in the filename before the command adds its own. Although a wildcard matching pattern will not put quotation marks around its resulting filenames, the batch program will still need the ~ operator in %%~a to remove any quotation marks you type around an individual filename. %1 is included in the REN command for the prefix you specify.

Now you are ready to test your batch program.

To add a prefix to filenames using your batch program:

1. Change to your **SolarWinds** directory and then set up your Command Prompt window by entering: Home

2. Change to the **Templates** directory.

3. Clear the **window** and enter: dir Five*

   This will display the names of the two files that begin with the word "Five".

4. Enter: AddPrefix Model Five*

   This will launch your batch program and add the word "Model" to every filename beginning with the word "Five".

5. Enter: dir Model*

   This will display the renamed files, now beginning with the word "Model". The order of the filenames displayed may differ from that shown in Figure 8-35.

Figure 8-35	TESTING A BATCH PROGRAM TO ADD A PREFIX TO FILENAMES USING A WILDCARD

6. Clear the **window** and enter: dir S*

   This will display the directory entry for files beginning with the letter "S".

7. Enter: AddPrefix SolarWinds "Savings Plan.xls"

   This will test your batch program on a quoted individual filename by adding the word "SolarWinds" to the filename "Savings Plan.xls".

8. Display the directory entry for a files beginning with the letter S again. Notice the new name "SolarWinds Savings Plan.xls", as in Figure 8-36.

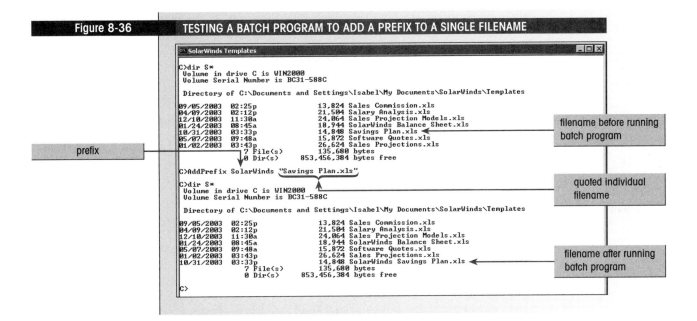

Figure 8-36 — TESTING A BATCH PROGRAM TO ADD A PREFIX TO A SINGLE FILENAME

prefix

filename before running batch program

quoted individual filename

filename after running batch program

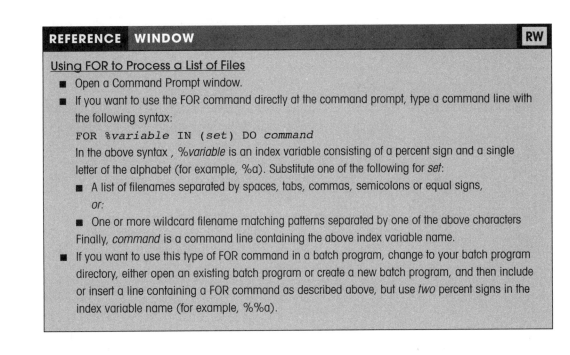

REFERENCE WINDOW — RW

Using FOR to Process a List of Files
- Open a Command Prompt window.
- If you want to use the FOR command directly at the command prompt, type a command line with the following syntax:

  FOR %*variable* IN (*set*) DO *command*

  In the above syntax, %*variable* is an index variable consisting of a percent sign and a single letter of the alphabet (for example, %a). Substitute one of the following for *set*:
  - A list of filenames separated by spaces, tabs, commas, semicolons or equal signs,
    or:
  - One or more wildcard filename matching patterns separated by one of the above characters
  Finally, *command* is a command line containing the above index variable name.
- If you want to use this type of FOR command in a batch program, change to your batch program directory, either open an existing batch program or create a new batch program, and then include or insert a line containing a FOR command as described above, but use *two* percent signs in the index variable name (for example, %%a).

The FOR command is a concise and powerful command for looping through a set of values and performing the same operations on each value.

Using FOR to Process Files in Different Directories

So you and other support staff can consistently rename similar files in different directories, Isabel recommends that you create a new version of your AddPrefix batch program, one that will add a prefix to filenames both within the current directory and in all of its subdirectories in one step. By itself, the REN command can rename files only in a single directory at a time.

You can use the FOR command with the **Recursive (/R)** switch to execute a command in every subdirectory within a directory folder, effectively "walking the tree," starting from the current directory or from another directory you specify and stepping down through each of the subdirectories. Within a batch program, the syntax of this form of the FOR command is as follows (the word "set" is sometimes used instead of "list"):

```
FOR /R %%A IN (list) DO command
```

If you want to begin in a directory folder other than the current one, specify the directory's path as follows:

```
FOR /R [drive:]path %%A IN (list) DO command
```

After examining the directory structure, you'll test the FOR command that you will eventually use in a batch program.

To determine whether your initial FOR command syntax will add a prefix to filenames in different directories:

1. Execute your **Home.bat batch program** to change to your **SolarWinds** directory by entering: Home

2. Enter: `tree /f | more`

   This will display filenames in the subdirectories under your SolarWinds directory. The order of the directories and filenames displayed may differ from that shown in Figure 8-37. After examining this tree listing, you decide to test your command line on two similar files: one named "Computer Basics.wk4" in the Presentations directory, and the other named "Computer Basics.doc" in the Memos directory.

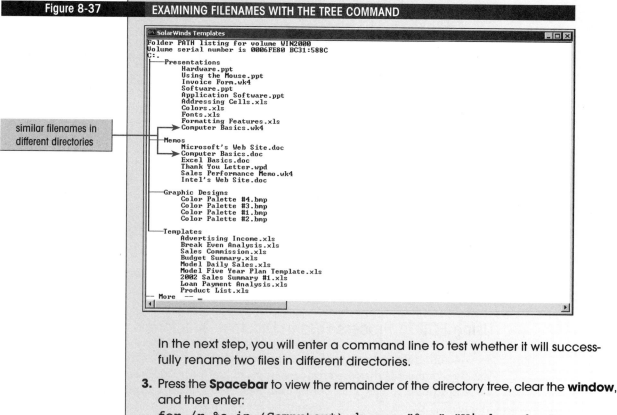

| Figure 8-37 | EXAMINING FILENAMES WITH THE TREE COMMAND |

similar filenames in different directories

```
SolarWinds Templates
Folder PATH listing for volume WIN2000
Volume serial number is 0006FE80 BC31:588C
C:.
    ├──Presentations
    │       Hardware.ppt
    │       Using the Mouse.ppt
    │       Invoice Form.wk4
    │       Software.ppt
    │       Application Software.ppt
    │       Addressing Cells.xls
    │       Colors.xls
    │       Fonts.xls
    │       Formatting Features.xls
    │   ──► Computer Basics.wk4
    │
    ├──Memos
    │       Microsoft's Web Site.doc
    │   ──► Computer Basics.doc
    │       Excel Basics.doc
    │       Thank You Letter.wpd
    │       Sales Performance Memo.wk4
    │       Intel's Web Site.doc
    │
    ├──Graphic Designs
    │       Color Palette #4.bmp
    │       Color Palette #3.bmp
    │       Color Palette #1.bmp
    │       Color Palette #2.bmp
    │
    └──Templates
            Advertising Income.xls
            Break Even Analysis.xls
            Sales Commission.xls
            Budget Summary.xls
            Model Daily Sales.xls
            Model Five Year Plan Template.xls
            2002 Sales Summary #1.xls
            Loan Payment Analysis.xls
            Product List.xls
-- More  ── _
```

In the next step, you will enter a command line to test whether it will successfully rename two files in different directories.

3. Press the **Spacebar** to view the remainder of the directory tree, clear the **window**, and then enter:

   ```
   for /r %a in (Computer*) do ren "%~a" "Windows %~a"
   ```

You used the same syntax as you did in your AddPrefix batch program, including tildes to remove any quotation marks around filenames that match the pattern you gave in parentheses, and adding the word "Windows" to each filename.

4. Observe the screen output. As shown in Figure 8-38, the FOR command produces two long REN command lines, both of which result in syntax errors. Rather than assigning just the names of the matching files to %a, the /R switch stores the full path of the matching names as part of the filename to rename.

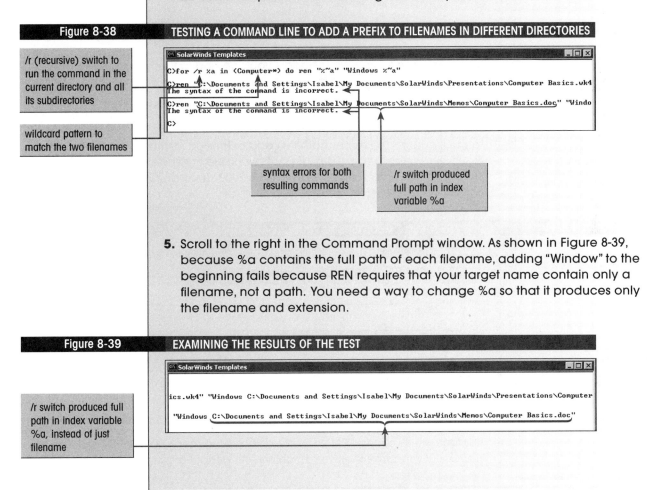

Figure 8-38   **TESTING A COMMAND LINE TO ADD A PREFIX TO FILENAMES IN DIFFERENT DIRECTORIES**

/r (recursive) switch to run the command in the current directory and all its subdirectories

wildcard pattern to match the two filenames

syntax errors for both resulting commands

/r switch produced full path in index variable %a

5. Scroll to the right in the Command Prompt window. As shown in Figure 8-39, because %a contains the full path of each filename, adding "Window" to the beginning fails because REN requires that your target name contain only a filename, not a path. You need a way to change %a so that it produces only the filename and extension.

Figure 8-39   **EXAMINING THE RESULTS OF THE TEST**

/r switch produced full path in index variable %a, instead of just filename

Again, Isabel suggests you revise your command line with an ECHO command to display just the contents of %~a in each repetition so you can see the FOR /R command's behavior with matching filenames in multiple directories.

To test the FOR /R command with full path names:

1. Clear the **window** and then enter:

```
for /r %a in (Computer*) do @echo "%~a"
```

This will test the appearance of filenames that match "Computer*". Notice that the @ECHO command displays the full path of each matching filename. Again, the @ (at sign) prevents the display of the ECHO command and shows just the results. See Figure 8-40.

Figure 8-40

TESTING THE FOR /R COMMAND WITH FULL PATH NAMES

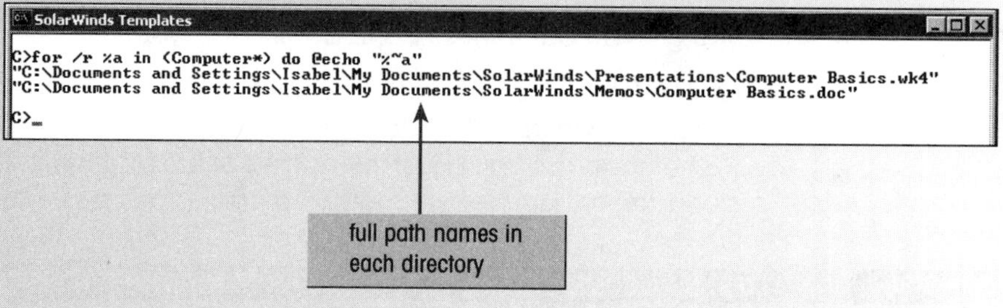

```
SolarWinds Templates                                                    _ □ ×

C>for /r %a in (Computer*) do @echo "%~a"
"C:\Documents and Settings\Isabel\My Documents\SolarWinds\Presentations\Computer Basics.wk4"
"C:\Documents and Settings\Isabel\My Documents\SolarWinds\Memos\Computer Basics.doc"

C>_
```

full path names in
each directory

Isabel now shows you two modifiers you can add to the %~a variable reference so it produces only the filename and extension, instead of the full path.

2. Enter: for /r %a in (Computer*) do @echo "%~nxa"

The n and x modifiers after the tilde (~) force the variable %a to expand only
to the filename (by the n modifier) and extension (by the x modifier). See
Figure 8-41. (These modifiers are not available in Windows or MS-DOS versions prior to Windows NT and Windows 2000. You can display a complete list
of modifiers by entering FOR /?.)

Figure 8-41

USING THE N AND X MODIFIERS TO PRODUCE ONLY THE FILE'S NAME AND EXTENSION

n and x modifiers

```
SolarWinds Templates                                                    _ □ ×

C>for /r %a in (Computer*) do @echo "%~a"
"C:\Documents and Settings\Isabel\My Documents\SolarWinds\Presentations\Computer Basics.wk4"
"C:\Documents and Settings\Isabel\My Documents\SolarWinds\Memos\Computer Basics.doc"

C>for /r %a in (Computer*) do @echo "%~nxa"
"Computer Basics.wk4"
"Computer Basics.doc"

C>_
```

only file's name and
extension produced
from index variable %a

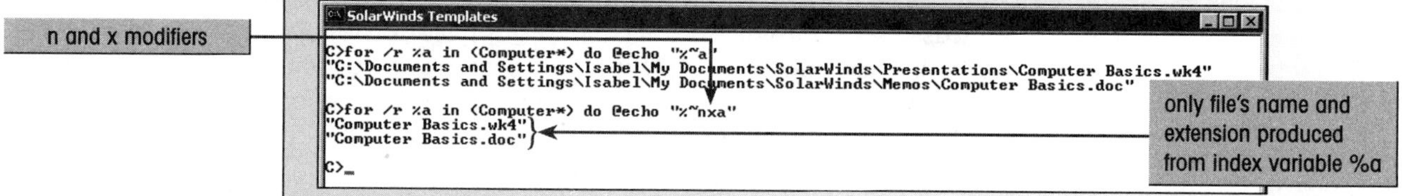

Isabel now suggests you re-enter your original FOR /R command line, using the
n and x modifiers.

3. Clear the **window** and then enter:
for /r %a in (Computer*) do ren "%~a" "Windows %~nxa"

This time, the two long REN command lines produced by your FOR command
successfully rename the two matching files without errors. See Figure 8-42.

Figure 8-42

TESTING A REVISED COMMAND LINE

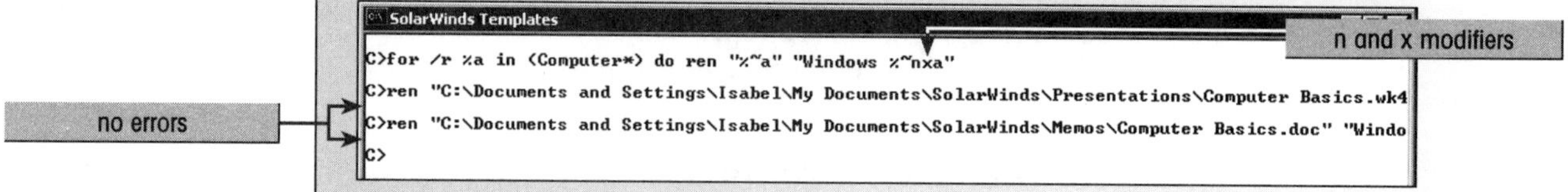

n and x modifiers

```
SolarWinds Templates                                                    _ □ ×

C>for /r %a in (Computer*) do ren "%~a" "Windows %~nxa"

C>ren "C:\Documents and Settings\Isabel\My Documents\SolarWinds\Presentations\Computer Basics.wk4

C>ren "C:\Documents and Settings\Isabel\My Documents\SolarWinds\Memos\Computer Basics.doc" "Windo

C>
```

no errors

4. Scroll to the right in your Command Prompt window. As shown in Figure 8-43,
the target filenames of the REN commands contain only the filenames and
extensions, as required by the REN command, because you added the n and x
modifiers to %~a in your command line.

Figure 8-43	EXAMINING THE SUCCESSFUL RENAME COMMANDS

n and x modifiers

filename and
extension only

5. Switch to the **Memos and Presentation** directories, and rename "Windows
   Computer Basics.doc" and "Windows Computer Basics.wk4" to their original
   "Computer Basics" names in preparation for repeating the name changes
   through a batch program.

Using the FOR /R command and the additional modifiers you have learned, you can now
create your new prefix-adding batch program.

To add a prefix to matching filenames throughout an entire directory branch using a batch program:

1. Change to your **batch program** directory.

2. Copy your batch program **AddPrefix.bat** to a new file named **AddPrefixSub.Bat**.

3. Use Notepad to edit AddPrefixSub.bat, changing or adding the lines shown
   in boldface:

```
@echo off

rem    Batch Program to Add a Prefix to Filenames in the Current
rem    Directory and its Subdirectories

rem    Name:  [Your Name]        Date:  [Today's Date]
rem    Filename:  AddPrefixSub.bat

rem    This batch program receives a prefix and a file
rem    specification as replaceable parameters,
rem    and for each matching file in the current directory
rem    and its subdirectories, renames it,
rem    adding the word to the beginning of the filename.

rem    Jump to error message if you did not type both
rem    a word and a filespec as parameters:
       if test%2 == test goto :ERR

rem    Rename each matching file, adding the word:
       for /r %%a in (%2) do ren "%%~a" "%1 %%~nxa"

rem    End the program:
       goto :EOF
```

```
:ERR
rem    Error message if you left out the prefix and filespec:
       echo Please include one prefix and one filespec,
       echo like this:
       echo AddPrefixSub prefix filespec
```

4. Save your new batch program and then exit **Notepad**.

In this batch program:

- You included the same type of error handling as in previous batch programs.
- You also included a FOR statement which uses the /R (Recursive) switch to search through the current directory and all its subdirectories for files matching the pattern you gave in the second parameter of the command line (%2). In each repetition for a matching filename, the FOR command stores the file's full path in the index variable %%a.
- After the FOR statement's DO clause, a REN command executes for each matching filename, including the n and x modifiers in the REN target %%~nxa to force the variable to expand to only the filename and extension.

To test your batch program that adds a prefix to filenames in multiple directories:

1. Change to your "SolarWinds" directory by entering: **home**

2. Clear the window, and then enter: **AddPrefixSub Windows Computer***

3. Enter: **tree /f | more**

This will verify the resulting filename changes, as in Figure 8-44.

Figure 8-44   **VIEWING THE RESULTS OF ADDING A PREFIX TO FILENAMES IN DIFFERENT DIRECTORIES**

```
SolarWinds Templates
Folder PATH listing for volume WIN2000
Volume serial number is 0006FE80 BC31:588C
C:.
───Presentations
        Hardware.ppt
        Using the Mouse.ppt
        Invoice Form.wk4
        Software.ppt
        Application Software.ppt
        Addressing Cells.xls
        Colors.xls
        Fonts.xls
        Formatting Features.xls
        Windows Computer Basics.wk4  ◄────
───Memos
        Microsoft's Web Site.doc
        Excel Basics.doc
        Thank You Letter.wpd
        Sales Performance Memo.wk4
        Intel's Web Site.doc
        Windows Computer Basics.doc  ◄────
───Graphic Designs
        Color Palette #4.bmp
        Color Palette #3.bmp
        Color Palette #1.bmp
        Color Palette #2.bmp
```

renamed files

4. View the remainder of the directory tree, and then return to the command prompt.

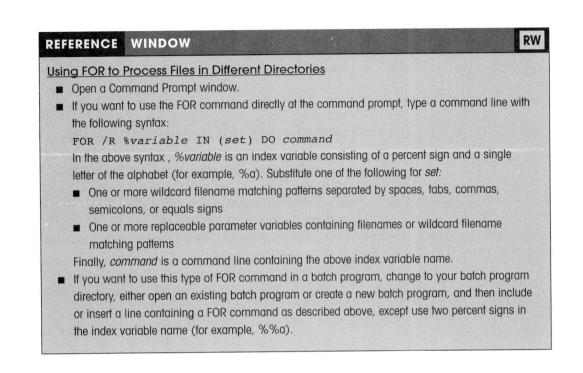

Besides using wildcard filename matching patterns in the parentheses set of FOR /R, you may instead specify just a single period (.). In that case, the command will enumerate the tree, that is, produce a list of subdirectories, rather than filenames, down through the directory tree branch. The FOR command would then repeat for each subdirectory, storing each name successively in the index variable.

Using FOR to Divide Lines of Text

Isabel asks you to produce a simple report that lists employees and their titles, using the contents of a text-only file downloaded to a diskette. The file is normally quite large and contains many pieces of information about each employee, so Isabel gives you a short section of the file with which to practice. She suggests that you use the **File parsing (/F)** switch of the FOR command for this purpose, which is used by the FOR command to process lines of text *inside* a file, rather than just a list of words or filenames on the command line. The FOR command with the /F switch **parses**, or divides, lines of text from the file or files you specify, according to rules you set as options.

The /F switch of the FOR command has many options. In this section, you will use the following syntax:

```
FOR /F "USEBACKQ DELIMS=delimiters TOKENS=tokenlist" %%variable IN ("file name set") DO command
```

Where:

- The first set of double-quotation marks ("") contains options for the /F switch: "USEBACKQ DELIMS=*delimiters* TOKENS=*tokenlist*".
- USEBACKQ specifies a more versatile syntax than Windows NT 4.0 permits in this command, so you can specify filenames containing spaces in the *file name set* by enclosing them in double quotation marks. The option is named USEBACKQ because it also allows you to use **back quotes** (`) around a command (such as DIR /S or FIND) to indicate that you want to process the output of that command, instead of the contents of a file—without having to go through the extra step of redirecting the output of the command

to a file and then specifying the filename. Enclose the command in back quotes in the parentheses after the IN clause (for example, `DIR /S` in place of "*file name set*" in the syntax line above).

- *delimiters* is a series of one or more characters that separate each line of text into parts called **tokens** (sometimes called "fields" or "values"). For example, **DELIMS=:/** would use either the colon character (:) or slash character (/) to divide text lines. If you leave out DELIMS=*delimiters*, then FOR /F divides text lines into tokens using the Space and Tab characters.

- *tokenlist* is a series of one or more numbers specifying which token or tokens on the text line to assign to %%*variable* and to new index variables whose names the command creates alphabetically after the one you specify. For example, using "**TOKENS=3,5**" %%J would store the third token in %%J, and the FOR command would then make a new index variable %%K and store the fifth token in it.

- *file name set* is a list of one or more names of text-only files, out of which FOR /F reads lines of text to process with the *command* at the end of the command line. If a filename contains spaces, you must enclose it in double-quotation marks (""), while specifying the USEBACKQ option.

First, you want to examine the contents of the data file you will process, so you can determine how you will divide it.

To inspect your data file's format:

1. Insert your copy of Data Disk #3 into drive A.

2. Change to your **batch program** directory.

3. Enter: `notepad a:\employees.csv`

   This will inspect the contents of the text-only data file you will parse.

4. Maximize the **Notepad** window so you can view a larger portion of the file. See Figure 8-45.

   a. Note that the first line is a list of field (or token) names separated by commas (,) and that the subsequent lines contain strings of text also separated by commas (the file type **CSV** stands for "Comma Separated Values"). Therefore, you will specify a comma as the delimiter between tokens.

   b. Note that the first name, last name, and job title are the second, third, and fourth items on each line. Therefore, you will specify token numbers 2, 3, and 4 in the FOR /F command options.

| Figure 8-45 | VIEWING THE CONTENTS OF THE COMMA SEPARATED VALUES FILE |

first line of field (token) labels

commas delimiting fields

```
Employees.csv - Notepad
File  Edit  Format  Help
SSN,First Name,Last Name,Job Title,Department,Salary,Date of Hire,Status,Benefits,Ph
826-40-3715,Jason,Falman,Accounts Receivable Clerk,Accounting,35300,12/6/1987,P,Yes,
833-14-4934,Lenore,Ruhling,Benefits Specialist,Personnel,87800,5/16/1989,S,No,(707)
762-88-4730,Renee,Bessone,Bookkeeper,Accounting,50000,3/12/1996,P,Yes,(707) 555-8788
832-14-8325,Deshi,Chiu,Clerk,Executive,39400,11/5/1993,P,Yes,(707) 555-5297
832-40-8571,Isabel,Navarro,Computer Systems Specialist,MIS,72600,3/22/1996,P,Yes,(70
966-13-3516,Rosemarie,Trevino,Computer Technician,MIS,63900,6/10/2003,P,Yes,(707) 55
773-32-3240,Takao,Yamakoa,Contracts Specialist,Finance,101100,4/19/1987,P,Yes,(707)
479-00-5338,Marci,Bauman,Corporate Accounts Manager,Marketing,123300,7/3/1995,P,Yes,
779-82-9183,Stefan,Drees,Database Systems Specialist,MIS,69100,2/14/2001,P,Yes,(707)
989-29-6959,Olivia,Serrano,Design Specialist,Research,74200,2/15/1982,P,Yes,(707) 55
```

5. Close the **Notepad** window and then return to the **Command Prompt** window.

Now that you have determined what you will specify in your batch program, you are ready to begin writing.

To create a batch program to display names and job titles:

1. Use **Notepad** to create the batch program EmpTitles.bat as shown below:

```
@echo off

rem    Batch Program to Extract Names and Job Titles from
rem    a Specified Text File

rem    Name:  [Your Name]          Date:  [Today's Date]
rem    Filename:  EmpTitles.bat

rem    This batch program receives as a replaceable parameter
rem    the name of an employee data text file with a
rem    predetermined format.  For each employee
rem    data line in the file, it extracts and displays
rem    the first name, last name, and job title.

rem    Jump to error message if you did not type
rem    a filename as a parameter:
       if test%1 == test goto :ERR

rem    Extract and display the first name, last name, and job title
rem    from each line in the file:
       for /f "usebackq delims=, tokens=2,3,4" %%a in ("%1") do echo %%a %%b, %%c

rem    End the program:
       goto :EOF


:ERR
rem    Error message if you left out the filename:
       echo Please include the employee data filename,
       echo like this:
       echo EmpTitles filename
```

2. Save your new batch program and then exit **Notepad**.

In this batch program, you included:

- the same type of error handling as in previous batch programs
- a comma as the specified delimiter, and tokens 2, 3, and 4: the first name, last name, and job title
- the index variable %%a, which will receive the first token you specified: number 2. Because you also specified tokens 3 and 4, the FOR command creates two new one-letter index variables to receive the tokens, in alphabetic sequence after your index variable name: %%b and %%c.

- a replaceable parameter variable, %1, for the name of the text file to parse (you will use Employees.csv in this case)
- an ECHO command that displays the three tokens from each line of text, using index variables: %%a (first name), a space, %%b (last name), a comma, and %%c (job title)

With your batch program written, you can now run it.

To run the batch program to extract first name, last name, and job title from an employee list:

1. Clear the **window** and enter: `EmpTitles a:\employees.csv`

   The batch program displays the second, third, and fourth fields from each line of the employee data file.

2. Enter: `EmpTitles a:\employees.csv | more`

   This will pipe the output of your batch program through the MORE filter and display it one full window at a time. See Figure 8-46.

| Figure 8-46 | EXTRACTING THE FIRST NAME, LAST NAME, AND JOB TITLE FROM A FILE |

SolarWinds Templates

```
First Name Last Name, Job Title
Jason Falman, Accounts Receivable Clerk
Lenore Ruhling, Benefits Specialist
Renee Bessone, Bookkeeper
Deshi Chiu, Clerk
Isabel Navarro, Computer Systems Specialist
Rosemarie Trevino, Computer Technician
Takao Yamakoa, Contracts Specialist
Marci Bauman, Corporate Accounts Manager
Stefan Drees, Database Systems Specialist
Olivia Serrano, Design Specialist
Donna Evans, Director
Michele Thomas, Director of Accounting
Matt Kirkland, Director of Finance and Administration
Nancy Zheng, Director of Marketing
Marna Tennyson, Director of Research
Adrienne Pirolle, Editor
Antonio Hernandez, Editorial Associate
Nina O'Brien, Equipment Technician
Cory Childers, Executive Director
Mirelle Rottiers, Executive Secretary
Josh Holmberg, Finance Manager
Brandon Ames, Financial Analyst
Sharon Cressler, Marketing Associate
Michael Egans, Network Administrator
Sharon Wainwright, Receptionist
Eileen Sanger, Recruiter
Jessica Thompson, Research Assistant
Janet Abrams, Research Assistant
Marcee Zimmerman, Research Associate
Istvan Kardos, Research Associate
Michael Kelsey, Research Associate
Shelby Harwick, Research Associate
Zhou Qiao, Research Associate
Jonathan Covington, Research Specialist
Timothy McKinlay, Research Specialist
Patrick Sydow, Research Technician
Francine Washington, Research Technician
Javier Rojas, Research Technician
-- More --
```

batch program extracts and outputs first name, last name, and job title from the Comma Separated Values file

3. Press the **Spacebar** to display the rest of the output.

4. Close the **Command Prompt** window.

You point out to Isabel that in addition to piping the output of your new batch program though the MORE filter for screen display, you can also redirect the output into a file for e-mailing, printing, or additional processing.

Using FOR to Divide Lines of Text

- Open a Command Prompt window.
- If you want to use the FOR command directly at the command prompt to divide lines of text, type a command line with the following syntax:

  `FOR /F "USEBACKQ DELIMS=delimiters TOKENS=tokenlist" %variable IN (set) DO command`

  In the above syntax, *delimiters* is a sequence of separator characters, *tokenlist* is a list of token (or field) numbers separated by commas, and *%variable* is an index variable consisting of a percent sign and a single letter of the alphabet (for example, %a).

  Substitute one of the following for *set*:
  - a pair of double quotes containing one or more wildcard filename matching patterns separated by spaces, tabs, commas, semicolons, or equals signs
  - a pair of double quotes containing one or more replaceable parameter variables containing filenames or wildcard filename matching patterns
  - a pair of single quotes containing a literal string to process
  - a pair of back quotes containing a command, whose lines of text output the FOR command will process

  Finally, *command* is a command line containing the above index variable name and any new index variables created by specifying more than one token.

- If you want to use this type of FOR command in a batch program, change to your batch program directory, either open an existing batch program or create a new batch program, and then include or insert a line containing a FOR command as described above, except use two percent signs in the index variable name (for example, %%a).

In addition to parsing lines from text files, you can use FOR /F to divide an immediate string literal in single quotes (which could come from a replaceable parameter), or you can directly process the output of a command in back quotes. Be sure to specify the USEBACKQ option for these alternatives.

The FOR command, when combined with replaceable parameters and other batch commands, is a powerful command for processing text and groups of files.

Windows Script Host

Now that you're familiar with the batch programming language used in the Windows 2000 command-line environment, Isabel asks you to enroll in an intensive workshop on the use of the Windows Script Host so the two of you can automate updates to the company network.

The **Windows Script Host (WSH)** is a Windows 2000 component that executes scripts from either the Windows 2000 desktop or from the command-line environment. A **script** is a program that is comparable to a batch program; however, it is written in the Visual Basic Scripting Edition (VBScript) with the "vbs" file extension, or in JScript (the Microsoft version of JavaScript) with the "js" file extension. You can use the Windows Script Host, Internet Information Server (IIS), and Microsoft Internet Explorer to run scripts. **Internet Information Services (IIS)** is a Windows component for publishing information on the Web. The Windows GUI version of the Windows Script Host is Wscript.exe, and the command-line version is Cscript.exe. The following listing illustrates a script from the Microsoft Windows Script Host Web site (http://msdn.microsoft.com/scripting/).

```
Set WshNetwork = WScript.CreateObject("WScript.Network")
Set oDrives = WshNetwork.EnumNetworkDrives
Set oPrinters = WshNetwork.EnumPrinterConnections
WScript.Echo "Domain = " & WshNetwork.UserDomain
WScript.Echo "Computer Name = " & WshNetwork.ComputerName
WScript.Echo "User Name = " & WshNetwork.UserName
WScript.Echo
WScript.Echo "Network drive mappings:"
For i = 0 to oDrives.Count - 1 Step 2
     WScript.Echo "Drive " & oDrives.Item(i) & " = " & oDrives.Item(i+1)
Next
WScript.Echo
WScript.Echo "Network printer mappings:"
For i = 0 to oPrinters.Count - 1 Step 2
     WScript.Echo "Port " & oPrinters.Item(i) & " = " & oPrinters.Item(i+1)
Next
```

To run the script above, you first would create it as a text file with a vbs extension. If you named the script file NetNames.vbs, you could execute it in a Command Prompt window by entering: `cscript NetNames.vbs`

This VBScript is designed to work with Cscript.exe and displays network information, such as the computer name, user name, drive mappings, and printer mappings, as shown in Figure 8-47.

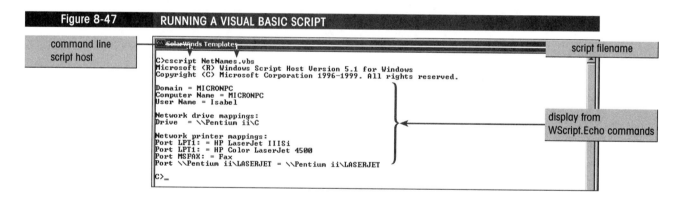

| Figure 8-47 | RUNNING A VISUAL BASIC SCRIPT |

The VBScript uses statements similar to those found in the Windows 2000 batch programming language, for example:

- Set performs a similar function to the SET command, and assigns a reference to an object to a variable.
- WScript.Echo performs a similar function to the ECHO command, and displays (or echoes) information on the console.
- For and Next form a loop structure, and perform a similar function to the FOR command by executing a set of commands for each item in a list.

Administrators can use scripts to automate routine tasks, such as customizing user environments after installing Windows 2000, creating logon scripts, updating the Windows 2000 registry, updating network access, and creating interactive Web pages.

You can create and use scripts under Windows 2000, Windows NT 4.0, Windows 98, and Windows 95; however, except in Windows 2000, you must install the Windows Script Host software first.

Restoring Your Computer

If you are working in a computer lab, you will need to remove the batch programs that you created in this lab. If you created a batch program directory on a computer in your computer lab, you will need to remove that directory also. Before you remove them, copy them to your "Batch Programs Backup" diskette in case you need them later. If your instructor assigns the Review Assignments or one or more Case Problems, then you will need copies of the batch programs that you created in this tutorial.

If you are working on your own computer and want to keep the batch program directory and the batch programs you created, then skip the remaining steps.

To restore your computer:

1. If necessary, create a **batch program directory** on a diskette labeled "Batch Programs Backup", switch to your **batch program directory** on drive C, and then copy the **batch programs** that you created in this tutorial so you can use them in the Review Assignments and Case Problems. Then, if you no longer need the batch programs on drive C, delete those batch programs. If you are working in a computer lab and you no longer need the batch programs you created in this tutorial, delete *only* the batch programs you created. An advantage of saving batch programs is that you can use an existing batch program as a template for creating a new one more quickly and easily.

2. If you no longer need your own batch program directory on the hard drive, use the Remove Directory command with the /S switch to remove the directory and any files that remain in that directory.

3. If you no longer need the SolarWinds directory, delete this directory and its contents.

4. Close the **Command Prompt** window.

By creating batch programs that perform conditional tests, check for operator errors in providing values for replaceable parameters to the batch programs, and which are capable of processing the same set of commands for multiple parameters, you have simplified and streamlined the process for providing templates to other employees at SolarWinds.

Session 8.3 QUICK | CHECK

1. The _____ command repeats the same operation, or operations, on each item in a list until it has processed all the items.

2. %a is an example of a(n) _____ used by the FOR command to store an item from a list temporarily so it can process that item.

3. You can use the _____ switch with the FOR command to examine files in different directories within the same branch of the directory tree.

4. You can use the _____ switch with the FOR command to parse or divide lines of text within a file.

5. _____ is an example of an environment variable that contains a list of items.

6. The _____ modifier removes quotation marks from a filename stored in an index variable such as %a.

7. The _____ and _____ modifiers force an index variable such as %a to expand to the filename and extension only.

8. If you named a script file NetNames.vbs, you could execute it in a Command Prompt window by entering: _____.

COMMAND REFERENCE

COMMAND	USE	BASIC SYNTAX	EXAMPLE
MODE	Sets the screen buffer width and height by specifying the number of columns and lines for the console (video display)	MODE CON: COLS=c LINES=n where *c* is the number of columns, and *n* is the number of lines	mode con: cols=300 lines=40
PROMPT	Changes the appearance of the command prompt	PROMPT [*text*] where *text* consists of one or more codes that determine the makeup of the command prompt	PROMPT $N PROMPT PG
CD	Displays the full path of the current directory	CD	CD
IF EXIST	Checks for the presence of a file or directory, and if true, executes a command	IF EXIST *filename command* IF EXIST *directory command*	if exist Cashflow.xls copy Cashflow.xls A: if exist %1 copy %1 a:
	Checks for the presence of a directory	IF EXIST *directory*\NUL *command*	if exist %1\nul copy %1 a:
IF NOT EXIST	Checks for the absence of a file or directory, and, if true, executes a command	IF NOT EXIST filename command IF NOT EXIST directory\NUL *command*	if not exist a: %1 copy %1 a: if not exist %1\nul md %1
IF	To perform a string comparison	IF *string1* == *string2 command*	if test%1 == test goto :err
GOTO	Branches to a target label in a batch program	GOTO *label*	goto :LOOP goto :ERR
	Branches to the end of a batch program		GOTO :EOF goto :EOF
SHIFT	Changes the position of replaceable parameters in a batch program	SHIFT	shift
FOR	Takes a list of items and repeats the same operation, or operations, on each item in turn until it processes all the items in the list	FOR %%A IN (*item1 item2 item3* ...) DO *command* %%A	for %%a in (a0,b0,c0,d0, e0,f0) do color %%a & pause for %%a in (%path%) do @echo %%a for %%a in (%2) do ren %%~a "%1%%a"
	To process files in different directories	FOR /R %%A IN (*list*) DO *command*	for /r %%a in (%2) do ren "%%~a" "%1 %%~a"
	To divide lines of text	FOR /F "*options*" %%A IN (*filename*) DO *command*	for /f "usebackq delims=, tokens=2,3,4" %%a in ("%1") do echo %%a %%b, %%c

Items shown in italics and *not* enclosed within square brackets are required parameters
Items shown in italics and enclosed within square brackets are optional parameters

Isabel asks you to enhance the functionality of your batch programs, adding documentation where needed.

Because you will be working with the same batch programs that you created in this tutorial, you will need to make sure the batch programs you need are in your batch program directory on drive C by following the steps below.

As you complete each step, record your answers to any questions so you can submit them to your instructor.

1. Open a Command Prompt window.

2. Check the computer you are using to make sure you have a batch program directory. If you have no batch program directory, then create one.

3. Change to your batch program directory.

4. If necessary, copy the batch programs that you created in this tutorial from your "Batch Programs Backup" diskette to your batch program directory on drive C.

5. Open the Reset.bat batch program that you created in this tutorial in Notepad (or the MS-DOS Editor), and then make the following changes:

   ■ At the beginning of the batch program, add @ECHO OFF and CLS commands.

   ■ Include documentation that identifies the purpose of the batch program. Include your own name as well as any other documentation that your instructor requests, such as the course section number, instructor's name, and date. *(Hint: Use the Clipboard in Notepad to copy the documentation you add to this batch program to each of the next batch programs you modify.)*

   ■ Include documentation that identifies the function and purpose of the PATH command in this batch program.

   ■ Save your changes to this batch program, and then test the batch program to make sure that the changes that you made work as you expect and do not alter the function of the batch program.

6. Open the UpdatePath.bat batch program that you created in this tutorial in Notepad (or the MS-DOS Editor), and then make the following changes:

   ■ Add an additional section (with documentation) at the end of the batch program that uses the PATH command to display the current search path after the batch program updates that path.

   ■ Save your changes to this batch program, and then test the batch program to make sure that the changes that you made work as you expect and do not alter the function of the batch program.

7. Open the Home.bat batch program that you created in this tutorial in Notepad (or the MS-DOS Editor), and then make the following changes:

   ■ Before the section for customizing the Command Prompt window, insert an additional section that specifies default settings for the Directory command by creating the DIRCMD environment variable and then specifying the Pause (or Page) and Sort Order switches.

   ■ Add an additional section (with documentation) before the TREE command that displays the name of the new current directory.

- Save your changes to this batch program, and then test the batch program to make sure that the changes that you made work as you expect and do not alter the function of the batch program.

8. Edit the DirCopy.bat batch program that you created in this tutorial and then make the following changes:

   - Add an additional section (with documentation) at the end of the batch program that tests for the existence of the new directory in drive A, and displays an error message if the directory is not present.

   - Save your changes to this batch program, and then test the batch program to make sure that the changes that you made work as you expect and do not alter the function of the batch program.

9. Edit the CopyCheck.bat batch program that you created in this tutorial and make the following changes:

   - Add an additional section (with documentation) that displays the name of each file before the batch program attempts to copy the file to drive A.

   - Save your changes to this batch program, and then test the batch program to make sure the changes you made work as you expect and do not alter the function of the batch program.

10. Document and test your ColorTest.bat batch program as you did for your batch program Reset.bat.

11. Edit the AddPrefixSub.bat batch program that you created in this tutorial and then make the following changes:

    - Edit the FOR statement, adding an additional command between DO and REN to display the full path of the filename to be changed. Follow the command with the & operator to link it with the REN command.

    - Revise the REM statement documentation to reflect the additional function.

    - Save your changes to this batch program, and then test the batch program to make sure the changes you made work as you expect and do not alter the function of the batch program.

12. Edit the EmpTitles.bat batch program that you created in this tutorial and then make the following changes:

    - Edit the FOR statement so it also displays each employee's department (the fifth field or token in each employee data line).

    - Revise the REM statement documentation to reflect the additional function.

    - Save your changes to this batch program, and then test the batch program to make sure the changes you made work as you expect and do not alter the function of the batch program.

13. Copy your updated batch programs to your batch program directory on your "Batch Programs Backup" diskette so you have a record of your work.

14. Submit copies of your batch program as your instructor requests, either as printouts, on diskette, or by e-mail, along with any other requested documentation.

CASE PROBLEMS

Case 1. Documenting Directory Structures at The Perfect Match   At the request of your department manager at The Perfect Match, a temporary employment agency, you had previously developed a batch program to print a directory tree of your "My Documents" directory so you could periodically evaluate its directory structure. She now asks that you update that batch program so you can use the batch program to document the directory structure of any subdirectory under your "My Documents" directory.

To complete this case problem, you will need your copy of Data Disk #3 and another diskette to which you can copy directories and files as you test your batch program.

1. Use the XCOPY command to copy the SolarWinds directory and its contents from your copy of Data Disk #3 to a subdirectory named PerfectMatch under the "My Documents" directory for your user account on drive C.

2. Make sure you have a batch program directory, and update your PATH to include its full path name.

3. In your batch program directory, use Notepad (or the MS-DOS Editor) to construct a batch program named DirDoc.bat that performs the following operations in the following order:
   a. Turns off the echo of all commands in the batch program, clears the window, and then produces three blank lines in the window.
   b. Displays the following message near the center of the screen:
      *** If necessary, insert a disk in drive A ***
   c. Produces three more blank lines, temporarily halts batch program processing so you can see the message, and then clears the window after resuming batch program execution.
   d. Changes to your "My Documents" directory. Include as part of that path the path for your user account stored in the USERPROFILE environment variable.
   e. Uses a single IF command to verify that a directory exists, and if so, redirects a directory tree of that directory to a file in the root directory of drive A named "Directory Structure.txt", and then appends to the same file another directory tree that shows the names of the files in each subdirectory below your "My Documents" directory.

4. Save your changes to this batch program.

5. Test your batch program by passing the PerfectMatch subdirectory of "My Documents" as a variable value for the batch program, and then verify that the batch program produced the correct output. If necessary, make any corrections to the batch program, and then test the batch program again.

6. Test the batch program on another subdirectory under your "My Documents" directory (such as SolarWinds, or by changing the name of PerfectMatch to "The Perfect Match" and then testing the batch program on the new subdirectory name), and then verify that the batch program produced the correct output.

7. Test the batch program on a nonexistent directory, and then verify that the batch program did not produce any output.

8. Once you are satisfied that the batch program is operating properly, document batch program operations within the batch program. Also include documentation in the batch program that identifies the purpose, filename, author, and date of the batch program.

9. Remove the "PerfectMatch" (or "The Perfect Match") subdirectory under your "My Documents" directory on drive C.

10. Submit a copy of your batch program, DirDoc.bat, as your instructor requests, either as a printout, on diskette, or by e-mail, along with any other requested documentation.

Case 2. Preparing Template Lists at Computer Troubleshooters Unlimited   Miles Biehler and the staff at Computer Troubleshooters Unlimited provide their customers with copies of template files. Since different customers request or need different types of templates, Miles wants you to create a batch program that will prepare an updated list of either all available templates or of templates for a specific application with a specific file type. He asks that your batch program show the full path to each file, that the path and filename be listed in alphabetical order, and that the results be output to a file named "Template Lists.txt." He also notes that you will have to pass two parameters—the directory name and the wildcard file specification—to the batch program.

To complete this case problem, you will need your copy of Data Disk #3 and another diskette to which you can copy directories and files as you test your batch program.

1. Use the XCOPY command to copy the SolarWinds directory and its contents from your copy of Data Disk #3 to a directory named CTU under the "My Documents" directory for your user account on drive C.

2. Make sure you have a batch program directory, and update your PATH to include its full path name.

3. In your batch program directory, use Notepad (or the MS-DOS Editor) to construct a batch program named ListTemplates.bat that performs the following operations in the following order:

   a. Turns off the echo of all commands in the batch program, and clears the window.
   b. Changes to the CTU subdirectory under your "My Documents" directory. Include as part of that path the path for your user account stored in the USERPROFILE environment variable.
   c. Uses an IF command to verify that the directory exists, and if so, changes to that directory. As noted, you will pass the directory name to the batch program when you invoke it.
   d. Uses another IF command to verify that there are files that match the wildcard specification that you provide and, if so, produces a directory listing that includes only the filenames, listed in alphabetical order, and then redirects the output to a file named "Templates List.txt" on the diskette in drive A. If the condition is false, use the ECHO command to display the message "No files found for this wildcard specification...". Use parentheses operators to identify the command that the batch program executes if the condition is true, and to identify the command that the batch program executes if the command is false. If necessary, use Windows 2000 Help and/or the Help switch to determine the correct syntax for this batch program command.

4. Save your changes to this batch program.

5. Test your batch program by passing variable values for the directory named Templates and the wildcard specification *.xls to the batch program, and then verify that the batch program produced the correct output. If necessary, make any corrections to the batch program, and then test the batch program again.

6. Test the batch program by passing variable values for the directory named Memos and the wildcard specification *.doc to the batch program, and then verify that the batch program produced the correct output.

7. Test the batch program by passing variables values for the directory named Templates and the wildcard specification *.doc to the batch program, and then verify that the batch program produced the correct output.

8. Test the batch program by passing variables values for the directory named "Training" (a nonexistent directory) and the wildcard specification *.doc to the batch program, and then verify that the batch program produced the correct output.

9. Once you are satisfied that the batch program is operating properly, document batch program operations within the program. Also include documentation within the batch program that identifies the purpose, filename, author, and date of the batch program.

10. Remove the CTU subdirectory under your "My Documents" directory on drive C.

11. Submit a copy of your batch program, ListTemplates.bat, as your instructor requests, either as a printout, on diskette, or by e-mail, along with any other requested documentation.

Case 3. Creating a Batch Program for Backing Up Important Files at Northbay Computers   At the end of a busy day, Jonathan Baum, an employee at Northbay Computers, manually copies files with customer orders to a diskette and Zip disk so he has backup copies of these files. To automate this task, he asks you to create a batch program to copy files stored on drive C to a floppy diskette. This batch program should first check to see if the file already exists on the diskette and, if the file does not exist, the batch program should then copy the file to the diskette.

To complete this case problem, you will need your copy of Data Disk #3. In the steps below, you will also make a new copy of Data Disk #1, to which you will copy files as you test your batch program.

1. Use the XCOPY command to copy the SolarWinds directory and its contents from your copy of Data Disk #3 to a directory named NorthBay under the "My Documents" directory for your user account on drive C.

2. Make a new copy of Data Disk #1 to use as a target diskette.

3. Make sure you have a batch program directory, and then update your PATH to include its full path name.

4. In your batch program directory, use Notepad (or the MS-DOS Editor) to construct a batch program named AddNewFiles.bat that performs the following operations in the following order:

   a. Turns off the echo of all commands in the batch program, and clears the window.
   b. Uses an IF command to test whether you included one replaceable parameter when you invoked the batch program, and then proceeds to an error handling routine if you did not do so.
   c. Changes to the NorthBay subdirectory under your "My Documents" directory. Include as part of that path the path for your user account stored in the USERPROFILE environment variable.
   d. Uses an IF command to verify the existence of the directory specified by the first (and only) replaceable parameter, and if the directory does exist, changes to that directory, but, if it does not exist, terminates the batch program.
   e. Executes a FOR command with:
      ■ a one-item set containing a wildcard matching all filenames in the current directory
      ■ a DO clause with an IF command which, if the file represented by the index variable does *not* exist on drive A, copies the file to drive A. Be sure to enclose the index variable in quotation marks for filenames containing spaces.
   f. Terminates the program.
   g. Includes an error-handling routine as described above with the first IF command.

5. Insert your copy of Data Disk #1 in drive A.

6. Test your batch program by specifying the Templates directory as a replaceable parameter to the batch program, and then verify that the batch program copies files when they are not already on the target diskette. If necessary, make any corrections to the batch program, and then test the batch program again.

7. Test your batch program by specifying the Memos directory as a replaceable parameter to the batch program, and then verify that the batch program copies files when they are not already on the target diskette.

8. Once you are satisfied that the batch program is operating properly, document batch program operations within the batch program. Also include documentation in the batch program that identifies the purpose, filename, author, and date of the batch program.

9. Remove the NorthBay subdirectory under your "My Documents" directory on drive C.

10. Submit a copy of your batch program, AddNewFiles.bat, as your instructor requests, either as a printout, on diskette, or by e-mail, along with any other requested documentation.

Case 4. *Extracting Payroll Information at Townsend & Sumner Publishing* Supervisor Mike Lyman at Townsend & Sumner Publishing in San Francisco needs a quick list of employee information for tax purposes. He gives you a diskette containing a Comma Separated Values data file of employee information and asks you to use it to produce a new list of employees. Each line of the new list should contain, in order, the employee's last name, first name, department, and Social Security number, all separated by commas.

1. Examine the Employees.csv file on Data Disk #3 to determine which fields (or tokens) contain the information you want to extract: last name, first name, department, and Social Security number. Note the field numbers and the delimiter separating the fields.

2. Make sure you have a batch program directory, and update your PATH to include its full path name.

3. In your batch program directory, create a batch program named SSNList.bat, containing a FOR command to extract fields from lines in a text data file. It should specify:
   a. an option for filenames containing spaces
   b. the delimiter used between tokens (or fields)
   c. which tokens to extract from each line
   d. a starting index variable
   e. a one-item set containing a replaceable parameter for the data filename to process
   f. a command to display the extracted fields, separated by commas, in this order: last name, first name, department, and Social Security number

4. At the beginning, turn off the echo of all commands in the batch program, and then clear the window.

5. Include error handling to display a usage message if you launch the batch program without a data filename parameter.

6. Include documentation that identifies the purpose of the batch program. Include your name as well as any other documentation that your instructor requests, such as the course section number, instructor's name, and date.

7. Test your batch program, using the name of the Employees.csv file on drive A as the parameter. If your batch program does not work properly, make any necessary changes with Notepad and then test it again until it works to your satisfaction.

8. In your batch program directory, redirect the output of your batch program to a new text file named EmpSSN.txt.

9. Submit a copy of your batch program, SSNList.bat, and your output file, EmpSSN.txt, as your instructor requests, either as a printout, on diskette, or by e-mail, along with any other requested documentation.

QUICK | CHECK ANSWERS

Session 8.1

1. PROMPT
2. IF
3. the null device (or NUL)
4. &
5. IF EXIST *filename command*

Session 8.2

1. string
2. GOTO, label
3. GOTO :EOF
4. error handling
5. SHIFT

Session 8.3

1. FOR
2. index variable
3. Recursive (R)
4. Parsing (F)
5. PATH *or* PATHEXT
6. ~ (tilde)
7. n, x
8. `cscript NetNames.vbs`

In this tutorial you will:

- Learn about the importance of the Windows 2000 Registry

- Open the Registry with the Windows 2000 Registry Editor

- Examine ways to back up and restore the Registry

- Export Registry settings

- Create and remove a registered file type

- Examine the structure and organization of the Registry

- Trace information on registered file types and their associated actions

- View information on Class Identifiers

- Examine the process for editing the Registry

THE WINDOWS 2000 REGISTRY

Using the Registry to Customize the Command-Line Environment at SolarWinds

CASE

SolarWinds

Isabel Navarro and her staff use the Windows 2000 tools built into the graphical user interface to specify, change, and update system settings whenever possible. Periodically, Isabel and her staff use the Windows 2000 Registry to change settings so that they can customize the operating environments of desktop workstations and portable computers used by staff working off-site, enhance the functionality of employees' computers, and troubleshoot configuration problems.

SESSION 9.1

In this session you will examine the importance of the Windows 2000 Registry. You will examine the types of hives (or files) that constitute the Registry, as well as where they are stored on disk, learn four different techniques for backing up the Registry, and update your Emergency Repair Disk. To back up your Registry settings, you will open the Registry and export the Registry settings to a registration file on disk. Finally, you will use the ASSOC and FTYPE commands to view information on the file type for specific file extensions, and also to define, and then later remove, a new file type.

The Role of the Windows 2000 Registry

Now that you've broadened your command line skills and become familiar with your job responsibilities as assistant network administrator, Isabel decides that it is time to introduce you to the Windows 2000 Registry.

Windows 2000 stores your computer's hardware, software, security, user settings (or profiles), and property settings for directories and programs in a database known as the **Registry**. When you perform a normal full boot of your computer, Windows 2000 processes the information in the Registry to configure your computer properly. For example, the Registry contains information on hardware devices and resources assigned to both Plug and Play and legacy devices. During booting, Windows 2000 uses this information to identify and configure hardware devices and to load device drivers for the installed hardware.

Windows 2000 updates the contents of the Registry when you change settings on your computer, such as when you:

- customize your desktop with the Display Properties dialog box
- install Plug and Play hardware or legacy hardware with the Add Hardware Wizard
- install or remove software with the Add/Remove Programs Wizard
- change settings using the Control Panel and Device Manager (a Windows tool that tracks hardware settings)
- modify file associations for registered files on the File Types property sheet (a **registered file** is a file that is associated with a specific application via its file extension)
- define user accounts and groups
- specify user rights and audit policies

In fact, Microsoft recommends that you use tools, such as Device Manager, the Control Panel, and property sheets, to make configuration changes to your computer rather than opening and editing the Registry. If you open the Registry and make a mistake while you are changing a configuration setting, you may not even be able to use your computer, or you may introduce errors into the configuration of your hardware and software so that they do not function properly. It's also important to note that if you open and make a change to the Registry, Windows 2000 does not warn you if the change you made is incorrect; rather, it attempts to apply the change to your computer system (even if the change creates problems). You should always make sure you have a backup copy of your computer's files and the Registry before you make a change to the Registry.

The Windows 2000 Registry database consists of a set of files named Default, SAM, Security, Software, and System. Each of these files (without any file extension) is referred to as a **hive**. Figure 9-1 lists the types of information stored in each hive. Each hive has a log file (Default.log, Sam.log, Security.log, Software.log, and System.log—with the file extension "log") that contains a list of changes made to a hive. Files with the "sav" file extension are copies of a hive made (when you are installing Windows 2000) at the end of the text mode phase of Setup before you see the graphical user interface. All of these hives are stored in the %SystemRoot%\System32\Config folder, where, as noted previously, the %SystemRoot% is the path to your Windows 2000 folder. Windows 2000 creates another Registry file, named NTUser.dat, along with its associated log file, NTUser.dat.log, in the folder for the user's account information. NTUser.dat contains information on a specific user's profile.

Figure 9-1	WINDOWS 2000 REGISTRY HIVES

HIVE	CONTENTS
Default	Default user settings
SAM (Security Account Manager database)	Information on users and group accounts
Security	Security information, such as user rights, password policy, and local group membership
Software	General configuration information on installed software
System	Information on installed hardware and startup configuration

Because these files are critical to the operation of Windows 2000 and your computer system, Windows 2000 stores backup copies of all or some of the hives. The backup copies have the same filename, but the file extension is "sav". For example, the backup copy of the Software hive is Software.sav. For the System hive, Windows 2000 keeps an additional backup copy in the file named System.alt. Figure 9-2 shows the hives on a computer.

Figure 9-2	VIEWING THE REGISTRY HIVES IN THE CONFIG DIRECTORY

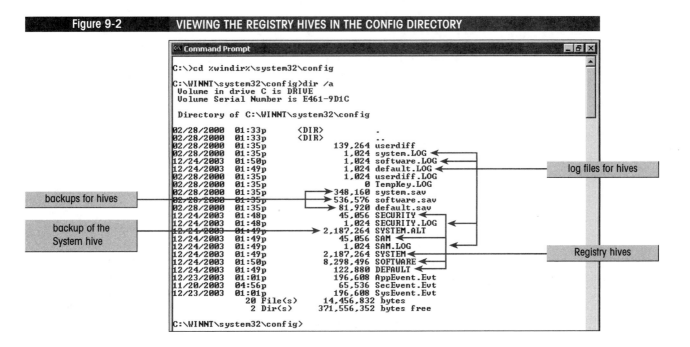

Windows 98 and Windows 95 have a Registry that is similar to the Windows 2000 Registry. The Windows 98 and Windows 95 Registries consist of two database files each—System.dat and User.dat—which contain hardware, software, and user settings. System.dat and User.dat are stored in the directory that contains the Windows 98 or Windows 95 operating system. Both Windows 98 and Windows 95 keep a backup copy of each file. After a successful boot, Windows 95 copies the settings in each of these two database files to files named System.da0 and User.da0. Windows 98 stores the five most recent versions of the Registry as cabinet files in the Windows Sysbckup folder. A **cabinet file** (with the file extension "cab") is a compressed file that contains operating system files. Windows 98 and Windows 95 also keep one other important file, named System.1st, in the root directory (C:\) of the hard disk. System.1st contains all the hardware settings detected by the Windows 98 or Windows 95 Setup program when Windows 98 or Windows 95 was installed on the computer. If you install Windows 2000 on your computer so that you have the option of dual booting with Windows 98 or Windows 95, then you will have a copy of both the Windows 2000 Registry and the Registry for Windows 98 or Windows 95.

As noted earlier, you generally make changes to the hardware configuration, installed software, user settings, and user preferences on your computer using tools provided with Windows 2000, such as the Control Panel. However, you may need to open the Registry periodically to view, change, add, or troubleshoot settings, so it's important to be familiar with its structure and use.

Backing Up and Restoring the Windows 2000 Registry

Isabel emphasizes to you the importance of backing up the Registry before making any changes to the Registry. Since the Windows 2000 Registry is crucial to the booting and functioning of your computer, the backup strategies that you develop for your computer system should also take into account the Registry. There are several ways in which you can back up the Registry:

- **Create an Emergency Repair Disk**. When you can create an Emergency Repair Disk (ERD) with the Windows 2000 Backup utility, you can specify that it also back up the Registry. The Backup utility will save your current Registry files in a directory named RegBack under the Windows Repair directory. Since your Windows 2000 settings change over time (when you upgrade Windows 2000, install new software, and reconfigure your system), you must make sure you have a recent copy of the Emergency Repair Disk and the Registry. Later, if you encounter problems with your computer, you can use the Emergency Repair Disk to repair the Windows 2000 system files (such as the Windows 2000 Registry), restore settings for dual-boot or multiple-boot systems, and repair the partition boot sector on your boot volume.

- **Export the Registry**. You can also open the Registry Editor, a utility for viewing the contents of, and making changes to, the Registry, and export (or transfer) a copy of the entire Registry or a copy of a hive to a file on disk.

- **Full System Backup**. With the Windows 2000 Backup utility, or any other backup utility, you can perform a full backup of your entire computer system. Then, if necessary, you can restore your entire system or selectively restore components, such as the Registry. If you intend to make a major change to the configuration of your computer, such as installing a new operating system, upgrading the operating system, or installing an office suite like Microsoft Office, then you should seriously consider a full system backup. If the installation or upgrade fails and you need to rebuild your computer, you may be able to use the full system backup to restore vital components. You should note that one disadvantage of relying only on this type of backup is that you might not be able to start Backup and restore the Registry because Backup relies on the availability of the graphical user interface.

- **Recovery Console.** You can also use the Recovery Console to restore the Registry, but only if you have made an Emergency Repair Disk for your computer system and choose the option for backing up the Registry. If you need to boot your computer with the Recovery Console, you can use the COPY command to copy backups of one or more Registry files from the Repair directory to the Config directory. If you use this approach, rename the file in the Config directory (under the System32 directory) that you intend to replace so that you have the original copy of that file in case you need it later. This strategy is commonly used by troubleshooters. Instead of overwriting a copy of an important configuration file, you rename it first, then you restore another copy of that same file (such as a previous version of that file, or a backup of the current Registry file) and determine whether that new copy works properly or not.

If you experience a problem starting Windows 2000, then you can use the Last Known Good Configuration (shown in Figure 9-3). Whenever Windows 2000 successfully loads all of its startup drivers and a user logs onto a computer, it copies these startup settings, referred to as the **Last Known Good Configuration**, to the Registry. To start your computer using the Last Known Good Configuration, reboot your computer, and when you see the message "Please select the operating system to start," press F8 and select Last Known Good Configuration. This approach provides a way for recovering from problems such as an improper driver for a hardware device, but it does not solve problems resulting from a corrupt or missing driver or file. If you are unable to boot your computer, then one or more of the hive files may be physically damaged, and you will need to replace them with a previous copy of the Registry.

Figure 9-3	LAST KNOWN GOOD CONFIGURATION

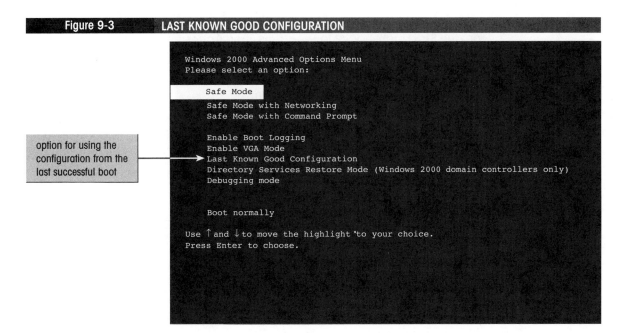

It's important to emphasize that before you make changes to the Windows 2000 Registry, make sure you have a backup copy of the Registry and an Emergency Repair Disk (ERD). If you accidentally or deliberately make a change to the Registry, and are not able to boot or use your computer, then you can use the Emergency Repair Disk to boot your computer so that you can restore the last good working copy of the Registry.

It is also a good idea to develop a strategy for working with the Windows 2000 Registry, including backing up the Registry and documenting any changes you make to it, so that you can effectively troubleshoot problems that may arise later.

Making an Emergency Repair Disk

Isabel recommends that you first update your copy of your Emergency Repair Disk before the two of you examine some important features of the Registry on your computer. *Do not skip the following steps.* Even though you have already performed the steps for making an Emergency Repair Disk (ERD) in Tutorial 6, you *must* repeat that process here so that you have an up-to-date copy of the ERD. As noted earlier, you should periodically update your ERD because your Windows 2000 settings change over time.

If you have not made a recent backup copy of your computer system and document files, then this is the time to do it. Make these backups before you proceed with the remainder of this tutorial.

In Tutorial 6, you worked from a Command Prompt window to make an Emergency Repair Disk. In the following steps, you will work from the desktop in the graphical user interface so that you are familiar with both approaches.

To create an Emergency Repair Disk:

1. Format a diskette in drive A. If a diskette contains defective sectors, do not use it as an Emergency Repair Disk, because you need as reliable a diskette as possible. Use a defect-free diskette, format it, and check to make sure all of the storage space is available (that is, no bad sectors are taking up space). Continue with the next step when you have a formatted empty diskette with no defective sectors.

2. From the **Start** menu, point to **Programs**, then **Accessories**, then **System Tools**, and finally click **Backup**. Windows 2000 displays a Backup window, and on the Welcome sheet is an option for making an Emergency Repair Disk.

3. Click the **Emergency Repair Disk** button.

4. After the Backup utility displays an Emergency Repair Diskette dialog box, which prompts for a formatted diskette in drive A, click the check box for the option to back up the Windows 2000 Registry to the Repair directory, and then click **OK**.

5. After the Backup utility displays another Emergency Repair Diskette dialog box informing you that the emergency repair diskette was successfully saved, click **OK**.

6. Close **Backup**.

7. Label your diskette "Emergency Repair Diskette" with today's date and any other pertinent information, such as the computer used to make the ERD.

You now have updated copies of the hives that constitute the Windows 2000 Registry in the %Systemroot%\Repair\RegBack folder, as well as updated copies of the Software and System hives in the %Systemroot%\System32\Config folders.

Opening **the Windows 2000 Registry**

Isabel explains that Windows 2000 has two different versions of the Registry Editor—Regedit and Regedt32—and the version you use will depend on what you want to do with the Registry.

If you want to search for and view information, then use Regedit. Although you can use either version to make changes to the Registry, Microsoft recommends that you use Regedit just to search for information and that you use Regedt32 to modify the Registry. Regedit is safer because of its built-in limitations. Unlike Regedit32, Regedit will not allow you to view or edit certain types of data stored in the Registry, and you cannot specify security settings.

Because there is no option on the Start menu for opening the Registry Editor, you can use either the Run option on the Start menu or a Command Prompt window to enter the command for opening the Registry Editor. Once you open the Registry, you can export or copy Registry settings to a file on disk so that you have an alternate backup to the one created by the Backup utility. You can then examine the structure and contents of the Registry and, if necessary, specify new settings or modify existing settings in the Registry.

Exporting Registry Settings

Isabel recommends that you start by opening the Registry with the Registry Editor and then export the Registry settings to a registration file on disk so that you have an additional backup. She also recommends that you use Regedit for viewing information in the Registry, as recommended by Microsoft.

If you open Regedit and export Registry settings, the Registry Editor creates a text file with the "reg" file extension that contains a copy of all the Registry settings. If necessary, you can restore the Registry from a registration file.

Both of the Registry Editors are designed for the more advanced user. *You must exercise* ***caution*** *when you use the Registry Editor*; closely follow any instructions you may have for navigating, viewing, and modifying the Registry; double-check and triple-check the changes you make; and be prepared to restore your computer and its Registry if you run into a problem. If your computer lab does not permit you to use either of the Registry Editors, or if you prefer not to use them on your computer until you first understand how they work, then read, but do not keystroke, the remainder of the steps in this tutorial.

In the next set of steps, you will open and export the Registry to a file on disk. Because of the large size of this file, you will have to store it either on the hard disk or on a removable disk, such as a Zip disk.

To open the Registry Editor:

1. Open a Command Prompt window, set background and foreground colors (if necessary), specify a default setting for the DIRCMD variable in the Windows environment so that directories and files are listed in alphabetical order by name, one screen at a time, and then clear the window.

2. Enter the command: `regedit`
   After the Registry Editor opens, you will see an Explorer-like pane with the Registry tree. See Figure 9-4. The information in the Registry tree is organized by **keys**, or branches, each of which stores a group of related settings in subkeys. Each key is represented by a folder icon. Even though the Regedit Registry Editor displays the Registry in the form of a single tree with subfolders, the Registry actually consists of a collection of separate files.

Figure 9-4

VIEWING THE CONTENTS OF THE REGISTRY WITH THE REGISTRY EDITOR

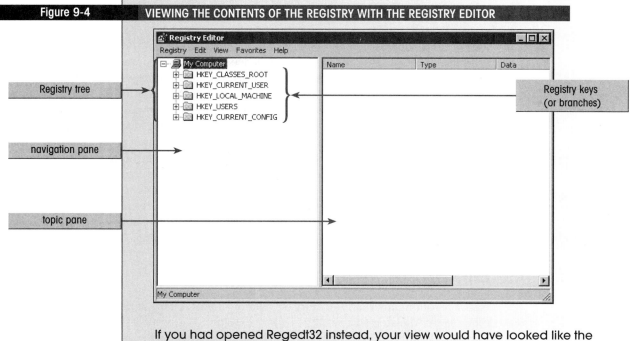

If you had opened Regedt32 instead, your view would have looked like the one shown in Figure 9-5. Notice that the different keys are each displayed in a different window, and you do not have a My Computer node at the top of a single Registry tree.

Figure 9-5

VIEWING THE REGISTRY WITH REGEDT32

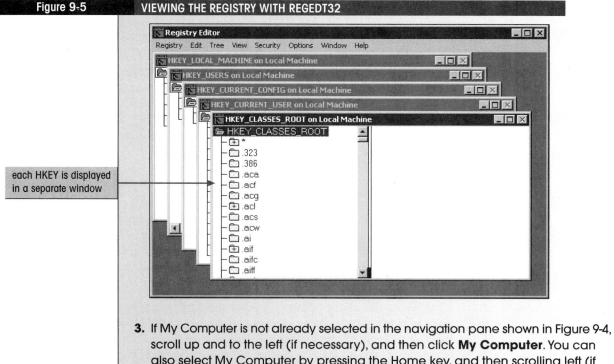

3. If My Computer is not already selected in the navigation pane shown in Figure 9-4, scroll up and to the left (if necessary), and then click **My Computer**. You can also select My Computer by pressing the Home key, and then scrolling left (if necessary). By selecting My Computer before performing the export, you are guaranteeing that the Registry Editor will export *all* the Registry settings to a registration file. If you select a specific key, rather than My Computer, the Registry Editor exports only that portion of the Registry.

4. Click **Registry** on the menu bar, and then click **Export Registry File**. Windows 2000 opens the Export Registry File dialog box. See Figure 9-6. Note that the file type is listed as Registration Files, and that it is set to export the entire Registry, not just a selected branch or key.

Figure 9-6   **EXPORTING THE REGISTRY TO A REGISTRATION FILE**

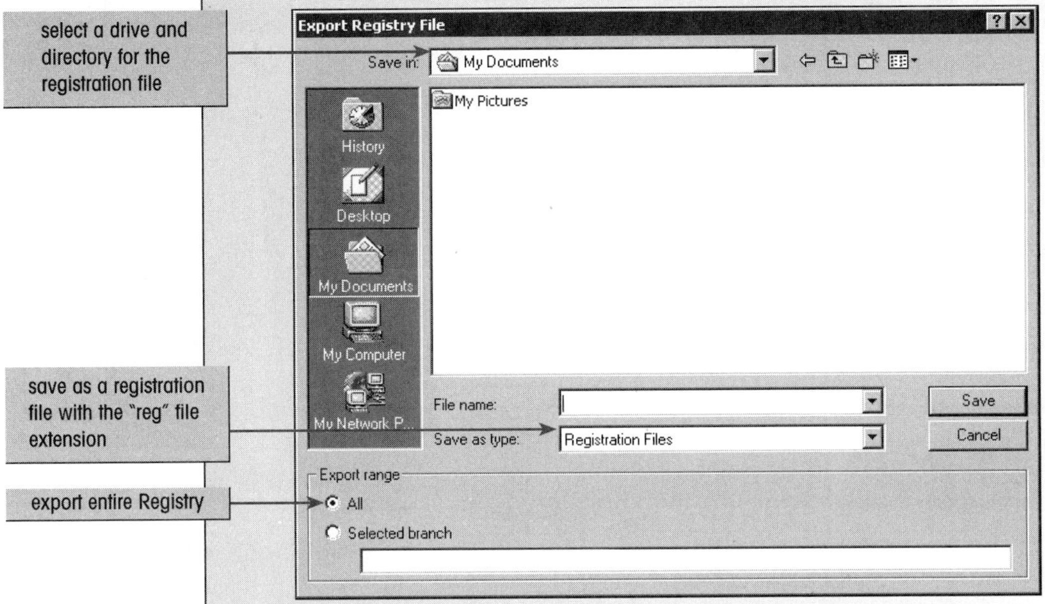

select a drive and directory for the registration file

save as a registration file with the "reg" file extension

export entire Registry

5. If the "My Documents" folder is not already displayed in the Save in list box, click the **Save in** list arrow, and then click **My Documents**. Click the **Create New Folder** button, type **Registry Backup**, press **Enter**, and then press **Enter** a second time to open the new Registry folder.

6. Click in the **File name** box, and then type **Registry Backup for** followed by the current date in the format yyyy-mm-dd in the File name box (for example, if the current date is May 16, 2003, then you would enter 2003-05-16 for the date), as shown in Figure 9-7.

Figure 9-7 | **SPECIFYING A FILENAME FOR THE REGISTRY BACKUP**

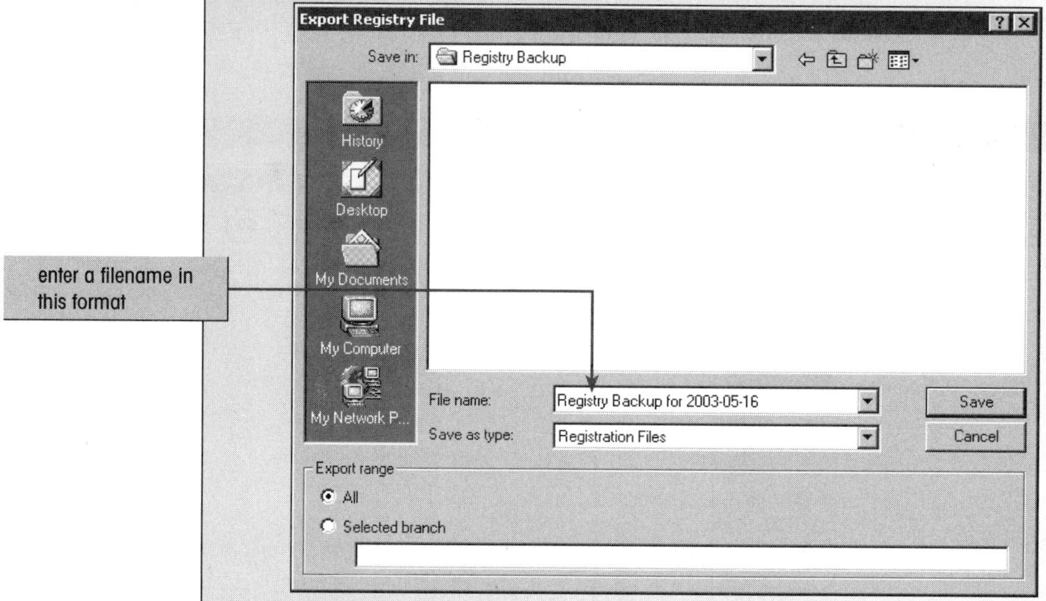

enter a filename in this format

7. Click **Save**, and then wait until the backup is complete.

8. Minimize the **Registry Editor** window and switch back to the **Command Prompt** window.

Next, you will examine the size of the registration file.

To view the size of the registration file:

1. Enter: `cd %userprofile%\My Documents\Registry Backup`
   The CD command changes to the directory for your account.

2. Display a directory listing. On the computer used for this figure, the registration file is 20,039,812 bytes (or approximately 19 MB). See Figure 9-8. The size of your registration file will differ.

Figure 9-8 | **VIEWING THE DIRECTORY WITH THE REGISTRATION FILE**

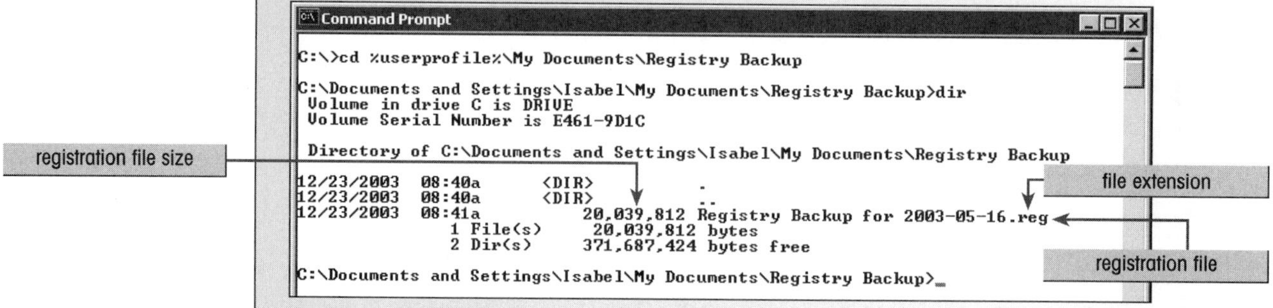

registration file size

file extension

registration file

If you open this registration file in Microsoft Word, the first page will be similar to that shown in Figure 9-9. If you used Microsoft Word to print the file shown in the figure, it would be 4,199 pages in length.

Figure 9-9 | **OPENING THE REGISTRATION FILE IN MICROSOFT WORD**

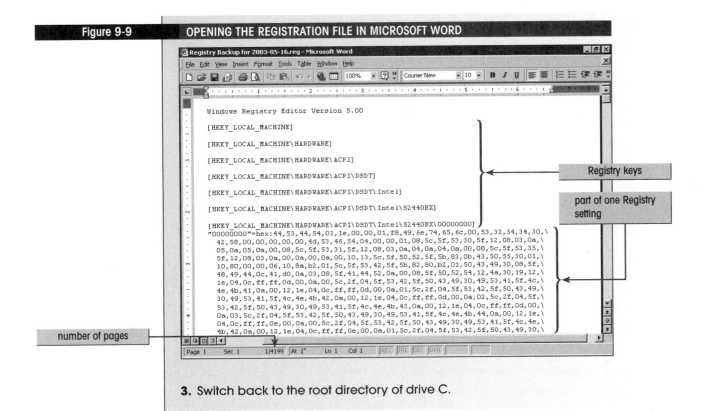

3. Switch back to the root directory of drive C.

REFERENCE WINDOW | **RW**

Exporting Registry Settings
- Open a Command Prompt window, type REGEDIT, and then press Enter. Or, from the Start menu, select Run, type REGEDIT in the Open box, and then press Enter.
- If it is not already selected, click My Computer in the navigation pane.
- Click Registry on the menu bar, and then click Export Registry File.
- In the Export Registry File dialog box, locate (or create) the folder where you want to store the exported Registry settings; then, in the File name box, type a name for your registration file and click OK.
- Close the Registry Editor.

If you need to restore the Registry from this registration file, open the Registry and use the Import Registry File command on the Registry menu. Then you would locate the registration file you want to use. Once you select that registration file, Windows 2000 will display an Import Registry File dialog box with a progress indicator. If the Registry Editor is unable to import all of the data to the Registry, it will display a Registry Editor dialog box explaining that some keys are open by the system or by other processes. You can also open the directory that contains the registration file, and then click or double-click the registration file to restore the Registry. If Windows 2000 will not load, you can use the Windows 2000 Setup disks and your Emergency Repair Disk to restore a working copy of the Registry (make sure it's a recent version; otherwise, you will lose settings).

If you open Regedt32 instead and want to export Registry settings, use the Save Subtree As command on the Registry menu to save the Registry settings for the top-level key in the current window to a text file on diskette. Repeat this process for each of the other top-level keys in each of the other windows.

Viewing **Information on Registered Files**

Before you proceed to examine information on file associations stored in the Windows 2000 Registry, Isabel recommends that you use the ASSOC and FTYPE commands to view information about commonly used file extensions.

One advantage of viewing information on file extensions from a Command Prompt window rather than from the Windows 2000 Registry is that you can locate the information you need much more quickly, and you do not run the risk of inadvertently changing the Registry.

Using the Associate Command

Isabel recommends that you use the Associate command to examine information on file types for three different, but common, file extensions—"bat", "bmp", and "doc"—so you know how to locate this information when you need it. She also notes that, although you can use the File Types property sheet to find information on file extensions, it's faster to use a Command Prompt window.

You can use the ASSOC (Associate) command to display or modify associations for file extensions. If you use the following syntax, the ASSOC command displays information on a single specified file extension:

ASSOC *.ext*

If you enter the ASSOC command without specifying a file extension, information on all file extensions is displayed.

In the next set of steps, you are going to examine information on the "bat", "bmp", and "doc" file extensions.

To view information on file extensions:

1. If necessary, switch back to the **Command Prompt** window, clear the window, and then maximize the **Command Prompt** window.

2. Enter: `assoc | more`
   The ASSOC command displays an alphabetical listing of file extensions and identifies the file type for some of the file extensions. See Figure 9-10. For example, files with the file extension "bat" are assigned the file type "batfile", and the file type for "bmp" files is "Paint.Picture". The associations for different file extensions will depend on the types of software installed on your computer, and therefore will vary.

Figure 9-10 | **USING ASSOC TO DISPLAY A LIST OF FILE EXTENSIONS AND FILE TYPES**

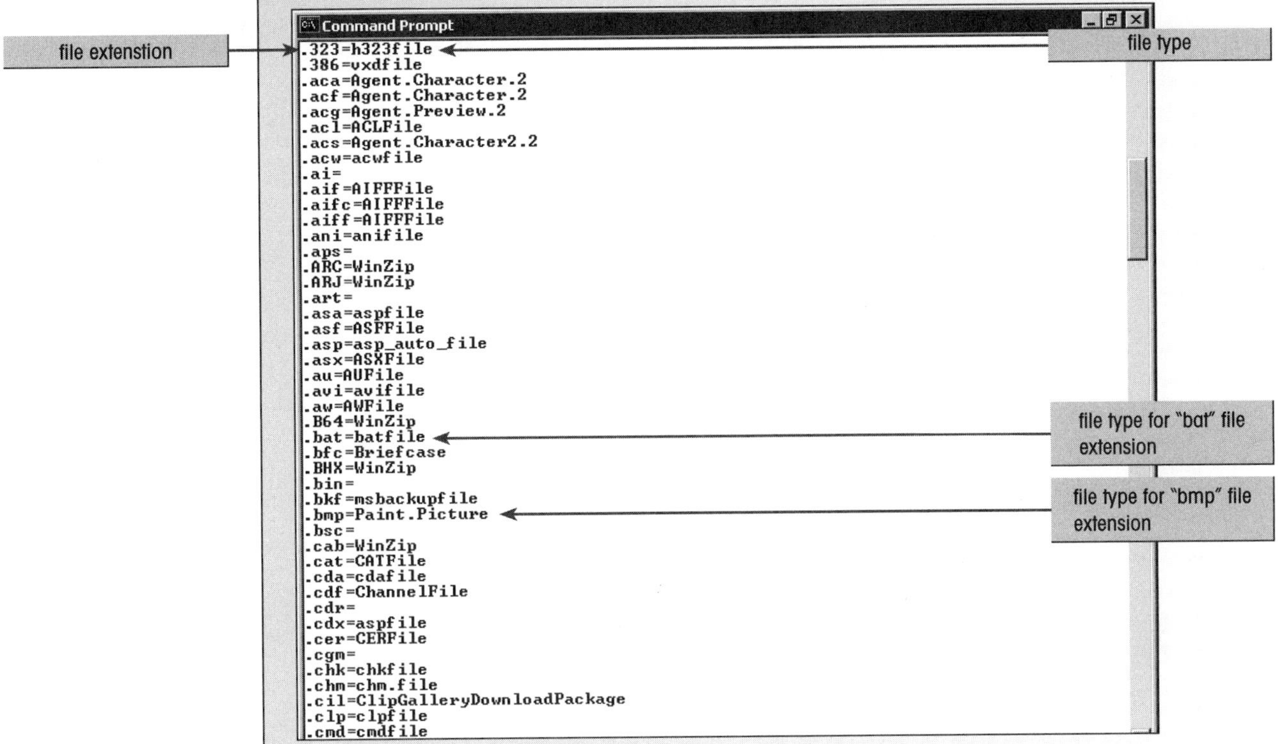

file extenstion

file type

file type for "bat" file extension

file type for "bmp" file extension

```
.323=h323file
.386=vxdfile
.aca=Agent.Character.2
.acf=Agent.Character.2
.acg=Agent.Preview.2
.acl=ACLFile
.acs=Agent.Character2.2
.acw=acwfile
.ai=
.aif=AIFFFile
.aifc=AIFFFile
.aiff=AIFFFile
.ani=anifile
.aps=
.ARC=WinZip
.ARJ=WinZip
.art=
.asa=aspfile
.asf=ASFFile
.asp=asp_auto_file
.asx=ASXFile
.au=AUFile
.avi=avifile
.aw=AWFile
.B64=WinZip
.bat=batfile
.bfc=Briefcase
.BHX=WinZip
.bin=
.bkf=msbackupfile
.bmp=Paint.Picture
.bsc=
.cab=WinZip
.cat=CATFile
.cda=cdafile
.cdf=ChannelFile
.cdr=
.cdx=aspfile
.cer=CERFile
.cgm=
.chk=chkfile
.chm=chm.file
.cil=ClipGalleryDownloadPackage
.clp=clpfile
.cmd=cmdfile
```

3. Press the **Spacebar** to view each successive screen of file type associations until you find the "doc" file extension. On the computer used for Figure 9-11, the file extension "doc" is assigned the file type "Word.Document.8". As just noted, the information provided by this command may vary, since it depends on the type of software installed on your computer system, the versions of those software products, and how your system is configured.

Figure 9-11   VIEWING THE NEXT SCREEN OF FILE EXTENSIONS

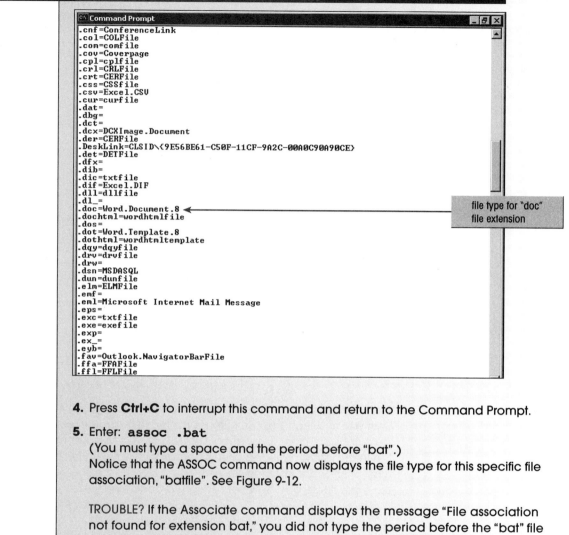

file type for "doc" file extension

4. Press **Ctrl+C** to interrupt this command and return to the Command Prompt.

5. Enter: **assoc .bat**
(You must type a space and the period before "bat".)
Notice that the ASSOC command now displays the file type for this specific file association, "batfile". See Figure 9-12.

TROUBLE? If the Associate command displays the message "File association not found for extension bat," you did not type the period before the "bat" file extension. Repeat Step 5.

Figure 9-12   DISPLAYING THE FILE TYPE FOR A SPECIFIC FILE EXTENSION

you must type the space and the period

command for displaying the file type of a specific file extension

file extension   file type

6. Enter: **assoc batfile**
The ASSOC command displays the description that Windows 2000 uses for this type of file, namely that it's an "MS-DOS Batch File". See Figure 9-13. Windows 2000 uses this description to arrange files in order by file type in a folder window. If you are working in Details view, Windows 2000 also displays "MS-DOS Batch File" in the Type column next to each file with a "bat" file extension.

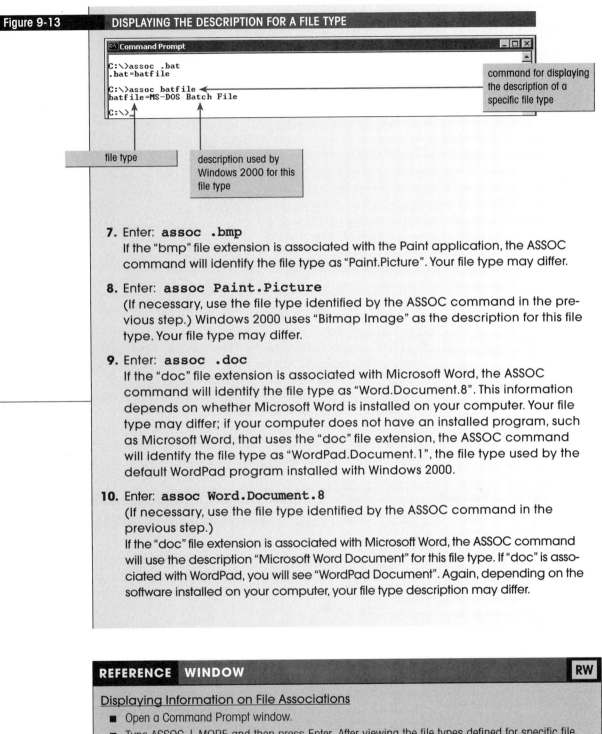

Figure 9-13 — DISPLAYING THE DESCRIPTION FOR A FILE TYPE

```
Command Prompt
C:\>assoc .bat
.bat=batfile

C:\>assoc batfile
batfile=MS-DOS Batch File

C:\>_
```

command for displaying the description of a specific file type

file type

description used by Windows 2000 for this file type

7. Enter: **assoc .bmp**
If the "bmp" file extension is associated with the Paint application, the ASSOC command will identify the file type as "Paint.Picture". Your file type may differ.

8. Enter: **assoc Paint.Picture**
(If necessary, use the file type identified by the ASSOC command in the previous step.) Windows 2000 uses "Bitmap Image" as the description for this file type. Your file type may differ.

9. Enter: **assoc .doc**
If the "doc" file extension is associated with Microsoft Word, the ASSOC command will identify the file type as "Word.Document.8". This information depends on whether Microsoft Word is installed on your computer. Your file type may differ; if your computer does not have an installed program, such as Microsoft Word, that uses the "doc" file extension, the ASSOC command will identify the file type as "WordPad.Document.1", the file type used by the default WordPad program installed with Windows 2000.

10. Enter: **assoc Word.Document.8**
(If necessary, use the file type identified by the ASSOC command in the previous step.)
If the "doc" file extension is associated with Microsoft Word, the ASSOC command will use the description "Microsoft Word Document" for this file type. If "doc" is associated with WordPad, you will see "WordPad Document". Again, depending on the software installed on your computer, your file type description may differ.

REFERENCE   WINDOW   `RW`

Displaying Information on File Associations

■ Open a Command Prompt window.

■ Type ASSOC | MORE and then press Enter. After viewing the file types defined for specific file extensions on the first screen, press the Spacebar to view each successive screen.

■ If you want to view the file type associated with a specific file extension, type ASSOC, press the Spacebar, type a period followed by the file extension (such as ASSOC .DOC), and then press Enter.

■ If you want to view the description of a specific file type, first display the file type for a specific file extension (see previous step); then type ASSOC, press the Spacebar, type the file type (such as ASSOC Word.Document.8), and press Enter.

You can improve your understanding of how your computer works by using the Associate command to display information for file extensions that you commonly use.

Using the FTYPE Command

The FTYPE command displays or changes file types used for file associations. If you use the FTYPE command with the following syntax, it will show the path to the program that Windows 2000 would open if you clicked a file with the file type associated with that program:

FTYPE *fileType*

The *fileType* parameter is the file type (such as "batfile" for files with the "bat" file extension) provided by the ASSOC command for a specific file extension.

To find the file type for use with the FTYPE command, you first need to use the ASSOC command to display the file type for a file extension (as you did earlier).

To display the file type for a file extension:

1. Clear the **Command Prompt** window, and enter: `assoc .bat`
   ASSOC displays the file type for files with the "bat" file extension.

2. Enter: `ftype batfile`
   The FTYPE command lists the file type you specified, and then shows the command line for opening this file type. In Figure 9-14, the command line is "%1" %*. This command line means that Windows 2000 uses "%1" as the replaceable parameter for the name of the batch program file. %* represents all the parameters that may be passed to the batch program when you execute the batch program. In contrast to document files, when you say you are "opening" a batch program, you are actually running or executing the batch program—not opening it in another application.

| Figure 9-14 | DISPLAYING THE COMMAND FOR OPENING A FILE TYPE |

command line for opening this file type

```
C:\>ftype batfile
batfile="%1" %*

C:\>_
```

3. Enter: `assoc .bmp`
   ASSOC displays the file type for files with the "bmp" file extension, Paint.Picture.

4. Enter: `ftype Paint.Picture`
   In Figure 9-15, the command line for opening this file type is "C:\WINNT\system32\mspaint.exe" "%1". Mspaint.exe is the name of the program file that Windows 2000 opens for files with the "bmp" file extension on this computer. The program, in this case, is Paint, a Windows 2000 accessory. The filename of the file icon that you click or double-click to open when working in the graphical user interface is inserted in the "%1" replaceable parameter. For example, if you double-click a file named "Seaside.bmp," then the command for opening this file is as follows:
   "C:\WINNT\System32\mspaint.exe" "Seaside.bmp".

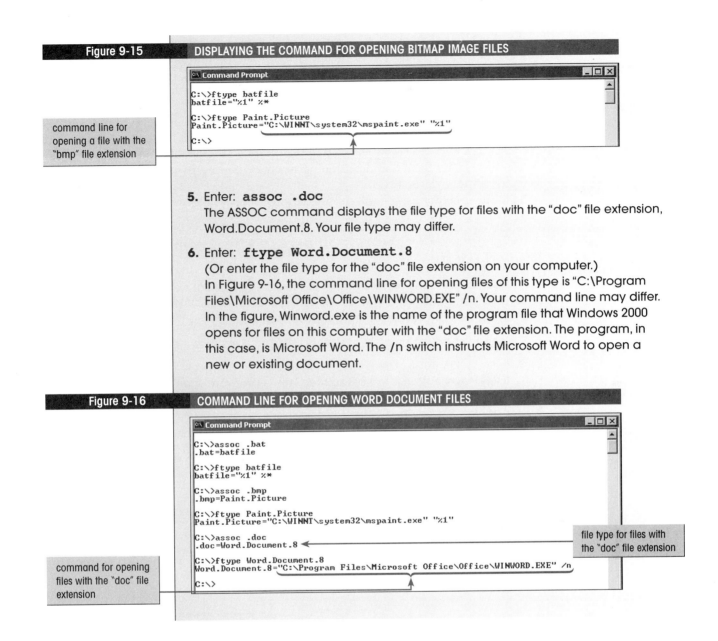

Figure 9-15 DISPLAYING THE COMMAND FOR OPENING BITMAP IMAGE FILES

command line for opening a file with the "bmp" file extension

5. Enter: **assoc .doc**
The ASSOC command displays the file type for files with the "doc" file extension, Word.Document.8. Your file type may differ.

6. Enter: **ftype Word.Document.8**
(Or enter the file type for the "doc" file extension on your computer.)
In Figure 9-16, the command line for opening files of this type is "C:\Program Files\Microsoft Office\Office\WINWORD.EXE" /n. Your command line may differ. In the figure, Winword.exe is the name of the program file that Windows 2000 opens for files on this computer with the "doc" file extension. The program, in this case, is Microsoft Word. The /n switch instructs Microsoft Word to open a new or existing document.

Figure 9-16 COMMAND LINE FOR OPENING WORD DOCUMENT FILES

file type for files with the "doc" file extension

command for opening files with the "doc" file extension

REFERENCE WINDOW | RW

Displaying the Command Line Used to Open a File Type
- Open a Command Prompt window.
- If necessary, use the Associate command to display the file type for a specific file extension (such as ASSOC .DOC).
- Type FTYPE followed by a space and the file type (such as FTYPE Word.Document.8) and then press Enter.

If you enter the FTYPE command and do not specify a file type, then FTYPE lists all of the file types associated with executable programs or command lines. If you try this use of FTYPE, pipe the output to the MORE filter so that you can control scrolling.

You can also use the ASSOC command to change or designate a file extension, and you can use the FTYPE command to change the associated command line to open the file type you specify. For example, you could assign "TempFile" as the file type for files with the "tmp" file extension, and then specify that Windows 2000 open these files in Notepad. Files with the "tmp" file extension are temporary files created by programs to process data. Normally, these files are deleted once you close the application; however, if a power failure occurs, or if your system locks up and you have to reboot, then these files remain on your hard disk and waste space. By associating them with a program like Notepad, you have the option of opening them and determining whether they are of any use before you decide whether or not to delete them.

In the next set of steps, you will create a file association for files with the "tmp" file extension.

To create a file association and specify a command for opening a file type:

1. Insert a new copy of Data Disk #1 in drive A, change the default drive to drive A, and then display a directory listing. The first file, ~WRC0070.tmp, is an actual temporary file created during a power failure.

2. View the next screen of the directory listing, and return to the command prompt.

3. Enter: `~wrc0070.tmp`
   If this file extension is not associated with a program, then Windows 2000 will display an Open With dialog box, and prompt you to choose the program for opening the file. See Figure 9-17.

| Figure 9-17 | OPTION FOR OPENING AN UNREGISTERED FILE TYPE |

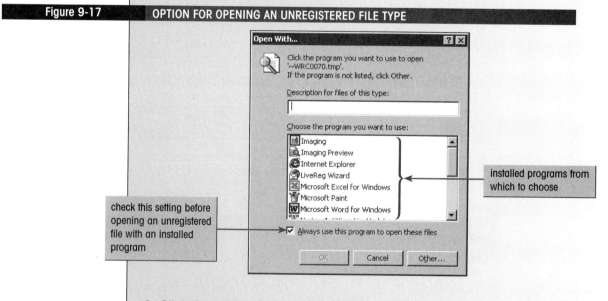

check this setting before opening an unregistered file with an installed program

installed programs from which to choose

4. Click **Cancel** to close the Open With dialog box without opening the file, and then, if necessary, click the **Command Prompt** button on the taskbar to return to the Command Prompt window.

5. Clear the window, and enter: `assoc .tmp`
   If no association is defined for this file extension, then you will see the message "File association not found for extension tmp." See Figure 9-18.

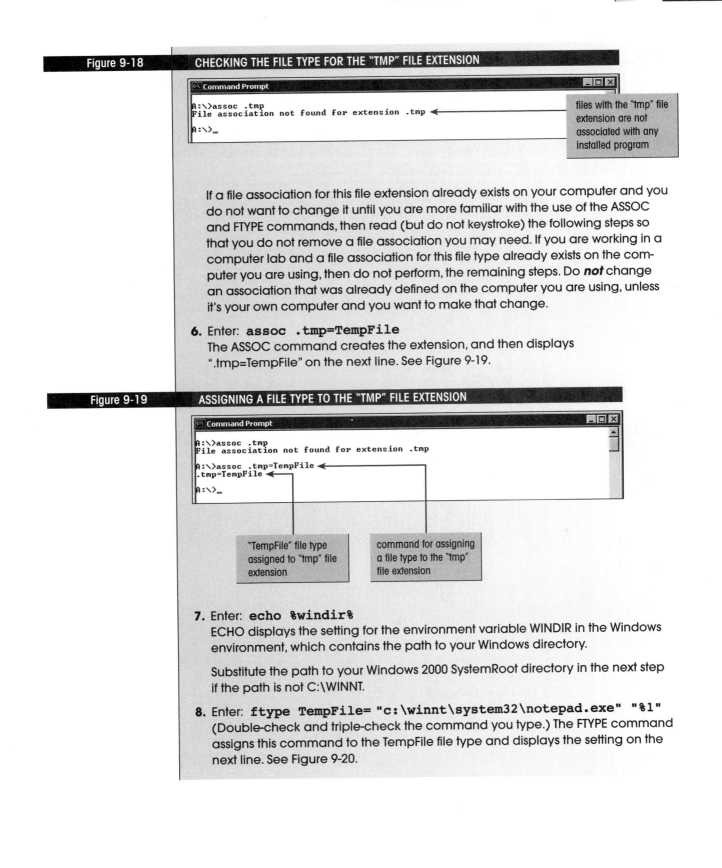

Figure 9-18   CHECKING THE FILE TYPE FOR THE "TMP" FILE EXTENSION

Command Prompt

```
A:\>assoc .tmp
File association not found for extension .tmp    ◄───
A:\>_
```

files with the "tmp" file extension are not associated with any installed program

If a file association for this file extension already exists on your computer and you do not want to change it until you are more familiar with the use of the ASSOC and FTYPE commands, then read (but do not keystroke) the following steps so that you do not remove a file association you may need. If you are working in a computer lab and a file association for this file type already exists on the computer you are using, then do not perform, the remaining steps. Do *not* change an association that was already defined on the computer you are using, unless it's your own computer and you want to make that change.

6. Enter: **assoc .tmp=TempFile**
   The ASSOC command creates the extension, and then displays ".tmp=TempFile" on the next line. See Figure 9-19.

Figure 9-19   ASSIGNING A FILE TYPE TO THE "TMP" FILE EXTENSION

Command Prompt

```
A:\>assoc .tmp
File association not found for extension .tmp

A:\>assoc .tmp=TempFile    ◄───
.tmp=TempFile    ◄───

A:\>_
```

"TempFile" file type assigned to "tmp" file extension

command for assigning a file type to the "tmp" file extension

7. Enter: **echo %windir%**
   ECHO displays the setting for the environment variable WINDIR in the Windows environment, which contains the path to your Windows directory.

   Substitute the path to your Windows 2000 SystemRoot directory in the next step if the path is not C:\WINNT.

8. Enter: **ftype TempFile= "c:\winnt\system32\notepad.exe" "%1"**
   (Double-check and triple-check the command you type.) The FTYPE command assigns this command to the TempFile file type and displays the setting on the next line. See Figure 9-20.

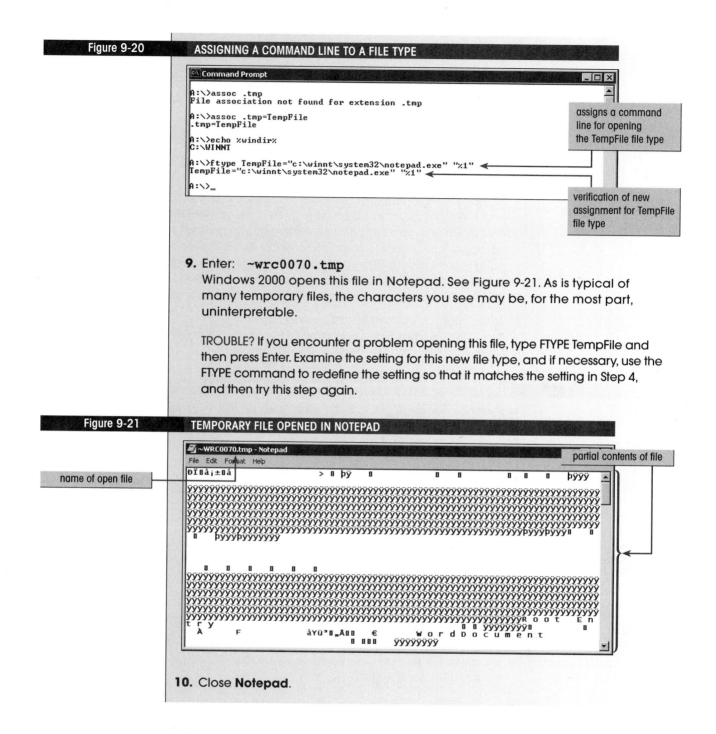

Figure 9-20   ASSIGNING A COMMAND LINE TO A FILE TYPE

```
A:\>assoc .tmp
File association not found for extension .tmp

A:\>assoc .tmp=TempFile
.tmp=TempFile

A:\>echo %windir%
C:\WINNT

A:\>ftype TempFile="c:\winnt\system32\notepad.exe" "%1"
TempFile="c:\winnt\system32\notepad.exe" "%1"

A:\>_
```

assigns a command line for opening the TempFile file type

verification of new assignment for TempFile file type

9. Enter: **~wrc0070.tmp**

Windows 2000 opens this file in Notepad. See Figure 9-21. As is typical of many temporary files, the characters you see may be, for the most part, uninterpretable.

TROUBLE? If you encounter a problem opening this file, type FTYPE TempFile and then press Enter. Examine the setting for this new file type, and if necessary, use the FTYPE command to redefine the setting so that it matches the setting in Step 4, and then try this step again.

Figure 9-21   TEMPORARY FILE OPENED IN NOTEPAD

partial contents of file

name of open file

10. Close **Notepad.**

REFERENCE   WINDOW `RW`

Associating a File Extension with a Program
- Open a Command Prompt window.
- Type ASSOC, press the Spacebar, type a period followed immediately by the file extension (such as ASSOC .TMP), and then press Enter to verify that no file association exists for files with that file extension.
- Type ASSOC, press the Spacebar, type a period followed immediately by the file extension, type an equals sign, type a name for the file type you want to use (such as ASSOC .TMP=TempFile), and then press Enter.
- Type FTYPE, press the Spacebar, type the file type, type an equals sign, type the command line you want to use to open files with this file extension (such as FTYPE TempFile= "C:\Winnt\System32\Notepad.exe" "%1"), and then press Enter.

By defining this association, you can now open all files with the "tmp" file extension in Notepad just by clicking the file icon or typing the filename at a command prompt.

Next, you will remove the association for this file extension. Perform this operation only if you want to remove the association or if the association did not exist previously. Do *not* change an association that was already defined on the computer you are using unless it's your own computer and you want to make that change.

To remove the association for the file extension:

1. Clear the window, and enter: `ftype TempFile=`
   If you do not specify a command line for opening the file type, you delete the previous command line assigned to the file type. The FTYPE command does not confirm the change. Unless you made an error, you see only another command prompt.

2. Enter: `ftype TempFile`
   (Or recall the previous FTYPE command and remove the equals sign.)
   FTYPE informs you that it did not find this file type and that there is no open command associated with it.

3. Enter: `assoc .tmp=`
   If you do not specify a file type for a file extension, then you delete the previous file type assigned to this file extension. Like FTYPE, the ASSOC command does not confirm the change.

4. Enter: `assoc .tmp`
   (Or recall the previous ASSOC command and remove the equals sign.)
   The ASSOC command informs you that it did not find a file association for the "tmp" file extension.

5. Close the **Registry Editor**, and then close the **Command Prompt** window.

REFERENCE	WINDOW	RW

Removing a File Extension's Association with a Program
- Open a Command Prompt window.
- Type FTYPE, press the Spacebar, type the file type immediately followed by an equals sign (such as FTYPE TempFile=), and then press Enter.
- Type ASSOC, press the Spacebar, type a period, type the file extension, and type an equals sign (for example, ASSOC .TMP=), and then press Enter.

Now you can see the importance and value of the ASSOC and FTYPE commands, as well as the power of associating file extensions with a program. Once you create (or define) a registered file type from the command prompt, that information is then stored in the Windows 2000 Registry.

Session 9.1 QUICK CHECK

1. When you boot your computer, Windows 2000 processes the information in the _____ to configure your computer properly.

2. A(n) _____ file is a file that is associated with a specific application via its file extension.

3. If you make changes to the configuration of Windows 2000, you must update your copy of the _____.

4. After you open the Registry Editor, you can export Registry settings to a(n) _____ file so that you have a backup of the Windows 2000 Registry.

5. The information in the Registry tree is organized by _____, each of which store groups of related settings in _____.

6. You can use the _____ command in a Command Prompt window to view the file type associated with files having the "url" extension.

7. You can use the _____ command in a Command Prompt window to display the command line that Windows 2000 uses to open files with the "url" file extension.

8. To assign a file type for a file extension that is not already associated with an application, use the _____ command.

9. To assign a command for opening a specific file type, use the _____ command.

10. A compressed file that contains operating system files and that has the "cab" file extension is called a(n) _____ file.

SESSION 9 .2

In this session you will examine the five major Registry keys, trace information on the same registered file types that you examined with the ASSOC and FTYPE commands in the previous session, examine important Registry subkeys, work with the Class-Definition for a registered file, examine the Class Identifiers (CLSIDs) examine the differences among the three types of values stored in the Registry, and then locate and edit a Registry key to simplify the process of entering commands in the Command Prompt window.

Examining the Structure of the Registry

Now that you're familiar with registered file types from working with the ASSOC and FTYPE commands in a Command Prompt Window, Isabel takes a few minutes to explain to you the specific types of information that each Registry key contains.

The Registry consists of five major keys, each of which starts with HKEY. The "H" in HKEY stands for "Handle," meaning each key is a handle for a specific group of settings. The HKEY branches are:

- HKEY_CLASSES_ROOT, which contains a subkey for each file extension, as well as information on system objects
- HKEY_USERS and HKEY_CURRENT_USER, which contain user profiles of all users and of the current user
- HKEY_LOCAL_MACHINE, with configuration information on the computer itself
- HKEY_CURRENT_CONFIG, which contains information on the hardware profile used at system startup

To view the contents of a Registry key:

1. From the Start menu, select **Run**, type `regedit` in the Open text box, press **Enter**, maximize the **Registry Editor** window, and then, if necessary, scroll up and to the left.

2. Click the **expand view** box ⊞ to the left of the HKEY_CLASSES_ROOT key. This key contains a subkey for each file extension. Each **Filename-File Extension subkey** contains the path to the program for opening that specific type of file. See Figure 9-22. Your subkeys will differ from those shown in the figure because the types of subkeys that you see under the HKEY_CLASSES_ROOT key depend on the types of software installed on the computer. This key also contains information on system objects, such as My Computer and the Recycle Bin, and OLE (Object Linking and Embedding) objects. HKEY_CLASSES_ROOT is actually another name for the HKEY_LOCAL_MACHINE\Software\Classes key. The operating system makes it available under the name HKEY_CLASSES_ROOT to provide backward compatibility with the Windows 3.1 registration database, which is used (and altered) by older 16-bit Windows programs.

Figure 9-22   EXPANDING THE HKEY_CLASSES_ROOT REGISTRY KEY

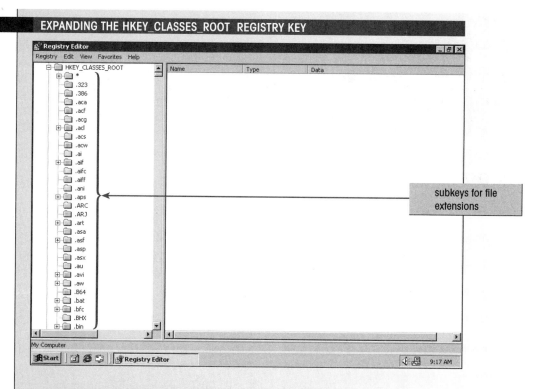

subkeys for file extensions

3. Click the **collapse view** box ▭ (E2) to the left of the HKEY_CLASSES_ROOT key.

4. Click the ⊞ box to the left of the HKEY_CURRENT_USER folder icon, and then click the ⊞ box to the left of the Control Panel subkey. This key and its subkeys contain the user profile, or configuration settings, for the current user logged on to the computer. The HKEY_CURRENT_USER key is derived from the HKEY_USERS key, which contains user profile settings for all users.

5. Click the **Mouse** subkey folder. In the topic pane on the right in Figure 9-23, Windows 2000 displays Registry settings that apply to the use of the mouse. For example, there is a setting called DoubleClickSpeed that determines how Windows 2000 recognizes a double-click, and another setting called SwapMouseButtons that determines whether the mouse is used for a right-handed person (a Data value of 0) or a left-handed person (a Data value of 1).

| Figure 9-23 | VIEWING REGISTRY SETTINGS FOR THE MOUSE SUBKEY |

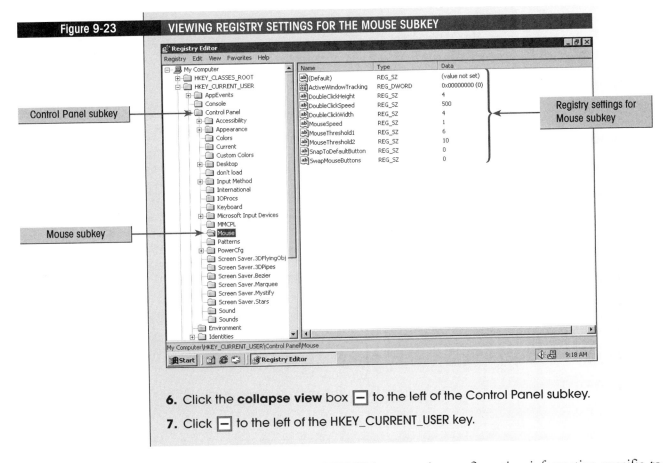

Control Panel subkey

Mouse subkey

Registry settings for Mouse subkey

6. Click the **collapse view** box ⊟ to the left of the Control Panel subkey.

7. Click ⊟ to the left of the HKEY_CURRENT_USER key.

The HKEY_LOCAL_MACHINE key contains configuration information specific to the computer, irrespective of the user. The HKEY_CURRENT_CONFIG key contains information on the hardware profile used on the computer at system startup.

As you can discern from examining just a small portion of the Registry, the Windows 2000 Registry contains a vast amount of data that is crucial to the startup and performance of your computer.

Tracing Information on Registered File Types

Isabel suggests that you next view information on file associations and registered file types so that you become familiar with the process of navigating around the Registry and locating information on registered file types.

To view information on registered file types:

1. If necessary, click the **expand view** box ⊞ to the left of the HKEY_CLASSES_ROOT key in the navigation pane.

2. Locate and double-click the **.bmp** folder subkey. Not only do you select this subkey and see its associated values in the topic pane on the right, but the Registry Editor also expands the .bmp folder subkey in the navigation pane and displays the subkeys located below the .bmp subkey. See Figure 9-24. The rows shown in the topic pane on the right are known as **value entries**, which define values for the currently selected key. Each value entry has three parts: the **name**, **data type**, and the **value** itself. For example, the first value entry in the topic name has the name "(Default)". Its data type is REG_SZ, which identifies the entry as a text string. As noted in Tutorial 8, a string is an entry that is treated exactly as it is typed or shown. The value for this entry is Paint.Picture. When you typed "assoc .bmp" in the previous session, the ASSOC command retrieved this file type value from this key of the Registry and displayed it. This value entry points to another subkey—a Class-Definition subkey (or FileType subkey)—by the same name. That Paint.Picture Class-Definition subkey contains additional information about this file association. You can change the program associated with a specific type of file extension, and that, in turn, changes the file type (or class definition).

Figure 9-24	VIEWING THE .BMP SUBKEY

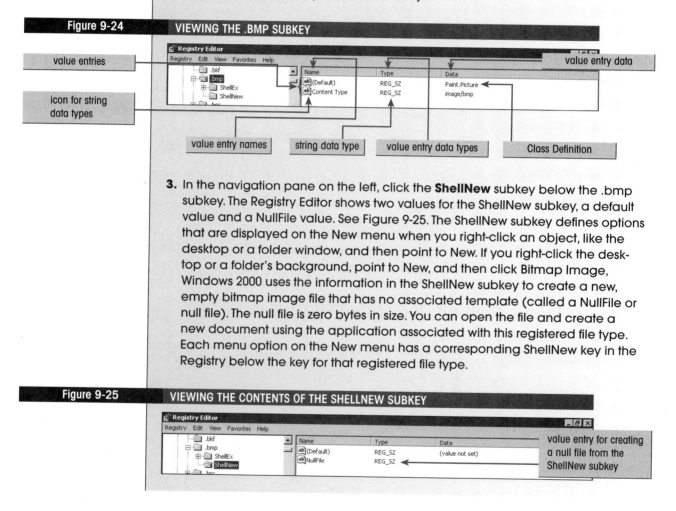

3. In the navigation pane on the left, click the **ShellNew** subkey below the .bmp subkey. The Registry Editor shows two values for the ShellNew subkey, a default value and a NullFile value. See Figure 9-25. The ShellNew subkey defines options that are displayed on the New menu when you right-click an object, like the desktop or a folder window, and then point to New. If you right-click the desktop or a folder's background, point to New, and then click Bitmap Image, Windows 2000 uses the information in the ShellNew subkey to create a new, empty bitmap image file that has no associated template (called a NullFile or null file). The null file is zero bytes in size. You can open the file and create a new document using the application associated with this registered file type. Each menu option on the New menu has a corresponding ShellNew key in the Registry below the key for that registered file type.

Figure 9-25	VIEWING THE CONTENTS OF THE SHELLNEW SUBKEY

Next, you are going to locate the Paint.Picture subkey. You could scroll through the Registry, but it is faster to use Find to search for the subkey.

To locate Paint.Picture:

1. Click **Edit** on the menu bar, and then click **Find**. The Registry Editor opens a Find dialog box.

2. Type **Paint.Picture** in the "Find what" box, remove the check marks from the Values and Data check boxes, add check marks to the Keys and "Match whole string only" check boxes (if necessary), click **Find Next**, and then wait for the result. See Figure 9-26. By limiting the search to just the keys with an exact match, you speed up your search for this subkey.

Figure 9-26   SEARCHING FOR THE PAINT.PICTURE CLASS-DEFINITION SUBKEY

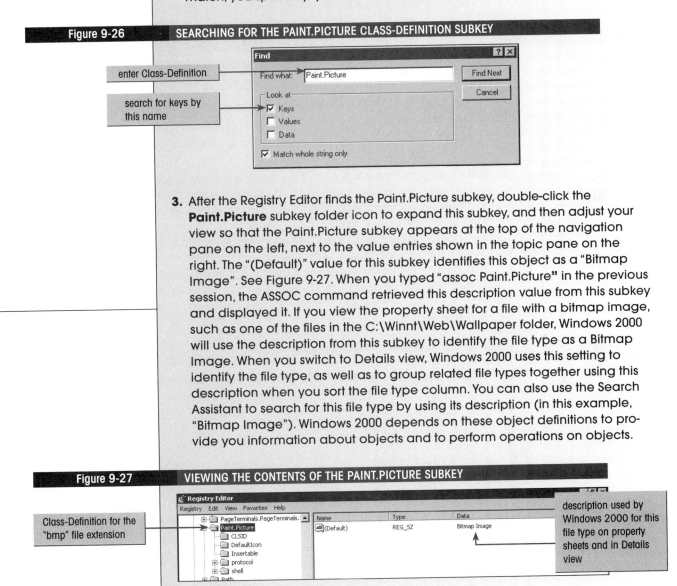

enter Class-Definition

search for keys by this name

3. After the Registry Editor finds the Paint.Picture subkey, double-click the **Paint.Picture** subkey folder icon to expand this subkey, and then adjust your view so that the Paint.Picture subkey appears at the top of the navigation pane on the left, next to the value entries shown in the topic pane on the right. The "(Default)" value for this subkey identifies this object as a "Bitmap Image". See Figure 9-27. When you typed "assoc Paint.Picture" in the previous session, the ASSOC command retrieved this description value from this subkey and displayed it. If you view the property sheet for a file with a bitmap image, such as one of the files in the C:\Winnt\Web\Wallpaper folder, Windows 2000 will use the description from this subkey to identify the file type as a Bitmap Image. When you switch to Details view, Windows 2000 uses this setting to identify the file type, as well as to group related file types together using this description when you sort the file type column. You can also use the Search Assistant to search for this file type by using its description (in this example, "Bitmap Image"). Windows 2000 depends on these object definitions to provide you information about objects and to perform operations on objects.

Figure 9-27   VIEWING THE CONTENTS OF THE PAINT.PICTURE SUBKEY

Class-Definition for the "bmp" file extension

description used by Windows 2000 for this file type on property sheets and in Details view

4. Click the **DefaultIcon** subkey in the navigation pane on the left. The topic pane on the right shows the name of the program file associated with this file type. See Figure 9-28. Various types of files, including executable files with the "exe" file extension, dynamic link library files with the "dll" file extension, and icon files with the "ico" file extension, contain one or more icons within the program file. You can choose which file type you want to use. On the computer used for this figure, Mspaint.exe (the Windows 2000 Paint program) is associated with this file type. The "1" after the path indicates that the file icon used for a Bitmap Image file is the second icon in the Mspaint.exe file. Since computers commonly start counting with the number 0 instead of the number 1, the first icon is 0, the second icon is 1, etc.

Figure 9-28   VIEWING INFORMATION ON THE DEFAULT ICON FOR BITMAP IMAGE FILES

5. In the navigation pane, double-click the **shell** subkey, double-click the **open** subkey, click the **command** subkey. If necessary, double-click the vertical borders between each column in the topic pane on the right so you can see all the information in the Data column. Below the shell key in the navigation pane, the Registry Editor lists subkeys that represent different actions that you can perform on this type of object: open, print, and printto (for "print to"). See Figure 9-29. The open and print options are displayed on the shortcut menu when you right-click a bitmap image file icon. The printto subkey provides Windows 2000 with information on how to handle this type of file when you drag and drop it on a printer icon.

Figure 9-29   VIEWING THE COMMAND FOR THE OPEN ACTION

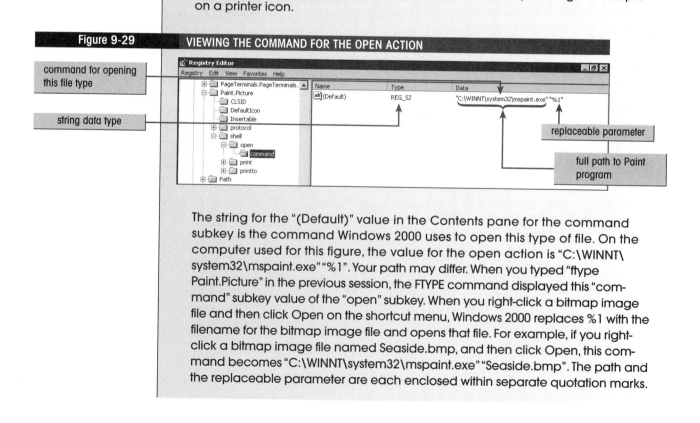

The string for the "(Default)" value in the Contents pane for the command subkey is the command Windows 2000 uses to open this type of file. On the computer used for this figure, the value for the open action is "C:\WINNT\system32\mspaint.exe" "%1". Your path may differ. When you typed "ftype Paint.Picture" in the previous session, the FTYPE command displayed this "command" subkey value of the "open" subkey. When you right-click a bitmap image file and then click Open on the shortcut menu, Windows 2000 replaces %1 with the filename for the bitmap image file and opens that file. For example, if you right-click a bitmap image file named Seaside.bmp, and then click Open, this command becomes "C:\WINNT\system32\mspaint.exe" "Seaside.bmp". The path and the replaceable parameter are each enclosed within separate quotation marks.

6. In the navigation pane on the left, double-click the **print** subkey folder icon, and then click the **command** subkey folder icon below the print subkey. The value assigned to the print action is "C:\WINNT\system32\mspaint.exe" /p "%1". See Figure 9-30. This command is similar to the one for opening a Bitmap Image file, except the /p switch instructs Paint to print the contents of the file you select. Your path may differ.

| Figure 9-30 | VIEWING THE COMMAND FOR THE PRINT ACTION |

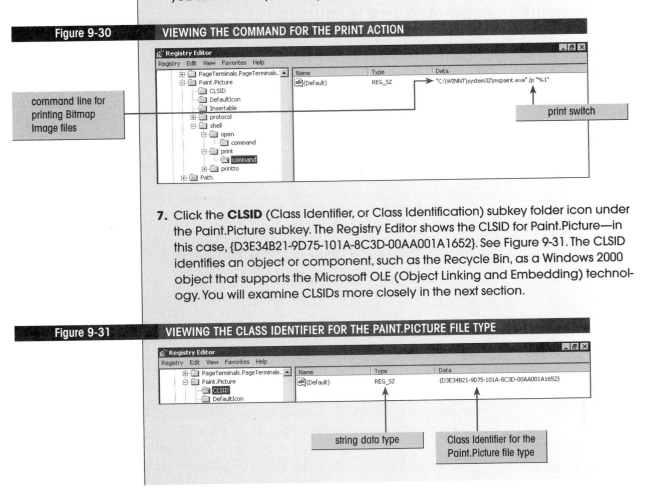

7. Click the **CLSID** (Class Identifier, or Class Identification) subkey folder icon under the Paint.Picture subkey. The Registry Editor shows the CLSID for Paint.Picture—in this case, {D3E34B21-9D75-101A-8C3D-00AA001A1652}. See Figure 9-31. The CLSID identifies an object or component, such as the Recycle Bin, as a Windows 2000 object that supports the Microsoft OLE (Object Linking and Embedding) technology. You will examine CLSIDs more closely in the next section.

| Figure 9-31 | VIEWING THE CLASS IDENTIFIER FOR THE PAINT.PICTURE FILE TYPE |

You can use the same strategy and approach to locate similar types of information on other types of registered files.

REFERENCE WINDOW   **RW**

Tracing Information on Registered File Types

- Open a Command Prompt window, type REGEDIT, and then press Enter. Or, from the Start menu, click Run, type REGEDIT in the Open box, and then press Enter.
- To locate the key for the file extension of a specific type of file (such as ".bmp"), click Edit on the menu bar, click Find, and then view the name of the Class-Definition subkey for the "(Default)" value in the topic pane.
- To locate the key with the same name as the Class-Definition subkey, click Edit on the menu bar, click Find, and then double-click that subkey to view information on the type of object and its subkeys.
- Close the Registry Editor.

If you open a folder window, such as My Documents, select Tools on the menu bar, select Folder Options, and then select the File Types property sheet in the Folder Options dialog box. Windows 2000 lists the names of all registered file types and provides the same type of information as shown in the Registry subkeys for file types. As you've seen earlier, it is easier to find this information using the ASSOC and FTYPE commands.

Viewing Information on Class Identifiers

To help you become familiar with the use of Class Identifiers for other types of objects, Isabel wants to show you how to locate the Class Identifier for the Recycle Bin.

Windows 2000 assigns CLSIDs or Class Identifiers to system objects, such as My Computer, Network Neighborhood, and the Recycle Bin. You can find the Class Identifier for these objects in the Registry's HKEY_CLASSES_ROOT key. To view or change properties of these objects, you need to work with Class Identifiers in the Registry. In some cases, the only way to change a property of a system object may be via the Registry.

To search for a specific type of object, like the Recycle Bin, you can search for "Recycle Bin", or you can search for part of the CLSID for the Recycle Bin (if you already know this value) since each object has its own unique CLSID. The CLSID for the Recycle Bin is {645FF040-5081-101B-9F08-00AA002F954E}.

To locate the Class Identifier for the Recycle Bin:

1. Press the **Home** key to go back to the top of the Registry. If My Computer is not highlighted, click **My Computer**. Your search will now start from this point in the Registry.

2. Click **Edit**, click **Find**, type **{645FF** in the "Find what" box, remove the check marks from the "Match whole string only," Values, and Data check boxes (if necessary), add a check mark to the Keys check box (if necessary), click **Find Next**, and then wait for the result. The Registry Editor finds the subkey for the Recycle Bin, {645FF040-5081-101B-9F08-00AA002F954E}. In the topic pane, the Registry Editor identifies this key as the Class Identifier for the Recycle Bin (note the "(Default)" value). See Figure 9-32. The InfoTip value shows the text that is displayed in the ToolTip when you hover over the Recycle Bin in Web style. If you want to change the message for this ToolTip, double-click the value entry's name in the topic pane, and then, in the Edit String dialog box, either edit the text for the ToolTip value data or replace it with text of your own choosing.

| Figure 9-32 | VIEWING SETTINGS IN THE CLASS IDENTIFIER SUBKEY FOR THE RECYCLE BIN |

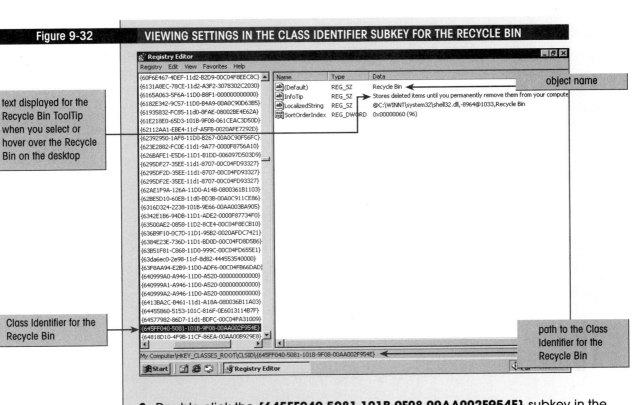

text displayed for the Recycle Bin ToolTip when you select or hover over the Recycle Bin on the desktop

Class Identifier for the Recycle Bin

object name

path to the Class Identifier for the Recycle Bin

3. Double-click the **{645FF040-5081-101B-9F08-00AA002F954E}** subkey in the navigation pane (the one with the open folder icon), and then click the **DefaultIcon** subkey in the left pane. The "(Default)" value entry name identifies the full path and name of the file (shell 32.dll) that contains the icon that Windows 2000 uses to represent the current status of the Recycle Bin. See Figure 9-33. The Empty value entry name likewise points to the icon for an empty Recycle Bin. The value entry name Full identifies the icon to use when the Recycle Bin contains deleted files. The values 31 and 32 represent the location of the icon in shell32.dll that Windows uses to represent the status of the Recycle Bin (empty or full). On the computer used for this figure, the Recycle Bin is currently empty, so Windows 2000 uses the icon specified by the Empty value. On your computer, you may not see the full path, but rather just the reference to shell32.dll.

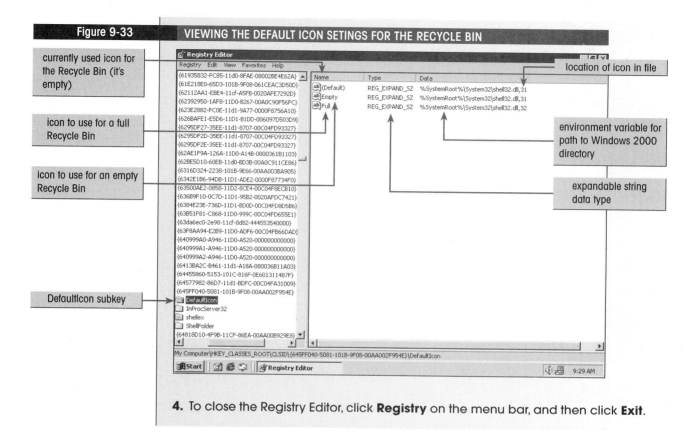

Figure 9-33   VIEWING THE DEFAULT ICON SETTINGS FOR THE RECYCLE BIN

currently used icon for the Recycle Bin (it's empty)

location of icon in file

icon to use for a full Recycle Bin

environment variable for path to Windows 2000 directory

icon to use for an empty Recycle Bin

expandable string data type

DefaultIcon subkey

4. To close the Registry Editor, click **Registry** on the menu bar, and then click **Exit**.

Figure 9-34 lists the CLSIDs for objects commonly found on a Windows 2000 computer. You can use these class IDs to locate the subkey in the Registry for the object so that you can customize your computer.

Figure 9-34   CLASS IDENTIFIERS FOR COMMONLY USED SYSTEM OBJECTS

OBJECT	CLASS ID
ActiveDesktop	{75048700-EF1F-11D0-9888-006097DEACF9}
Briefcase	{85BBD920-42A0-1069-A2E4-08002B30309D}
Control Panel	{21EC2020-3AEA-1069-A2DD-08002B30309D}
Desktop	{00021400-0000-0000-C000-000000000046}
Internet Explorer	{871C5380-42A0-1069-A2EA-08002B30309D}
My Computer	{20D04FE0-3AEA-1069-A2D8-08002B30309D}
My Documents Folder	{450D8FBA-AD25-11D0-98A8-0800361B1103}
My Network Places	{208D2C60-3AEA-1069-A2D7-08002B30309D}
Printers Folder	{2227A280-3AEA-1069-A2DE-08002B30309D}
Recycle Bin	{645FF040-5081-101B-9F08-00AA002F954E}
Scheduled Tasks	{D6277990-4C6A-11CF-8D87-00AA0060F5BF}

Figure 9-34	CLASS IDENTIFIERS FOR COMMONLY USED SYSTEM OBJECTS (CONTINUED)

OBJECT	CLASS ID
Shortcut	{00021401-0000-0000-C000-000000000046}
Start Menu	{4622AD11-FF23-11d0-8D34-00A0C90F2719}
SysTray	{35CEC8A3-2BE6-11D2-8773-92E220524153}
The Internet	{3DC7A020-0ACD-11CF-A9BB-00AA004AE837}

REFERENCE WINDOW   **RW**

Locating Information on Class Identifiers:

- Open a Command Prompt window, type REGEDIT, and then press Enter. Or, from the Start menu, select Run, type REGEDIT in the Open box, and then press Enter.
- Click Edit on the menu bar, click Find, type part of the CLSID for the object you want to find (you need to know the object's CLSID), remove the check marks from the "Match whole string only," Values, and Data check boxes, add a check mark to the Keys check box, and then click Find. Or, if necessary, expand the HKEY_CLASSES_ROOT key, scroll until you locate the CLSID subkey, and then click the CLSID for the object you want to examine.

As you select and examine subkeys for registered file types and objects, you will discover that you are already familiar with some or many of the settings, because you access and work with these settings using Windows 2000 tools, property sheets, and dialog boxes, as well as commands in the Command Prompt window.

Editing the Registry

After discussing features of the Command Prompt environment with Isabel, you discover that you can change the default color settings for the Command Prompt window by editing the Registry. She also notes that you can simplify the process for entering directory names in commands by enabling the Tab key to complete directory names. After you start to type a directory name, you can press the Tab key and let the command interpreter locate and complete the directory name, thereby saving typing. (UNIX command interpreters typically contain this feature.)

To make these changes, you have to locate the correct subkeys in the Registry and then change the existing values for those value entries. Because changes to the Registry can adversely affect the performance of a computer, you must be careful when you change it. In a computer lab, the network administrator and technical support staff will more than likely restrict access to the Registry so unauthorized users cannot modify the configuration of the network connection and potentially cause problems with that computer and the network itself. If this is the case in your situation, or if you are working on your own computer but prefer to wait until you are more familiar with the process for changing a Registry setting, then read, but do not keystroke, the following steps.

If you decide to keystroke the next set of steps, make sure you have the necessary backups you would need to restore your entire computer system. Also make sure you have a recent copy of the Windows 2000 Setup Disks and the Emergency Repair Disk, as well as a recent backup of the Registry. If you decide to edit the Registry on your computer and then you run into a problem, you can boot your computer with the Windows 2000 Setup Disks, and restore the Registry with your Emergency Repair Disk.

Locating the Correct Registry Key

Isabel reminds you that you can use either the 32-bit version of the Registry Editor (Regedt32) or the 16-bit version (Regedit) to edit settings in the Registry; however, as noted earlier, Microsoft recommends that you use the 16-bit version so you do not inadvertently modify security and user settings. After opening the Registry, the first step is to locate the correct subkeys that contain the settings you want to change. Before you can edit the Registry, you must know the correct name and path to those subkeys. You also have to know the name of the values that you want to edit and, if they are not present, how to add them to the Registry. You also have to know the settings that you are going to assign to those values. Many articles in computer magazines, online newsletters, and reference books on Windows 2000, as well as the Microsoft Online Support Web site and other Web sites, provide you with step-by-step details on how to change the Registry so you can customize or troubleshoot your computer.

To change default color settings and also enable support for the use of the Tab key in completing directory names and filenames, you have to make changes to two different value entries in the Command Processor subkey under the HKEY_CURRENT_USER key. The complete path to this subkey is "My Computer\HKEY_CURRENT_USER\Software\ Microsoft\Command Processor".

To locate the Command Processor subkey:

1. From the Start menu, select Run, type **regedit** in the Open box, press **Enter**, maximize the **Registry Editor** window, and then, if necessary, scroll up and to the left to select **My Computer** at the top of the Registry tree (the beginning of your path).

2. Search for the subkey using the following steps:

   a. Click **Edit** on the menu bar.
   b. Click **Find**.
   c. Type **Command Processor** in the "Find what" text box.
   d. Add a **check mark** to the Keys check box in the "Look at" section (if necessary).
   e. Delete **check marks** from the Values and Data check boxes in the "Look at" section (if necessary).
   f. Add a **check mark** to the "Match whole string only" check box (if necessary).
   g. Click **Find Next**, and wait for the result. The Registry Editor locates and highlights the Command Processor subkey.

3. If necessary, double-click the **borders** between the Name, Type, and Data columns in the topic pane on the right so you can see the settings for the value entries in this subkey.

4. Check the path on the status bar to verify that you have found the correct key. The path should read "My Computer\HKEY_CURRENT_USER\Software\Microsoft\ Command Processor". Figure 9-35 shows the Command Processor subkey and its values.

   TROUBLE? If the path to your subkey is different than that shown in this step and Figure 9-35, then repeat Steps 1-4 in this section to locate the correct subkey. If you cannot locate this subkey, ask your instructor or technical support staff for assistance.

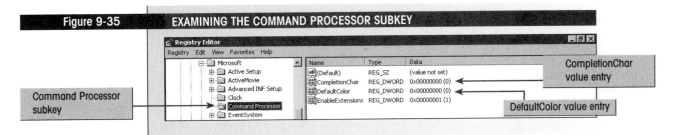

Figure 9-35   **EXAMINING THE COMMAND PROCESSOR SUBKEY**

REFERENCE WINDOW   **RW**

Locating a Registry Key

- Open a Command Prompt window, type REGEDIT, and then press Enter. Or, from the Start menu, click Run, type REGEDIT in the Open box, and then press Enter.
- If necessary, click any subkey in the navigation pane on the left, and then press the Home key to return to My Computer at the top of the Registry tree (the beginning of your path).
- Click Edit on the menu bar, click Find, type the name of the Registry key you want to locate in the Find what box, add a check mark to the Keys check box in the "Look at" section (if necessary), remove check marks from the Values and Data check boxes in the "Look at" section (if necessary), add a check mark to the "Match whole string only" check box (if necessary), click Find Next, and wait for the result.
- If you already know the path to the subkey that contains the value entry you want to change, then you can check the path on the status bar to verify that you have found the correct key.

It is important that you know the path to the key that you want to change and that you verify this path after you locate the key. Microsoft Support, online tips, magazines, and newsletters may provide you the path to the subkey that contains the value entry you want to change.

Changing a Value for a Registry Key

Isabel notes that the settings you want to change are the ones for the DefaultColor and CompletionChar value entries.

There are three basic data types used in the Registry. As noted earlier when you examined the .bmp subkey, a string value is a text entry, such as Paint.Picture (a Class-Definition, or FileType), Bitmap Image (an object description), mspaint.exe,1 (a program name that also identifies the position of the default icon within the program file), "Stores deleted items until you permanently remove them from your computer" (the ToolTip text for the Recycle Bin, shown without the quotation marks), or %SystemRoot%\System32\shell32.dll,31 (a path to a program file and an icon within that program file). String values are identified using the REG_SZ (text string), REG_EXPAND_SZ (an expandable text string with a variable), or REG_MULTI_SZ (a multiple-line text string) data types. An **expandable string** contains text but it also contains a reference to a variable value, such as %SystemRoot% (the environment variable with the path to the Windows 2000 directory).

The second type of value is a binary value. Binary value entries are identified as REG_BINARY, and the value data is represented using a code in binary (a base-2 number system that uses combinations of 0s and 1s to encode data) or in hexadecimal (a base-16 number system that uses the digits 0 through 9 and the uppercase and lowercase letters A through F to encode data). An example of a binary value is 00 00 00 00, the value data for the EnableAutodial feature under the Internet Settings subkey.

The third type of value is a DWORD, which stands for "double word." It is identified in the Registry as a REG_DWORD data type (as, for example, the value data for the DefaultColor and CompletionChar value entries). A **double word** consists of two binary words of 16 bits, but it is expressed in decimal form (base 10). A DWORD, such as 0x00000409 (1033), which identifies the language version for Microsoft Office 2000 (in this case, English), is represented as a four-byte hexadecimal sequence followed by the decimal equivalent in parentheses.

Isabel recommends that you change the default color settings for your Command Prompt window first, since you are already familiar with specifying color attributes for the COLOR command, and since it is also the simpler of the two types of changes you are going to make.

To change the Data value for the DefaultColor value entry:

1. Note that the current value of the DefaultColor value entry is 0x00000000 (0).

2. Single-click the **DefaultColor** value entry name in the topic pane on the right, click **Edit** on the menu bar, and then click **Modify**. As shown in Figure 9-36, the Registry Editor then displays an Edit DWORD Value dialog box with the Value name "(DefaultColor)", the Value data (0), and the Base (how you want to represent the value), which in this case is Hexadecimal.

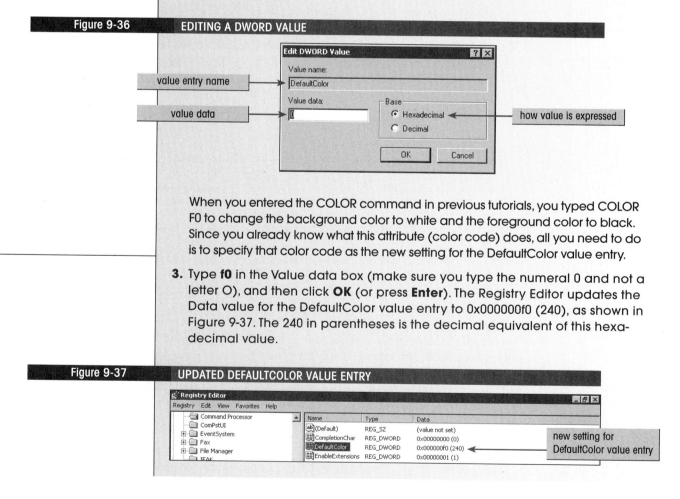

Figure 9-36   EDITING A DWORD VALUE

When you entered the COLOR command in previous tutorials, you typed COLOR F0 to change the background color to white and the foreground color to black. Since you already know what this attribute (color code) does, all you need to do is to specify that color code as the new setting for the DefaultColor value entry.

3. Type **f0** in the Value data box (make sure you type the numeral 0 and not a letter O), and then click **OK** (or press **Enter**). The Registry Editor updates the Data value for the DefaultColor value entry to 0x000000f0 (240), as shown in Figure 9-37. The 240 in parentheses is the decimal equivalent of this hexadecimal value.

Figure 9-37   UPDATED DEFAULTCOLOR VALUE ENTRY

4. With the Registry Editor window still open, open a **Command Prompt** window. Note that the Command Prompt window automatically has a white background with a black foreground (for text). See Figure 9-38. Windows 2000 immediately applied the change to your computer. This change applies only to your local user account profile. Any other users who log on to your computer with different user names will still see a black background and light gray foreground (for text) when they open Command Prompt windows.

| Figure 9-38 | NEWLY OPENED COMMAND PROMPT WITH NEW COLOR SETTINGS |

```
Command Prompt
Microsoft Windows 2000 [Version 5.00.2195]
(C) Copyright 1985-1999 Microsoft Corp.

C:\>_
```

5. Close the **Command Prompt** window, but keep the Registry Editor window open for the next change you will make.

Whenever you open a Command Prompt window, Windows 2000 will always use the new setting that you specified in the Registry, so you no longer have to enter the COLOR command manually and change the background and foreground colors before you start working.

Now that you're familiar with how to make a simple change to the Registry, using a value with which you are already familiar from working with the COLOR command at the command prompt, you are ready to make another change that is slightly more complicated—the setting for the CompletionChar value entry.

Notice that the setting for the CompletionChar value entry is 0x00000000 (0). The value in parentheses (0) for the REG_DWORD 0x00000000 (0) is the decimal equivalent of the hexadecimal value assigned to the CompletionChar value entry. The ASCII code for the Tab key is the number 9; therefore you have to change the decimal value of the CompletionChar value entry to 9 to enable the feature for completing directory names and filenames with the Tab key.

To change the Data value for the CompletionChar value entry:

1. Double-click the **CompletionChar** value entry name in the topic pane on the right. The Registry Editor then displays an Edit DWORD Value dialog box, as shown in Figure 9-39. The dialog box shows the Value name (CompletionChar), the Value data (0), and the Base (the numeric base in which the value is represented); in this case it is Hexadecimal.

| Figure 9-39 | CHANGING A DWORD VALUE |

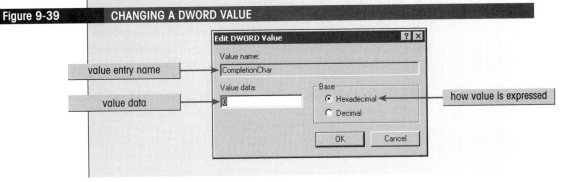

2. Type **9** in the Value data box, and then click **OK** (or press **Enter**). The Registry Editor updates the Data value for the CompletionChar value entry to 0x00000009 (9), as shown in Figure 9-40.

Figure 9-40   UPDATED COMPLETIONCHAR VALUE ENTRY

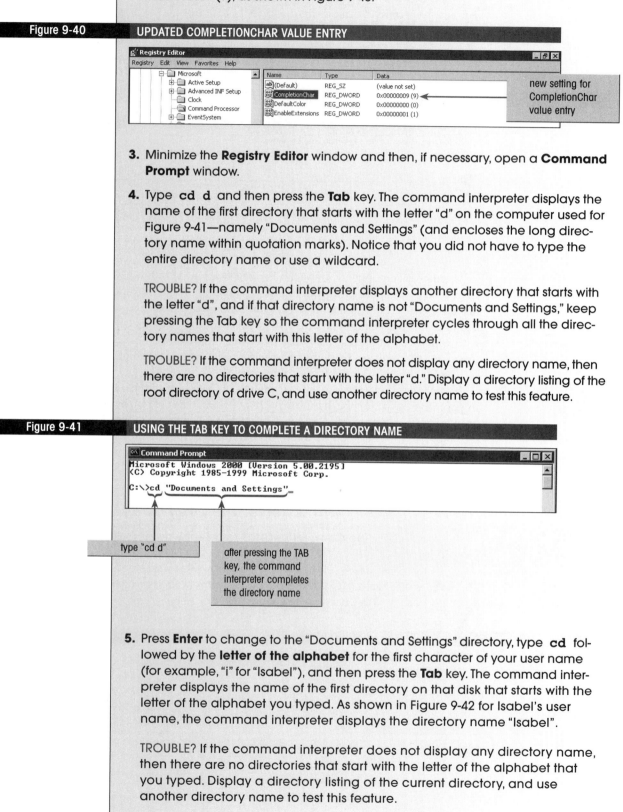

3. Minimize the **Registry Editor** window and then, if necessary, open a **Command Prompt** window.

4. Type **cd d** and then press the **Tab** key. The command interpreter displays the name of the first directory that starts with the letter "d" on the computer used for Figure 9-41—namely "Documents and Settings" (and encloses the long directory name within quotation marks). Notice that you did not have to type the entire directory name or use a wildcard.

TROUBLE? If the command interpreter displays another directory that starts with the letter "d", and if that directory name is not "Documents and Settings," keep pressing the Tab key so the command interpreter cycles through all the directory names that start with this letter of the alphabet.

TROUBLE? If the command interpreter does not display any directory name, then there are no directories that start with the letter "d." Display a directory listing of the root directory of drive C, and use another directory name to test this feature.

Figure 9-41   USING THE TAB KEY TO COMPLETE A DIRECTORY NAME

5. Press **Enter** to change to the "Documents and Settings" directory, type **cd** followed by the **letter of the alphabet** for the first character of your user name (for example, "i" for "Isabel"), and then press the **Tab** key. The command interpreter displays the name of the first directory on that disk that starts with the letter of the alphabet you typed. As shown in Figure 9-42 for Isabel's user name, the command interpreter displays the directory name "Isabel".

TROUBLE? If the command interpreter does not display any directory name, then there are no directories that start with the letter of the alphabet that you typed. Display a directory listing of the current directory, and use another directory name to test this feature.

Figure 9-42   USING THE TAB KEY TO COMPLETE A SUBDIRECTORY NAME

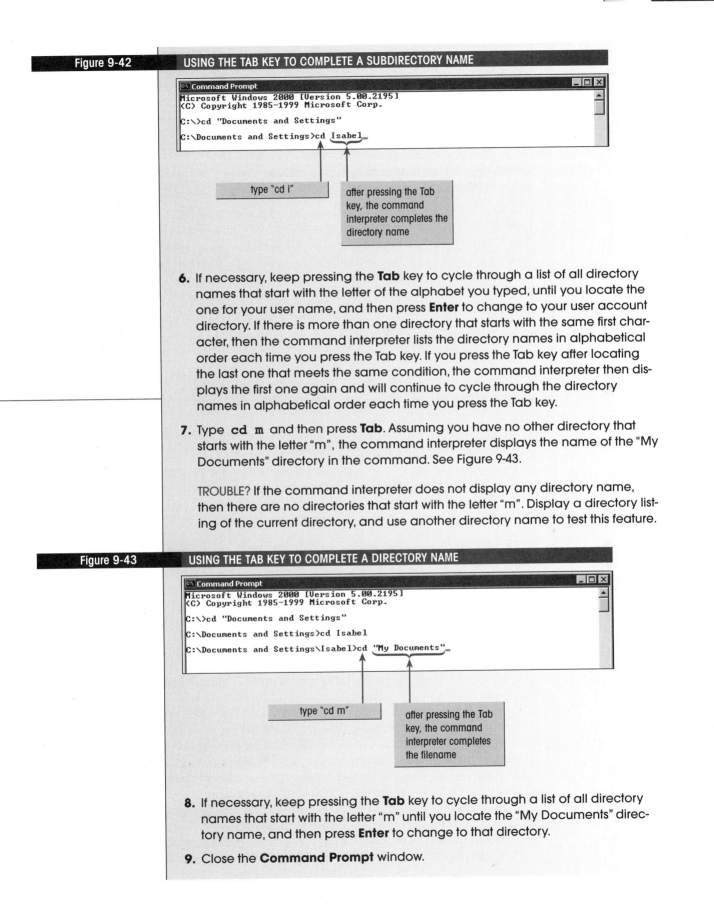

```
Command Prompt                                              _ □ ×
Microsoft Windows 2000 [Version 5.00.2195]
(C) Copyright 1985-1999 Microsoft Corp.

C:\>cd "Documents and Settings"

C:\Documents and Settings>cd Isabel_
```

type "cd i"

after pressing the Tab key, the command interpreter completes the directory name

6. If necessary, keep pressing the **Tab** key to cycle through a list of all directory names that start with the letter of the alphabet you typed, until you locate the one for your user name, and then press **Enter** to change to your user account directory. If there is more than one directory that starts with the same first character, then the command interpreter lists the directory names in alphabetical order each time you press the Tab key. If you press the Tab key after locating the last one that meets the same condition, the command interpreter then displays the first one again and will continue to cycle through the directory names in alphabetical order each time you press the Tab key.

7. Type **cd m** and then press **Tab**. Assuming you have no other directory that starts with the letter "m", the command interpreter displays the name of the "My Documents" directory in the command. See Figure 9-43.

TROUBLE? If the command interpreter does not display any directory name, then there are no directories that start with the letter "m". Display a directory listing of the current directory, and use another directory name to test this feature.

Figure 9-43   USING THE TAB KEY TO COMPLETE A DIRECTORY NAME

```
Command Prompt                                              _ □ ×
Microsoft Windows 2000 [Version 5.00.2195]
(C) Copyright 1985-1999 Microsoft Corp.

C:\>cd "Documents and Settings"

C:\Documents and Settings>cd Isabel

C:\Documents and Settings\Isabel>cd "My Documents"_
```

type "cd m"

after pressing the Tab key, the command interpreter completes the filename

8. If necessary, keep pressing the **Tab** key to cycle through a list of all directory names that start with the letter "m" until you locate the "My Documents" directory name, and then press **Enter** to change to that directory.

9. Close the **Command Prompt** window.

This Tab completion character feature also works with filenames. Type a command that operates on files, followed by the first character of the filename, and then press the Tab key. The command interpreter will display the first filename that starts with the letter of the alphabet you type. Each time you press the Tab key, it will list the next filename (in alphabetical order).

You have successfully made a change to the Registry—a change that customizes and simplifies the use of the command-line environment.

REFERENCE WINDOW   **RW**

Changing a Setting in the Registry

■ Open a Command Prompt window, type REGEDIT, and then press Enter. Or, on the Start menu, click Run, type REGEDIT in the Open box, and then press Enter.

■ If necessary, select My Computer at the top of the Registry tree (the beginning of your path) in the navigation pane on the left.

■ Click Edit on the menu bar, click Find, type the name of the Registry key you want to locate in the "Find what" box, add a check mark to the Keys check box in the "Look at" section (if necessary), remove check marks from the Values and Data check boxes in the "Look at" section (if necessary), add a check mark to the "Match whole string only" check box (if necessary), click Find Next, and then wait for the result.

■ Check the path on the status bar to verify that you have found the correct key.

■ Click the value entry name in the topic pane on the right, click Edit on the menu bar, and then click Modify.

■ In the dialog box for changing the value for a value entry, enter the setting you want to use in the Value data box, and then click OK (or press Enter).

■ Close the Registry Editor. If necessary, restart your computer, or log off and then log on again, to apply the change to your computer.

Depending on the type of change that you make to the Registry, you might need to restart your computer, or just log off and then log back on for Windows 2000 to apply the change to your computer.

Adding and Removing Registry Keys and Value Entries

If you need to add a new subkey to the Registry, or a new value entry to an existing key, first locate and select the key below which you want to add a new key or new value entry. For example, if you want to add a new key or new value entry below the Command Processor subkey, you would first locate and select the Command Processor subkey. Then select the Edit menu, point to New, and indicate whether you want to add a new key under the currently selected subkey or add a string value, binary value, or DWORD value in the currently selected subkey. If you add a new key, then the Registry Editor will create the key, name it "New Key #1," and then highlight this name so that you can type the name you want to use. If you create a new value entry, the Registry Editor creates a new value entry with the name "New Value #1," assigns a default setting for the Data value, and then highlights the value entry name so that you can type the name you want to use. If you are adding a new value entry, then you would step through the process that you used earlier to modify the setting for a value entry. During this process, check, double-check, and triple-check all the changes you make. Windows may apply the change immediately, or you may need to restart your computer for them to take effect.

As an example, you may want to add an option to the Windows Explorer shortcut menu to open a Command Prompt window by right-clicking a directory folder. To make this change, you would:

- open the Registry Editor and locate the HKEY_CLASSES_ROOT\Directory\shell subkey

- before you make a change, back up this subkey by exporting this branch of the Registry to a registration file on disk

- create a new key named "Command Prompt" (without the quotes and with the required space between the two words)

- create a new key named "command" (again without the quotes) under the new "Command Prompt" subkey, and then

- store the string "c:\winnt\system32\cmd.exe" (again without the quotes, and substituting your System Root directory for "c:\winnt", if necessary) in the "(Default)" key

When you open a Windows Explorer or a My Computer window and right-click on a directory folder, the shortcut menu will now contain a menu item named "Command Prompt." After you select "Command Prompt", Windows opens a Command Prompt window and automatically places you in that directory, so you no longer need to change directories at the command prompt.

If you need to remove a Registry key or value entry, you first locate and select the subkey or value entry that you want to remove, press the Delete key or click Delete on the Edit menu, and then confirm that you want to delete the subkey or value.

Restoring Your Computer

If you are working in a computer lab, or if you want to restore your own computer, you will need to delete the Registry folder and registration file in the "My Documents" folder that you created in the first session. If you decide that you want to keep the Registry folder and registration file on your computer, then you can skip the steps for removing this folder and file. You will also need to restore the default setting for the CompletionChar and DefaultColor value entries.

To restore your computer:

1. Open the "**My Documents**" folder, select and delete the **Registry Backup** folder with the registration file, and then empty the **Recycle Bin**.

2. If necessary, select **Run** on the Start menu, type **regedit** in the Open box, and then click **OK** (or press **Enter**) to open the Registry Editor.

3. If the CompletionChar value entry under the Command Processor subkey is not already highlighted:

   a. Select a **subkey** in the navigation pane on the right.
   b. Press the **Home** key, or select **My Computer** in the navigation pane on the left.
   c. Click **Edit** on the menu bar.
   d. Click **Find**.
   e. Type **Command Processor** in the "Find what" box.
   f. Add a **check mark** to the Keys check box in the Look at section (if necessary).
   g. Remove **check marks** from the Values and Data check boxes in the "Look at" section (if necessary).
   h. Add a **check mark** to the "Match whole string only" check box (if necessary).

i. Click **Find Next**.

j. After the Registry Editor locates and highlights the Command Processor subkey, check the path on the status bar to verify that you have found the correct key.

The path should read:
"My Computer\HKEY_CURRENT_USER\Software\Microsoft\Command Processor".

4. If necessary, single-click the **CompletionChar** value entry name in the topic pane on the right, click **Edit** on the menu bar, and then click **Modify**. The Registry Editor then displays an Edit DWORD Value dialog box for this value entry.

5. Type **0** (a zero, not the letter "O") in the Value data box, and then click **OK** (or press **Enter**).

6. If necessary, single-click the **DefaultColor** value entry name in the topic pane on the right, click **Edit** on the menu bar, and then click **Modify**. The Registry Editor then displays an "Edit DWORD Value" dialog box for this value entry.

7. Type **0** (a zero, not the letter "O") in the Value data box, and click **OK** (or press **Enter**).

8. Close the **Registry Editor**.

Isabel recommends that you implement this change to the Registry on other computers at SolarWinds, so employees who use the command line environment will have standard color settings and can enter commands that specify folders and files more quickly and easily, and thereby improve their productivity.

Session 9.2 QUICK CHECK

1. The "H" in HKEY stands for _____.

2. Each setting in a Registry subkey, such as the Command Processor subkey, is called a(n) _____.

3. The REG_SZ, REG_EXPAND_SZ, and REG_MULTI_SZ data types represent _____.

4. In the Registry, Paint.Picture is an example of a(n) _____.

5. If you want to change a setting for a system object, such as My Computer, My Network Places, and the Recycle Bin in the Registry, you need to know the object's _____.

6. In the Data value %SystemRoot%\System32\shell32.dll,3 for the DefaultIcon subkey under the Directory subkey, 3 identifies the location of the _____ in the program file.

7. In the Data value Word.RTF.8 for the "(Default)" value entry in the .rtf subkey, Word.RTF.8 identifies the _____ assigned to files with the "rtf" file extension.

8. In the Data value %SystemRoot%\system32\NOTEPAD.EXE %1 for the "(Default)" value entry in the command subkey under the open key, %1 is a replaceable parameter that represents a(n) _____.

9. The HKEY_CLASSES_ROOT Registry key contains information on
_____.

10. Each value entry in a Registry key has a(n) _____, _____, and _____.

REVIEW ASSIGNMENTS

Isabel mentions to you that staff members frequently encounter problems when they open files with the "doc" file extension. In certain cases, Windows 2000 opens documents originally produced in WordPad with Microsoft Word instead. Since Microsoft Word is the most commonly used word-processing application at SolarWinds, Isabel recommends that you open the Windows 2000 Registry and examine information on "doc" file associations so you can decide on a course of action for fixing this problem. Isabel also suggests that you use the Registry to customize the Command Prompt window.

As you complete this exercise, answer the questions about the operations you perform so you can submit them to your instructor.

1. Do you have Microsoft Office suite or Microsoft Word installed on your computer? If so, what version of Microsoft Office or Microsoft Word is installed?

2. Make sure you have a recent copy of the Windows 2000 Setup Disks and an Emergency Repair Disk, as well as a recent backup of the Registry.

3. Create a Registry Backup folder on drive C. Open the Registry and export all of its settings to a registration file in the Registry Backup folder.

4. Open the Registry Backup folder and examine the registration file. What is its file size? Assuming Microsoft Word would require approximately 4,200 pages to print a 19 MB registration file, how many pages would you estimate your registration file to be?

5. Open a Command Prompt window, and use the Associate command to identify the file type associated with the "doc" file extension. What file type is defined for the "doc" file extension on your computer?

6. Use the Associate command to view the description for this file type. What description does Windows 2000 use for files with the "doc" file extension?

7. What file type and description does Windows 2000 use and associate with the "dot" file extension?

8. Use the FTYPE command to identify the command line that Windows 2000 uses for opening files with the "doc" file extension. What command line does Windows 2000 use on your computer?

9. What command line does Windows 2000 use for opening files with the "dot" file extension?

10. Open the Regedit Registry Editor from the Command Prompt window.

11. Expand the HKEY_CLASES_ROOT key, and locate and double-click the ".doc" subkey. What is the default Class-Definition for this file type? Is this value a string, binary, or DWORD value?

12. Open the Class-Definition subkey below the doc subkey, and then open the ShellNew subkey. What is the name of the template (or document file type) assigned to the Filename value entry?

13. From the Command Prompt window, use the Directory command and its Subdirectory switch to search your computer for this FileName value. Is there a file by this name stored on your computer? If so, in which directory is it stored?

14. Switch back to the Registry, and use Find on the Edit menu to locate the default Class-Definition subkey that you identified in Step 3 for the ".doc" subkey (not the subkey located below the .doc subkey). You can use the F3 key to continue the search. What is the default string value that Windows 2000 uses to identify this type of file on a property sheet or in a folder listing?

15. Open the shell subkey. What types of actions can you perform on this file type? What is the command assigned to the "(Default)" value entry for creating a new document of this type?

16. Click the key or subkey in the navigation pane on the left, and then press the Home key to select My Computer.

17. Click Edit on the menu bar, click Find, and then in the Find what box, type DefaultColor (one word, no space). In the "Look at" area, remove check marks from the Keys and Data check boxes (if necessary), and add check marks to the Values check box (if necessary). Add a check mark to the "Match whole string only" check box (if necessary), and then click Find Next.

18. After the Registry Editor locates the DefaultColor value entry, check the path on the status bar, and verify that your path is "My Computer\HKEY_CURRENT_USER\Software\Microsoft\Command Processor". As a double-check, the value entries in the topic pane on the right should include the CompletionChar value entry with which you worked in the tutorial.

19. Select the Command Processor subkey in the navigation pane on the left, and use the Export Registry File on the Registry menu to copy the contents of this subkey to a registration file named Command Processor.reg on your Data Disk in drive A.

20. What is the current Data value for the DefaultColor value entry?

21. Double-click the DefaultColor value entry, change the Value data from 0 to b (the letter "b"), and then click OK. What is the new Data value setting for the DefaultColor value entry? (*Note*: To obtain color settings to test, you can use the Help switch with the COLOR command to view the color codes for setting background and foreground colors.)

22. From the Start menu, select Run, and then open a new Command Prompt window. How does this change in the DefaultColor setting change the Command Prompt window?

23. Close the Command Prompt window.

24. Double-click the DefaultColor value entry, change the Value data from b to e (the letter "e"), and then click OK. What is the new Data value setting for the DefaultColor value entry?

25. Open a new Command Prompt window, and describe how this change in the DefaultColor setting changes the Command Prompt window.

26. To restore your computer, double-click the DefaultColor value entry, change the Value data from e to 0 (the number "0"), or to the default setting that you identified in Step 20, and then click OK.

27. Close the Registry Editor.

28. Open a Command Prompt window, and verify that you have restored the Command Prompt window to its default setting.

29. Use the Help switch to view Help information on the COLOR command. When you changed the setting for the DefaultColor value entry in the Registry, what values were you actually entering for the new setting?

30. Close the Command Prompt window.

CASE PROBLEMS

Case 1. Preparing a Handout on File Associations at Fast Track Trainers Most of Fast Track Trainer's corporate customers in St. Paul, Minnesota, have upgraded their computers and purchased new computers with Windows 2000, and they now want to provide customized training for their employees. Samantha Kuehl, Fast Track Trainer's lead training specialist, recently hired you to design and develop a series of workshops for these corporate customers. Because one of the workshops focuses on registered file types, Samantha recommends that you develop a handout that lists information on file types important to individuals who provide technical and troubleshooting support.

1. Open a Command Prompt window.

2. Prepare a table similar to the one shown in Figure 9-44, and use the ASSOC and FTYPE commands to locate information on these file extensions so you can include that information in the table. An example for the "hlp" file extension is shown in the table.

Figure 9-44	IMPORTANT REGISTERED FILE TYPES		
FILE EXTENSION	**FILE TYPE**	**DESCRIPTION**	**COMMAND LINE**
chk			
cmd			
com			
cpl			
csv			
dll			
drv			
dun			
exe			
gif			
hlp	hlpfile	Help File	hlpfile=%SystemRoot%\System32\winhlp32.exe %1
htm			
ico			
inf			

Figure 9-44	IMPORTANT REGISTERED FILE TYPES		
FILE EXTENSION	**FILE TYPE**	**DESCRIPTION**	**COMMAND LINE**
jpg			
lnk			
log			
ocx			
pif			
ppt			
reg			
rtf			
shb			
shs			
sys			
txt			
xls			
zip			

3. Is there any other way you might have found this same information? If so, explain.

4. Submit a copy of the completed table in the format requested by your instructor, either as a printout, on diskette, or by e-mail, along with any other requested documentation.

Case 2. Customizing Folder Shortcut Menus at HiPerform Systems James Everett, the owner of HiPerform Systems in Ipswich, Massachusetts, would like to be able to launch a Command Prompt window from a selected directory folder in Windows Explorer or My Computer, instead of opening a Command Prompt window and then navigating to it. He asks you to change the Registry to add a "Command Prompt" shortcut menu item to Explorer and My Computer, and then create a "Command Prompt.reg" registration file he can use to apply these changes to other computers.

1. Launch Regedit.

2. Navigate to HKEY_CLASSES_ROOT\Directory\shell.

3. Make a backup copy of the HKEY_CLASSES_ROOT\Directory\shell key branch using the Export Registry File function. Save the resulting file as "Default Directory shell.reg" on a blank diskette.

4. Create a new key named "Command Prompt" (without the quotes).

5. Under "Command Prompt", create a new key named "command" (again without the quotes).

6. In the "(Default)" key, store the string "c:\winnt\system32\cmd.exe" (again without the quotes, and substituting your own SystemRoot directory for "c:\winnt", if necessary).

7. Open a Windows Explorer or My Computer window, then right-click on the "Documents and Settings" directory folder. The shortcut menu should contain the item "Command Prompt". If it doesn't, go back and check the contents of the Registry keys you created above, make sure they are correct, and try again.

8. Click "Command Prompt". You should see a Command Prompt window open, titled with the string that you entered for the "(Default)" value entry above. If this doesn't occur, check your Registry keys to make sure they are correct, and try again.

9. In Regedit, export a registry file to your drive A diskette named "Command Prompt.reg" containing the new "HKEY_CLASSES_ROOT\Directory\shell\Command Prompt" subkey branch you created.

10. Remove your "Command Prompt" branch from the Registry.

11. Submit a copy of Command Prompt.reg in the format requested by your instructor, either as a printout, on diskette, or by e-mail, along with any other requested documentation.

Case 3. *Compiling Information from a Registration File at Computer Troubleshooters Unlimited* Miles Biehler at Computer Troubleshooters Unlimited plans to analyze the Windows 2000 Registry to find entries related to the MS-DOS subsystem. He asks you to prepare a list of all entries in the Registry containing the word "dos".

1. If you have not already done so, use Regedit to export a complete backup of the registry.

2. From a Command Prompt window, use the FIND command to locate all lines containing the "dos" string, without regard to uppercase or lowercase, in the registration file. Pipe the command to the SORT filter and redirect the final output into a file named "DOS Registry Entries.txt" on a diskette in drive A.

3. Submit a copy of the "DOS Registry Entries.txt" file and the command line you used to create it in the format requested by your instructor, either as a printout, on diskette, or by e-mail, along with any other requested documentation, including the command line that you used to search the registration file.

Case 4. *Making a Better Command Prompt Shortcut at InTime Troubleshooting* Christopher Heathcote, a small business computer consultant, recently hired you to assist him in his office at InTime Troubleshooting. Christopher asks you to create a Command Prompt shortcut on the desktop to customize the Command Prompt window so it uses black-on-white colors and supports file and directory name completion. He also requests that you describe how to use file and directory completion and the corresponding Registry changes for both functions.

1. Open a Command Prompt window, and use the Help switch to display Help information on the use of the CMD command, which opens the command processor. Examine the Help information for ways in which you can customize the command line when you run CMD.

2. Click the Start button and navigate to the Command Prompt item under Accessories. Right-drag the Command Prompt menu item to the desktop, and then click Copy Here to create a duplicate shortcut.

3. Right-click on your new Command Prompt shortcut, and then click Properties.

4. Change the shortcut's Target command line to add switches to set the colors to black text on a white background, and to enable filename and directory name completion characters.

5. Test your new shortcut, particularly the file and directory completion feature. Make sure control characters for both file and directory completion work as described in the Help text for the CMD command.

6. Describe how to use the control characters, and how to change their corresponding Registry keys, both for filename completion and directory name completion.

7. Submit a copy of the shortcut's Target command line and your description of the file and directory name completion characters and Registry keys in the format requested by your instructor, either as a printout, on diskette, or by e-mail, along with any other requested documentation.

QUICK CHECK ANSWERS

Session 9.1

1. Registry
2. registered
3. Emergency Repair Disk or ERD
4. registration
5. keys, subkeys
6. ASSOC *or* assoc .url
7. FTYPE *or* ftype InternetShortcut
8. ASSOC
9. FTYPE
10. cabinet

Session 9.2

1. Handle
2. value entry
3. strings
4. Class-Definition
5. Class Identifier (or CLSID)
6. icon
7. file type
8. filename
9. registered file types
10. name, data type, and value

In this tutorial you will:

- Examine network concepts and features, and the process for creating a network connection

- View information on network settings, activity, resources, and user accounts

- Map a drive letter to a shared directory

- Share your "My Documents" directory

- Examine the process for creating an Internet connection

- View properties of a dial-up connection

- Work with the TCP/IP commands IPCONFIG, PING, and TRACERT

- Use FTP commands to examine and download files from a Web site

- Create a network connection to an FTP site

CONNECTING
TO NETWORKS AND THE INTERNET

Using Network, TCP/IP, and FTP Commands at SolarWinds

CASE

SolarWinds Unlimited

SolarWinds, like other businesses, relies on a computer network to provide employees with access to the resources they need for their jobs. The network also provides employees with access to the Internet and the World Wide Web so they can communicate both with co-workers located in branch offices and with customers. Isabel Navarro and her staff help employees connect their computers to the network and the Internet, and also provide training on the use of networking features within the graphical user interface, as well as in the Command Prompt environment. Because technology changes so rapidly and employees increasingly need access to new tools for their jobs, Isabel and her staff are constantly improving and upgrading their networking skills.

SESSION 10.1

In this session, you'll examine basic network concepts and features, including the difference between client/server and peer-to-peer networks. You will also examine the process for setting up a peer-to-peer network and then compare the process of viewing and changing network settings using tools in the graphical user interface or commands in a Command Prompt window. You will examine how to create a new network connection with the Make New Connection Wizard. Finally, you will enter network commands that allow you to view information on network resources, map a drive letter to a shared directory, share a directory on a network, and examine information on user accounts.

Introduction to Networks and Networking

Over the past several months, SolarWinds has hired additional technical support staff to provide support for their rapid growth and the ever-increasing needs of their customers. Isabel and her staff set up network connections for new employees so they can access the resources they need for their jobs.

Windows 2000 Professional, like its predecessor Windows NT Workstation 4.0, is a network operating system designed for use in networked business environments. With a network operating system, you can connect your computer to one or more computers, so each computer can share resources such as hardware and software. For example, in a typical college computer lab, computers are networked so students can use any computer in the lab to access the same printer (or printers). If these computers were not networked, then each computer would have to have its own printer (a prohibitive and unnecessary cost), or one computer would have to be devoted exclusively to printing, and students would have to swap stations to print. Another benefit of networking is that users can share directories and files (with the caveat that network administrators routinely apply security settings that limit access to certain directories and files).

If the networked computers and other hardware devices, such as printers, are located within the same general area, then the network is called a **local area network,** or **LAN**. If the networked computers are located in different geographical areas and connected together through some type of telecommunications link, then the network is called a **wide area network**, or **WAN**. The Internet is an example of a wide area network.

Although there are different ways to connect and network computers, the two most common approaches are client/server networks and peer-to-peer networks.

In a **client/server network**, a computer known as the **server** manages the operation of the network, provides access to network resources (such as printers and software) and also can provide files for users. The network operating system on the server maintains network security and verifies user passwords. The other computers on the network are called **clients**. They access and use resources provided by the server.

Client/server networks rely on network administrators to set up, configure, monitor, and troubleshoot the network. Corporations and businesses commonly use client/server networks to manage network resources reliably, create a common security database, and support hundreds or thousands of users. To set up a computer as a Windows 2000 server for a client/server network, you must use either the Windows 2000 Server or Advanced Server editions.

In contrast, a **peer-to-peer network**, or **workgroup**, is a small network that does not require a central server and usually consists of two to ten computers located within the same general area. Each computer functions as a peer or equal on the network, communicates with all the other computers, and accesses and uses resources designated as shared resources (such as printers, drives, directories, and files). Each computer can also act as a server, sharing specified resources on the network. Depending on the user's level of permission, a specific user may or may not be able to make changes to shared resources. Peer-to-peer networks are simpler, but less secure, than client/server networks. Nevertheless, peer-to-peer networks are more useful and more common in smaller businesses, including home-based businesses, because of their simplicity, ease of setup, and lower cost (no server required, a less expensive operating system, and fewer administrative personnel needed) for both initial setup and ongoing maintenance. You cannot use Windows 2000 Professional as a server in a client/server network, but you can set it up as a server sharing its resources in a peer-to-peer network.

Windows 2000 Server and Advanced Server support more command line functions than does Windows 2000 Professional; however, this tutorial covers only the Command Line functions used by Windows 2000 Professional in peer-to-peer networks.

Peer-to-Peer Network Setup

To create a peer-to-peer network, you must install a network adapter in each computer. The **network adapter**, or **Network Interface Card (NIC)**, is an add-in card that provides a physical interface and circuitry that enable a computer to access a network and exchange data. Before you connect the computers together by cable, you have to decide which type of physical layout you want to use for the network. One common approach is to connect each computer to a **hub**, a hardware device that contains a port for connecting each computer on the network. Once data arrives from a computer to its port on the hub, the hub transmits a copy of the data to the other ports so the data is available to the other computers on the network.

After installing network adapters, deciding on the network configuration, and cabling the computers together, you will need to log on under an account with Administrator privileges and configure the network connection for each computer. Then you install a protocol so the networked computers can communicate with each other. A **network protocol** specifies the rules for transmitting data over a network. If Windows 2000 detects a network adapter in your computer when you install it, it will automatically install support for **Transmission Control Protocol/Internet Protocol (TCP/IP)**, an Internet protocol that enables computers with different types of hardware architectures and different types of operating systems to communicate with each other. The **Transmission Control Protocol (TCP)** manages the transmission of packets of data around the Internet and their reassembly on your computer. The **Internet Protocol (IP)** manages the way each packet is addressed so it arrives at the correct destination. In the past, a commonly used network protocol for LANs with up to 200 clients was **NetBIOS Extended User Interface (NetBEUI)**, a Microsoft networking protocol. Because NetBEUI does not support the transmission of data between networks or over the Internet, TCP/IP is now the more logical choice for a network protocol.

As you set up a peer-to-peer network, you label each computer with a unique name and join the computer to a workgroup so other users can access it. After installing all the network components, each user specifies which resources they want to share (such as printers, drives, directories, and files), and you can implement a security system for the entire network and specific resources. The Administrator typically creates a user account for each user, and assigns each user to a group account. **Group accounts** define a set of rights and permissions for users in that group. For example, an Administrator may assign the Power Users group (a predefined Windows 2000 group) rights and permissions so all members of that group can change system settings and install software. The Administrator may also implement a scheme for **auditing**, or tracking, events, such as attempts to log onto a computer and to access files and other network components, so there is a record of all operations that affect the network.

For many users, network access is an important part of their jobs because the network provides access to the applications, documents, and hardware devices (such as printers) required for their work. Furthermore, individuals can commonly access the Internet and World Wide Web through their company networks. In the future, more and more individuals will be able to set up simple peer-to-peer networks at home so these networks can interface with other home computers, as well as interface with consumer devices (such as VCRs, telephones, and appliances) in the home itself.

Examining Your Computer's Network Settings

Isabel recommends that you first examine the network settings on your computer, verify whether those settings are correct, and then decide if you want to make any changes to your network settings.

If you want to view or change your current network settings, open the Network and Dial-up Connections folder and view the properties of your Local Area Connection. You will also need to log on your computer under an account with Administrator privileges, or as Administrator, if you want to make changes to network settings. If you log on as a Power User, you can view many of the settings but not make changes.

If you are working on a non-networked computer, perform Step 1, and then read, but do not perform, the remainder of the session.

To view your computer's network settings:

1. Right-click **My Network Places** on the desktop, and then click **Properties**. Windows 2000 opens the Network and Dial-up Connections folder. See Figure 10-1. The Make New Connection Wizard will help you create new network connections as needed. If you are already connected to a network, you can use the Local Area Connection tool to view information about that network connection. The Network and Dial-up Connections folder may also contain a dial-up connection, such as the one shown for MSN (The Microsoft Network) in the figure. A **dial-up networking (DUN)** connection is a connection to a network that relies on the use of the telephone network and is commonly used to connect to an online service (such as AOL) or an ISP. In the left pane, you can click the Network Identification link to access the Network Identification property sheet in the System Properties dialog box. Then you can use the Add Network Components link to open the Windows Optional Networking Components Wizard dialog box and add Windows networking components.

Figure 10-1 | **VIEWNG THE CONTENTS OF THE NETWORK AND DIAL-UP CONNECTIONS FOLDER**

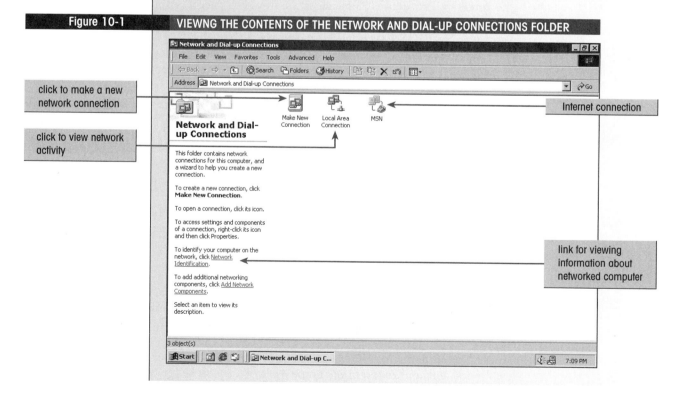

2. Right-click the **Local Area Connection** icon, and then click **Properties**. Windows 2000 opens the Local Area Connections Properties dialog box, which contains information about the network components installed on your computer. See Figure 10-2. If the Install, Uninstall, and Properties buttons are dimmed, and if the check boxes in the "Components checked are used by this connection" box have a dark gray background, then you cannot change network components or settings without logging on first with Administrator privileges.

TROUBLE? If Windows 2000 displays a Local Network dialog box and informs you that the controls on this property sheet are disabled because you do not have sufficient privileges to access them, then your user account does not include Administrator privileges. Click OK to close the Local Network dialog box. You can still view information on the installed components, but you cannot install, uninstall, or view properties of specific components.

TROUBLE? If your Network and Dial-up Connections folder does not contain a Local Area Connection icon, then your computer does not have a network connection. Read, but do not perform, the steps in this section of the tutorial.

Figure 10-2	VIEWING NETWORK SETTINGS

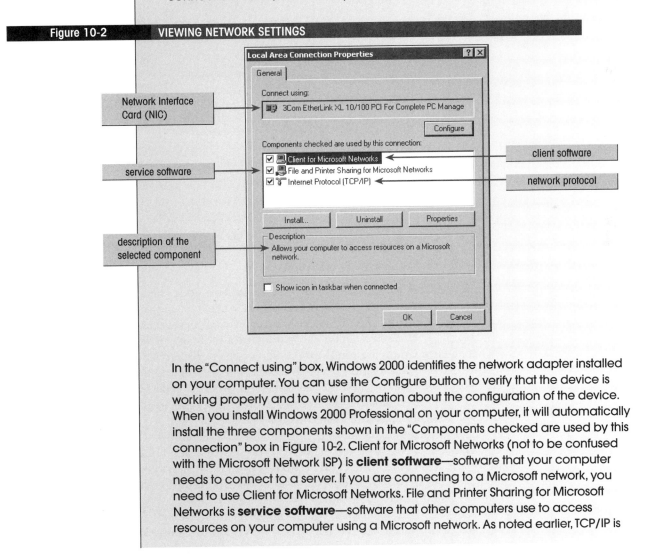

In the "Connect using" box, Windows 2000 identifies the network adapter installed on your computer. You can use the Configure button to verify that the device is working properly and to view information about the configuration of the device. When you install Windows 2000 Professional on your computer, it will automatically install the three components shown in the "Components checked are used by this connection" box in Figure 10-2. Client for Microsoft Networks (not to be confused with the Microsoft Network ISP) is **client software**—software that your computer needs to connect to a server. If you are connecting to a Microsoft network, you need to use Client for Microsoft Networks. File and Printer Sharing for Microsoft Networks is **service software**—software that other computers use to access resources on your computer using a Microsoft network. As noted earlier, TCP/IP is the default **network protocol** used by Windows 2000—a wide area network protocol that supports communication with different types of interconnected networks. If you upgrade to Windows 2000, rather than performing a clean install, other network components may remain installed (such as the NetBEUI protocol).

3. Click **Internet Protocol (TCP/IP)**, and then click the **Properties** button. Windows 2000 displays the Internet Protocol (TCP/IP) Properties dialog box where you can check, specify, or change IP settings. See Figure 10-3.

TROUBLE? As noted earlier, if the Install, Uninstall, and Properties buttons are dimmed, then you are not logged on under an account with Administrator privileges. Do not perform Step 3, but read it and the explanation that follows.

Figure 10-3   VIEWING TCP/IP SETTINGS

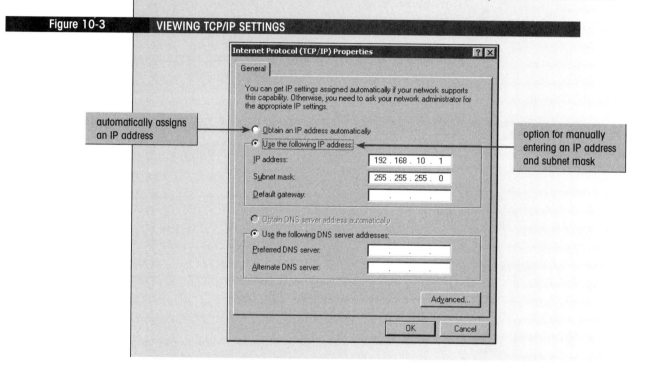

An **IP address** is a 32-bit address that identifies a node (such as a computer) on a network. A **node** is a device that is connected to a network and that can communicate with other network devices. The IP address is represented in dotted-decimal notation, such as 169.254.73.147. Windows 2000 can automatically obtain an IP address from a DHCP (Dynamic Host Configuration Protocol) server on your local network, if one is available, or by using APIPA (Automatic Private IP Addressing), or you can manually specify one in the "Use the following IP address" section. A **Dynamic Host Configuration Protocol (DHCP) server** maintains a database of IP addresses, assigns those IP addresses to computers on the network on an as-needed basis (as a **lease**), and reclaims IP addresses that are no longer needed so it can make them available to other computers.

If Windows 2000 does not detect the presence of a DHCP server, then it will use **Automatic Private IP Addressing (APIPA)** to automatically assign an IP address to a computer or other network device from among the Microsoft-reserved IP addresses, ranging from 169.254.0.1 to 169.254.255.254, to configure TCP/IP.

In addition to the IP address, you can specify a **subnet mask**, which is a set of four numbers, like an IP address, used to split a local network into subdivisions. (The creation and use of subnet masks is beyond the scope of this book.) In a small local area network, your computer may ignore this number, or the system may set the number automatically. In a larger subdivided network, your network administrator will most likely assign the subnet mask.

You may also need to specify a default gateway address. A **gateway** is a device that translates protocols between separate networks. However, in TCP/IP systems, *gateway* usually refers to the address of a **router**, which is a hardware device that forwards data to destinations outside the local network and most commonly to the Internet at large.

IPv4 (Internet Protocol Version 4) addresses use 32 bits and permit around 4.3 billion (4.3×10^9, or 2^{32}) potential IP addresses. As the result of the rapid growth of the Internet and the need for more IP addresses, IPv6 (Internet Protocol Version 6) uses 128 bits, potentially creating about 340 undecillion (340×10^{36}, or 2^{128}) IP addresses.

On a computer where the IP and subnet address is manually configured, the network Administrator or a member of your technical support staff will configure your computer with the correct settings.

To continue your examination of network settings:

1. Click **Cancel** to close the Internet Protocol (TCP/IP) Properties dialog box (if necessary), and then click **Cancel** (or **Close**) to close the Local Area Connection Properties dialog box without making any changes.

2. In the menu bar of the Network and Dial-up Connections window, click **Advanced**, and then click **Network Identification**, or click the **Network Identification** link. Windows 2000 opens the System Properties dialog box and then immediately displays the Network Identification property sheet. See Figure 10-4. As noted on the property sheet, Windows 2000 uses the Full computer name and Workgroup to identify your computer on the network.

   TROUBLE? If you do not see the Network Identification link, your system may be set up in Windows Classic style instead of Web style. Minimize the Network and Dial-up Connections window, and any other open windows, until you see the My Computer icon on the desktop. Right-click the My Computer icon and then click Properties. In the System Properties dialog box, click the Network Identification tab.

Figure 10-4   **VIEWING NETWORK ID SETTINGS**

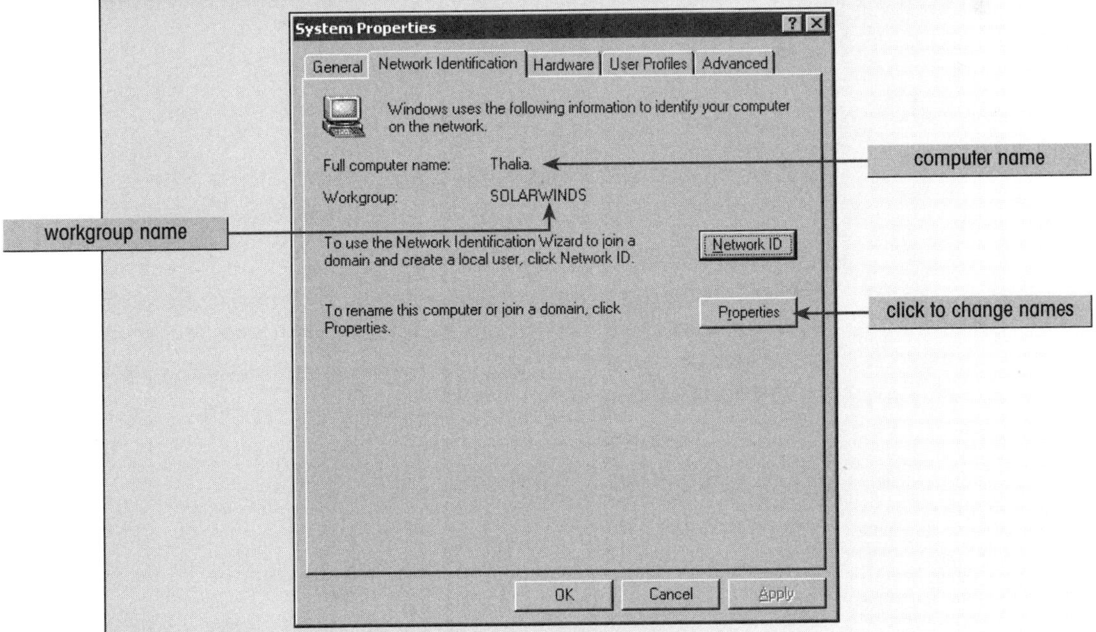

3. Click the **Properties** button on the Network Identification property sheet. Windows 2000 displays the Identification Changes dialog box. See Figure 10-5. You can change the computer's name in the Computer name box; however, Windows 2000 warns you that changes may affect your access to network resources. Windows 2000 also shows if your computer is a member of a domain or a workgroup. A **domain** is a group of computers on a client/server network that share a common directory database. The network Administrator creates a computer account for each computer that is part of a domain. Your user account gives you access to all of the domain resources, such as printers, for which you have permissions. You can change or specify a domain name for your computer account. If you specify the name of your domain, you will also be prompted for your domain user name and password. In contrast, a **workgroup** is a group of computers that share information on a peer-to-peer network in which a server is not required. Figure 10-5 shows the workgroup name as "SOLARWINDS." Windows 2000 defaults to the name WORKGROUP, but you or your network Administrator should use a different name, as it can otherwise present a security risk through your Internet connection.

TROUBLE? If the Properties button is dimmed, then you are not logged on under an account with Administrator privileges. Do not perform this step, but read it and the explanation that follows.

Figure 10-5   **CHANGING NETWORK ID SETTINGS**

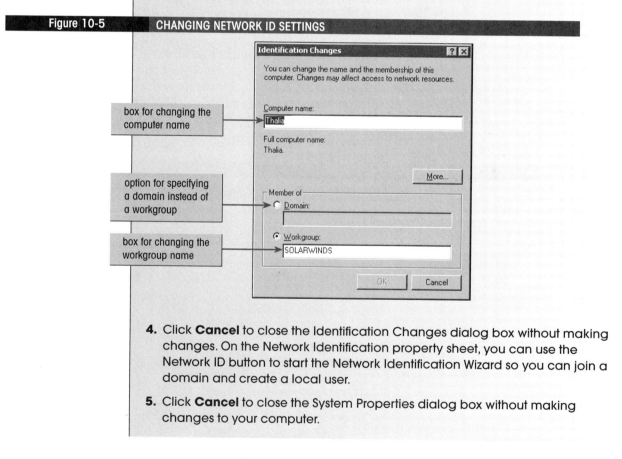

4. Click **Cancel** to close the Identification Changes dialog box without making changes. On the Network Identification property sheet, you can use the Network ID button to start the Network Identification Wizard so you can join a domain and create a local user.

5. Click **Cancel** to close the System Properties dialog box without making changes to your computer.

From the Network and Dial-up Connections window, you can also view information on network activity.

To view information on network activity:

1. Double-click the **Local Area Connection** icon. Windows 2000 opens the Local Area Connection Status dialog box. See Figure 10-6. In the Connection section, Windows 2000 displays the speed of the network connection. In this figure, the data transmission speed is 100.0 Mbps (millions of bits per second). In the Activity section, Windows 2000 reports on the number of packets sent and received over the network. A **packet** is a set of data that is transmitted as a discrete unit from one computer to another. From this dialog box, you can also click the Properties button to display the Local Area Connection Properties dialog box you examined earlier.

   TROUBLE? If your Network and Dial-up Connections folder does not contain a Local Area Connection icon, then your computer does not have a network connection. Read, but do not perform, the steps in this section of the tutorial.

   TROUBLE? If Windows 2000 displays a Local Area Connection Properties dialog box rather than a Local Area Connection Status dialog, then there may be a problem with your network connection, such as an unplugged or loose network cable. Click Cancel to close the Local Area Connection Properties dialog box and, if possible, correct the problem, and then repeat this step. If you are using a computer in your college's computer lab, notify your instructor or lab staff.

Figure 10-6	VIEWING NETWORK ACTIVITY

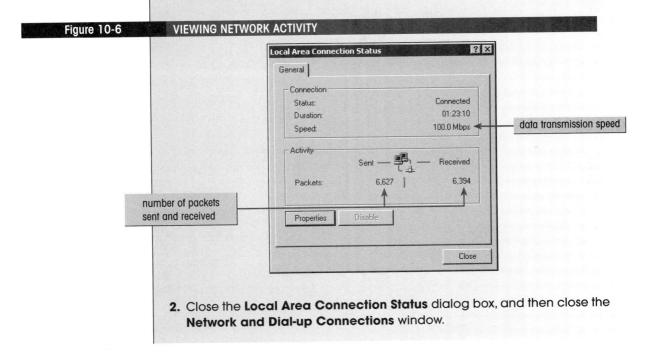

2. Close the **Local Area Connection Status** dialog box, and then close the **Network and Dial-up Connections** window.

REFERENCE WINDOW   **RW**

<u>Viewing Network Settings on a Computer</u>

- If you want to make changes to network settings or view certain types of network settings, you must log on to your computer using an account with Administrator privileges or as Administrator; otherwise, you will be limited to only viewing some of the settings.
- Right-click My Network Places on the desktop, and then click Properties.
- After Windows 2000 opens the Network and Dial-up Connections folder, right-click the Local Area Connection icon (if you are connected to a network), and then click Properties.
- After Windows 2000 opens the Local Area Connection Properties dialog box, examine the local area device (such as a network adapter) in the Connect using box and the installed network components in the "Components checked are used by this connection" box.
- If you want to view settings for, or configure, the local area device in the Connect using box, click the Configure button, check the Device status area on the General property sheet to verify that the device is working properly, and then examine the configuration settings on the property sheets for this device. After you are finished, click Cancel to close the property sheet for the local area device without making changes, or, if you have made changes that you want to keep, click OK.
- If you want to view properties of, or configure network components such as client software, service software, or network protocols listed in the "Components checked are used by this connection" box, select the network component first, and then click the Properties button.
- If you want to install a network component, such as client software, service software, or network protocols, click the Install button, select the type of component you want to install, and then specify the specific service or protocol you want to use.
- If you want to uninstall a network component, select that network component in the "Components checked are used by this connection" box, and then click the Uninstall button.
- If you want to display a network connection icon in the status area (also known as the system tray), next to the time of day in the lower-right corner of the screen on the taskbar, click the "Show icon in taskbar when connected" check box.
- Click Cancel to close the Local Area Connection Properties dialog box without making any changes to your network settings, or, if you want to keep changes that you have made, click OK instead.
- If you want to view information that identifies your computer on the network, click the Network Identification link in the Network and Dial-up Connections window. If you want to rename the computer or join a domain, click the Properties button. If you want to use the Network Identification Wizard to join a domain and create a local user, click the Network ID button and complete the steps for using that wizard.
- Click Cancel to close the System Properties dialog box without making changes to your computer, or click OK to save changes that you have made to your Network Identification settings.
- Close the Network and Dial-up Connections window.

If your computer is part of a network, familiarize yourself with the network settings for your computer so you can find them when you need to examine them. Be sure to document the current settings in case you need to verify or restore them later.

Creating a New Network Connection

If you want to create a new network connection, you can use the Make New Connection Wizard in the Network and Dial-up Connections folder. If you click the Make New Connection icon, then Windows 2000 displays the Network Connection Wizard dialog box and informs you that you can use this wizard to create a connection to other computers and other networks, as well as to enable applications such as e-mail, Web browsing, file sharing, and printing. See Figure 10-7.

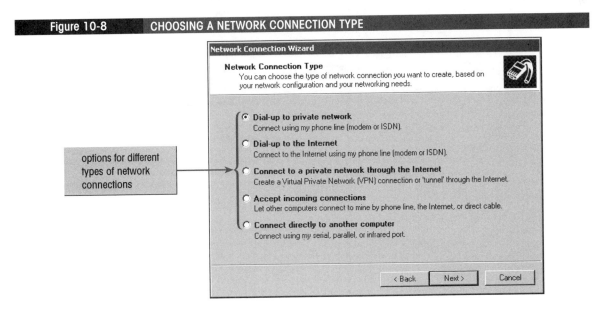

If you go to the Network Connection Wizard's next step, you can use it to create one of five different types of network connections, as shown in Figure 10-8. You can create a dial-up connection to a private network, the Internet, and a private network through the Internet, or you can create a dial-up connection for accepting incoming connections or connecting directly to another computer. A **Virtual Private Network (VPN)** is a network that uses both public and private networks for a network connection. This type of network connection is made via a direct connection to the Internet, or via an ISP, and is used by businesses to establish network connections to the Internet for company computers at reduced cost. At the same time, VPNs support the most common network protocols and enhance security by using authentication and encryption protocols to protect sensitive data and IP addresses.

Now that you have examined your network setup, you are ready to try some networking commands.

Using Basic Network Commands

Isabel would like you to become familiar with two ways for managing shared network resources (such as directory folders and printers), first by using programs from the Windows 2000 desktop and then by using command line utilities. She asks you to perform some basic network tasks and compare each approach, pointing out that you will need to use command line network utilities to automate network tasks with batch programs.

In each of the tasks below, you first will use the GUI approach, and then follow it with an equivalent command-line approach, using a NET subcommand.

Viewing Network Resources

Using Windows Explorer, you can find out what shared resources are available on your computer by opening My Network Places, then opening Computers Near Me. This provides you with a list of networked computers in your workgroup. If you don't see any computers in the list, try opening Entire Network and then opening the network icons you find until you see a list of networked computers.

To view network resources using Windows Explorer:

1. Right-click **My Network Places**, and then click **Explore**.

2. Click the **expand view** box ⊞ next to Computers Near Me. If you are on a network, you should see the name of your own computer and the name of at least one other computer on the network.

   TROUBLE? If you do not see a "Computers Near Me" icon, either you or your system administrator can create one by temporarily changing your computer's Workgroup name, and then changing it back. Each time you change the Workgroup name, Windows 2000 will prompt you to restart the computer. However, you do not need to restart in this case, and you can just click No each time.

3. Click the name of another computer on the network. The names of any shared resources, including printers and shared directory folders, will appear in the contents pane on the right-hand side of the window. See Figure 10-9. Your display will differ.

Figure 10-9   **VIEWING SHARED RESOURCES ON ANOTHER NETWORK COMPUTER**

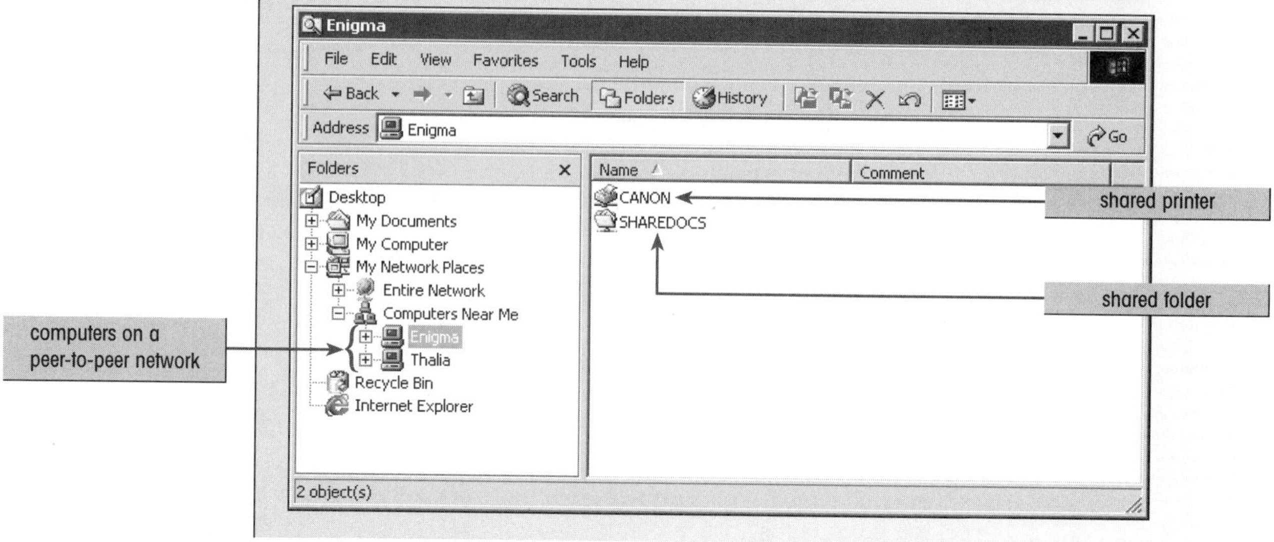

computers on a peer-to-peer network

shared printer

shared folder

4. Click the **expand view** box ➕ next to the name of the other computer. Any shared directory folders will also appear below the computer name in the Folders pane.

5. Click a directory folder to view the contents in the right-hand pane. See Figure 10-10. Again, your display will differ.

| Figure 10-10 | VIEWING THE CONTENTS OF A SHARED FOLDER |

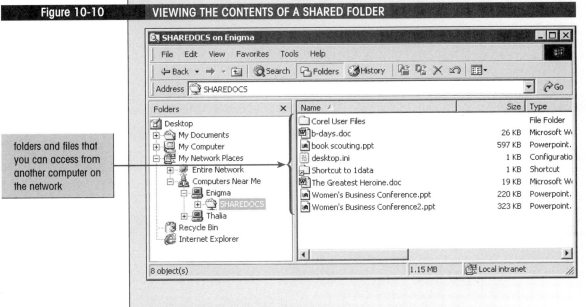

folders and files that you can access from another computer on the network

6. Close the **Explorer** window.

When you select another computer on your network, you can see what directory folders and printers that computer shares with other users on the network. You can get the same information from the command line; first, however, you want to get an overview of network commands and get help in how to use them.

Using NET Commands

At the command line, you can perform many network management tasks using commands beginning with the word net. These commands use the syntax **net** *command* in which you specify one of the NET subcommands in place of the word *command*. To get a list of net subcommands, type "net help". You can then get detailed help on any of the NET commands by typing "net help *command*", replacing *command* with the appropriate NET command. You can also get brief syntax help on any NET command by typing **net** *command* **/?**.

To display help text for NET commands:

1. Open a **Command Prompt** window, set colors (if necessary), and then clear the window.

2. Enter: `net help`

   The command interpreter displays a detailed list of NET subcommands, as shown in Figure 10-11.

Figure 10-11 VIEWING HELP ON THE NET COMMANDS

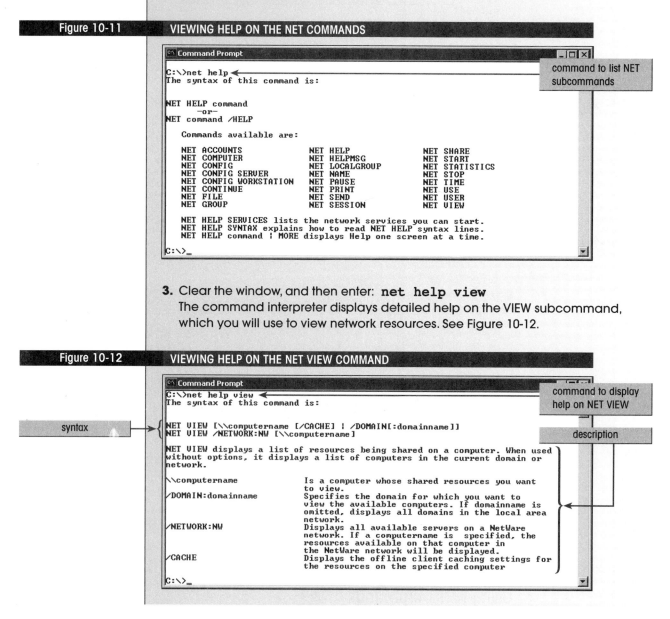

3. Clear the window, and then enter: `net help view`

   The command interpreter displays detailed help on the VIEW subcommand, which you will use to view network resources. See Figure 10-12.

Figure 10-12 VIEWING HELP ON THE NET VIEW COMMAND

Viewing Help Information on NET Commands
- Open a Command Prompt window.
- Type NET HELP and then press Enter to view a detailed list of NET subcommands.
- To view Help information on a specific command, type NET HELP, press the Spacebar, type the command with which you want Help, and then press Enter.

As you learn more about networking and working in a Command Prompt window, you will find the Help feature invaluable. Now you're ready to view information about network resources.

To view network resources at the command line:

1. Clear the window, and then enter: **net view**

   The NET VIEW command displays a list of local networked computers. See Figure 10-13. Your display will differ. A networked computer name always begins with two backslashes (\\ ), as in the name \\ENIGMA in the figure. This format is called the **Universal Naming Convention** (or **UNC**) and it identifies the path to a network resource.

Figure 10-13	VIEWING A LIST OF LOCAL COMPUTERS ON A NETWORK

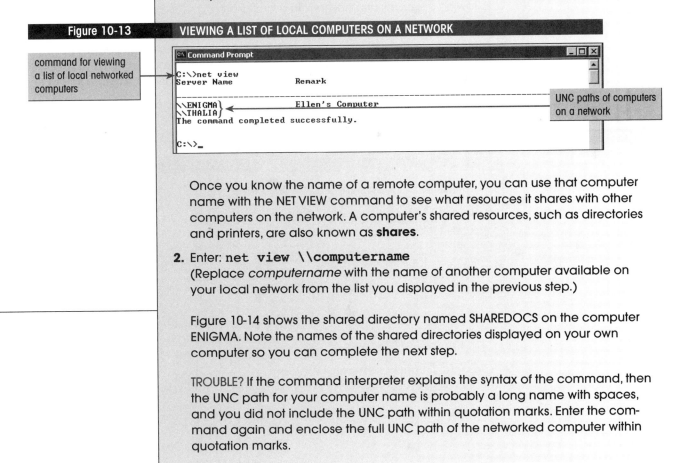

command for viewing a list of local networked computers

UNC paths of computers on a network

   Once you know the name of a remote computer, you can use that computer name with the NET VIEW command to see what resources it shares with other computers on the network. A computer's shared resources, such as directories and printers, are also known as **shares**.

2. Enter: **net view \\computername**
   (Replace *computername* with the name of another computer available on your local network from the list you displayed in the previous step.)

   Figure 10-14 shows the shared directory named SHAREDOCS on the computer ENIGMA. Note the names of the shared directories displayed on your own computer so you can complete the next step.

   TROUBLE? If the command interpreter explains the syntax of the command, then the UNC path for your computer name is probably a long name with spaces, and you did not include the UNC path within quotation marks. Enter the command again and enclose the full UNC path of the networked computer within quotation marks.

TROUBLE? If NET VIEW did not display any server names in the previous step, then your computer does not have any local network connections, and you will not be able to complete this step. Read, but do not perform, the next two steps.

| Figure 10-14 | DISPLAYING A LIST OF SHARED RESOURCES ON A NETWORKED COMPUTER |

UNC path for a computer on the network

shared resources on networked computer

When you know the name of a shared directory folder on another computer, you can use it with a command in the Universal Naming Convention (UNC) by following the computer name with a backslash (\) and the shared directory folder name.

3. Clear the window, and then enter: dir \\computername\directory (Replace *computername* with the name of another computer in the network, and *directory* with the name of a shared directory folder on that computer.)

Figure 10-15 shows a directory listing of the shared directory SHAREDOCS.

| Figure 10-15 | VIEWING THE CONTENTS OF A SHARED DIRECTORY ON ANOTHER COMPUTER |

UNC path to a shared directory on another computer in the network

directories and files in shared directory

4. Close the **Command Prompt** window.

RW

REFERENCE WINDOW

Viewing Network Resources from the Command Prompt

- Open a Command Prompt window.
- To display a list of local computers on the network, type NET VIEW and then press Enter.
- To display shared resources on a specific computer, type NET VIEW, press the Spacebar, type two backslashes followed immediately by the name of another computer on the network, and then press Enter.
- To view the contents of a shared directory, type DIR, press the Spacebar, and then type the UNC path of that directory.

You can also use the UNC format to open or copy files at the command prompt. For example, you could open the file b-days.doc in Figure 10-15 by entering "\\enigma\sharedocs \b-days.doc" at the command prompt. If you entered "copy \\enigma\sharedocs \b-days.doc" instead, you would copy the same file to the current directory.

Mapping a Drive Letter to a Shared Directory Folder

At the command prompt, you cannot use the Universal Naming Convention format with the CD command to switch to a shared directory folder on another computer. To address this problem, you can **map**, or assign, a drive letter (such as F:) to a shared directory folder. You can then use the drive letter in place of the UNC specification at the command prompt and in other programs.

To map a drive letter to a shared directory with Windows Explorer:

1. Right-click **My Network Places**, click **Explore**, and then navigate down to a shared directory folder on another computer, as you did in the previous steps. In the Folders pane, Windows Explorer displays the names of the networked computers and the shared resources on the network computer you select.

2. Right-click the **shared directory folder** to open a context menu, and then click **Map Network Drive**, as shown in Figure 10-16. Windows 2000 displays a Map Network Drive dialog box where you can specify a drive letter for the shared directory folder. See Figure 10-17. The drive letter defaults to the next available letter, but you can use the drop-down list and select a different letter, if you wish. Because you right-clicked a shared folder (rather than selecting the folder and then selecting Map Network Drive on the Tools menu), the Folder text box contains the folder's name grayed out, so you cannot change it. In the Map Network Drive dialog box, you can also specify whether you want Windows 2000 to reconnect to the mapped drive during logon.

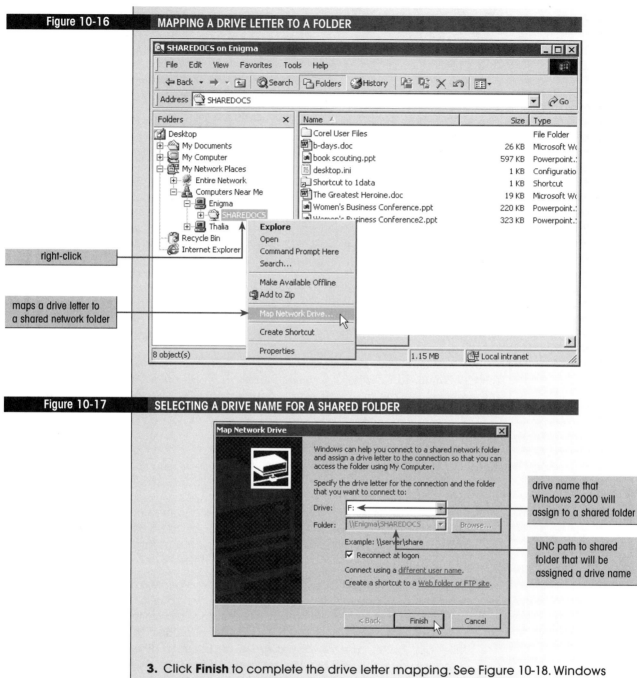

Figure 10-16   MAPPING A DRIVE LETTER TO A FOLDER

right-click

maps a drive letter to
a shared network folder

Figure 10-17   SELECTING A DRIVE NAME FOR A SHARED FOLDER

drive name that
Windows 2000 will
assign to a shared folder

UNC path to shared
folder that will be
assigned a drive name

3. Click **Finish** to complete the drive letter mapping. See Figure 10-18. Windows opens a My Computer window onto the newly mapped drive.

Figure 10-18	WINDOW OF A NEWLY MAPPED DRIVE

shared folder name

mapped drive letter

Sharedocs on 'Enigma' (F:)

File   Edit   View   Favorites   Tools   Help

⇐ Back ▾ ⇒ ▾ 🖹 | 🔍 Search 🗂 Folders 🕘 History | 🖺 🖺 ✕ ✕ | 🖽▾

Address 🖳 F:\   ▾   🔗 Go

Name	Size	Type	Modified
📄 symbols.doc	19 KB	Microsoft Word Document	8/8/200
📄 b-days.doc	25 KB	Microsoft Word Document	8/3/200
📄 Shortcut to 1data	1 KB	Shortcut	6/28/20
📄 book scouting.ppt	597 KB	Powerpoint.Show.7	5/15/20
📄 The Greatest Heroine.doc	19 KB	Microsoft Word Document	5/13/20
📄 Women's Business Conference2.ppt	323 KB	Powerpoint.Show.7	3/31/20
📄 Women's Business Conference.ppt	220 KB	Powerpoint.Show.7	3/27/20
📄 desktop.ini	1 KB	Configuration Settings	3/4/200
📁 Corel User Files		File Folder	3/8/200

9 object(s)   1.17 MB   🖳 Local intranet

4. Close the **mapped drive** window.

5. Click the **expand view** box ⊞ next to My Computer in the Folders pane. Windows Explorer displays the mapped drive as a drive that you can access after you open My Computer. See Figure 10-19.

Figure 10-19	NEWLY MAPPED DRIVE

SHAREDOCS on Enigma

File   Edit   View   Favorites   Tools   Help

⇐ Back ▾ ⇒ ▾ 🖹 | 🔍 Search 🗂 Folders 🕘 History | 🖺 🖺 ✕ ✕ | 🖽▾

Address 🖳 \\Enigma\SHAREDOCS   ▾   🔗 Go

Folders   ✕

📁 Desktop
  ⊞ 📁 My Documents
  ⊟ 🖳 My Computer
    ⊞ 💾 3½ Floppy (A:)
    ⊞ 🖴 WIN2000 (C:)
    ⊞ 💿 Compact Disc (D:)
    ⊞ 🖴 Removable Disk (E:)

newly mapped drive ⊞ 🖳 Sharedocs on 'Enigma' (F:)
    ⊞ 🖴 CYBELE (G:)
    ⊞ 🖴 Control Panel
  ⊟ 🖳 My Network Places
    ⊞ 🌐 Entire Network
    ⊟ 🖳 Computers Near Me
      ⊟ 🖥 Enigma

shared network folder ⊞ 📁 SHAREDOCS
      ⊞ 🖥 Thalia
  📁 Recycle Bin
  🌐 Internet Explorer

Name ▲	Type	Size
📁 Corel User Files	File Folder	
📄 b-days.doc	Microsoft Word Doc...	25 KB
📄 book scouting.ppt	Powerpoint.Show.7	597 KB
📄 desktop.ini	Configuration Settings	1 KB
📄 Shortcut to 1data	Shortcut	1 KB
📄 symbols.doc	Microsoft Word Doc...	19 KB
📄 The Greatest Heroine.doc	Microsoft Word Doc...	19 KB
📄 Women's Business Conference.ppt	Powerpoint.Show.7	220 KB
📄 Women's Business Conference2.ppt	Powerpoint.Show.7	323 KB

9 object(s)   1.17 MB   🖳 Local intranet

You can now use this new mapped drive letter as you would any other drive on your system.

In preparation for mapping a drive letter at the command line, you first want to remove the existing mapping you just created with Windows Explorer.

To remove a drive letter mapping with Windows Explorer:

1. If necessary, right-click **My Network Places**, and then click **Explore**.

2. Click the **expand view** box ⊞ next to My Computer (if necessary), and locate the mapped drive you created previously. It will display the drive letter you selected in parentheses after the name (for example, F:).

3. Right-click the **mapped drive**, and then click **Disconnect**. See Figure 10-20. Windows 2000 removes the drive letter mapping.

| Figure 10-20 | REMOVING A DRIVE MAPPING |

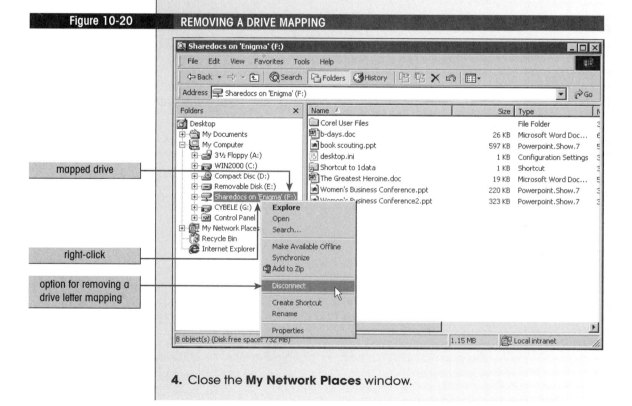

4. Close the **My Network Places** window.

Removing a Mapped Drive with Windows Explorer
■ Right-click My Network Places, and then click Explore.
■ Click the expand view box ⊞ next to My Computer, and then locate the mapped network drive
for which you want to remove the drive mapping.
■ Right-click the mapped drive, and then click Disconnect.
■ Close the My Network Places window.

Mapping a Drive from the Command Line

Now you are ready to map a drive letter at the command line.

To map a drive letter to a shared directory folder at the command line:

1. Open a **Command Prompt** window and then clear the window.

2. Enter: **net use**

   The NET USE command displays a list of shared network resources that are
   already mapped. Figure 10-21 shows no mapped resources. Your network
   setup may display mapped drives.

Figure 10-21   DISPLAYING MAPPED NETWORK RESOURCES

```
Command Prompt                                              _ □ ×

C:\>net use
New connections will be remembered.

There are no entries in the list.

C:\>_
```

3. Clear the window again, type **net use** followed by a space, the same **drive
   letter** you used in the previous set of steps, a **colon** (:), a **space**, the **UNC
   path** of the shared directory folder you used previously (for example,
   \\engima\sharedocs), and then press **Enter**. Figure 10-22 shows an example of this form of the NET USE command. After displaying the message "The
   command completed successfully," Windows 2000 opens a My Computer
   window onto the newly mapped drive, as it did previously when you mapped
   a drive with Windows Explorer.

   TROUBLE? If the NET USE command reports a system error and indicates that it
   cannot find the network name, then your UNC path probably includes a computer name or directory name with spaces. Repeat this step, but enclose the
   UNC path within quotation marks.

Figure 10-22   MAPPING A DRIVE NAME TO A SHARED DIRECTORY

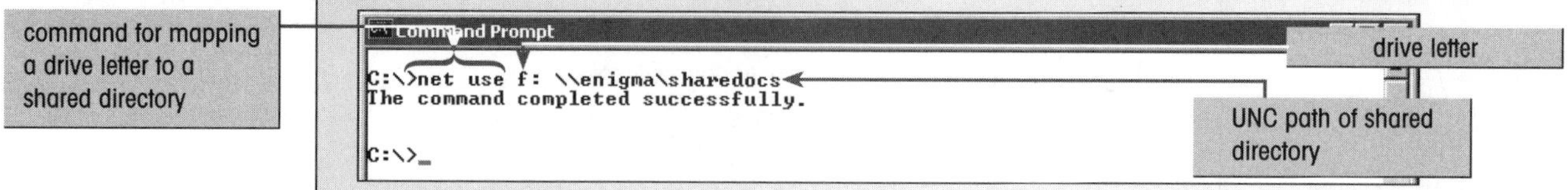

command for mapping a drive letter to a shared directory

drive letter

```
Command Prompt

C:\>net use f: \\enigma\sharedocs
The command completed successfully.

C:\>_
```

UNC path of shared directory

4. Close the **My Computer** window of your newly mapped drive, and then switch back to the **Command Prompt** window, if necessary.

5. Enter: `net use`
NET USE displays your new drive mapping. See Figure 10-23.

Figure 10-23   VERIFYING A DRIVE MAPPING

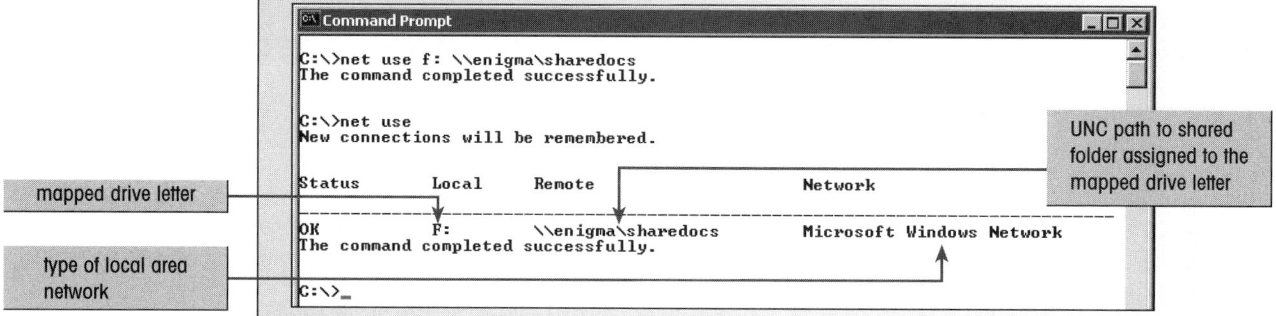

```
Command Prompt                                                    _ □ ×

C:\>net use f: \\enigma\sharedocs
The command completed successfully.

C:\>net use
New connections will be remembered.

Status       Local      Remote                        Network
-------------------------------------------------------------------
OK           F:         \\enigma\sharedocs    Microsoft Windows Network
The command completed successfully.

C:\>_
```

mapped drive letter

type of local area network

UNC path to shared folder assigned to the mapped drive letter

6. Clear the window. Type **net use** followed by a **space**, the **drive letter** you just specified, and a **colon** (for example, net use f:), and then press **Enter**. This form of the command shows details of the drive mapping. See Figure 10-24.

Figure 10-24   VIEWING DETAILS OF A DRIVE MAPPING

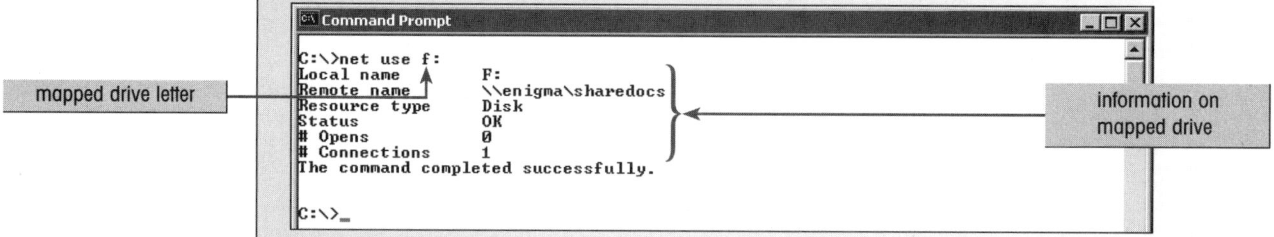

```
Command Prompt                                                    _ □ ×

C:\>net use f:
Local name        F:
Remote name       \\enigma\sharedocs
Resource type     Disk
Status            OK
# Opens           0
# Connections     1
The command completed successfully.

C:\>_
```

mapped drive letter

information on mapped drive

7. Clear the window, type your new **drive letter**, a **colon** (for example, f:), and then press **Enter** to switch to the newly mapped directory.

8. Display a directory listing of the mapped directory. Figure 10-25 displays a directory of a mapped drive.

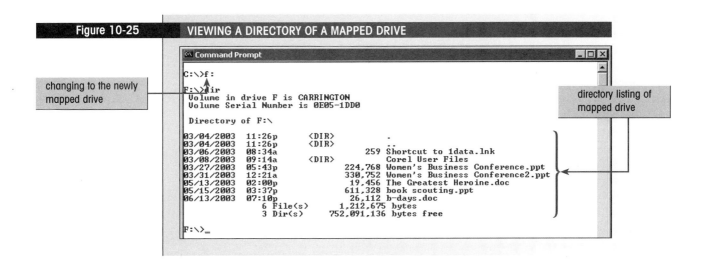

Figure 10-25   VIEWING A DIRECTORY OF A MAPPED DRIVE

changing to the newly mapped drive

directory listing of mapped drive

REFERENCE WINDOW   **RW**

Mapping a Drive Letter to a Shared Directory from the Command Prompt

- Open a Command Prompt window.
- Type NET USE, press the Spacebar, type the drive letter you want to use (followed by a colon), press the Spacebar, type the name of the shared directory folder, and then press Enter.
- Close the My Computer window for the newly mapped drive.
- Type NET USE and then press Enter to view the newly mapped drive.
- To view details of a drive mapping, type NET USE, press the Spacebar, type the drive letter (with a colon) of the mapped drive, and then press Enter.
- To change to a newly mapped drive, type the drive letter (followed by a colon) of the mapped drive, and then press Enter.

If you want to remove a mapped drive so you can assign the drive letter to another network resource, you can use the NET USE command to remove the current driving mapping.

To remove a mapped drive letter from the command line:

1. Clear the **window** and then change to drive **C**.

2. Type `net use` followed by your **mapped drive letter**, a **colon**, a **space**, and then **/delete** (for example, `net use f: /delete`). NET USE verifies that it deleted the mapped drive name, as shown in Figure 10-26.

Figure 10-26   REMOVING A MAPPED DRIVE

mapped drive letter

switch for removing a mapped drive

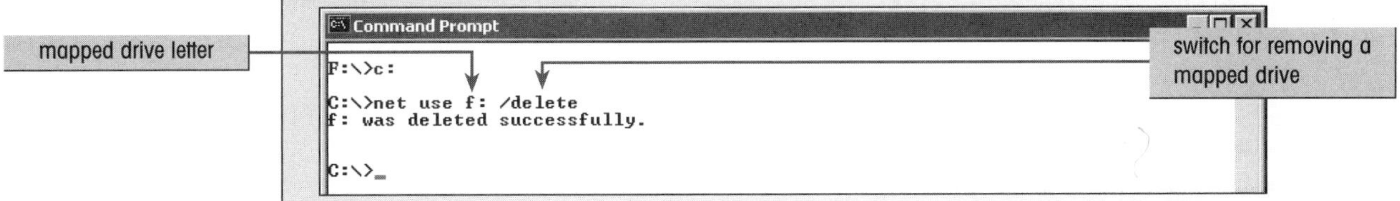

TROUBLE? If you receive the message "There are open files and/or incomplete directory searches pending on the connection to (*your mapped drive name*). Is it OK to continue disconnecting and force them closed? (Y/N) (N):", the mapped drive letter you are trying to delete may still be your current default drive. You cannot delete a mapped drive letter while you are working from it. Press Enter, switch to drive C:, and try again.

3. Close the **Command Prompt** window.

REFERENCE WINDOW   **RW**

Removing a Mapped Drive from the Command Prompt
- Open a Command Prompt window.
- Type NET USE, press the Spacebar, type the mapped drive letter (followed by a colon), press the Spacebar, type /DELETE, and then press Enter.

Not only is it easy to create a mapped drive quickly from the Command Prompt window, but you can also switch to a mapped drive easily and quickly by using its drive name rather than having to type a long UNC path name.

Sharing the "My Documents" Folder on a Network

You can share folders on a network so other co-workers within your work group can access and use your files.

To share your "My Documents" directory folder using My Computer:

1. Open **My Computer**, and navigate to the folder for your user account (check in the "Documents and Settings" folder on drive C).

2. Right-click the "**My Documents**" folder icon, and then click **Sharing**. Windows 2000 displays the Sharing property sheet in the "My Documents Properties" dialog box. See Figure 10-27.

   TROUBLE? If you don't see a Sharing item in your menu, you may not have permissions to share resources on the network. Read, but do not perform, the rest of the steps in this section.

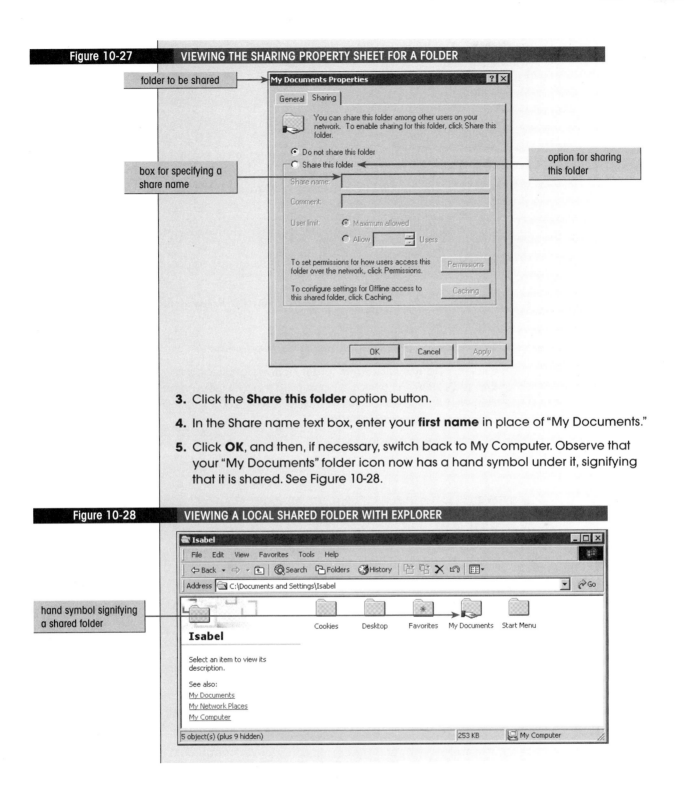

Figure 10-27   **VIEWING THE SHARING PROPERTY SHEET FOR A FOLDER**

folder to be shared

box for specifying a
share name

option for sharing
this folder

3. Click the **Share this folder** option button.

4. In the Share name text box, enter your **first name** in place of "My Documents."

5. Click **OK**, and then, if necessary, switch back to My Computer. Observe that
your "My Documents" folder icon now has a hand symbol under it, signifying
that it is shared. See Figure 10-28.

Figure 10-28   **VIEWING A LOCAL SHARED FOLDER WITH EXPLORER**

hand symbol signifying
a shared folder

> **REFERENCE WINDOW**   **RW**
>
> Sharing the "My Documents" Folder Using My Computer
> - Open My Computer, and then navigate to the folder for your user account (check in the "Documents and Settings" folder on drive C).
> - Right-click the "My Documents" folder icon, and then click the Sharing tab.
> - Click the "Share this folder" option button.
> - In the Share name text box, specify a name for the shared folder, and then click OK.

If you no longer want to share a folder, you can remove the option for sharing it from the General property sheet for that folder.

Now remove the sharing from your "My Documents" folder.

To remove sharing from your "My Documents" folder using My Computer:

1. Right-click the "**My Documents**" folder icon, and then click **Sharing**.

2. Click the **Do not share this folder** option button, and then click **OK**. Note that Windows 2000 removes the hand from the "My Documents" folder icon to show that the folder is no longer shared. Windows 2000 also removes the name you assigned to the shared folder.

3. Close the **My Computer** window.

> **REFERENCE WINDOW**   **RW**
>
> Removing Sharing from the "My Documents" Folder Using My Computer
> - Open My Computer, and then open the folder for your user account (check the "Document and Settings" folder on drive C).
> - Right-click the "My Documents" folder icon, and then click the Sharing tab.
> - Click the "Do not share this folder" option button, and then click OK.

Using Windows Explorer, you can quickly view shared resources, create new shares, and remove shares.

Sharing the "My Documents" Directory from the Command Prompt

Next, you will share your "My Documents" folder from the command prompt. Sharing a directory from the command prompt is as easy as sharing it from the graphical user interface.

To share your "My Documents" folder from the Command Prompt:

1. Open a **Command Prompt** window, and then clear the **window**.

2. Enter: `net share`

NET SHARE displays the current shares on your computer. See Figure 10-29. Your shares may differ.

TROUBLE? If you see the message, "System error 5 has occurred. Access is denied," you may not have permissions to share resources on the network. Read, but do not perform, the rest of the steps in this section.

Figure 10-29	VIEWING THE SHARES ON A LOCAL COMPUTER

command for viewing shared resources →

```
Command Prompt                                                    _ □ ×
C:\>net share

Share name    Resource                         Remark
-----------------------------------------------------------------
print$        C:\WINNT\System32\spool\drivers   Printer Drivers  ⎫
ADMIN$        C:\WINNT                          Remote Admin     ⎮
G$            G:\                               Default share    ⎮
C$            C:\                               Default share    ⎬ current shared devices
IPC$                                            Remote IPC       ⎮
Cybele        G:\                                                ⎮
Win2000       C:\                                                ⎮
LaserJet      LPT1:              Spooled  HP LaserJet IIIP       ⎭
The command completed successfully.


C:\>_
```

3. Clear the **window** and then enter:
   net share *firstname*="**%userprofile%\My Documents**" (Replace *firstname* with your own first name and enclose quotation marks around the path to the "My Documents" folder.)

   NET SHARE reports that "(your name) was shared successfully."

4. Enter: **net share**

   NET SHARE lists the "My Documents" directory folder as one of your shared directories. See Figure 10-30.

Figure 10-30	SHARING A DIRECTORY

name to assign to new share →

```
Command Prompt                                                    _ □ ×
C:\>net share Isabel="%userprofile%\My Documents"
Isabel was shared successfully.              ← path of directory to share

C:\>net share

Share name    Resource                         Remark
-----------------------------------------------------------------
print$        C:\WINNT\System32\spool\drivers   Printer Drivers
C$            C:\                               Default share
G$            G:\                               Default share
IPC$                                            Remote IPC
ADMIN$        C:\WINNT                          Remote Admin
Cybele        G:\
Isabel        C:\Documents and Settings\Isabel\My Documents       ← new share

Win2000       C:\
LaserJet      LPT1:              Spooled  HP LaserJet IIIP
The command completed successfully.


C:\>_
```

REFERENCE WINDOW   **RW**

Sharing the "My Documents" Directory from a Command Prompt

- Open a Command Prompt window.
- Type NET SHARE and then press Enter to view the current shares on your computer.
- Switch to the directory for your user account under the "Documents and Settings" directory.
- Type NET SHARE, press the Spacebar, type a name for the shared directory, type an equals sign (=), type "%userprofile%\My Documents", and then press Enter.
- Type NET SHARE and then press Enter to check the shared directories on your computer.

If you need to remove a shared directory, you can use a variation of the NET SHARE command.

Next, you will remove sharing from your "My Documents" directory.

To remove sharing from your "My Documents" directory at the Command Prompt:

1. Clear the **window**, and then enter: **net share** *firstname* **/delete**
   (Replace *firstname* with your own first name, which is now the share name.)

   NET SHARE reports that, "(your shared directory name) was deleted successfully." This does not mean your directory was deleted, only that the shared status is deleted.

2. Enter: **net share**

   Note that the previously shared directory is no longer shown in the share list. See Figure 10-31.

Figure 10-31	REMOVING SHARING FROM A DIRECTORY

name assigned to share —— switch for deleting share

```
Command Prompt

C:\>net share Isabel /delete
Isabel was deleted successfully.


C:\>net share

Share name    Resource                                Remark

-------------------------------------------------------------------------------
print$        C:\WINNT\System32\spool\drivers  Printer Drivers
ADMIN$        C:\WINNT                                Remote Admin
G$            G:\                                     Default share
C$            C:\                                     Default share
IPC$                                                  Remote IPC
Cybele        G:\
Win2000       C:\
LaserJet      LPT1:                          Spooled  HP LaserJet IIIP
The command completed successfully.


C:\>_
```

share no longer listed for the "My Documents" directory

3. Close the **Command Prompt** window.

Removing a Shared Directory from the Command Prompt Window
- Open a Command Prompt window.
- Type NET SHARE, press the Spacebar, type the name of the shared directory, press the Spacebar, type /DELETE, and then press Enter.
- Type NET SHARE and then press Enter to check the shared directories on your computer.

When working in a Command Prompt window, you can use the NET SHARE command to view shared resources, assign new shares, and remove shares just as quickly as you can in the graphical user interface.

Working with User Account Commands

Only the Administrator, or a member of the Administrators' group, can open Users and Passwords in the Control Panel and view information about user accounts, or make changes to those accounts. However, even if you do not have Administrator privileges, you can open the Computer Management console and view (but not change) information about user accounts. If you open a Command Prompt window, you can use network commands to view information on user accounts without having to log on as a member of the Administrators' group, and you can print this information, which cannot be done under the GUI.

To display user information from the desktop:

1. Right-click **My Computer**, and then click **Manage** to open the Computer Management window for your local computer.

2. Under System Tools in the console tree pane, click the **expand view** box ⊞ for Local Users and Groups.

3. Click the **Users** folder to display a list of users for your computer in the contents pane on the right-hand side of the window. See Figure 10-32.

Figure 10-32   VIEWING LOCAL USERS USING THE COMPUTER MANAGEMENT TOOL

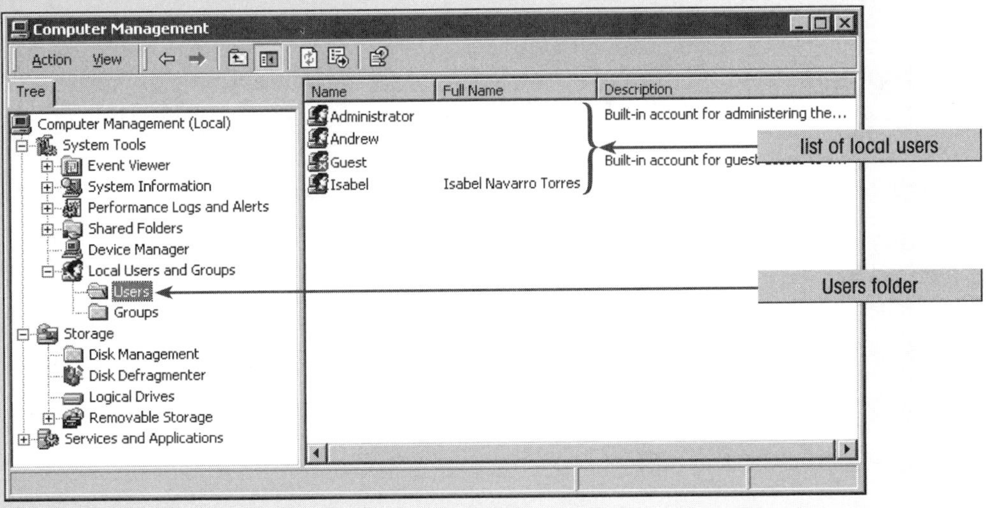

4. Locate and double-click your **user name** to display the Properties dialog box for your user account. See Figure 10-33. On the General property sheet, the Administrator can specify password and account options for a user. On the Member Of property sheet, Windows 2000 displays the group or groups to which the member belongs. On the Profile property sheet, the Administrator can specify a home folder for the user on the local computer, or specify that Windows 2000 uses a shared network directory as the home directory for that specific user.

Figure 10-33 | **VIEWING USER PROPERTIES**

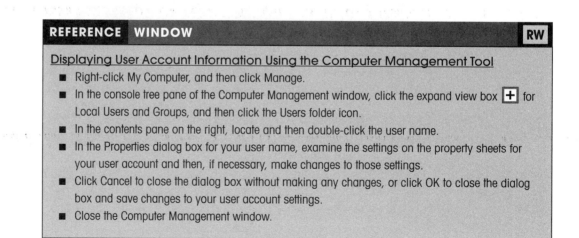

5. After examining the settings for your user account, click **Cancel** to close the Properties dialog box without making any changes.

6. Close the **Computer Management** window.

REFERENCE WINDOW | **RW**

Displaying User Account Information Using the Computer Management Tool

- Right-click My Computer, and then click Manage.
- In the console tree pane of the Computer Management window, click the expand view box ⊞ for Local Users and Groups, and then click the Users folder icon.
- In the contents pane on the right, locate and then double-click the user name.
- In the Properties dialog box for your user name, examine the settings on the property sheets for your user account and then, if necessary, make changes to those settings.
- Click Cancel to close the dialog box without making any changes, or click OK to close the dialog box and save changes to your user account settings.
- Close the Computer Management window.

You can display comparable information on user accounts within a Command Prompt window.

To display user information at the Command Prompt window:

1. Maximize the **Command Prompt** window, and then clear the **window**.

2. Enter: `net user`

   NET USER displays a list of users for your computer.

3. Maximize the **Command Prompt** window, clear the **window**, type `net user` followed by a space and then your user name (enclose your user name in quotation marks if it contains spaces), and then press **Enter** to display information about your user account. See Figure 10-34. Notice that the information is comparable to what you would see if you used the Computer Management administrative tool.

Figure 10-34	VIEWING LOCAL USERS FROM THE COMMAND PROMPT WINDOW

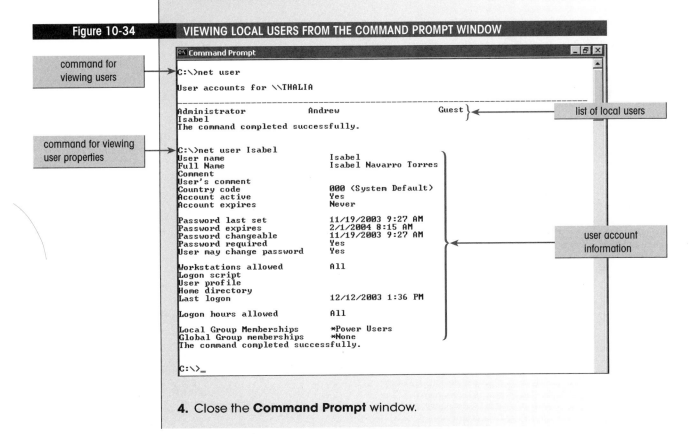

4. Close the **Command Prompt** window.

If you redirect the output of the Net User command, you can document account settings for a specific user even if you do not have Administrator privileges. This option is not available in the graphical user interface.

REFERENCE WINDOW	RW

Viewing User Account Information from a Command Prompt Window
- Open a Command Prompt window.
- To display a list of users on your computer, type NET USER, and then press Enter.
- To view information on a specific user's account, type NET USER, press the Spacebar, type that user's account name, and then press Enter.
- Close the Command Prompt window.

Because networking is such an important component of each employee's job, and because employees may need to use both the graphical user interface and the command-line environment, Isabel and her staff strongly encourage employees to participate in regular network training sessions to develop these necessary skills.

Session 10.1 QUICK CHECK

1. A(n) _____ is a small network that consists of 2 to 10 computers located within the same general area and does not require a central server to manage the network.

2. The _____ is an add-in card that provides a physical interface and the circuitry that enables a computer to access a network and exchange data.

3. _____ is the Windows 2000 default network protocol that enables computers with different types of hardware architectures and different types of operating systems to communicate with each other.

4. A(n) _____ is a 32-bit address that identifies a node (such as a computer) on a network.

5. A path notation starting with two backslashes (\\) followed by the name of another computer on the network is called the _____ format.

6. To simplify access to a shared directory on another computer, you can assign, or _____, a drive letter to that shared directory.

7. In a Command Prompt window, you can use the _____ to display a list of local network computers, as well as a list of shared resources on a specific computer in the network.

8. To map a drive letter to a shared directory folder in a Command Prompt window, use the _____ command.

9. You can use the _____ command to share a directory folder when working in a Command Prompt window.

10. If you want to display information about a user in a Command Prompt window, use the _____ command.

SESSION 10.2

In this session you'll work with three TCP/IP commands: IPCONFIG, to check the IP address for your network adapter and your dial-up connection; PING, to test the connection with another computer on your local network and a server at a Web site; and TRACERT, to view a list of routers on a subnetwork and the Internet. You will connect to an FTP site on the Internet and use FTP commands to navigate the directory structure of that site and download files. Additionally, you will create a network connection to an FTP site using the Add Network Connection Wizard and compare the graphical user interface with the command line environment for accessing and downloading files from an FTP site.

Using TCP/IP Commands

As members of Isabel's staff set up network connections, they need to assign IP addresses to networked computers, check network connections, and troubleshoot problems with the transmission of data to Web sites. Windows 2000 includes a set of TCP/IP commands that provides staff members with the tools they need—including some command line tools not available in the graphical user interface.

Using IPCONFIG to Display Information on IP Addresses

If you want to view information on the configuration of your network adapter or your dial-up Internet connection, you can use the IPCONFIG command in a Command Prompt window. If your computer uses DHCP (Dynamic Host Configuration Protocol) or APIPA (Automatic Private IP Addressing), then the IPCONFIG command displays the TCP/IP configuration values that are automatically assigned by the DHCP server or by APIPA. If you or your network administrator manually assigned the IP address and subnet mask, then IPCONFIG displays those settings.

If you connect to the Internet using a dial-up connection and use the IPCONFIG command, this utility will display the IP address for your dial-up connection. ISPs and online services assign this temporary address when you connect to the Internet.

Note: if your computer is not part of a local area network, the steps below may not display all of the described information.

> *To display your IP settings:*
>
> 1. Open a **Command Prompt** window, set **colors** (if necessary), and then clear the **window**.
>
> 2. Enter: `ipconfig`
>
>   IPCONFIG displays your computer's IP settings, which will be in the same format as those shown in Figure 10-35.

If you type IPCONFIG with no switches, the command displays a heading and four items for each network adapter in your computer:

- A heading specifying the type of adapter (Ethernet in Figure 10-35) and the name of the adapter (Local Area Connection in Figure 10-35).
- Connection-specific DNS Suffix: When you specify a computer name (in a UNC path, for example), this optional field contains one of the suffixes added to the name (for example, course.com) to help locate the computer on your local network or on the Internet.

- IP Address or Autoconfiguration IP Address: This is the permanent or temporary network address of your computer.
- Subnet Mask: This set of numbers defines how to divide your IP address between the network number and the host number for your particular computer.
- Default Gateway: This optional field contains the IP address of a specially designated computer or device used to connect to addresses outside your local network.

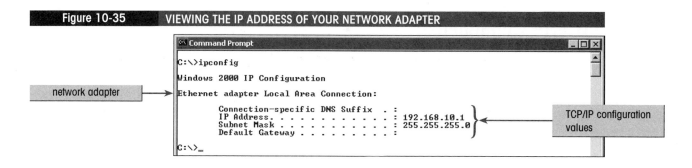

Figure 10-35   VIEWING THE IP ADDRESS OF YOUR NETWORK ADAPTER

```
C:\>ipconfig

Windows 2000 IP Configuration

Ethernet adapter Local Area Connection:

        Connection-specific DNS Suffix  . :
        IP Address. . . . . . . . . . . : 192.168.10.1
        Subnet Mask . . . . . . . . . . : 255.255.255.0
        Default Gateway . . . . . . . . :

C:\>_
```

network adapter

TCP/IP configuration values

To view more information about your IP configuration:

1. Clear the **window**.

2. Enter: `ipconfig /all`

As shown in Figure 10-36, if you use the /ALL switch with IPCONFIG, it provides information about your Windows 2000 IP configuration (including the host name, which is the name of your computer), as well as more detail on your Local Area Connection.

Figure 10-36   VIEWING A MORE DETAILED SUMMARY OF YOUR IP CONFIGURATION

```
C:\>ipconfig /all

Windows 2000 IP Configuration

        Host Name . . . . . . . . . . . : Thalia
        Primary DNS Suffix  . . . . . . :
        Node Type . . . . . . . . . . . : Broadcast
        IP Routing Enabled. . . . . . . : No
        WINS Proxy Enabled. . . . . . . : No

Ethernet adapter Local Area Connection:

        Connection-specific DNS Suffix  . :
        Description . . . . . . . . . . : 3Com EtherLink III ISA (3C509b-TPC)
        Physical Address. . . . . . . . : 00-60-08-8E-7C-D9
        DHCP Enabled. . . . . . . . . . : No
        IP Address. . . . . . . . . . . : 192.168.10.1
        Subnet Mask . . . . . . . . . . : 255.255.255.0
        Default Gateway . . . . . . . . :
        DNS Servers . . . . . . . . . . :

C:\>_
```

switch to show detailed information

You can also use the IPCONFIG to view information about your dial-up connection. Depending on how your computer is set up, you might have a dial-up connection to the Internet and perhaps one to a corporate network as well.

To view information about a dial-up connection:

1. If you have dial-up networking installed, connect to the **Internet** or your **corporate network**, clear the **Command Prompt** window, and then enter: `ipconfig`

IPCONFIG now displays IP information about your dial-up networking connection, labeled PPP adapter, and an identification label, as in Figure 10-37. **Point-to-Point Protocol (PPP)** is a commonly used protocol for remote access that provides stability and error-correcting features and is supported by Windows 2000 and Windows NT Server. ISPs generally use this type of protocol to provide Internet access to their users. Windows 2000 allows you to set up other protocols for special situations. **Serial Line Interface Protocol (SLIP)** is an older, remote-access standard for connecting to servers, including UNIX servers. **Compressed SLIP (C-SLIP)** compresses data prior to transmission.

Figure 10-37	VIEWING THE IP ADDRESS OF YOUR DIAL-UP CONNECTION

```
C:\>ipconfig

Windows 2000 IP Configuration

Ethernet adapter Local Area Connection:

        Connection-specific DNS Suffix  . :
        IP Address. . . . . . . . . . . . : 192.168.10.1
        Subnet Mask . . . . . . . . . . . : 255.255.255.0
        Default Gateway . . . . . . . . . :

PPP adapter <E217EF2C-BAB5-4CD8-A4FD-9CB0F546F853>:  ◄───── dial-up connection

        Connection-specific DNS Suffix  . :
        IP Address. . . . . . . . . . . . : 209.204.136.113
        Subnet Mask . . . . . . . . . . . : 255.255.255.255
        Default Gateway . . . . . . . . . : 209.204.136.113

C:\>_
```

2. Maximize the **Command Prompt** window, clear the **window**, and then enter: `ipconfig /all`

With the /ALL switch, IPCONFIG also provides additional information about your dial-up connection. See Figure 10-38. Under Description, note that you are connected to a WAN.

Figure 10-38   **VIEWING A MORE DETAILED SUMMARY OF YOUR DIAL-UP CONNECTION**

switch to show
detailed information

```
C:\>ipconfig /all

Windows 2000 IP Configuration

        Host Name . . . . . . . . . . : Thalia
        Primary DNS Suffix  . . . . . :
        Node Type . . . . . . . . . . : Broadcast
        IP Routing Enabled. . . . . . : No
        WINS Proxy Enabled. . . . . . : No

Ethernet adapter Local Area Connection:

        Connection-specific DNS Suffix  . :
        Description . . . . . . . . . . : 3Com EtherLink III ISA (3C509b-TPC)
        Physical Address. . . . . . . . : 00-60-08-8E-7C-D9
        DHCP Enabled. . . . . . . . . . : No
        IP Address. . . . . . . . . . . : 192.168.10.1
        Subnet Mask . . . . . . . . . . : 255.255.255.0
        Default Gateway . . . . . . . . :
        DNS Servers . . . . . . . . . . :

PPP adapter {E217EF2C-BAB5-4CD8-A4FD-9CB0F546F853}:

        Connection-specific DNS Suffix  . :
        Description . . . . . . . . . . : WAN (PPP/SLIP) Interface
        Physical Address. . . . . . . . : 00-53-45-00-00-00
        DHCP Enabled. . . . . . . . . . : No
        IP Address. . . . . . . . . . . : 209.204.136.113
        Subnet Mask . . . . . . . . . . : 255.255.255.255
        Default Gateway . . . . . . . . : 209.204.136.113
        DNS Servers . . . . . . . . . . : 208.201.224.11
                                          208.201.224.33
        NetBIOS over Tcpip. . . . . . . : Disabled

C:\>_
```

detailed dial-up
connection information

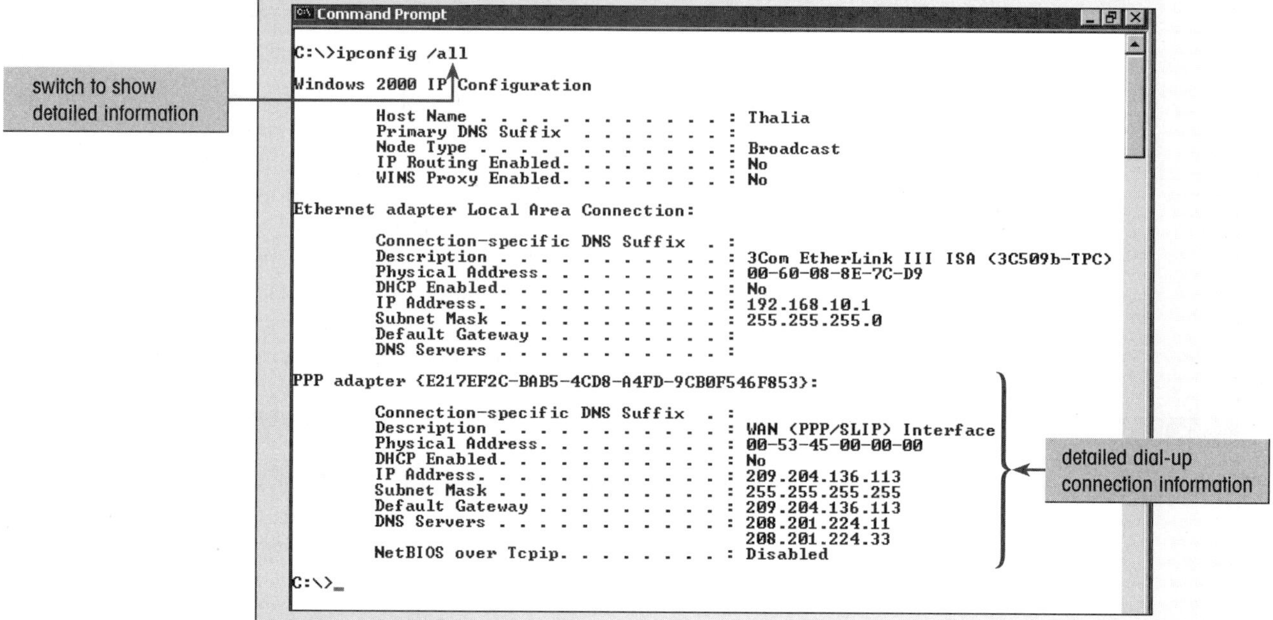

3. Restore the **Command Prompt** window to normal size.

REFERENCE WINDOW   **RW**

Displaying IP Configuration Settings
- Open a Command Prompt window.
- Type IPCONFIG and press Enter to view summary information about the Windows 2000 IP configuration for your Local Area Connection. If you want to view all settings, type IPCONFIG /ALL and then press Enter.
- If you want to view information about your dial-up connection, use your dial-up connection to connect to the Internet or your corporate network, type IPCONFIG, and then press Enter to view a summary of your configuration settings. If you want to view all settings, type IPCONFIG /ALL and then press Enter.

You can use the IPCONFIG to verify that the settings for your IP address and subnet mask settings for your network adapter and Internet connection are correct and unique within your network (that is, they do not conflict with corresponding settings assigned to another computer on your network). If another computer uses the same settings, then a conflict exists and neither computer will be able to connect to the network or Internet. You will need to change the IP host address of one of the computers.

Using PING to Test an IP Connection

You can use the **Packet Internet Groper (PING)** command to check connections to a computer on a local network, or to a remote computer on the Internet; however, for this command to work, the TCP/IP protocol discussed earlier must be installed on your computer.

When you ping another computer, you test whether or not you can communicate with it and determine the reliability of the connection. You can refer to the target computer by its computer name or by using its IP address. If you ping a computer with its computer name, the PING command also reports the IP address of the computer. You can also ping your own computer to test whether or not your TCP/IP configuration is set up correctly; if it isn't, you will not get a response to the PING command.

To test an IP connection with the PING command:

1. Clear the Command Prompt window, and then enter: **net view**

   NET VIEW displays a list of computers in your local network. See Figure 10-39.

   TROUBLE? If NET VIEW does not display any server names, then you are not connected to a network and cannot complete this section of the tutorial. Read, but do not perform, the following steps.

| Figure 10-39 | VIEWING THE COMPUTERS IN YOUR LOCAL AREA NETWORK |

```
Command Prompt                                          _ □ ×

C:\>net view
Server Name              Remark
--------------------------------------------------------
\\ENIGMA                 Ellen's Computer
\\THALIA
The command completed successfully.

C:\>_
```

computers on your local area network

2. Select a **target computer** (other than your own) on your network, and then enter: `ping computername` (using just the target computer's name, without backslashes, in place of *computername*)

   The PING command sends four inquiry packets to the target computer, receives replies, and then presents the resulting statistics, as in Figure 10-40. Note that the PING command reports on whether or not any packets were lost during transmission.

   TROUBLE? If the PING command displays an "Unknown host" error message, then your computer can't locate the target computer using the name you typed. Make sure you have entered the name *without* backslashes (\\ ). If you know the target computer's IP address, try using that instead of the name (for example, PING 192.168.10.2).

Figure 10-40 PINGING A COMPUTER ON A PEER-TO-PEER NETWORK

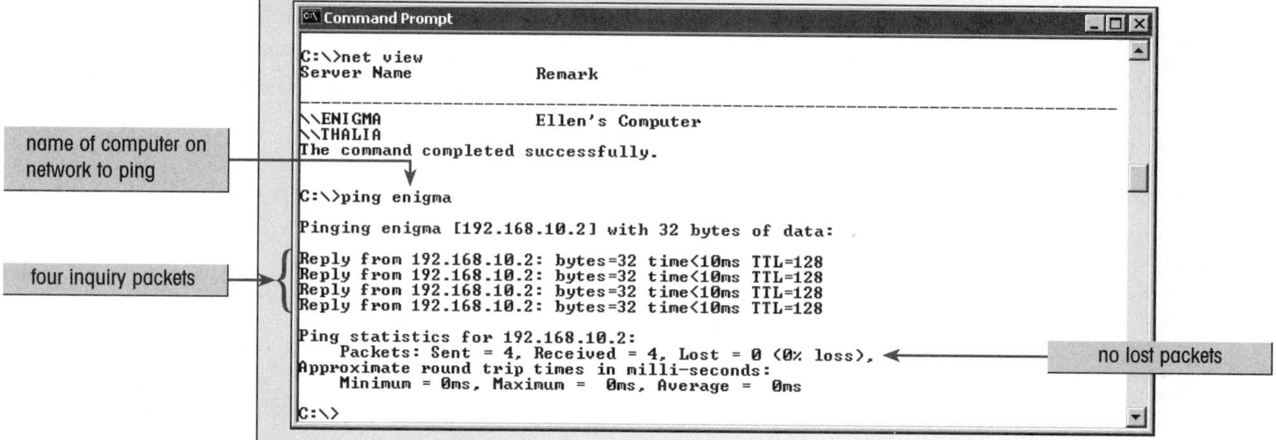

```
Command Prompt                                                    _ □ ×

C:\>net view
Server Name             Remark

---------------------------------------------------------------
\\ENIGMA                Ellen's Computer
\\THALIA
The command completed successfully.

C:\>ping enigma

Pinging enigma [192.168.10.2] with 32 bytes of data:

Reply from 192.168.10.2: bytes=32 time<10ms TTL=128
Reply from 192.168.10.2: bytes=32 time<10ms TTL=128
Reply from 192.168.10.2: bytes=32 time<10ms TTL=128
Reply from 192.168.10.2: bytes=32 time<10ms TTL=128

Ping statistics for 192.168.10.2:
    Packets: Sent = 4, Received = 4, Lost = 0 (0% loss),
Approximate round trip times in milli-seconds:
    Minimum = 0ms, Maximum =  0ms, Average =  0ms

C:\>
```

name of computer on network to ping

four inquiry packets

no lost packets

3. If you logged off your ISP earlier, connect to the **Internet** again to test a dial-up connection.

4. Clear the **window**, and then enter the PING command with an Internet host name: `ping course.com`

This time, PING's statistics reflect a longer round-trip time, as shown in Figure 10-41, because your computer is querying a computer on the Internet rather than a local computer.

Figure 10-41 PINGING A WEB SITE

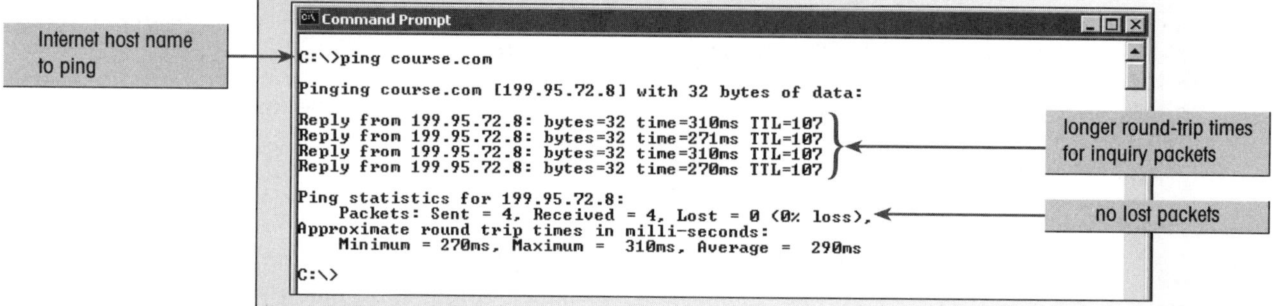

```
Command Prompt                                                    _ □ ×

C:\>ping course.com

Pinging course.com [199.95.72.8] with 32 bytes of data:

Reply from 199.95.72.8: bytes=32 time=310ms TTL=107
Reply from 199.95.72.8: bytes=32 time=271ms TTL=107
Reply from 199.95.72.8: bytes=32 time=310ms TTL=107
Reply from 199.95.72.8: bytes=32 time=270ms TTL=107

Ping statistics for 199.95.72.8:
    Packets: Sent = 4, Received = 4, Lost = 0 (0% loss),
Approximate round trip times in milli-seconds:
    Minimum = 270ms, Maximum =  310ms, Average =  290ms

C:\>
```

Internet host name to ping

longer round-trip times for inquiry packets

no lost packets

5. Clear the **window**, and then enter: `ping localhost`

The name *localhost* is associated with the **loopback address** 127.0.0.1, which always points to your own computer. This is a basic test you can use on any machine to make sure TCP/IP is installed correctly. See Figure 10-42.

TROUBLE? If the above step produces error messages, you may need to reinstall TCP/IP on your computer. If you are using a computer in your college's computer lab, notify your instructor or lab staff.

Figure 10-42	PINGING YOUR COMPUTER

loopback name for
your computer

loopback address

```
Command Prompt                                              _ □ X

C:\>ping localhost

Pinging Thalia [127.0.0.1] with 32 bytes of data:

Reply from 127.0.0.1: bytes=32 time<10ms TTL=128
Reply from 127.0.0.1: bytes=32 time<10ms TTL=128
Reply from 127.0.0.1: bytes=32 time<10ms TTL=128
Reply from 127.0.0.1: bytes=32 time<10ms TTL=128

Ping statistics for 127.0.0.1:
    Packets: Sent = 4, Received = 4, Lost = 0 (0% loss),
Approximate round trip times in milli-seconds:
    Minimum = 0ms, Maximum =  0ms, Average =  0ms

C:\>_
```

check to verify that
TCP/IP is installed
correctly

REFERENCE WINDOW   **RW**

Using PING to Test an IP Connection
- Type NET VIEW and then press Enter to view a list of computers on your network.
- Type PING computername (replace computername with the target computer's name, without backslashes), and then press Enter.
- If you want to test a dial-up connection, first use your dial-up connection to connect to the Internet or your corporate network, type PING, press the Spacebar, type the Internet computer address you want to check (for example, course.com), and then press Enter.
- If you want to test whether TCP/IP is properly installed on your computer, type PING LOCALHOST and then press Enter.

If you are experiencing problems with the transmission of data (in packets) over a network connection, you can use the PING command to check the data transmission. If PING reports lost packets for a specific network computer, then you have identified the source of the problem and your network administrator can troubleshoot the network connection.

You can also use PING to test Internet Connection Sharing (ICS), a recent Windows feature that allows multiple computers on a home or small office network to connect to the Internet through one computer on the network. ICS is useful if you have only one external line to use for an Internet connection. Install Internet Connection Sharing on the computer that has the Internet connection, and then, once you enable automatic IP addressing, all other computers networked to that computer can access the Internet through the computer. To ping the computer installed with Internet Connection Sharing, use the address 192.168.0.1, because Internet Connection Sharing automatically sets up that address to identify the ICS host.

Using TRACERT to Trace the Route to Another Computer

The TRACERT command (called *traceroute* in UNIX) documents the pathway that IP packets take to reach another computer. It displays a list of routers (also called gateways) between different networks on the way to the target computer, with timing information for each router. Because the route to another computer may vary from time to time, you may see different lists of routers at different times.

To display the route statistics between your computer and another:

1. Clear the **window**, and then enter: *tracert computername* (Replace *computername* with the name of the target computer used with the PING command in the previous section, again with *no* backslashes.)

   The TRACERT command will show a short route to the target computer. Figure 10-43 shows just the other computer, with no router computers between you and your target.

   TROUBLE? If TRACERT displays the message, "Unable to resolve target system name," along with the name of the computer you specified, then your computer can't locate the target computer using the name you provided. As in the previous section, make sure you entered the name with *no* backslashes (\\ ). If you know the target computer's IP address, try using that instead of the computer name (for example, tracert 192.168.10.2).

Figure 10-43	VIEWING ROUTE STATISTICS FOR ANOTHER NETWORK COMPUTER

```
Command Prompt                                              _ □ ×

C:\>tracert enigma

Tracing route to enigma [192.168.10.2]
over a maximum of 30 hops:

  1    <10 ms    <10 ms    <10 ms   ENIGMA [192.168.10.2]

Trace complete.

C:\>_
```

name of computer to trace route

2. If you require dial-up networking to connect to the Internet, launch it if you have not done so already.

3. Clear the **window**, and then enter: **tracert www.thomsonlearning.com**

   The list of intermediate router computers between your computer and www.thomsonlearning.com will differ from that shown in Figure 10-44.

Figure 10-44	TRACING THE ROUTE TO A WEB SITE

name of Web site to trace route

computers through which packets are routed

```
Command Prompt                                              _ □ ×

C:\>tracert www.thomsonlearning.com

Tracing route to www.THOMSONLEARNING.com [199.95.73.12]
over a maximum of 30 hops:

  1    181 ms   160 ms   180 ms   nas21.sonic.net [208.201.224.185]
  2    150 ms   151 ms   150 ms   mega-100BT.sonic.net [208.201.224.1]
  3    160 ms   201 ms   170 ms   aar2-serial5-1-0-0.SanFranciscosfd.cw.net [206.2
4.221.217]
  4    180 ms   191 ms   160 ms   bpr1.pax.cw.net [206.24.210.8]
  5    180 ms   171 ms   180 ms   p6-0.paix-bi1.bbnplanet.net [4.0.2.105]
  6    170 ms   191 ms   170 ms   p7-0.paix-bi2.bbnplanet.net [4.0.3.142]
  7    180 ms   201 ms   190 ms   p6-0.paloalto-nbr1.bbnplanet.net [4.0.6.97]
  8    230 ms   261 ms   240 ms   p3-0.chcgil1-br2.bbnplanet.net [4.24.6.97]
  9    231 ms   240 ms   250 ms   p4-0.chcgil1-br1.bbnplanet.net [4.24.5.225]
 10    231 ms   250 ms   250 ms   p3-0.bstnma1-br1.bbnplanet.net [4.24.6.86]
 11    220 ms   250 ms   251 ms   p4-0.cambridge1-nbr2.bbnplanet.net [4.0.5.158]
 12    230 ms   270 ms   251 ms   p4-1-0.cambridge1-colo2.bbnplanet.net [4.0.5.250
]
 13    220 ms   251 ms   260 ms   www.thomsonlearning.com [199.95.73.12]

Trace complete.

C:\>_
```

Each line in the TRACERT display in Figure 10-44 shows:

- The sequential number (for example, 1, 2, 3, etc.) of the router computer along the path to your target
- Three columns showing the time in milliseconds (ms) it took between routers for three successive tries. The report provides information about the round-trip time (RTT).
- The name and IP address of the router computer. Each router connection in this sequence is referred to as a **hop**.

An asterisk (*) in place of the time in milliseconds indicates that the router timed out —that is, it took too long to reply — so the TRACERT command proceeded to its next inquiry.

REFERENCE WINDOW　　　　　　　　　　　　　　　　　　　　**RW**

Using TRACERT to Trace the Route to Another Computer
- Type NET VIEW and then press Enter to view a list of computers on your network.
- Type TRACERT *computername* (replace *computername* with the name of a target computer, without backslashes), and then press Enter.
- If you want to trace the route to a computer on the Internet, use your dial-up connection to connect to the Internet, type TRACERT, press the Spacebar, type the target Internet computer address you want to check (for example, www.thomsonlearning.com), and then press Enter.

Not only does the TRACERT command provide you with a mechanism for understanding how packets of data are routed on the Internet, but it also identifies routers that affect the transmission of data.

Using FTP

Isabel asks you to download some files that you and other staff members will need to build new templates. The files are currently located on the company's FTP site. Isabel would like you first to become familiar with the command-line form of FTP, because it is used by earlier versions of Windows, as well as UNIX. Then, she would like you to create a connection to an FTP site using the Add Network Place Wizard found in My Network Places.

Using **File Transfer Protocol (FTP)**, you can download files from, and upload to, FTP sites on the Internet. These FTP sites are running an FTP server service (also known as a **daemon** in UNIX) that creates a subenvironment in which you can issue FTP commands. Under Windows 2000, FTP is a command line subsystem with a set of 52 of its own commands.

FTP is particularly useful if you need to send or receive large files, such as program files. You can use FTP to download and upload files so you do not need to attach large files to e-mail messages and create lengthy download times for the individual to whom you sent the message. Furthermore, e-mail attachments are frequently subject to size limitations by ISPs. Instead, you can post the file at an FTP site, and then the recipient can download the file at his or her convenience. You may have FTP space assigned to your personal account on that server, or the system administrator will give you a password.

You can use FTP either from the command prompt, or by using My Network Places on the desktop; each method has advantages and disadvantages.

To complete this section of the tutorial, you will need an e-mail address so you can log onto an FTP server. If you do not have an e-mail address, read, but do not perform, the steps in this section of the tutorial.

If the remote host (the FTP server) closes your connection before you complete these steps, you will need to log back onto the FTP server and repeat the steps from the beginning.

If, for some reason, you are not able to connect to ftp://ftp2.course.com, you can use another FTP site and adapt the following instructions to that site. Ask your instructor about possible alternate FTP sites you might use.

To connect to an FTP site from a Command Prompt window:

1. If necessary, connect to your **ISP** or **online service**.

2. Insert an empty, formatted diskette into drive A, and then switch to the root directory on drive A.

3. Enter: `ftp ftp2.course.com`

   FTP connects you to the FTP site at ftp2.course.com, and the FTP server prompts you for your user name.

4. Enter: `anonymous`

   The FTP server verifies that Anonymous access is allowed, and prompts you for your e-mail address.

5. When the FTP server prompts you for a password, enter your **e-mail address** (it does not display on the monitor). You are now connected to the FTP server, and FTP displays the ftp> command prompt. See Figure 10-45.

Figure 10-45	LOGGING ONTO AN FTP SERVER

FTP site

```
C:\>ftp ftp2.course.com
Connected to ftp2.course.com.
220 ice Microsoft FTP Service (Version 4.0).
User (ftp2.course.com:(none)): anonymous
331 Anonymous access allowed, send identity (e-mail name) as password.
Password:
230-Welcome to Course Technology's FTP2 Backup site
230 Anonymous user logged in.
ftp>
```

anonymous logon

enter e-mail address (not shown on screen)

Public FTP servers use your e-mail address to track site usage. Many public FTP sites will allow you to type "ftp" instead of "anonymous" as your user name, and you can often skip the password completely by pressing the Enter key at the password prompt.

REFERENCE WINDOW | **RW**

Connecting to an FTP Site from a Command Prompt Window

- If necessary, connect to your ISP or online service.
- Open a Command Prompt window and specify any default settings that you want to use.
- Type FTP, press the Spacebar, type the address of an FTP site, and then press Enter.
- Enter your user name when prompted, or if the site supports an anonymous logon, type Anonymous and then press Enter.
- When prompted for a password, enter that password. Or, if the site supports an anonymous logon and prompts for an e-mail address, type your e-mail address, and then press Enter.

Many different FTP sites support the use of an Anonymous logon with the option of providing your e-mail address as the password.

Displaying and Changing Directories

Once you connect to an FTP site, you can start by orienting yourself to your location on that FTP server by using the DIR command.

> *To view the current directory and navigate the directory structure of an FTP server:*
>
> **1.** Enter: `dir`
>
> The DIR command displays a directory listing with the name of one directory, "course." See Figure 10-46. Since FTP sites, like Web sites, change over time, your directory listing may differ. Like the Windows 2000 DIR command, the FTP DIR command displays file and directory names at the right side of each line. Instead of DIR, you can also use the LS —list— command, which may produce a different display, depending on the type of FTP host computer.

Figure 10-46	VIEWING A DIRECTORY LISTING OF AN FTP SITE

```
Command Prompt - ftp ftp2.course.com

C:\>ftp ftp2.course.com
Connected to ftp2.course.com.
220 ice Microsoft FTP Service (Version 4.0).
User (ftp2.course.com:(none)): anonymous
331 Anonymous access allowed, send identity (e-mail name) as password.
Password:
230-Welcome to Course Technology's FTP2 Backup site
230 Anonymous user logged in.
ftp> dir
200 PORT command successful.
150 Opening ASCII mode data connection for /bin/ls.
09-26-00  01:42PM       <DIR>          course
226 Transfer complete.
ftp: 47 bytes received in 0.01Seconds 4.70Kbytes/sec.
ftp>
```

directory name

> **2.** Enter: `cd course`
>
> The CD command changes to the course directory. See Figure 10-47. Although the DIR command verifies that the operation was completed successfully, the ftp> command prompt does not change appearance. CWD, an alternate CD command, stands for "Change Working Directory."

Figure 10-47	CHANGING TO ANOTHER DIRECTORY AT AN FTP SITE

```
Command Prompt - ftp ftp2.course.com

C:\>ftp ftp2.course.com
Connected to ftp2.course.com.
220 ice Microsoft FTP Service (Version 4.0).
User (ftp2.course.com:(none)): anonymous
331 Anonymous access allowed, send identity (e-mail name) as password.
Password:
230-Welcome to Course Technology's FTP2 Backup site
230 Anonymous user logged in.
ftp> dir
200 PORT command successful.
150 Opening ASCII mode data connection for /bin/ls.
09-26-00  01:42PM       <DIR>          course
226 Transfer complete.
ftp: 47 bytes received in 0.01Seconds 4.70Kbytes/sec.
ftp> cd course
250 CWD command successful.
ftp>
```

changing to a directory at an FTP site

3. Enter: `pwd`

In UNIX, the PWD (Print Working Directory) command identifies the name of the current directory. See Figure 10-48. The term "Print" in "Print Working Directory" was originally used to describe the process of displaying output, whether printed on a teletype or displayed on a video monitor. Note that the path uses UNIX syntax with a forward slash (not a backslash) to separate directory names.

Figure 10-48	VIEWING THE PATH OF THE CURRENT DIRECTORY

```
Command Prompt - ftp ftp2.course.com                              _ □ ×
C:\>ftp ftp2.course.com
Connected to ftp2.course.com.
220 ice Microsoft FTP Service (Version 4.0).
User (ftp2.course.com:(none)): anonymous
331 Anonymous access allowed, send identity (e-mail name) as password.
Password:
230-Welcome to Course Technology's FTP2 Backup site
230 Anonymous user logged in.
ftp> dir
200 PORT command successful.
150 Opening ASCII mode data connection for /bin/ls.
09-26-00  01:42PM       <DIR>          course
226 Transfer complete.
ftp: 47 bytes received in 0.01Seconds 4.70Kbytes/sec.
ftp> cd course
250 CWD command successful.
ftp> pwd
257 "/course" is current directory.
ftp>
```

path of current directory

4. Use the DIR command to display a directory listing of the current directory. As you can tell from the directory listing, the "course" directory contains many different subdirectories. See Figure 10-49.

Figure 10-49	DISPLAYING A DIRECTORY LISTING

```
Command Prompt - ftp ftp2.course.com                              _ □ ×
10-05-00   09:05AM    <DIR>        Computer_Concepts
07-10-00   11:03AM    <DIR>        CP_MODS
10-10-00   02:46PM    <DIR>        Database
07-10-00   11:04AM    <DIR>        Demos
07-10-00   11:04AM    <DIR>        Finance_Accounting
10-10-00   03:56PM    <DIR>        Graphic_Design
07-10-00   11:05AM    <DIR>        Help_Desk
10-10-00   02:47PM    <DIR>        Integrated_Apps
10-13-00   05:09PM    <DIR>        Internet
07-10-00   11:08AM    <DIR>        MIS
07-10-00   11:08AM    <DIR>        Networking
10-13-00   04:52PM    <DIR>        Operating_Systems
07-10-00   11:09AM    <DIR>        Other
07-10-00   11:10AM    <DIR>        Presentation
10-04-00   03:49PM    <DIR>        Presentation_DTP
10-10-00   02:48PM    <DIR>        Programming
08-31-00   10:51AM    <DIR>        project_mgmt
07-10-00   11:13AM    <DIR>        Software
09-26-00   01:43PM    <DIR>        Spreadsheets
07-10-00   11:14AM    <DIR>        Updates
10-04-00   03:39PM    <DIR>        Word_Processing
09-26-00   01:42PM    <DIR>        Wordprocessing
226 Transfer complete.
ftp: 1246 bytes received in 0.15Seconds 8.31Kbytes/sec.
ftp>
```

partial directory listing

5. To clear the window, enter: `!cls`

Although the FTP program does not have its own command to clear the screen, you can issue any MS-DOS subsystem command by prefixing it with an exclamation point (!). FTP temporarily invokes the CMD command interpreter to process your command, then immediately returns to the ftp> command prompt. If you type ! by itself, FTP will launch a new command interpreter session; typing EXIT will then return you to the ftp> prompt.

6. To change to one of the listed subdirectories, enter: `cd Operating_Systems`

7. To step down one more directory, enter: `cd 1976-x`

8. Display a directory listing of the current directory. This directory contains a set of self-extracting binary zip files with the "exe" and "zip" file extensions, and ASCII text files with the "csv," "prn," and "txt" file extensions. See Figure 10-50.

| Figure 10-50 | VIEWING THE CONTENTS OF THE 1976-X DIRECTORY |

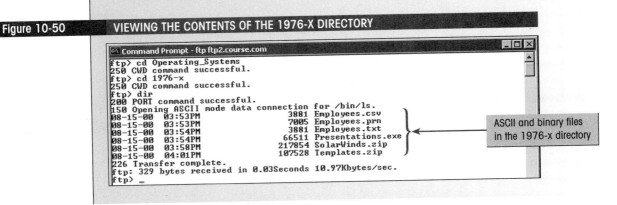

ASCII and binary files in the 1976-x directory

REFERENCE WINDOW   **RW**

Displaying and Changing Directories on an FTP Site

■ After connecting to an FTP site, type DIR and then press Enter to view a directory listing, or type LS (the UNIX list directory command), and then press Enter to display a directory with only the directory names and filenames. Depending on the type of host computer, you may get the same results from both LS and DIR.

■ To view the contents of a directory, type DIR, press the Spacebar, type the directory name, and then press Enter.

■ To change to a directory, type CD, press the Spacebar, type the directory name, and then press Enter.

■ To view the path and name of the current directory, type PWD and then press Enter.

■ To clear the window, type !CLS and then press Enter.

If you need to change the directory on your local computer, you can use the LCD (Local Change Directory) command, and then specify the path to that directory. Otherwise, FTP uses the current directory on your local computer before issuing the FTP command to connect to the FTP server. For example, if you want to change from the root directory of drive C to the A:\Downloads directory, you would enter: LCD A:\Downloads as the command.

Downloading a File from an FTP Site

Before you download a file from an FTP site using the GET command, you need to specify whether the file type is ASCII (a text file) or a binary image (such as an executable file, a zip file, or a Word document). The default setting is typically ASCII, so you will need to change it if you want to download a binary image. When downloading a file in binary mode, FTP copies the file unchanged. You can also check the current setting for the file transfer type by using the TYPE command. On FTP sites that permit you to upload files, you can use the PUT command to copy files from your local computer to the FTP site.

To download a file from an FTP server:

1. To clear the window, enter: `!cls`

2. Enter: `type`

FTP reports that it is using ASCII mode to transfer files. See Figure 10-51. Because the first file you want to download is a text file, you do not need to change the file type.

Figure 10-51   **DISPLAYING THE CURRENT FILE TRANSFER MODE**

```
Command Prompt - ftp ftp2.course.com
ftp> type
Using ascii mode to transfer files.
ftp> _
```

> command for
> displaying the current
> file transfer mode

3. Enter: `get Employees.txt`

After the download is complete, you will see the message "Transfer complete." See Figure 10-52.

Figure 10-52   **DOWNLOADING AN ASCII TEXT FILE**

```
Command Prompt - ftp ftp2.course.com
ftp> type
Using ascii mode to transfer files.
ftp> get Employees.txt
200 PORT command successful.
150 Opening ASCII mode data connection for Employees.txt(3881 bytes).
226 Transfer complete.
ftp: 3881 bytes received in 0.74Seconds 5.24Kbytes/sec.
ftp> _
```

> command for
> downloading an ASCII
> text file

The next file you want to download is a binary image, so you will need to change and then verify the file transfer type.

4. Clear the **window** as you did in the step above.

5. Enter: `binary`

6. Enter: `type`

FTP changes the file transfer type to I (Image), and then reports that it used binary mode to transfer files. See Figure 10-53.

Figure 10-53   **CHANGING TO BINARY TRANSFER MODE**

```
Command Prompt - ftp ftp2.course.com
ftp> binary
200 Type set to I.
ftp> type
Using binary mode to transfer files.
ftp> _
```

> current transfer mode

> command for changing
> to binary transfer mode

As was evident when you downloaded the "Employees.txt" file, FTP does not provide any indicator on the progress of the download. However, if you issue the HASH command before downloading a file, FTP will display the pound sign (#), also known as a **hash mark**, to represent each block of data that it transfers. Not only can you get a general idea of the progress of the download, but you also have a way of verifying that a download is actually occurring.

7. Enter: `hash`

The HASH command reports that hash mark printing is now on, and that each hash mark represents 2,048 bytes. See Figure 10-54.

Figure 10-54   **ENABLING HASH MARK PRINTING**

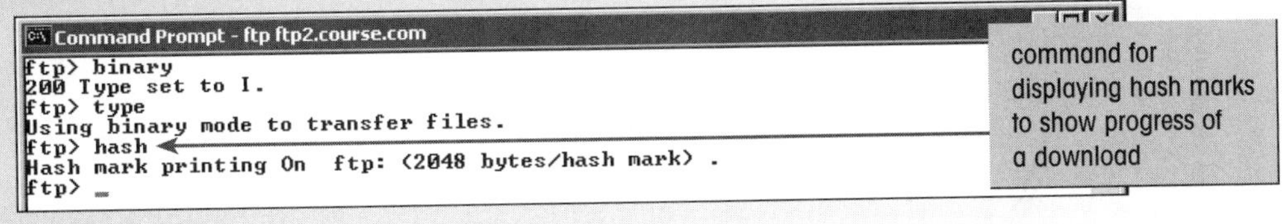

command for displaying hash marks to show progress of a download

Now you're ready to download a file.

8. Enter: `get Presentations.exe`

The FTP service displays a hash mark as a progress indicator, and after the download is complete, you see the message "Transfer complete." See Figure 10-55. Remember, if a filename contains spaces, you will need to enclose the long filename within quotation marks (otherwise, the space is interpreted as a delimiter).

Figure 10-55   **DOWNLOADING A BINARY FILE**

hash marks

command for downloading a binary file

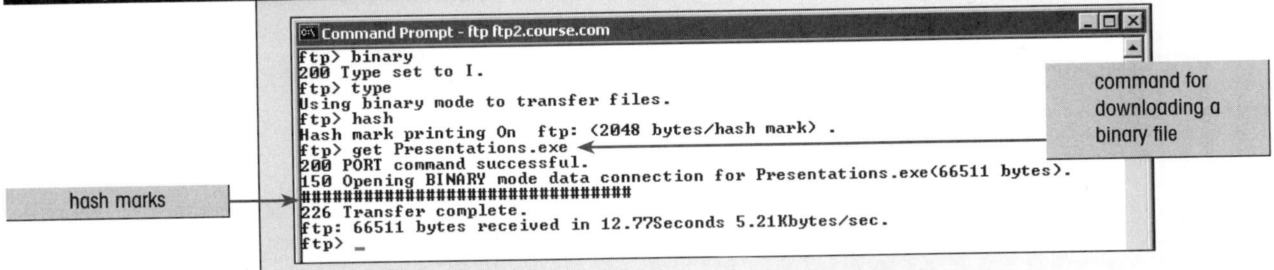

Now that you have downloaded the file you need, you can log off the FTP server and close FTP.

9. Enter: `bye`

10. Close the **Command Prompt** window.

REFERENCE WINDOW **RW**

Downloading a File from an FTP Site

- Type TYPE and then press Enter to view the current mode used for transferring files.
- If you want to download an ASCII file, type ASCII and then press Enter to change to ASCII mode. ASCII is generally the default transfer mode if you do not specify another mode.
- If you want to download a binary image file, type BINARY, and then press Enter to change to binary mode.
- If you want hash mark printing to show the progress of the download, type HASH and then press Enter.
- If you want to download a single file, type GET, press the Spacebar, type the filename (use quotation marks around long filenames with spaces), and then press Enter.

If the FTP site permits you to perform uploads, change to the local directory that contains the file you want to upload, start FTP, connect to the FTP server you want to use, change to binary mode if the file is not an ASCII file, then use the PUT command and specify the filename you want to upload. As illustrated in the previous steps, you might want to use hash marks so you have a general idea of the progress of the upload.

Creating a Network Connection to an FTP Site

Using a feature new to Windows 2000, you can also create a network connection to an FTP site so you can download and upload files using My Network Places instead of the command-line environment. You can then take advantage of drag-and-drop to download and upload files. This approach for connecting to an FTP site can perform only binary-mode transfers, and you cannot transfer ASCII text files. Instead, you must use the command-line FTP utility to download or upload such text files.

To create an FTP connection using the Add Network Place Wizard:

1. If necessary, connect to your **ISP** or **online service**.

2. From the desktop, open **My Network Places**. In the "My Network Places" window, you will see an Add Network Place icon, an Entire Network icon, and a Computers Near Me icon. See Figure 10-56. You may also see one or more icons for network connections to shared resources (such as the "C on Pentium ii" icon in this figure).

Figure 10-56 VIEWING THE CONTENTS OF MY NETWORK PLACES

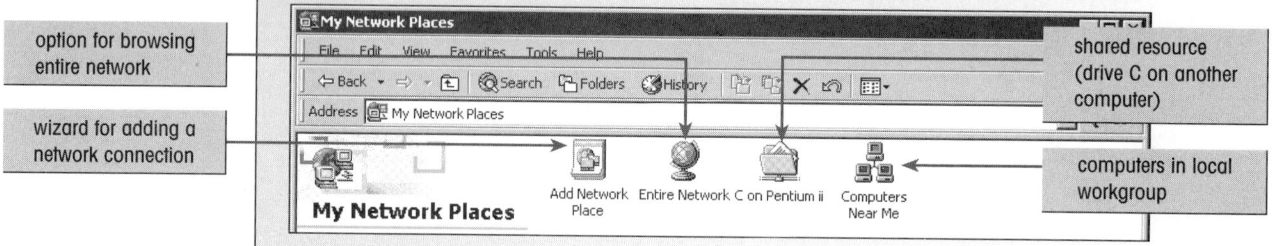

3. Open **Add Network Place**. Windows 2000 displays an Add Network Place Wizard dialog box and explains that you can add a link to a Network Place where you can store documents. See Figure 10-57. A Network Place can be a shared folder, a Web folder on the Internet, or an FTP site.

| Figure 10-57 | STARTING THE ADD NETWORK PLACE WIZARD |

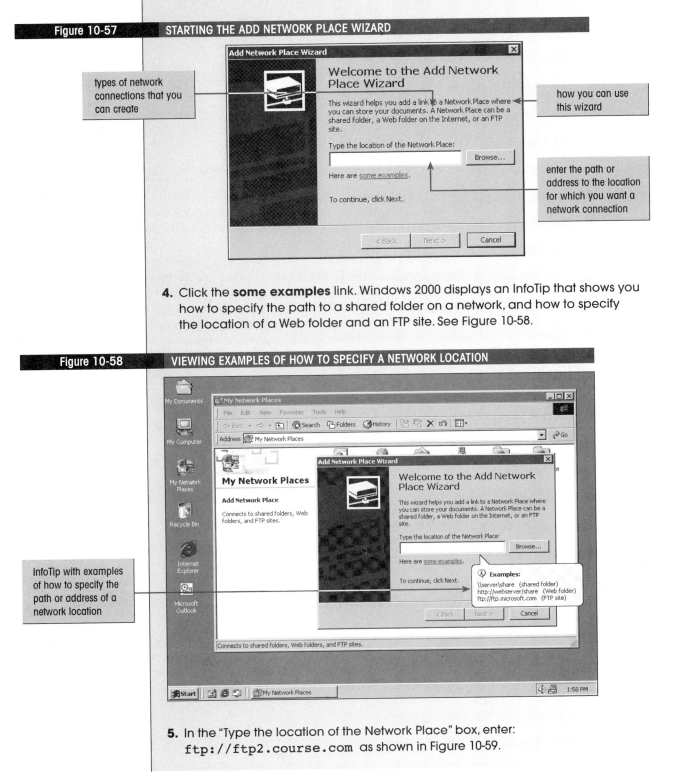

types of network
connections that you
can create

how you can use
this wizard

enter the path or
address to the location
for which you want a
network connection

4. Click the **some examples** link. Windows 2000 displays an InfoTip that shows you how to specify the path to a shared folder on a network, and how to specify the location of a Web folder and an FTP site. See Figure 10-58.

| Figure 10-58 | VIEWING EXAMPLES OF HOW TO SPECIFY A NETWORK LOCATION |

InfoTip with examples
of how to specify the
path or address of a
network location

5. In the "Type the location of the Network Place" box, enter: `ftp://ftp2.course.com` as shown in Figure 10-59.

| Figure 10-59 | SPECIFYING THE FTP SITE |

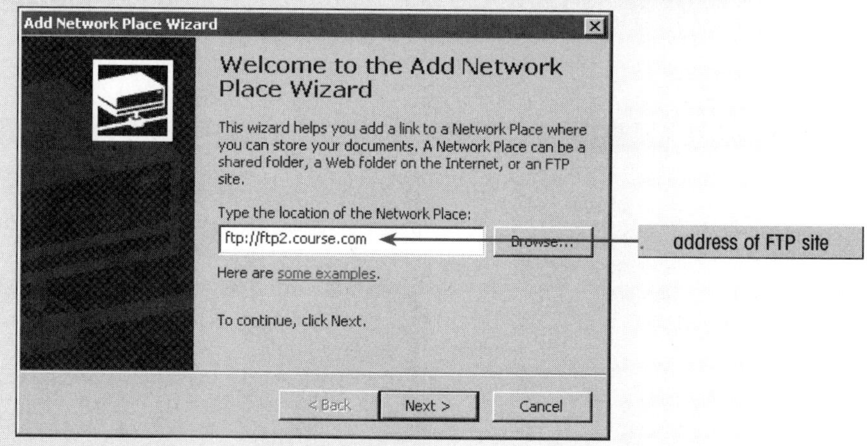

address of FTP site

6. Click **Next**. In the next dialog box, you have the option of specifying whether or not to log on anonymously. See Figure 10-60. The Add Network Place Wizard notes that most FTP servers permit users to log on anonymously, but with limited access to the FTP server. If this option is enabled, then the User name box is dimmed, and Windows 2000 will use "Anonymous" as the logon name. If you remove the check mark from the "Log on anonymously" check box, you can specify a different user name for an FTP site. For example, if you need to transfer files to or from a remote server in order to manage your Web site, you would normally do so with a private user name and password.

| Figure 10-60 | OPTION FOR AN ANONYMOUS LOGON |

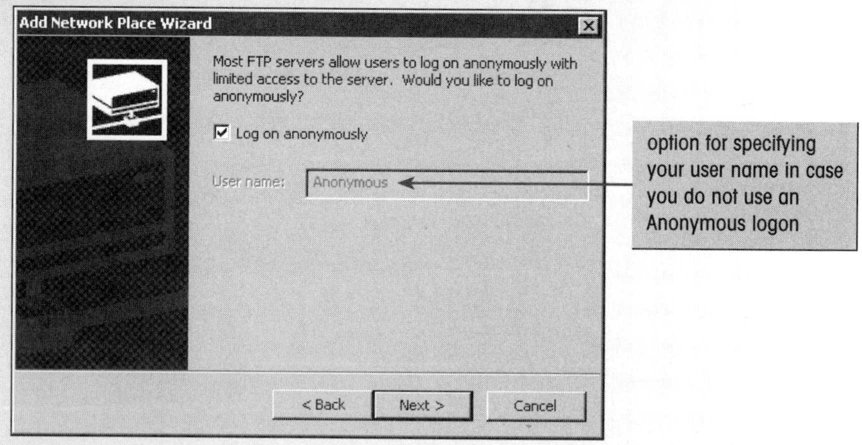

option for specifying your user name in case you do not use an Anonymous logon

7. Make sure there is a **check mark** in the "Log on anonymously" check box, and then click **Next**. The Add Network Place Wizard is now ready to connect to the FTP site you specified. The next step asks for your own name for the FTP site, but defaults to the site's Internet name. See Figure 10-61. You can specify any name for this Network Place.

Figure 10-61   COMPLETING THE NETWORK CONNECTION

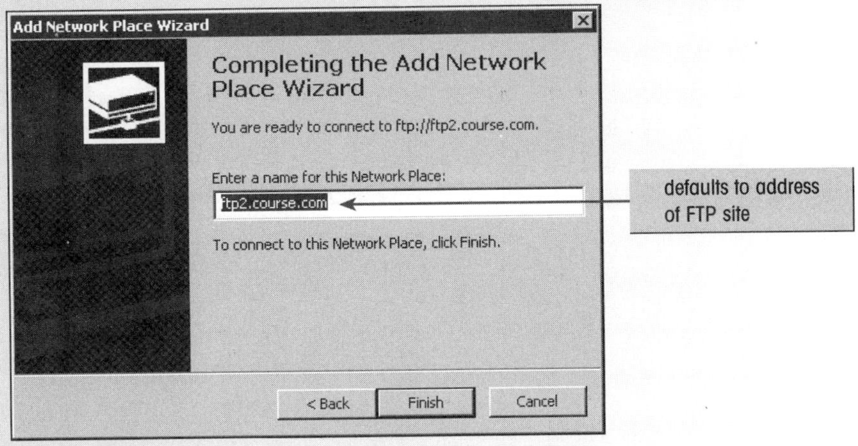

defaults to address
of FTP site

8. In the "Enter a name for this Network Place" box, enter: `CTI FTP Site`

9. Click the **Finish** button in the Add Network Place Wizard dialog box, and then wait a moment. After Windows 2000 displays a CTI FTP Site window, it displays the message "Getting contents of folder" on the status bar, and then you will see the "course" folder in the CTI FTP Site window. See Figure 10-62.

Figure 10-62   VIEWING THE CONTENTS OF AN FTP SITE

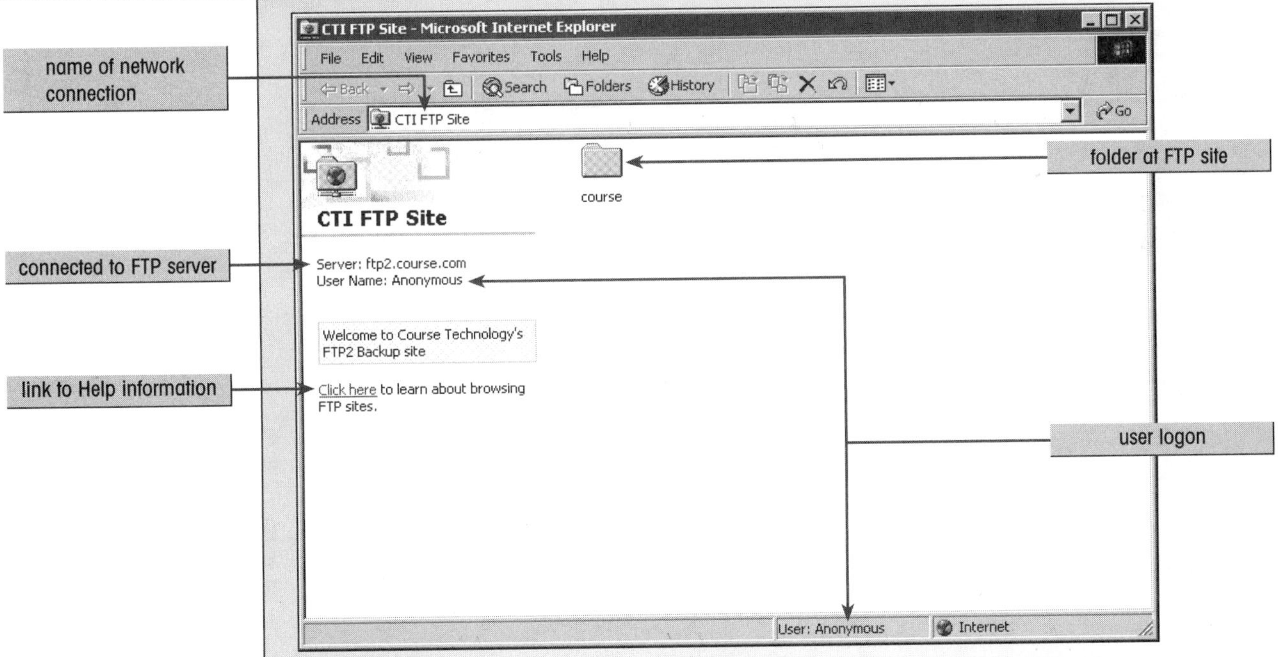

name of network
connection

folder at FTP site

connected to FTP server

link to Help information

user logon

Now that you've created this network connection, and have actually connected to the FTP site, you can open the course folder and download a file.

1. Right-click the **My Network Places** taskbar button, and then click **Minimize**.

2. Open the **course** folder, and then wait a moment. Windows 2000 displays the subfolders within the course folder. See Figure 10-63.

| Figure 10-63 | VIEWING THE CONTENTS OF THE "COURSE" FOLDER |

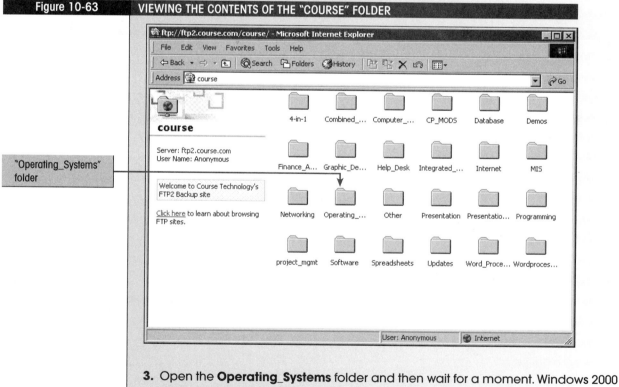

"Operating_Systems" folder

3. Open the **Operating_Systems** folder and then wait for a moment. Windows 2000 displays the folders within this folder. See Figure 10-64.

Figure 10-64 VIEWING THE CONTENTS OF THE "OPERATING_SYSTEMS" FOLDER

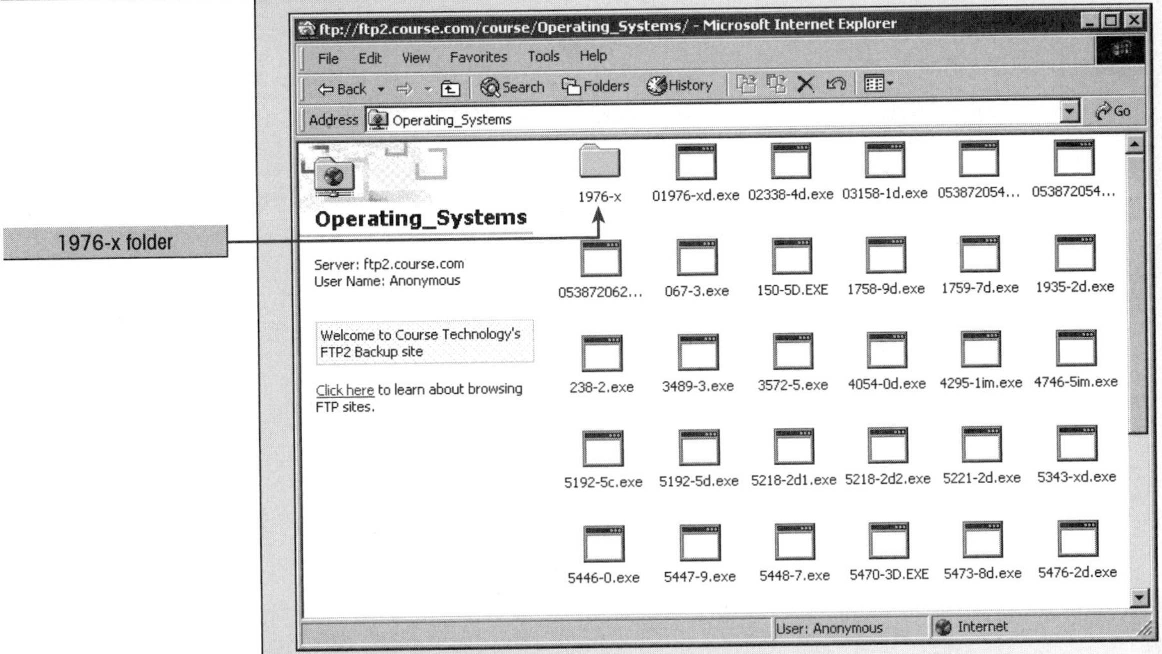

1976-x folder

4. Open the **1976-x** folder, and then wait a moment. Windows 2000 displays the files within this folder. The icons in your display might differ from Figure 10-65.

Figure 10-65 VIEWING THE CONTENTS OF THE "1976-X" DIRECTORY

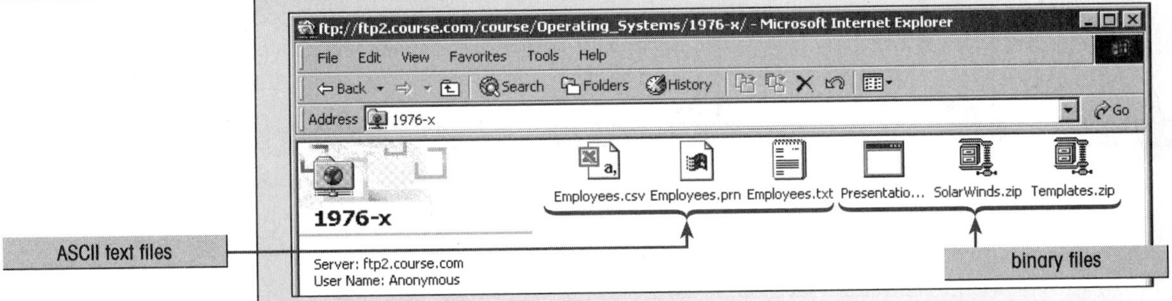

ASCII text files

binary files

5. Use My Computer to open a window on drive A.

6. Click the **ftp://ftp2.course.com** taskbar button to bring the window to the foreground, right-click an empty area of the taskbar, and then click **Tile Windows Vertically**. Windows 2000 arranges the two windows side-by-side. See Figure 10-66.

Figure 10-66 TILING WINDOWS VERTICALLY

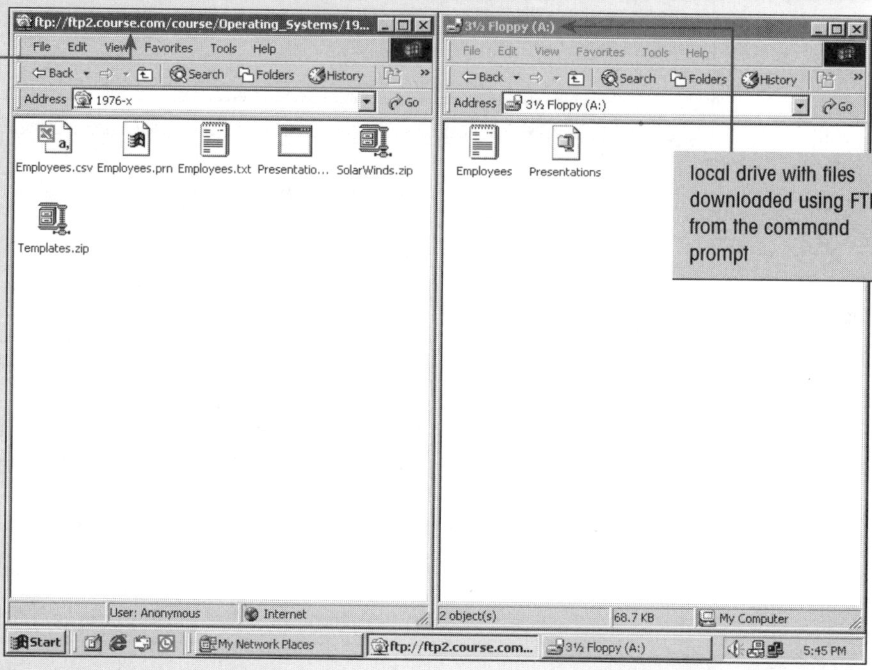

FTP site window with downloadable files

local drive with files downloaded using FTP from the command prompt

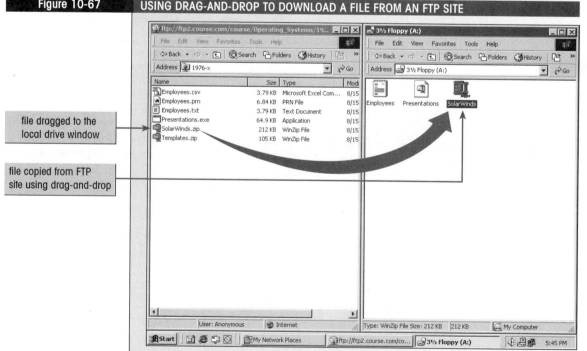

7. In the ftp://ftp2.course.com window, click **View**, and then click **Details**. By switching to Details view, you can see file sizes and make sure the diskette you are going to use for the download contains enough space for the file or files you want to download.

8. Drag the **SolarWinds.zip** file from the ftp://ftp2.course.com window to the 3½ Floppy (A:) window, and then wait a moment. Windows 2000 displays a Copying dialog box and then copies the binary file to drive A. See Figure 10-67.

Figure 10-67 USING DRAG-AND-DROP TO DOWNLOAD A FILE FROM AN FTP SITE

file dragged to the local drive window

file copied from FTP site using drag-and-drop

9. Close the **drive A** window, and then close the **ftp://ftp2.course.com** window.

10. Click the **My Network Places** taskbar button. In the My Network Places folder window, you now have an icon for connecting to this FTP site. See Figure 10-68.

| Figure 10-68 | NETWORK CONNECTION FOR AN FTP SITE |

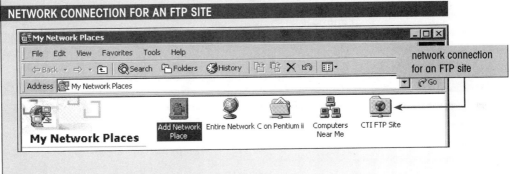

11. Close the **My Network Places** window.

Downloading a Binary File from an FTP Site Using a Network Connection in the My Network Places Window

- Open My Network Places, and then click the icon for the FTP site that you want to access.
- After Windows 2000 connects to the FTP site, locate and then open the folder that contains the file you want to download.
- Minimize the window onto the FTP site, and then open a window onto the local folder into which you want to download the file.
- Click the taskbar button for the FTP site, right-click an empty area of the taskbar, and then click Tile Windows Vertically.
- Drag the file you want to download from the window for the FTP site to the window for your local folder.
- Close the window for the FTP site, and then close the My Network Places window.

You can also perform a similar process from a Windows Explorer window and drag remote files into a local directory folder or drive in the Explorer left-hand *Folders* pane.

If you regularly download and upload files from FTP sites, you may want to simplify the process of connecting, downloading, and uploading files by using the Add Network Place Wizard to create a link for each FTP site in the My Network Places folder.

Using **Telnet**

Many employees need to access SolarWinds' corporate network from their home computers, so Isabel prepares and distributes a memo to all staff on how to use Telnet.

The Windows 2000 Telnet Client uses the Telnet Protocol to open a text-only interactive session with a remote computer over a network, network device, or private TCP/IP network. Telnet users most commonly open command-line sessions on remote computers with operating systems such as Windows NT, Windows 2000, or some variety of UNIX or GNU/Linux. You must have a user account and password on the remote computer to run a command-line session.

Unlike the Telnet Client in previous versions of Windows, the Windows 2000 Telnet Client is a command-line program like that found in UNIX, rather than a separate GUI program running in its own window. To use Telnet, use the following syntax from the command prompt:

TELNET *hostname*

where *hostname* is the name or IP address of the remote computer to which you want to connect.

Figure 10-69 shows the command line to access a college's GNU/Linux server. Telnet shows a "Connecting To" message, and, if it makes a connection, immediately clears the window for the login display. Figure 10-70 shows the beginning of the Telnet command line session.

Figure 10-69   LAUNCHING A TELNET SESSION

host computer name

command line to start Telnet session

```
C:\>telnet gracie.santarosa.edu
Connecting To gracie.santarosa.edu...
```

Figure 10-70   LOGGING IN TO A REMOTE COMPUTER WITH TELNET

login prompt

system indentification

command prompt

user name

password hidden

opening display

command to list remote directory

```
Gracie

gracie.santarosa.edu login: ericdemo
Password:

=============== DISK QUOTA ====================

326        .

==============================================

[ericdemo@gracie ericdemo]$ ls -F
0524.01/     VILEARN/     elm.faq.txt   labs@        names10
2853.01/     atest        flotsam       llfile       perm1/
Hints.txt    bin/         home1.tar     lsfile       test
Mailbox      dead.letter  jetsam.txt    mail/        testlink@
[ericdemo@gracie ericdemo]$ _
```

To change the way Telnet operates, press Ctrl +] to switch to the Telnet control console. As shown in Figure 10-71, entering help displays a list of control commands. To return to your online session, just press Enter without typing anything else.

Figure 10-71   USING THE TELNET CONTROL CONSOLE

help command

available control commands

press Enter to return to session

```
Microsoft (R) Windows 2000 (TM) Version 5.00 (Build 2195)
Welcome to Microsoft Telnet Client
Telnet Client Build 5.00.99201.1

Escape Character is 'CTRL+]'

Microsoft Telnet> help

Commands may be abbreviated. Supported commands are:

close            close current connection
display          display operating parameters
open             connect to a site
quit             exit telnet
set              set options (type 'set ?' for a list)
status           print status information
unset            unset options (type 'unset ?' for a list)
?/help           print help information
Microsoft Telnet> _
```

Hundreds of libraries and other computers on the Internet host Telnet services, comprising a valuable information resource. For example, Figure 10-72 shows the opening menu of the Telnet service of the United States Library of Congress.

| Figure 10-72 | ACCESSING THE LIBRARY OF CONGRESS WITH TELNET |

```
Command Prompt - telnet locis.loc.gov                              _ □ ×
          L O C I S:  LIBRARY OF CONGRESS INFORMATION SYSTEM

            To make a choice: type a number, then press ENTER

     1   Copyright Information     -- files available and up-to-date

     2   Braille and Audio         -- files frozen mid-August 1999

     3   Federal Legislation       -- files frozen December 1998

*    *    *    *    *    *    *    *    *    *    *    *    *    *    *

                The LC Catalog Files are available at:
                  http://lcweb.loc.gov/catalog/

*    *    *    *    *    *    *    *    *    *    *    *    *    *    *

     8   Searching Hours and Basic Search Commands
     9   Library of Congress General Information
    10   Library of Congress Fast Facts

    12   Comments and Logoff
         Choice:
    ▬
```

In her memo, Isabel points out that the standard Telnet Client in Windows 2000 is not secure; it transmits everything you type, including your password, as regular text. Therefore, anyone with the appropriate software could wiretap your connection, steal your password, and commandeer your account. To prevent such a security compromise, other third-party secure Telnet programs that use the SSH (Secure Shell) protocol are available. These programs require that the host computer use SSH protocol as well.

Restoring Your Computer

You will need to remove the network connection that you created to Course Technology's FTP site.

To restore your computer:

1. Open **My Network Places**.

2. Right-click the **CTI FTP Site** network connection icon, click **Delete** and, in the Confirm File Delete dialog box, click **Yes**.

3. Close the **My Network Places** window.

By building a strong understanding of basic network concepts and skills, members of Isabel's staff are in a better position to provide support services to other staff members and to improve those employees' understanding of networks and the benefits of network connectivity in the 21st century.

Session 10.2 QUICK CHECK

1. _____ is a Windows 2000 feature that is used by other computers on a small office or home network to connect to the Internet through one computer.

2. In a Command Prompt window, you can use the _____ command to display information on the configuration of your network adapter and dial-up connection.

3. If you want to test your connection with another computer on the same network or with a remote computer on the Internet from a Command Prompt window, you can use the _____ command.

4. _____ is a command-line diagnostic utility that displays information on the route to an Internet destination.

5. _____ is a command-line subsystem that allows you to connect to a site on the Internet and download or upload files.

6. If you want to download a binary image file from an FTP site, you need to use the _____ command in the FTP command-line subsystem to change from ASCII mode to binary mode.

7. To display the current mode used on an FTP site from the FTP command-line subsystem, use the _____ command.

8. Prior to downloading a file from an FTP site, you can use the _____ command in the FTP command-line subsystem to display pound signs (#) that represent each block of data during the transfer.

9. To download a single file from an FTP site, use the _____ command in the FTP command-line subsystem.

10. Many FTP sites use a(n) _____ log on, and ask you to specify your _____.

11. To change the way Telnet operates, press _____ to switch to a Telnet control console.

COMMAND REFERENCE

COMMAND	USE	BASIC SYNTAX	EXAMPLE
DIR	Displays directories and files on a networked computer	DIR \\computername\ directory	dir \\enigma\sharedocs
FTP	Transfers files to or from a remote computer	FTP hostname (see FTP command summary below)	ftp ftp2.course.com
IPCONFIG	Displays a computer's IP configuration settings; if used with the /ALL switch, displays a detailed summary of these settings	IPCONFIG IPCONFIG /ALL	ipconfig ipconfig /all
NET SHARE	Displays the current shares on your computer	NET SHARE	net share
	Shares, and assigns a share name, to a directory	NET SHARE sharename=	net share Isabel="%userprofile%\My Documents
	Removes sharing, and the share name, from a directory	NET SHARE sharename /DELETE	net share Isabel /delete
NET USE	Displays a list of shared network resources	NET USE	net use
	Maps a drive letter to a shared directory on a networked computer	NET USE drive \\computername\directory	net use f: \\enigma\ sharedocs
	Displays details of a drive mapping	NET USE drive	net use f:
	Removes a drive mapping	NET USE drive /DELETE	net use f: /delete
NET VIEW	Displays a list of local networked computers	NET VIEW	net view
	Displays shared resources on a networked computer	NET VIEW \\computername	net view enigma
NET USER	Displays user information	NET USER	net user

COMMAND REFERENCE (CONTINUED)

COMMAND	USE	BASIC SYNTAX	EXAMPLE
PING	Checks connections to a computer on a network, or to a remote computer; checks your own computer when used with LOCALHOST	PING *computername*	ping enigma ping course.com ping localhost
TELNET	Opens a text-only interactive session with a remote computer	TELNET *hostname*	telnet locis.loc.gov
TRACERT	Displays a list of routers between subnetworks on the way to a target computer	TRACERT *computername*	tracert enigma tracert www.course.com

FTP COMMAND SUMMARY

COMMAND	USE	BASIC SYNTAX	EXAMPLE
ASCII	Changes to the ASCII file transfer mode	ASCII	ascii
BINARY	Changes to the binary file transfer mode	BINARY	binary
BYE	Logs off an FTP server and closes FTP	BYE	bye
CD	Changes to another directory	CD *directoryname*	cd course
DIR	Displays a directory listing	DIR	dir
FTP	Connects your computer to an FTP site	FTP *computername*	ftp ftp2.course.com
GET	Downloads a file from an FTP site to the current directory on a local computer	GET *filename*	get Employees.txt get Presentations.exe
PWD	Displays the path of the current directory	PWD	pwd
TYPE	Displays the current file transfer mode	TYPE	type

Items shown in italics and not enclosed within square brackets are required parameters
Items shown in italics and enclosed within square brackets are optional parameters

REVIEW ASSIGNMENTS

So that the staff members in her department know how to assist other company employees with the company's local area network, Isabel asks you to show all the department staff members how to obtain information on the company's network and its network configuration settings. Since most of her staff members are already familiar with the Windows graphical user interface, she asks you to use the command line environment where possible to improve everyone's understanding of network, TCP/IP, and FTP commands.

The following Review Assignments assume that your computer is part of a network and that you can at least view network settings.

As you complete each step, record your answers to any questions so you can submit them with your lab assignment.

1. Is the computer that you are using part of a network? If so, is it a peer-to-peer network, or a client/server network?

2. Right-click the My Network Places desktop icon, and then select Explore.

3. What options and network components does Windows 2000 display under My Network Places? Are any of these components shared resources? If so, briefly describe what they represent and their purposes.

4. Expand Entire Network, expand Microsoft Windows Network and, if your computer is part of a workgroup, expand the workgroup. What are the names of the local computers connected to your network?

5. Expand the view onto the shared resources of the computer you are using. What resources does Windows 2000 identify as shared resources?

6. Expand the view onto the shared resources of another computer on the network. What resources does Windows 2000 identify as shared resources?

7. Expand "Computers Near Me." What does Windows 2000 display under "Computers Near Me"? (*Note*: If you do not see a "Computer Near Me" icon, either you or your system administrator can create one by temporarily changing your computer's Workgroup name, and then changing it back. Each time you change the Workgroup name, Windows 2000 will prompt you to restart the computer. However, you do not need to restart in this case, and you can just click **No** each time.)

8. Right-click My Network Places, and select Properties. Does Windows 2000 display icons in the Network and Dial-up Connections window for network and dial-up connections? If so, briefly identify each connection and describe its purpose.

9. Right-click the Local Area Connection icon and select Properties. If Windows 2000 displays a Local Network dialog box informing you that some of the controls on the property sheet are disabled because you do not have sufficient privileges to access them, click OK.

10. Click the Configure button under the "Connect using" box with the name of your network adapter. What type of network adapter is installed on your computer?

11. Verify that the network adapter is working properly, and then close the network adapter dialog box without making any changes to the settings.

12. What types of components are installed for this network connection? Identify which components are client software, service software, and protocols.

13. Select the Internet Protocol (TCP/IP) component and, if the Properties button is not dimmed, then click that button. Does Windows 2000 automatically obtain an IP address, or did you or someone else manually specify an IP address? If the latter is the case, what is the IP address and subnet mask on this computer?

14. Close the Internet Protocol (TCP/IP) Properties dialog box, close the Local Area Connection Properties dialog box, click the background of the Network and Dial-up Connections window, and then click the Network Identification link. If the window displays no such link, display the desktop, right-click on My Computer, click Properties, and then click the Network Identification tab. What is the full name of the computer you are using? What is the workgroup name of the computer?

15. Close the System Properties dialog box, and then double-click the Local Area Connection icon in the Network and Dial-up Connections window. What is the speed of your network connection?

16. Close the Local Area Connection Status dialog box, close the Network and Dial-up Connections window, and then close the My Network Places window.

17. Open a Command Prompt window.

18. Use the NET VIEW command to display a list of the computers on your network. What is the UNC path for each of these computer (or server) names? (*Note:* If you need help with the NET VIEW command, you can use the Help switch or NET HELP VIEW to display Help information.)

19. Use the NET VIEW command to display a list of shared resources on another computer in the network. What command did you enter to perform this operation? Are there any shared resources and, if so, what are the share names and share types?

20. Use the NET USE command to assign a drive letter to one of the shared folders on the other computer. What command did you enter to perform this operation?

21. Change to the newly mapped drive, and then display a directory of the contents of the shared folder.

22. Remove the drive mapping that you just created. What command did you enter to perform this operation?

23. Use the NET SHARE command to display a list of shared resources on your computer. List the share names, and the resources that are shared.

24. Select a drive within your computer (such as a zip drive, drive A, or drive C), and use the NET SHARE command to assign the share name CTI to the drive. What command did you enter to perform this operation?

25. Use NET SHARE to verify that the drive is now a shared drive, and then use NET SHARE to remove the CTI share name. What command did you enter to perform this operation?

26. Use the NET USER command to examine information about the Guest user account. What command did you enter for this operation? Is the Guest account active? Is a password required for this account?

27. Use the IPCONFIG command to display configuration information on your network adapter. What is its IP address? Is the IP address configured manually or automatically? What is the subnet mask for the network adapter?

28. Use your dial-up connection to connect to your ISP, and then use the IPCONFIG command to display configuration information on your Internet connection. What is the IP address for your dial-up connection? What is the subnet mask?

29. Insert an empty, formatted diskette into drive A.

30. Use the PING command to ping the address of your college's Web site. Repeat the command, and redirect the output to a file on your diskette.

31. Use the TRACERT command to show information on how data is routed to the address of your college's Web site. Repeat the command again, and append the output to the file you used in the previous step.

32. Use the FTP command to connect to Course Technology's ftp2.course.com Web site.

33. Display a directory listing, and then switch to the Operating_Systems directory.

34. Change the file transfer mode from ASCII to BINARY.

35. Use the TYPE command to verify that the file transfer mode is now BINARY.

36. Turn on Hash mark printing.

37. Download a copy of one of the files to your Data Disk.

38. After the download is complete, exit the FTP subsystem.

39. Submit the output of the PING and TRACERT commands and the answers to the questions above in the format requested by your instructor, either as a printout, on diskette, or by e-mail, along with any other requested documentation.

CASE PROBLEMS

Case 1. Documenting User Information at The Perfect Match Corey Tanner recently supervised the installation and setup of a peer-to-peer network at The Perfect Match, a temp agency. The company wants a record of all the changes that have been made to the computers in the office, and Corey has carefully documented all the changes made to each computer and to the network itself. Because other employees use your computer, Corey asks you to document user account information on your computer in case another user changes the settings and you need to restore them.

As you complete each step, record your answers to any questions so you can submit them to your instructor.

1. Insert a blank diskette into drive A.

2. Open a Command Prompt window and then switch to drive A.

3. Enter a command to list the defined users on your computer.

4. Enter the command again, this time redirecting the output into the file UserStats.txt on drive A. What command did you use?

5. For each of the defined users, enter a command to list the user account information, using redirection to append the output to UserStats.txt. Give an example of one of the command lines you used.

6. Examine the contents of UserStats.txt to make sure they contain all of the necessary output, and then repeat any steps necessary to correct missing information.

7. Edit UserStats.txt to include documentation that identifies the purpose of the file. Include your name, as well as any other documentation that your instructor requests, such as the course section number, the instructor's name, and the date.

8. If the User Profile and Home Directory items are blank in a list of user account information, what command line or lines could you use to obtain this information? Give an example and describe how to interpret the output.

9. Submit the answers to the questions above, and a copy of UserStats.txt, either as a printout, on diskette, or by e-mail, as your instructor requests, along with any other requested documentation.

Case 2. Sharing Data on the Network at Computer Troubleshooters Unlimited Miles Biehler hired a college student as a summer intern at Troubleshooters Unlimited to assist with customer and technical support. Miles asks you to show the intern how to share resources on Troubleshooters Unlimited's peer-to-peer network.

To complete this case problem, your computer must be on a network, and you must have at least Power User or Administrator level privileges on your computer.

As you complete each step, record your answers to any questions so you can submit them to your instructor.

1. Use the Help switch from the command line and the Windows 2000 Help system to learn how to share a drive or directory folder on the network using the NET SHARE command.

2. Insert a copy of Data Disk #3 into drive A.

3. Open a Command Prompt window and switch to drive A.

4. Enter a command to display the shared network resources on your computer. What command did you use?

5. If drive A is already shared, enter a command to remove the share, and then issue the command in the previous step again to make sure drive A is not shared.

6. Enter the command to display the shared network resources on your computer again, and this time redirect the output into a file on your diskette called ShareDisk.txt.

7. Enter a command to share drive A on the network, using the share name DriveA. What command did you use for this operation?

8. To check your work, display the shared network resources on your computer.

9. Repeat this command, but this time use redirection to append the command's output to your ShareDisk.txt file on drive A. What command did you use to perform this operation?

10. Enter a command to display a directory listing of drive A, using UNC format. What command did you use?

11. Enter the above command again but, this time, append its output to ShareDisk.txt on drive A.

12. Enter a command to remove sharing of drive A. What command did you use?

13. Finally, to check your work, enter a command to display shared resources, then issue it again, appending the output to ShareDisk.txt on drive A.

14. Edit ShareDisk.txt to include documentation that identifies the purpose of the file. Include your name as well as any other documentation that your instructor requests, such as the course section number, the instructor's name, and the date.

15. Submit the answers to the questions above and a copy of ShareDisk.txt in the format requested by your instructor either as a printout, on diskette, or by e-mail, along with any other requested documentation.

Case 3. Diagnosing Network Connections at Stratton Graphics To guarantee that its employees can provide Stratton Graphics' corporate customers with the highest quality service and the fastest turnaround times, owner Eve Stratton asks you to perform a diagnostic check of the company's network to ensure that it is performing optimally.

As you complete each step, record your answers to any questions so you can submit them to your instructor.

1. In the Windows 2000 Help system index, type *ping* and then open the section labeled "testing TCP/IP configuration" to learn how to use a series of PING commands to test the setup and connections of your local network.

2. If your computer is not connected to a local network with a router connection to another network or the Internet, launch a dial-up networking connection. If neither is available, specify that information where applicable in your answers to the questions below.

3. Insert a blank diskette into drive A, open a Command Prompt window, and then switch to drive A.

4. Use the IPCONFIG /ALL command to obtain IP addresses necessary to complete the steps described in Windows Help. Issue the command again, this time redirecting the command's output into the file PingDiag.txt on drive A.

5. Complete the steps described in Windows Help. In each step, enter the step's PING command a second time, using redirection to append the command's output to the file PingDiag.txt on drive A. To test a remote host, first use the name *course.com*, then repeat the command using course.com's IP address.

6. Edit PingDiag.txt to include documentation that identifies the purpose of the file. Include your name, as well as any other documentation that your instructor requests, such as the course section number, the instructor's name, and the date.

7. Submit a copy of PingDiag.txt in the format requested by your instructor, either as a printout, on a diskette, or by e-mail, along with any other requested documentation.

Case 4. Downloading a Group of FTP Files at Townsend & Sumner Publishing A client of Townsend & Sumner Publishing in San Francisco just posted a set of templates at one of the FTP sites. Your supervisor, Mike Lyman, asks you to download specific files from that FTP site so you can adapt those templates for use by employees at Townsend & Sumner.

If, for some reason, you are not able to connect to ftp://ftp2.course.com, you can use another FTP site specified by your instructor and adapt the following instructions to that site.

1. In the Windows 2000 Help system index, type *ftp commands*, and then open the section labeled "subcommands," and read about the subcommands "mget" and "prompt".

2. Connect to your ISP.

3. Insert a blank diskette into drive A.

4. Open a Command Prompt window, and then switch to the root directory folder of drive A.

5. Launch a command-line FTP connection to ftp2.course.com (or another site if ftp2.course.com is not available). What command did you use?

6. Change to the course directory, change to the Operating_Systems directory, and then change to the 1976-x directory. What commands did you use?

7. Verify that you are in the 1976-x directory by displaying the path to the current directory. What command did you use? What is the path to the current directory?

8. Change the file transfer type to download binary files. What command did you use?

9. Display a directory listing. What command did you use?

10. Using the directory listing, choose a set of small files whose names begin with the same first character.

11. Using a single command line and a wildcard specification, download to drive A the set of files you chose in the previous step. What command did you use?

12. What did FTP display during the file download, and what responses did you have to make?

13. Turn off prompting for multiple file transfers. What command did you use?

14. Exit FTP and remove your diskette.

15. Submit a copy of your answers to the above questions in the format requested by your instructor, either as a printout, on diskette, or by e-mail, along with any other requested documentation.

QUICK | CHECK ANSWERS

Session 10.1

1. peer-to-peer
2. network adapter *or* NIC
3. TCP/IP
4. IP address
5. UNC
6. map
7. NET VIEW
8. NET USE
9. NET SHARE
10. NET USER

Session 10.2

1. Internet Connection Sharing (ICS)
2. IPCONFIG
3. PING
4. TRACERT
5. FTP
6. BINARY
7. TYPE
8. HASH
9. GET
10. Anonymous, e-mail address
11. Ctrl +]

WINDOWS XP COMMAND-LINE UPDATE

Overview

The Windows XP Appendix provides you with the information you need to complete the tutorials in the Microsoft Windows 2000 MS-DOS Command Line book using Windows XP Professional or Windows XP Home Edition. This appendix includes new features, describes key differences between Windows 2000 and Windows XP, and provides additional Help for you to complete the tutorial steps. The Appendix uses the following icons to help you quickly find the information you need.

 A new topic that expands on the coverage in a tutorial and focuses on new features of Windows XP and operating system software, or that replaces the comparable section for completing a set of steps, such as starting Windows XP.

 An update to tutorial steps that describes differences between Windows 2000 and Windows XP.

Additional information to help you complete a step or resolve a problem you might encounter.

New Topics

Working in the Windows XP command-line environment is remarkably similar to that for Windows 2000 Professional. Because Windows XP is an upgrade to Windows 2000, improvements have been made to the GUI (graphical user interface), some features have been replaced, and features have been added. This appendix includes the following additional topics on new features of Windows XP Professional and Windows XP Home Edition that extend the coverage provided in the previous version of this book:

TUTORIAL	NEW TOPICS
Tutorial 1: Opening Command-Line Sessions	PC Operating Systems: The Windows Me Operating System The Windows XP Operating System The Convergence of the Windows 9x and Windows NT Product Lines Starting Windows XP The Windows XP Desktop Changing to Windows Classic Style Changing to Web Style Logging Off, or Turning Off, Your Computer
Tutorial 5: Managing and Backing Up a Hard Disk	Moving the My Documents Folder to Another Location
Tutorial 6: Using Troubleshooting Tools	Overview of Remote Desktop and Remote Assistance Making a Windows MS-DOS Startup Disk Using the Automated System Recovery Wizard Multiple-Boot Configurations Understanding File Fragmentation The New Windows XP Command-line Disk Defragmenter Utility Analyzing a Disk for Fragmentation Defragmenting a Disk Logging into the Recovery Console (Resolving an Administrator Password Problem) Case Problem: Analyzing a Volume for Fragmentation at Amalgamated Insurance
Tutorial 9: The Windows XP Registry	The System Restore Utility Examining System Restore Settings Creating a Restore Point Using a Restore Point to Roll Back a Computer Undoing a Restoration
Tutorial 10: Connecting to Networks and the Internet	Network Bridges Internet Connection Firewall Internet Connection Sharing

TUTORIAL 1   OPENING COMMAND LINE SESSIONS

Session 1.1

This session provides an overview of the role of operating system software, the types of operating systems used on PCs, and the importance of developing a skill set that enables you to work with different operating systems in today's dynamic business environments. This additional section expands on Tutorial 1 and provides information about the Windows Me and Windows XP operating systems, as well as the convergence of Microsoft's two product lines for desktop operating systems.

Because individuals who use this updated book may be new to Windows XP or may not have taken a comprehensive course that covers features of Windows XP, this tutorial provides an overview of the new Windows XP GUI, describes how to perform basic operations that are different than previous versions of Windows, such as logging onto your computer, switching between Web style and Windows Classic view, and shutting down your computer, and describes how to work with basic Windows tools, such as the Start menu, taskbar, folder windows, and task-oriented dynamic menus. In addition, although most of your work will be in a Command Prompt window, some tutorials cover related features of the GUI for comparison.

PC Operating Systems

After the introduction of Windows 2000 Professional, Microsoft developed and released the Windows Me and Windows XP operating systems, which built on the successes of previous versions of Windows and also introduced many new and important features. Like other operating systems, Windows Me, Windows XP Professional, and Windows XP Home Edition complete the startup process, configure and customize your computer, display a user interface, provide support services to programs, handle input and output, manage the file system and system resources (such as memory), resolve system errors and problems (if possible), provide Help, and include utilities for optimizing and troubleshooting your computer.

The Windows Me Operating System

The Windows Me operating system, or Millennium Edition (Windows Version 4.900.3000), was designed as an upgrade for Windows 98 users and incorporated features of Windows 2000 Professional, and marked the next step in the development of the Windows 9x product line. Windows Me was also intended to be a bridge for upgrading to the Windows NT product line from Windows 95 and Windows 98. **Windows 9x** refers to the operating system product line that includes Windows 95, Windows 98, and Windows Me. See Figure A1-1. This product line was designed primarily for the home user. In contrast, the Windows NT product line includes Windows NT Workstation 4.0 and Windows 2000 network operating systems that are more commonly used in business environments. Over the years, Microsoft has indicated it would eventually combine the two different product lines into a single product line. If you start with Windows 95 in *Figure A1-1* and navigate from right to left down the table, you are looking at the order in which the products in the two different lines were released. Also, there were prior versions of the Windows NT product line before Windows NT Workstation 4.0.

Figure A1-1	WINDOWS DESKTOP OPERATING SYSTEM PRODUCT LINES
WINDOWS 9x PRODUCT LINE	**WINDOWS NT PRODUCT LINE**
Windows 95	Windows NT Workstation 4.0
Windows 98	Windows 2000
Windows Me	Windows XP

One of the important features introduced in Windows Me is the System Restore feature. This feature creates **system checkpoints** that save changes to system files, device drivers, and system settings on your computer system. If you run into a problem, you can "roll back" your computer system and restore it to an earlier working, or trouble free, state. For example, if you encounter problems when installing a new application or modifying a hardware configuration, you can roll back your computer to the point just before you installed the software or modified the hardware configuration, and restore a previous configuration that worked without any problems.

Another new component in Windows Me is the **Home Networking Wizard** which is designed to step a user through the process of setting up a home network, enabling Internet Connection Sharing so that networked computers connect to the Internet via one computer, and choosing which files and printers to share on a network.

Windows Me includes **Windows Movie Maker** for editing and enhancing video and home movies; an enhanced **Windows Media Player** for listening to music CDs with on-screen visualizations of sounds, creating music libraries, playing movies, listening to Internet radio stations, and customizing the appearance of Windows Media Player with the use of **skins** (a design scheme for changing the look of Windows Media Player); **WebTV** for viewing television programs broadcast over the Internet with a TV tuner card (a feature originally introduced in Windows 98); and the **Windows Image Acquisition** technology for obtaining images from a scanner or digital camera. Not surprisingly, these technologies are also incorporated into the Windows XP operating system.

The Windows XP Operating System

The Windows XP (for "Experience") operating system marks another important and major change in the development of the Windows operating system. Windows XP supports and enhances many of the features included in previous versions of Windows, includes major changes to the graphical user interface, and introduces many new features.

In October 2001, Microsoft released the following versions of Windows XP:

- **Windows XP Professional Edition** (Windows Version 2002, or Windows Version 5.1.2600) for business users and for advanced users who prefer to use it on their home computer system,
- **Windows XP Home Edition** (Windows Version 2002, or Windows Version 5.1.2600) for home users and users of entertainment-based computer systems, and
- **Windows XP 64-Bit Edition** for scientific, engineering, business, and other types of resource-intensive applications, such as those required for creating special effects in movies and 3D animation.

Windows XP 64-Bit Edition is designed for use with Intel's new Itanium processor that supports up to 16 GB (gigabytes) of RAM, and up to 16 TB (terabytes) of virtual memory. The **Itanium** processor performs up to 20 operations simultaneously, and can preload data into virtual memory for faster access and processing.

For users of earlier Windows versions, the most obvious change in Windows XP Professional and Windows XP Home Editions is the redesign of the GUI. For new installations of Windows XP, Microsoft has simplified the desktop by removing all icons except the Recycle Bin. The Start menu is now the primary way by which you access resources on your computer system. In addition to e-mail and Internet access links, the Start menu lists the five most recently used programs. You still access installed software through the All Programs menu on the Start menu. In addition, you can open the My Documents, My Computer, My Pictures, My Music, and Control Panel folders as well as the enhanced Help and Support Center from the Start menu. You will also see My Network Places and Printers and Faxes on the Start menu in Windows XP Professional, but not Windows XP Home Edition. However, you can modify the Start Menu to display these two options, and you can add Favorites to the Start menu in both versions of Windows XP.

The Control Panel is organized into a new view called **Category view** that provides links to common tasks for customizing and configuring your computer. When you are working in a folder window, Windows XP uses **dynamic menus** to display menu options related to your current task, and links to other places on your computer where you might want to work. For example, if you are working in a folder that contains document files, the dynamic menus list options for working with files, such as copying, moving, renaming, and deleting files. Also, **Tiles view** (Large Icons view in previous versions of Windows), when combined with the **Arrange Icons by Type** and the **Show in Groups** options, organizes the contents of a folder window by file type. If a folder contains Microsoft Word and Microsoft Excel files, Windows XP can group all the Word document files together and all the Microsoft Excel files together so that you can easily locate what you need to use. Within the My Pictures folder and other folders designated for images, **Filmstrip view** displays thumbnail views of images contained within the files in the folder as well as a full-screen view of whichever thumbnail you select.

Rather than setting aside a taskbar button for each document you open in each application, Windows XP uses **taskbar grouping** to provide access to all open documents of a certain type (such as Word documents) under one taskbar button. For example, if you open different documents with the same application, Windows XP combines all the documents' taskbar buttons into one taskbar button labeled with the name of the application. When you click this taskbar button, Windows XP displays a pop-up list of the document names so you can select the document you want to use. Another advantage of taskbar grouping is that you can perform the same operation on all documents that you open with the same application. For example, you can right-click a taskbar button, and then close all documents opened in the same application.

Here are some of the other new features available in both the Windows XP Professional and Home Editions:

- ■ **Dynamic Update**—The Setup program used to install Windows XP can now check Microsoft's Windows Update Web site for important system updates and download them before it installs Windows XP. This guarantees that the operating system files on your computer are current.

- ■ **Performance enhancements**—Windows XP starts up more quickly, performs better, uses system resources and memory more efficiently, and shuts down faster than other versions of Windows.

- ■ **Fast User Switching**—You do not need to log off if someone else needs to use the computer. Instead, another user can log onto their user account while you remain logged onto your account. After the other user logs off, you can switch back to your user account and continue working with any open applications and documents.

■ **Enhanced multimedia features and capabilities with Windows Movie Maker**—You can capture, edit, and organize video clips from a digital video camera or an analog camera so you can create and share home movies on your computer. You can use the **Scanner and Camera Wizard** to scan images or download them from a camera and automatically store those images in your My Pictures folder. Within the enhanced **My Pictures** folder, you can organize and preview digital photos as well as order prints using a Web service. You can use the enhanced **Windows Media Player** to play CDs and DVDs, burn CDs, and organize music files in the **My Music** folder.

■ **Internet Explorer 6**, an enhanced and improved version of Microsoft's Web browser, and **Windows Messenger**, an instant messaging application that allows you to find out who is online, send an instant message, engage a group of friends in an online conversation, invite someone who is online to play a game, dial a contact's computer, send one or more files to someone else, and, if you have a HotMail account, receive a notification when new e-mail arrives.

■ **Credential Manager**—This tool secures and automatically provides your user name and password to applications (such as e-mail software), services (such as your ISP), and Web sites that request that information so that you do not have to repeatedly specify the same information.

■ **System Restore**—As noted earlier, Windows XP periodically saves information regarding changes to the configuration of your computer system, operating system files, and device drivers, so that if you make a change to your computer and then encounter a problem, you can roll back your computer system to an earlier functioning state.

■ **Device Driver Rollback**—This tool replaces a newly installed device driver that does not work properly with a previously working version of that same device driver.

■ **Side-by-side DLLs**—Windows XP maintains different versions of the same DLL (Dynamic Link Library) program files used by different applications. This feature prevents problems caused by replacing a DLL file used by several different applications when installing a new application.

■ **Internet Connection Firewall**—This feature protects your computer from intruders and hackers while you are connected to the Internet.

■ **Remote Assistance**—A technical support person, colleague, or friend can remotely connect to your computer to assist you with a project or to troubleshoot a problem. Note that both systems must be using Windows XP.

■ **Network Setup Wizard**—This feature steps you through the process of creating a home network so your computers can share peripherals (such as a printer), software, files, and use Internet Connection Sharing to share a single Internet connection.

■ **Help and Support Center**—Microsoft has expanded and enhanced the Help system in Windows XP so that you can find information on your local computer or on the Web.

Here are some additional features and capabilities of Windows XP Professional:

■ **Remote Desktop**—This tool allows you to access and use another computer from a computer running Windows 95 or later. For example, you can use Remote Desktop to access your office computer from your home computer, or vice versa.

- **Encrypting File System**—This feature, introduced in Windows 2000 Professional, augments the NTFS file system and enables you to encrypt files with a randomly generated key. This feature provides a high level of security.

- **Network Location Awareness**—This new Windows XP service allows the operating system and applications to determine when a computer has changed its network location.

- **User State Migration Tool**—Administrators can use this tool to migrate a user's data, operating system settings, and application settings from one computer to another computer with Windows XP Professional.

- **Wireless 802.1x networking support**—This feature improves performance for wireless networks.

- **Enhanced processor and memory support**—Window XP Professional now supports two symmetric processors and up to 4 GB of RAM. In a computer that uses **symmetric multiprocessing**, programs or tasks can be processed simultaneously by multiple microprocessors.

Not surprisingly, Windows XP Professional and Windows XP Home Edition provide increased performance and support for setting up, configuring, securing, administering, and troubleshooting networks. In addition, Windows XP Professional and Windows XP Home Edition offer enhanced Internet and Web technologies, and protection for the Windows XP operating system and operating environment, which are important factors in providing the best possible support in a business environment.

The Convergence of the Windows 9x and Windows NT Product Lines

As noted earlier, the different versions of the Windows operating systems fall into two major product lines: Windows 9x and Windows NT (see *Figure A1-1*). Each of these product lines reflects the differences in the needs of Microsoft's home user base and its business user base. Over the years, Microsoft has worked to merge the two product lines into a single Windows operating system. This transition not only requires successfully merging technologies in the different product lines, but also meeting the more complex networking and security needs of businesses, while appealing to home users who want simplicity and access to entertainment-oriented multimedia technologies. With the development of Windows XP, Microsoft is moving much closer to that goal.

The rapid changes in hardware technologies and in the Internet and World Wide Web are reflected in changing operating system technologies. *Figure A1-2* illustrates the introduction of operating systems and operating environments over a 20-year period from 1981-2001. As *Figure A1-2* shows, the primary operating system used by PCs over this time period was DOS, having been used for more than twice as long as the different versions of the Windows operating systems. In contrast, there were six major upgrades of the DOS operating system over a 14-year period, and Microsoft has upgraded the Windows operating system six times in a six-year period. The pace of development and change in operating system technology in the future will be as rapid as it was in the past, and coincide with rapid changes in the Internet, World Wide Web, and hardware technologies.

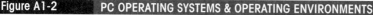

Figure A1-2   **PC OPERATING SYSTEMS & OPERATING ENVIRONMENTS**

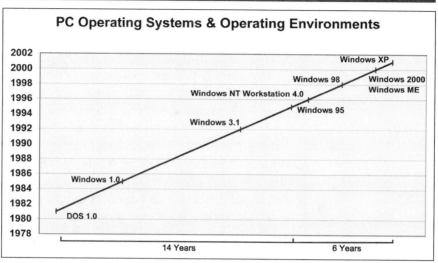

Session 1.2

The second session leads you through the process of opening a command-line session and using basic commands. Although Windows XP Professional and Windows XP Home Edition provide new features and no longer include certain features found in Windows 2000 Professional, the command-line environment in both versions is almost identical to that of Windows 2000. However, because the process for logging on your computer, working with the Windows XP desktop and Start menu, using Web style, opening a command-line session, and logging off your computer can differ from that for Windows 2000, the following material describes how to complete these operations using Windows XP. This section also explains differences that you can encounter when working within the Windows XP command-line environment.

Starting Windows XP

If you are using Windows XP Professional or Windows XP Home Edition, complete the following steps to log onto your computer, and then read the subsequent sections that describe the Windows XP desktop and how to switch between Web style and Windows Classic style.

To log on to your computer:

1. Power on your computer, and if you have a dual-boot or multiple-boot system, select Windows XP Professional or Windows XP Home Edition from the OS Choices startup menu. While starting up, your computer might briefly display information about startup operations and technical specifications for your computer, or you might see a splash logo for your computer's manufacturer. Eventually, Windows XP displays a Welcome screen and prompts you to select your user name, as shown in *Figure A1-3*, or it might display a Log On to Windows dialog box instead.

   TROUBLE? If you are working in a computer lab, your instructor and lab support staff will supply you with a user name and password.

TROUBLE? If you do not see a Welcome screen or a Log On to Windows dialog box, then Windows XP has automatically logged you onto your computer.

TROUBLE? If you do not see the Welcome screen, this feature is turned off, and you log onto your computer using the standard Log On to Windows dialog box.

TROUBLE? If you are working on a network domain, you might need to press Ctrl+Alt+Del before you can log onto your computer.

Figure A1-3	WINDOWS XP WELCOME SCREEN

2. If Windows XP displays a Welcome screen, click your **user account** icon, and if Windows XP prompts you for your password, type your **password**, and then press the **Enter** key or click the **Next** button. If Windows XP displays a Log On to Windows dialog box, enter your **user name** (if necessary), type your **password** (if you use a password), and then press the **Enter** key, or click the **OK** button. Windows XP loads your personal settings and then displays the desktop. See *Figure A1-4.* If you purchased a computer that was customized by the manufacturer, or if you or someone else has already customized your computer, your desktop will differ from the one shown in this figure.

TROUBLE? If you do not remember your password, and if you are logging onto your computer from the Welcome screen, you can click the Password Hint button, and Windows XP will display a hint to remind you of your password if you specified a hint or provided one to your network administrator.

TROUBLE? If Windows XP displays an MSN Explorer dialog box informing you that no one is set up to use MSN Explorer on your computer and prompting you to click "Add New User" to create a user account, click the Close (x) button in the MSN Explorer dialog box, and then click the Close [x] button in the MSN dialog box. Unfortunately, Windows XP might continue to redisplay these dialog boxes periodically, and you might need to close them to continue working with your computer. If Windows XP displays a "Take a tour of Windows XP" informational Help balloon, click its Close button [×].

Figure A1-4 | WINDOWS XP DESKTOP

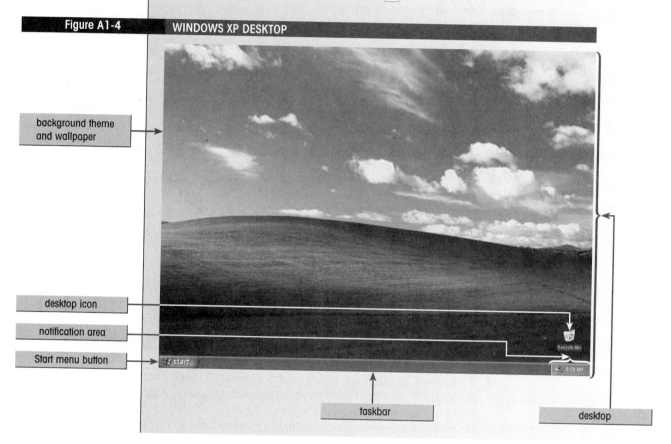

If your computer is a member of a network **domain**, a group of computers on a network that share a common directory database, each user is assigned to a group, which in turn provides each user with rights and permissions granted to the group by the network administrator. Each domain has a unique name and is administered as a unit with common rules and procedures. A **group** can consist of a set of users, computers, contacts, and even other groups. A **right** is a task that a user can perform on a computer or within a domain. For example, the administrator might grant a user the right to log onto a computer locally. A **permission** is a rule that determines which users can access an object and how they can access that object. For example, a network administrator might grant some users the permission to use a printer and others the permission to use and manage the printer.

In a domain, a user can belong to any of the following groups: Administrators, Power Users, Users, Backup Operators, Guests, or Replicator.

- **Administrators Group**—Users have full access to the computer and can install an operating system, update or upgrade the operating system, configure and troubleshoot the operating system, manage the security of the computer system, and back up and restore the computer system.

- **Power Users Group**—Users can install software that does not modify the operating system, customize or make changes to some system settings and system resources (such as power options), and create and manage local user accounts and groups.
- **Users Group**—Users cannot modify the operating system, its settings, or data belonging to other users, and therefore this account is considered the most secure.
- **Backup Operators Group**—Users can back up and restore files on a computer, but cannot change security settings.
- **Guests Group**—Users can log onto a computer and use the computer, but with limits.
- **Replicator Group**—Users can replicate files across a domain.

The same types of user groups are also found in Windows 2000 Professional.

Instead of belonging to a domain, users might belong to a **workgroup**, which consists of a group of computers that provide users with access to printers and other shared resources, such as shared folders, on the network. Or a user might have a user account on a standalone computer that is not connected to other computers within a network. On a workgroup or standalone computer, there are three types of user accounts: Computer Administrator, Limited, and Guest.

- **Computer Administrator**—Users can make changes to the computer system, including creating and removing other user accounts, install software, and access all files on a computer. Windows XP creates a Computer Administrator account for you during installation, and uses the Administrator password you provide during setup.
- **Limited**—Users cannot install hardware or software, or change the account name or account type. A member with this type of account can use software already installed on the computer, and can make some changes to their account, such as changing their password or picture.
- **Guest**—An account that allows users who do not already have a user account to log onto and use the computer. There is no password for a Guest account.

If you are the only user for a computer, your user account is a Computer Administrator account that gives you full access to that computer. If you create multiple accounts when you install Windows XP, each account is a Computer Administrator account. However, it is a good idea to create another account with limited access, and to use that account, especially when you connect to the Internet, in order to prevent unauthorized access and changes to your system. If you log onto your computer as an Administrator and then connect to the Internet, a hacker who gains access to your computer has full access to your computer system. You are also vulnerable to **Trojan horses**, programs that appear to be *bona fide* programs, but which are designed to retrieve information from your computer, such as user names and passwords, and then transmit that information to others who then can subsequently access your computer via an Internet connection.

To further protect your computer, use a password that contains at least 7 to 14 characters, and that contains letters of the alphabet (both uppercase and lowercase), numerals, and symbols. Use at least one symbol as the second through sixth character. Your password should not be a common name or word, and you should not repeat previously used passwords. Although Windows XP supports passwords that are up to 127 characters long, use passwords that are 7 to 14 characters long if you have other computers in your network that are running either Windows 95 or Windows 98, because they do not support longer passwords.

The Windows XP Desktop

Windows XP uses the desktop as the starting point for accessing and using the resources and tools on your computer. With previous versions of Windows, the desktop contained icons for My Computer, My Documents, My Network Places (called Network Neighborhood in Windows 95, and Network in Windows 98), Internet Explorer, Microsoft Outlook, and the Recycle Bin. If you upgrade from a previous version of Windows, your Windows XP desktop contains the same icons as before. If you purchase a new computer with Windows XP Professional or Home Edition, the Recycle Bin is the only icon on the desktop, unless the manufacturer customized the desktop. However, you can still place the standard desktop icons found in previous versions of Windows on the desktop, and you can add shortcuts to the desktop. As you install software and hardware, icons for those products might also be placed on the desktop.

Microsoft has reorganized the Start menu in Windows XP so that the Start menu consists of two panels, each separated into groups. See *Figure A1-5*. On the left panel of the Start menu shown in *Figure A1-5*, Internet MSN Explorer and E-mail with Microsoft Outlook are listed above the separator line in an area called the **pinned items list**. Items in this area always remain on the Start menu. Your e-mail option might indicate that you use MSN Explorer instead of Microsoft Outlook.

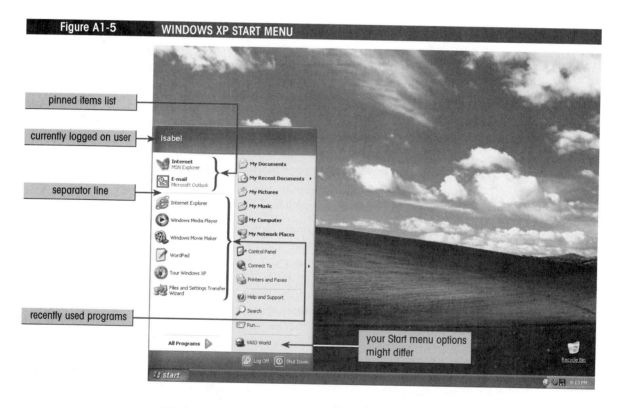

Figure A1-5   WINDOWS XP START MENU

Under the separator line, Windows XP lists the most frequently used programs in an area called the **most frequently used programs list**. Located at the bottom of the left panel, you can display the All Programs menu from which you can choose a system tool, such as Windows Update, or open an application.

From the right panel, you can open the My Documents, My Pictures, My Music, My Computer, or My Network Places folders, or use My Recent Documents, if displayed, to open a recently used document. You can also open the Control Panel or Printers and Faxes folders, connect to MSN Explorer, or display all connections. With Windows XP Home Edition, you might not have a Connect To option (though it can be added to the Start menu).

You can open the Help and Support Center, which has been expanded to provide you with access to not only Help but also system settings. Search has been expanded so that you can search for pictures, music, video, documents, files, folders, computers, people, or even information in the Help and Support Center. As with previous versions of Windows, you can use Run to open a program, folder, document, or Web site.

You can also log off and turn off your computer from the Start menu. As you can see with this new release, the focal point has shifted from the desktop to the Start menu.

In addition to displaying the Start button and **notification area** (formerly called the system tray), the taskbar retains the same features and functions found in earlier versions of Windows. The notification area contains not only the current time, but also icons for programs loaded in the background. If you have not used an icon in the notification area for a period of time, Windows XP hides the icon. You can click the Show Hidden Icons ◀ button to display icons that are hidden from view.

Although Microsoft has redesigned the desktop, Start menu, and taskbar, you should feel at home with Windows XP, because you still have access to the same basic Windows GUI and the same features found in previous versions of Windows.

Changing to Windows Classic Style

Windows XP provides you with a new way of interacting with your computer called **Web style**. With Web style, you can navigate your computer as you would navigate the World Wide Web using hypertext links. You select an object by pointing to the object (you do not need to click the object to select it) and you open an object with a single click as you would with a hypertext link.

In contrast, earlier versions of Windows defaulted to the Windows Classic view or style originally found in Windows 95. That meant you clicked an object to select it, and you double-clicked an object to open it.

Although these two different styles do not affect the way in which you work within a command-line environment, you should be familiar with them so that you can choose the style that best suits your needs.

If you or the organization for which you work prefer that you use the Windows Classic style, you can switch to that style by making four changes to the user interface:

■ Apply the Windows Classic theme
■ Change the Start menu style to the Windows Classic Start menu
■ Apply the Windows Classic folders option
■ Select the option for double-clicking icons to open objects

As you perform the following tutorial steps, you might discover that your computer already uses certain settings, but not other settings, and your original view of the user interface was a mix of Web style and Windows Classic style. Remember which settings your computer uses so that you can restore those settings at the end of the tutorial.

If you are working in a computer lab, make sure you have permission to change desktop settings. If necessary, ask your instructor or technical support staff before you complete these steps. If you are not allowed to change desktop settings, read, but do not complete, the steps in this section. However, review the figures so that you are familiar with the features described in these steps.

If your computer already uses the Windows Classic style, you can still work through the following tutorial steps to determine whether all four types of changes have been made to the user interface.

To apply the Windows Classic theme:

1. Right-click an empty area of the desktop, and then click **Properties** from the shortcut menu. Windows XP opens the Display Properties dialog box as shown in *Figure A1-6*. The name of the current theme is shown in the Theme list box. Note which theme is used on your computer.

| Figure A1-6 | CHOOSING A DESKTOP THEME |

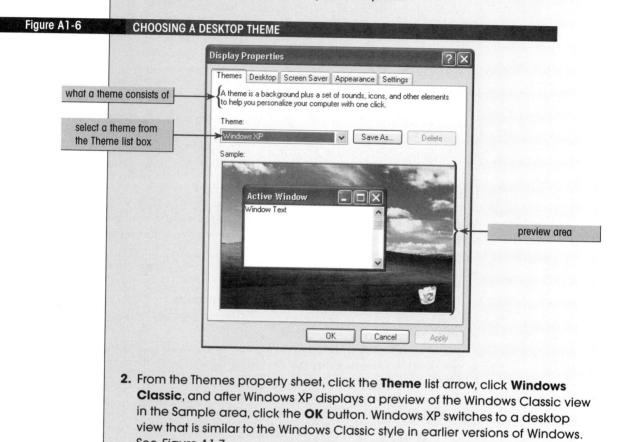

what a theme consists of

select a theme from the Theme list box

preview area

2. From the Themes property sheet, click the **Theme** list arrow, click **Windows Classic**, and after Windows XP displays a preview of the Windows Classic view in the Sample area, click the **OK** button. Windows XP switches to a desktop view that is similar to the Windows Classic style in earlier versions of Windows. See *Figure A1-7*.

Figure A1-7   WINDOWS CLASSIC DESKTOP THEME

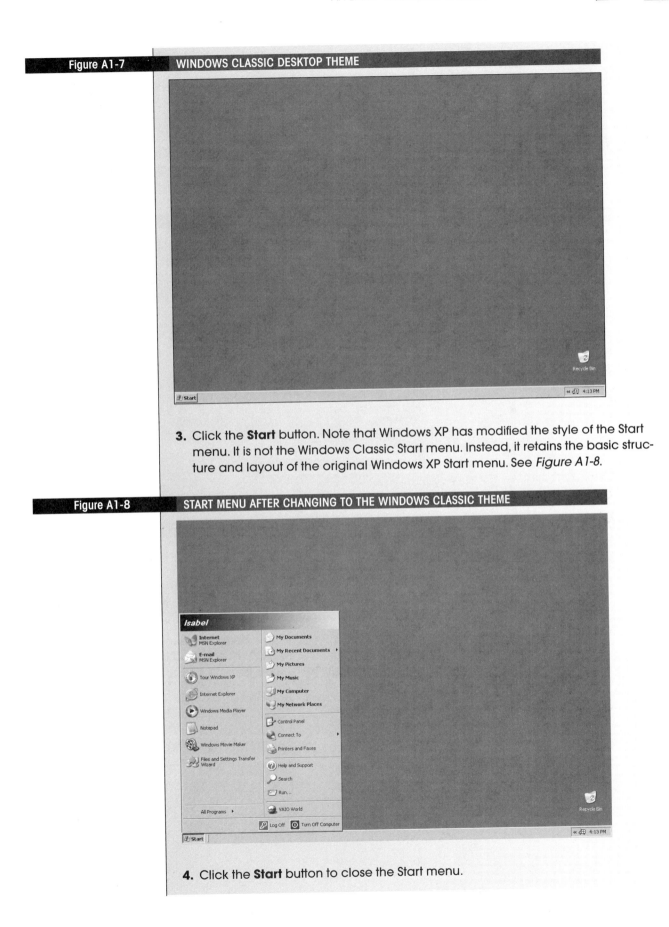

3. Click the **Start** button. Note that Windows XP has modified the style of the Start menu. It is not the Windows Classic Start menu. Instead, it retains the basic structure and layout of the original Windows XP Start menu. See *Figure A1-8*.

Figure A1-8   START MENU AFTER CHANGING TO THE WINDOWS CLASSIC THEME

4. Click the **Start** button to close the Start menu.

The next step is to change the Start menu style to the Windows Classic Start menu. You can use the Start Menu property sheet to switch between the Windows XP Start menu style and the Windows Classic Start menu, and to customize the appearance of the Start menu.

To change the Start menu style:

1. Right-click the **Start** button, click **Properties**, and after Windows XP opens the Taskbar and Start Menu Properties dialog box, click the **Start Menu** tab if it is not already selected. See *Figure A1-9*.

Figure A1-9	START MENU PROPERTY SHEET

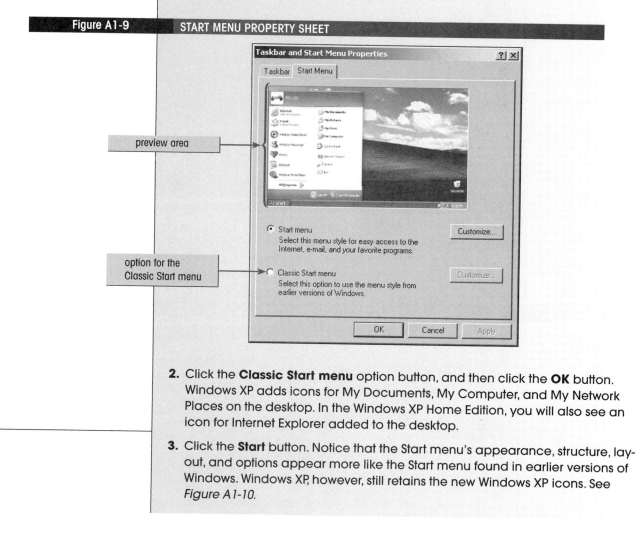

preview area

option for the Classic Start menu

2. Click the **Classic Start menu** option button, and then click the **OK** button. Windows XP adds icons for My Documents, My Computer, and My Network Places on the desktop. In the Windows XP Home Edition, you will also see an icon for Internet Explorer added to the desktop.

3. Click the **Start** button. Notice that the Start menu's appearance, structure, layout, and options appear more like the Start menu found in earlier versions of Windows. Windows XP, however, still retains the new Windows XP icons. See *Figure A1-10*.

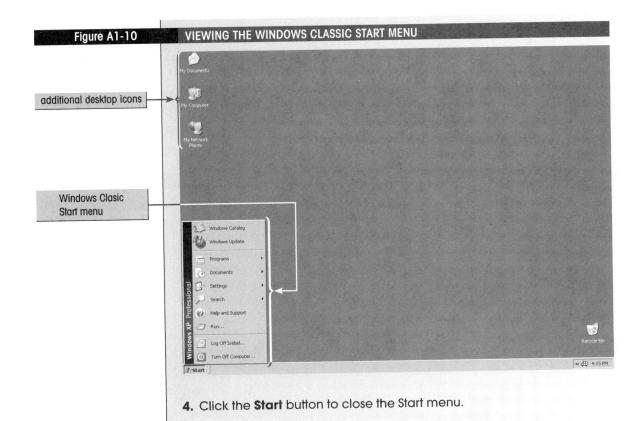

Figure A1-10 | VIEWING THE WINDOWS CLASSIC START MENU

additional desktop icons

Windows Clasic Start menu

4. Click the **Start** button to close the Start menu.

Before you change to the Windows Classic folders view, examine the My Documents folder so that you can compare the task-oriented view found in Web style with the Windows Classic folders view. In the **task-oriented view**, Windows XP uses dynamic menus to display links to common folder tasks and other locations on your computer.

To change to Windows Classic folders and enable double-clicking:

1. Double-click the **My Documents** icon on the desktop. Windows XP displays the contents of the folder in task-oriented view. For this folder, Windows XP provides links to common File and Folder Tasks, as well as links to Other Places on your computer. See *Figure A1-11*.

Figure A1-11 | TASK-ORIENTED VIEW WITH DYNAMIC MENUS

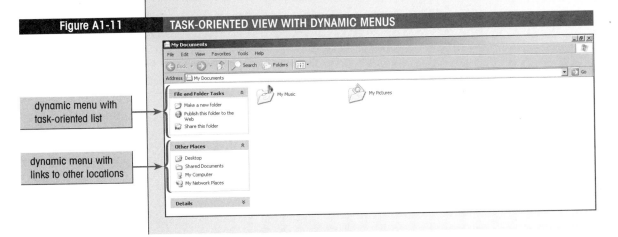

dynamic menu with task-oriented list

dynamic menu with links to other locations

2. Close the My Documents window.

3. Click the **Start** button, point to **Settings**, click **Control Panel**, and after Windows XP opens the Control Panel window, click **Switch to Classic View** in the Control Panel dynamic menu. Windows XP retains the dynamic menus so that you can switch back to Category View.

4. Double-click the **Folder Options** icon. Windows XP opens the Folder Options dialog box. *See Figure A1-12.*

Figure A1-12   **FOLDER OPTIONS DIALOG BOX**

option for displaying task-oriented view

option for Windows classic folders

double-click option

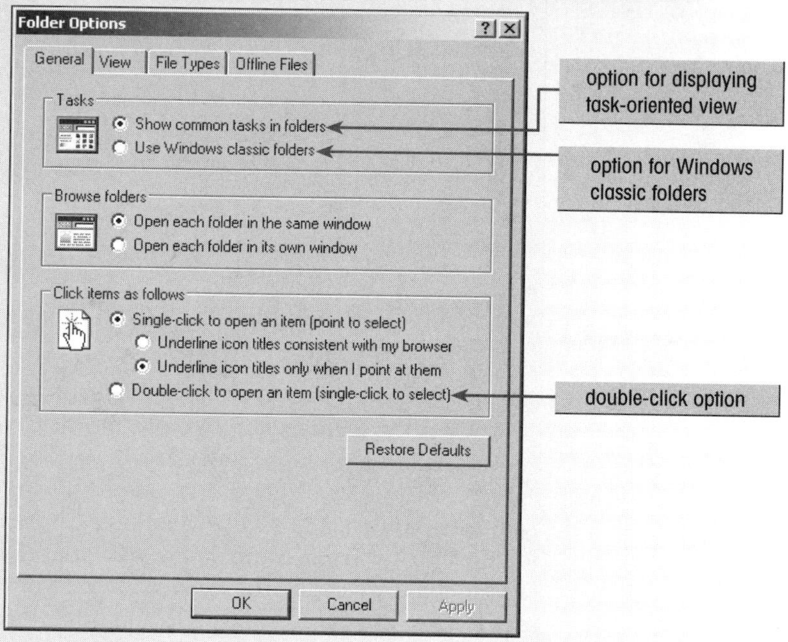

5. On the General property sheet, click the **Use Windows classic folders** option button under Tasks, click the **Double-click to open an item** option button under the "Click items as follows" section if it is not already selected, and then click the **OK** button. You no longer see dynamic menus in the Control Panel.

6. Close the Control Panel, and then double-click the **My Documents** folder icon on the desktop. Windows XP no longer displays the task-oriented list and the links to Other Places on your computer in the folder window. *See Figure A1-13.*

Figure A1-13   **WINDOWS CLASSIC FOLDERS VIEW**

7. Close the My Documents window.

REFERENCE WINDOW   **RW**

Changing to Windows Classic Style

- Right-click an empty area of the desktop, and then click Properties on the shortcut menu.
- After Windows XP opens the Display Properties dialog box, click the Theme list box arrow on the Themes property sheet, click Windows Classic, and then click the OK button.
- Right-click the Start button, click Properties, and after Windows XP opens the Taskbar and Start Menu Properties dialog box, click the Start Menu tab if it is not already selected.
- Click the Classic Start menu option button, and then click the OK button.
- Click the Start button, point to Settings, and then click Control Panel.
- After Windows XP opens the Control Panel window, click the "Switch to Classic View" link in the Control Panel dynamic menu.
- Double-click the Folder Options icon, and after Windows XP opens the Folder Options dialog box, click the "Use Windows classic folders" option button under Tasks on the General property sheet, click the "Double-click to open an item" option button under the "Click items as follows" section if it is not already selected, and then click the OK button.
- Close the Control Panel.

You've modified the user interface so that it more closely resembles the Windows Classic view found in Windows 2000. Depending on your individual preferences, you might combine elements of Web style and Classic view.

Changing to Web Style

To change your computer from Windows Classic style to Web style, you must reverse the changes you've made, namely:

- Apply the Windows XP theme
- Change the Start menu style
- Change to a task-oriented view of folders
- Select the option for single-clicking to open objects

If your computer originally used Web style (the default), you will likely want to switch back to that style. If your computer originally used Windows Classic style, you may want to read, but not complete, the following steps so that you can continue to work in Windows Classic style.

If you are working in a computer lab, make sure you have permission to change desktop settings. If necessary, ask your instructor or technical support staff before you continue with this tutorial. If you are not allowed to change desktop settings, read, but do not complete, the following steps. However, you should review the figures so that you are familiar with the features described in these steps.

To apply the Windows XP theme:

1. Right-click an empty area of the desktop, and then click **Properties** from the shortcut menu.

2. After Windows XP opens the Display Properties dialog box, click the **Theme** list arrow on the Themes property sheet, click **Windows XP**, and then click the **OK** button. Windows XP applies the Windows XP theme to the desktop.

   TROUBLE? If Windows XP does not display the original desktop wallpaper used on your computer, right-click an empty area of the desktop, click Properties, click the Desktop tab in the Display Properties dialog box, locate and select that desktop wallpaper in the Background list box, and then click the OK button.

Now you can change the Windows Classic Start menu style back to the Windows XP Start menu style.

To change the Start menu style:

1. Right-click the **Start** button, click **Properties**, and after Windows XP opens the Taskbar and Start Menu Properties dialog box, click the **Start Menu** tab if it is not already selected.

2. Click the **Start menu** option button, and then click the **OK** button. Windows XP removes the My Documents, My Computer, My Network Places, and Internet Explorer icons (if previously displayed) from the desktop and switches to the Windows XP Start menu style.

Next, change the Windows Classic folders view back to a task-oriented view and enable single-clicking.

To change to a task-oriented view of folders and enable single-clicking:

1. Click the **Start** button, click **Control Panel**, and then double-click the **Folder Options** icon in the Control Panel window. Windows XP opens the Folder Options dialog box.

2. On the General property sheet, click the **Show common tasks in folders** option button under Tasks, click the **Single-click to open an item** option button if it is not already selected, click the **Underline icon titles only when I point at them** option button if it is not already selected, and then click the **OK** button. Note that Windows XP has restored the dynamic menus in the Control Panel window.

3. Click the **Switch to Category View** link in the Control Panel dynamic menu, and then close the Control Panel.

<u>Changing to Web Style</u>

- Right-click on an empty area of the desktop, and then click Properties on the shortcut menu.
- After Windows XP opens the Display Properties dialog box, click the Theme list box arrow on the Themes property sheet, click Windows XP, and then click the OK button. *Note*: If you want to apply a different desktop wallpaper option, choose that wallpaper option from the Background list box on the Desktop property sheet in the Display Properties dialog box before closing it.
- Right-click the Start button, click Properties, and after Windows XP opens the Taskbar and Start Menu Properties dialog box, click the Start Menu tab if it is not already selected.
- Click the Start menu option button, and then click the OK button.
- Click the Start button, click Control Panel, and then double-click the Folder Options icon in the Control Panel window.
- After Windows XP opens the Folder Options dialog box, click the "Show common tasks in folders" option button under Tasks on the General property sheet, click the "Single-click to open an item" option button if it is not already selected, click the "Underline icon titles only when I point at them" option button if it is not already selected, click the OK button, and then close the Control Panel.
- Click the "Switch to Category View" link in the Control Panel dynamic menu, and then close the Control Panel.

Now you've restored your computer to the default Windows XP Web style. As you've seen, Web style simplifies the way you work with Windows XP, and allows you to use your Web browsing skills within the Windows XP user interface.

[UPDATE] Opening a Command-Line Session

The process for opening a Command Prompt window is slightly different with Windows XP. The command interpreter displays a different Windows version number in the Command Prompt window, and the command prompt shows the full path to your user account directory instead of the root directory:

- **Page 24, Step 1**: The Programs menu is now listed on the Start menu as "All Programs". After you open a Command Prompt window, the command interpreter identifies the version of Windows XP you are using. In addition, the default operating system prompt or command prompt shows the path for the directory for your user account instead of the path for the root directory. *Figure A1-14* shows that Isabel is using the original version of Windows XP Professional, Version 5.1.2600. The path to Isabel's user account directory is located under the Documents and Settings directory. Yours will differ. So that your screen more closely matches the figures shown in the text, type CD \ and then press the Enter key to change to the root directory. CD is the Change Directory command, and you will learn more about it in Tutorial 4.

Figure A1-14	COMMAND PROMPT WINDOW

path to Isabel's user account directory

command for changing to the root directory

root directory

Microsoft Windows XP [Version 5.1.2600]
(C) Copyright 1985-2001 Microsoft Corp.

C:\Documents and Settings\Isabel>CD \

C:\>_

- **Page 30, Step 1**: The Version command (VER) reports that you are using Windows XP and a specific version of Windows XP. As noted in the last bullet, Version 5.1.2600 is the original version of Windows XP.

Logging Off, or Turning Off, Your Computer

Once you have finished working with Windows XP, you can do one of two things: You can shut your computer down, or if you are connected to a network, you can log off your user account. If you are working on a company network, on a network in a computer lab, or on your own home network, you can use the Log Off option to display the Welcome screen or the Log On to Windows dialog box. Then you or someone else can log onto the computer and network later.

If you are working in a computer lab, do not shut down your computer unless your instructor or technical support staff has specifically requested you to do so. If you are unsure of what to do, check with your instructor or technical support staff. *Most computer labs prefer that you do not turn off the computers for any reason.* Typically, the computer lab support staff is responsible for turning the computer systems on and off.

To log off, or turn off, your computer:

1. If you want to log off your own computer, or if you are working in a computer lab and want to log off the computer you are using, click the **Start** button, click the **Log Off** button, and then click the **Log Off** button in the Log Off Windows dialog box. Windows XP displays the Welcome screen or a Log On to Windows dialog box.

2. If you are using your own computer and want to turn off the computer, open the Start menu, click the **Turn Off Computer** button, and in the Turn off computer dialog box, click the **Turn Off** button.

If you are working on a company network, it is a good idea to log off when you finish your work so that no one else can access files via your account. Also, when you are ready to shut down a computer at the end of the day, it is important to use the Turn Off Computer option so that Windows XP can save important settings to disk and properly shut down your computer.

TUTORIAL 2 | DISPLAYING DIRECTORIES

Session 2.1

The first session in Tutorial 2 describes how to use the Directory command to display information about the directories and files stored on a disk. Because Windows XP defaults to a different directory when you open a Command Prompt window, you must change directories.

`UPDATE` Displaying a Directory Listing

So that the view in your Command Prompt window matches those shown in the figures, complete the following operation after you complete Step 2 on Page 53:

- **Page 53, Step 3** and **Figure 2-1**: You must first switch to the root directory. Type CD \ and then press the Enter key to change to the root directory. Then, complete Step 3 on Page 53. Also, the Windows directory is likely to be named "Windows" instead of "Winnt".

Session 2.2

The second session in Tutorial 2 covers advanced command-line switches and the use of wildcards in file specifications. As described in the next section, there are some minor differences.

`HELP` Using Sort Order Parameters

Note the following differences when examining Figure 2-12 and Figure 2-15:

- **Page 67, Step 2,** and **Page 68, Figure 2-12**: Although files are still organized by file extension, the order in which files are listed differs from that shown in the figure. For example, files with the "bmp" file extension are listed in the order "Palette #1.bmp," "Color Palette.bmp," "Colors of the Rainbow.bmp," and "Palette #2.bmp," instead of the order "Palette #2.bmp," "Palette #1.bmp," "Colors of the Rainbow.bmp," and "Color Palette.bmp" (as shown in the figure).
- **Page 70, Step 1,** and **Figure 2-15**: For files that are the same size, the file order differs. For example, the three files with a file size of 24,064 bytes are listed as "File0000.chk," "Break Even Analysis.xls," and "Sales Projection Models.xls" instead of "Break Even Analysis.xls," "Sales Projection Models.xls," and "File0000.chk" (as shown in the figure).

`HELP` Displaying Short Filenames

Note the following minor difference when examining Figure 2-18:

- **Page 74, Figure 2-18**: In this figure, there are blank lines between some of the entries in the directory listing. These blank lines are caused by filenames that are longer than the width of the window and that wrap to the next line. You may see additional files displayed in the Command Prompt window.

UPDATE Displaying a Directory Using File Attributes

You might note the following differences when examining these figures:

- **Page 76, Figure 2-21**: You will not see a RECYCLER folder.
- **Page 77, Figure 2-22**: You will not see a RECYCLER folder, and if your computer does not have the MS-DOS startup configuration files Config.sys and Autoexec.bat, they do not appear in the directory listing.

TUTORIAL 3   WORKING WITH FILES

Session 3.1

As you work through Session 3.1 and Session 3.2 in Tutorial 3, you will discover that Windows XP is remarkably similar to Windows 2000 when performing file operations. However, you might notice several differences when using Windows XP or Windows 2000.

UPDATE Piping Output to the MORE Filter

The following note provides additional information on Readme files that are included with software products:

- **Page 103, paragraph following the Reference Window**: If you use the Type command to view the contents of a Readme file with an "htm" or "html" file extension, such as Readme.htm located in the root directory of the Windows XP CD, you will see the HTML code in the text-based HTML file.

HELP Sorting ASCII Text Files

You might notice that one of the files shown in the directory listing for Figure 3-13 is in a different location:

- **Page 108π Step 2**, and **Figure 3-13**: Because the date of your Templates.txt file will probably differ from that shown in the figure, this file will appear at a different position in the redirected input.

HELP Redirecting Output to the Printer

The command interpreter and your printer might not respond when redirecting output to your printer port:

- **Page 115, Step 4**: If you enter this command and nothing happens, complete these steps:
  1. Close the Command Prompt window.
  2. Open the Command Prompt window.
  3. Change the background and foreground colors.

4. Switch to the root directory, and then switch to drive A.

5. Complete the directions in the first Trouble to print a copy of the directory listing.

■ **Page 116, Reference Window**: If you redirect output of the Directory command to PRN and nothing happens, close the Command Prompt window, open it again, redirect output of the Directory command to a file on disk, and use Notepad to print the contents of the file.

TUTORIAL 4   USING DIRECTORIES AND SUBDIRECTORIES

Session 4.2

As you step through both Session 4.1 and Session 4.2 in Tutorial 4, you will discover that Windows XP is remarkably similar to Windows 2000 when working with directories and subdirectories. If your Windows directory is named Windows instead of Winnt, you will see "Windows" in the command prompt path when working in that subdirectory or when viewing a directory listing for the Windows directory.

Stepping Down a Directory Tree

You will observe the following difference between the contents of your Windows directory and the one shown for Windows 2000:

■ **Page 157, Step 6** and **Figure 4-31**: Your System32 directory might contain approximately twice as many directories and files as compared to Windows 2000.

Case 4: Investigating Advertising Images at Turing Enterprises

Because the total size of the files in the Wallpaper directory exceeds the capacity of a floppy disk, you must modify one step in this case problem:

■ **Page 168, Step 10**: The collective size of all the files in the Windows XP Wallpaper directory exceeds the storage capacity of a floppy disk. In addition, Bliss.bmp, which is used by Windows XP as the default desktop wallpaper, will fill a floppy disk. Instead of copying all the files in the Wallpaper directory, copy five files of your choosing that are each less than 100 KB in size to the Windows Images directory on your floppy disk.

TUTORIAL 5   MANAGING AND BACKING UP A HARD DISK

Session 5.1

As you step through Session 5.1 in Tutorial 5, you will discover that Windows XP is remarkably similar to Windows 2000 when working with and reorganizing the directory structure of a disk.

Organizing Files on a Hard Disk

As you would expect, the Windows directory for Windows XP Professional is more extensive than that for Windows 2000 Professional, and might contain over 500 folders, close to 19,000 files, and occupy nearly 2 GB of space on the hard disk. If you also count the system folders and files within the root directory, as well as those within the Program Files subdirectory, then the total number of folders can approach 1,000, the total number of files can be as many as 22,000, and the total capacity used by the operating system can be nearly 2.5 GB. As you download updates to Windows XP, the number of folders and files, as well as the storage capacity, used by the operating system will increase.

Documenting the Directory Structure

When viewing a directory tree with files listed by subdirectory, you may notice the following difference:

- **Page 186, Figure 5-16**: The order of subdirectories under the My Documents directory can be different than that shown in the figure.

Session 5.2

Although you will find that Windows XP is remarkably similar when backing up a hard disk using the commands and features covered in Session 5.2, you will notice some differences in using the Windows XP GUI. In addition, bitmap image files with the "bmp" file extension are now associated with the Windows Picture and Fax Viewer.

Organizing Folders and Files for Backups (Moving the My Documents Folder to Another Location)

If your computer has two drives—for example, a drive C and drive D, and if you prefer to store all your document files on drive D to simplify backups, you should also move the My Documents directory and its contents to that drive. By default, the My Documents directory is stored under the Documents and Settings directory on the drive where Windows XP is installed (usually drive C). If you right-click the My Documents folder icon on the desktop or Start menu and then select Properties from the shortcut menu, the Target property sheet within the My Documents Properties dialog box shows the current path to the My Documents directory. See *Figure A1-15*. You can then use the Move button to select another location for the My

Documents directory. However, you should first create the subdirectory that will become the new target for the My Documents directory. Although you can specify any subdirectory on drive D as the target, you might want to create a directory structure similar to that on drive C, so that the new path for the My Documents folder on drive D is similar to the original path Windows XP used for drive C. For example, you could create a Documents and Settings directory on drive D, then a directory with your user account name (Isabel, for example) within the Documents and Settings directory, and finally a My Documents directory in your user account directory. Once you choose the option to move the My Documents directory, Windows XP prompts you as to whether or not you want to move all the files in the My Documents directory to the new location. Then, when you are ready to perform a backup of all your document files, you can select drive D and the contents of your My Documents directory is included in the backup. This same feature is available in Windows 2000 Professional.

Figure A1-15	VIEWING THE PATH TO THE MY DOCUMENTS DIRECTORY

My Documents Properties

Target | General | Sharing

The My Documents folder is a shortcut to the target folder location shown below.

Target folder location

Target: C:\Documents and Settings\Isabel\My Document

Restore Default | Move... | Find Target...

path to Isabel's My Documents directory

OK | Cancel | Apply

Selecting the Appropriate Backup Media

As noted at the end of this section, backup tape technologies and other types of technologies are constantly changing and improving. DVD disks currently have a storage capacity of 17 GB, and high-capacity tape drives can backup as much as 2.2 TB of data.

Documenting the Directory Structure

You might need to open the My Documents Properties dialog box using the My Documents icon on the Start menu:

■ **Page 202, Step 1** (bottom of the page): If you do not have a My Documents folder icon on the desktop, click the Start button, right-click the My Documents folder icon on the Start menu, and then click Properties.

HELP Performing a Normal Backup with XCOPY

As you complete this section, you may notice two differences, and you may have to adapt one of the steps for opening bitmap image files:

- **Page 213, Step 7** and **Figure 5-36**: The order of your subdirectories within the SolarWinds Normal Backup directory may differ.
- **Page 216, Step 2**: If Windows XP opens your file using the Windows Picture and Fax Viewer application instead of the Paint application, close the window, and enter the following command at the command prompt: mspaint "Color Palette.bmp"

TUTORIAL 6   USING TROUBLE SHOOTING TOOLS

Session 6.1

As you step through Session 6.1 in Tutorial 6, you will find both similarities and differences between Windows XP and Windows 2000. The major difference is that Windows XP does not include an option for making an Emergency Repair Disk. However, it does include a new Automated System Recovery Wizard and an option for making an MS-DOS Startup Disk, both of which are discussed in this section of the Appendix.

UPDATE Developing a Troubleshooting Strategy

Instead of using PC Anywhere or Microsoft NetMeeting, you can use two new GUI tools in Windows XP for assisting others and for troubleshooting problems: Remote Desktop and Remote Assistance. These new tools are briefly described in the next section.

Overview of Remote Desktop and Remote Assistance

Remote Desktop is a new feature available with Windows XP Professional, but not Windows XP Home Edition. Using Remote Desktop, you can access a computer running Windows XP Professional (called the remote computer) from another computer that has any version of Windows (called the client computer). For example, you can connect to your office computer from home or while traveling as long as your office computer is running Windows XP Professional. You can also use Remote Desktop to connect to another computer, and troubleshoot problems on that other computer. However, the computer to which you connect must have Remote Desktop Connection installed on it.

You can establish the remote connection via a dial-up, ISDN, DSL, or virtual private network connection, via the Internet, or using a local area network (LAN) or wide area network (WAN). A **virtual private network (VPN)** is an extension of a private network to include public or shared networks, such as the Internet. Once you make a connection to another computer, that computer is locked, and any operations you perform on the locked computer are not visible on that computer's monitor. In addition, no one can use the keyboard or mouse on the computer to which you've connected. Once the Remote Desktop connection is established, you have access to the remote computer's file system, software, and hardware; you can use applications from the remote computer on your computer; and you can redirect video, audio, and print jobs to your computer.

Remote Assistance is a new feature in Windows XP Professional and also Windows XP Home Edition. You can use Remote Assistance to allow another person to connect to your computer system remotely. Likewise, you can connect to another person's computer. Unlike Remote Desktop, both computers must be running a version of Windows XP. Also, both individuals must be present at their computers and must work with each other. The person requesting help extends an invitation and is referred to as the **novice**, and the person who accepts the invitation and provides assistance is referred to as the **expert**. You can establish the remote connection via the Internet or using a local area network (LAN). The connection works even if either of the computers are behind a firewall.

The Importance of CMOS

The process for restarting your computer may differ under Windows XP:

■ **Page 237, Step 2**: Depending on how your computer is set up, you can restart Windows XP using one of two methods. If there is a Turn Off Computer option on the Start menu, click that button, and then click Restart. If there is a Shut Down option on the Start menu, click Restart in the "What do you want the computer to do?" list box in the Shut Down Windows dialog box, and then click the OK button.

Windows XP Booting Options

Although the booting process in Windows XP is similar to that in Windows 2000, there are differences in the Windows XP startup menu and the use of Safe Mode:

■ **Page 243, Figure 6-8**: The Windows XP startup menu is called the "Windows Advanced Options Menu" and the "Boot Normally" option is called "Start Windows Normally". Also, Windows XP has a Reboot option, and if you have multiple operating systems installed on your computer, you will see a "Return to OS Choices Menu" option.

■ **Pages 244-245, Steps 2, 3, & 4**: In Windows XP, these steps are in a different order. Before Windows XP prompts you to select an operating system, it displays the Windows Advanced Options Menu and highlights the Start Windows Normally boot option, instead of the Safe Mode option. You can then select the Safe Mode with Command Prompt boot option. Next, you are prompted to select an operating system. Select your version of Windows XP from the OS Choices menu. Windows XP then displays a list of files that it loads when booting in this mode.

■ **Page 245, Step 5**: After logging on to Windows, your command prompt shows the path to your logon directory.

■ **Page 246, Step 8 Trouble**: After you press Ctrl+Alt+Del in Windows XP Home Edition, click Shut Down on the menu bar of the Windows Task Manager dialog box, and then click Restart.

Making Windows XP Setup Disks

You cannot make Windows XP Setup Disks from your Windows XP CD. To make Setup Disks, you must download a Win32 Cabinet Self-Extractor program from Microsoft's Download Center on the Web (*www.microsoft.com/downloads*). Also, there is a different program for making Windows XP Professional Setup Disks and Windows XP Home Edition Setup Disks.

Once you locate this Web site, select Keyword Search in the Search for a Download section of the Web page, enter Setup Disks in the Keywords box, select Windows XP from the Operating System list box, and then click the Find It button. If you scroll down the page, you will see the search results and two links, one for Windows XP Professional and the other for Windows XP Home Edition. After selecting a link, you will see the Web page for downloading the utility for making Setup Disks for that version of Windows XP. *Figure A1-16* shows the Web page for Windows XP Professional.

Figure A1-16	MICROSOFT'S DOWNLOAD CENTER

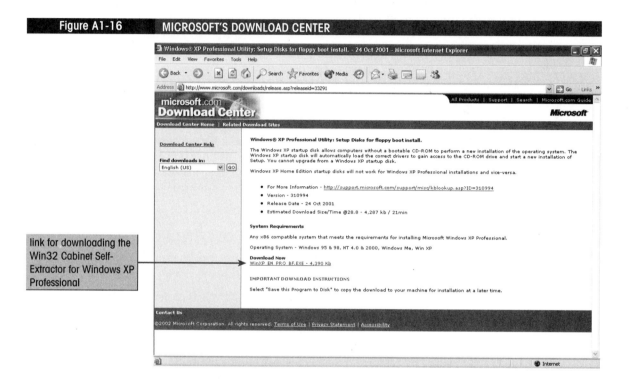

link for downloading the Win32 Cabinet Self-Extractor for Windows XP Professional

If you decide to download the Win32 Self-Extractor for either Windows XP Professional or Windows XP Home Edition, you must adapt the following tutorial steps to create Windows XP Setup Disks:

- **Page 248, Step 2**: Because Windows XP requires six disks and not four, you will need two additional diskettes. Label your diskettes Windows XP Setup Boot Disk, Windows XP Setup Disk #2, Windows XP Setup Disk #3, Windows XP Setup Disk #4, Windows XP Setup Disk #5, and Windows XP Setup Disk #6.

- **Page 248, Step 3**: You will not need your Windows XP CD to make Setup Disks. You will only need the Win32 Self-Extractor program file that you downloaded from the Microsoft Web site.

- **Page 248, Steps 4-5**: Because you are not using your Windows XP CD, skip these steps.

■ **Page 248, Step 6**: The easiest way to run Makeboot.exe is to open the folder where you downloaded the Win32 Self-Extractor program, click the file icon, and then follow the instructions displayed by the program. Or, if you are working in a Command Prompt window, change to the directory that contains the program file downloaded for making Setup Disks, and then type the name of the file to run the MakeBoot program. If you downloaded the Win32 Self-Extractor program file for making Setup Disks for Windows XP Professional, you will need to type the following command to start the Makeboot.exe program: WinXP_EN_PRO_BF.EXE If you downloaded the Win32 Self-Extractor program file for making Setup Disks for Windows XP Home Edition, type the following command to start the Makeboot.exe program: WinXP_EN_HOM_BF.EXE

The information and prompts displayed by Makeboot.exe are similar to the one for Windows 2000 (see *Figure A1-17*).

Figure A1-17	CREATING WINDOWS XP PROFESSIONAL SETUP DISKS

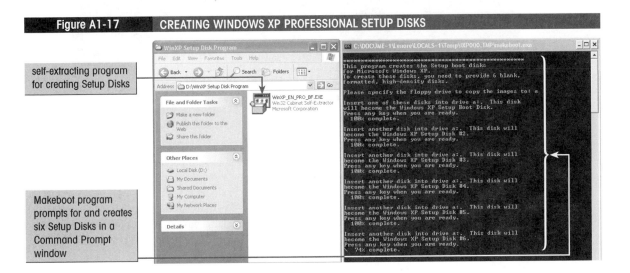

self-extracting program for creating Setup Disks

Makeboot program prompts for and creates six Setup Disks in a Command Prompt window

■ **Page 249, Step 9**: Because Windows XP requires six floppy disks, you will need to repeat this process for the Windows XP Setup Disk #5 and Windows XP Setup Disk #6.

Like Windows 2000, if you need to use these Setup disks, insert the Windows XP Setup Boot Disk (the first disk) in drive A, and then restart Windows XP. If your computer is set up to boot from drive A instead of drive C, you will see a message informing you that Setup is inspecting your computer's configuration. After loading components from the first setup disk, the Setup program prompts you for each of the next disks and loads device drivers and other Windows XP components, including support for the different Windows XP file systems. During this process, Setup displays information on which Windows XP components are being loaded in the status bar at the bottom of the screen. After loading the contents of the sixth disk, you see a Windows Setup screen like the one shown in *Figure A1-18* from which you can install Windows XP, or repair your computer using the Recovery Console (covered later in Tutorial 6 and also covered in Tutorial 7).

| **Figure A1-18** | **SETUP OPTIONS FOR REINSTALLING OR REPAIRING WINDOWS** |

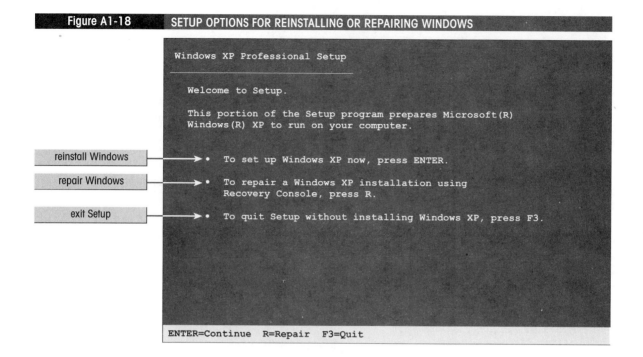

reinstall Windows

repair Windows

exit Setup

Newer computer systems allow you to boot directly from your Windows CD, so you no longer need to make Windows XP Setup Disks unless you want an extra backup.

Making an Emergency Repair Disk

Windows XP does not have an option for making an Emergency Repair Disk, so you will not be able to complete the steps in this section of Tutorial 6. Microsoft has replaced this option with an option for using the Automated System Recovery Wizard that is covered after the next section on making an MS-DOS Startup Disk.

So that you are familiar with the process for making an Emergency Repair Disk in Windows 2000, read this section and the tutorial steps, and examine the figures, but do not complete the steps.

Making an MS-DOS Startup Disk

The Windows XP **MS-DOS startup disk** is a floppy disk that contains the core operating system files needed to boot your computer from drive A. The MS-DOS startup disk does not contain any additional troubleshooting utilities. However, you can add utilities or diagnostic programs to the disk so that you can use them after you boot your computer with this disk. You cannot use this disk to access the contents of NTFS volumes, but you can use it to examine and navigate FAT volumes, or use troubleshooting utilities to diagnose problems on FAT volumes. In the unlikely event your computer has more than one floppy disk drive, you must make the MS-DOS startup disk using drive A. You cannot use drive B because the BIOS (Basic Input/Output) routine that looks for the operating system files during the booting process checks drive A and drive C—not drive B—for a boot disk.

If a disk contains defective sectors, do not use the disk as a MS-DOS startup disk, or for any other type of boot disk or system disk for any version of Windows. You need as reliable a disk as possible should a problem develop later. A disk with defective sectors could prove to be unreliable. You can use the Check Disk utility (covered in Session 6.2) to check for defective sectors on a newly formatted disk.

You cannot make an MS-DOS Startup Disk from a Command Prompt window. Instead, you must open My Computer and choose the option for formatting a floppy disk. In the Format options section of the Format 3½ Floppy (A:) dialog box, shown in *Figure A1-19*, click the "Create an MS-DOS startup disk" check box before you format the diskette. Since an MS-DOS Startup Disk may prove to be an important troubleshooting tool, you should know how to make one, especially if your boot volume is a FAT volume.

Figure A1-19   CHOOSING FORMATTING SETTINGS

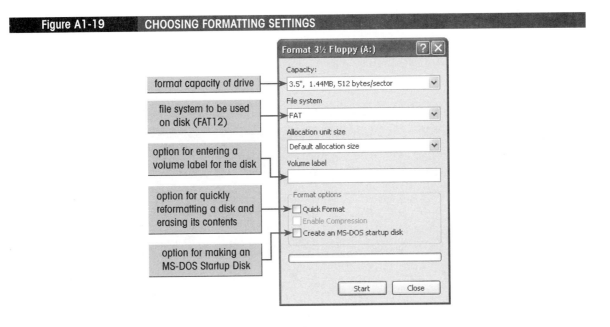

After you create an MS-DOS startup disk, or any other type of boot disk or startup disk, it is a good idea to test the disk to make sure that it works properly. You do not want to wait until a problem arises, only to discover that the boot disk does not work.

Before you test the MS-DOS startup disk, you need to know which file system drive C uses. You can open My Computer, right-click the drive C icon, click Properties on the shortcut menu, and then check the File system setting on the General property sheet within the Properties dialog box for drive C. As noted earlier, an MS-DOS Startup Disk can only read FAT volumes, not NTFS volumes.

To test the disk, open CMOS and choose the option for booting from your floppy disk drive. Save your updated CMOS settings, and then boot your computer from the MS-DOS startup disk and wait for an operating system prompt (A:\>) that indicates the computer successfully booted and that the operating system is now using drive A as the default drive and the top-level folder, or root directory, (\ ) as the default directory. If you use the Version command (VER) to check the version of Windows used on the MS-DOS Startup Disk, you will discover that the Windows version is reported as Windows Millennium [Version 4.90.3000], not Windows XP.

You can use the Directory command with the Attribute switch (/A) to display a directory listing of all the files stored on the MS-DOS Startup Disk. See *Figure A1-20*. An MS-DOS Startup Disk contains the hidden protected operating system files Io.sys, Msdos.sys, and Command.com.

■ Io.sys is responsible for booting the computer from the MS-DOS startup disk.

■ Msdos.sys contains a remark (;W98EBD) that identifies the disk as a Windows 98 Emergency Boot Disk (EBD).

■ Command.com is the command interpreter (like Cmd.exe), and is responsible for displaying the command-line user interface (the operating system prompt, or command prompt) so you can interact with the operating system, for interpreting commands that you enter at the command prompt, and for locating and loading programs for those commands.

The startup configuration files, Config.sys and Autoexec.bat (if available) are empty. However, under previous versions of Windows and under DOS, **directives**, or commands, included in Config.sys modified the operating system as it loaded into memory. For example, device drivers for hardware devices, such as a CD-ROM drive, might have loaded along with the operating system. Also, commands were included in Autoexec.bat for customizing a computer.

| Figure A1-20 | DISPLAYING THE CONTENTS OF AN MS-DOS STARTUP DISK |

Directory command →

switch →

```
A:\>DIR /A

 Volume in drive A has no label
 Volume Serial Number is 2A87-6CE1
 Directory of A:\
```

filename →

file extension →

file size →

file date →

file time →

```
MSDOS    SYS           9  04-07-01  1:40p
IO       SYS     116,736  05-15-01  6:57p
EGA2     CPI      58,870  06-08-00  5:00p
EGA3     CPI      58,753  06-08-00  5:00p
EGA      CPI      58,870  06-08-00  5:00p
KEYB     COM      21,607  06-08-00  5:00p
KEYBOARD SYS      34,566  06-08-00  5:00p
KEYBRD2  SYS      31,942  06-08-00  5:00p
KEYBRD3  SYS      31,633  06-08-00  5:00p
KEYBRD4  SYS      13,014  06-08-00  5:00p
MODE     COM      29,239  06-08-00  5:00p
COMMAND  COM      93,040  06-08-00  5:00p
DISPLAY  SYS      17,175  06-08-00  5:00p
CONFIG   SYS           0  01-31-05 11:42a
```

total number of files →

```
      14 file(s)         565,454 bytes
       0 dir(s)          889,344 bytes free

A:\>_
```

total storage space used by files →

The other files with the "sys" and "cpi" (for "Code Page Information") file extensions are device drivers for the video display and keyboard. The different versions of these driver files provide support for different countries and regions. Mode.com is a multi-purpose program for configuring system devices, and Keyb.com allows you to set up a keyboard for use with another language. Both programs work with code page information files to specify a character set for use with a device.

If drive C is a FAT volume, you can use the MS-DOS startup disk to examine the contents of that drive. If you try to examine an NTFS volume with this disk, Windows Millennium displays the message "Invalid drive specification".

Like any other boot disk, you should write-protect the MS-DOS startup disk so that a computer virus cannot gain access to the disk.

Using the Automated System Recovery Wizard

You can use the **Automated System Recovery (ASR)** Wizard in Windows XP Professional to back up the system state, system services, and the system volume of your computer so that you have the system files and settings required to rebuild that computer. Note that the Automated System Recovery is not available in the Home Edition of Windows XP. The **system state** consists of the operating system components that define the current state of the operating system, and includes Registry settings for user accounts, applications, hardware, and software, as well as files in the top-level folder and Windows folder that Windows XP needs to boot the computer. The **system volume** contains the hardware-specific files for loading Windows XP on x86-based computers that contain a BIOS. The system volume might be the same volume as the boot volume that contains the Windows operating system and its support files. **x86-based computers** are systems based on the architecture of the Intel 8086 processor.

The Windows XP Professional Automated System Recovery Wizard can back up the contents of your system volume (i.e., drive C) to tape or another hard disk, but not to a network drive, and your system settings to a floppy disk. Because of the volume of data, using other types of removable media, such as rewritable CDs or Zip disks, is impractical for backing up.

You can start the Automated System Recovery Wizard in one of two ways:

■ If you are already at the desktop, click the Start button, point to All Programs, point to Accessories, point to System Tools, click Backup, and after the Backup or Restore Wizard dialog box opens, click the Advanced Mode link. You can then start the Automated System Recovery Wizard from the Welcome sheet in the Backup Utility window. See *Figure A1-21*.

Figure A1-21	STARTING THE AUTOMATED SYSTEM RECOVERY WIZARD

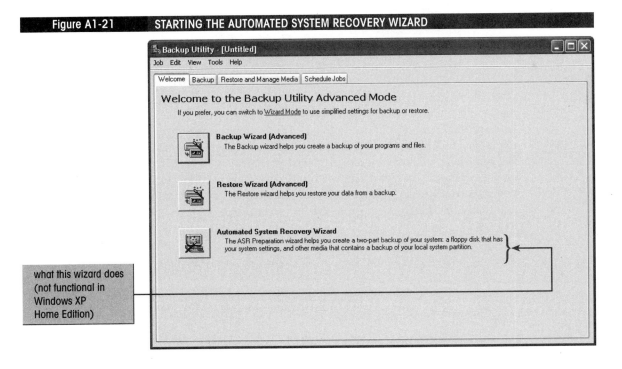

what this wizard does
(not functional in
Windows XP
Home Edition)

■ Alternately, if you are working in a Command Prompt window, you can type the command NTBACKUP and then press the Enter key to open the Backup Utility window.

As noted next to the Automated System Recovery Wizard button on the Welcome sheet, the ASR Preparation Wizard creates a two-part backup of your computer system: a floppy disk with your system settings, and a backup of your local system partition on other media. Although the Windows XP Home Edition includes an Automated System Recovery Wizard button on the Welcome sheet in the Backup Utility window, the Automated System Recovery feature does not work. Also, the Backup Utility is not automatically installed in Windows XP Home Edition.

After you click the Automated System Recovery Wizard button, an Automated System Recovery Preparation Wizard dialog box explains the importance of making an ASR disk and backup of system files in the event of a system failure. See *Figure A1-22*. The wizard also emphasizes the importance of backing up your data separately.

Figure A1-22   **ASR WIZARD WELCOME SCREEN**

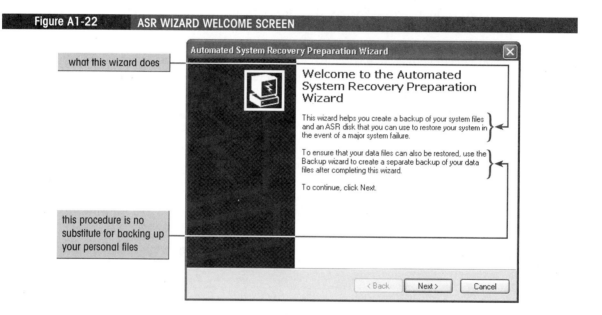

In the next Automated System Recovery Preparation Wizard dialog box, you specify the backup destination, namely, the location and name of the tape device or file for storing the backup. See *Figure A1-23*. In the Backup media or file name box, it proposes to use the file-name Backup.bkf (the default filename) or the filename of your last backup, and under the Backup media or file name box, the wizard informs you that it also needs a floppy disk to create a recovery disk. You can use the Browse button to locate the drive and folder where you want to store the backup, then you type a name for the backup file in the File name box, and then click the Save button in the Save as dialog box.

Figure A1-23	SELECTING THE BACKUP MEDIA AND FILE

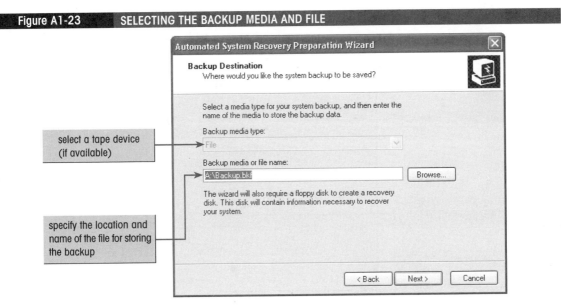

select a tape device (if available)

specify the location and name of the file for storing the backup

In the next and last Automated System Recovery Preparation Wizard dialog box, the wizard informs you that it will create a backup of your system files, and that you will be prompted to insert a floppy disk. See *Figure A1-24.*

Figure A1-24	COMPLETING THE PREPARATION FOR AN ASR BACKUP

what will happen

how and when you should use this backup

After you click the Finish button, the Automated System Recovery Wizard examines all the files on your computer, and then a Backup Progress dialog box displays the status of the backup. See *Figure A1-25.* In the figure example, the backup utility selected 8,927,167,284 bytes, or approximately 8.3 GB of data for the backup. The backup operation, initially estimated at close to 3 hours by the Backup Utility, actually took 45 minutes, because the data was backed up to another volume.

Figure A1-25	PROGRESS OF THE ASR BACKUP

volume being backed up

estimated duration for this backup

total size of files scheduled for this backup (8.3 GB)

After backing up the system volume, you are prompted to insert a formatted floppy disk in drive A. After creating the ASR Disk, the Backup Utility asks you to remove the floppy disk, place a specific label on the disk to identify the backup set, and then keep it in a safe place. See *Figure A1-26*.

Figure A1-26	ASR DISK COMPLETED

add this label to the disk

what to do with this disk

Before you close the Backup Utility, you can print and save a summary report. To print the report, click the Report button in the Backup Progress dialog box to open the report in Notepad, click File on the menu bar, click Print, choose the correct printer, and then click the Print button. To save the report, click File on the menu bar, click Save As, click the Save in list arrow, open the folder where you want to store the report, enter a filename in the File name box, and then click the Save button. You can then close Notepad, the Backup Progress dialog box, and the Backup Utility window.

Because system settings and the contents of your system volume change over time, you should develop a schedule for updating the backup created by the Automated System Recovery Wizard. Because it is comparable to a normal backup in terms of the time and amount of media required, you might want to schedule it on as frequent a basis as you schedule a normal backup of your document files. After you download and install operating system updates, or reconfigure Windows XP, you must update your ASR backup.

The contents of the backup media include:

- A backup of files in the Documents and Settings, My Music, Program Files, Recycle Bin, System Volume Information, and Windows folders, as well as a backup of operating system files in the top-level folder of drive C. That means this backup not only includes any files stored in your My Documents, My Pictures, and My Music folders, but also the corresponding folders for all other user accounts.

■ A System State backup that includes boot files, the COM+ Class Registration Database, and the Registry. The **COM+ Registration Database** stores information about COM+ components, or operating system services for applications and components in a networking environment.

The ASR Disk contains Windows NT Setup files with the file extension "sif" (for Setup Installation File) and a Setup Log file. See *Figure A1-27*. The Automated System Recovery State Information File (Asr.sif) contains information about the operating system, disks, partitions, and buses on your computer. The Setup.log file contains a copy of the Setup.log file first created when Windows XP was installed on your computer, which in turn contains information on the location of Windows XP system files and settings.

| Figure A1-27 | VIEWING THE CONTENTS OF THE ASR DISK |

If you experience a system failure, and after you have tried other troubleshooting options such as Safe Mode, you can attempt to restore your computer using the Automated System Recovery tool, your most recent ASR Disk, your most recent ASR backup, and your Windows XP CD. After inserting your Windows XP CD into a bootable CD drive, restart your computer from the Windows XP CD or using the Windows XP Setup Disks. When you see the message "Press F2 to run Automated System Recovery," press F2, insert your ASR Disk and backup media to start the system recovery, and then follow the instructions for restoring your computer. You are prompted for the name of the Windows folder, and after the system recovery is complete, you must restore your document files from your most recent backup sets because the Automated System Recovery formats the system partition during the restore process. As noted earlier, Microsoft has designed the Automated System Recovery as a last resort measure in case other troubleshooting methods do not resolve a problem.

Session 6.2

Session 6.2 focuses on Windows 2000 file systems and the use of the command-line Check Disk utility. Windows XP supports the same file systems as Windows 2000, and like Windows 2000, its native file system is NTFS.

Another utility commonly used with the Check Disk utility in prior versions of Windows is Disk Defragmenter. In earlier versions of Windows, you opened and used this utility via the graphical user interface. In contrast, Windows XP also has a command-line version of this utility and it is designed to solve a problem known as file fragmentation.

This section of the Appendix includes a discussion on multiple-boot configurations, as well as file fragmentation and tutorial steps for using the command-line Windows Disk Defragmenter utility to defragment a disk.

Multiple-Boot Configurations

You can create dual-boot or multiple-boot configurations with Windows XP Professional, Windows XP Home Edition, Windows 2000 Professional, Windows NT Workstation 4.0, Windows Me, Windows 98, Windows 95, and MS-DOS.

Like Windows 2000, each operating system must be installed on a different partition. You can create up to four partitions on a hard disk, each functioning as a logical drive with a different drive letter and each supporting a different operating system. For example, you can create a multiple-boot configuration with Windows XP Professional, Windows XP Home Edition, Windows 2000, and Windows 98 or Windows 95. You can create the partitions with the FDisk utility as described earlier, or you can use Advanced Options during Setup while installing Windows XP.

Each partition can use a different file system. As is the case with Windows 2000, the operating system that you install might dictate the file system you use for a partition. For example, MS-DOS, Windows 95 (original version), and Windows 95a can only be installed on a FAT16 partition. Windows 95b and Windows 95c must be installed on a FAT32 partition. Windows 98 and Windows Me can be installed on a FAT16 or FAT32 partition. If you are creating a multiple-boot configuration with Windows XP and an operating system that uses FAT16 or FAT32, you should install the other operating system on the system partition (the first partition, drive C), and you should use FAT16 or FAT32 on that partition. Even with Windows NT Workstation 4.0, which supports NTFS, Microsoft recommends that the system partition use the FAT file system.

By installing each operating system on a different partition, you do not run the risk of one operating system overwriting files needed by another operating system. However, if you intend to use the same application with different operating systems, you must install that application on each partition.

You also must install the operating systems in a specific order. For example, if you want to create a dual-boot between Windows XP and Windows 2000 Professional, install Windows 2000 Professional before you install Windows XP. If you want to create a multiple-boot configuration with Windows XP, Windows 2000 Professional, Windows Me, and Windows 98, install them in the following order: Windows 98, Windows Me, Windows 2000 Professional, and finally Windows XP.

If you are considering a dual-boot or multiple-boot configuration, you should examine the Resource Kit Documentation for Microsoft Windows XP Professional, or visit the Microsoft Web site and examine the information it provides on multiple-boot configurations. The process for creating a multiple-boot configuration can be complex and varies with the types of operating systems included in the multiple-boot configuration, the partition used to install a specific operating system, the file system used on each partition, the file system used on the system partition (usually the first partition), and the implementation of more advanced Windows XP features, such as dynamic disks.

You can also use a third-party software product such as Partition Magic to partition your hard disk and set up a multiple-boot configuration while, at the same time, retaining your files and settings.

Understanding File Fragmentation

As you create, modify, and save files to a hard disk, Zip disk, or floppy disk, Windows XP attempts to store the different parts of each file in **contiguous** or adjacent clusters. However, as you add, delete, and modify files, Windows XP might need to store different parts of the same file in **non-contiguous**, or non-adjacent, clusters that are scattered across the surface of a disk because the disk does not have enough space to store the file in contiguous clusters. Windows XP saves updates to a file in the largest continuous space on a disk, and that space is often in a different location than other parts of the file. The file is then called a **fragmented file**. As file fragmentation builds up on a disk, you need to use a defragmenting utility such as Windows' Disk Defragmenter to rearrange the files on the disk so that the different clusters for the same file are stored in consecutive clusters.

Each time you retrieve a file from a hard disk, the read/write heads that retrieve data from the surface of the disk must locate each cluster for a file and reassemble its contents so that the application you are using can work with the entire file or part of the file. If the read/write heads attempt to retrieve a fragmented file from disk, it takes your drive longer to locate and read the different parts of that file. Likewise, when you issue a command to save a new or modified file to a disk, Windows XP must locate available clusters for that file on disk. If a file is stored in non-contiguous clusters, it takes the read/write heads longer to write the file to the disk. Clearly, the problem is compounded if all or most of the files on a disk are fragmented. Because the access time of a hard disk is over 120,000 times slower than RAM, you spend more time waiting as the hard drive locates and reads file clusters into RAM. Furthermore, as fragmentation builds up on a disk, it results in more disk access, and that in turn causes increased wear-and-tear on the drive and reduces the useful lifetime of the disk.

To give you a better understanding of how file fragmentation occurs, let's consider a simple example. Assume that over the last six months, you added, deleted, and modified files on the disk. *Figure A1-28* shows a part of the disk that contains three files on the disk.

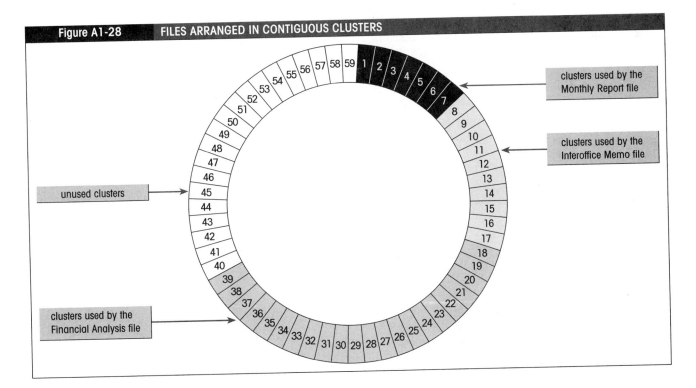

Figure A1-28   FILES ARRANGED IN CONTIGUOUS CLUSTERS

clusters used by the Monthly Report file

clusters used by the Interoffice Memo file

unused clusters

clusters used by the Financial Analysis file

The file with the Monthly Report occupies seven clusters, the file with the Interoffice Memo occupies the next ten clusters, the file with the Financial Analysis occupies the next 22 clusters, and the next 20 clusters are not currently used. You decide you no longer need the file with the Interoffice Memo, so you delete this file. By removing this file, you have freed ten clusters, as shown in *Figure A1-29*.

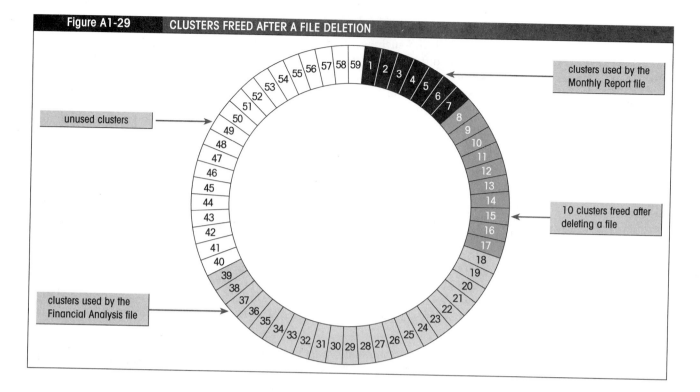

Figure A1-29   **CLUSTERS FREED AFTER A FILE DELETION**

clusters used by the Monthly Report file

unused clusters

10 clusters freed after deleting a file

clusters used by the Financial Analysis file

Now you prepare a bid proposal and save it to the same disk. Assume that this file requires ten clusters and that Windows XP uses the clusters that were previously occupied by the letter. Later, you open the file again and add a new section to the bid proposal so that the final size is 28 clusters. When Windows XP saves the file to disk, the additional 18 clusters might be stored in the next available set of contiguous sectors, right after the report, as shown in *Figure A1-30*.

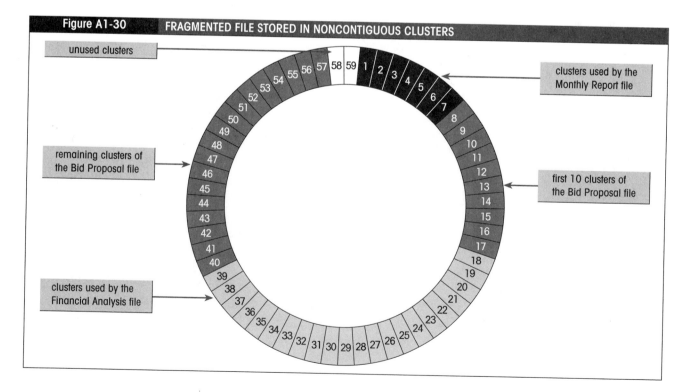

Figure A1-30   **FRAGMENTED FILE STORED IN NONCONTIGUOUS CLUSTERS**

unused clusters

clusters used by the Monthly Report file

remaining clusters of the Bid Proposal file

first 10 clusters of the Bid Proposal file

clusters used by the Financial Analysis file

The file with the bid proposal is now a fragmented file because it is stored in non-contiguous clusters. From this example, you can see that if you continue to reduce the size of files or delete files from a disk, you free clusters that Windows XP might use later for parts of a different file. If you increase the size of files or add new files to a disk and the disk does not contain enough consecutive clusters to hold the entire file, Windows XP might store the files in non-contiguous clusters.

Windows XP contains two defragmenting utilities. The GUI utility is called Disk Defragmenter, and the command-line version is called Windows Disk Defragmenter. These defragmenting utilities can reorganize the clusters assigned to a file so that they are located together, rather than scattered across the disk. They also record the clusters for one file right after the clusters for another file, and in the process, remove free space (or empty space) between files that would result in more fragmentation later. After using these defragmenting utilities on a disk, all the files are stored in contiguous clusters starting from the outer edge of the disk, and as a result, all unused disk space is consolidated near the inner edge of the disk. Once all of the clusters of a file are stored in adjacent clusters, the read/write heads can more quickly retrieve the contents of that file, thus improving the response time and performance of your computer, and preventing deterioration of your hard disk. By using these defragmenting utilities on a regular basis, you can eliminate or reduce file fragmentation and also free space fragmentation. **Free space fragmentation** occurs when the available free space is scattered around the disk, rather than consolidated in adjacent clusters in one part of the disk.

Before you run these defragmenting utilities, you should close all other programs and applications that you are using, turn off your screen saver, and possibly disable your antivirus software and adjust power management settings. Because the primary function of these defragmenting utilities is to rearrange data stored on disk, you do not want to have any open programs accessing data in clusters that a defragmenting utility needs to move to another location.

You should not use a defragmenting utility designed for DOS or a version of Windows before Windows 95 because you can corrupt long filenames. If that occurs, you might discover that your programs do not work properly, or not at all. Furthermore, you should only use a defragmenting utility included with Windows XP, or one that has been developed by a third party specifically for use with Windows XP.

It is a good idea to run Check Disk before you run the defragmenting utility so that it can repair errors in the file system that might interfere with the defragmenting utility. Because file fragmentation does not build up as fast as errors to the file system (such as lost clusters), you probably need to use a defragmenting utility less frequently than Check Disk, perhaps only once every month or every few months. Plus, defragmenting a hard disk takes time.

Analyzing a Disk for Fragmentation

The first time you optimize your hard disk with one of the defragmenting utilities, it may take a long time to defragment the hard disk, but it is well worth it. The time it takes to defragment a hard disk depends on the size of the hard disk, the number of folders and files on the disk, how much of the hard disk's storage space is used, the amount of fragmentation that already exists on the volume, the available system resources (such as memory), and how often you run a defragmenting utility. If you run one of the defragmenting utilities frequently, it takes less time to defragment the disk because most of the disk is already optimized. If disk fragmentation builds up quickly, the amount of time required to defragment the disk increases.

Before you defragment a disk, you can analyze the disk to determine whether you need to defragment the disk and what you will gain if you do. These defragmenting utilities will recommend that you defragment your disk when fragmentation is 10% or greater; however, you can still defragment the disk if fragmentation is less than 10%.

The defragmenting utilities in Windows XP do not operate on floppy disks, so in the next section of the tutorial, you will use the command-line defragmenting utility to examine a hard disk drive or, if you prefer, a Zip disk. This process typically consists of two phases. First, you analyze a disk to determine the level of fragmentation, and then you defragment the disk if the fragmentation is high. The analysis is fairly quick; however, as noted earlier, defragmenting a hard disk can take time, so plan accordingly. For example, on the computer used for the steps in this section and the next section, it took 5.25 hours to defragment a 16 GB drive with 58% of the drive used to store files and with 8% file fragmentation. If you have a Zip drive, you might want to analyze and then defragment a Zip disk instead of drive C to save time. Also, these defragmenting utilities require that the drive contain more than 15% free space for sorting file fragments. If a drive has less than 15% free space, the defragmenting utility only partially defragments the drive. If there is a problem with the file system on a drive, you must first use Check Disk or the Error-checking tool to correct the problem before you can use a defragmenting utility.

Isabel recommends that you show employees how to analyze a disk for fragmentation and how to defragment the disk. She also notes that, because defragmenting a disk can be a time-consuming process, employees should know in advance whether their disk really needs defragmentation. Then they can plan their time more effectively, and schedule the defragmentation when their schedule permits.

To complete the following tutorial steps, you must be logged on as Administrator or logged on under an account with Administrator privileges. If you are working in a computer lab, ask your instructor or technical support staff whether you have permission to analyze and defragment one of the hard disk drives. If you do not have permission to use the command-line defragmenting utility, read the steps and examine the figures so that you are familiar with how this utility works, but do not complete the following steps.

To analyze disk defragmentation on drive C or a Zip disk:

1. Close any applications or windows you may have open on your computer, and temporarily turn off your screen saver, power management options, and antivirus software so that they do not interfere with Disk Defragmenter.

2. If necessary, open a Command Prompt window, type **cd ** and press the **Enter** key to switch to the root directory, type **color f0** to change the background and foreground colors, and then clear and maximize the Command Prompt window.

3. Type **defrag c: -a -v** and then press the **Enter** key. Then wait while Disk Defragmenter examines the drive. After that examination is complete, Windows Disk Defragmenter displays an Analysis Report that shows volume, file, pagefile, and folder fragmentation. See *Figure A1-31*. Your results will differ. The Analyze switch (-a) analyzes the disk for fragmentation, and the Verbose switch (-v) produces verbose output (rather than abbreviated output).

Figure A1-31	DISK DEFRAGMENTER ANALYSIS REPORT

```
C:\>defrag c: -a -v
Windows Disk Defragmenter
Copyright (c) 2001 Microsoft Corp. and Executive Software International, Inc.

Analysis Report

    Volume size                      = 15.97 GB
    Cluster size                     = 4 KB
    Used space                       = 8.14 GB
    Free space                       = 7.83 GB
    Percent free space               = 49 %

Volume fragmentation
    Total fragmentation              = 4 %
    File fragmentation               = 8 %        volume fragmentation
    Free space fragmentation         = 0 %

File fragmentation
    Total files                      = 75,047
    Average file size                = 106 KB      number of fragmented
    Total fragmented files           = 308         files
    Total excess fragments           = 1,150
    Average fragments per file       = 1.01

Pagefile fragmentation
    Pagefile size                    = 384 MB
    Total fragments                  = 70

Folder fragmentation                              number of fragmented
    Total folders                    = 5,794       folders
    Fragmented folders               = 136
    Excess folder fragments          = 497
```

TROUBLE? If Windows XP informs you that you must have Administrator privileges to defragment a volume, you are not logged on as an Administrator or you are not logged on under an account with Administrator privileges. Close the Command Prompt window, log off the computer, log on under an account with Administrator privileges, and then repeat these steps. Or, if you prefer to not log off, read the steps and examine the figures, but do not complete the remaining steps.

In the figure example, Disk Defragmenter reports that there is a total of 15.97 GB of storage space on the disk, and that 7.83 GB or 49% of that storage space is free. The total fragmentation on the disk is 4%, there is 8% file fragmentation on the disk, and the free space fragmentation is 0%. There are a total of 308 fragmented files and 136 fragmented folders. The average number of fragments per file is 1.01. A value of 1.00 indicates that all the files (or nearly all) are contiguous. If the value were 1.10, then 10% of the files, on average, are stored as two fragments. If the value were 1.20, then 20% of the files, on average, are stored as two fragments. On this computer, 1% of the files, on the average, are stored as two fragments. The virtual memory paging file (identified in the report as Pagefile) contains 70 fragments. However, because Windows XP requires access to this file at all times, it cannot be defragmented.

Defragmenting a Disk

When defragmenting utilities optimize a disk, they rearrange clusters on the disk so that all the clusters for a file are stored contiguous to each other (where possible), and they consolidate free space to reduce the rate at which file fragmentation builds up after the defragmentation.

Even if one of the defragmenting utilities reports that defragmentation is less than 10%, you can still defragment the disk if you want, or you can read, but not complete, the following steps. Also, because defragmentation can take hours, you might want to read, but not complete, the following steps. Also, as noted earlier, you must be logged on as Administrator or logged on under an account with Administrator privileges. Your instructor will inform you whether you can perform these steps and, if so, how you should log on. If you do not have these privileges, read the steps and examine the figures so that you are familiar with how Windows Disk Defragmenter works, but do not complete the following steps.

If you are working in a computer lab, make sure you have permission to use the Disk Defragmenter to defragment one of the hard disk drives.

Now that you have demonstrated to Isabel's staff how to properly analyze a disk for fragmentation, Isabel asks you to defragment the disk and then determine the effectiveness of the defragmentation.

To defragment drive C:

1. So that you have a general idea of how long it takes for Disk Defragmenter to defragment drive C on your computer, note the time you started the defragmentation.

2. Clear the window, type **defrag   c: -v** and press the **Enter** key. Then, wait patiently.

   Windows Disk Defragmenter analyzes the disk again, displays an Analysis report, and then starts the defragmentation. After Windows Disk Defragmenter displays a Defragmentation Report, note the time the defragmentation was completed, and compare it with the time you started the defragmentation. You can then use this information to schedule future defragmentations of your hard disk. *Figure A1-32* shows a Defragmentation Report for drive C. If necessary, adjust the view within the Command Prompt window so that you can see the Defragmentation Report.

Figure A1-32 | **DISK DEFRAGMENTER DEFRAGMENTATION REPORT**

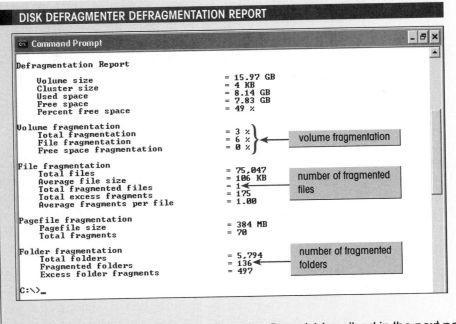

3. After you evaluate the Defragmentation Report (described in the next paragraph), close the Command Prompt window.

For the example in *Figure A1-32*, Windows Disk Defragmenter reports 3% total fragmentation (a decrease of 1%), 6% file fragmentation (a decrease of 2%), and 0% free space fragmentation (no change). Also, Windows Disk Defragmenter reports only 1 fragmented file (as compared to 308 prior to defragmentation), 136 fragmented folders (no change), and an average of 1.00 fragments per file (almost perfect defragmentation for a volume this size). There was no change in pagefile fragmentation or folder fragmentation. Windows XP must have access to the paging file at all times, so the Disk Defragmenter cannot defragment this file. Although the percentage of total fragmentation and file fragmentation decreased only slightly, overall file fragmentation was substantially reduced.

If you now perform operations on your computer, such as opening, creating, modifying, and saving files, and then analyze the disk for defragmentation, you will discover more fragmented files. Obviously, the number of fragmented files will be lower than if you had not defragmented the disk, because there is more contiguous space available; therefore, it is easier for the operating system to store all the clusters for one file together in contiguous clusters.

Certain operating system files, such as the paging file (for virtual memory) and the hibernation file (for power management), are excluded from the defragmentation, so you can never achieve 100% defragmentation. You can, however, purchase a defragmenting utility from another company, such as Executive Software International's Diskeeper, to provide more information about the organization of your disk, dramatically improve the amount of defragmentation, and substantially reduce the amount of time required to perform a defragmentation. The Windows XP Disk Defragmenter utilities were also developed by Executive Software International.

REFERENCE WINDOW | **RW**

Defragmenting a Disk

- Log on as Administrator or under an account with Administrator privileges.
- If necessary, open a Command Prompt window, type CD \ and press the Enter key to switch to the root directory, type COLOR F0 to change the background and foreground colors, and then clear and maximize the Command Prompt window.
- Note your starting time.
- Type DEFRAG C: -V and then press the Enter key. Then wait patiently while Disk Defragmenter examines the drive. After the examination is complete, Windows Disk Defragmenter displays an Analysis Report that shows volume, file, pagefile, and folder fragmentation. Note the time the defragmentation was completed, and compare it to the time you started so that you can plan future defragmentations.

Although Disk Defragmenter optimizes the arrangement of files on a drive and reduces free space fragmentation, it does not consolidate all of the free space on the volume, but may leave some free space scattered around the volume.

You should optimize disks, especially your hard disk, on a regular basis, such as monthly or weekly. If you are working with graphics applications and creating and removing large image files, or if you work with a large number of files (creating, modifying, deleting, copying, and moving files) everyday, you should defragment your disk at least weekly. If you do not optimize your hard disk with one of the Windows defragmenting utilities, your hard disk's performance will gradually decline. In fact, if you spend too much time waiting for applications and documents to load, that is a good sign you need to use a defragmenting utility. Also, as you use more of your hard disk's storage space, it becomes increasingly difficult for a defragmenting utility to optimize your disk, because the disk contains only a limited area of storage space for rewriting clusters as it defragments the disk. As a result, the amount of time that one of the Windows defragmenting utilities takes to optimize a disk increases substantially. You might have to temporarily remove files from the hard disk so that you can optimize the disk, and then copy those files back to the drive later. Before you "defrag" a disk, you should review which data files remain on disk and which can be deleted or archived (moved off the disk for long-term storage).

Session 6.3

The Recovery Console in Windows XP is very similar to that in Windows 2000; however, there are some minor differences that you need to be aware of. Also, this section of the Appendix includes additional information to help you if the Windows XP Professional Recovery Console will not accept your Administrator password.

UPDATE Installing Recovery Console

If you boot your computer from your Windows XP CD, you will see options for continuing your current upgrade, installing a new version of Windows, or exiting Setup, but not one for launching the Recovery Console. You can, however, use your Windows XP Setup Disks.

- **Page 284, Step 1:** Click the Start button, click Log Off, click the Log Off button in the Log Off Windows dialog box, select the Administrator account, enter the proper password, and then click OK.

- **Page 284, Steps 4 and 5**: If the command interpreter reports that the system cannot find the path specified, use the Change Directory (CD) command to change to the i386 directory on your Windows XP CD, and then enter the following command: winnt32 /cmdcons
- **Page 285, Reference Window**: If the command in the fourth bullet does not work, and if the command interpreter reports that the system cannot find the path specified, use the Change Directory (CD) command to change to the i386 directory on your Windows XP CD, and then enter the following command: winnt32 /cmdcons

Logging into the Recovery Console

When you successfully log into the Recovery Console, the command prompt may show Windows as the name of the Windows directory. However, on some computers, you might have difficulty logging into the Recovery Console. If you attempt to log into the Recovery Console with either Windows XP Professional or Windows XP Home Edition, the Recovery Console might display an error message indicating that your Administrator password is not valid, even if you enter the correct Administrator password. The Recovery Console will then prompt you to retype your Administrator password. If you try to log into the Recovery Console again, you will still encounter this same problem. If you reboot your computer, log on as Administrator, change your Administrator password, reboot your computer, and then try to log into the Recovery Console again, you will still experience this problem.

This problem can occur if Windows XP was originally installed using the System Preparation Tool (Sysprep) image, or if Sysprep 2.0 was run on the computer. The Sysprep utility, which allows someone to create a disk image of one computer and then copy that disk image to other computers to reduce the time and effort for setting up other computers, changes the way password keys are stored in the Registry, and these changes are not compatible with the Recovery Console.

Microsoft recommends you wait for the next Windows XP service pack upgrade to fix this problem, and then download and install that update. If you need to resolve the problem immediately, you can contact Microsoft to obtain a hot fix, or operating system update. This hot fix updates the Cmdcons folder where the Recovery Console is installed. If you reinstall the Recovery Console, you also need to reinstall the hot fix. Alternatively, you can download one of two files to create floppy disks that allow you to make repairs using the Recovery Console. These floppy disks are the Windows XP Setup Disks that you created earlier.

If you want more information about this problem, you can visit Microsoft's Knowledge Base on the Web and locate a Knowledge Base article entitled "Cannot Log On To Recovery Console After Running Sysprep in Windows XP (Q308402)". To locate the Web page for searching the Knowledge Base, go to Microsoft's home page (*www.microsoft.com*), click Support at the top right of the Web page, and then click Knowledge Base. To use the Knowledge Base Search, you specify the product for which you want to locate information, and the keyword or keywords (a word or phrase) you want to use for the search. If you know the article number, you can search by that item of information and locate the article more quickly.

Launching Recovery Console from Setup Disks or a CD

If you boot your computer from your Windows XP CD, you will see options for continuing your current upgrade, installing a new version of Windows, or exiting Setup, but not one for launching the Recovery Console. You can, however, use your Windows XP Setup Disks.

- **Page 287, Step 2**: You will need to insert and boot with your Windows XP Setup Disks.
- **Page 287, Steps 4-5**: Step 5 is unnecessary. The Recovery Console automatically loads once you type R to repair a Windows installation.

HELP Using Recovery Console Commands

As you complete this section, you will see that the output of certain commands is different than that shown in the figures. Also, the Recovery Console requires that you adhere strictly to the syntax for using commands.

- **Pages 291-292, Steps 4-5**: If the Recovery Console displays the message "The system cannot find the file or directory specified", enter the command again and make sure you spell the filename correctly. If the Recovery Console displays the same message and if your computer does not have an NtBtLog.txt file, then read but do not keystroke these steps.
- **Page 292, Figure 6-58**: The contents of your NtBtLog.txt file (if present) will differ.
- **Page 292, Step 6**: You must press the Spacebar before typing the backslash (\). If you do not leave a space between "cd" and "\", you will see the error message: "The command is not recognized. Type HELP for a list of supported commands."
- **Page 294, Figure 6-61**: If your volume is a FAT volume, you might also see the message: "CHKDSK is performing additional checking or recovery..."

NEW Recovery Console Commands

Windows XP Professional and Windows XP Home Edition contain two additional Recovery Console commands not found in Windows 2000 Professional:

- **BOOTCFG**: Scans a hard disk or disks and uses the information it collects to modify the Boot.ini file or build a new copy of Boot.ini.
- **NET**: Maps a network share point to a drive letter (covered in Tutorial 10 of the textbook).

HELP Restoring Your Computer

The Windows XP Help system, now called the Help and Support Center, is more extensive than that found in Windows 2000, and is structured differently than the Help systems in previous versions of Windows.

- **Page 294, Step 2**: After you open the Help and Support Center, enter "recovery console" in the Search box, and click the Search button. In the Search Results panel, click the Recovery Console overview Help link, click the Related Topics Help link, and then click the "Delete the Recovery Console" Help link to locate the steps for removing the Recovery Console from your computer.

UPDATE Command Reference

There are some differences in the commands listed in the Command Reference table on Page 295:

- **MAKEBOOT**: You cannot make Windows XP Setup Disks from the Windows XP CD. Instead, you must download a Windows XP Professional or Windows XP Home Edition Win32 Cabinet Self-Extractor program from Microsoft's Download Center, as described earlier in this Appendix tutorial, to make Setup Disks.
- **NTBACKUP**: You cannot make an Emergency Repair Disk using the Backup utility.

✓REVISED Review Assignments

Because the process for making Windows XP Setup Disks is different than that for Windows 2000, and because you cannot make an Emergency Repair Disk with Windows XP, complete the following revised Review Assignments steps rather than those in the textbook if you are using Windows XP Professional or Windows XP Home Edition:

Isabel asks you to show a new intern how to set the boot sequence in CMOS, make and test an MS-DOS Startup Disk, make Windows XP Setup Disks, boot to Safe Mode with Command Prompt, check a disk for errors, defragment a disk, and use Recovery Console commands.

If you are working in a computer lab and if the lab restricts access to CMOS, you might not be able to complete all the steps. For those steps that include questions about CMOS, note whether the lab restricts access to CMOS.

As you complete each step, record your answers to any questions so that you can submit them to your instructor.

1. Restart your computer, log onto Windows, open My Computer from the Start menu or from a desktop icon (if available), insert an empty floppy disk in drive A, right-click the drive A icon in the My Computer window, click Format on the shortcut menu, click the "Create an MS-DOS startup disk" check box in the Format options section, click the Start button, and then click the OK button in the Format 3½ Floppy (A:) dialog box. After the format is complete, click the OK button in the Formatting 3½ Floppy (A:) dialog box, click the Close button in the Format 3½ Floppy (A:) dialog box, and then close the My Computer window.

2. Open and maximize a Command Prompt window, and then display a directory of all files (including hidden system files) on the MS-DOS Startup Disk in drive A in alphabetical order by filename. What are the core operating system files on the MS-DOS Startup Disk, and which file is the command interpreter?

3. With your MS-DOS Startup Disk in drive A, close the Command Prompt window, restart your computer, open the CMOS Setup utility, and change the boot sequence (if necessary) so that your computer will check drive A first for a boot disk. What key(s) did you press to access CMOS? What boot sequence does your computer now use?

4. Some computers contain an option in CMOS for write-protecting the fixed disk boot sector to protect it from computer viruses. Examine the Security settings in CMOS. Is there an option for write-protecting the fixed disk boot sector? What is that setting? What types of computer viruses would attempt to access the fixed disk boot sector?

5. Examine the other settings in CMOS. Are there any other settings that you might want to change? If so, what are they and why would you want to change them? Do not make these changes unless you are sure you want to implement them now.

6. Exit CMOS and save your settings. After your computer boots from the MS-DOS Startup Disk, what version of Windows does it report as the operating system that loaded from the disk? Use the Version command to display the Version number? What Version number does the Version command report?

7. Now that you've successfully tested your MS-DOS Startup Disk, remove the disk from drive A, press Ctrl+Alt+Del to reboot your computer, boot your computer to the desktop, and log onto your computer.

8. If you have not yet downloaded the Win32 Cabinet Self-Extractor program for making Windows XP Setup Disks from Microsoft's Web site, connect your computer to your ISP (if necessary), and then use your Web browser to locate Microsoft's Download Center (*www.microsoft.com/downloads*).

9. Once you locate this Web site, select Keyword Search in the Search for a Download section of the Web page, enter Setup Disks in the Keywords box, select Windows XP from the Operating System list box, and then click the Find It button. If you then scroll down the page, you will see the search results and two links, one for Windows XP Professional and the 6ther for Windows XP Home Edition.

10. Select the link for the version of Windows used on your computer, download the Win32 Cabinet Self-Extractor program for making Setup Disks for your version of Windows XP and store it in a folder within your Documents folder, and then disconnect from your ISP (if necessary).

11. Open a Command Prompt window, and format six high-density diskettes for use as Windows XP Setup Disks. *Note*: If you are using the same diskettes as you used in the tutorial, and if you recently formatted those diskettes, you can use the Quick switch (/Q) with the FORMAT command to quickly reformat the diskettes. Also, if you want to label those diskettes, use the following labels: Windows XP Setup Boot Disk, Windows XP Setup Disk #2, Windows XP Setup Disk #3, Windows XP Setup Disk #4, Windows XP Setup Disk #5, and Windows XP Setup Disk #6.

12. Change to the directory where you downloaded the Win32 Self-Extractor program, and then type the name of the Win32 Self-Extractor program file, as follows: If you downloaded the Win32 Self-Extractor program file for making Setup Disks for Windows XP Professional, type WinXP_EN_PRO_BF.EXE If you downloaded the Win32 Self-Extractor program file for making Setup Disks for Windows XP Home Edition, type WinXP_EN_HOM_BF.EXE When prompted by the Makeboot.exe program, insert each of your formatted floppy disks.

13. Make a duplicate copy of Student Data Disk #1.

14. Restart your computer, display the Windows Advanced Options menu, and choose the option for booting in Safe Mode with Command Prompt, choose your version of Windows XP, and then log onto Windows under an account with Administrator privileges. What program does Windows XP start after you log on your computer?

15. Execute the Check Disk program with the Fix option on your duplicate diskette. What information does Check Disk report? Next, execute the Check Disk program with the Repair option on your duplicate diskette. What information does Check Disk report?

16. Use the Windows Disk Defragmenter utility to analyze a Zip disk or one of the hard disk drives within your computer. What command did you enter for this operation? What results did the Windows Disk Defragmenter report? (*Note*: You may want to repeat the command and redirect the output to a text file on disk.)

17. Use Ctrl+Alt+Del to restart your computer, and then log on your computer under an account with Administrator privileges.

18. Briefly compare and contrast the use of an MS-DOS Startup Disk, Windows XP Setup Disks, Safe Mode with Command Prompt, and the Recovery Console. In your comparison, describe any advantage(s) or disadvantage(s) of each feature or tool. (*Note*: In addition to examining the discussion on the Recovery Console, you may want to complete the following steps using the Recovery Console first.)

Note: The following steps use the Recovery Console, and are optional.

19. If the Recovery Console is not installed on your hard drive, and if you want to install the Recovery Console now, insert your Windows XP CD, and then follow the steps described earlier for installing the Recovery Console.

20. Reboot your computer, choose the Recovery Console from the OS Choices Menu, type the number of the Windows installation you want to use, and then log into the Recovery Console with your Administrator password.

21. In Recovery Console, change to the SystemRoot directory (if necessary), change to the System32 directory, and then change to the Config directory.

22. Execute the DIR command. How many files does DIR list, and what are their attributes? (*Note*: You do not need to list all the files, just summarize the types of attributes assigned to those files.)

23. Execute the Check Disk command on your hard drive. What information does Check Disk report?

24. Exit the Recovery Console, reboot your computer, and log onto Windows.

UPDATE Quick Check Answers

■ **Page 300, Question 5**: The answer to this Quick Check question should be "boot record" or "boot sector".

TUTORIAL 7   USING BATCH PROGRAMS

Session 7.1

Windows XP is remarkably similar to Windows 2000 in creating and using batch programs. However, there are some differences when using Windows XP in the following situations:

■ Your starting directory after opening a Command Prompt window
■ The name of your Windows directory

UPDATE Creating a Batch Program

There are minor differences between Windows XP and Windows 2000 in this section:

■ **Page 303, Step 1** (bottom of page): You do not need to complete this step because you are already placed in the directory for your user account after you open a Command Prompt window. If you changed to another directory after opening a Command Prompt window, then complete this step. If you want to try the command in this step so that you are familiar with its use, type CD \ and press the Enter key to switch to the root directory, and then complete this step.

■ **Page 304, Step 2** and **Figure 7-2**: You may also see a Windows directory in the directory listing.

UPDATE Viewing the Search Path

Your search path might differ:

■ **Page 313, Step 2**: Your path may differ from that shown in the figure, and the name of your Windows directory in the search path might differ.

Session 7.2

The process for creating, testing, and documenting batch programs is identical to that in Windows XP. However, you will see the following differences as you complete this section of the tutorial:

- The starting directory that Windows XP uses after opening a Command Prompt window
- How Windows XP opens the Address Book program
- How shortcuts are named (also applies to Windows 2000)
- How you display the Administrative Tools menu on the Start menu

UPDATE   Defining the Steps for a Batch Program

Because Windows XP uses a different default directory when you open a Command Prompt window, you may need to change directories:

- **Page 323, Step 1**: If you want your screen to match the figures in this section, change to the root directory.

HELP   Testing the Batch Program

When opening the Address Book program in Windows XP, you might need to complete an additional step:

- **Page 326, Step 3**: You may see an Address Book dialog box asking whether you want to make the Address Book your default vCard viewer. Before you click the No button, you may also want to add a check mark to the "Do not perform this check when starting the Address Book" check box so that you are not constantly prompted every time you or your batch program opens the Address Book.
- **Page 326, Step 4**: The Address Book may not have completely opened, but might instead have displayed an Address Book dialog box asking whether you want to make the Address Book your default vCard viewer. If so, click the No button, and then close the Address Book window.

Documenting Batch Program Operations

When opening the Address Book program in Windows XP, you might need to complete an additional step:

- **Page 335, Step 5**: The Address Book may not have completely opened, but might instead have displayed an Address Book dialog box asking whether you want to make the Address Book your default vCard viewer. If so, click the No button.

Making a Shortcut to a Batch Program

You might encounter minor differences in using Windows XP and Windows 2000 Professional:

- **Page 336, Step 3**: You may also need to resize the Command Prompt window so that you can see the desktop.

- **Page 337, Step 6** and **Figure 7-33**: Your desktop shortcut might not include the phrase "Shortcut to" as part of the shortcut name.
- **Page 338, Step 7**: If your shortcut name is 3app.bat, change its name to just 3app (without the file extension).
- **Page 338, Step 9**: The Address Book may not have completely opened, but might instead have displayed an Address Book dialog box asking whether you want to make the Address Book your default vCard viewer. If so, click the No button.

Session 7.3

Configuring, starting, entering commands, and using batch programs in the Recovery Console is similar to that in Windows XP Professional. However, if you are using Windows XP Home Edition, you will not be able to complete this section of the tutorial, because Windows XP Home Edition does not contain the Security Configuration and Analysis snap-in found in Window XP Professional. Therefore, you cannot take advantage of all the features in the Recovery Console. For example, you cannot set Local Security Policy in Windows XP Home Edition, and therefore you cannot change settings of the environment variables in the Recovery Console either manually or with the use of a batch program.

Expanding the Recovery Console's Capabilities

There are minor differences between Windows XP Professional and Windows 2000 Professional in displaying the Administrative Tools menu and in using the Local Security Policy Setting dialog box. As noted in the preface to this section, Windows XP Home Edition users will not be able to complete Session 7.3, but instead should read this section so that they are familiar with this process in Windows XP Professional and Windows 2000 Professional.

- **Page 340, Step 2**: If you are using Windows XP Home Edition, you will not find a Local Security Policy option on the Administrative Tools menu. Instead, read this section so that you are familiar with how to specify these settings in Windows XP Professional and Windows 2000 Professional.
- **Page 340, Step 2 Trouble**: The process for displaying the Administrative Tools option on the All Programs menu is slightly different: Right-click the taskbar, click Properties on the shortcut menu, click the Start Menu tab in the Taskbar and Start Menu Properties dialog box, click the Customize button to the right of Start menu, click the Advanced tab in the Customize Start Menu dialog box, locate System Administrative Tools in the Start menu items box (the last option in that box), click the "Display on the All Programs menu" option button, click the OK button to close the Customize Start Menu dialog box, click the OK button to close the Taskbar and Start Menu Properties dialog box, and then try Step 2 again.
- **Page 341, Step 5** and **Figure 7-36**: The title of the dialog box is now the same as the policy setting you just selected, and within the dialog box, there is a Local Security Setting tab with the option for enabled or disabling this setting. Click the Enabled option button if it is not already selected.

[UPDATE] Writing a Recovery Console Batch Program

You will need to use the Windows Advanced Options Menu or your Windows XP Setup Disks to launch the Recovery Console. If you are using Windows XP Home Edition, you can create the batch program described in this section of the textbook; however, you will not be able to execute the program in the Recovery Console because you cannot change the Local Security Policy setting for using the SET command in the Recovery Console. As noted earlier, Windows XP Home Edition users should read this section so that they are familiar with the features described in the textbook for Windows XP Professional and Windows 2000 Professional.

■ **Page 343, Step 1**: If you boot from your Windows XP CD, you will see options for continuing your current upgrade, installing a new version of Windows, or exiting Setup, but not one for launching the Recovery Console. However, if you boot with the Windows XP Setup Disks, the Recovery Console automatically loads once you type R to repair a Windows installation.

[HELP] Review Assignments

When designing your batch program, you will need to specify the path to one of two copies of the WordPad and Character Map programs:

■ **Page 348, Step 10**: Both Windows 2000 Professional and Windows XP will locate two copies of wordpad.exe and charmap.exe in the following directories:

wordpad.exe   C:\Windows\System32\Dllcache
                                       C:\Program Files\Windows NT\Accessories

charmap.exe   C:\Windows\system32
                                         C:\ Windows\System32\Dllcache

When you design your batch program, specify the path to the wordpad.exe program in the Accessories directory and the charmap.exe program in the System32 directory.

[HELP] Case 1: Documenting the Directory Tree of the My Documents Folder at The Perfect Match

You may need to adapt one of the instructions for your batch program so that it works properly under Windows 2000 Professional and Windows XP:

■ **Page 349, Step 1h**: Because you may not be able to redirect output to PRN, modify your batch program so that it redirects output to a text file on your diskette that you can then print with Notepad. Also, modify the message block so that instead of prompting you to check the status of the printer, you are prompted to insert a diskette where the redirected output will be stored.

[HELP] Case 3: Running Dual Graphics Programs at Stratton Graphics

Because the Imaging program is not available in Windows XP Home Edition, you will need to design your batch program to use another Windows program. Instead of the Imaging program, you can use another graphics program of your choosing, or if you prefer, you can use Windows Media Player, which is available on the All Programs menu.

TUTORIAL 8   ENHANCING THE POWER OF BATCH PROGRAMS

Session 8.1

As you step through Sessions 8.1, 8.2, and 8.3 in Tutorial 8, you will discover that Windows XP is remarkably similar to Windows 2000 when working with batch programs.

UPDATE Creating a Batch Program Directory

There is one minor difference in Windows XP which saves you a step:

■ **Page 355, Step 4**: You do not need to complete this step because you are already in the directory for your user account after you open a Command Prompt window. If you changed to another directory after opening a Command Prompt window, then complete this step. If you want to try the command in this step so that you are familiar with its use, type CD \ and press the Enter key to switch to the root directory, and then complete this step.

UPDATE Checking for the Presence of a Directory

In both Windows XP and Windows 2000, IF EXIST does not need the NUL device to find a directory. In the example on Page 368, you can use the following command instead:

```
IF EXIST %1 COPY %1 A:
```

where %1 is a directory name.

However, if you are using a previous version of Windows, such as Windows 98 or Windows 95, you will need to include the reference to the NUL device in the syntax for the IF EXIST command.

Session 8.3

Microsoft has improved the capabilities and features of the Windows Script Host in Windows XP.

UPDATE Windows Script Host

The Windows XP Script Host is similar to that in Windows 2000. In the original version of Windows XP, the Windows Script Host version is Version 5.6, and it includes new functionality that simplifies its use, increases its capabilities, and makes it safer to use.

TUTORIAL 9 | THE WINDOWS XP REGISTRY

Session 9.1

The Windows XP Registry is very similar to the Windows 2000 Registry. However, you will see differences in Registry settings that result from new features incorporated into Windows XP.

Backing Up and Restoring the Windows Registry

As noted in the Appendix for Tutorial 6, Windows XP no longer contains an option for making an Emergency Repair Disk. You can use the Automated System Recovery Wizard in Windows XP Professional (covered in Tutorial 6 of the Appendix) to back up the system state, system services, and the system volume of your computer so that you have the system files and settings required to rebuild that computer. As you may recall, the system state consists of the operating system components that define the current state of the operating system, and includes Registry settings for user accounts, applications, hardware, and software, as well as files in the top-level folder and Windows folder that Windows XP needs to boot the computer. The Automated System Recovery is not available in the Home Edition of Windows XP. Windows XP Professional and Windows XP Home Edition include a System Restore Utility (covered in the next section) that you can use to back up the Registry and other system settings.

The System Restore Utility

The **System Restore** utility, first introduced in Windows Me and not available in Windows 2000, is a Windows XP component that allows you to restore your computer to a previous working state if you encounter a problem after installing an operating system upgrade, installing or upgrading an application or utility, installing or upgrading a device driver for a hardware device, restoring files from a backup, experiencing damage caused by a virus infection or file corruption, or making changes to system settings. System Restore creates restore points periodically in response to system events, or at the request of the user. System Restore also creates a restore point every 24 hours, or when 24 hours have elapsed since the last restore point. Each **restore point** contains a snapshot of the Registry as well as information on the system state, and represents a "picture" of the state of your computer at a given point in time. These restore points do not include user files (such as those found in the My Documents folder), files with file extensions known to be common document file extensions (such as "doc"), shortcuts (such as Internet shortcuts found in the user's Favorites folder), e-mail, graphics files, passwords, or the Windows paging file.

The System Restore utility is not a command-line utility, so you need to work in the Windows GUI to create restore points, restore your computer to an earlier point in time, or undo a restoration.

System Restore creates the following types of restore points:

- **Initial system checkpoints**. System Restore creates a system checkpoint when you first start a new computer with Windows XP or after you upgrade a computer to Windows XP. A **system checkpoint** is a scheduled restore point that System Restore automatically creates.

- **System checkpoints**. System Restore creates a system checkpoint after every 24 hours of calendar time.

■ **Program name installation restore points**. System Restore creates a restore point before you install a program using an installer such as InstallShield or Windows Installer. If you need to revert to this restore point, System Restore removes installed files and Registry settings for the newly installed program and restores programs and system files that were altered during the installation of the new program. If you roll back your computer to a state that existed before a program was installed, the program will not work after the roll back, and you will need to reinstall the program.

■ **Automatic update restore points**. If you use the automatic update feature to download operating system updates, System Restore creates a restore point before you install any updates.

■ **Unsigned device driver restore points**. If you install a device driver that has not been digitally signed or certified by Microsoft's Windows Hardware Quality Labs (WHQL), System Restore creates a restore point before installing the driver. If a problem arises after installing the updated device driver, you can use the restore point to roll back your computer and restore your previous device driver.

■ **Microsoft Backup Utility restore points**. If you restore files from a backup using the Microsoft Backup Utility, System Restore creates a restore point before the restore operation.

■ **Restore operation restore points**. If you need to roll back your computer using a restore point, System Restore creates a new restore point first so that if a problem develops after the restore, you can roll your computer forward to its original state before the restore.

■ **Manual restore points**. You can manually create restore points before you make changes to your computer. For example, before you manually make changes to Registry settings or other system settings, or before you install a downloaded program that does not use an InstallShield wizard or Windows XP Professional Installer, you can create a restore point in the event a problem develops later.

System Restore is enabled on all drives when you first power on a new computer or after you install Windows XP unless there is less than 200 MB of hard disk space available on the partition that contains the Windows operating system folder. You have to make sure that you do not run out of disk space; otherwise, System Restore becomes inactive.

Using the information stored in Filelist.xml, System Restore monitors changes to operating system and application files, and either records changes to the original files or backs them up. Filelist.xml lists files, directories, and file extensions that are either included or excluded from the restore checkpoints. If your Windows folder is named Windows, then the path to this file is C:\Windows\System32\Restore\Filelist.xml.

[UPDATE] Making an Emergency Repair Disk

You will not be able to complete the steps in this section of Tutorial 9 because Windows XP does not have an option for making an Emergency Repair Disk. However, you can create a restore point with the System Restore utility and back up the Registry before you continue with this tutorial.

■ **Page 422, Steps 1-7**: Read, but do not complete, these tutorial steps so that you are familiar with the process for creating an Emergency Repair Disk in Windows 2000.

Examining System Restore Settings

Because System Restore is such an invaluable tool for troubleshooting problems on employees' computers, Isabel and her staff check the System Restore settings on all new computer systems with Windows XP and on all existing computers upgraded to Windows XP.

Before you create a restore point, you will examine the System Restore settings on the computer you are using. You must log on to your computer under an account with Administrator privileges. If you do not have Administrator privileges on the computer you are using, read the steps and examine the figures, but do not complete the steps.

As noted earlier, when you use the System Restore utility, you work in the GUI rather than in a command-line environment.

To view System Restore settings:

1. Log on under an account with Administrator privileges.

2. From the Start menu, right-click **My Computer**, click **Properties** on the shortcut menu, and in the System Properties dialog box, click the **System Restore** tab. From the System Restore property sheet, shown in *Figure A1-33*, you can turn off the System Restore feature for all drives, or examine drive settings used by System Restore; however, if you do, System Restore deletes all existing restore points and you cannot track or undo changes to your computer. On the computer used for this figure, System Restore is currently monitoring drive C and drive D.

   TROUBLE? If you do not see a System Restore tab in the System Properties dialog box, you did not log on under an account with Administrator privileges. You must log out of the current account, and log on under another account with Administrator privileges.

Figure A1-33   **VIEWING SYSTEM RESTORE PROPERTIES**

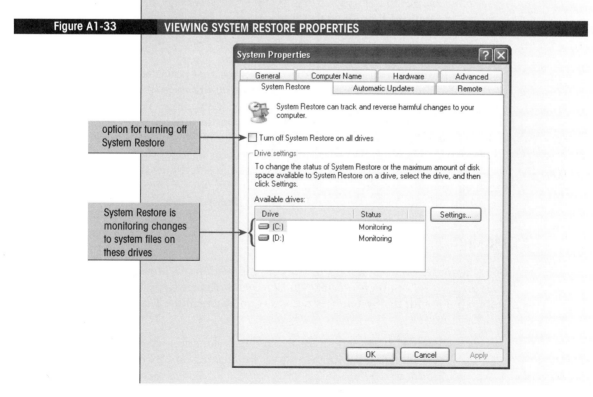

3. Under Available drives, click **(C:)**, and then click the **Settings** button. In the Drive (C:) Settings dialog box, Windows XP notes that it is monitoring drive C. It also notes that you cannot turn off System Restore on this drive (the system volume) without turning it off on all drives. See *Figure A1-34*. If your computer has another disk drive, as is the case for the computer used for the figure, you can turn off System Restore for that volume. In the Disk space usage section, Windows XP automatically allocates approximately 12% of a volume over 4 GB for storing restore points. For the computer used for this figure, that translates into 1,962 MB, or approximately 1.9 GB of storage space. If you do not want to keep older restore points or if you need to conserve the use of storage space on a drive, you can reduce the amount of disk space used for restore points, but if you decrease the available storage space, that reduces the number of restore points that System Restore can create and store on the disk.

TROUBLE? If you cannot click the icon for drive C, and if you do not have a Settings button, read this step and the next step and examine the figure.

Figure A1-34   **VIEWING SYSTEM RESTORE DRIVE SETTINGS**

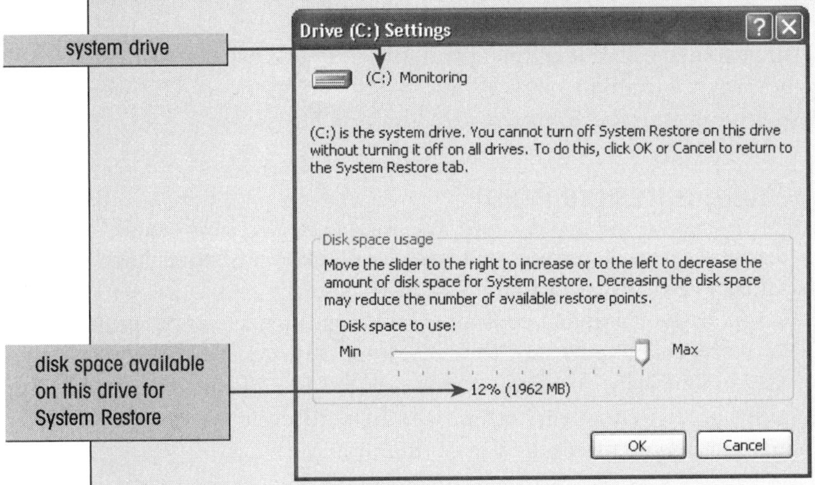

4. Click the **Cancel** button to close the Drive (C:) Settings dialog box without making any changes, and then click the **Cancel** button to close the System Properties dialog box without making any changes.

REFERENCE WINDOW   **RW**

<u>Checking System Restore Settings</u>

■ Log on under an account with Administrator privileges.

■ From the Start menu, right-click My Computer, click Properties, and in the System Properties dialog box, click the System Restore tab.

■ If you want to turn off System Restore for all drives, click the "Turn off System Restore on all drives" check box (and add a check mark). Precaution: System Restore then deletes all existing
restore points, and you cannot track or undo changes to your computer.

■ If you want to view System Restore settings for a drive, click a drive in the Available drives box,
and then click the Settings button. If you want to turn off System Restore for just that drive, and if
that option is available, click the "Turn off System Restore on this drive" check box in the Drive
Settings dialog box. If you want to adjust the storage space used by System Restore, use the
slider bar under Disk space to use, and then click OK.

■ Click OK to close the System Properties dialog box.

Although System Restore is automatically enabled, you should check the System Restore
settings to make sure it is functioning the way you expect. Also, if you have a dual-boot configuration, for example, with Windows 98 and Windows XP, System Restore will also create
restore points on the volume with Windows 98.

Creating a Restore Point

In the next set of steps, you will manually create a restore point so that you have an additional backup of your computer's Registry settings.

If you are working in a computer lab, make sure you have permission from your instructor or technical support staff to use System Restore to create a restore point.

As you and Isabel upgrade computers for Windows XP and provide new computers to
employees, you show each employee how to create a restore point before they make a
change that might affect the use of their computer.

To create a restore point:

1. Make sure you are logged on under an account with Administrator privileges.

2. From the Start menu, point to **All Programs**, point to **Accessories**, point to
   System Tools, and then click **System Restore**. In the first System Restore dialog
   box, Windows XP explains the value of System Restore, the use of restore points,
   and notes that any changes you make to your computer with System Restore
   are completely reversible because System Restore creates a new restore point
   before restoring your computer to a previous state with a previously made
   restore point. See *Figure A1-35*. Windows XP also notes that before you change
   your system, you can manually create a restore point so that you can reverse
   any changes you make. If you decide to check or make changes to System
   Restore settings, you can also use the System Restore Settings link in this dialog
   box to open the System Properties dialog box and select the System Restore
   property sheet.

Figure A1-35	CHOOSING A SYSTEM RESTORE TASK

System Restore

Welcome to System Restore

? Help

what System Restores does and how it works →

You can use System Restore to undo harmful changes to your computer and restore its settings and performance. System Restore returns your computer to an earlier time (called a restore point) without causing you to lose recent work, such as saved documents, e-mail, or history and favorites lists.

Any changes that System Restore makes to your computer are completely reversible.

Your computer automatically creates restore points (called system checkpoints), but you can also use System Restore to create your own restore points. This is useful if you are about to make a major change to your system, such as installing a new program or changing your registry.

System Restore Settings

System Restore tasks →

To begin, select the task that you want to perform:

◉ Restore my computer to an earlier time

○ Create a restore point

To continue, select an option, and then click Next.

[Next >]   [Cancel]

3. Click the **Create a restore point** option button, and then click the **Next** button. In the Create a Restore Point window, you can provide a description for this restore point. See *Figure A1-36*. A description is useful so that you know why you manually created a specific restore point.

Figure A1-36	ENTERING A RESTORE POINT DESCRIPTION

System Restore

Create a Restore Point

? Help

Your computer automatically creates restore points at regularly scheduled times or before certain programs are installed. However, you can use System Restore to create your own restore points at times other than those scheduled by your computer.

Type a description for your restore point in the following text box. Ensure that you choose a description that is easy to identify in case you need to restore your computer later.

enter a description for this new restore point →

Restore point description:

The current date and time are automatically added to your restore point.

This restore point cannot be changed after it is created. Before continuing, ensure that you have typed the correct name.

[< Back]   [Create]   [Cancel]

4. In the Restore point description box, type **RP** (for Restore Point), press the **spacebar**, type your last name (for example, Isabel Navarro would type "RP Navarro"), and then click the **Create** button. System Restore informs you that it has created a restore point, and it identifies the date, time, and name of the restore point. See *Figure A1-37*.

Figure A1-37	RESTORE POINT CREATED

information on the restore point you just created

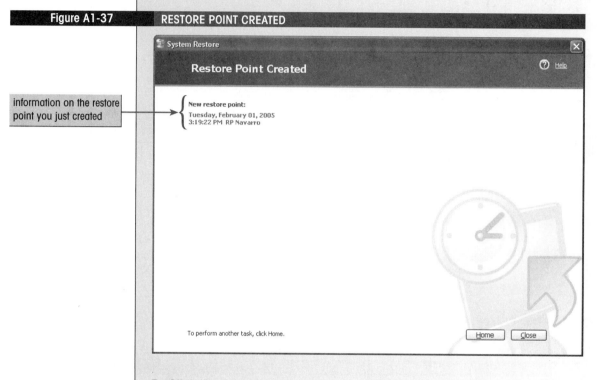

5. Click the **Close** button to close System Restore.

REFERENCE   WINDOW   **RW**

<u>Creating a Restore Point</u>
- Log on under an account with Administrator privileges.
- From the Start menu, point to All Programs, point to Accessories, point to System Tools, and then click System Restore.
- Click the "Create a restore point" option button, and then click the Next button.
- When prompted to provide a description for this restore point, type the description in the "Restore point description" text box, and then click the Create button.
- Close the System Restore dialog box.

Because System Restore works in the background to create restore points when you make changes to your computer, you are free to work on your computer with the knowledge that you can roll it back to an earlier point in time if a problem should develop.

Using a Restore Point to Roll Back a Computer

To roll back your computer to a restore point, you open System Restore, and then choose the option for restoring your computer to an earlier time. In the Select a Restore Point window, you select a restore point from a system calendar that includes all of the dates for which restore points are available. See *Figure A1-38*. The system calendar displays in bold all of the dates for which restore points are available. When you select a date, the list on the right displays the restore points for that particular date.

Figure A1-38	SELECTING A RESTORE POINT

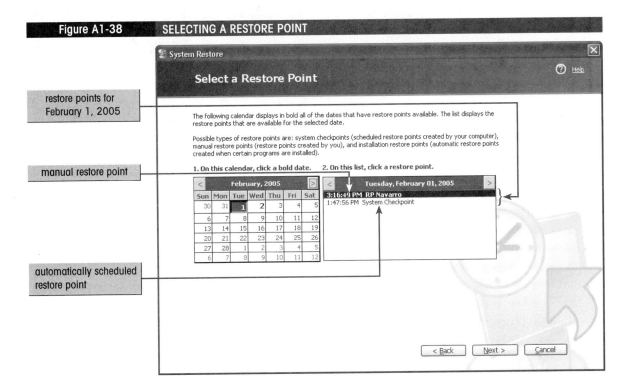

After you select the restore point you want to use and click the Next button, you are then prompted to confirm the restore point. See *Figure A1-39*. After you click the Next button, System Restore shuts down Windows XP during the restoration, and then restarts using the settings from the restore point you just made. As your system shuts down, a System Restore dialog box appears with a progress indicator showing how far the restore process has progressed. After your computer restarts and you log on under your user account. System Restore displays a System Restore dialog box verifying that the restoration is complete. It also notes that if the restoration did not correct the problem, you can choose another restore point, or undo this restoration. To complete the booting process and display the desktop, you click the OK button in the System Restore dialog box.

Figure A1-39   CONFIRMING THE RESTORE POINT SELECTION

is this the correct restore point?

creating a restore point is reversible

what will happen

precaution

System Restore

Confirm Restore Point Selection   ? Help

Selected restore point:
Tuesday, February 01, 2005
3:19 PM RP Navarro

This process does not cause you to lose recent work, such as saved documents or e-mail, and is completely reversible.

During the restoration, System Restore shuts down Windows. After the restoration is complete, Windows restarts using the settings from the date and time listed above.

Important: Before continuing, save your changes and close any open programs.

System Restore may take a moment to collect information about the selected restore point before shutting down your computer.

To restore your computer to this date and time, click Next.   [< Back] [Next >] [Cancel]

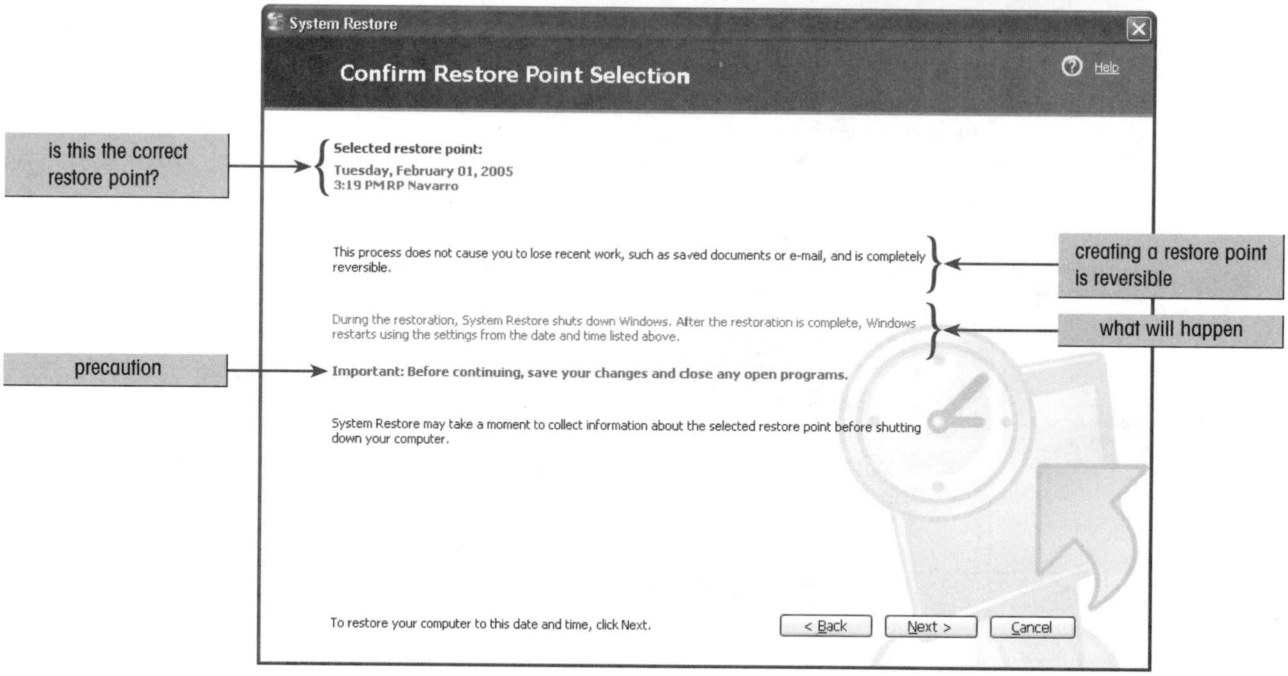

After you roll back your computer using a restore point, you should examine your computer and the applications you use to make sure that everything is working properly and that you have access to the resources you need.

Undoing a Restoration

If you decide that you want to return to your original configuration before you used the restore point, you can undo that restoration.

To undo a restoration, you open the System Restore utility, and you will find that the System Restore dialog box lists an additional option to indicate that you can undo the last restoration. See *Figure A1-40*.

Figure A1-40 | SYSTEM RESTORE TASK OPTIONS

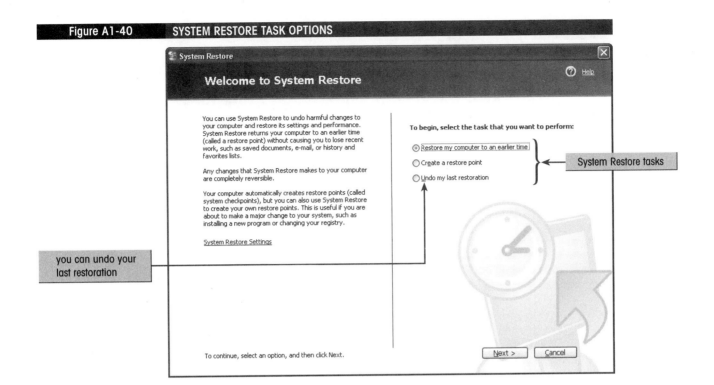

you can undo your last restoration

System Restore tasks

If you want to undo the last restoration, you click the Undo my last restoration option button, and then click the Next button. System Restore then informs you that it will undo the restoration you just performed, and asks you for confirmation. See *Figure A1-41*. After you click the Next button, System Restore restores your files and settings, shuts down Windows XP, and then restarts the computer. After your computer restarts, you log on again under your user account. Then a System Restore dialog box verifies that it has successfully reversed the previous restoration operation. To complete the booting process and display the desktop, you click the OK button in the System Restore dialog box.

Figure A1-41   CONFIRMING AN UNDO OF A SYSTEM RESTORATION

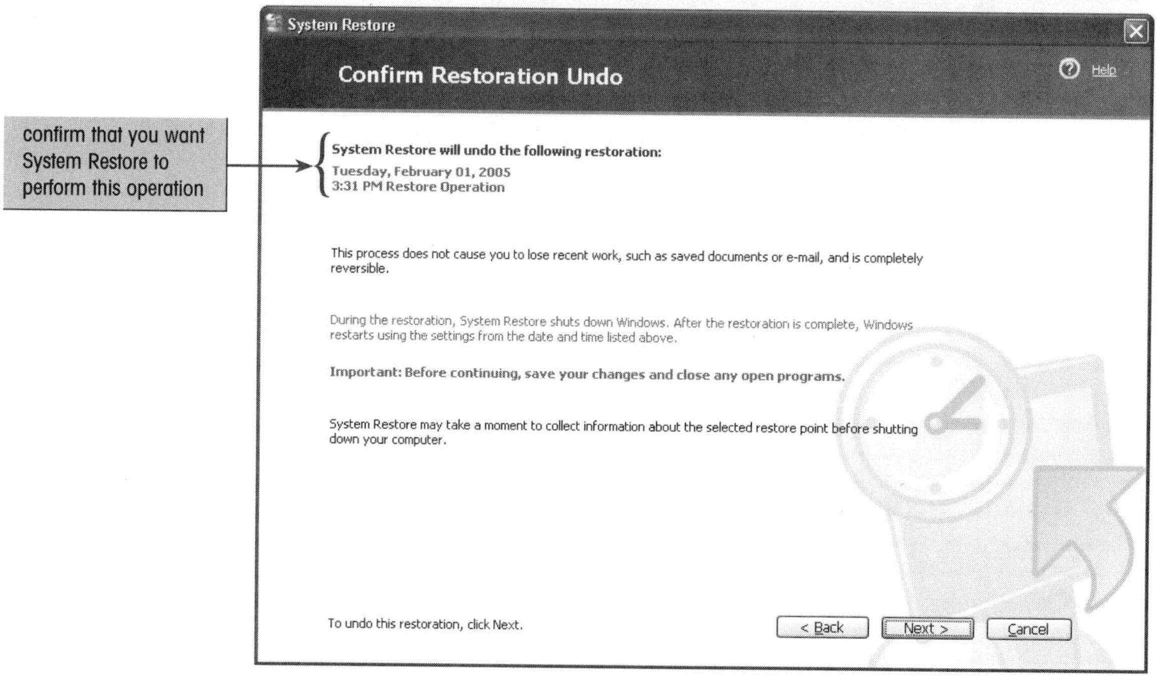

confirm that you want System Restore to perform this operation

If you open System Restore and choose the option for restoring your computer to an earlier date, and then select the date for which you created a restore point, roll back your computer to that restore point, and then undo the restoration, you will find that System Restore lists both restore operations along with your restore points for that date, so that you have a record of the changes you've made to your computer.

The hidden System Volume Information folder on your system volume (most likely drive C) contains a _Restore folder, which in turn contains folders with different restore points for your computer. See *Figure A1-42*. These restore points are identified by the label RP followed by a number. System Restore periodically purges older restore points from this folder to make room for new restore points. Purging is on a **first in, first out (FIFO)** basis, and Fifo.log keeps track of this information.

Figure A1-42   VIEWING THE CONTENTS OF THE _RESTORE FOLDER

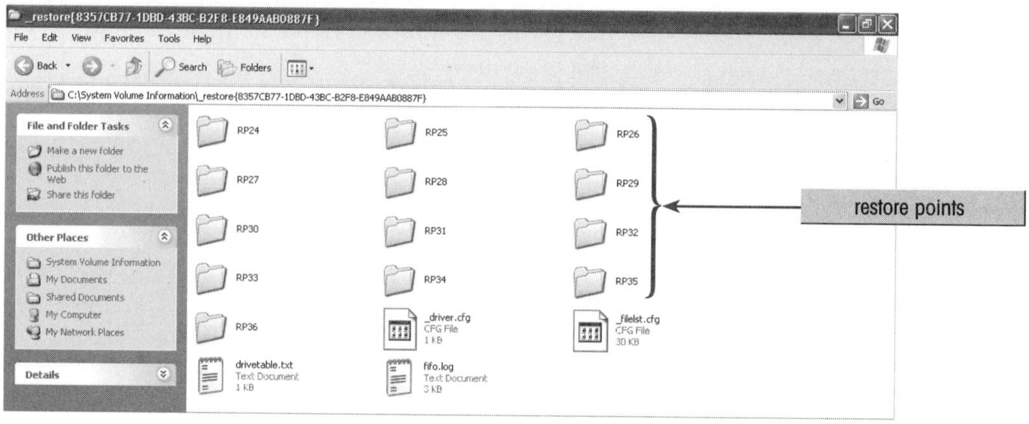

restore points

If you open the most recent restore point folder, you see a Snapshot folder that contains information on Registry settings, and you also see files with configuration settings (the ones with the "ini" file extension) as well as log, configuration, and ID files with information about the restore point. See *Figure A1-43*. Your files will differ from the ones shown in the figure.

| Figure A1-43 | VIEWING THE CONTENTS OF A RESTORE POINT FOLDER |

System Restore provides you with a powerful tool for reversing changes that affect the performance of your computer system. Although System Restore is designed to create restore points prior to operations that affect the use of your computer, such as installing new software, you can use System Restore to manually create restore points before you make changes to your computer. Furthermore, although System Restore is invaluable, it does not substitute for backups, so you still must back up your important documents on a regular basis.

Exporting Registry Settings

Microsoft has made changes to the Registry Editor menu and the use of the Regedt32 command in Windows XP:

- **Pages 423–424, Step 2** and **Figure 9-4**: The Registry option on the menu bar has been replaced with the File menu option.
- **Page 424, Step 2** and **Figure 9-5**: The Registry Editor that ships with Windows XP is Regedit.exe. However, if you use the command REGEDT32 rather than REGEDIT, Windows XP will open the Registry, and your view onto the Registry will appear like that shown in Figure 9-4 in the textbook. You will not see multiple windows as shown in Figure 9-5 of the textbook.
- **Page 425, Step 4**: To complete this step, click File on the menu bar, and then click Export.
- **Page 426, Step 2** and **Figure 9-8**: The file with the backup of your Windows XP Registry settings will be much larger in size than that shown for Windows 2000 in Figure 9-8 in the textbook (perhaps by two-and-a-half times).

Using the FTYPE Command

You will see differences when using the FType command in Windows XP because of new features that result in different file associations. Also, Microsoft has changed the process for opening files not associated with a program.

- **Pages 432–433, Step 4** and **Figure 9-15**: Files with the "bmp" file extension are now associated with the Windows Picture and Fax Viewer in

Windows XP instead of the Paint application (or applet), so the command line differs as follows:

rundll32.exe C:\WINDOWS\System32\shimgvw.dll, ImageView_Fullscreen %1

The RunDLL program opens a dynamic link library file with the "dll" file extension in the System32 folder. A **dynamic link library** is a program file that contains program code that is loaded only when needed by a program. Different programs can share the same dynamic link library file.

- **Page 433, Step 6**: If you are using Office XP (also called Office 2002), your path for the Word program may differ, may include a reference to the Office10 subdirectory (instead of Office) under the Microsoft Office directory, and may also include the /dde switch (for Dynamic Data Exchange). Your path may then appear as:

"C:\Program Files\Microsoft Office\ Office10\WINWORD.EXE" /n /dde

Dynamic Data Exchange (DDE) is a form of interprocess communication found in the Windows family of operating systems, and programs that support DDE can exchange information and commands.

- **Page 434, Step 3**: When you attempt to open a file that is not associated with a program, Windows XP displays a Windows dialog box instead of an Open With dialog box, as shown in *Figure A1-44*. In addition to informing you that it cannot open this file, the Windows dialog box also informs you that it needs to know what program created the file in order to open it. Windows XP notes that it can go online to look up that information, or you can select the program from a list of programs available on your computer.

Figure A1-44	ATTEMPTING TO OPEN AN UNREGISTERED FILE TYPE

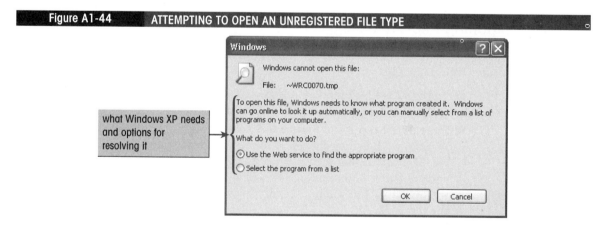

what Windows XP needs and options for resolving it

If you choose the "Use the Web service to find the appropriate program" option button, click the OK button, and then connect to your ISP, you will see a Microsoft Application Search window with the title "Microsoft Windows .NET File Extensions." Microsoft identifies the file type as a "Temporary File" with the file extension .tmp (notice it includes the dot or period), and it explains that applications create this type of file to store information temporarily. See *Figure A1-45*. This Web page also contains links to Web sites for related software and information. Because this approach does not provide you with the information you need, you can search for the information you need by using links to various Web sites from this Web page, or try some other approach.

Figure A1-45	USING MICROSOFT'S WEB SERVICE TO LOCATE A PROGRAM FOR A FILE TYPE

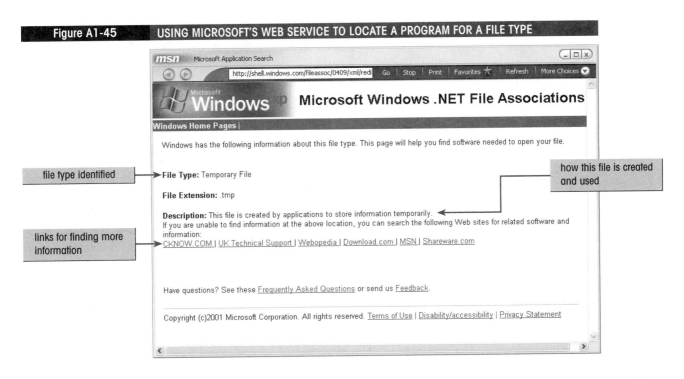

file type identified

how this file is created and used

links for finding more information

If you instead choose the "Select the program from a list" option button in the Windows dialog box, and then click the OK button, Windows XP will open an Open With dialog box where you can choose a program for opening this file. See *Figure A1-46*. If you have previously attempted to open a file of this same type with one of the programs on the computer you are using, the list of programs will be subdivided into two categories—a Recommend Programs category and an Other Programs category.

Figure A1-46	OPENING AN UNREGISTERED FILE TYPE

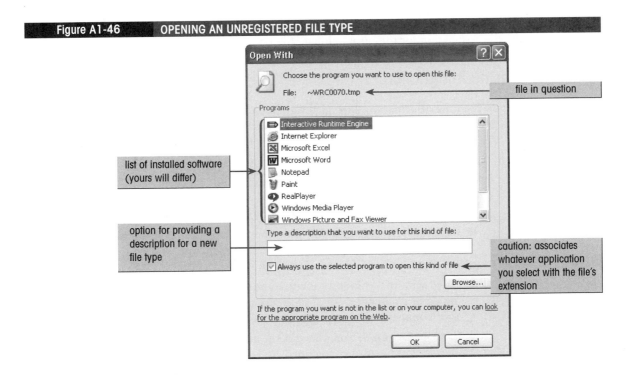

file in question

list of installed software (yours will differ)

option for providing a description for a new file type

caution: associates whatever application you select with the file's extension

- **Page 434, Step 5** and **Figure 9-18**: If the Registry does not contain a key for a file extension, you will see the message displayed in Figure 9-18 for both Windows 2000 and Windows XP. If the Registry contains a key for a file extension, but no Class Definition has been assigned to that file extension, then Windows 2000 and Windows XP will not display a message, but will instead display the file extension you specified followed by an equals sign to indicate that there is no defined file type for this file extension. You will see the following on the screen: .tmp=

- **Page 435, Step 8**: The path for Notepad under Windows XP is different than that for Windows 2000, and the Windows directory name may also vary. If your Windows directory is named "Windows", then enter this command: ftype TempFile="c:\windows\notepad.exe"

- **Page 437, Step 1**: After you enter the command in this step, you will see the message "File type 'TempFile' not found or no open command associated with it."

- **Page 437, Step 2**: If the command interpreter displays TempFile="c:\windows\notepad.exe" "%1" after you enter this command, repeat Step 1 and press the Spacebar after you type the equals sign and before you press the Enter key. Then repeat this step.

- **Page 437, Step 4**: After you complete Steps 1-4, you will have removed the key for the "tmp" file extension from the Windows XP Registry. To add that subkey back to the Windows XP Registry (and restore your computer to its original state), enter the following command, press the spacebar, and then press the Enter key: assoc .tmp=
  For this to work properly, you must press the spacebar after the equals sign.

Session 9.2

The primary differences you will notice in this section of the tutorial result in a change in the file association for the bitmap image file type.

Tracing Information on Registered File Types

As you examine information on registered file types, you will see different types of subkeys and value entries in Windows XP and Windows 2000. If bitmap images are associated with the Windows Picture and Fax Viewer, then some of the actions will be associated with ACDSee:

- **Page 442, Step 2**: You will see a third value entry (PerceivedType), your list of subkeys will also include "OpenWithList, OpenWithProgids, and PersistentHandler," and you will not see a ShellEx subkey.

- **Page 443, Step 3**: In addition to the (Default) value entry, you will see three other value entries: EditFlags, FriendlyTypeName, and ImageOptionFlags.

- **Page 444, Step 4**: Because files with the "bmp" file extension are now associated with the Windows Picture and Fax Viewer in Windows XP instead of the Paint application (or applet), the name of the program file will differ. Your command line may appear as: shimgvw.dll,1

- **Page 444, Step 5**: You may not see a subkey for the print action, but instead there might be a subkey labeled ACDPrint. Also, you may see options for ACDEdit and ACDView. These actions are displayed on a shortcut menu for a bitmap image file as ACD Photo Enhance, Print with ACDSee, View with ACDSee, Edit, and Print. ACDSee is an image viewer from ACD Systems, and it is integrated into Windows XP. Or you might only see a printto subkey.

- **Page 444, Step 5**: Because files with the "bmp" file extension are now associated with the Windows Picture and Fax Viewer in Windows XP instead of the Paint application (or applet), the command line will differ. Your command line may appear as:

  rundll32.exe C:\WINDOWS\System32\
  shimgvw.dll,ImageView_Fullscreen %1

- **Page 445, Step 6**: If you have an ACDPrint subkey, but not a print subkey, double-click the ACDPrint subkey, and then click the command subkey under the ACDPrint subkey. The path for this program may be shown with short filenames or alias instead of long filenames, and may appear as: "C:\PROGRA~1\ACDSYS~1\ACDSEE\ACDSEE.EXE" /p "%1"
  If you have only a printto subkey, then read this step and examine the figure but do not keystroke it.

Viewing Information on Class Identifiers

You will see some minor differences between Windows XP and Windows 2000:

- **Page 446, Step 2**: If the Registry Editor does not find this key, repeat this step and make sure you type the correct search string. The search string starts with a curly brace (not a parenthesis or square bracket). You can also just search for: 645FF

- **Pages 446-447, Step 2** and **Figure 9-32**: The InfoTip value entry does not show the text that displayed in the ToolTip for the Recycle Bin.

- **Page 448, Step 4**: Windows XP's Registry Editor does not have a Registry menu option on the menu bar. Instead, click the File menu option, and then click Exit.

Changing a Value for a Registry Key

You may see some minor differences between Windows XP and Windows 2000:

- **Page 453, Step 1**: The Value data for the CompletionChar value entry may not be 0 (zero), but might be another value, such as 9.

- **Page 454, Step 2**: If the Value data for the CompletionChar value entry is already 9, you will not need to change this value.

- **Page 454, Steps 3**: After you open a Command Prompt window, type CD \ and then press the Enter key to change to the root directory so that you can test the feature in Step 4.

- **Page 454, Step 4**: If the command interpreter displays "cd Desktop" instead of the results shown in the step, type CD \ and then press the Enter key to change to the root directory so that you can test the feature in this step.

Restoring Your Computer

When you restore your computer's original settings, you may need to use your original settings instead of those described in the steps:

- **Page 458, Step 5**: If the value for the CompletionChar value entry was a value other than 0, enter that value instead.

Review Assignments

Because Windows XP no longer has an option for making an Emergency Repair Disk, you must modify one of the steps in the Review Assignments:

- **Page 459, Step 2**: Use the System Restore utility to create a restore point if you have not already created a recent restore point on your computer.

 ## Case 2: Customizing Folder Shortcut Menus at HiPerform Systems

To complete this case problem under Windows XP, you must log on under an account with Administrator privileges.

TUTORIAL 10   CONNECTING TO NETWORKS AND THE INTERNET

Session 10.1

As you complete Session 10.1 in Tutorial 10, you will see differences in the way in which you access information on network resources and how those resources are organized under Windows XP, but the same basic principles still apply. Also, as covered in the next section, Windows XP supports the use of network bridges and includes a new component, Internet Connection Firewall, for protecting your computer while you are connected to the Internet.

Examining Your Computer's Network Settings

The contents of the Windows XP Network Connections folder (comparable to the Network and Dial-up Connections folder in Windows 2000) differs and depends on the types of networking components included in your computer and the configuration of your network:

- **Page 468, Step 1 (Windows 2000 Professional)**: To view the contents of the Network and Dial-up Connections folder, click the Start button, point to Settings, and then click Network and Dial-up Connections.

- **Page 468, Step 1 (Windows XP)**: If you do not have a My Network Places icon on the desktop, click the Start button, right-click My Network Places on the Start menu, and then click Properties. If the Start menu does not contain My Network Places, right-click the taskbar, click Properties on the shortcut menu, click the Start Menu tab in the Taskbar and Start Menu Properties dialog box, click the Customize button for the Start menu option, click the Advanced tab in the Customize Start Menu dialog box, locate and click the My Network Places check box in the Start menu items box, click OK to close the Customize Start Menu dialog box, click OK to close the Taskbar and Start Menu Properties dialog box, click the Start button, right-click My Network Places on the Start menu, and then click Properties. When you choose the shortcut menu option for viewing Properties of My Network Places, Windows XP opens a Network Connections folder window rather than a Network and Dial-up Connections folder window. Also, your view of the contents of the Network Connections folder will differ. As shown in *Figure A1-47*, you might see a Local Area Connection icon under a category labeled LAN or High Speed Internet or, as shown in *Figure A1-48*, you might see a Network Bridge category with a Local Area Connection icon. When you install Windows XP, or when you use the Network Setup Wizard, Windows XP automatically creates a Local Area Connection if it detects a network adapter. A **network bridge** consists of connections between computers using different types of network adapters, or between different types of network adapters on the same computer. A network bridge replaces the need for special equipment, and simplifies the process of setting up and configuring a network. Although you can create only one network bridge on a computer, that bridge can support any number of network connections. On the computer used for *Figure A1-48*, the network bridge creates a connection between the Ethernet adapter for the Local Area Connection and the IEEE 1394 network adapter for the 1394 Connection on a Windows XP Professional workstation. This figure also shows a dial-up connection for MSN Explorer under Connection Manager. Your Network Connections window will more than likely differ.

Figure A1-47	LOCAL AREA CONNECTION ON A COMPUTER WITH WINDOWS XP HOME EDITION

Figure A1-48	NETWORK BRIDGE ON A COMPUTER WITH WINDOWS XP PROFESSIONAL

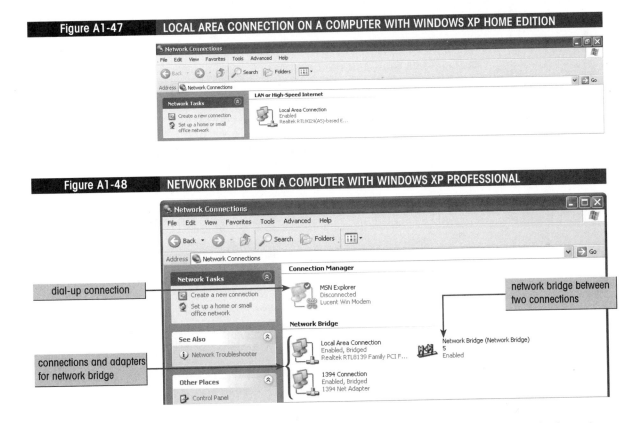

You can use the "Create a new connection" link in the Network Tasks dynamic menu to start the New Connection Wizard, which can then help you connect to the Internet or to a private network (such as your company's network), or help you set up a home or small office network. You can use the "Set up a home or small office network" link in the Network Tasks dynamic menu to start the Network Setup Wizard, which can then help you set up Internet Connection Sharing, set up Internet Connection Firewall, share files and folders, and share a printer.

Internet Connection Firewall (ICF) is a Windows XP security system that tracks and stores information on all outbound communications from your computer in a table, and then compares that information with all inbound communications arriving to your computer from the Internet to determine whether it is safe for the data to pass. If the ICF table contains a matching entry, indicating that the communication is a response to a communication you originated, it allows the incoming data to reach your computer; otherwise, the incoming communication is silently discarded. The net effect is that you do not receive unsolicited communications, and ICF blocks hackers who use programs to probe the ports on your computer in an attempt to find and exploit a weakness in your computer. Internet Connection Firewall provides this protection for a single computer whether you are connected to the Internet via a cable modem, DSL modem, or a dial-up modem.

You can use Internet Connection Firewall with or without Internet Connection Sharing. With **Internet Connection Sharing (ICS)**, individuals who use different computers on a small home or office network can all connect to the Internet via one connection on one of the computers in the network. When Internet Connection Sharing is enabled on a computer, that computer becomes the ICS host for all other computers on the network. Internet Connection Sharing is also available in Windows 2000, Windows Me, and Windows 98 Second Edition.

If the ICS host uses an external DSL or cable modem to connect to the Internet, you need to install two network adapters—one that connects to the DSL or cable modem and that provides the Internet connection, and one for communicating with the other computers in your home or small business network. If the ICS host has an internal modem, you only need one network adapter.

■ **Page 469, Step 2**: If the Local Area Connection Properties dialog box informs you that your adapter is part of a network bridge, close the Local Area Connection Properties dialog box, right-click Network Bridge, and then click Properties. Under Adapters, you will see a list of the adapters within the network bridge. See *Figure A1-49*. In the "This connection uses the following items" box, you may also see **QoS (Quality of Service) Packet Scheduler**—a component that controls network traffic, including rate-of-flow and prioritization services.

Figure A1-49 **VIEWING NETWORK BRIDGE PROPERTIES**

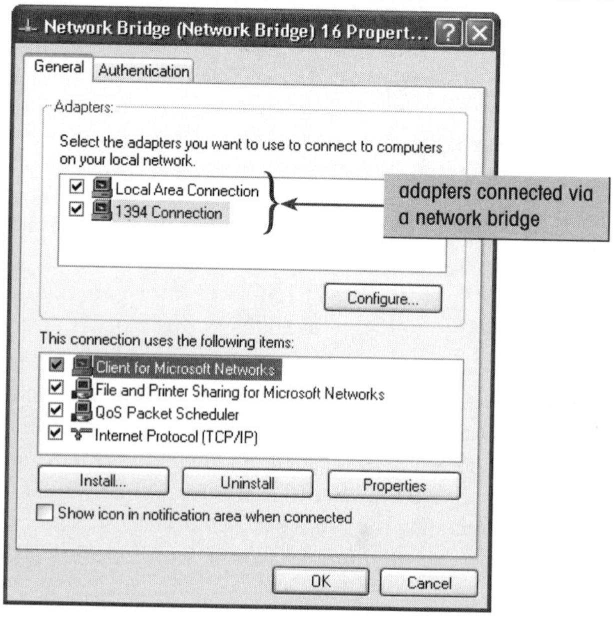

■ **Page 470, Step 3**: If your computer obtains an IP address and DNS server address automatically, then the settings for IP address and DNS server addresses are dimmed.

- **Page 471, Step 2**: The Network Identification sheet is now named "Computer Name". Also, you will see a Computer description box where you can enter a label that clearly identifies the computer on your network.
- **Page 472, Step 3**: There is no Properties button; instead, click the Change button. The dialog box that you open now has the name "Computer Name Changes". Also, your Windows XP workgroup name may have a different name, such as MSHOME.
- **Page 473, Step 1**: If you have a network bridge, the Properties button will open the Local Area Connection Properties dialog box, not the Network Bridge Properties dialog box that you examined earlier.

[UPDATE] Viewing Network Resources

You can see changes in the way in which resources are organized under My Network Places:

- **Page 476, Step 1**: If you do not have a My Network Places icon on the desktop, click the Start button, right-click My Network Places on the Start menu, and then click Explore. If the Start menu does not contain My Network Places, right-click the taskbar, click Properties on the shortcut menu, click the Start Menu tab in the Taskbar and Start Menu Properties dialog box, click the Customize button for the Start menu option, click the Advanced tab in the Customize Start Menu dialog box, locate and click the My Network Places check box in the Start menu items box, click OK to close the Customize Start Menu dialog box, click OK to close the Taskbar and Start Menu Properties dialog box, click the Start button, right-click My Network Places on the Start menu, and then click Explore.
  You will not see a Computers Near Me icon or option under My Network Places. Instead, click the expand indicator for Entire Network, click the expand indicator for Microsoft Windows Network, and then click the expand indicator for the name of your workgroup (such as MSHOME). You may also see shared resources such as shared folders and drives listed under My Network Places. Also, if Windows XP does not display the names of other networked computers under your workgroup, you can still view the shared resources on your local computer.

[HELP] Using NET Commands

When completing this section with the NET command, you may notice small differences:

- **Page 478, Step 1**: After you open a Command Prompt window, you must change to the root directory if you want your computer screen to more closely match the figures in the book.
- **Page 478, Steps 2-3**: Part of the syntax of a command may appear on the line following the command, rather than on one line as shown in Figure 10-11 and Figure 10-12 of the textbook.
- **Page 479, Step 1**: The Net View command may show only one server name.
- **Page 479, Step 2**: If the previous step only displays one computer name, and if you know the name of one of the other computers on your network, you can view the shared resources on that other computer. You can also view the shared resources on the computer you are currently using.
- **Page 480, Step 3**: If you see the message "Access is denied," try the name of another shared folder.

[UPDATE] Mapping a Drive Letter to a Shared Directory Folder

To map a drive letter to a shared folder, you may have to use the Tools menu instead of the shortcut menu:

- **Page 481, Step 1**: If you do not have a My Network Places icon on the desktop, click the Start button, right-click My Network Places on the Start menu, and then click Explore. If the Start menu does not contain My Network Places, right-click the taskbar, click Properties on the shortcut menu, click the Start Menu tab in the Taskbar and Start Menu Properties dialog box, click the Customize button for the Start menu option, click the Advanced tab in the Customize Start Menu dialog box, locate and click the My Network Places check box in the Start menu items box, click OK to close the Customize Start Menu dialog box, click OK to close the Taskbar and Start Menu Properties dialog box, click the Start button, right-click My Network Places on the Start menu, and then click Explore.

- **Page 481, Step 2**: If the shortcut menu, or context menu, does not have a Map Network Drive option, make sure the shared folder on another computer is still selected, click Tools on the menu bar, and then click Map Network Drive. The drive letter will not default to the next available drive letter, and the Folder box may not contain the UNC path to the shared folder. You may have to enter that path or use the Browse button to locate the shared folder before you can go to the next step.

[UPDATE] Mapping a Drive from the Command Line

You will see a minor difference when performing this operation:

- **Page 485, Step 3**: Windows XP does not automatically open a window onto the newly mapped drive.

[UPDATE] Sharing the My Documents Folder on a Network

You will notice differences in the Windows XP Sharing property sheet:

- **Pages 488-489, Steps 2-3**: If your My Documents folder is already shared and if you do not want to change the share name, select another unshared folder (such as the Desktop folder) for the steps in this section.

- **Page 488, Step 2**: The shortcut menu now displays "Sharing and Security" instead of just "Sharing." The Sharing property sheet is organized differently than for Windows 2000, and contains two sections—one for Local sharing and security and one for Network sharing and security. In addition, the options differ and you may see a Customize and Web Sharing property sheet.

- **Page 488, Step 3**: The "Share this folder" option button may now appear as a check box labeled "Share this folder on the network," or there may be no option at all. If the latter is true, the Network Sharing and Security section may display the following message: "As a security measure, Windows has disabled remote access to this computer. However, you can enable remote access and safely share files by running the Network Setup Wizard". If the option for sharing this folder is not available, then you will not be able to complete the remainder of this section of the tutorial. Instead, read the steps and explanatory discussion, and examine the figures, but do not complete the steps.

■ **Page 490, Step 2**: If there is no "Do not share this folder" option button, click the "Share this folder on the network" check box and remove the check mark.

[UPDATE] Sharing the My Documents Directory from the Command Prompt

You may want to use an alternate folder instead of the My Documents folder:

■ **Pages 491, Step 3**: If your My Documents folder is already shared and if you do not want to change the share name, select another unshared folder for the steps in this section.

[UPDATE] Working with User Account Commands

Windows XP Home Edition differs from Windows 2000 and Windows XP Professional in how you access information on user accounts. Because Computer Management does not contain the Local Users and Groups component under System Tools, you must use a different approach to examining information on your user account:

■ **Pages 493-494, Steps 2-6**: If you are using Windows XP Home Edition, there is no Local Users and Groups folder. Close the Computer Management window, click the Start button, click Control Panel, and click User Accounts to view information about local users. If you click your user logon name, you will see a list of options for changing your name, changing or removing your password, changing your picture, changing your account type, and setting up your account to use a .NET Passport. When you have finished examining settings for your user account, close the User Accounts window.

Session 10.2

As you view information on your network, you may see additional information about your network configuration. In addition, the process for downloading files from an FTP site in the Windows XP GUI may differ.

Using IPCONFIG to Display Information on IP Addresses

Windows XP also displays information on network bridges:

■ **Pages 497-498, Step 2** and **Figure 10-35**: If you have a network bridge on your computer, you will see information for that bridge.
■ **Pages 498, Step 2** and **Figure 10-36**: If you have a network bridge on your computer, you will see information for that bridge.

[HELP] Using PING to Test an IP Connection

You might need to specify the name of another computer on your network to ping that computer:

■ **Page 501, Step 2**: If the previous step only displays one computer name, and if you know the name of one of the other computers on your network, you can specify that computer name with the PING command.

[UPDATE] Creating a Network Connection to an FTP Site

You may see differences in how you create a network connection to an FTP site:

- **Page 512, Step 2**: You will not see an Add Network Place icon, but there is an "Add a network place" link in the Network Tasks dynamic menu that you can use instead.

- **Page 513, Step 3** and **Figure 10-57**: Click the "Add a network place" link on the dynamic menu. The first Add Network Place Wizard dialog box is different than that for Windows 2000. See *Figure A1-50*. After reading the information in the dialog box, click the Next button.

| Figure A1-50 | OPENING THE ADD NETWORK PLACE WIZARD |

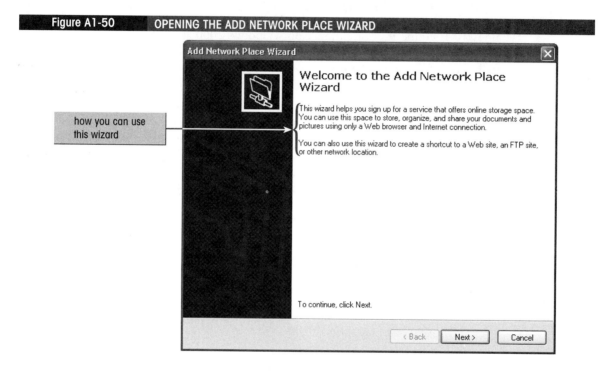

The next Add Network Place Wizard dialog box asks you where you want to create this network place. As shown in *Figure A1-51*, you can choose another network location in the Service providers box.

| Figure A1-51 | CHOOSING THE NETWORK LOCATION |

option for creating a shortcut to another network connection

If necessary, select "Choose another network location," and then click the Next button. The next dialog box is comparable to the one shown in Figure 10-57 of your textbook.

■ **Page 513, Step 4** and **Figure 10-58**: Your computer may be set up so that you do not see an InfoTip when you click the "View some examples" link. Instead, examine Figure 10-58 in the textbook.

■ **Page 513, Step 5**: In the "Internet or network address" box, enter the Internet address shown in this step.

■ **Page 515, Steps 8-9**: You will need to click the Next button before you can complete Step 9.

■ **Page 515, Step 9** and **Figure 10-62**: Your FTP window may show links rather than folders, as shown in *Figure A1-52.*

| Figure A1-52 | FTP SITE |

■ **Page 516, Step 2**: To open the course folder, you might need to click the course link. In the subsequent steps, you may need to click the links for each directory.

■ **Page 518, Step 7:** You will not be able to complete this step if you see links rather than folders in the FTP directory window.

■ **Page 518, Step 8:** If you drag SolarWinds.zip to the 3½ Floppy (A:) window and if Windows XP does not copy the file, but instead creates a shortcut to this file, then delete the new shortcut, right-click the SolarWinds.zip link, click Save Target As on the shortcut menu, select 3½ Floppy (A:) from the Save in list box, and then click the Save button to download the file. After the download is complete, click the Close button in the Download complete dialog box. The downloaded copy of SolarWinds.zip is now a Windows XP Compressed (zipped) folder that you can open and use like any other folder. You do not need to extract the contents of the folder first (as you would a WinZip file). When you copy or move a Compressed (zipped) folder to a computer with a prior version of Windows, it functions like a Zip file instead of a folder.

[HELP] Review Assignments

As noted earlier, My Network Places does not contain Computers Near Me, there is no Network Identification link, and your computer may contain a network bridge, so you will need to modify some of the steps:

■ **Page 524, Step 7:** Because Windows XP does not contain Computers Near Me, click the expand indicator for Entire Network, click the expand indicator for Microsoft Windows Network, and then click the expand indicator for the name of your workgroup (such as MSHOME). You may also see shared resources listed under My Network Places. If you can see only the name of the local computer you're using under your workgroup, you can still view its shared resources.

■ **Page 524, Step 12:** If you have a Network Bridge category with a Network Bridge icon, right-click the Network Bridge icon, and then click Properties to view information about components for your network connection.

■ **Page 524, Step 14:** If you have a Network Bridge, then you will also have to close the Network Bridge Properties dialog box. Because there is no Network Identification link in the Network Connections window, you will have to right-click My Computer in the Other Places dynamic menu, click Properties, and then click the Computer Name tab in the System Properties dialog box. As noted earlier, the Network Identification sheet is now named "Computer Name," and you will see a Computer description box where you can enter a label that identifies the computer on your network.

[HELP] Case 3: Diagnosing Network Connections at Stratton Graphics

Finding Help information is slightly different in the Windows XP Help and Support Center:

■ **Page 527, Step 1:** After you open the Windows XP Help and Support Center from the Start menu, use Search and the search string "ping" to locate Help information, In the Search Results, use the link "Test a TCP/IP configuration using the ping command" to locate Help information on testing the setup and connections of your local network.

Case 4: Downloading a Group of FTP Files at Townsend & Sumner Publishing

Finding Help information is slightly different in the Windows XP Help and Support Center:

- **Page 527, Step 1**: If you are using Windows XP Professional, open the Windows XP Help and Support Center from the Start menu, use Search and the search string "ftp commands" to locate Help information. In the Search Results, use the link "Ftp subcommands" to locate Help information on using the mget and prompt commands. Windows XP Home Edition's Help and Support Center does not contain information on the use of FTP subcommands. Instead, use the following information to complete this case problem:

  - **mget** *Files*   Copies files from a remote computer to your local computer, where *Files* is the file specification you want to use for selecting the files.
  - **prompt**   Toggles between prompt mode on and off; by default, prompt mode is on.

Extra Case Problem: Using PATHPING to Diagnose Network Problems at InTime Troubleshooting

Unless you are familiar with the use of the PathPing command and know how to interpret is results, you must use Windows XP Professional or Windows 2000 to complete this case problem because Windows XP Home Edition's Help and Support Center does not contain information on the use of PathPing or information on analyzing the results of a PathPing command.

A

Automated System Recovery (ASR) Wizard

A Windows XP Professional component for backing up the system state, system services, and system volume of your computer so that you have the system files and settings required to rebuild that computer

auditing

Tracking events, such as attempts to log onto a computer and to access files and other network components, so there is a record of all operations that affect the network

C

Category view

A Windows XP view that organizes components in a window into related categories

COM+ Registration Database

A Windows component that stores information about COM+ components, or operating system services for applications and components in a networking environment

contiguous clusters

Adjacent clusters on a disk

Credential Manager

A Windows component that secures and automatically provides your user name and password to applications (such as e-mail software), services (such as your ISP), and Web sites that request that information so that you do not have to repeatedly specify the same information

D

Dynamic Data Exchange (DDE)

A form of interprocess communication found in the Windows family of operating systems. Programs that support DDE can exchange information and commands.

Device Driver Rollback

A Windows component that replaces a newly installed device driver that does not work properly with a previously working version of that same device driver

directive

A command included in Config.sys for modifying and configuring the operating system during booting

dynamic menu

A new Windows XP component of folder windows that displays a menu of options related to your current task or the contents of the window, and that provides links to other places on your computer

Dynamic Update

The process of downloading updates to Windows XP during the installation of Windows XP on a computer

E

expert

The person who accepts an invitation and provides help during a Remote Assistance session

F

Fast User Switching

A new Windows XP feature that enables a user to remain logged onto their user account with open applications and documents while another user logs onto their user account on the same computer

FIFO

First in, first out

Filmstrip view

A new Windows XP view that displays thumbnails of images contained within the files in the folder at the bottom of a window and that also displays a full-screen view of the currently selected thumbnail

fragmented file

A file that is stored in non-contiguous clusters on a disk

free space fragmentation

A state in which free space is scattered around a disk, rather than being consolidated in adjacent clusters in one part of the disk

G

group

A set of users, computers, contacts, and other groups within a network domain

H

hop

One of a sequence of router connections between networked computers

I

Internet Connection Firewall

A new Windows XP component that protects your computer from intruders and hackers while you are connected to the Internet

Itanium

A processor that can perform up to 20 operations simultaneously, and that can preload data into virtual memory for faster access and processing

M

most frequently used programs list

The bottom portion of the left panel of the Windows XP Start menu that contains a list of the most frequently used programs you have used

MS-DOS Startup Disk

A Windows XP floppy disk that contains the core operating system files needed to boot a computer from drive A

N

network bridge

Connections between computers using different types of network adapters, or connections between different types of adapters on the same computer

Network Location Awareness

A new Windows XP service that allows the operating system and applications to determine when a computer has changed its network location

Network Setup Wizard

A Windows XP component that steps you through the process of creating a home network so that your networked computers can share peripherals (such as a printer), software, and files, and use Internet Connection Sharing to share a single Internet connection

non-contiguous clusters

Non-adjacent clusters that are scattered across the surface of a disk because the disk does not have enough space for storing files in contiguous clusters.

Notification area

The right-hand area of the Windows XP taskbar with the digital clock and icons for applications loaded during booting (formerly called the system tray)

novice

The individual who extends an invitation and requests help during a Remote Assistance session

P

pinned items list

The upper portion of the left panel on the Windows XP Start menu that contains options for accessing the Internet and using your e-mail software, and that might also contain shortcuts to other tasks

Q

Qos (Quality of Service) Packet Scheduler

A component that controls network traffic, including rate-of-flow and prioritization services

R

Remote Assistance

A new Windows XP component that enables another user who also uses Windows XP to remotely connect to your computer to assist you with a project or to troubleshoot a problem

Remote Desktop

A new Windows XP component that allows you to access and use another computer from a computer running Windows 95 or later

restore point

(1) A representation of the state of your computer system at a specific point in time that includes changes to system files, device drivers, and system settings; (2) a snapshot of the Registry as well as information on the system state of a computer

right

A task that a user can perform on a computer or within a domain, such as logging onto a computer locally

S

Show in Groups

A new Windows XP view that organizes the contents of a folder window in groups

Side-by-side DLLs

A new Windows XP feature that maintains different versions of the same DLL (Dynamic Link Library) program file used by different applications

skin

A design scheme for changing the look of Windows Media Player

system checkpoint

A scheduled restore point that the System Restore utility automatically creates

System Restore

A Windows component that periodically saves information regarding changes to the configuration of your computer system, operating system files, and devices drivers, so that if you make a change to your computer and then encounter a problem, you can "roll back" your computer system to an earlier functioning state

system state

The operating system components that define the current state of the operating system, and that includes Registry settings for user accounts, applications, hardware, and software, as well as the files in the top-level folder and Windows folder that Windows XP needs to boot a computer

system volume

The volume or drive that contains the hardware-specific files for loading Windows XP on x86-based computers with a BIOS

T

taskbar grouping

A new Windows XP feature that combines all the taskbar buttons for documents opened with the same application into one taskbar button labeled with the name of the application

task-oriented view

A view in which Windows XP uses dynamic menus to display links to common folder tasks and other locations on your computer

Tiles view

Large Icons view in previous versions of Windows

Trojan horse

A program that appears to be a bona fide program, but which is designed to retrieve information from your computer, such as user names and passwords, and then transmit that information to others who then can access your computer via an Internet connection

U

User State Migration Tool

A new Windows XP Professional tool for migrating a user's data, operating system settings, and application settings from one computer to another computer

W

WebTV

A Windows technology for viewing television programs broadcast over the Internet with a TV tuner card

Windows 9x

The operating system product line that includes Windows 95, Windows 98, and Windows ME

Windows Image Acquisition

A Windows technology for obtaining images from a scanner or digital camera

Windows Media Player

A Windows component for listening to music CDs with on-screen visualizations of sounds, creating music libraries, playing movies, and listening to Internet radio stations

Windows Messenger

A Windows instant messaging application that allows you to find out who is online, send an instant message, engage a group of friends in an online conversation, invite someone who is online to play a game, dial a contact's computer, send one or more files to someone else, and, if you have a HotMail account, receive a notification when new e-mail arrives

Windows Movie Maker

A Windows component for editing and enhancing video and home movies

x86-based computer

A computer based on the architecture of the Intel 8086 processor

APPENDIX TASK REFERENCE

TASK	PAGE #	RECOMMENDED METHOD
Disk, analyzing fragmentation on a	574	See Reference Window "Analyzing a Disk for Fragmentation"
Disk, defragmenting a	576	See Reference Window "Defragmenting a Disk"
Fragmentation, analyzing a disk for	574	See Reference Window "Analyzing a Disk for Fragmentation"
Restore point, creating a	592	See Reference Window "Creating a Restore Point"
System Restore settings, checking	590	See Reference Window "Checking System Restore Settings"
Web style, changing to	549	See Reference Window "Changing to Web Style"
Windows Classic style, changing to	547	See Reference Window "Changing to Windows Classic Style"

Windows XP File Finder

As you complete the tutorials in the textbook with Windows XP, you will use the same data disks, folders, and files, and you will create the same folders and files as listed in the Windows 2000 File Finder at the end of the textbook. However, for the following end-of-chapter exercises, you will work with a different set of files or with additional files.

Location in Tutorial	Name and Location of Data File	Student Creates New File
Tutorial 4 Case 4	C:\Windows\Web\Wallpaper [Five files that are each less than 100 KB in size]	Windows Images (directory) [Directory Structure.txt]

Tutorial 6 Review Assignments	Data Disk #1
	  WinXP_EN_PRO_BF.EXE (downloaded file for Windows XP Professional)
	  WinXP_EN_HOM_BF.EXE (downloaded file for Windows XP Home Edition)	

A

* (asterisk wildcard)

A symbol used as part of a directory or file specification to substitute for any number of characters in the directory name, filename, or file extension, starting from the position of the asterisk

. ("dot") 1

A symbol for the current directory in a directory listing , which can be used as a shortcut to specify the current directory

. . ("dot dot")

A symbol for the parent directory of the current directory in a directory listing, which can be used as a shortcut to specify the parent directory of the current directory

:EOF

End of file label line used in a batch program; you must include the colon

? (question mark wildcard)

A symbol used as part of a file specification to substitute for a single character in the directory name, filename, or file extension

\ (backslash symbol)

A symbol for the root directory, or top-level folder, on a disk

< (input redirection operator)

An operator that uses input from a source other than the keyboard, such as a file

> (output redirection operator)

An operator that redirects the output of a command to a file, the printer port, or another device, instead of to the monitor

>> (append output redirection operator)

An operator that appends the output of a command to an existing file

A:

The device name for the first floppy disk drive in a computer

absolute path

The use of the full path to identify the exact location of a folder or file, starting from the root directory

access time

The amount of time it takes for a device to locate an item of data from disk or memory and make it available to the rest of the computer system

active content

Web content that changes periodically

algorithm

A formula or procedure for calculating or producing a result, such as determining an alias or MS-DOS name from a long name

allocation unit

(1) One or more sectors used by an operating system as the minimum storage space for a file or part of a file when it allocates storage space on a drive to the file; (2) a cluster

ANSI (American National Standards Institute)

(1) A character set that supports characters from different languages; (2) an organization that sets computer standards in the United States

APIPA (Automatic Private IP Addressing)

A process used by Windows 2000 and Windows XP to assign IP addresses if they do not detect the presence of a DHCP server for automatically assigning an IP address to a computer or other network device from among the Microsoft-reserved IP addresses, ranging from 169.254.0.1 to 169.254.255.254

append output redirection operator (>>)

An operator that appends the output of a command to an existing file

application-oriented

An operating mode in which you open the software application you want to use, then you locate and open the document you want to use

archive

(1) To store less frequently used files on a storage medium such as diskettes, recordable CDs, or Zip disks; (2) a file that contains one or more other files within it

Archive attribute or **Archive bit**

A setting associated with a file that Windows operating systems turn on when you create or modify a file and that determines whether or not a file is included in certain types of intermediate backups performed by a backup utility

ASCII (American Standard Code for Information Interchange)

A seven-bit coding scheme for representing 128 character codes, including the uppercase and lowercase letters of the American alphabet, digits, and a limited set of symbols and control codes.

ASCII code

The numerical code for an ASCII character

ASCII text file

A simple file format in which data is stored as text
ASCII value see "ASCII code"

asterisk wildcard (*)

A symbol used as part of a directory or file specification to substitute for any number of characters in the directory name, filename, or file extension, starting from the position of the asterisk

attribute

(1) An optional parameter for the COLOR command; (2) a special characteristic, such as System, Hidden, Read-Only, Archive, Directory, Compress, Encrypt, or Index, assigned to a folder or file by the operating system

B

back quotes (`)

Used under the USEBACKQ option of the FOR command to process the output of a command instead of the contents of a file (without having to go through the extra step of redirecting the output of the command to a file and then specifying that file's name)

back up

To make a duplicate copy of an entire disk volume, a directory branch, or individual directories or files.

backslash (\)

A symbol for the root directory, or top-level folder, on a disk

backup cycle

A periodic cycle used to back up files on a hard disk and which starts with a full backup, includes additional backups of selected files, and then ends with the next full backup

backward compatibility

The ability of an operating system to handle hardware and software designed for earlier types of computers, microprocessors, and operating systems

batch program or **batch file**

A user-defined program file with the file extension "bat" that contains a set of commands for performing a set of operations which the operating system can execute. A batch program used in the Recovery Console can have any file extension.

binary file

A file that can contain any kind of data, rather than just ASCII text

BIOS (Basic Input/Output System)

The component of an Intel-based computer system board that contains routines executed by the microprocessor at startup; see also ROM-BIOS

boot disk

A disk, such as a hard disk or a diskette in drive A, that contains the core operating system files needed to start a computer

boot loader

A program in the Master Boot Record that locates the boot partition and then starts the process of loading the operating system

boot record (boot sector)

A hidden table that contains information about the version of the operating system used to format a disk and the physical characteristics of the disk, such as the number of bytes per sector, sectors per cluster, maximum number of files per disk, total number of sectors, and sectors per track

booting

The process of powering on a computer system and loading the operating system into memory so it can configure the computer system and manage the basic processes of the computer, including providing support for applications

branching

Bypassing lines in a batch program with the use of the GOTO command and a target label

byte

(1) The storage space required on disk or in memory for one character; (2) a combination of eight binary digits, or bits, used to encode commonly used characters, including letters of the alphabet, numbers, and symbols

C

C:

The device name for the first hard disk drive in a computer

cabinet file

A compressed file that contains operating system files and that has the "cab" file extension

chain

A connected sequence of clusters belonging to a single file

client

A computer, device, or program in a network that requests and uses services provided by another computer, device, or program called a server

client software

Software that a computer needs to connect to a server

client/server network

A type of network in which a central computer provides file, printer, user authentication, and communications support to other computers on the network

Clipboard

An area of memory where Windows operating systems temporarily store data for copy or move operations

clock speed or **clock rate**

The speed at which a microprocessor executes instructions, measured in megahertz (MHz)—millions of cycles per second

clone

(1) an IBM-compatible computer that works like an IBM computer; (2) a computer program on one platform that works like another computer program on another platform

cluster

(1) One or more sectors used by an operating system as the minimum storage space for a file or part of a file when it allocates storage space on a drive to the file; (2) an allocation unit

CMOS (Complementary Metal Oxide Semiconductor)

A special type of computer chip, or integrated circuit, that requires less power and that, with the use of a battery backup, retains important computer settings after you turn off the power to your computer

command

An instruction to perform a task, issued by a user to a program

command history

An area of memory where Windows 2000 and Windows XP keeps track of the last 50 commands entered at the command prompt

command interpreter or **command processor**

a program that displays a command prompt, interprets commands entered at the command prompt, locates and loads the appropriate program from memory or disk, and then executes the program

command line interface

A text or character-based user interface, with an operating system prompt at which you type commands in order to interact with the operating system and instruct it to perform a task

command line session

A window in which you use the command prompt and MS-DOS commands

command prompt

The operating system prompt (for example, C:\>) displayed on the screen or in a Command Prompt window to identify the current drive and directory and used as an interface for interacting with the operating system

command stack

A small area of memory used by the command processor to store the command history

Compress attribute

A setting associated with an NTFS directory or file indicating that it is compressed to use less disk space

compressed file

(1) A copy of a file whose size has been reduced using an algorithm, or special formula; (2) a file that contains one or more other compressed files

computer virus

A program that gains access to your computer, makes copies of itself, and that can adversely affect the use or performance of a computer system, or even damage the computer

CON:

The device name for the console (the screen for output and the keyboard for input); can be used without the colon

conditional test

A test that examines a condition and then performs an operation if the condition meets a criterion that is specified

configure

The process by which the operating system loads and installs the software that it needs to interact with the hardware and software on your computer

console

(1) A video display device, or monitor; (2) an administrative program, or snap-in, for managing the hardware, software, and network components of your computer system.

control code

An ASCII code for the use of the Ctrl (Control) key with another key; e.g. Ctrl+I for the Tab code

controller

A circuit board or card that controls a peripheral device, such as a hard disk or floppy disk

conventional memory

The first 640 KB of memory—the most important part of memory for DOS and DOS applications

copy backup

A type of backup that includes all the files you select for a backup and that does not affect other types of backups that you perform during a backup cycle

corrupted file

A program or document file whose contents have been altered as the result of a hardware, software, or power failure, or a computer virus infection

cross-linked file

An error condition in which a file contains at least one cluster that belongs to, or is shared by, at least one other file

C-SLIP (Compressed SLIP)

A standard for compressing data prior to transmission by SLIP (Serial Line Interface Protocol)

CSV (Comma Separated Values)

A file type in which a comma is the delimiter between tokens or fields

current directory

In a Command Prompt window, the directory in which you are currently working, which is identified in the command prompt and which becomes the default directory for commands that do not specify an alternate directory

cursor

A blinking underscore character (_) or a small solid rectangle that identifies your current working position on the screen and marks where the next typed character will appear on the screen

customize

To set up a computer system to meet a specific set of user needs, such as loading antivirus software during booting

cylinder

In a hard drive, a set of tracks all with the same track number across multiple sides of the drive's disk platters, which the hard drive can access without moving the read/write heads

D

daemon

A service running as a background program on a UNIX host

daily backup

A type of backup that includes selected files that have been created or modified the day you perform the backup and that does not affect other types of backups that you perform during a backup cycle

DAT (Digital Audio Tape)

A helical scan recording technology that increases the storage capacity of tapes used for backups and that supports storage capacities from 2 GB to 40 GB

date stamp

The date assigned to a file by the operating system

default directory

(1) The starting directory used by the operating system; (2) the directory in which a command operates unless the user specifies a different directory

default drive

(1) The starting drive used by the operating system; (2) the drive Windows uses to locate commands and files if no other drive is specified; (3) the current working drive

destination disk

The disk to which files are copied

destination file

A new file produced by the operating system during a copy operation

device

A hardware component

device driver

A file with program code that enables the operating system to communicate with, manage, and control the operation of a specific hardware or software component

device driver

A file with program code that enables the operating system to communicate with, manage, and control the operation of a hardware or software component

device name

A name Windows assigns to a hardware component or "device"

DHCP (Dynamic Host Configuration Protocol) server

A server that maintains a database of IP addresses, assigns those IP addresses to computers on the network on an as-needed basis (as a lease) and reclaims IP addresses that are no longer needed so it can make them available to other computers

dialog box

A component of the graphical user interface that displays information, lists objects properties and settings, or that provides options from which to choose as you perform a command operation

dial-up networking (DUN)

A subsystem used to establish a network connection by modem and telephone line to an Internet Service Provider (ISP)

differential backup

A type of backup performed during a backup cycle that includes all new or modified files since the last normal, or full, backup

DIP (Dual In-Line Package) switches

A set of toggle switches that are mounted on a chip, which is in turn mounted on an add-in board, and that are used to specify the configuration for a hardware device

directory

A specialized file that contains information about files or other directories; also known as a folder

Directory attribute

An attribute assigned to a file by the operating system to indicate a directory or subdirectory

directory listing

A list of directory and filenames, file sizes, file dates, and file times, and other information displayed by the DIR command

directory space

The storage space available on a disk volume for tracking filenames and information about directories and files

directory table

A table, or file, that keeps track of the folders and files stored in the top-level folder, or root directory of a disk that uses the FAT12, FAT16, or FAT32 file system

directory tree

A diagrammatic representation of the directory structure of a disk

disk order

The order in which the file system keeps track of files on a diskette or hard disk

DLT (Digital Linear Tape)

A tape technology that supports capacities of 15 to 70 GB, and that is faster than most other types of tape drives

document-oriented approach

An approach, or operating mode, in which you locate and open the document you want to use, and then the operating system automatically opens the program originally used to produce that document or the program currently associated with that document type

domain

A group of computers on a client/server network that share a common directory database

DOS (Disk Operating System)

(1) A common term for the primary operating system software used on IBM and IBM-compatible microcomputers from 1981 to 1995; varieties include MS-DOS, PC-DOS, and IBM DOS; (2) a generic term for a computer operating system that uses disk storage

DOS prompt

The command line interface for interacting with DOS

double word

Two binary words of 16 bits expressed in decimal form (base 10); used in Registry settings

dual-boot computer or **dual-boot configuration**

A computer with two installed operating systems, one of which you choose during booting

dual-boot system

A computer configuration for starting one of two different operating systems installed on the computer

dynamic link library

A file with executable program code that is used by one or more software applications and that has the file extension "dll"

E

Encrypt attribute

A setting associated with an NTFS directory or file indicating that it has been encrypted, preventing access by any person other than the Administrator and the user who encrypted the directory or file

end-of-file code (EOF) or **end-of-file marker**

(1) A control code, [Ctrl][Z], that marks the end of an ASCII file; (2) the code in the File Allocation Table that identifies a cluster as the last cluster in use by a specific file

environment variable

A symbolic name associated with a setting or sequence of characters (such as the name of the operating system), and stored in the Windows environment to make information available to programs

executable or **executable file**

A file that contains program code which the operating system can load into memory and run

expandable string

A string that contains text and a reference to a variable value

extended ASCII

A variation of the ASCII code that uses 8 bits to encode characters and contains values ranging from 0 (zero) to 255

extended memory

All memory above 1 MB

extended partition

A partition that does not contain operating system files, but that can be divided into additional logical drive volumes

external command

A command whose program code is stored in a file on disk

F

FAT (File Allocation Table)

A file on a disk that uses the FAT12, FAT16, or FAT32 file system that contains a list of each allocation unit or cluster on a disk along with information on whether each allocation unit or cluster is available, in use, defective (i.e., contains a bad sector), or reserved for use by the operating system

file

(1) A collection of data, such as a program or document, stored in a folder on disk; (2) the storage space on a disk that is set aside for the contents of a program, document, or data file

file extension

One or more characters included after a period at the end of the main part of a filename, typically used to identify the type of data in the file

file record segment (FRS)

A unique ID assigned to each folder and file in the NTFS Master File Table

file specification

The use of a drive name, path, directory name, filename, and wildcards to select one or more directories or files

file system

The features built into an operating system, and the data structures used by the operating system, for naming, organizing, storing, and tracking folders and files on disks

Filename-File Extension subkey

A Registry subkey under HKEY_CLASSES_ROOT that contains the path to the program for opening a specific type of file

files area

The area of a disk that follows the system area and that contains any folders and files created or copied onto the disk

filter

A command that modifies the output of another command

folder

The graphical user interface term for a directory. See "directory"

format capacity

The storage capacity of a drive or disk

FTP (File Transfer Protocol)

A protocol for connecting to a host computer via Internet Protocol and sending or receiving files

full format

A type of format used on new or formatted diskettes that defines the tracks and sectors on the disk; creates a boot sector, new File Allocation Tables, and a new directory file; and performs a surface scan for defects in the disk

full path (also called the **MS-DOS** path)

A notation that identifies the exact location of a file or folder on a disk by specifying the drive and folders (and, if needed, the filename) that lead to the desired folder or file

full system backup

A backup that includes all the files stored on your computer system, including operating system, application software, and data files

G

gateway

(1) A device that translates protocols between separate networks; (2) the address of a router

group accounts

Accounts which can be established to define a set of rights and permissions for users in the group

GUI (Graphical User Interface)

An interface that operates in graphics mode and that provides a pictorial method for interacting with the operating system through the use of icons, multiple windows, menus with task-related lists, dialog boxes, and a mouse

H

Hard Disk Partition Table

A table within the Master Boot Record on a hard disk which contains information that identifies where each hard drive starts and which drive on the hard disk is the boot drive

hardware

The physical components of a computer system

Hardware Abstraction Layer (HAL)

The component of the Windows 2000 or Windows XP operating system that contains the machine-specific program code for a particular type of microprocessor

hash mark

A mark (#) that represents each block of data transferred via FTP if the HASH command is issued before downloading a file

head

A mechanism on one side of a disk or platter in a disk drive used to read or write data

helical scan recording

A process by which data is recorded in diagonal stripes across a tape in order to increase the storage capacity of the tape

Help switch

An optional parameter (/?) which, when used with the command for an operating system or program, displays any available Help information included with the program

Help system

Information included within an operating system or program on its use and features

hexadecimal digit

A value in the hexadecimal, or base 16, numbering system

Hidden attribute

An attribute which indicates that the icon and name of a folder or file should not be displayed in a directory listing

hive

A file that stores specific Registry settings

hub

A hardware device that contains a port for connecting each computer on a network segment

hyperlink

A link between one object and another on a computer or the Web

I

icon

An image or picture displayed on the screen to represent hardware and software resources (such as drives, disks, applications, and files) as well as system tools (such as "My Computer") on your computer that you can open and use

IDE (Integrated Drive Electronics)

A hard disk drive interface in which the electronics for the controller are included in the drive itself

IIS (Internet Services)

A Windows component for publishing information on the Web

incremental backup

A type of backup performed during a backup cycle that includes only those files that you created or changed since your last normal or last incremental backup

Index attribute

A setting associated with an NTFS directory or file indicating that its contents and properties are indexed so you can search for text or properties within the file or directory

index variable

A symbol consisting of a percent sign (%) and a single alphabetic letter, such as %a, representing a storage location in which the FOR command sequentially stores items from a list

initialization file

A file that contains system settings or settings used by the operating system or by a specific program when it loads into memory

input

The process of providing program instructions, commands, and data to a computer system so that it can accomplish a specified task

input redirection operator (<)

An operator that uses input from a source other than the keyboard such as a file

insert mode

The default keyboard mode, in which characters typed at the command prompt are inserted at the position of the cursor, and characters to the right of the cursor are shifted to the right

internal command

A command whose program code is contained in the command interpreter program (such as Cmd.exe or Command.com) and is available once the command interpreter loads into memory; also known as a built-in command

Internet Connection Sharing (ICS)

A feature of certain versions of Windows that allows other computers on a local network to access the Internet through a connection on one main computer

IP (Internet Protocol)

The network protocol used by the Internet, which manages the way each packet is addressed so that it arrives at the correct destination

IP address

A 32-bit Internet Protocol address that identifies a node on a network; usually represented as four numbers separated by dots, e.g. 192.168.0.1

J

jumper

A small metal block that completes a circuit by connecting two pins on a circuit board and, in the process, controls a hardware configuration

K

kernel

The portion of the operating system that resides in memory and

provides services for applications, as distinguished from operating system programs run temporarily for specific purposes

L

LAN (Local Area Network)

A collection of computers and other peripherals joined by direct cable (or sometimes wireless) links and located relatively close to each other, usually in the same building, so that users can share hardware and software resources and files

Last Known Good Configuration

A booting option in which Windows 2000 or Windows XP boots with the configuration saved by the operating system from the last successful boot

lease

To temporarily assign IP addresses to computers on a network on an as-needed basis

legacy devices

Hardware devices that do not support the Plug and Play standards defined by Microsoft Corporation and hardware manufacturers, and which require manual installation, including, in many cases, setting jumpers or DIP switches; also now known as non-Plug and Play devices

literal text string

Consists of a word or sequence of characters that is processed without treating any of the characters as a variable

lock

(1) A function of the Check Disk utility that prevents access to a drive; (2) a setting which prevents access to a drive, directory, or file

logical structure of the disk

The combination of the File Allocation Tables, the file system, the folder or directory structure, and filenames that the operating system uses to track allocation of space to files on FAT volumes, and the data structures used on an NTFS volume to track information on files

long filename

A folder name or filename of up to 255 characters, which can contain spaces as well as uppercase and low-ercase letters and certain symbols

loopback address

An IP address (127.0.0.1) which always points back to your own computer

lost chain

An error condition in which a connected sequence of clusters is defined but is no longer associated with a file

lost cluster

An error condition in which a still-allocated cluster on a disk contains data that once belonged to a program, document, or some other type of file, such as a tempo-rary file, but is no longer associ-ated with that file

LPT1 or LPT1:

The device name for the first Line Printer Port in a computer; also known as PRN

LPT2 or LPT2:

The device name for the second Line Printer Port in a computer

M

macro

A set of stored keystrokes or commands that can execute an operation or set of operations automatically

Master Boot Record (MBR)

The first sector on a hard disk that contains information about the partitions on the disk

Master File Table (MFT)

An NTFS system file that contains entries on all the infor-mation that Windows NT, Windows 2000, and Windows XP tracks on a file, including its size, date and time stamps, permissions, and data content

media descriptor byte

A byte in the File Allocation Table that identifies the type of disk on a computer that uses the FAT16 or FAT32 file system

memory leak

A gradual decrease in available memory caused by program code that remains in memory after you exit an application and that ties up that memory so the operating system and other applications cannot use it

menu

A list of command choices or task-related options presented by a program

MORE filter

An external command that dis-plays one screen of output, pauses, and then displays a prompt that permits the user to view subse-quent screens when ready

MS-DOS mode

A shell that emulates the MS-DOS operating environment using the Windows 2000 MS-DOS subsystem

MSN (The Microsoft Network)

An Internet Service Provider (ISP)

multimedia

The integration of video, audio, animation, graphics, and text

multiple-boot system

A computer configuration for starting one of several different operating systems installed on the computer

multitasking

An operating system feature that permits the user to open and run more than one program simultaneously

multithreading

The ability of an operating system to execute more than one opera-tion within a single application simultaneously, or to execute the same operation multiple times

N

NetBEUI (NetBIOS Extended User Interface)

A Microsoft networking protocol for local networks only, which does not support the transmission of data between networks or over the Internet

network adapter (also Network Interface Card or NIC)

An add-in card that provides a physical interface and circuitry that enables a computer to access a network and exchange data

network protocol

An internal language that specifies the rules for transmitting data over a network, enabling computers and devices to communicate

node

A device that is connected to a network and that can communi-cate with other network devices

non-Plug and Play devices

See legacy devices

normal backup (full backup)

A type of backup that marks the start of a backup cycle and that includes all or part of the contents of a hard disk (in other words, all selected files)

NTFS (NT File System)

The native file system for Windows NT, Windows 2000, and Windows XP that uses a Master File Table (MFT) to track infor-mation about files on disk, sup-ports large storage media, long filenames and object-oriented applications that treat objects with user-defined and system-defined properties, disk compression, encryption, and indexing, and the use of security permissions for folders and files

NUL or null device

A special device that behaves like a perpetually empty file to which data can be copied or redirected and then discarded by the operat-ing system

O

object

A component of your computer system, such as a hardware device, software application, document, or part of a document

object-oriented operating system

An operating system that treats each component of the computer as an object and that manages all the actions and properties associated with an object

operating environment

A software product that performs the same functions as an operating system except for booting the computer and storing and retrieving data in files on a disk

operating system

A software product that manages the basic processes that occur within a computer, coordinates the interaction of hardware and software so that every component works together, and provides support for the use of other software, such as application software

operating system prompt

A set of characters displayed on the monitor to provide an interface for interacting with the computer. See command prompt.

orphaned file

A file that has a valid file record segment in the NTFS Master File Table, but which is not listed in any directory

output

To transmit the results of a computer process to the screen or to storage media; also, the results of a computer process

output redirection operator (>)

An operator that redirects the output of a command to a file, the printer port, or another device, instead of to the monitor

overtype mode

A keyboard mode in which new characters overwrite existing text as they are typed in

P

packet

A set of data that is transmitted as a discrete unit from one computer to another

paging file

See swap file

parallel directories

Directories located at the same level within the directory tree

parameter

An optional or required item of data for a command, entered as part of the command line

parent directory

The directory located one level above the current directory

parse

To divide lines of text from a file or files, according to specified rules

partition

(1) All or part of the physical hard disk that is set aside for a drive volume or set of logical drives; (2) to divide a hard disk into one or more logical drive volumes

partition boot sector

A portion of the hard disk partition that contains information about the disk's file system structure and a program for loading an operating system

path

The sequence of drive, folder, and file names that identifies the location of a folder, a file, or object on a computer. See absolute path and relative path.

PCMCIA (Personal Computer Memory Card International Association)

An organization that sets standards for connecting peripherals to portable computers

peer-to-peer network

A simple type of network in which each computer can access and share the same printer(s), hard disk drives, removable storage devices (such as CD-ROM, Zip, and DVD drives) and other drives, as well as software, folders, and files on any other computer

permission

A rule associated with an object to regulate which users can gain access to the object and in what manner

PING (Packet Internet Groper)

A TCP/IP command or protocol used to check connections to a computer on a local network, or a to a remote computer on the Internet

pipe operator

A symbol (|) that indicates that the output of one command is to be used as the input for another command

pipe or piping

To use the output of one command as the input for another command

pipeline

A command line containing a sequence of commands and that uses a pipe operator to transfer the output of one command so that it becomes the input for another command

platter

A disk within a hard disk drive that is made of aluminum or glass and that provides all or part of the storage capacity of the entire hard disk drive

PNP (Plug and Play)

A set of specifications for designing hardware so that the device is automatically detected and configured by the operating system when the computer boots or when it is attached to, or inserted in, the computer

POST (Power-On Self-Test)

A set of diagnostic programs executed during start-up and used to test the system components—including memory—for accessibility and for errors

Power Users

Advanced users who have developed a broad base of skills useful for many different situations, such as designing and automating the use of custom programs, troubleshooting problems, providing support for other users, and setting up computer systems from scratch; (2) members of the Windows 2000 or Windows XP Power Users Group who are authorized to install software and change some system settings

PPP (Point-to-Point protocol)

A commonly used protocol for remote access using modems and telephone lines that provides stability and error-correcting features

primary partition

The bootable partition on a hard disk that contains the operating system (such as drive C in Windows operating systems)

print queue

A list of all the documents that are scheduled to print, along with information about each print job

PRN or PRN:

The device name for the first printer port in a computer; also known as LPT1

program-oriented approach

An approach or operating mode in which you open the software application you want to use, then locate and open the document you want to use

property

A setting associated with an object (for example, the Windows version shown on the General property sheet in the System Properties dialog box for My Computer)

protected mode

A operating mode in which the microprocessor can address more than 1 MB of memory, support the use of virtual memory (a technique for supplementing memory by using unused storage space on a hard disk as memory), provide memory protection features for applications (so that one application does not attempt to use the memory space allocated to another application), use 32-bit (rather than 16-bit) processing, and support multitasking

Q

QIC (Quarter-Inch Cartridge)

A standard type of tape cartridge technology commonly used for backing up data on desktop computers

question mark wildcard (?)

A symbol used as part of a file specification to substitute for a single character in the directory name, filename, or file extension

Quick format

A type of format in which the formatting program erases the contents of the File Allocation Tables and directory file but does not lay down new tracks or sectors and does not verify the integrity of each sector on a previously formatted disk

R

RAM (Random-Access Memory)

(1) Temporary, or volatile, computer memory used to store program instructions and data; (2) the computer's working memory

Read-Only attribute

An attribute assigned to a file to indicate that you can read from, but not write to, the file

read-only mode

A diagnostic mode of operation in which the Check Disk utility checks a drive and, if it finds errors, reports the presence of these errors and simulates how it would correct the problem

real mode

An operating mode used by 8088 and 8086 microcomputers in which the microprocessor can only address 1 MB of memory

redirect

To change the source of input or the destination of output

registered file

A file that is associated with a specific application via its file extension

Registry

A system database that consists of a set of files where Windows 2000 or Windows XP stores your computer's hardware, software, and security settings, as well as user settings or profiles, and property settings for folders and programs.

relative path

A sequence of directory names that identifies the location of a file relative to the current directory.

replaceable parameter variable

A symbol consisting of a percent sign (%) and a single digit, such as %1, used in batch programs to represent one of the strings of characters the user types at the command line after the batch program name when launching a batch program. %1 represents the first string, %2 the second, and so on. Also known as a command-line argument.

Restricted User

A user who is part of the Windows 2000 or Windows XP Users Group, but who cannot install software or change system settings

robustness

The stability associated with an operating system and the system resources that it manages and protects

ROM-BIOS (Read Only Memory Basic Input Output System)

A computer chip that contains the program routines for running the Power-On Self Test, identifying and configuring Plug and Play devices, communicating with peripheral devices, and locating and loading the operating system

root directory

(1) The first directory created on a disk during the formatting of the disk; (2) the name of the top-level directory on a disk

router

A hardware device that forwards data to destinations outside the local network and most commonly to the Internet at large

routine

(1) A discrete subsection of a computer program that performs a particular well-defined function; (2) A program executed during the booting process to check the availability and functioning of hardware components or to locate and load the operating system from disk

routine

A program executed during the booting process to check the availability and functioning of hardware components or to locate and load the operating system from disk

S

scan code

A code that is produced from pressing a key on the keyboard and that is, used by the operating system to determine which character to display on the monitor

script

A program that is comparable to a batch program, but which is written in a scripting language such as Visual Basic Scripting Edition (VBScript), which has the "vbs" file extension

scrolling

A process by which a program adjusts the screen view

sector

(1) A division of a track that provides storage space for data; (2) the basic unit of storage space on a disk, typically 512 bytes of data

security descriptor

NTFS settings associated with a file, directory, or device about the owner, permissions granted to users and groups, and information on security events to be audited

server

A high-performance computer that manages a computer network with the use of network operating system software, and that provides access to software, hardware, and files on a network

server software

Software that other computers use to access resources on your computer using a network

service

A program, routine, or process that provides support to other programs

shares

A computer's shared resources on a network, such as directories and printers

shell

The interface provided by a program so that a user can communicate with the program. In the case of Windows operating systems, the graphical user interface and the command line interface are shells employed by a user to communicate commands, or requests for actions, that the operating system will then carry out

short filename

An MS-DOS folder name or filename (also called an MS-DOS-Readable filename, or alias) that follows the rules and conventions for 8.3 filenames (that is, names that allow up to 8 characters for the main part of the filename and then up to 3 characters for the file extension, all using capital letters only)

slack

Part of the last cluster allocated to a file, but not used to store data

SLIP (Serial Line Interface Protocol)

An older, remote-access standard for connecting to servers by serial connections such a telephone lines

sort order parameters

One-character codes used with the DIR command and Order switch to control the way in which the DIR command displays a directory listing

source code

The original, non-executable code in which a program was written

source disk

The disk that contains files you want to copy

source file

The original file copied by the operating system during a COPY operation

spool

To store print jobs on disk until the printer is ready to process the print request

spool file

A temporary file that contains a processed print job request, complete with printer formatting codes

spooling

The process of storing a document for printing in a temporary file on disk and transferring the document to the printer as a background operation

standard input device

The device the operating system uses for input; by default, the keyboard

standard output device

The device the operating system uses for output; by default, the monitor

Standard User

A user who is part of the Power Users Group and who can modify computer settings and install software

startup environment

Configuration settings that specify which operating system to start and how to start each operating system

string

A set of characters that is treated exactly as entered

string comparison

A test that a form of the IF command performs to see whether two pieces of text are identical

subdirectory

A directory that is contained within, and subordinate to, another directory; also known as a subfolder

subnet mask

A set of four numbers, like an IP address, used to split a computer's IP address into network and host computer numbers

surface scan

(1) A part of the formatting process in which the formatting program records dummy data onto each sector of a disk and reads it back to determine the reliability of each sector; (2) the phase during which the operating system examines the surface of a disk for defects

swap file

A special file created on a hard disk by the operating system for use as supplemental RAM; also known as a paging file

switch

An optional parameter, or piece of information, that is added to a command to modify the way in which a program operates

syntax

The proper format for entering a command, including how to spell the command, required parameters (such as a drive), optional parameters (such as a switch), and the spacing between the command, the required parameters, and any optional parameters

system architecture

The internal design and coding of an operating system

system area

The area of a disk that contains the boot sector, File Allocation Tables, and directory table

System attribute

An attribute that identifies an operating system file or folder

system disk

A disk that contains the core operating system files needed to start a computer; also known as a boot disk

system files

Files that Windows operating systems use to load, configure, and run the operating system

SystemRoot

The directory that contains the installed version of the Windows 2000 or Windows XP operating system

systems software

The programs that manage the fundamental operations within a computer, such as starting the computer, loading or copying programs and data into memory, executing or carrying out the instructions in programs, saving data to a disk, displaying information on the monitor, and sending information through a port to a peripheral device

T

tape drive

A backup drive unit using high-capacity magnetic tape cartridges

target disk

The disk that receives a duplicate copy of the contents of another disk

target file

A new file that results from a copy operation

taskbar

A gray horizontal bar on the desktop that displays a Start button for starting programs or opening documents, a Quick Launch toolbar, buttons for currently open software applications and folder windows, and a system tray with the current time and icons for programs loaded into memory during booting

task-switching

The process of changing from an open task, or process, in one window to another task in another window

TCP/IP (Transmission Control Protocol/Internet Protocol)

An Internet protocol that enables computers with different types of hardware architectures and different types of operating systems to reliably communicate with each other

template

A file that contains the structure, general layout, formatting, and some of the contents of a specific type of document, such as spreadsheet templates for analyzing a company's performance and projected growth

temporary file

A file used by the operating system, application, or utility to store a copy of the data that it is processing until it completes the operation

text file

A simple file type consisting of lines of ASCII characters, each terminated with an end-of-line code, and, in MS-DOS and Windows, typically a pair of codes -- CR (Carriage Return) and LF (Line Feed)

text mode

A simple and fast video display mode for displaying text, including letters, numbers, symbols, and a small set of graphics characters using white characters on a black background

thread

A segment, or unit, of program code within an application which Windows can execute more than once at a time, or at the same time as other segments of program code in the same program

throughput

The speed with which a device processes and transmits data

time stamp

The time assigned by the operating system to a file

toggle key

A key that alternates between two related uses or functions each time you press the key

tokens

Parts (sometimes called "fields" or "values") that are separated by delimiter characters in a line of text

top-level folder (root directory)

The first folder or directory created on a disk volume by the operating system or a formatting utility to track information on the directories and files on the volume

track

A concentric recording band around the inner circumference of a disk that stores data and which the operating system creates when formatting the disk,

Travan

A type of tape drive and tape technology that supports storage capacities in the range of 400 MB to 8 GB, and that also supports the use of QIC tapes

U

UNC (Universal Naming Convention)

The notation used to Identify a server, computer (such as \\Pentium), printer, or other resource on a network

Unicode

A 16-bit coding scheme that can represent 65,536 character combinations, which can represent all the characters within the alphabets of most of the world's languages

USB (Universal Serial Bus)

A computer interface with fast data transfer rates and which supports connections to multiple devices

user interface

The combination of hardware and software that lets the user interact with a computer

utility

An auxiliary program included with operating system software for performing common types of tasks, such as searching the hard disk for files that can be safely deleted, or for monitoring or optimizing the performance of your computer

V

value entry

An entry in the Windows Registry that consists of a **value name** (a name assigned to a setting), its **data type**, and its **value data** (the setting itself)

VFAT (Virtual File Allocation Table)

The virtual device driver that Windows 98 and Windows 95 use with the FAT file system

virtual device driver

A special type of device driver that Windows 98 or Windows 95 uses when it operates in protected mode and uses the full capabilities of 80386 and later microprocessors to address memory above 1 MB and also provide memory protection features

virtual DOS machine (VDM)

A complete operating environment for one program that is created each time a user opens a DOS program

virtual memory

(1) Space on a hard disk that an operating system uses as extra memory to supplement the memory available in RAM; (2) the combination of RAM and the swap file used as memory

Virtual Private Network (VPN)

A network that encrypts its transmissions across a public network to simulate a private network connection

volatile

Dependent on the availability of power, and therefore temporary (such as RAM)

volume

A physical storage device, such as a diskette, or a logical storage device, such as a drive partition on a hard disk

volume label

An electronic label or name assigned to a disk

W

WAN (wide area network)

A collection of computers located in different geographical areas and connected together through some type of telecommunications link

Web style

A Windows user interface and operating environment that allows you to work on your local computer in the same way that you work on the Web

wildcard

A symbol in a directory or file specification that substitutes for all or part of the directory or filename

window

A bordered working area on the screen for organizing your view of an application, document, drive, folder, or file

Windows environment

An area of memory that stores information in environment variables for use by programs

wizard

A program tool that asks a series of questions about what problem you are experiencing, or what you want to do and the settings you want to use, then provides suggestions to solve the problem, or completes the operation or task for you

workgroup

A group of computers that share information on a network

write-protect

A technique for protecting a disk so the operating system or any other program cannot record data onto it

WSH (Windows Script Host)

A Windows 2000 and Windows XP component that executes scripts from either the Windows 2000 or Windows XP desktop or from the command-line environment

INDEX

TASK REFERENCE

TASK REFERENCE

TASK REFERENCE

TASK REFERENCE

TASK	PAGE #	RECOMMENDED METHOD
Share the My Documents folder, using Windows Explorer to	490	See Reference Window: Sharing the My Documents Folder Using Windows Explorer
Shared directory, using the Command Prompt to remove a	493	See Reference Window: Removing a Shared Directory from the Command Prompt window
Sharing, remove from the My Documents folder using Windows Explorer	490	See Reference Window: Removing Sharing from the My Documents Folder Using Windows Explorer
Short filenames, displaying in a directory listing	74	See Reference Window: Displaying Short Filenames in a Directory Listing
Start Windows 2000	22	See Reference Window: Powering on Your Computer and Starting Windows 2000
String comparisons in a batch program, performing	377	See Reference Window: Performing String Comparisons and Branching in a Batch Program
Text strings, using FOR with simple	388	See Reference Window: Using FOR with Simple Text Strings
Text, using FOR to divide lines of	405	See Reference Window: Using FOR to Divide Lines of Text
Time, viewing or changing the	33	See Reference Window: Viewing or Changing the Date and Time
Trace the route to another computer, using TRACERT to	505	See Reference Window: Using TRACERT to Trace the Route to Another Computer
User account information, using the Command Prompt to view	496	See Reference Window: Viewing User Account Information from a Command Prompt window
User account information, using the Computer Management tool to display	494	See Reference Window: Displaying User Account Information using the Computer Management Tool
User logon directory, changing to your	6	At the command prompt, type CD %USERPROFILE% and press Enter
Wide directory listing, displaying a	64	See Reference Window: Viewing a Wide Directory Listing
Wildcard, using the asterisk	82	See Reference Window: Using the Asterisk Wildcard in a File Specification
Wildcard, using the question mark	84	See Reference Window: Using the Question Mark Wildcard in a File Specification
Windowed view, change to	25	Press Alt+Enter
Windows environment, viewing and changing settings in the	87	See Reference Window: Viewing and Changing Settings in the Windows Environment
Windows search path, viewing, saving, and changing the	316	See Reference Window: Viewing, Saving, and Changing the Windows Search Path
Windows version, display the	30	Type VER and then press Enter

File Finder

Location in Tutorial	Name and Location of Data File	Student Creates New File
Tutorial 1	Data Disk #1	
Review Assignments	Data Disk #1	
Tutorial 2	Data Disk #1	
Review Assignments	Data Disk #1	
Case Problem 1	Data Disk #1	
Case Problem 2	Data Disk #1	
Case Problem 3	Data Disk #1	
Case Problem 4	Data Disk #1	
Tutorial 3	Data Disk #1	Templates.txt Sales Templates.txt Five Year Plan Draft.xls Computer Training Proposal.doc 2003 Sales Summary #1.xls 2003 Sales Summary #2.xls
Review Assignments	Data Disk #1	Spreadsheet Solutions.txt Spreadsheet Solution Files.txt Backup of Spreadsheet Solution Files.txt
Case Problem 1	Data Disk #1	Stratton Graphics.txt
Case Problem 2	Data Disk #1	Bayview Travel.txt Financial Analyses.txt
Case Problem 3	Data Disk #1	Five Year Sales Projection.xls Company Balance Sheet.xls Loan Analysis.txt Bank Loan Analysis.txt
Case Problem 4	Data Disk #1	Turing Balance Sheet.xls Turing Client Invoices.xls Turing Weekly Worklog.xls 2003 Trips Summary #1.xls 2003 Trips Summary #2.xls Turing Budget Projection.xls Mediterranean Excursions.ppt
Tutorial 4	Data Disk #1 ~WRC0070.tmp File0000.chk Data Systems Budget.xls Hardware.ppt Application Software.ppt Software.ppt Using the Mouse.ppt Colors of the Rainbow.bmp Color Palette.bmp Palette #1.bmp Palette #2.bmp Addressing Cells.xls Fonts.xls Format Code Colors.xls Formatting Features.xls Andre's Employee Payroll.xls Loan Payment Analysis.xls Invoice Form.wk4 Weekly Worklog.xls Daily Sales.xls Savings Plan.xls Product List.xls Sales.wk4 Balance Sheet.xls Commission on Sales.xls Client Invoices.xls 2002 Sales Summary #1.xls 2002 Sales Summary #2.xls	Presentations (directory) Designs (directory) Training (directory) Business Records (directory) Company Projections (directory) 2003 Sales Summary #1.xls 2003 Sales Summary #2.xls Treefile.txt
Review Assignments	Data Disk #1 File0000.chk ~WRC0070.tmp Colors of the Rainbow.bmp Color Palette.bmp Palette #1.bmp Palette #2.bmp Projected Growth Memo.doc Proposal.doc Hardware.ppt Application Software.ppt	Images (directory) Word Templates (directory) Presentations (directory) Lotus Templates (directory) Excel Templates (directory) [Directory Structure.txt]

File Finder

Location in Tutorial	Name and Location of Data File	Student Creates New File
	Software.ppt	
	Using the Mouse.ppt	
	Invoice Form.wk4	
	Sales.wk4	
	Commission on Sales.xls	
	Client Invoices.xls	
	Weekly Worklog.xls	
	Software Quotes.xls	
	Andre's Employee Payroll.xls	
	Daily Sales.xls	
	2002 Sales Summary #2.xls	
	Advertising Income.xls	
	Break Even Analysis.xls	
	2002 Sales Summary #1.xls	
	Data Systems Budget.xls	
	Five Year Growth Plan.xls	
	Five Year Plan Template.xls	
	Product List.xls	
	Product Sales Projection.xls	
	Regional Sales Projections.xls	
	Sales Projection Models.xls	
	3 Year Sales Projection.xls	
	Savings Plan.xls	
	Loan Payment Analysis.xls	
	Fonts.xls	
	Formatting Features.xls	
	Format Code Colors.xls	
	Addressing Cells.xls	
	Balance Sheet.xls	
	Sales Projections.xls	
	Employees.xls	
Case Problem 1	Data Disk #1	Spreadsheet Templates (directory)
	File0000.chk	Business Records (directory)
	~WRC0070.tmp	Projections (directory)
	Colors of the Rainbow.bmp	Sales Summaries (directory)
	Color Palette.bmp	Training (directory)
	Palette #1.bmp	[Directory Structure.txt]
	Palette #2.bmp	
	Projected Growth Memo.doc	
	Proposal.doc	
	Hardware.ppt	
	Application Software.ppt	
	Software.ppt	
	Using the Mouse.ppt	
	Invoice Form.wk4	
	Sales.wk4	
	Balance Sheet.xls	
	Client Invoices.xls	
	Commissions on Sales.xls	
	Daily Sales.xls	
	Data Systems Budget.xls	
	Employees.xls	
	Loan Payment Analysis.xls	
	Product List.xls	
	Software Quotes.xls	
	Weekly Worklog.xls	
	3 Year Sales Projection.xls	
	Advertising Income.xls	
	Break Even Analysis.xls	
	Five Year Growth Plan.xls	
	Five Year Plan Template.xls	
	Product Sales Projection.xls	
	Regional Sales Projections.xls	
	Sales Projection Models.xls	
	Sales Projections.xls	
	2002 Sales Summary #1.xls	
	2002 Sales Summary #2.xls	
	Addressing Cells.xls	
	Andre's Employee Payroll.xls	
	Fonts.xls	
	Format Code Colors.xls	
	Formatting Features.xls	
	Savings Plan.xls	
Case Problem 2	Data Disk #1	FY 2002 (directory)
	Colors of the Rainbow.bmp	2002 Sales Projections.xls
	Color Palette.bmp	FY 2003 (directory)

File Finder

Location in Tutorial	Name and Location of Data File	Student Creates New File
	Palette #1.bmp Palette #2.bmp File0000.chk Projected Growth Memo.doc Proposal.doc Hardware.ppt Application Software.ppt Software.ppt Using the Mouse.ppt ~WRC0070.tmp Invoice Form.wk4 Sales.wk4 2002 Sales Summary #1.xls 2003 Sales Summary #2.xls Sales Projections.xls	2003 Sales Projections.xls 2003 Sales Summary #1.xls 2003 Sales Summary #2.xls [Directory Structure.txt]
Case Problem 3	Data Disk #1 Projected Growth Memo.doc Proposal.doc File0000.chk ~WRC0070.tmp Invoice Form.wk4 Sales.wk4 Hardware.ppt Application Software.ppt Software.ppt Using the Mouse.ppt Fonts.xls Software Quotes.xls Colors of the Rainbow.bmp Color Palette.bmp Palette #1.bmp Palette #2.bmp	Computer Courses (directory) Images (directory) [Directory Structure.txt]
Case Problem 4	C:\Winnt\Web\Wallpaper Boiling Point.jpg Chateau.jpg Fall Memories.jpg Fly Away.jpg Gold Petals.jpg Ocean Wave.jpg Paradise.jpg Purple Sponge.jpg Snow Trees.jpg Solar Eclipse.jpg Water Color.jpg Windows 2000.jpg	Windows Images (directory) [Directory Structure.txt]
Tutorial 5	Data Disk #2 My Documents (directory) New Folder (2) (directory) New Folder (directory) Training (directory) Meeting (directory) Overhead Transparencies (directory) New Folder (directory) Application Software.ppt Excel Basics.doc Computer Basics.doc Using the Mouse.ppt Company Logo Design.bmp Designs (directory) Microsoft's Web Site.doc ~WRC0070.tmp Sales.wk4 My Documents (directory) Training (directory)	Hdtree.txt Beforetree.txt Memos (directory) Company Templates (directory) Aftertree.txt SolarWinds (directory) SolarWinds Normal Backup SolarWinds Incremental Backup #1 Company Templates (directory)
Review Assignments	[Reorganized Data Disk from Session 5.1]	Cash Flow (directory) Company Budget.xls Personnel (directory) Portfolio (directory Products (directory) Projections (directory) Sales (directory) Accounting (directory) Reorganized Disk.txt SolarWinds Templates (directory)

File Finder

Location in Tutorial	Name and Location of Data File	Student Creates New File
		SWT Normal Backup (directory)
		Sales Summary #3.xls
		SWT Differential #1
		SolarWinds Templates.txt
Case Problem 1	Data Disk #2	[DirectoryTree.txt]
Case Problem 4		Directory Organization.txt
Tutorial 6	Data Disk #2	
Review Assignments	Data Disk #1	
Case Problem 3	Data Disk #1	
Tutorial 7		Batch Programs for [Your Name] (directory)
		FormatDisk.bat
		Reset.bat
		VolumeLabel.bat
		3app.bat
		setrc.txt
Review Assignments		[Batch programs directory]
		[Batch program file]
Case Problem 1		[Batch program file]
Case Problem 2		[Batch program file]
Case Problem 3		[Batch program file]
Case Problem 4		[Batch program file]
Tutorial 8	Data Disk #3	Batch Programs for [Your Name] (directory)
		Reset.bat
		UpdatePath.bat
		SolarWinds (directory)
		Home.bat
		CopyCheck.bat
		DirCopy.bat
		ColorTest.bat
		AddPrefix.bat
		AddPrefixSub.bat
		EmpTitles.bat
Review Assignments	[Batch programs from Sessions 8.1 and 8.2]	[Batch programs directory]
Case Problem 1	Data Disk #3	PerfectMatch (directory)
		DirDoc.bat
Case Problem 2	Data Disk #3	CTU (directory)
		ListTemplates.bat
Case Problem 3	Data Disk #3	Northbay Computer (directory)
	Data Disk #1	AddNewFiles.bat
Case Problem 4	Data Disk #3	SSNList.bat
		EmpSSN.txt
Tutorial 9	Data Disk #1	Registry Backup (folder)
		Registry Backup for [Date].reg
Review Assignments		[Registration File].reg
		Command Processor.reg
Case Problem 2		Default Directory Shell.reg
		Command Prompt.reg
Case Problem 3		DOS Registry Entries.txt
Tutorial 10		Employees.txt [Downloaded]
		Presentations.exe [Downloaded]
		CTI FTP Site (shortcut)
		SolarWinds.zip [Downloaded]
Review Assignments		[Downloaded file]
Case Problem 1		UserStats.txt
Case Problem 2	Data Disk #3	ShareDisk.txt
Case Problem 3		PingDiag.txt
Case Problem 4		[Downloaded files]